From Ambivalence to Betrayal

The Left, the Jews, and Israel

Studies in Antisemitism

Series Editor, Robert S. Wistrich

Vadim Rossman, *Russian Intellectual Antisemitism in the Post-Communist Era* (2002)

Anthony D. Kauders, *Democratization and the Jews: Munich, 1945–1965* (2004)

Cesare D. De Michelis, *The Non-Existent Manuscript: A Study of the* Protocols of the Sages of Zion (2004)

Robert S. Wistrich, *Laboratory for World Destruction: Germans and Jews in Central Europe* (2007)

Graciela Ben-Dror, *The Catholic Church and the Jews: Argentina, 1933–1945* (2008)

Andrei Oişteanu, *Inventing the Jew: Antisemitic Stereotypes in Romanian and Other Central-East European Cultures* (2009)

Olaf Blaschke, *Offenders or Victims? German Jews and the Causes of Modern Catholic Antisemitism* (2009)

This book is dedicated to the memory of my former history teacher at Kilburn Grammar School in London,

Dr. Walter Isaacson

a refugee from Nazi Germany

who first taught me how to think independently.

"If you can look into the seeds of time,
And say which grain will grow and which will not. . . ."

Macbeth, I, iii

Table of Contents

Preface

The main title of this book may raise a few eyebrows. To what "betrayal" is the author referring? Surely neither antisemitism nor hostility to Israel can be seen as prerogatives of leftism; and if they do exist in some quarters of the Left, is that not an example of "legitimate criticism" of Israel—a country regularly pilloried in international forums as one of the last remaining bastions of Western colonialism?

I have been hearing such arguments for over forty years, ever since (as a young radical) I myself participated in the student revolts of 1968, in both America and France. True, for most of my contemporaries (born like me after the end of World War II) the "Jewish Question" still seemed marginal at that time.

However, in my case, it was something more than mere background noise. Perhaps, because I had been born in the Muslim Republic of Kazakhstan, in Stalin's Soviet Union at the height of the Great Dictator's prestige, following the victory over Hitler's hordes; perhaps because my father's experience as a wartime prisoner of the NKVD (secret police) meant that from the outset there was great ambivalence in my own mind concerning the "fatherland of socialism." My father, who in pre-1939 Kraków had been a fellow-traveler of the illegal Polish Communist Party, nourished some bitter memories of Soviet mendacity after the war and the cruelty of a totalitarian system that ruthlessly crushed all individuality. My mother was slightly more inclined to socialist ideas. Her negative experiences of bourgeois Catholic antisemitism in interwar Poland had been much worse than anything she encountered in Stalin's USSR, though she, too, had no illusions about the "Communist paradise."

I grew up in 1950s England, seemingly far removed from these totalitarian nightmares. Nevertheless, during my adolescence I was becoming radicalized at grammar school, at the very time that Great Britain was beginning to definitively shed its colonial Empire. In 1961 I first visited Israel, spending a month on a far left kibbutz—fascinated but also slightly repelled by its intense collectivist ethos. It was also the time of the Eichmann trial which made me even more intensely aware (at the age of 15) of the Holocaust—in which so many of my own relatives had been killed. I would return to Israel in 1969 after two years of study and radical protest (mainly in Stanford,

California) against the "capitalist alienation," racism, and militarism of the West. I had already read the Marxist classics while still a pupil at Kilburn Grammar School in London and then at Cambridge University where I found most of my fellow-students to be far more conservative than I was. My own "ideology" at that time was somewhat eclectic—a mixture of the Frankfurt Freudo-Marxist School of Sociology (especially Erich Fromm and Herbert Marcuse), Sartrian existentialism, the French "situationist" school, and a dose of Guevarist Third World mythology thrown in for good measure.

My first *adult* encounter with the Jewish State in 1969 was by no means easy or painless. The intellectual baggage I came with did not predispose me to any special sympathy with a country that struck me then as being dangerously intoxicated with its stunning military victory of June 1967. The result had been to greatly expand Israel's borders from the frighteningly narrow dimensions of the ceasefire lines after the 1948 war, to something that seemingly offered secure and defensible boundaries. The other side of that coin was a certain degree of hubris which seemed to me frankly alarming. As the literary editor of the peace-oriented left-wing magazine *New Outlook* (in Tel Aviv) I found myself at the age of twenty-four suddenly and unexpectedly thrust into the internal political debates of the Israeli Left. I did not get on with the principal editor of the journal, Simha Flapan, who came from the left wing of the Mapam movement—a Marxist-Zionist party whose power base was in the *kibbutzim*. He was a strange kind of debunking "post-Zionist" before the term even existed. Though no Communist fellow-traveler, his view of the Cold War and the Soviet Union struck me as naïve. Even at the height of my own anti-American feelings in the late 1960s as a result of the Vietnam War, I had never seen the United States as being morally equivalent to the U.S.S.R. Having been trapped in Prague for two weeks as a tourist during the Soviet invasion of Czechoslovakia in August 1968, it was obvious to me, even then, that "real socialism" as practiced in the Communist bloc was the complete negation of anything resembling humanist ideals. Moreover, during visits to Poland and Czechoslovakia in the late 1960s, I had not failed to notice the cynical use by the Communist regimes of anti-semitism—under the guise of anti-Zionism—to repress any trace of intellectual or personal dissent.

By the time I left the Middle East during the month of "Black September" 1970 (when King Hussein summarily crushed the PLO challenge to his rule) I had begun to crystallize the theme of my future doctoral research on Socialism and the "Jewish Question" in Central Europe. The idea had arisen in conversations that I had in Jerusalem, earlier in 1970, with Israeli historian

Jacob Talmon and Professor George Mosse (then a visiting professor from Wisconsin at the Hebrew University) whose courses I had been taking. They both felt that it would be better for me to do my dissertation at University College, London, where I would enjoy easier access to the relevant sources, especially those in France, Germany, and East-Central Europe. During the next three years I traveled widely, learned a number of new languages, and focused on my research. I also became aware of the Soviet Jewish self-awakening—the first real crack in the Iron Curtain. At that time, the cause of Soviet Jewry—including the demand for "repatriation" to Israel—even enjoyed some support on the non-Communist Left, which condemned the growing manifestations of Soviet antisemitism.

Forty years on, I have to say that the *classical* Marxist Left whose ideology and politics I studied during the early 1970s seems to me to belong to a very different political universe from the pro-Palestinian leftism of our own time. True, there are a number of theoretical continuities between today and the anti-Zionism of prewar European Social Democrats like Karl Kautsky or Otto Bauer. There is even a connection between the hostility to the "separatist" Jewish labor movement exhibited by Lenin, Trotsky, and Stalin, and the ideological negation of Israel on the contemporary Marxist Left. Outwardly at least, there is also a common language of socialist "internationalism" that still animates the radical anti-Zionist discourse.

Yet even in the mid-1970s when I became more directly involved in debates on British campuses with pro-Palestinian leftists, there was a sharp edge to anti-Israel sentiment which went beyond theory. Though I well understood Palestinian resentment towards Israel, it was more difficult to comprehend why so many on the new Left had turned against the Jewish State with such vehemence. After all, British leftists were physically far removed from the Middle East conflict, and many seemed to have not even the faintest grasp of either Arab or Jewish culture. The "progressive" take on the Middle East stuck me as extraordinarily simplistic—dividing the conflict into "good" and "bad" guys—the "oppressive" Israelis against the "oppressed" Palestinians.

At one level, this is less surprising when one recalls that much of the Western Left (especially the Communists) had for decades applauded "revolutionary" dictators like Stalin, Mao, Pol Pot, Colonel Qaddafi, Saddam Hussein, and Castro. Today, it still remains either supportive, indifferent, or silent about populist dictators like Ahmadinejad, Mugabe, or Chávez while rallying its militants on behalf of Hezbollah and Hamas. At the same time, the anti-Zionist Left systematically demonizes Israel—which in terms of its civil society, democratic norms, freedom of criticism and rule of law is light-years ahead of the Arab world. One might well ask if this is not an "anti-colonialism" of frauds and fools.

Can we seriously imagine Marx, Engels, Kautsky, or Rosa Luxemburg remaining silent about the advocacy of sharia law, censorship, female genital mutilation, honor killings, suicide bombings, or making the world safe for Allah's rule? Can we conceive of any circumstances in which they would have envisaged an alliance with Sheikh al-Qaradawi and the Muslim Brotherhood—along the lines of British leftists like Ken Livingstone or George Galloway? The question almost answers itself. But neo-Stalinists or neo-Trotskyists—not to mention post-modern leftists—have no such difficulty. A key element in this emerging Red-Green axis is the rampant anti-Israel and anti-Jewish mythology, especially in the Muslim-Arab world and among anti-American leftist leaders like Daniel Ortega or Hugo Chávez. The type of conspiratorial thinking currently dominant on the pro-Islamic Left is, I would argue, a complete betrayal of the Enlightenment legacy and a caricature of socialist internationalism masquerading under the banner of "anti-globalism."

In this book, I have tried to explain what went wrong while suggesting that the degeneration was already prefigured in the 19th-century seedbed of antisemitic socialism. A poisonous anti-Jewish legacy can be found in Marx, Fourier, and Proudhon, extending through the orthodox Communists and "non-conformist" Trotskyists to the Islamo-Leftist hybrids of today who systematically vilify the so-called racist essence of the Jewish State. Twentieth-century Marxism had no trouble in rationalizing the crimes of the Soviet gulag with the help of convoluted Hegelian dialectics. Similarly, the propagandists of the radical Left have in many cases proved adept at justifying the elimination of Israel in favor of the Palestinian "revolution"—whose most authentic representatives today are the Islamist antisemites of the Hamas.

From Karl Marx to Sheikh al-Qaradawi, via Ken Livingstone (former leftist Mayor of London), it would appear that the Jews (whoops, sorry, the "Zionists") are always "guilty" of something bad. It is also worth noting that this is a language that neither the radical Right nor the Nazis and the Islamo-fascists have any pangs of conscience in warmly embracing. European fascists, no less than leftists, regularly identified the Jews with capitalism and western imperialism. Today, rather than denouncing the "Jewish-Bolshevik" alliance (as Hitler and the prewar fascists continually did), the extreme Right focuses on attacking the "American-Zionist axis." This is the consensual point where it meets with the "anti-Zionist" Left and the Islamists; where neo-Marxists or liberal "progressives" find common cause with Islamic revolutionists from Haj Amin al-Husseini to Arafat, or from Hassan al-Banna to Khomeini, Ghadaffi, and al-Qaradawi. This is the place where "Islamo-fascism" merges with "Islamo-Marxism" in an empty "progressivism" without progress, driven by a convulsive hatred of Western modernity, of Jews, and bourgeois liberalism.

But why are Jews still the scapegoats at the heart of this jihad? Why does a whole section of the Left—which has almost abandoned Marx (except for his "Jewish" antisemitism)—flirt with a counter-Enlightenment so fundamentally alien to its self-proclaimed core value of human emancipation? I can still remember young French students chanting "We are all German Jews" in the streets of Paris in May 1968—their way of protesting against the Gaullists, the Communists, and police brutality. Today, such a march in the streets of Europe would be more likely to echo to calls of "Death to Israel," "End the Holocaust in Gaza," or "Hamas, Hamas, Jews to the Gas!" In such demonstrations, radical leftists frequently join hands with pro-Palestinian jihadists in their relentless campaign to defame, delegitimize and ultimately to destroy the Jewish State of Israel.

It is as if the Holocaust had never happened for much of the Left except as a cynically manipulated metaphor enabling it to brand Israel with the mark of Cain as *the* ultimate symbol of evil; as the "little Satan" carrying out the imperialist will of the "Great Satan" (America) or else as the conspiratorial mafia that determines U.S. foreign policy. For the European Left, still unhinged by the fall of Communism after 1989, anti-Americanism and anti-Zionism appear as the last two ideological pillars still standing in the debris of the collapsed Soviet Empire. When Leftists evoke America, nowadays they often mean "Jewish power"—"domination" of Hollywood, the media, high finance, the Congress, the Pentagon, and the White House by American Jewry. They are talking antisemitism, only now it is wrapped in the more politically correct euphemism of the "Zionist lobby." Even a "progressivist," more or less pro-Palestinian American President like Barack Obama, has not been able to escape the potency of such myths by which he, too, is judged. Anti-Americanism, like antisemitism, has truly become the "anti-imperialism" of fools.

This book is (among other things) an attempt to get to grips with the paranoid conspiracy-mongering on the Left, which invariably parades as a *humanitarian* endeavor and a compassionate defense of the "oppressed" or powerless against the might of the "Zionist-Crusader" axis. Already in

September 2001, there was a foregleam of the new century in Durban, South Africa. In the streets and in various forums one could hear chants of "One Jew, one bullet," voiced by leftist, Third Worldist, and Islamist advocates of the Palestinian cause at a UN-sponsored conference of NGOs. The UN event, ostensibly organized to condemn slavery, racism, hunger, and war, soon degenerated into an ugly hate-fest of the "new antisemitism." The "anti-racists" of the contemporary Left had found their *chosen* target by proclaiming what they have never ceased to do ever since—that there is only one "criminal" state in the whole world—and its name is Israel.

Thirty-five years ago it had been the Soviet Union (together with the Arab states) which initiated the UN Big Lie that Zionism-is-racism. Today there is no longer any need for a totalitarian Stalinist apparatus to perpetuate such a major moral and intellectual fraud. For it is "freedom-loving" intellectuals in the West (some of them Jews) who *voluntarily* lend their hands to the "anti-racist" masquerade which declares Israel to be an "apartheid State"—whose disappearance is *the* precondition for peace in the Middle East. On campuses throughout Britain and North America "Israel Anti-Apartheid Week"—often led by publicity-conscious Israeli and Jewish leftists—has now become an increasingly institutionalized fixture for spreading the "anti-Zionist" poison. So, too, have the continual leftist and Palestinian calls for the boycott of Israel in the scientific, technological, commercial, and academic spheres. All of this radical agitation is no longer directed at the "Christ-killers," the "Jewish usurers" of the Middle Ages, the Bourse Jews, or an inferior race of *Untermenschen,*" but against the so-called perpetrators of a (fictional) "genocide" against the Palestinians. Never mind that this grotesque libel is contradicted by all available empirical evidence, never mind that Israel is increasingly threatened by the genocidal antisemitism promoted by Iran, the Muslim Brotherhood, Hamas, Hezbollah, and the global jihad. Such minor details do not for one moment disturb the sleep of left-wing activists (including the Jews among them) whose "humanist" posture evidently does not extend to the idea that Israelis might also be victims. In truth, the Left today is a mere shadow of its former self— not least because it is so deeply mired in the muck of antisemitic lies and anti-Zionist delusions, many of them focused on the "monstrosity" of Israel as the most racist, fascist, and criminal state on earth. This book goes to the heart of what has become a serious mental derangement in the hope that it may help the Left (and others afflicted by the same malady) to regain their sanity.

This is no doubt an uphill struggle and the prospects of a cure may seem remote. On the other hand, the Arab world is currently in the midst of a historic revolutionary upheaval, which has exposed the emptiness of the claim (so often heard in the West) that Palestine is the eternal source of all unrest in the Middle East—for which Israel is predictably to blame. But the rising of the Arab citizenry against their corrupt and often tyrannical rulers—who have always used antisemitism as the "opium of the masses," proves exactly the opposite. Israel is *not* the real issue except for those driven by malice, bigotry, cynical self-interest, power-seeking, or an irrevocably distorted world-view. It is still far too early to say how the Arab revolutions of 2011 will finally play themselves out. Israel, as well as the West, certainly has serious grounds for concern at the possible negative fallout for its own security. Yet a ray of light has already pierced the thick propaganda barrage of anti-Israelism and antisemitism—whether it be Muslim, leftist, liberal, or neo-fascist in origin. Much will depend on whether this small window of hope can be extended or not.

The Islamist war against Israel (spearheaded by Iran) which is itself a war for expanding the global jihad would, if successful, ultimately endanger not only the existence of Israel but of civilization itself. It would also destroy any prospect of enhanced freedom or democracy for Palestine and the Arab world. At the same time, the defense of Israel's right to exist in peace and security is rapidly becoming a litmus-test of the boundaries between jihadists and democrats, extremists and moderates. By focusing attention so obsessively on the "sins" of Israel and its so-called crimes, most of the Left has completely missed the wider picture and will continue to condemn itself to irrelevance until or unless it awakens from its self-induced stupor.

Robert Solomon Wistrich
Jerusalem
11 March 2011

Acknowledgments

This book represents the closing of a circle after four decades of reflection about the complex interaction between Socialism and the Jews, the Jewish involvement in radical movements, and the phenomenon of antisemitism as well as anti-Zionism on the Left. It began exactly forty years ago, in 1971, when I started work on my doctoral dissertation at University College, London (UCL) under the supervision of Professor Chimen Abramsky. My doctorate dealt at some length with the "Jewish Question" in Central Europe before 1914 as seen through the prism of the German, Austrian, and Polish labor movements. It was completed in 1974 with the aid of a German Academic Exchange Scholarship (DAAD) and a stipendium from the Austrian Ministry for Science and Research. These grants enabled me to spend time at the Archives of the Friedrich-Ebert Stiftung in Bonn—Bad Godesberg, at the Institute of Social History (IISH) in Amsterdam, as well as examining many relevant sources in Vienna. Two years later I received an award from the British Academy which permitted an extensive stay in Paris to research the response of the French Left to the Dreyfus Affair. In the early 1980s, soon after my arrival in Israel, I extended my work to the examination of a wide range of Soviet materials relating to Israel and Zionism. Fortunately, I was able to benefit from the rich holdings of the Jewish National Library in Jerusalem and the Soviet and East European Research Centre at the Hebrew University as well as the Central Zionist Archives in Jerusalem. This was supplemented by several visits to New York (to the Yivo Institute and the Bund Archives), to the Leo Baeck Archives, and the Library of Congress in Washington, D.C. While holding the Jewish Chronicle Chair for Modern Jewish History at UCL in the 1990s, my forays continued at the IISH in Amsterdam, the Austrian National Library, the British Library in London, and the Bibliothèque Nationale in Paris.

After 2001, as Director of the Vidal Sassoon International Center for the Study of Antisemitism (SICSA) at the Hebrew University of Jerusalem, I became more oriented towards studying left-wing attitudes in the present towards Zionism and Israel. The last third of this book reflects that updated contemporary focus. Thanks to the assistance of the late Simon Wiesenthal, to Felix Posen, and also the Memorial Foundation for Jewish Culture in New York, I was able to pursue these researches to their completion. In that context it is a pleasure to thank the indefatigable Esther Rosenfeld and my much esteemed colleague Alifa Saadya for their typing and editorial skills. Without their help this huge labor might never have seen the light of day in its present form. My colleagues at SICSA, in particular Sara Grosvald, also deserve my thanks for tracking down some of the more elusive contemporary sources on the internet. I also want to acknowledge the following distinguished individuals with whom over the past forty years I discussed certain aspects of this subject. Some of them have since departed to another (hopefully better) world. In alphabetical order they include Hannah Arendt (New York), Pierre Birnbaum (Paris), Gerhard Botz (Linz), Julius Braunthal (London), Francis Carsten (London), Shmuel Ettinger (Jerusalem), Alain Finkielkraut (Paris), Bill Fishman (London), Jonathan Frankel (Jerusalem), Manfred Gerstenfeld (Jerusalem), Georges Haupt (Paris), Jeffrey Herf (Washington DC), Helmut Hirsch (Düsseldorf), Jack Jacobs (New York), James Joll (London), Annie Kriegel (Paris), Peter Loewenberg (Los Angeles), Susanne Miller (Bonn), George Mosse (Wisconsin), Fiamma Nirenstein (Rome), Arnold Paucker (London), Peter Pulzer (Oxford), Alvin Rosenfeld (Bloomington, Indiana), Boris Sapir (Amsterdam), Zeev Sternhell (Jerusalem), Pierre-André Taguieff (Paris), Jacob Talmon (Jerusalem), Jacques Tarnero (Paris), Shmuel Trigano (Paris), Feliks Tych (Warsaw), and Stephen J. Whitfield (Brandeis).

In the course of my research I have read sources in twelve different languages—English, French, German, Dutch, Italian, Spanish, Hebrew, Yiddish, Czech, Polish, Ukrainian, and Russian. That has been no easy task and took years of diligent study and endurance. I do not believe that such a *comprehensive* study of this historical phenomenon has been previously attempted in a global perspective. I present it to the scholarly and general public in the belief that it will illuminate the fascinating, though often painful encounter between Jews, Zionism, and the radical Left.

Robert Solomon Wistrich
The Hebrew University of Jerusalem
6 March 2011

Introduction
Jews, Zion, and Revolution

For approximately thirty years after the end of the Second World War there was a widespread belief that antisemitism and the "Jewish Question" were things of the past. After Auschwitz, a repetition of the murderous Jew-hatred of the Nazis and their European collaborators seemed inconceivable. The "antifascist" consensus in Europe appeared solid. A "post-national" European community claimed to have learned the lessons of history and to be shaping its postwar identity in opposition to the evils of Nazism and fascism.[1] To the extent that antisemitism still existed it was treated somewhat condescendingly as an obsolescent relic of the European far Right and its imitators on other continents. In recent decades, however, it has become apparent that antisemitism has assumed multiple new forms and adopted a new "anti-Zionist" discourse, which owes much of its inspiration to the Left and its view of the conflict in the Middle East, to pro-Palestinian propaganda and the formidable rise of militant Islam.[2] Moreover, as I have indicated elsewhere, the proposition that Jew-hatred seriously declined after 1945 is itself largely a myth.[3] Antisemitism has been intensely active across the Arab world for the past sixty years, was revived as a political weapon in the Soviet-dominated Communist bloc after 1948 and has found many echoes (direct and indirect) in the western democracies since the Second World War. Today it is no longer expressed primarily in the form of a direct assault upon the rights of Jews to live as equal members of the non-Jewish societies which they inhabit. Rather, the "new" antisemitism involves the denial of the rights of the Jewish people to live as an equal member within the family of nations. In that sense contemporary antisemitism above all targets Israel as the "collective Jew" among the nations.

In this book we are primarily concerned with the Left and its complex history of interaction with the Jews since the emergence of modern socialism in the 1830s. We intend to show that in its early history the European Left (especially in France and Germany) was profoundly antisemitic as part of its atheistic critique of religion and its populist anti-capitalism. Judaism was essentially treated as a fossil; its concept of "chosenness" denounced as an absurdly egoistic form of "separatism"; Jews were accused of misanthropy, fanaticism, and inveterate opposition to science and progress. Their religion was deemed to be trivial, clannish, and utterly "non-historical"—"utilitarian" in the narrowest sense and well suited to the exploitation of other peoples. Jews were a "phantom" people—usurious, avaricious, and materialistic, who had become influential through the power of money. For the early 19th-century socialists—like some of their Enlightenment and Young Hegelian forerunners—Judaism stood, therefore, beyond the pale of human development. It was backward, ethnocentric, vengeful, and obstinately reactionary in its rejection of universal "progress.[4]

Some of these negative stereotypes have revived in more contemporary leftist claims that Judaism is intrinsically *racist,* that Zionists eagerly collaborated with the Nazis, that Israel itself is a "Nazi State," or that a sinister Jewish/Israeli lobby currently dominates world politics. Left-wingers like the crusading journalist John Pilger write with unmitigated hatred of "the Biblio-ethnic cleansers in Israel"; Nobel Prize laureate, the late José Saramago (a veteran Portuguese Communist), denounced Judaism's "monstrous doctrines"—which are "racist not just against the Palestinians, but against the entire world, and which it seeks to manipulate and abuse."[5] Jostein Gaarder, the Norwegian author, writing in 2006, insisted like Saramago that Jewish doctrines of "election" or "chosenness" were inherently racist; and that Israel's actions against the Palestinians meant it had forfeited its right to exist.[6] This is a typical offshoot of the new form of antisemitism which negates the Jewish right to an independent national existence.

On the left (and in parts of the European liberal mainstream) it has become almost *de rigueur* to vilify Zionism (the national liberation movement of the Jewish people) as a *criminal* project without the slightest proof or on the flimsiest of evidence. These denunciations often come from the same people who claim to be humanists, to repudiate (right-wing) antisemitism much as they do racism, nationalism, war-mongering, power politics, and Auschwitz.[7] They think they have overcome this apparent contradiction of being "anti-racist" and discriminating *against* Israel, by almost exclusively projecting the evils of racism on the tiny Jewish State and its main protector, the United States of America. At the same time, in the name of progressive "anti-racism" the anti-Zionist Left inexcusably rationalizes Islamist terror, Palestinian suicide bombers, genocidal Iranian threats against Israel, and antisemitic attacks by Muslim immigrants on Jewish targets in Europe or on other continents.

Some of the most extreme anti-Zionist vitriol today undoubtedly has its origins among the Israeli and Diasporic Jewish ultra-Left. Many in this group of "critics" have embraced an ideology that obstinately rejects the right of the Jewish people to self-determination and statehood, while blindly accepting the excesses of Palestinian integralist or fundamentalist nationalism as well as the Palestinian "right of return."[8] The anti-Zionist Israeli left, in particular, seeks not only to *de-Judaize* and *de-Zionize* the State of Israel but systematically vilifies and demonizes it. For them (and their many allies abroad) anti-Zionism is purely political and supposedly devoid of any trace of antisemitism.[9] Factually this is simply not true. The effects of "anti-Zionist" actions such as the attempted boycott of Israeli academics, universities, and commerce are exclusionary, racist, and discriminatory towards Jews. Actions designed intentionally to cause real damage to Israeli citizens and the Jewish people can hardly qualify as mere "criticism"; nor can the mendacious attempt to brand Israel as an illegitimate criminal entity even worse than apartheid South Africa be considered as legitimate criticism. The advocacy by a broad section of the contemporary Left of such *defamatory* propositions is a betrayal of its own egalitarian principles and supposed respect for democratic values. Worse still, by identifying with Islamist organizations like Hamas or Hezbollah which advocate and act upon an openly *annihilatory* form of antisemitism, radical leftists have in effect become complicit in what is a symbolic form of genocide.

There is an especially bitter irony in the fact that large sections of the Left today should have become so infected with anti-Jewishness as well as being anti-Zionist. For if we cast our minds back a century ago, we would see not only that Jews played a major role in the emergence of modern Socialism but that the Jewish world was itself permeated by socialist influences. A left-wing political culture forged by the Russian-Jewish intelligentsia and radical youth together with educated, politically conscious Jewish workers spread in the late 19th century from the Tsarist Empire to America, Britain, France, Argentina, and other diaspora communities. At a popular level, the Yiddish language was its lingua franca, the clothing industry and sweatshop its economic base, trade-union politics, ideologically committed socialist parties and self-defense units its hallmarks. This pattern also extended to the Ottoman backwater of early 20th-century Palestine where Jewish socialism would, however, develop in a Hebrew-speaking agricultural context. In this book I have reconstructed some of these debates among Jewish radicals before 1917, who were seeking a new identity based on a synthesis of secular Jewish nationalism and socialism. This was an unusually restless energetic generation of radical Jewish youth torn between the prospect of socialist revolution in Russia, mass emigration abroad (especially to America), the settlement of Zion as a national goal, and the fight for cultural autonomy in Europe. It is simply not possible to understand either the roots or the huge impact of the Bolshevik Revolution and the establishment of Israel on Jewish life without knowledge of this crucial formative period.[10]

Modern Socialism, whose initial raison d'être was the overthrow of capitalism, owed much, as we will show, to militant Jews who were among its initial creators, leading practitioners, and most fervent apostles. Jewish intellectuals, in particular, brought to the Socialist ranks their acute critical intelligence, unabashed rationalism, devotion to justice, and high ethical ideals.[11] As outsiders, who suffered intensely from the *numerus clausus* (especially in Russia and eastern Europe), it was natural enough for upwardly aspiring Jews to contest the semi-feudal Christian established order. Their carefully cultivated aptitude for mental gymnastics made them as well equipped for jousting in Marxist or Freudian theoretical debates as for excelling in the stock exchange wars of the era. Their secularized heritage of Hebraic messianism enabled Jewish intellectuals to provide a new sense of urgency to the fashionable liberal ideals of modern Progress.[12]

The American sociologist, Thorstein Veblen, writing in 1919 about the "intellectual preeminence of Jews in modern Europe," discerned its secret in the ability to break free of dogmatic religious tradition and the dead weight of the past. Jews, he observed, were inveterate disturbers of the intellectual peace, insatiable wanderers "in the intellectual no-man's-land"; their main advantage lay precisely in their homelessness, rootlessness and lack of patriotic attachments.[13] However, Zionism (which aimed to "cure" Jewry of its pathological *wanderlust*) would mean, according to Veblen, the end of this striking intellectual dominance. Socialism, he forgot to add, was no less determined than Zionism to lay Ahasverus ("the wandering Jew") to rest in the Promised Land of "fraternal" internationalism. Nor could Veblen anticipate the brutal pathology of Hitler's National Socialism which sought to simultaneously smash liberal capitalism, Bolshevism, and modern urban civilization by killing off millions of European Jews in a scientifically planned, cold-blooded "Final Solution." Hitler was an ultra-nationalist socialist who learned a great deal from Marxism including organizational techniques, propaganda methods, the need for a coherent world-view, and the imperative of obtaining mass support.

Hitler's utopian vision of the *Volksgemeinschaft* (people's community) combined Marxian collectivism with pre-capitalist *völkisch* myths into what he believed was a true German Socialism. State control and a planned economy would be achieved without civil war on the Leninist-Stalinist model; without destroying the entrepreneurial spirit or individual initiative. National Socialism consciously aimed to transform the German people into a real community without leveling down or completely wiping out the existing social order and its class divisions. At the same time, Nazism was an unmistakably *militarized* socialism in which racial ideology and antisemitism were absolutely integral elements. In August 1920, speaking in Munich, Hitler declared: "If we are socialists, then we must definitely be anti-Semites—and the opposite, in that case, is Materialism and Mammonism, which we seek to oppose."[14] German National Socialism was an anti-Jewish mutation of the socialist idea which the European Left was singularly ill-equipped to confront.

Jewish radicals, whether because of or despite repeated waves of racial antisemitism, often embraced modern Socialism or Communism with the fervour of neophytes, eager to throw off the unwanted residues of an anachronistic tribal past. Not for them the limited horizons of blood, soil, tribe, the "organic community," the fatherland, or an antiquated religious faith. Nor would they be content with the material satisfactions of bourgeois liberalism, which in the 19th and early 20th centuries had often seemed like the most promising of all "Jewish" options for the future. The liberal system did indeed offer individual liberty, the rule of law, the intellectual appeal of Reason, science, and enlightenment. It also conjured up for a time the seductive dream of painless assimilation and a new civic religion predominantly based on human rights which would definitively disregard the claims of blood, descent, and aristocratic privilege.[15] But secular liberalism also had serious drawbacks, not least of which (especially in East-Central Europe) was its unavoidable "Jewish" colouring and the antisemitic *ressentiment* that it swiftly brought in its wake. In fin-de-siècle Europe, "progressive" liberalism had already become far too "cosmopolitan" for the taste of increasingly nationalistic middle-class strata whose status was threatened from within and without.

Socialism, at least, appeared after 1900 to propose a way out of this impasse for many aspiring and educated Jewish professionals. They were generally middle-class themselves, yet also conscious of the subtle discrimination which they still suffered. Jewish woes, so they felt, should be subsumed in seeking to correct the broader injustice of a class-divided society. By the turn of the 20th century, Socialism—along with Nationalism—had clearly emerged as one of the dominant charismatic ideologies of the New Age. This was a decisive period when the Jewish intelligentsia and an emerging Jewish proletariat (especially in Russia) sought ways to synthesize the ethical Socialist ideal with their own version of Jewish nationalism—Zionist and non-Zionist.[16] The hybrid national socialisms of this pre–First World War "age of innocence," it should be stressed, did not yet have the sinister connotations they would later acquire. Rather they could best be seen as a brave effort to resolve the deep fissures in secular Jewish identity—personal or collective—provoked by the stresses of the modernization process itself and the breakdown of tradition.

Nationalism—increasingly exclusivist, organic, and *völkisch* by the turn of the 20th century—began to pose an acute dilemma for many Jews. In the West it offered the hope of social integration for patriotic Jewish citizens who passionately identified with their recently adopted homelands. But in its blood-and-soil incarnation, nationalism inevitably tended to exclude Jews as *the* strangers par excellence. Socialism, too, was not immune to the Janus-face of modern nationalism. It remained hostile towards most immigrant ethnic and religious minorities, often advocating economic protectionism in favor of the native working-class. The nationalist varieties of socialism were rarely empathetic towards "cosmopolitan" Jews. On the other hand, international socialism also had its Achilles heel, denying any legitimacy to Jews *as* Jews—looking instead to a classless future where "the Jews will have become *impossible*" (Marx).

The Jewish participation in Communism, Socialism, and revolutionary movements—whether as theoreticians, teachers, parliamentarians, journalists, orators, or propagandists—is still a controversial and sensitive issue in some parts of the world. It is also an incontrovertible fact. István Deák once noted that in Weimar Germany, "Jews were responsible for a great part of leftist literature" in their capacity as publishers, editors, intellectuals, or journalists.[17] They played "a decisive role in the pacifist and feminist movements, and in the campaigns for sexual enlightenment." Not for the first or last time "Jews created the left-wing intellectual movement" whether it was in Germany in the 1920s, in Soviet Russia, Hungary or in the United States and France forty years later.[18] The "critical theorists" of the Frankfurt School (Theodor Adorno, Max Horkheimer, Erich Fromm, Walter Benjamin, Herbert Marcuse, and others) all came from German-Jewish bourgeois families.[19] However, their skeptical, elitist theories which tried to combine Marx and Freud, lacked any strong social base or transformational dynamic in the context of Weimar Germany. They were also curiously reluctant to discuss their own Jewishness or to go beyond a highly psychologized view of antisemitism as a "delusion" or "projection" of modern false consciousness. Horkheimer, who came from a conservative upper-middle-class Jewish background, had already moved towards socialism as a young man, during the abortive Communist revolution of 1918–19 in Munich. Influenced by German idealist philosophy as well as by Marx, Horkheimer pioneered Critical Theory at the Frankfurt Institute in the early 1930s. At that time he was still convinced that Socialism would sweep away the "relics" of antisemitism. No specialized therapy would therefore be required. Evidently, Horkheimer and his circle—armed with their socialist dogmas—had no feelings of insecurity regarding their own ethnic descent, even as late as 1932. The "Jewish" aspect of the Hitlerian menace was, in fact, grossly underestimated by them. Only in 1939, when he was already well established in New York, did Max Horkheimer finally address the issue of antisemitism in an essay called "Die Juden und Europa" (The Jews and Europe). Horkheimer now claimed that Fascism/Nazism was the "legitimate" heir to "liberalistic" society which had bred it. Moreover, he added that he "who does not want to talk of capitalism should also remain silent about Fascism"—which later became a favorite slogan of the 1968 West German student revolt. Horkheimer was extraordinarily harsh about his fellow German-Jewish refugees, implying that they deserved their fate for courting the powers of reaction "as long as they were not too openly anti-Semitic." Jews were now paying the price for having identified with an unjust social system.[20] Horkheimer would substantially modify such views in the late 1940s, while working with Adorno and others, on the pathbreaking *Studies in Prejudice* series in America that gave birth to *The Authoritarian Personality*. After his return to West German academia in the 1950s, he also found his way back to a "reborn" Judaism. Abandoning his earlier opposition to Zionism, he even expressed a qualified solidarity with the State of Irael as a necessary refuge for a homeless and traumatized people.

Horkheimer's "critical theory" seems in retrospect like a perfect reflection of Jewish social marginality and spiritual restlessness during the interwar years. Undoubtedly the social psychology of borderline existences did play a role in Jewish radicalism, much as they did in academia, journalism, and the liberal professions. Adaptability, mobility, intellectual agility, a gift for abstract thought, and the sense of being social outsiders were obviously factors potentially conducive not only to scholarly or business success but also to the Jewish affinity for socialism or Communism. The question of messianism is more controversial. Nicholas Berdyaev stressed, for example, the Hebraic messianic element in Judaism itself—which aspired to implement the Kingdom of God *on earth.* Socialism had simply transmuted this characteristic (according to Berdyaev) into worldlier channels in modern times. What Isaiah and the prophets of Israel had envisioned more than 2000 years ago—a universal reign of social justice and the definitive overcoming of evil—had been renewed through the secular Marxist dream of collective redemption. Only this time, the messianic idea had been transferred by Marx from the Jews (as God's chosen people) to the industrial proletariat as History's chosen class.[21] Much as the Jewish "apostate" followers of Jesus Christ had once sought to theologically *internationalize* God, so Marx and Trotsky had done the same for secular history in constructing the Communist utopia.[22] But neither Christ nor Marx could in practice succeed in expelling "the moneylenders" from the Temple. Analogies to Berdyaev's messianic view of Biblical Judaism can also be found in the writings of some Jewish anarchists like the French Dreyfusard Bernard Lazare or Gustav Landauer, the short-lived commissar of culture in the Munich Soviet republic—murdered by counter-revolutionary forces in 1919. For the martyred Landauer, Judaism itself contained the seeds of permanent Revolution and the exiled Jews were destined "to be the Messiah of the nations."

A Hebraic prophetism, derived from the Old Testament, did undoubtedly influence some modern Jewish radicals as it had the German Anabaptists of the Protestant Reformation or Cromwell's Puritan revolutionaries in 17th-century England.[23] In a more subtle sense, one might perhaps add that there was also a *post-biblical* "Talmudic style" of disputation over the meaning of canonical texts—their commentary and interpretation—which often re-appears in the work of "Jewish" radicals. This hair-splitting quality sometimes found in the writings of Communist ideologues of Jewish background can, however, be exaggerated. Easier to demonstrate is the youthful social revolt of Jewish sons and daughters against the tribal patriarchal and commercial world of their fathers. There were those like the famous literary critic Georg Lukaçs (later an orthodox Stalinist) who rebelled in Budapest around 1910 against his wealthy banking family and its close ties to the Habsburg Empire and official Hungary.[24] There was the intellectually outstanding Rosa Luxemburg, growing up in Tsarist-ruled Warsaw, who felt constantly embarrassed by her parents' petty-bourgeois tastes and self-evident Jewishness.[25] The Frankfurt Marxist Leo Löwenthal also reacted sharply in Weimar Germany against what he termed the "shoddy liberalism, shoddy *Aufklärung* (Enlightenment), and double standards" of his own family environment.[26] Then there was the anarchist leader of the American Yippie movement in the late 1960s, Jerry Rubin, who had this to say about his

Jewish background, growing up in a country (America) which he liked to spell with a "K" in order to better "Nazify" it:

> I know it [Jewishness] made me feel like a minority or outsider in Amerika from my birth and helped me become a revolutionary."[27]

Such examples are legion in the biographies of children from upwardly mobile Jewish families who became radicalized—whether in backward Tsarist Russia, middle-class Central Europe or ultra-modern affluent America.

A different kind of revolt against the world of their fathers (still stuck in the Russian or East European shtetls) led directly to the Hebrew-based revolutionary nationalism of the Zionist socialists.[28] They were secularists driven by a quasi-religious pioneering fervor to transform the "Promised Land" into a Jewish "national home." The essence of the Zionist Revolution in their eyes was to turn Diaspora Jews away from their traditional middlemen occupations or petty commerce into becoming primary producers on the land. They revolted against the bourgeois cult of individual success in favor of building up a *national* society. From a condition of virtual powerlessness they aspired to one where Jews could again become sovereign masters of their own fate. In the Zionist socialist dispensation, this drive for Jewish national self-determination had a *pioneering* dimension that demanded physical rootedness in the land of Zion (Palestine). Zionism was intended to be a social, spiritual and political revolution against the very condition of Jewish Exile, against the predominant current of Jewish history for 2,000 years and against the "yoke of the Gentiles." Only by redeeming the Jewish people in their own homeland could Jews hope to "normalize" their status among the nations and fully participate in transforming the destiny of mankind.[29] From A. D. Gordon, Nachman Syrkin, and Ber Borochov to David Ben-Gurion, the Labour Zionists saw Jewish *national rebirth* as the core-aim of their socialism; it could only be achieved, however, by a socio-economic and psychological self-transformation. Even a Marxist Zionist like Borochov insisted that proletarian internationalism would have to pass through the crucible of Hebrew nationalism, if it was ever to achieve its aims. Jewish involvement in the universal class-struggle would forever remain a fiction as long as the Jewish people lacked its own national framework and soil under its feet.[30]

Nevertheless, before the First World War Russian Zionists (the numerically strongest section of the worldwide Zionist movement) found it difficult to compete with Bundism—a Yiddish-speaking Marxism which aimed its agitation at the "Jewish street" in the Russian Pale of Settlement.[31] Zionists felt even more blocked by the growing Russification of Jewish youth which seemed to be leading as early as 1900 towards world revolution rather than the Zionist national cause. The young Chaim Weizmann anxiously reported to Theodor Herzl in 1903 that

> almost all those now being victimized [by Tsarism] in the entire Social Democratic movement are Jews, and their number grows every day. They are not necessarily young people of proletarian origin; they also come from well-to-do families, and incidentally not infrequently from Zionist families.[32]

Through revolutionary conviction, a large part of this Russian-Jewish younger generation (according to Weizmann) had already become *anti-Zionist*. He deplored this "mass-sacrifice" of Jews on the altar of the Russian revolutionary movements. It was a trend that had begun in the Jewish fold and had already consumed "much Jewish energy and heroism." But in their attitude to Jewish nationalism, revolutionary Jews displayed "antipathy, swelling at times to fanatical hatred."[33] The young Weizmann bitterly noted that the "children are in open revolt against their parents." This was a pattern that had significantly increased with the rise of Russian Marxism in the 1890s. But even in the 1870s and 1880s Jews had already made up around 20% of the activists in the radical Populist (People's Will) movement.[34]

As Chaim Weizmann's comments suggest, Jewish radicalism in Russia (and elsewhere) involved a rejection not only of autocratic Tsarism and of parental authority but also of Jewishness itself. The embrace of internationalism meant the repudiation of tradition, religion, Jewish family attachments, "petty-bourgeois "acquisitiveness" (Trotsky), or what Marx had contemptuously derided as "practical, real Judaism" (haggling). Jews clearly did not fit into the traditional Orthodox Christian society of Imperial Russia and (as yet) they still lacked a strong ethnic nationalism of their own. Hence, social revolution around 1900 appeared as a particularly attractive option. The pervasiveness of antisemitism among Tsarist officialdom, in the native middle class and the Russian peasant masses, further reinforced Jewish motivation. Jewish urban commercial skills and their status as perennial "strangers," to quote Anatoly Lunacharsky (Bolshevik commissar for education)—made Jews both a "natural target" of Russian hatred and transformed them into "instinctive" revolutionaries.[35] This view was broadly shared by Lenin, whose maternal grandfather happened to be Jewish—a tightly-kept state secret in the Soviet Union—though constantly asserted by antisemites and anti-Communists around the world. Lenin was on record as admiring the tenacity, smartness and "progressive" outlook of the Jews with whom he surrounded himself—so unlike the boorish, "thick-skulled" Russian or Ukrainian peasants.[36]

Even more than Lenin, the outstanding Russian proletarian writer, Maxim Gorky, highlighted this binary opposition very explicitly. The Jew was "almost always a better worker than the Russian" and invested more passion in his labor. He was a far "better European" and "culturally superior to, and more beautiful than, the Russians." According to the philosemitic Gorky, the anarchic Russians were drowning in alcoholism, "in the swamp of oriental stagnation" and primitive brutality, whereas the Jews were endowed with a "heroic idealism," energy, enthusiasm and drive for "the tireless pursuit of truth." Maxim Gorky openly glorified the Jews as the only force capable of releasing Promethean energies in the somnolent and slothful Russians. In his eyes, Jews had unquestionably been "the greatest revolutionaries in history"; they constituted "the old, thick yeast of humanity" constantly stirring noble ideas and "inspiring people to seek a better life."[37] Antisemitic antipathy to Jews ultimately arose from the envious realization of sluggish, self-satisfied Russians and Ukrainians that the Jew "is obviously better, more dexterous, and more capable than they are."[38]

Jews would indeed play an important role in the Bolshevik Revolution of 1917. At the first All-Russian Congress of Soviets nearly one-third of Bolshevik delegates were Jews; at the Bolshevik Central Committee meeting that voted on 23 October 1917 to carry out an armed rising, Jews made up five out of the twelve members present. Three out of the seven Politbureau members (Trotsky, Zinoviev, Sokolnikov) who led the uprising were Jewish. So, too, were the first two heads of the Soviet State, Lev Kamenev and Yaacov Sverdlov. Kamenev also ran the Moscow Party, while Zinoviev was the first President of the Communist International and Bolshevik Party chief in Petrograd. According to Yuri Slezkine, over 50% of leading Party officials in Petrograd in 1918 were Jews, as well as 45% of city and provincial Bolshevik officials. In Moscow, in 1923, the figures were not much different. Jews made up 29 percent of the Bolshevik "leading cadres." At that time Jews also represented 15 percent of all leading secret police officials and half of the top echelon of the Cheka Secretariat.[39] If that were not enough, many of the leading non-Jewish Bolsheviks (including Bukharin, Dzierżyńnski, Lunacharsky, Kirov, Rykov, Voroshilov, and Molotov) were married to Jewish women.

The bloody Russian Civil War would greatly exacerbate use of "Judeo-Bolshevism" as an antisemitic trope not only by the White counter-revolutionaries but by conservatives and nationalists across the globe. The notion that Jews were the backbone of the Communist Party, the Soviet state, and the world-revolutionary project would become a major demagogic slogan in Hitler's Germany, Fascist Italy, Francoist Spain, and in various Catholic authoritarian regimes throughout the interwar period. It gave new life to the Tsarist antisemitic fabrication, *The Protocols of the Elders of Zion,* about a Jewish plan for world conquest. It inspired incitement against Jews from the paranoid effusions of industrialist Henry Ford in America to the annihilationist rhetoric of Haj Amin al-Husseini, leader of the Arab national movement in Palestine. Long before the post-Communist hysteria of the 1990s, Jews were held responsible for all Bolshevik "crimes against humanity, for the Red Terror, the Soviet Gulag, and "genocide" against the Russian people.[40] The prominence of individual Bolshevik Jews like Leon Trotsky at the head of the Red Army and the unprecedented entry of Jews into the institutions of the Soviet State, provoked endless antisemitic diatribes —especially *outside* the U.S.S.R. Linking Jews with the Russian revolution and its worldwide repercussions, made the myriad enemies of Communism in the West feel greatly empowered. The fact that virtually all Jewish revolutionaries had ostentatiously left their Jewishness behind, was totally irrelevant to antisemites whether past or present.

In Soviet Russia itself, the official ideology proclaimed that Communism was determined to abolish *all* racial, religious, and class distinctions; and that it had definitively *solved* the "Jewish Question" through economic and national equality. At the same time, the Bolsheviks (especially Jewish Communist officials in the Yevsektsiia) insisted that their fight to uproot Jewish tradition, religion, patriarchy, and all other residues of the *shtetl,* was indispensable both to achieving full assimilation and the Communist goal of a classless society. When viewed from this perspective, Palestinocentric Zionism seemed like an abomination to the Yevsketsiia; yet in the 1920s and 1930s labor Zionism had some resemblances to the Soviet experiment. It, too, sought to create a new world and a New Man, on a secular collectivist basis—only this time in Palestine. There was the same incorrigible romanticism, a sense of youthful adventure, pioneering on the land, a cult of muscular virility, and a veritable worship of manual labor. Both Communism and Zionism idealized the conquest of nature, advocated revolutionary Puritanism, and promoted the spirit of group self-sacrifice in the name of a higher ideal.[41] The Zionist effort in Palestine was, of course, on a much smaller scale than in Soviet Russia and had to confront an antagonistic Palestinian Arab national movement which sought to completely destroy the project from birth. Before 1948, moreover, the Zionist movement was still dependent on the British Mandatory Power, whose policies after 1939 had become increasingly hostile to its objectives. Nevertheless, the socialist Zionist experiment (carried out in the *kibbutzim* and through the trade unions) achieved some remarkable successes without any of the bloodstained purges or calculated state terrorism that irremediably blighted the Stalinist revolution from above.

However, on the eve of the Second World War, such a conclusion would still have seemed premature to many observers. In the Soviet Union, Jews were not yet subject to persecution or discrimination; and they were the most educated "nationality" within the Communist State. Though less than 2% of the total Soviet population in 1939, Jews made up 17 percent of all university students in Moscow, 19 percent in Leningrad, and just over 35% in Kiev.[42] Thanks to their remarkable literacy rates, and political loyalty, they still constituted a core element of the Soviet bureaucracy. In Leningrad on the eve of World War II, Jews were as prominent in the "liberal" professions as they had once been in pre-Hitler Central Europe. Jews in the city represented 69% of all dentists, 58% of all pharmacists, 39% of all doctors, 35% of all legal consultants, 31% of all writers, journalists, and editors, as well as 18% of all university professors and scientists. They stood at the apex of the cultural elite in Moscow and Leningrad, not least among the literary or artistic avant-garde. In fields like chess and classical music, Jews were often among the most celebrated of all the Soviet maestros.[43] For many members of the new Soviet Jewish intelligentsia, this still seemed like a time of revolutionary hope.

To this success story we must add the extraordinarily heroic role played by Soviet Jews in the Red Army during the fierce battles of the Great Patriotic War (1941–1945). Half a million Soviet Jewish soldiers fought the Nazis and 40 percent died in combat—the highest percentage of all the U.S.S.R.'s ethnic groups. Nevertheless there were warning signs even in 1939 of a negative shift in Soviet policy towards the Jews. Maxim Litvinov (one of the Old Guard Jewish Bolsheviks) was replaced in May 1939 as Foreign Minister by Molotov—a signal of the coming rapprochement with Hitler Germany. In the top echelon of the NKVD (secret police) by 1939 there were only 4 percent of Jews compared to 38 percent only a few years earlier. During the war years, too, the Soviet government—aware of Nazi antisemitic propaganda and hostility to Jews among different nationalities in the U.S.S.R.—chose to play down or ignore the unique dimensions of the Holocaust.

The assault on the Jewish position in the cultural elite intensified in 1949 with the campaign against "rootless cosmopolitans" in the theater and literature. A year earlier, Stalin had begun to wage a parallel war against Zionism and Jewish bourgeois nationalism. Though supporting the establishment of Israel, he did not let up on his determination to purge the ranks of Soviet Jewry of all those he deemed to have "dual loyalties." Antisemitism—in the form of "anti-Zionism"—became for the first time around 1950 a legitimate official tool of Soviet Communist domestic and foreign policy. From being an *anti-antisemitic* State in the early 1930s, the USSR would henceforth steadily turn into a powerhouse for the new-style anti-Jewishness and delegitimation of the Jewish homeland. This was linked to the fact that by the early 1970s Soviet internationalist ideology had begun to irrevocably crumble. The failed leap into Communism had produced only crude efforts at Russification and a xenophobic ethnic nationalism that literally oozed with vulgar antisemitism. For the first time in Soviet history, Jews found themselves unequivocally attacked as *ethnic* outsiders and "alien" elements. The "grand alliance" between Communism, Jewish revolutionaries, and the Soviet State had finally come to an end. Stalin proved after 1945 to be its pioneering gravedigger. Khrushchev and Brezhnev completed his work. In this new post-Shoah reality, many Jews—from America to Palestine—were also belatedly cooling their past enthusiasm for Communism. Significantly, in the United States during the 1950s, a democratic liberalism sometimes mixed with a suitably diluted Freudianism began to supplant the fashionable Marxist credo so prevalent among an earlier generation of Jewish intellectuals.

The drawn-out death-agonies of Soviet communism did not, however, mean the end of Jewish radicalism as a motivating ideology. It would revive again towards the end of the 1960s especially in Argentina, France, and the United States where young Jewish radicals became prominent in *gauchiste* (leftist) movements—whether Trotskyist, Maoist, anarchist, or new Leftist. Initially they were often split over the conflict between Israel and the Arab countries and were especially divided by the Palestinian question. Some even championed unconditionally the cause of the Palestinian guerrillas as part of their "fraternal" internationalist sympathy for the oppressed masses of the underdeveloped countries. Like the rest of the White New Left, the PLO, Third Worldists, and black radicals, they attacked Zionism as a reactionary tool of Western imperialism and Israel as a stooge for American domination in the Middle East. Anti-Zionism soon became an integral part of this anti-American New Leftist outlook. In Argentina, a significant number of the Jewish revolutionary youth from the late 1960s openly supported some version of "Third World Marxism," "revolutionary Peronism," or Palestinian organizations like Al-Fatah. Unlike North America, there were virtually no organized frameworks in which radical pro-Zionist Argentine Jews could find a place within the new Left.

In the United States, some of the more radical Jewish students during the 1960s unreservedly identified with Third World causes—with the iconic Che Guevara and the Cuban Revolution under Fidel Castro, with the Vietnamese Communists, or with indigenous American Indians and rebellious Afro-Americans in their own country. They opposed what they saw as an arrogant "fascistic" American Empire, despised rampant Western materialism and felt increasingly alienated from their own affluent Jewish middle-class *milieux*. In France, the red-haired anarchist leader of the 1968 student revolt, Daniel Cohn-Bendit, typically defined himself as "neither French nor German, Jewish or non-Jewish"—adopting a hybrid and provocatively "rootless" internationalist identity.[44] More than half of the key leaders in the Parisian revolt were indeed of Jewish descent—*gauchistes* who could perhaps be considered as existential or involuntary Jews in the Sartrian sense—their identities defined by the "anti-Semitic other."[45]

There were also maverick individuals like the anarchist revolutionary, Pierre Goldman who had been imprisoned in France on charges of armed robbery. The son of Polish-Jewish antifascist rebels (he was assassinated by French neo-Nazis in 1979), Goldman—*unlike* many of his comrades on the far Left in France—supported Israel's right to exist. Shortly before his murder he stated in an interview: "To be Jewish is to convey the past. And why is this so important? Because of anti-Semitism, because of the hatred. The only answer to the question of what it means to be a Jew is Auschwitz. The Holocaust has renewed Jewish identity for centuries."[46] Goldman despised the playacting rebels of the 1968 Parisian student revolt, some of whom openly identified with the "liquidationist" anti-Zionism of al-Fatah. Their heirs today seem, at times, no less determined than the Palestinian Hamas to see an end to the State of Israel.[47] They have focused much of their energy on a relentless anti-Israel boycott movement in academia and within the trade unions, which has achieved some success, particularly in Great Britain. These "new" anti-Zionists indignantly deny that their pro-boycott position has anything to do with antisemitism. They insistently claim that this accusation is itself an act of bad faith, a means of deflecting criticism from Israel. They are quite unable to see anything discriminatory in their compulsive singling out of Israel for vilification while glossing over massive and infinitely graver human rights abuses like the Arab-Islamist genocide of black Africans in Darfur.[48] For such radical Leftists, double standards, moral blindness, and self-righteous narcissism appear to have become a way of life. The illegal Turkish occupation of Northern Cyprus, mass rapes in the Congo, the tyrannical rule of Mugabe in Zimbabwe, the repression in Iran, Chinese imperialism in Tibet, or Muslims slaughtering fellow Muslims in Iraq are totally unimportant in comparison with the "crimes" of Israeli occupation.

Left-wing antisemitism is *not* a new phenomenon as I have documented at considerable length throughout the first third of this book. It is, however, a neglected issue which has revived today through the constantly proliferating anti-Zionist discourse which includes vociferous calls for excluding Israel and the demand that Jews must dissociate themselves from the Jewish State if they wish to be part of "progressive mankind." Conspiracy theories, too, which endlessly fantasize about "Jewish power" or secret Jewish lobbies that control America and Western governments more generally, are also back in vogue on the contemporary Left.[49] As with the Rothschild myth in the 19th century, the current trend on the anti-Zionist Left presupposes the existence of powerful shadowy forces in the democratic West, manipulating the financial strings which supposedly guarantee Jewish Zionist power in the international arena. In this rapidly mushrooming conspiracy literature there appears to be no limit to the insidiously manipulative and all-pervasive influence of the "Zionist lobby" which purportedly controls the mass media and world politics.[50] The "anti-racist" leftists who repeat such hoary myths about the Jewish "Hidden Hand" obviously regard the Zionist State as wholly illegitimate. Its iniquity and essential wickedness are as self-evident to them as was the "cursed" condition of the Jewish people in medieval Christian demonology. At bottom, the State of Israel, whatever its borders or political complexion, is perceived by many so-called critics as at best a "historical mistake" to be rectified or at worst as an intolerable and cancerous presence in the region. In the rhetoric of the current Iranian leadership, of Hezbollah and Hamas, the "Zionist entity" must be definitively cut out like a "racist tumor" in the Middle East. Radical Leftists who sympathize with militant Islam appear to take this genocidal language about the State of Israel all-too-easily in their stride.

There are also icons of the contemporary Left like the famous Greek composer Mikis Theodorakis, who claim to be "friends of Israel" even as they, too, deride its "evil stubbornness" and self-importance. Sly, masochistic, exploiting their "victimhood" to dominate and control, the Jews have, according to Theodorakis, embraced Fascism in the name of their Biblical chosenness. Their superiority complex and cultural dominance have led them (especially the arrogant Israelis) to adopt "Nazi behavior." Such ravings, first uttered in 2003, are now fairly commonplace among Europe's left-wing intellectuals and also among those Jews whose main source of pride is to loudly proclaim to the Gentiles their *shame* at being "Jewish." Since anti-Zionism is currently *the* litmus-test of "progressive" politics for a significant segment of left-wing opinion, Israel-bashing is clearly the contemporary key to acceptance in this milieu. In Israel itself, this type of self-incrimination is a growing trend in the universities, providing the perfect alibi for antisemites and anti-Zionists outside the country to step up the pressure. Indeed, there are veteran Israeli leftists, like Uri Avnery, who have made a profession out of confirming the most insipid anti-Jewish slanders like the accusation that "the pro-Israel lobby pushed the American administration to start the [Iraq] war." It goes without saying for Avnery and his pro-Palestinian friends that Israel as well as American Jews are mainly responsible for "the resurrection of anti-Semitism." Indeed, he openly lambasted the Sharon government as "a giant laboratory for growing the anti-Semitism virus. It exports it to the whole world."[51]

Jews themselves, it must be said, have played a central role in the framing of anti-Zionist thought ever since the time of Theodor Herzl. One hundred years ago, the Jewish leftist opposition to Zionism was especially strong in the secular socialist Bund. For the Bund in Russia and Poland, Zionism was an intrinsically reactionary movement which legitimized the demands of the local antisemites that Jews must emigrate. Moreover, as the Bund liked to insist, Palestine could never absorb the millions of Jews in the Diaspora, let alone solve the social problems of the Jewish masses. After 1917, the Soviet Union, the Communist International (Comintern) and the Communist parties under Moscow's control, would institutionalize such ideological hostility to the Zionist project, which was branded as being "counter-revolutionary" to the core. In 1931 the Comintern further blackened Zionism as the oppressive and exploitative ideology of the international Jewish bourgeoisie—politically allied to the British imperialists in order to suppress the Arab national movement. The Palestine Communist Party in the mid-1930s went further still. It publicly called for the cessation of any Jewish immigration to Palestine and the *liquidation of all Zionist settlement* in the country. It strongly backed the Arab revolt against the British Mandate led by the pro-Nazi Mufti of Jerusalem Haj Amin al-Husseini, who had he been victorious would certainly have tried to wipe out the Jewish community in Palestine.[52] Nevertheless, for reasons of Soviet *Realpolitik* in the Middle East, Stalin did support the establishment of Israel in 1948, even as he launched a domestic antisemitic campaign against Jews living *inside* the U.S.S.R.[53]

Ever since German labor leader August Bebel's definition in 1893 of antisemitism as the "socialism of fools," there has been a disturbing complacency on the Left regarding Judeophobia, which we have subjected to depth analysis throughout this book. Equally, there has been a tendency to persistently underestimate the broad impact of antisemitism as an ideology, its uniqueness, specificity, and longevity. Rare indeed are the examples of socialists who have even attempted to address the fundamentally demonic view of the world held by Judeophobes or the mythical power of antisemitic archetypes of "the Jew" like Judas, Satan, or the Antichrist.[54] No less fleeting have been the efforts at deciphering the phantasmagoric conspiracy theories at the heart of so many antisemitic beliefs. This failure was a factor in the conceptual impotence with which much of the American, French, British or German Left confronted Nazi antisemitism in the 1930s. Very few socialists, anarchists or Communists (apart from isolated mavericks like Wilhelm Reich) showed much grasp of the mass psychology of fascism, let alone seriously addressed the Manichean world-view of the antisemites before the Holocaust.

This dismal failure of imagination both before, during and after the Holocaust has made it ever harder for the Left to take the ever-mutating radical or genocidal forms of antisemitism with the seriousness that they require.[55] In the case of the German Social Democracy (SPD), the roots of this impaired understanding, as we show in this book, go back well before the First World War and they continued unabated throughout the Weimar years.[56] After the Nazi seizure of power in 1933, the SPD studiously played down the issue of antisemitism in their underground and propaganda activity, generally avoiding any direct attacks on it.[57] This crippling paralysis of thought went far beyond mere ambivalence towards the "Jewish Question;" or the opportunistic fear of challenging the prejudices of German workers inside the Third Reich who were exposed on a daily basis to Nazi antisemitic appeals. The problem lay much deeper. Even the leading expert on Nazism of the interwar Frankfurt Marxist School, Franz L. Neumann (widely admired by "functionalist" political scientists to this day) completely failed to grasp the genocidal intent of Nazi antisemitism as late as 1942. In that same year, (writing from his American exile) when the mass murder of European Jews was already well under way, Neumann published his classic work on National Socialism—confidently asserting that the Nazis would "never allow a complete extermination of the Jews." His reasoning was based on the deeply flawed assumption (especially common among liberals, leftists and in some mainstream Jewish organizations) that antisemitism was only a means to other political ends—such as the destruction of free and democratic institutions.[58] For Neumann, like so many academic analysts, it was simply inconceivable that the "Jewish Question" could be anything but secondary to the overall Nazi project. Hannah Arendt was one of the few German-Jewish exiles in the United States to challenge this conventional wisdom during the 1940s.

It has proven equally difficult for most left-wing thinkers since that time to comprehend the centrality of the paranoid antisemitic world-view based on radical conspiracy theories which lay at the heart of Hitler's politics.[59] The fact that such violently irrational antisemitism could move millions of ordinary Germans and other Europeans to follow the Nazi creed and to act upon total fabrications appears to have been altogether too much to digest for many leftists. Nor do most Marxist believers—any more than most liberals and conservatives in the West, really grasp the appeal of religious fanaticism—one of the key components in Protestant, Catholic, fascist, Nazi, and contemporary Islamist forms of antisemitism.[60] The Left has evaded this issue much as it sought to downplay the fact that the Nazis really did fixate their attention on the Jews. Instead, since the 1930s, leftists have preferred to de-emphasize everything unique about the Jewish fate during the Holocaust or regarding Nazism itself. The focus was generally placed on the common ground between the Nazis and other fascist regimes, while pointing to the economic roots of fascism in a decaying liberal-capitalist system. Even Arno Mayer's important work of 1988 (the first by an American left-wing historian to deal seriously with the mass murder of the Jews) treated the Holocaust as if it were primarily the by-product of Hitler's reactionary right-wing anti-Communism and his failed *Glaubenskrieg* (holy war) for living-space in the Soviet Union.[61] For Mayer, there would have been no Holocaust without the Nazi crusade to eradicate the Soviet regime and Bolshevik ideology. This ideological-political goal had to be viewed within the perspective of what Mayer problematically called the "General Crisis and Thirty Years War of the Twentieth Century."[62]

Mayer's universalist approach was not without merit, though one might with equal plausibility argue that Hitler's anti-Bolshevism was the function of his antisemitism rather than the other way around. The work of Mayer was undoubtedly a step forward from the silence of veteran Trotskyists like the late Ernest Mandel—who had for decades conspicuously ignored the subject.[63] Mayer did, at least, abandon the Left's general amnesia regarding the Holocaust and jettison its absurdly mechanical interpretations of Marxism which reduced the "Jewish Question" to a marginal offshoot of moribund capitalism. But Mayer's book has remained the exception rather than the rule. The Holocaust for many leftists is still what it has generally been since 1945—a mere *epiphenomenon* of capitalism—ancillary and almost incidental to the permanent "fascist" temptation that reputedly arises from the crisis of capitalist economies. This was, for example, the prevailing view in Stalinist East Germany almost until its demise in 1990.[64]

There have, of course, been a few exceptions on the postwar intellectual Left to this mind-boggling picture of conceptual sterility since the end of World War II. Most prominent among them was the French existentialist Marxist, Jean-Paul Sartre.[65] Nobody could accuse Sartre—a distinguished novelist, playwright and philosopher – of lacking imagination. His *Refléxions sur la Question Juive* (1946) was indeed a courageous and perceptive essay. Yet even Sartre's combative opposition to antisemitism was not free of racial stereotypes.[66] Almost incredibly, he could still believe after the Holocaust that a socialist revolution would "solve" the "Jewish Question." At the time Sartre was a Communist fellow-traveller. In a society without classes, he imprudently predicted, antisemitism would be definitively cut off at the roots. It was, he thought, essentially a "petty-bourgeois" and "poor white" phenomenon which had no echo in the working-class.

Sartre's closest collaborator, Simone de Beauvoir, was much freer of such illusions and far more emotionally committed to Israel than her long-term companion-in-arms. Originally from an upper-middle-class provincial Catholic family where conventional antisemitism was almost "normal," de Beauvoir had been profoundly shocked by the Holocaust and moved by Israel's postwar struggle for national rebirth against an obstructive British colonialism. Her pioneering feminist engagement had made her especially sensitive to the humiliating situation of Jews in the Diaspora, subject to continual antisemitic insult and social exclusion. Even more than Sartre, she saw Israel's battle for survival as a heroic drive for liberation from the yoke of exile. By their ceaseless labor, creativity, courage, and attachment to the land of Israel, Zionist Jews had in her eyes truly earned their indisputable right to an independent State. Although a personality of the Left and not uncritical of Israel's policies, de Beauvoir sharply disagreed with the anti-Zionist positions of some of her more militant French comrades. Already in 1973 she expressed her consternation at a growing strand of ideological antisemitism masked as "anti-Zionism" that was taking root on the French Left. She was also fiercely critical of Arab efforts to annihilate Israel and the support they were receiving from the Soviet Union. For de Beauvoir, the *fundamental* justice of the Israeli cause was a matter of deep personal conviction which transcended the political cleavages between Right and Left.[67]

Like Sartre, Simone de Beauvoir unequivocally opposed the new totalitarian "anti-Zionism" which had rapidly emerged in the Soviet bloc after the Six-Day War and was to be a valuable subsidiary tool of Soviet foreign policy in the Arab world.[68] Antisemitic "anti-Zionism" in the U.S.S.R. certainly appealed to latent xenophobic, ethnocentric, and populist sentiments against Jews in the lower classes as well as to the wider resentment at the prominent position of "Muscovite" (pro-Soviet) Jews during the early postwar years of Communist domination in Eastern Europe. After 1967 it also served as a valuable *demoralizing* agent used by the Soviet Communist State and Party machine to discourage liberalization, dissent and crush dissident intellectuals, especially in the U.S.S.R., Czechoslovakia, or Poland. For example, in order to discredit the Solidarity resistance movement in Poland in 1981, its activities were blamed on the alleged machinations of "Zionists," freemasons, and cosmopolitan liberals in the West.[69]

There has, of course, also been a tradition of Marxist anti-Zionism relatively untainted by antisemitism. Militants like the young Belgian Trotskyist, Abram Leon (martyred in Auschwitz at the age of 26) were fierce opponents of antisemitism while adamantly opposing Zionism as a "petty-bourgeois" utopia. Leon's narrowly materialist analysis of Jewish history led him, however, to the wildly mistaken hypothesis (originating with the Austro-Marxist Otto Bauer) that the disappearance of the Jewish economic functions as a "people-class" had inexorably led to the demise of the Jews as a nation. Like other Trotskyists of Jewish origin, Leon blamed the cataclysmic Jewish tragedy in the 20th century almost solely on the "decay of world capitalism" which, he overconfidently predicted, would also doom the "puerile dreams of Zionism."[70] Shortly before his deportation to the death camps in Poland, Leon concluded his study (written while in the Belgian underground resistance) with the poignant if pathetic words:

> We still cannot foresee exactly what the "offspring" of present Judaism will be; socialism will take care that the "birth" will take place under the best possible conditions."[71]

Though never overtly antisemitic, Marxists like Abram Leon all-too-dismissively assumed that any retention of Jewish cultural uniqueness or special Jewish traits was deleterious—an outlook clearly in conflict with contemporary notions of pluralism or liberal multiculturalism. Even non-Zionist or Bundist forms of Jewish nationalism (which had favoured cultural-national autonomy in the Diaspora) were consistently repudiated by the rigorously "assimilationist" school of Marxism. Indeed, there has never been any question of orthodox Marxists recognizing a diasporic Jewish nation any more than one which was rooted in the soil of Zion. The handful of Jewish radicals in the West, like the French anarchist Bernard Lazare—who had cogently argued the Jewish autonomist case in the late 1890s—were almost totally isolated among their comrades. As for the Bundists, they were told in no uncertain terms well before 1914 by international Marxists like Lenin, Trotsky, or Rosa Luxemburg that they would have to obliterate their identity as Jews if they sought to be fully emancipated. With a truly remarkable intransigence the anti-Zionist Bundists were denounced as "separatists," "chauvinists," and "isolationists" for even raising the question of an autonomous Jewish culture. Georgii Plekhanov (the father of Russian Marxism) contemptuously and characteristically mocked the Bundists as "Zionists afraid of sea-sickness."

We need to remember that a century ago, none of the founding fathers of Marxism had ever dreamed that Zionism could one day become a *major world problem*. Convinced as they were that the emancipation of the Jews meant the dissolution of any Jewish group identity, they were unable for the most part to envisage that Israel might one day emerge as a Jewish nation-state. Israel's creation and continued survival has in effect been one massive slap in the face for the entire Marxist tradition of theorizing on the "Jewish Question."[72] The current defamation of Israel as an *inherently* racist colonialist, militarist, or fascist state needs to be seen in this context of consistently *failed* Marxist prognoses—both then and now. For radical anti-Zionists the conflict has never really been about the territorial contours of the Jewish State—a land which even today is completely dwarfed in size and population by all of its Arab neighbours. But for much of the Left, Palestine has become an issue that concerns the "de-Zionizing" and "de-Judaizing" of Israel. If ever implemented, such a policy would rapidly lead to the loss of Israel's viability and raison d'être. No doubt that is one goal of the perverse campaign to relentlessly stigmatize Israel with the "original sin" of Western racism.

It generally turned out to be "old Left" intellectuals like Jean-Paul Sartre, Simone de Beauvoir, Claude Lanzmann, Max Horkheimer, or Herbert Marcuse who resisted the cruder Manichean efforts to link Israel exclusively with "imperialist" interests and the Arab States with the socialist, "peace-loving" camp. For this pre-Holocaust generation of thinkers it appeared to be self-evident that Israel was the only nation in the Middle East whose very existence was constantly threatened by its neighbours. In 1967, Marcuse—then the guru of Western radicals—recalled, for example, in a discussion with left-wing German students, that Jews had for centuries "belonged to the persecuted and oppressed" peoples; that "not too long ago six million of them were annihilated"; and that Israel was designed as a refuge where Jews would no longer need to fear persecution. Sartre, for his part, emphasized Israel's geo-political and existential vulnerability along with the fact that the Israeli-Arab conflict was a clash between two equally legitimate national rights. While publicly neutral and insistently refusing to offer his own solution, Sartre nonetheless regarded the 1973 Yom Kippur War as a clear-cut case of Arab aggression—animated by a desire to destroy Israel which he denounced as "criminal."[73]

In the 1970s in Britain, too, there were still some older Labour MPs like Prime Minister Harold Wilson, the left-wing Ian Mikardo, Sydney Silverman, and Richard Crossman who retained a marked sympathy for Israel, though this was notably less visible among English academics and intellectuals. However, from the early 1980s the British Labour Left would come under the spell of ideologically driven anti-Zionist positions far removed from reformist Labour politics and much closer to Trotskyism.[74] Indeed, despite the pro-Israel instincts of former New Labour Prime Ministers Tony Blair and Gordon Brown, the "anti-racist" anti-Zionism of the present-day British Left has brought it to the edge of a nasty whirlpool of antisemitic innuendo.[75] As elsewhere in the West, anti-Zionist British Leftists vehemently deny any responsibility for this state of affairs, while pillorying Israel for causing Arab hatred and the rise in antisemitism. Whether the appointment of a radical English Jew, Ed Milliband, as the new Labour leader, will change this state of affairs remains to be seen. Similarly, in the United States, there is no shortage of left-wing intellectuals (not a few of them Jewish) who depict the "new" antisemitism as a straightforward and understandable response to Israeli occupation policies. In their view, the Jews themselves are most definitely to blame for the aggression against them—itself a classic anti-semitic proposition.[76]

American leftist radicalism, it should be said, has retained a distinctive trajectory, featuring among its advocates some highly diverse groups of Marxists, social democrats, Communists, anarchists, radical liberals, and new leftists.[77] It has adopted a highly critical attitude over decades towards U.S. foreign policy, inequalities in American society, white racism, and many other burning conflicts that are the subject of legitimate debate. In the economically depressed 1930s (the heyday of the Soviet utopian myth) American academics, intellectuals, and artists were drawn in not insignificant numbers towards communism. The mass liquidations of peasants during the forced collectivization campaign and the murderous purges in Stalin's U.S.S.R. during the 1930s were usually defended by American Communists on "utilitarian" grounds as being economically "necessary" or politically "progressive," when they were not being denied outright. Even the Nazi-Soviet pact found its left-wing apologists in the United States, as it did in Europe. During the war years, a flurry of American films, books, and newspaper articles openly indulged in glorifying the Soviet Union as a "peace-loving" and democratic nation. Only after 1945, did the star of American Communism gradually begin to wane. The Cold War as well as the onset of McCarthyism and its fallout contributed to this change.

The Communists were, however, soon replaced by a new generation of leftist radicals in the 1960s whose anti-Americanism was, if anything, even more overt than that of their Old Left forerunners.[78] Issues like the Vietnam war, nuclear disarmament, black civil rights, free speech, drugs, and the student rebellion now assumed centre stage. A sweeping anti-American agenda took root in which the United States was relentlessly denounced *from within* as being an "imperialist" predator and accused of seeking hegemony over Third World nations. At the same time, the crimes of its communist adversaries were systematically whitewashed. Prominent in these anti anti-communist campaigns were a number of Jewish academics, among them Noam Chomsky and Richard Falk. They strongly supported the Vietnamese Communists against the United States—whose own military actions were vilified as amounting to "genocide."[79] Not surprisingly, perhaps, similarly hyperbolic charges would later be laid against Israel by Falk and other left-wing academics, who identify with the Palestinian cause. Falk, however, proved to be so pro-Hamas that even the Palestinian Authority was unhappy with his role as special rapporteur to the UN on Palestinian human rights.[80]

This was consistent with the position taken by Falk and a number of other Western leftists after the victory of the Ayatollah Khomeini's Islamic Revolution of 1979 in Iran. There was no question of condemning its repressive authoritarian theocracy or its human rights record. On the contrary, radical leftists in the West supported the Khomeinist revolution while maintaining that the U.S. remained the major global obstacle to peace and progress. Falk, for example, could find no evidence of religious and ethnic intolerance, let alone discrimination against women in the Islamic Republic of Iran. However, he did suggest that the Islamic Revolution had much to offer to Third World nations as "an example of non-authoritarian governance."[81] Nearly thirty years later (while noticeably silent about Iran's brutal repression of its own citizens) Falk proclaimed at a symposium held in

Los Angeles that America and Israel continue to practice "genocidal geopolitics." In February 2009 he added (as a Jew) that Israel's three-week incursion into the Gaza Strip had evoked "the worst kind of international memories of the Warsaw Ghetto."[82] This utterly misleading comparison of Nazi Germany's deliberate starvation and murder of Warsaw's Jews in 1942 with the war between Israel and the terrorist Hamas regime in Gaza, has, however, become increasingly common in a whole swathe of the liberal-left Western media mainstream in our own day.

Underlying such perverse inversions of reality in the worldview of the radical Left there is a truly Manichean dualism. Visceral hatred for America, the West and Israel is beatifically wrapped up in a radiant vision of human rights and social justice. Belief in this utopia has not prevented the cause of the "oppressed" from being incarnated by Communist or Third World dictators like Stalin, Mao Tse-Tung, Ho Chi Minh, Fidel Castro, Khomeini, Saddam Hussein, or Yasser Arafat. These tyrants have been worshipped as defenders of so-called Third World peoples against the yoke of Western imperialism and Zionism. International solidarity with the Palestinians has given a new and utterly bogus halo of respectability to all those—including totalitarian tyrants—who have hijacked or milked the cause of the "toiling" masses for their own ends. The Islamists are only the latest in a long line of manipulative exploiters of Palestinian or Third World misfortunes that began with the Nazis and Stalinists. All have indulged in the demonization of Israel as a "genocidal state" engaged in "ethnic cleansing from the day of its birth"—a thesis now put forward by growing numbers of self-flagellating and attention-seeking anti-Zionist Israeli academics.[83] Such hysterical rhetoric, totally divorced from any semblance of historical truth or geo-political realities, offers no constructive possibility of reform or redressment of genuine grievances.

There is a destructive and nihilist hatred exhibited in much contemporary left-wing discourse about Israel and the Jewish people (especially that which stems from Jewish sources) which patently lacks any credible perspective for social transformation. In the "post-Zionist" narratives of Israeli historians like Ilan Pappé (formerly an active member of the Israeli Communist Party, Hadash), the entire Jewish national project has been distorted into a nightmarish tale of occupation, expulsion, discrimination, and institutional racism perpetrated by alien and demonic Zionist invaders.[84] In such stunningly partisan accounts, the Palestinians are always the permanent victims, Israelis are forever the "brutal colonizers." According to Pappé, the "Zionist" ethnic cleansing of Palestine was already in full swing in 1948. It was a long-premeditated crime which has been escalating ever since. Since such dogmatic black-and-white views are increasingly widespread among radical left-wing Jews—in Israel and the Diaspora—it is not surprising to see these anti-Zionists so ostentatiously issuing their certificates of divorce from the Jewish state; or to find them squarely in the forefront of petitions against Israel's "apartheid wall" (a security fence to defend against Palestinian suicide bombers) and denouncing its allegedly "racist" oppression of local Arabs.[85] At the same time so-called progressive Jews (like their far more numerous non-Jewish admirers) seem astonishingly indifferent to the suffering of Israeli *civilians*—the innocent victims of often savage Palestinian atrocities. The "progressives" shed tears for Palestinian children (which is certainly understandable) but they invariably turn their heads away from the dead of their own people, the Jews. This is a bizarrely selective humanism in which the systematic, bitter, and overwrought denigration of Israel coexists alongside a highly romanticized and abstract "Palestinophilism" which often seems to have taken the place of any critical thought or attempt at objectivity.[86]

Left-wing animus toward Israel most emphatically did not disappear with the collapse of the Communist bloc. Nor was there any rethinking or re-evaluation by most leftist intellectuals of their Marxist worldview, not to mention their attitudes towards American capitalism and Western liberal democracy.[87] A perfect illustration of this petrification of thought can be found in the writings of Eric Hobsbawm, the veteran icon of the British Left whose membership of the Communist Party only lapsed after the fall of the Berlin wall in 1989. In 1995 Hobsbawm published his much-acclaimed effort to understand the 20th century, *The Age of Extremes*—about which he proved to have been so desperately wrong in his own political choices. What emerges from this singularly overrated work and his subsequent autobiography is the "indulgence and tenderness" (*his* words) with which he still treats the murderous legacy of the Soviet Union, for which he had over many decades acted as such a tireless and dedicated apologist.[88] Long after the great Communist "experiment" had stained itself forever with the blood of millions of innocent victims, Hobsbawn still felt genuine nostalgia for the dream of the October Revolution which was "still there somewhere inside me." Instead of wrestling with his own responsibility in this human debacle, Hobsbawm continued to exude a fierce unabated hostility to the capitalist democracies of the West, whose academies masochistically insisted on honoring his work. In comparison with the inherent wickedness of capitalism, it was clear to Hobsbawm that the brutal Communist tyrannies were the *lesser* evil.[89] Such hollow judgements make for melancholy reading, indicating that even today, Hobsbawn has not fathomed the scale of the gigantic delusion in which he believed. As for Zionism, it was deserving of no more than the occasional derisory (and crassly ignorant) footnote in his general *oeuvre*. Like most Communists who came from a Central European Jewish background, the Jews were, for Hobsbawm, at best a phantom people—whose contemptible (Israeli) nation-State merely illustrated the latent proto-fascist features of all reactionary nationalisms. Naturally, it did not occur to Hobsbawm that in comparison with the massive crimes committed by the Soviet empire at its peak (which he was such a past master at explaining away), Israel has remained a shining beacon of freedom and hope. Having failed to address the Soviet experience except in the most evasive fashion, Hobsbawn remains a singularly untrustworthy guide to anything concerning the Jewish State whch he treats with the level of accuracy and insight of a second-rate Stalinist hack.

Equally revealing is the case of the late Howard Zinn, Boston University historian and author of the best-selling *A People's History of the United States*. Zinn, a self-proclaimed Marxist and admirer of Mao and Fidel Castro, never disguised his view of America as a deeply repressive, racist, and imperialist nation guilty of repeated genocide. His opinion of Israel was scarcely more balanced, though he had been brought up in a working-class Jewish home in Brooklyn and served as a bombardier in World War II. Zinn acknowledged that until 1967 Israel did not loom large in his consciousness, which was also true of many other American Jews. But by the time of the 1982 Lebanon War he had become thoroughly "ashamed" of the Jewish State and convinced that its establishment was "a mistake"—indeed "the worst thing that the Jews could have done." Israel, like the United States, was aggressive, violent, bigoted and driven by a nationalistic frenzy. It had turned its back on what was best in the Jewish tradition—its internationalism, creativity, and emphasis on cultural achievement. Indeed, it was Israel's existence and its actions which had become the main source of antisemitism in the world. Zinn, like many left-wing Jewish anti-Zionists, insisted on describing the subjugation of the Palestinians as a form of "ethnic cleansing," while ignoring the actual causes of the Six-Day War. For him it was self-evident that Israel had betrayed the essential nature of Judaism by its preoccupation with security, borders, military power, and geo-political strategy. Nowhere in his account is there the slightest recognition of the jingoistic, racist nature of Arab nationalism or the genocidal threat posed by radical Islam. Nor have Jewish intellectuals like Howard Zinn had anything to say about the bankruptcy of their own Marxist creed, whose practitioners in recent years have begun to form a de facto alliance with the Islamists. This is perhaps the final stage of decomposition in the slow death of Socialism and Communism.[90]

Marxists and Islamists share a curiously similar apocalyptic agenda of earthly redemption that envisages the installment of absolute "social justice" through violent means. For both of these extremes (and for parts of the neo-fascist Right) Palestinian martyrdom in the name of Allah has become a glowing symbol of "resistance" not only to Israel but to globalization and the "corrupt" West. At the heart of such radical utopias, there is the quasi-religious belief that the world will only be "liberated" by the downfall of America and the defeat of the Jews.[91] This chiliastic fantasy has today emerged as a notable point of fusion between the radical anti-Zionist Left in the West and the global jihad. Revolutionary antisemitism has become an increasingly important factor in cementing this anti-capitalist populism much as it was during the birthpangs of modern socialism over 150 years ago.

NOTES

1. Yves Pallade, "Delegitimizing Jews and the Jewish State: Antisemitism and Anti-Zionism after Auschwitz," *Israel Journal of Foreign Affairs* 3, no. 1 (2009): 63–69.

2. Robert S. Wistrich, *A Lethal Obsession. Anti-Semitism from Antiquity to the Global Jihad* (New York, 2010).

3. Anthony Julius, *Trials of the Diaspora. A History of Anti-Semitism in England* (Oxford, 2010).

4. Shmuel Ettinger, "The Young Hegelians—A Source of Modern Antisemitism?," *Jerusalem Quarterly* 28 (Summer 1983): 73–82; also Robert S. Wistrich, "Radical Antisemitism in France and Germany (1840–1880)," *Modern Judaism* 15 (1995): 109–35; and Michael Mack, *German Idealism and the Jew* (Chicago, 2003).

5. Wistrich, *Lethal Obsession,* 7–8.

6. Assaf Uni, "Norway Up In Arms after Author Insists Israel Has Lost Right to Exist," *Ha'aretz,* 12 Aug. 2006.

7. Alain Finkielkraut, "In the Name of the Other: Reflections on the Coming Anti-Semitism," *Azure* (2004): 21–33.

8. Elhanan Yakira, *Post-Zionism, Post-Holocaust* (Cambridge, U.K., 2010), 303–14.

9. Ibid., 306.

10. Judith Butler, "No, It's Not Anti-Semitic," *London Review of Books,* 21 Aug. 2003.

11. Robert S. Wistrich, *Revolutionary Jews from Marx to Trotsky* (London, 1976); idem, "The Jews and Socialism," *Jewish Spectator* (Winter 1976): 13–22.

12. Yuri Slezkine, *The Jewish Century* (Princeton, 2004), 50–104.

13. Thorstein Veblen, "The Intellectual Pre-eminence of Jews in Modern Europe," *Political Science Quarterly* 34, no. 1 (Mar. 1919): 33–42.

14. Robert S. Wistrich, *Hitler's Apocalypse. Jews and the Nazi Legacy* (New York, 1985), 27–88; see also George Watson, "Hitler and the Socialist Dream," *The Independent on Sunday,* 22 Nov. 1998.

15. On the liberal-Jewish nexus, see Steven Beller, *Vienna 1867–1938. A Cultural History* (Cambridge, U.K., 1989); also Gerald Stourzh, *From Vienna to Chicago and Back* (Chicago, 2007), 204–23.

16. Jonathan Frankel, *Prophecy and Politics. Socialism, Nationalism and the Russian Jews 1862–1917* (Cambridge, U.K., 1981).

17. István Deák, *Weimar Germany's Left-Wing Intellectuals: A Political History of the Weltbühne and Its Circle* (Berkeley, 1968); Walter Z. Laqueur, "The Tucholsky Complaint," *Encounter* (Oct. 1969): 76–80; and Michael Löwy, *Redemption and Utopia: Jewish Libertarian Thought in Central Europe* (Stanford, Calif., 1992).

18. Deák, *Weimar Germany,* 28–29; see also Robert S. Wistrich, *Socialism and the Jews. The Dilemmas of Assimilation in Germany and Austria*-Hungary (London, 1982), 83–85 and for the postwar era, Stanley Rothman and S. Robert Lichter, *Roots of Radicalism: Jews, Christians and the New Left* (New York, 1982), 83ff.

19. See Martin Jay, *Dialectical Imagination: A History of the Frankfurt School and the Institute of Social Research 1923–1950* (Boston, 1973), 31–36. Unfortunately, this book is not very illuminating on the Jewishness of the Frankfurt School. The joint work by its two leading theorists, Max Horkheimer and Theodor W. Adorno, *Dialektik der Aufklärung* (Frankfurt a.M., 1969)—which first appeared in 1947—was an important postwar landmark in addressing antisemitism.

20. Eva G. Reichmann, "Max Horkheimer the Jew. Critical Theory and Beyond," *Leo Baeck International Yearbook* (hereafter *LBIYB*) 19 (1974): 181–95; see also Lars Rensmann, *Demokratie und Judenbild in der politischen Kultur der Bundesrepublik Deutschland* (Frankfurt a.M., 2005).

21. Slezkine, *Jewish Century,* 92–93.

22. Ibid., 93.

23. See Christopher Hill, *Puritanism and Revolution* (London, 1968).

24. Lewis S. Feuer, "Generations and the Theory of Revolution," *Survey* 18, no. 3 (Summer 1972): 161–88.

25. Elżbieta Ettinger, *Rosa Luxemburg: A Life* (London, 1986), 24.

26. Löwy, *Redemption and Utopia,* 33.

27. Jerry Rubin, *We Are Everywhere* (New York, 1971), 74–76. Also Robert S. Wistrich, *A Lethal Obsession,* 527–30.

28. Gideon Shimoni, *The Zionist Ideology* (Hanover, 1995), 155–235.

29. Shlomo Avineri, *The Making of Modern Zionism. The Intellectual Origins of the Jewish State* (New York, 1981), 198–227.

30. Ibid., 139–50. For a hyper-critical view of Labour Zionism, see Zeev Sternhell, *The Founding Myths of Israel. Nationalism, Socialism, and the Making of the Jewish State* (Princeton, 1998), 3–46.

31. Ezra Mendelsohn, *Class Struggle in the Pale: The Formative Years of the Jewish Workers' Movement in Tsarist Russia* (Cambridge, U.K., 1970); Yoav Peled, *Class and Ethnicity in the Pale. The Political Economy of Jewish Workers' Nationalism in Late Imperial Russia* (New York, 1989).

32. Chaim Weizmann, *The Letters and Papers of Chaim Weizmann* (London, 1971), vol. 2, series A (Nov. 1902–Aug. 1903): 306–7.

33. Ibid.

34. Erich Haberer, *Jews and Revolution in Nineteenth-Century Russia* (Cambridge, U.K., 1995), 79–94.

35. A. Lunacharsky, *Ob antisemitizme* (Moscow, 1929), 17.

36. Slezkine, *Jewish Century,* 163.

37. Ibid., 164–65.

38. Ibid.

39. Ibid., 176–77.

40. Wistrich, *A Lethal Obsession,* 154–64.

41. See Amos Elon, *The Israelis: Founders and Sons* (New York, 1971).

42. Mordechai Altschuler, *Soviet Jewry on the Eve of the Holocaust* (Jerusalem, 1988), 118–27.

43. Slezkine, *Jewish Century,* 224–26.

44. Daniel Cohn-Bendit, *Le Grand Bazar* (Paris, 1975), 9–-20.

45. Hervé Hamon and Patrick Rotman, *Génération. Les années de rêve* (Paris, 1987).

46. Wistrich, *A Lethal Obsession,* 528–29.

47. Anthony Julius, *Trials of the Diaspora,* 447–521.

48. Denis MacShane, "'Kauft nicht bei Juden' will worsen the Israeli-Palestinian conflict," *Jerusalem Post,* 30 Nov. 2010.

49. Wistrich, *A Lethal Obsession,* 385–87, 400–15.

50. Julius, *Trials of the Diaspora,* 486–90.

51. See Alvin Rosenfeld, "Modern Jewish Intellectual Failure," *Society* (Nov.–Dec. 2005): 8–18; idem, *"Progressive" Jewish Thought and the New Anti-Semitism* (American Jewish Committee Publication, New York, 2006).

52. Laurent Murawiec, *The Mind of Jihad* (Cambridge, U.K., 2008), 235–39.

53. Arkady Vaksberg, *Stalin against the Jews* (New York, 1995), 175–77, 196–97.

54. Steve Cohen, *That's Funny You Don't Look Anti-Semitic. An Anti-Racist Analysis of Left Anti-Semitism* (Leeds, 1984) makes a useful stab at exposing some of these failings.

55. See Philip Spencer, "The Left, Radical Antisemitism, and the Problem of Genocide," in *Journal for the Study of Antisemitism* 2, no. 1 (2010): 133–51.

56. Donald Niewyk, *Socialist, Anti-Semite and Jew—German Social Democracy Confronts the Problem of Anti-Semitism, 1918–1933* (Baton Rouge, La., 1971).

57. David Bankier, "German Social Democrats and the Jewish Question," in *Probing the Depths of German Anti-Semitism: German Society and the Persecution of the Jews 1933–1941* (Oxford, 2001), 521.

58. Franz L. Neumann, *Behemoth: The Structure and Practice of National Socialism 1933–1941* (London, 1942), 551.

59. See Robert S. Wistrich, *Hitler and the Holocaust* (London, 2002); Jeffrey Herf, *The Jewish Enemy: Nazi Propaganda during World War II and the Holocaust* (Cambridge, Mass., 2006); Saul Friedländer, *The Years of Extermination: Nazi Germany and the Jews, 1939–1945* (London, 2007).

60. See Robert Michael, *Holy Hatred: Christianity, Anti-Semitism and the Holocaust* (Basingstoke, U.K., 2006).

61. Arno Mayer, *Why Did the Heavens Not Darken? The "Final Solution in History* (New York, 1988), 3–35.

62. Ibid., 462.

63. Ernest Mandel, *The Meaning of the Second World War* (London, 1986); also the critique of Mandel's thinking by Norman Geras, *The Contract of Mutual Indifference* (London, 1998); and Mandel's theses, published as "Prémisses Matérielles, Sociales et Idéologiques du Génocide Nazi," in *Le Marxisme d'Ernest Mandel,* edited by G. Achcar (Paris, 1999).

64. Andrei S. Markovits, "Coping with the Past. The West German Labor Movement and the Left," in *Reworking the Past. Hitler, the Holocaust, and the Historians' Debate,* edited by Peter Baldwin (Boston, 1990), 262–73.

65. Jean-Paul Sartre, *Réflexions sur la question juive* (Paris, 1954); also Jonathan Judaken, *Jean-Paul Sartre and the Jewish Question* (Lincoln, Neb., 2006), 123–46. For his view on Israel, see ibid., 184–207.

66. See Susan Suleiman, "The Jew in Jean-Paul Sartre's *Réflexions sur la Question Juive*: An Exercise in Historical Reading," in *The Jew in the Text: Modernity and the*

Construction of Identity, edited by Linda Nochlin and Tamar Garb (London, 1995), 208–15.

67. Denis Charbit, "Simone de Beauvoir, "Israel et les Juifs: Les Raisons d'Une Fidelité," *Les Temps Modernes* (2001): 163–84.

68. Robert Wistrich, "Der alte Antisemitismus in neuem Gewand," in *Neuer Antisemitismus?,* edited by Doron Rabinovici et al. (Frankfurt a.M., 2004), 250–70.

69. *Trybuna Ludu* 22/3 (Dec. 1981); see also Joanna Beata Michlic, *Poland's Threatening Other* (Lincoln, Neb., 2006), 259–61. On the 1968 Polish campaign, see Dariusz Stola, "Anti-Zionism as a Multipurpose Policy Instrument: The Anti-Zionist Campaign in Poland, 1967–1968," *Journal of Israeli History* 25, no. 1 (Mar. 2006): 175–201.

70 Abram Leon, *The Jewish Question. A Marxist Interpretation* (New York, 1970), 225–63.

71. Ibid., 266.

72. Robert S. Wistrich, "Left-Wing Anti-Zionism in Western Societies," in *Anti-Zionism and Antisemitism in the Contemporary World,* edited by idem (London, 1990), 46–52.

73. Judaken, *Jean-Paul Sartre,* 203.

74. See Robert S. Wistrich, "Cruel Britannia," *Azure,* no. 21 (Summer 2005): 100–24.

75. David Hirsh, *Anti-Zionism and Antisemitism. Cosmopolitan Reflections* (Yale Initiative for the Study of Antisemitism, Working Paper, 2007).

76. See the essay by Martin Jay, "Ariel Sharon and the Rise of the New Antisemitism," *Salmagundi* (Spring 2003): 14–21. For a biting commentary, see Edward Alexander, "The Warped Case for Jew-Hatred: Martin Jay 'Explains' how Jews cause Antisemitism," *Midstream* (Feb–Mar. 2004): 5–8.

77. Edward Walter, *The Rise and Fall of Leftist Radicalism in America* (Westport, Conn., 1992).

78. Wistrich, *A Lethal Obsession,* 543–67.

79. Walter, *Rise and Fall,* 134–39.

80. Jordana Horn, "Falk: Population Transfer Could Be War Crime," *Jerusalem Post,* 1 July 2010.

81. See Richard Falk, *Human Rights and State Sovereignty* (New York, 1981) for his views on the 1979 Islamic Revolution. Also Walter, *Rise and Fall,* 147–55.

82. Wistrich, *A Lethal Obsession,* 514.

83. A good example is Ilan Pappé, *A History of Modern Palestine: One Land, Two Peoples* (Cambridge, U.K., 2004) and the review by Benny Morris, "Politics by Other Means," *The New Republic,* 22 Mar. 2004, 25–30; Pappé's subsequent book, *The Ethnic Cleansing of Palestine* (New York, 2006) is more brazen.

84. Ibid. See also "Nations and Narratives," *Economist,* 4 Nov. 2006, 108–9.

85. See the collective work *Antisémitisme: L'intolérable chantage* (Paris, 2003), written by French leftists—mainly of Jewish origin. Also important are some of the essays in Edward Alexander and Paul Bogdanor, eds., *The Jewish Divide Over Israel: Accusers and Defenders* (New Brunswick, N.J., 2006).

86. Anne Roiphe, "Jews Who Call Each Other 'Nazi,'" *Jerusalem Report,* 21 Mar., 2005, 46.

87 David Horowitz, *Unholy Alliance. Radical Islam and the American Left* (Lanham, Md., 2004).

88. Eric Hobsbawm, *The Age of Extremes* (London, 1995);see also idem, *Interesting Times: A Twentieth Century Life* (New York, 2002) and his recent *How to Change the World: Tales of Marx and Marxism* (New York, 2011). Also the critique by John Gray, "Following a False Prophet," *New Statesman,* 17 Jan. 2011.

89. Hobsbawm, *Interesting Times,* 280. Also idem, "After the Fall," in *After the Fall: The Failure of Communism and the Future of Socialism,* edited by Robin Blackburn (London, 1991), 122–23. For a glimpse of his ignorance and bias towards Israel, see Eric Hobsbawm, with Antonio Polito, *On the Edge of the New Century* (New York, 2000), 26, where he makes the absurd statement that "Israel, like Zionism, has no historical foundation." Among other pearls of wisdom, Hobsbawm insists that Orthodox Jews "completely rejected" Israel before the 1967 war and offers a pathetic caricature of what the Temple and Jerusalem have meant for Judaism and Jewish history.

90. See the interview with Howard Zinn in *Moment Magazine* (Mar.–Apr. 2010): 74–77; also http://frontpagemag.com/2009/10/21collaborators-in-the-campus-war-against-israel-and-the-jews-howard-zinn.

91. David Horowitz, *Unholy Alliance,* 123–45; also Paul Berman, *Terror and Liberalism* (New York, 2003), 121–60; and Wistrich, *A Lethal Obsession*, 400–28.

PART I

The Antisemitic Question

CHAPTER 1

The Racist Temptation in the Labor Movement

It is generally recognized that antisemitism as a modern ideology and as an organized political movement first emerged in Europe in the latter half of the 19th century. There is, however, far less agreement as to the nature and cause of this phenomenon, the significance of the term "antisemitism" itself and to what extent it can be seen as expressing a coherent world-view, let alone a consistent policy or platform—at least in the conventional framework of 19th-century political parties. If by "ideology" we imply the search for a total explanation of history and society, a system of belief which, without necessarily being "rational," seeks to account for fundamental changes in the world and, more specifically, to articulate the sense of an existing or impending social crisis, then antisemitism can indeed be included under this heading. By the end of the 19th century, without always assuming the form of a systematic philosophy, antisemitism had nonetheless become a recognizable *Weltanschauung*—an interconnected way of thinking, feeling and acting in the world, a distinctive cultural code and at the same time a vehicle for the expression of all kinds of economic and political grievances.[1]

We are concerned here with the process of crystallization of this "ideology" and with its origins and content as well as with its subsequent manifestations as they emerged in the 20th century. In particular, I want to examine how far modern antisemitism, in its early phases (i.e., before 1900) was a movement of the left or right, radical or conservative—or whether it belongs to some more heterogeneous, hybrid category. In attempting to answer this question my angle of approach will be to examine its credentials as a species of radicalism and to consider in what ways it derives from, resembles and differs from other "leftist" ideologies in 19th-century Europe.

For this purpose it is necessary to consider the earlier part of the 19th century, before the term *antisemitism* with all its ambiguities and subsequent associations had become a fixed part of the European political vocabulary. This period of raw Jew-hatred preceded the absorption of antisemitism into the whole cultural matrix of fin-de-siècle nationalism, *völkisch* racism, conservatism and aggressive imperialism, especially in Germany and Austria-

Hungary. In considering antisemitism as a form of political radicalism, in re-examining its *social* dimension and its claims to have been a vehicle for anti-establishment protest, I do not, of course, wish to deny the strong elements of traditional-conservative and Christian influences inherent both in the genesis of the ideology and in the mass organizations that it subsequently produced. Thus, in predominantly Catholic countries such as France, Poland, and Austria there is no doubt that believing Catholics provided the bulk of the leadership and the main support for the 19th-century antisemitic parties as well as contributing to the elaboration of the ideology. On the other hand, the Berlin movement in Germany—the first example of organized political antisemitism—was founded and led by the Protestant court-preacher, Adolf Stöcker. Theological concerns were important here but secondary to the socio-political features of the Christian-Social parties in the late 19th century. It was predominantly the urban lower middle classes, the peasantry and the lower clergy rather than the ecclesiastical hierarchy which provided wholehearted support for antisemitism. At the same time, the leadership from Adolf Stöcker in Germany to Karl Lueger in Austria or the Abbé Garnier in France exploited all the resources of radical populist, anticapitalistic demagogy to revive the fortunes of the Church in an era of rapid dechristianization, secularism and rampant anticlericalism.

Catholic and Protestant antisemites in the late 19th century did not, however, abandon any of the traditional religious accusations against the Jews—such as the diatribes against the Talmud or deicide and blood libel charges—especially potent in Russia and the Habsburg Empire. But these medieval superstitions owed their power to essentially *modern* techniques of mass agitation and to the crisis of insecurity, afflicting lower middle-class rural and urban strata whose imminent proletarization made them more receptive to such demagogy. What was novel and significant about Lueger's Christian-Social Party in Austria was precisely the way it blended such indigenous clerical traditions of Judeophobia (which had existed for centuries) with concrete *social* protest—with the revolt of the Viennese "little man" in the 1880s against liberalism, high finance and the so-called *Judenherrschaft* (Jew-rule). The Habsburg loyalist and Catholic "traditionalist" image of Karl Lueger—once he had conquered Vienna in 1897—should not disguise the social radicalism which enabled him to successfully mobilize the mass of small-scale producers, craftsmen, tradesmen, and shopkeepers in the Austro-Hungarian capital. Lueger's exploitation of what his liberal rival Ferdinand Kronawetter perceptively called "the socialism of fools," in order to win political power was successful partly because of favorable local conditions and his own charismatic leadership—but also because Christian-Social antisemitism so perfectly expressed the vacillating radicalism of the Viennese *Kleinbürger* (petty-bourgeois). Antisemitism was both *anti-capitalist* (against the modern manufacturing methods which were indeed swamping skilled craftsmen and small business), *anti-liberal* (the Jews were invariably seen as the backbone of the liberal establishment in Austria) and *anti-immigrant*—directed against the unwelcome competition of poor immigrant Jewish peddlers from Galicia, Hungary and Russia.[2]

In addition Christian Socialism in Vienna held out the promise of a more democratic social order which would protect the interests of the lower middle-classes against a narrow and unrepresentative liberal-capitalist oligarchy. Of course, the ideology on which Lueger's Christian Socialism was based (formulated by Karl Freiherr von Vogelsang two decades earlier) also contained a strong conservative, neo-feudal element with its dream of a corporatist society, a restoration of the guilds and its emphasis on the Catholic prohibition of "usury." Similarly, the attack on the materialist, anti-clerical and subversive ethos of modern bourgeois civilization was fundamentally conservative. Yet even here, in the aristocratic critique of social atomism, *laissez-faire* capitalism and the "Jewish spirit," there are parallels between Karl von Vogelsang and the young Marx, as well as with later Austro-Marxist theoreticians like Karl Renner and Otto Bauer.

The romantic *anti-modernist* outlook of Catholic antisemites like von Vogelsang in Austria or René La Tour de Pin in France clearly represented a hostile reaction to the growth of the industrial civilization. They were dreaming of a pre-capitalist way of life, reflecting nostalgia for the dissolution of the traditional Christian order. Hence many Social Democrats (especially in Germany, where the working classes were more effectively mobilized against the antisemitic groups) tended to dismiss the "radicalism" of the antisemites as merely representing a backward-looking utopian folly, directed to the past, not the future. They were sometimes compared to the machine-breaking Luddites or to the early anarchists—primitive rebels lacking any social theory, training in dialectics, or understanding of technological development. Marxian socialism, especially as it developed in Germany after 1880, proudly regarded itself as standing at the opposite pole to the antisemites—representing an optimistic emancipatory creed which shared the liberal belief in education, progress, and interracial tolerance. It paraded as an internationalist revolutionary movement based on class identification and opposed in principle to *all* forms of national or religious discrimination. By comparison, antisemites appeared to be concerned not with more emancipation but with less, with the interests of traditional, not of new classes, with the primacy of the *national* and the *integral* over the universal. But this distinction was by no means universally valid. Moreover, it should not lead one to assume an a priori, inborn immunity to antisemitism within the Socialist movement.[3] It also seriously underestimates the social and political radicalism of the antisemites. In both Austria-Hungary and France, where they organized a more formidable political movement than in the Second German Reich, antisemites could and did nourish themselves on a radical leftist tradition. Even in Germany before 1880 one can observe a similar phenomenon.

Nor is it an adequate explanation to present modern antisemitism as being primarily a reaction to the economic depression after 1873 or to the political crisis of post-1879 liberalism in Germany. The corollary view propounded by Reinhard Rürup that modern antisemitism was essentially "a post-emancipation phenomenon" directed by its proponents "against an influential powerful Jewry at the very center of that society" is also somewhat misleading, because it takes too literally the claims of the antisemites themselves. While plausibly seeing the decline of bourgeois liberalism in Central Europe in the 1870s as a crucial turning point in the emergence of modern political antisemitism, this approach does not adequately explain *why* the Jews were selected as scapegoats. Antisemitism was not the only possible reaction to the stock-exchange crash of 1873, the socio-economic crisis of capitalism and the backlash against liberal political culture. The implication in Rürup's argument seemed to be that in Berlin at least, the Jews really were *the* representatives of capitalist economy and culture; therefore German antisemites might perhaps be justified in regarding themselves as the organizers of a "defensive movement" opposed to "Jewish rule." This is not to be dismissed out of hand. Certainly many contemporaries did see the new antisemitism of the 1870s as a movement against an emerging "Jewish domination" in cultural and economic life. So, too, did their imitators in Austria and France a few years later. On this point conservative, Catholic, radical, and even socialist critics of "Manchester" liberalism could unite. Ironically, although the radical antisemites made much of the running in the 1880s, it would be clerical and conservative elements who would reap the fruits in the following decade.

Otto Glagau, the petit-bourgeois German pamphleteer, who initiated the new antisemitic assault in the 1870s, explicitly linked Jewry with "applied Manchesterism carried to extremes." He called for emancipation *from* the Jews, just like his fellow journalist Wilhelm Marr—the German originator in

1879 of the novel political concept *antisemitism*. Along with other initially obscure publicists of the 19th century who achieved unexpected fame with their revelations (like Drumont in France and August Röhling in Austria), they gave a sensational journalistic expression to anti-Jewish feelings that had emerged in the overheated post-emancipation climate of social aggression and racist nationalism. Glagau's originality was to explicitly identify the "Jewish question" with the social question and to rouse the embittered German *Mittelstand* with his revelations concerning the stock-exchange swindles of the *Gründerzeit* (promoter's era). There are more than a few echoes of early socialism in Glagau's denunciation of the cash-nexus, the bourse-wolves, the plight of the ruined artisan class and the iniquities of "Manchester liberalism." In identifying the Jewish merchant and banker with *homo capitalisticus,* Glagau and other radical antisemites of the 1870s were in fact continuing the communist tradition that began with Marx, admittedly without the intellectual sophistication of Hegelian dialectics. In the same way, Edouard Drumont could draw on the anti-Jewish writings of prominent 19th-century utopian socialists in France such as Charles Fourier, Alphonse Toussenel, and Pierre-Joseph Proudhon.

There are a number of continuities between Young Hegelian anti-Judaism in the early 1840s and the emergence of the new antisemitism in France and Germany three decades later. One important link in this chain was the secular tradition of anticlericalism, which goes back to the French *philosophes* of the 18th century. The German radical Wilhelm Marr himself emerged from this background and it is not surprising that he so vehemently emphasised that his antisemitism was *not* motivated by religious hatred. A veteran radical democrat of 1848, convinced by his reading of Voltaire, Feuerbach, and Daumer that Hebrew monotheism was "a malady of human consciousness" and the root of all tyranny and evil, Wilhelm Marr's antisemitism was also virulently anti-Catholic. Together with Karl-Eugen Dühring, himself an ex-socialist (and the most influential ideologist of radical antisemitism in Central Europe in the 1880s), Wilhelm Marr believed that no Christian could be a genuine antisemite since Christianity was itself based on Jewish racial tradition. Marr's radical negation of monotheistic religion was paralleled in France by the Blanquist socialists and continued in Germany by Dühring and Theodor Fritsch. Already in his socialist phase, Dühring presented Christianity as a doctrine that negated the life-force, sundering man from nature, sapping his vitality and his spontaneous attachment to his native land. By the time he broke with the German labor movement, Dühring was calling for the complete emancipation of the modern "Aryan" peoples from the Judeo-

Christian yoke. He based his argument for the renewal of German culture on the total repudiation of both the Old and the New Testaments.

The *völkisch* anti-Christian antisemitic tradition in 19th-century Germany and Austria led by Theodor Fritsch, Otto Böckel, and Georg von Schönerer following in Dühring's wake, found expression in a plebeian populist agitation that claimed to be above party and religious denominations. The social radicalism of Dr. Otto Böckel's Hessian peasant movement in the late 1880s, was typical of this trend. It went together with a racist, neo-pagan *Blut und Boden* romanticism, denunciations of Jews, Junkers, and clerics as well as with serious efforts to establish producer and consumer self-help organizations in the Hessian countryside to eliminate the Jewish middleman and trader. Böckel's Antisemitische Volkspartei, which won a number of parliamentary seats in the 1890s, expressed a burgeoning plebeian revolt against the existing parliamentary system in the Second Reich, against metropolitan Berlin culture, big business, the world of industry, the Jews, and the Prussian aristocracy. At the same time, Böckel's anti-modernist nostalgia embodied the conservative side of modern German antisemitism—its romantic *völkisch* aspirations for a pre-industrial culture. However, as a follower of Glagau and Dühring, Dr. Böckel viscerally rejected the Judeo-Christian outlook and strongly defended *Mittelstand* interests against the Junkers, capitalists, and Jews. In other words, Böckel was a populist radical as well as a reactionary anti-modernist. Even the title of one of his best-known pamphlets, *Die Juden—Die Könige unsere Zeit* (1887), which inter alia attacked the Rothschilds, consciously recalled the antisemitic work by the French socialist Alphonse Toussenel written in 1845—*Les Juifs, Rois de l'Époque* (The Jews—kings of the epoch).

Georg von Schönerer in Austria stood even more clearly in the radical camp as the undisputed leader of the leftist opposition in the Habsburg Monarchy during the early 1880s. His populist attacks on the Austrian Rothschilds in 1884 accusing them of transport usury (a campaign denounced by the liberal *Neue Freie Presse* as "communistic") was the high point of his career as the anti-capitalist *Führer* of the Austro-German masses. Von Schönerer at this time still enjoyed the support of the future leaders of Austrian Social Democracy, Victor Adler and Engelbert Pernerstorfer, as well as of the later Christian Socialists Karl Lueger and Ernst Schneider, not to mention the Pan-German nationalists. Anti-liberalism, anti-capitalism, and anti-clericalism were unifying threads in Von Schönerer's national-socialist ideology already expressed in the Linz Program of 1882. Ironically enough, it had been formulated with the help of two assimilated Germanized Jews—

Heinrich Friedjung and Victor Adler. Von Schönerer's *anti-capitalist* rhetoric in favor of productive classes, his call for universal suffrage, a progressive income tax, a tax on stock-exchange transactions, as well as the nationalizing of railways and insurance companies, and the limitation of working hours, marked him out as the natural leader of the radical opposition in Austrian politics. In 1885, he added the notorious "Jew paragraph"—calling for the removal of Jewish influence from all areas of public life—regarded as "indispensable for realizing these reforms." Thus antisemitic populism became the hallmark of his campaign of social reform and effort to democratize an antiquated semi-feudal political system.

The growing emphasis on the racial gulf between "Aryan" and Jew now began to fuse with an extremely militant anti-liberal and quasi-socialist platform. Von Schönerer, no less than Wilhelm Marr in Germany, saw himself as the descendant of the radical-liberal generation of 1848 with its republican, anti-clerical, romantic nationalist ideals. He, too, called for the destruction of the Catholic Church and Jesuit influence as well as demanding an end to the "Semitic" domination of banking, credit institutions, and the press. His intense hostility to the Catholic Church was summed up in the popular Pan-German slogan, "Without Judah, Without Rome, We will build Germany's dome" (*Ohne Juda ohne Rom wird gebaut Germaniens Dom*).[4] The radical racist dynamic behind Austrian Pan-Germanism, all-too-evident in Schönerer's insistence on the eternal, *biological,* necessity of combating the Jew, would become a key source for Adolf Hitler's National Socialist ideology. In *Mein Kampf,* Hitler expressed admiration for both of his two pre-1914 Austrian role models. He was greatly impressed by Karl Lueger's grasp of the social question and flair for mass politics which decisively shaped the young Hitler's views on propaganda. It was from Lueger's electoral triumphs that Hitler learned the *political* significance of antisemitism as a weapon for mobilizing the masses against a *single* enemy—one who simultaneously symbolized liberalism, capitalism, socialism, and the dominant political system to be overthrown. But it was from Georg von Schönerer that Hitler adopted a world-view based on race, blood and biological antisemitism—which his mentor described in 1888 as the "greatest ideological achievement of the 19th century."[5]

This type of Judeophobia involved far more than simple rejection of Jews and Judaism. It was anti-Catholic, anticapitalist, anti-modernist, neo-pagan, and pan-German as well as purporting to represent the disenfranchised masses. The antisemites claimed, of course, to be reacting defensively to the "Jewish peril" and advocated all kinds of measures for banning Jewish immigrants, reducing or abolishing Jewish employment in certain professions (especially banning Jews from public office), withdrawing citizenship, restoring the ghetto, encouraging the expropriation of Jewish fortunes, favoring repatriation, or even the physical elimination of the Jews. But most of this agitation in Western and Central Europe (as opposed to the pogromist barbarism of Tsarist Russia) tended to remain at a purely verbal level before 1918—however violent the rhetoric. The "fantasy" element was no less strong in this emerging genre of modern plebeian antisemitism than in its medieval antecedents. Its mythical quality was strengthened by the new emphasis on "race"—a concept which notoriously lent itself to all kinds of mystification in spite of its modern "scientific" ring. The very abstractness of the "antisemitic" ideology—itself largely a creation of semi-radicalized, frustrated intellectual misfits and sensation-mongering journalists—succeeded in reactivating the sense of an *ideal* world beyond social atomization, class antagonisms, and the "decadence" of modern bourgeois culture. The diffuse radicalism expressed by this antisemitic mythology offered a new kind of anchor for the psychologically unhinged, the economically insecure, social misfits, unemployed intellectuals, bankrupt aristocrats, as well as serving the material interests of the "respectable" professional middle-classes, confronted by unwelcome Jewish competition.[6]

In Austria, during the late 1880s the radical democrat, Ferdinand Kronawetter, had somewhat contemptuously branded antisemitism as "the socialism of fools." The leader of the German Social Democrats, August Bebel, would borrow the phrase in 1893 in order to signal that it was primarily a symptom of lower middle-class distress. Bebel already understood that the rise of Jew-baiting was a potentially dangerous "deviation" from the class struggle. On the other hand, for the French Catholic writer Anatole Leroy-Beaulieu, antisemitism was better described as the socialism of "snobs" and "clubmen" rather than as a "socialism" of petty-bourgeois fools. It had already demonstrated alarming efficacy in bringing together the aristocracy and the mob, the men of capital and honest laboring artisans, exploited peasants, and the disaffected, culturally disorientated *Mittelstand* in a national front against the alleged domination of an "alien" race. One might add that this political utility of antisemitism along with its *protean* quality and ability to fuse with other social or national issues is what distinguished it from traditional Jew-hatred and gave it a distinctively *modern* quality. By the 1890s antisemitism had clearly emerged as an identifiable world-view, as an ideology and a political movement able to compete with conservatism, liberalism or socialism.

A similar assessment was also made by the prominent French writer and politician Maurice Barrès, who noted in 1890, the ability of antisemitic appeals to tap into the inequalities of modern bourgeois society and exploit the xenophobic mood of economic protectionism. First, as a "national" socialist Boulangist and then as a chauvinist anti-Dreyfusard in the late 1890s, Barrès would himself cynically play on this exclusivist rejection of Jews. So, too, did conservative German nationalists like Heinrich von Treitschke or Protestant clerics like Adolf Stöcker, as well as aristocrats like the "Red Prince," Alois von Liechtenstein, in Catholic Austria. Their task was made easier by the long list of illustrious German thinkers and artists from Luther, Kant, Goethe, and Fichte to Hegel, Feuerbach, Schopenhauer, and Richard Wagner whose derogatory views of Jews and Judaism were often drawn upon to legitimize antisemitic opinions in the second half of the 19th century.

In France the tradition of literary antisemitism was no less "distinguished" than in Germany and contributed its share towards making the new ideology socially respectable by the end of the 19th century. Indeed, in France, antisemitism had been part of the rationalist, anti-clerical, and socialist traditions well before the 1870s, giving it a certain credibility and intellectual prestige. Voltaire's contempt for the Jews and Judaism would be frequently cited with approval by a later generation of French socialists and free thinkers. The Fourierist critique of commercialism, mercantile parasitism, and Jewish "usury" added a nasty secular edge to French antisemitism in the first half of the 19th century. The anarchist Proudhon's visceral diatribes "against this race [the Jews] which poisons everything, by meddling everywhere without ever joining itself to another people" were by no means unrepresentative for the French Left. In 1847 he wrote: "One must send this race back to Asia or exterminate it"—which made even Karl Marx's notorious remarks on the subject seem like a model of cool objectivity. For all his anti-clericalism, Proudhon felt obliged to point out that it is not for nothing that the Christians called them [the Jews] "deicides." Proudhon added that "hatred of the Jew like Anglophobia must be an article of our political faith."[7]

The socialist anti-Jewish tradition of Fourier, Proudhon, and Blanqui absorbed popular feeling against the Jews-as-usurers into its mainstream rhetoric. No doubt, this was made easier by the prominence of the Rothschilds and a number of other Jews (as well as Protestants) in the French banking oligarchy. Indeed, modern antisemitism in France first developed primarily as an offshoot of the early radical attack on the *féodalité financière*—the new financial feudalism, which had established its hegemony under the bourgeois Orleanist Monarchy (1830–48). French socialist stereotypes of the Jew as the incarnation of Mammon and the mercantile spirit retained a noticeably Christian tinge in the writings of Charles Fourier, Pierre-Joseph Proudhon, Pierre Leroux, and Alphonse Toussenel. The latter's book *Les Juifs, Rois de l'Époque* directly related the iniquities of the Protestant capitalist ethic to "biblical" morality and "Jewish" racial traits—particularly those exemplified by cosmopolitan Jewish financiers. The Pope of modern French antisemitism, Edouard Drumont, had a ready-made model before him when he came to compose *La France Juive,* forty years later. Not for nothing did Drumont refer to the "wonderful book" of the Fourierist Alphonse Toussenel, "the work of a poet, of a thinker, of a prophet." Indeed, he declared his sole ambition to be that his own work would stand alongside that of Toussenel "in the libraries of those who would understand the causes which have brought ruin and shame to our country." Toussenel's work was undoubtedly one of the primary sources of modern French antisemitism, admiringly quoted not only by Drumont but also by the integral socialists writing in Benoît Malon's *La Revue Socialiste* in the 1880s, and by the integral nationalists around Action Française in the 1900s. They all shared Toussenel's hatred of *la haute banque,* of the "unproductive" [Jewish] middleman and merchant, of Protestantism, Anglo-Saxon capitalism, and the ethics of the Hebrew Bible.

A section of the labor movement in France also proved receptive to the "Aryan" myth, first developed during the 1850s primarily by French scholars like Count de Gobineau and the polymath Ernst Renan. Proudhon reflected this race-based antisemitism when he wrote that the Jew "is the evil element, Satan, Ahriman, incarnated in the race of Shem." Proudhon had, for example, argued in *De la justice dans la revolution et dans l'église* (1858) that "monotheism is a creation of the Indo-Germanic spirit, and could not have arisen from any other source." Elsewhere he blamed the Jews, this "*race insociable, obstinée, infernale*" for the "*superstition malfaisante*" called Catholicism. It was the influence of this "Jewish" element which (following Voltaire) Proudhon held responsible for Christian intolerance and fanaticism. These racist diatribes in Proudhon seem to have been grafted on as a pseudo-scientific appendix to justify his visceral hatred of Jews and Judaism. His violent prejudices were shared by the Russian revolutionary anarchist Mikhail Bakunin who, in the late 1860s, called the Jews "an exploiting sect, a bloodsucking people, a unique devouring parasite, tightly and intimately organized. . . ." Bakunin agreed with Proudhon's primitive view that only peasants and workmen were real producers. He identified with Proudhon's bitter hatred of Marx and Marxism—pointing out that "the communism of Marx wants a mighty centralization by the state, and where this exists there must nowadays be a central State Bank and where such a bank exists, the parasitical Jewish nation, which speculates on the labor of the peoples, will always find a means to sustain itself."

On the issue of Jewish "parasitism," it is clear that Bakunin's Russian revolutionary populism, Proudhon's French anarchism, and early German Marxism found considerable common ground. The French socialists were particularly susceptible to this crude anticapitalist antisemitism, which reflected the role of the *haute banque* in French economic and political life during the first half of the 19th century. This fact also coincided with the extensiveness of small-scale enterprise in France and the dominance of its predominantly agrarian peasant Catholic culture. Moreover, the lack in French socialism of a developed "scientific" theory to compare with Marxism, made it easier to equate the Jew with the banker and graft this stereotype on to the pre-existing traditional image of the usurer. Above all, there was the all-pervasive myth of the Rothschilds. For most left-wing radicals (and for the mass of French shopkeepers, artisans and workers), the Rothschild family was and would remain *the* embodiment of big capital. Hence the extensive propaganda against banking capital in France was all too easily diverted into antisemitic channels. Among some of the followers of the revolutionary insurrectionist Louis-Auguste Blanqui, this hostility towards the Jew as the incarnation of swindling, usury, and rapacity was further intensified by their acceptance of the "Aryan" racial myth and "Semitic" inferiority. This obsession took on pathological proportions in the work of the French Blanquist Gustave Tridon (notably in his *Du Molochisme Juif*). He did not shrink from accusing biblical Jews of cannibalism and of originating human sacrifice. This malevolent and utterly false charge was already to be found in Voltaire and in the writings of some left Hegelian radicals in Germany such as Friedrich Daumer. But it was left to the French Blanquists to demonstrate that the prime task of modernity and of revolutionary radicalism was to sweep away the last particle of the "Semitic spirit" from the face of the earth.

What distinguished France from most European societies was the potency of this left-wing Judeophobia. By the 1890s, political journalists like Drumont and Barrès, radical populists like Henri Rochefort, and agitators like the Marquis de Morès and Jules Guérin had learned to blend this tradition of socialist Judeophobia with integral nationalism. During the Dreyfus Affair this version of national socialism became the most sophisticated conceptualization of antisemitism yet achieved in modern Europe. It was to take another thirty years before the full destructive potential of such "radical" late 19th-century ideology would become apparent. Ironically, the ultimate synthesis would not happen in Paris, its original laboratory, but rather in Munich, Berlin, and Vienna where antisemitism emerged as an absolutely key element in the National Socialist onslaught against liberal-bourgeois democracy and the Marxist labor movement. The dynamic role played by racist antisemitism in German Nazism would not, however, have been possible without the radical intellectual framework which first developed in fin-de-siècle bourgeois Europe.

One of the dominant themes in post-1918 Nazi and fascist antisemitism would be the accusation that Jews were responsible for the wave of revolutionary radicalism in Russia, Europe, and the New World. The German-Italian sociologist Roberto Michels had already remarked in 1913 that "in many countries, in Russia and Romania for example, but above all in Hungary and in Poland, the leadership of the working-class parties (the Russian Social Revolutionary Party excepted) is almost exclusively in the hands of Jews, as is plainly apparent from the examination of the personality of the delegates to the international congresses."[8] This was by no means a wild exaggeration, though a little overstated. But the individual examples were indeed legion. Karl Marx and Ferdinand Lassalle, both German Jews by birth, were the twin icons of the most powerful labor movement in the world, the German Social Democratic Party (SPD), founded by Lassalle in 1863. Marx's centrality as the inventor of modern Communism would, of course, be decisively important in the history of the 20th century. Eduard Bernstein, a friend of Marx and Engels, would become the spiritual godfather of West European social democracy and the most important "revisionist" Marxist in Imperial Germany. Rosa Luxemburg, a unique blend of German, Polish, and Russian influences and endowed with a fiery Jewish temperament, was his antithesis within the SPD. The co-founder of the German Communist Party (KPD) in 1918, an ardent international socialist and the most formidable feminine personality in the annals of the workers' movement, Luxemburg was brutally murdered in the counter-revolutionary backlash of 1919. Other leading German Communists of Jewish origin in 1918 included Luxemburg's successor, Paul Levi, and her lover Leo Jogiches, who came from a Litvak-Russian milieu. At the head of the short-lived Munich revolutionary Republic at the end of 1918 was another ill-fated Jewish intellectual, the independent socialist Kurt Eisner—a neo-Kantian pacifist and a Berliner with a bohemian life-style. Among the other prominent Jewish revolutionaries who swiftly rose to the top in Germany in the fateful year of 1918 one should add the anarcho-Communist mystic Gustav Landauer and the Russian Jewish émigré Eugen Leviné. Like Luxemburg and the leading independent Socialist in Germany, Hugo Haase, all of these radical Jews were deliberately "liquidated" in 1919 in the German counter-Revolution.[9] They were all "chosen" targets of radical right circles, ultra-conservatives and enemies of the new Republic.

The leaders of Austro-Marxism, both before and after the First World War were also overwhelmingly Jewish middle-class intellectuals, beginning with the founder of the Party, Victor Adler. The Party's leading theoretician, Otto Bauer, along with intellectuals like Friedrich Adler, Robert Danneberg (who would later die in Auschwitz), Wilhelm Ellenbogen, Friedrich Austerlitz, Julius Deutsch, and Max Adler all unwittingly contributed to the Austrian clerical and bourgeois identification of "Reds" with Jews. Though such intellectuals rarely disguised their own antipathy to Judaism and Jewry (*das Judentum*), this did not prevent their nationalist or clerical opponents from branding the Austrian Socialist Party as thoroughly *verjudet* (judaized).[10] This was particularly ominous because the antisemitic movement in Austria proved to be sturdy and politically robust.[6] Victor Adler, who had founded Austrian Social Democracy in 1889, set the tone for the movement by adopting from the outset a position of official neutrality in the battle between liberal "philosemites" and populist antisemites in Vienna. Adler was adamant that the workers of Austria must never "allow themselves to be used as a battering-ram either for or against the Jews."[11] It was imperative to prove to the masses that the Socialist Party would under no circumstances serve as a *Judenschutztruppe* (a Jewish protective guard).[12]

In the late 1890s, as the Christian-Social antisemites under Dr. Karl Lueger swept all before them, Victor Adler began to align his party much more vigorously against the liberals than the Luegerites. One of his more dubious tactics against the rising antisemitic wave was to brand Christian-Social leaders as *Judenknechte* (Jew-lackeys). The antisemites were accused of acting as accomplices of the Rothschilds and finance capitalism rather than of seeking to expropriate their "Jewish" enemies. As one delegate, Jakob Brod, complained at the 1897 Party Congress, Victor Adler's policy seemed designed to avoid at all costs "the impression of [Social Democracy] being a Jewish party."[13] Brod was convinced that Victor Adler's approach stemmed from his own "prejudices" against Jews (he had in fact converted to Protestantism at the age of 26) and reflected a misguided willingness to pander to the xenophobic prejudices of the petty-bourgeois Austrian masses.

Like his close friend and chief lieutenant Engelbert Pernerstorfer, Victor Adler had once been a militant pan-German nationalist during his student days. In 1898, both Adler and Pernerstorfer would evoke the ghost of Karl Marx and his notorious anti-Jewish essay of 1844 ("Zur Judenfrage") as if it was the last word in wisdom on the "Jewish Question."[14] Marx's diatribe provided a convenient rationalization for the anti-Jewish bias that Adler and Pernerstorfer had already exhibited in the early 1880s when they were briefly allied with the Austrian pan-German *Führer* (and racial antisemite) Georg von Schönerer.[15]

The Jewish Marxist intelligentsia around Victor Adler certainly shared his undisguised antipathy towards *Ostjuden* (the traditionalist caftan-clad Jews of Galicia), his ambivalent attitude toward the *völkisch* antisemites, and his firm belief that the development of capitalism would finally bring about the extinction of a "Jewish nation." Zionism, according to this view, was nothing but an impractical, romantic, and ultra-reactionary utopia—the ridiculous attempt of backward-looking intellectuals to revive the defunct corpse of a people doomed to self-dissolution.[16] This was the position of prominent "Jewish" Austro-Marxists like Otto Bauer and Friedrich Austerlitz, as it was of Karl Kautsky (the leading theorist of the Second International), Rosa Luxemburg, and Lenin. Even in 1949, it would still be the attitude expressed by Friedrich Adler (son of Victor Adler), who wrote in a Swiss socialist paper:

> I, like my father, always considered the complete assimilation of the Jews not only desirable but also possible, and even the bestialities of Hitler have not shaken my view that Jewish nationalism is bound to lead to reactionary tendencies—namely, to the resurrection of a language which has been dead for almost two thousand years and to the rebirth of an antiquated religion.[17]

The Adlerian legacy would be inherited after World War II by Austria's Socialist Chancellor, Bruno Kreisky, who was both anti-Zionist and anti-Jewish. But long before Kreisky, Victor Adler had told the celebrated Belgian Socialist Camille Huysmans in 1917: "One must have Jews, comrade, but not too many."[18] To some extent this was a case of proverbial Jewish "self-hatred"—the internalization by assimilated Jews of antisemitic attitudes prevalent in the Christian and secular societies of the modern era. Self-hatred has indeed existed among a significant number of Jewish writers and journalists, academics, artists, and even some Zionists in modern times. It is not always easy to draw the boundary between this ugly phenomenon and legitimate criticism of a given culture, society, or human group that one seeks to change.[19] Gifted individuals within a minority, especially those with a markedly critical outlook, are probably more prone than others to self-hatred. In the case of Jews, if they operate within a highly antisemitic society yet seek to fully assimilate into its ranks, the temptation to displace their latent aggression or frustration against members of their own minority group, must be so much the greater. Fin-de-siècle Vienna was one striking example of a propitious terrain for this kind of self-accusation which was especially common among converted intellectuals or artists such as Otto Weininger, Gustav Mahler, and Karl Kraus.[20]

Already in pre-unification Germany during the 1830s and 1840s one can find radical Jews like the journalist Ludwig Boerne or Karl Marx (both converts), who identified Jews with capitalism and equated the "Jewish spirit" with the "universal dominion" of money. Indeed, Jewish radicals who insisted on the social *de-judaization* of the Jew as being intrinsic to the fulfillment of universal human emancipation were usually among the most extreme in their hostility to Judaism.[21] Their antipathy went far beyond the rejection of organized religion, loathing for tribalism, or mere dislike of cultural particularism. There is a noticeably nasty edge to the anti-Judaic contempt displayed by socialists of Jewish origin such as Karl Marx, Ferdinand Lassalle, Rosa Luxemburg, Victor Adler, Friedrich Austerlitz, Otto Bauer, the young Bernard Lazare, Chaim Zhitlovsky, or Leon Trotsky. It was as if they were determined to kill the "Jew" in themselves, usually wrapping this ethnic death-wish in the more idealistic mantle of the universal brotherhood of man. Among the various methods employed one can find the denigration of Jewish religious practices and customs like circumcision or *kashrut* (observance of the Jewish dietary laws); mocking Jewish "tactlessness," "vulgarity" and "pushiness"; focusing on the allegedly "barbarous" qualities of the Yiddish language; or castigating haggling and cut-throat exploitation which supposedly characterized Jewish merchants. There were many disturbing similarities between this "socialist" vocabulary and the lexicon of the antisemites.[22] In both cases the ultimate goal appeared to be the disappearance of the Jews. For such left-wing Judeophobes, the "elimination" of Jewry was a necessary pre-requisite for the "redemption" of humanity.[23] Ironically, the more that Jewish radicals sought *not* to be identified as Jews, thereby displaying their *ostentatious indifference* to the "Jewish Question," the more it came to haunt them and to nourish antisemitic obsessions about a hidden Jewish conspiracy for "world domination."[24]

Jewish Socialists and Communists invariably saw matters very differently.[25] They believed their assimilationist philosophy to be entirely "progressive" in the spirit of the French Revolution of 1789 which had demanded the *dissolution* of Jewry as a distinctive group or corporate entity. Leaving the ghetto behind, Jews were expected to fully merge as individuals into their non-Jewish environment and to disappear. No longer definable as an independent or separate nation, they would graciously be permitted to become Englishmen, Frenchmen, Germans, Americans, or Poles of the "Mosaic persuasion."[26] For all his contempt towards the liberal bourgeoisie, the Bolshevik leader, Lenin, fully embraced this classical *emancipationist* ideology of the 19th century. He approvingly quoted the radical deputy Alfred Naquet—an assimilated French anti-Zionist Jew—who had insisted in 1903 that Jewish nationalism was, by definition, artificial and regressive. Like many liberal, radical and socialist Jews of the time, Naquet tended to equate Zionism and antisemitism as if they were mirror images of one another—opposite sides of the same "petty-bourgeois" reactionary coin. This distorted perception would later be revived with a vengeance by Soviet East European and German Communists after World War II.[27] During the past forty years it has unfortunately become a widespread conventional wisdom in western democratic societies.[28]

Contemporary left-wing efforts to stigmatize or defame Zionism as "racist" or symmetrical with antisemitism have indeed a long history dating back for over a century. Today, the focus is on the politicidal call to dismantle Israel despite its being a fully legitimate State recognized by the United Nations since 1949. Evidently to "cleanse" the world of Israel, in the name of human rights, is held by many on the Left to be a *historically* "progressive" political project.[29] This goes some way beyond the intense polemics about Zionism that characterized public debate before 1948. Much of the contemporary negation of Zionism likes to denounce Israel as a state born of the "original sin" of displacing, expropriating, or expelling an "aboriginal" population—namely the Palestinians—who (unlike the Israelis) are deemed to have an *absolute* right to national self-determination. In the contemporary literature of the radical Left, Zionism alone among national movements is considered "immoral" and "illegitimate." Worse still, character traits of cruelty, bloodthirstiness, duplicity, greed, and brutality are routinely attributed by much of the Left to Israel in a language of secularized dogma that echoes the discourse of classical antisemitism.[30]

Already in the 1930s the seeds of this perverse world-view were present, though usually in a more latent form. For example, antisemitism was frequently reduced to a mere by-product of capitalist crisis or imperialism. Its connection to German (and other) nationalisms was downplayed; as was its longevity, religious roots, and linkage to the specific historical conditions of Diasporic existence. Socialists also tended to ignore the persistence in their own ranks of a cultural system of norms, a vocabulary, and associations that were hostile to Jews as a social group.[31] There was a disturbing willingness to recognize a kernel of truth in antisemitism by highlighting negative features in the Jewish contribution to finance-capitalism. Even when condemning or mocking their political rivals, the socialist and Communist press would virtually never defend Jews *qua* Jews. The emphasis was far more on the hypocrisy of racist, antisemitic or Nazi leaders who themselves engaged in dishonest or dubious ("Jewish") business practices, fraud, embezzlement, and rapacious exploitation of others.[32] These were hardly arguments that were likely to counteract the deeper layers of social, racial, or cultural prejudice against the Jews. Socialists and anarchists alike also tended to assume that antisemitism (insofar as it was anti-capitalist, populist, or "democratic") was ultimately useful to the revolutionary cause. This was the argument of the French-Jewish anarchist Bernard Lazare on the eve of the Dreyfus Affair. He wrote:

> Such is the irony of things that antisemitism which everywhere is the creed of the conservative class, of those who accuse the Jews of having worked hand-in-hand with the Jacobins of 1789 and the Liberals and Revolutionists of the nineteenth century, this antisemitism is acting, in fact, as an ally of the Revolution. Drumont in France, Pattai in Hungary, Stoecker and von Boeckel in Germany are cooperating with the very demagogues and revolutionists whom they believe they are attacking. . . . Antisemitism stirs up the middle class, the small tradesmen, and sometimes the peasant, against the Jewish capitalist, but in so going it gently leads them toward Socialism, prepares them for anarchy, infuses in them a hatred for all capitalists, and more than that, for capital in the abstract. And thus, unconsciously, antisemitism is working for its own ruin, for it carries in itself the germ of destruction.[33]

Lazare was, of course, dramatically wrong about the imminent self-destruction of antisemitism as a movement or its "contribution" to the revolutionary cause. Indeed, the Dreyfus Affair which began a few months after the appearance of Lazare's book, raised antisemitism to a new fever pitch as he himself would subsequently acknowledge. Ironically, leading French antisemites from Edouard Drumont to Charles Maurras were generous in their praise of his highly informative work. It was indeed described in Drumont's book review as being "dominated from beginning to end by a fine effort at impartiality" and a determination "not to yield to the impulses of the race."[34] Like many Jewish revolutionists of his generation, the young Bernard Lazare was, it should be said, far from being immune in the early 1890s to a virulent distaste for "ghetto" Jewry, loathing for the Talmud, dislike of unassimilated East European Jewish immigrants, and antipathy towards all forms of Jewish huckstering or petty commerce. Lazare's own Dreyfusard commitment might indeed best be seen as a "passionate rewriting" *in action* of the highly problematic book he had authored in 1894.

Not all leftists—whether Jewish or Gentile—succumbed to the racist temptation of internalizing the antisemitic stereotypes of European Christian and bourgeois society. Friedrich Engels, the co-founder of Communism (with Karl Marx), managed to overcome his own personal prejudices when confronted with the rising tide of political antisemitism. In 1890, he would confidently proclaim that antisemitism was primarily a phenomenon of backward, semi-feudal societies which would be rendered obsolete by the development of full-blooded capitalism.[35] Engels was, of course, no less mistaken than Lazare in his prognosis. But his visible contempt for the reactionary "medieval" nature of fin-de-siècle European antisemitism helped to shield mainstream Social Democracy from some of the worst temptations in appeasing modern political antisemitism before the Shoah. Nonetheless, some leading German Social Democrats like August Bebel and Wilhelm Liebknecht were by no means free of troubling ambivalences. For example, Bebel embraced at times unsavory echoes of antisemitic rhetoric about "Jewish exploitation" or the quasi-Darwinian notion that (negative or positive) *racial* traits can be transmitted over time. Thus "the natural inclination and disposition of the Jews to trade" was matter-of-factly presented by Bebel as if it were a hereditary characteristic heightened by historical development. Darwin fused with Marx in Bebel's appeal to racial as well as class logic in explaining antisemitism.[36]

The physical appearance of Jews ("the characteristic nose"), along with their conspicuous middleman role and ubiquitousness in capitalist economic development were seen by the SPD leader as major social causes of antisemitism. Bebel's main objection to the agitation of the German antisemites was his belief that nothing would substantially change even if "one could remove all Jews from Germany" since "tomorrow the so-called Christians will take their place." Like other SPD leaders, he accepted the essentially fatalistic belief that the antisemitic peasants, artisans, and small business people would inevitably gravitate towards the socialist orbit once it became apparent that their real enemy was *capitalism in general*. Their anti-

Jewish sentiments were not in his eyes irrational, but merely myopic and ultimately futile. In 1906 Bebel even echoed Marx by describing all of modern society as *verjudet* ("judaized")—a vulgar term with decidedly antisemitic connotations.[37] Bebel further evoked and even radicalized Marx's conclusions by suggesting that with "the demise of bourgeois society the particular nature of the Jew will also disappear."[38]

Similar ambiguities, mixed with an unpleasant streak of contempt for Jewry, can be found in the writings of Rosa Luxemburg, who angrily complained in 1917 when her friend Mathilde Wurm evoked the pogroms in Russia: "Why do you come to me with your special Jewish sorrows?" Luxemburg despised all forms of Jewish nationalism, including Zionism, as "petty-bourgeois" deviations from international Socialism.[39] Admittedly, she was also a militant adversary of all nationalist and "progressive" antisemitism—especially in her native Poland. Her vehement articles on the subject of antisemitism (which were first analyzed by me in the early 1970s) have a more resolute and unapologetic tone than the awkward polemics of most German and Austrian Social Democrats.[40] Luxemburg, it should be remembered, was responding to the macabre horrors of the Russian pogroms in 1905 and their ideological justification by Polish "free-thinking" antisemites. Since the authority of Marx had been specifically invoked by Polish intellectuals like Andrzej Niemojewski, in defense of their own position, Luxemburg felt obligated to vigorously defend *Zur Judenfrage*. Yet it was far from imperative to present this youthful anti-Jewish work of Karl Marx as a profoundly *anti-antisemitic* text, which it most certainly was not. Though Luxemburg strongly repudiated Polish middle-class intellectual demagogy on the "Jewish Question," she could never seriously come to terms with her own Jewish identity or with the reality of antisemitism in *German* society.

Nor did the German Communist Party, which Luxemburg co-founded, ever truly grasp the racist core of Nazi policies. Instead, it mendaciously presented big Jewish capitalists as financiers of Hitler's party and falsely accused German Zionists of "collaborating" with the National Socialist regime.[41] Moreover, as one secret report in 1936 by intelligence agents of the SPD noted, the German working class itself was far from immune to the general antisemitic psychosis in the Third Reich. The agent observed that the proletariat (which before 1933 had generally voted for the Socialists and Communists) "agrees to a large extent with Hitler."[42] The Crystal Night onslaught against German Jewry did, it is true, prompt a robust denunciation of the "shameful pogrom" by the German Communist leaders abroad.[43]

Immediately after World War II this anti-Nazi tradition briefly continued but it would come to a sharp halt with the anti-Jewish turn in Stalin's domestic policy after 1948. With the exception of mavericks like the East German Communist Paul Merker (who spent the war years in Mexican exile), the "Jewish Question" would be ruthlessly subordinated by Stalinist ideologues throughout the Soviet bloc to the requirements of the Cold War.

For the next forty years, Communist East Germany—ruled with an iron fist by the Socialist Unity Party (SED)—would shamelessly engage in the most malicious "anti-Zionist" propaganda. Initially, as in the Soviet Union from early 1949, this campaign was conducted under the umbrella of attacks on "bourgeois cosmopolitanism," on "rootless money men" and (mainly Jewish) Communists who had allegedly kowtowed to the West or were accused of espionage for Britain and America. Furthermore, the East German Communist regime since 1950 rigidly opposed any restitution of Jewish property seized by the Nazis. At the same time, it linked Zionism to "cosmopolitanism" and the penetration of American finance capital into postwar Germany.[44] Moreover, in the 1960s, East German ties with the Arab states were being consistenly strengthened, reinforcing the vilest Soviet rhetoric against Israel as well as Zionism. This propaganda barrage reached a paroxysm following the 1967 Six Day War victory of Israel over the Arab States. The Israeli "imperialists" were now systematically accused of imitating Hitler and his barbaric policies. Significantly, in the next twenty years the East German Communists would become key suppliers and supporters of Palestinian terrorism. Not only did the East German regime back the Arab adversaries of the Jewish State to the hilt; but in 1982 it falsely accused Israel of carrying out a "criminal genocide" of the Palestinian people.[45] Only in the last two years of its existence (1988–90) did the German Democratic Republic repent and begin to acknowledge its moral and material obligations to the victims of the Holocaust as well as seeking normalization of its relations with Israel. In one of its last acts, the GDR parliament (following the first free elections) in April 1990 unanimously adopted a statement that "asked the Jews of the world to forgive us." The parliament also asked forgiveness from the people of Israel "for the hypocrisy and hostility of official East German policies toward Israel and for the persecution and degradation of Jewish citizens also after 1945 in our country."[46]

In the Soviet Union, government attitudes towards Israel (at least until 1955) ranged from neutral to supportive, despite the official anti-Zionist ideology and the increasingly antisemitic domestic policies of Stalin's last years.[47] The Soviet dictator, as part of his Cold War against the West, was determined to seal off the "socialist paradise" from any foreign contamination. This was not only an expression of Stalin's personal paranoia but also reflected a rising tide of postwar Russian nationalism and xenophobia.[48] The Stalinist regime now began to depict international Jewry as an occult power or hidden hand manipulating the mass media, the banking system in the capitalist West, the intelligence services of the world, and foreign governments. At the same time, the Jewish State and its helpers were increasingly demonized as part of a shadowy, well-organized cabal, a freemasonry of international financiers and monopolists with an immensely ambitious plan to achieve global domination. Like Hitler before him, Stalin now saw the political usefulness of inventing an invisible, omnipotent enemy like the Jews to justify his calls for a policy of eternal vigilance and internal repression.

The deliberate assassination in January 1948 of Solomon Mikhoels, head of the wartime Jewish Anti-Fascist Committee (JAF), was the first shot in Stalin's new war against the Jews.[49] It was followed by the Slańsky trial in Prague (1952), in which thirteen Czech Communist leaders (overwhelmingly of Jewish origin) were falsely accused and then executed for working on behalf of foreign intelligence services. This was a significant escalation of the Soviet antisemitic campaign to Eastern Europe, which tightened its grip on Czechoslovakia. The pejorative label of "Zionism" (already synonymous with "treason against the Socialist fatherland") was cynically exploited against Jewish Communist leaders like Slańsky, even though throughout his career he had been firmly anti-Zionist. Then, in the spring and summer of 1952, Stalin stage-managed the secret trial of a large group of Soviet Jews connected, in some way, to the activities of the Jewish Anti-Fascist Committee.[50] They were charged with the "crime" of Jewish bourgeois nationalism, and espionage on behalf of American intelligence agencies. In August 1952, thirteen of the defendants—many of them Yiddish writers belonging to the cream of the Soviet Jewish intelligentsia—were summarily executed.

This annihilation of the remnants of an independent Jewish culture in the U.S.S.R. was formally covered by a smokescreen of Marxist-Leninist verbiage. In reality, however, there was a considerable difference between Lenin's earlier assimilationist vision of the Communist future (which had envisaged Jews eventually relinquishing their separate identity after the revolution) and Stalin's tyrannical methods of coercion in dealing with the "national question."[51] Perhaps for this reason, Stalin was careful (even after 1945) when carrying out his purge of Jews to avoid too open an expression of antisemitic prejudice. In 1931 Stalin had proclaimed to the Jewish Telegraph Agency that: "Anti-Semitism is an extreme expression of racial chauvinism and as such is the most dangerous expression of cannibalism."[52] In the interwar period, Stalin and much of the Soviet leadership had even encouraged Jewish settlements in the Crimea, established the Jewish autonomous region in Birobidzhan (as a counterweight to Zionism) and promoted a Soviet framework for developing a secular socialist Yiddish-speaking culture. It seemed plausible to many observers that the Soviet leader and his closest colleagues were against antisemitism and not opposed to the Jews becoming a "normal," territorialized national minority within the U.S.S.R. Those, like Leon Trotsky, who disputed this assessment, found themselves accused of bias.

However, by 1939, it appeared increasingly evident that Stalin was indeed moving towards eliminating most Soviet Jews (except those blindly loyal to him) from leading positions in the State or the Communist Party. Only the German invasion of the U.S.S.R. in 1941 delayed this decision for a few years. But even during the "great patriotic war" against Nazi Germany, antisemitism was raising its ugly head alongside Russian chauvinism and growing envy at the high visibility of Jews in the Soviet academy, sciences, artistic culture, the professions, and industrial enterprises. By 1945, Stalin's own paranoia about the Jews and Zionism was also becoming increasingly evident. Nonetheless, this did not prevent the articulation of vigorous Soviet support for the partition of Palestine into a Jewish as well as an Arab State at the UN from May to November 1947. Nor did it affect Stalin's authorization of arms supplies (through Czechoslovakia) to the fledgling Jewish State during the Israeli War of Independence in 1948–49. At the same time, the Soviet regime nonetheless encouraged a truly poisonous campaign of antisemitic invective to accompany the secret arrests, detentions, trials and executions of prominent Jewish personalities after 1948. On 1 December 1952 Stalin even declared during a meeting of the ruling Presidium that: "every Jew is a nationalist and an agent of American intelligence."[53] The ground was now set for the Doctors' Plot in which a number of leading Soviet physicians (mostly Jews) were grotesquely accused of conspiring with American intelligence agencies, the Zionists, and the American Jewish Joint Distribution Committee (the "Joint") to assassinate the Soviet leadership.[54]

However, the real plot was not that allegedly concocted by mythical "Zionists" but of Stalin against the Jewish doctors. This Soviet State conspiracy threatened to devastate the surviving remnant of Soviet Jewry. It would have led to the organized repression of intellectuals and artists as well as to mass deportations of Soviet Jews to Siberia and Kazakhstan. The rabid antisemitic character of this KGB-organized scenario, devised at Stalin's behest, went well beyond the suppression of Jewish intellectuals during the "anti-cosmopolitan" campaign of 1948–49 or even beyond the 1952 trial of the Jewish Anti-Fascist Committee. Hundreds of doctors were arrested between October 1952 and February 1953; antisemitic libels rapidly spread to the effect that Jewish physicians were poisoning Russian children and killing newborn infants in maternity hospitals.[55] Large-scale concentration camps, too, had allegedly been put in place as part of Stalin's planned "final solution" of the "Jewish Question" in the U.S.S.R. A great public trial, it was rumored, was intended for the end of March 1953 against the dastardly spies who had "plotted" to overthrow the Soviet government. Fortunately, on 5 March 1953 Stalin unexpectedly died (on Purim) and within less than a month the Ministry of Internal Affairs recommended that the arrested doctors be freed.[56]

Between 1948 and 1953, Stalin came to believe that Soviet Jewry was a potential fifth column in the event of what seemed like an increasingly "hot" war with the United States. He had already been dismayed in September 1948 by the pro-Israel fervor displayed by many Soviet Jews following the foundation of the Jewish State. He became convinced that Soviet Jews would side with America as the Cold War intensified and that Jews were already part of an "international conspiracy" directed from Washington against the U.S.S.R. The result was the relentless interrogation of thousands of Jewish Communists, State Security personnel, scientists, artists, and private persons of Jewish origin, who lost their positions, suffered threats and imprisonment, or endured public pillorying. All the Jewish theaters in the U.S.S.R. were closed down. Between 1949 and 1951, there were massive dismissals of Jews from public health positions and other professions across the country, especially in journalism, education, the arts and sciences. By early 1953 Soviet Jewry was being collectively demonized as "enemies of the State" by the Ministry of Security and the Soviet government. It was alleged that Jews were anti-Soviet and poisoned by bourgeois nationalism; that they controlled the foreign and domestic policies of the United States; and that they even believed themselves to be "chosen" to rule the world.[57]

Following Stalin's providential death, the Soviet and East European Communist vilification of the Jews and Israel did not disappear though it was somewhat muted. Stalin's successor, Nikita Khrushchev, liked to claim that antisemitism was the remnant of a "reactionary past" but he was nonetheless ready to justify discrimination against Jews. He told visiting foreign delegations concerned about Soviet Jews that the U.S.S.R. required "new cadres"; that the "indigenous inhabitants" of the various Soviet republics would take it amiss if Jews received top positions; and, in any case, when a Jew was appointed to an important post, "he surrounds himself with Jewish collaborators," thereby provoking antisemitic hostility.[58] Khrushchev's own racist prejudices were further revealed in a 1958 interview in *Le Figaro,* blaming the failure of Birobidzhan on Jewish individualism. They were, he said, "incapable of collective work" or any agricultural labor. As a good Communist, Khrushchev naturally denied that antisemitism had ever existed in the U.S.S.R., even during the Doctors' Plot. He did not hesitate to brazenly lie to Bertrand Russell in February 1963, blandly asserting:

> There has never been and there is not any policy of antisemitism in the Soviet Union, since the very nature of our multi-national socialist state precludes the possibility of such a policy.[59]

Yet, it was during Khrushchev's regime that the Ukrainian Academy of Sciences would publish in 1963 Trofim Kichko's vile antisemitic text depicting Judaism as a religion encouraging greed, bribery, hypocrisy, and usury. The Jewish religion, according to this work, was inextricably linked to Zionism, Israel, and Western capitalism in a global conspiracy.[60] Kichko, it is worth noting, extensively used Karl Marx's identification of Judaism and Jewry with huckstering (*torgachestvo* in Russian).[61] Initially withdrawn, Kichko's book was once again reissued after 1968, heralding the gradual incorporation of antisemitism into official Soviet Marxist-Leninist ideology.[62]

The Six Day War of 1967 with its massive defeat by Israel of several Arab States (armed by the Soviet Union) sparked an unprecedented public campaign of anti-Zionism and antisemitism emanating directly from the U.S.S.R. Henceforth the Soviet media related to "world Zionism" as a sinister international network controlling thousands of publications around the world. This "Mafia" supposedly had unlimited resources (used in the service of American imperialism) which were being mobilized to dominate the Arab world, Asia, Africa, and Latin America. "Zionism" would now be branded as Public Enemy No. 1 by the vast Soviet propaganda apparatus which expended seemingly endless amounts of money and vitriol in bracketing it with the unholy trinity of racism, imperialism, and colonialism. "World Zionism" was now being endowed by Communist propaganda with extraordinary satanic powers. It was invariably presented as the embodiment of the forces of darkness, as a truly *monstrous* force aspiring to global domination. A never-ending stream of surrealistic depictions emerged in the following decades of the Zionist enemy as "an invisible but huge and mighty empire of financiers and industrialists"; as a giant octopus whose tentacles extended into almost seventy countries around the globe.[63] In the fantasy world of Soviet journalism after 1967, the "Zionists" already had an iron grip on the Western mass media, on the big banks and publishing houses in the United States, not to mention its armaments industry. There were close to 25 million [*sic*] Zionists in America, including a majority of physicists and lawyers in the country.

In Communist Eastern Europe, too, the mythical theme of a "world Zionist conspiracy" was activated during the Polish antisemitic campaigns of 1968 and following the successful effort (imposed by Soviet tanks) to bring down Alexander Dubcek's innovative Czech experiment in humanizing "real" Socialism. In both cases, Moscow employed the time-honored techniques of racist and diversionary antisemitism to crush internal dissent, suppress trends towards democratization and channel smouldering East European nationalism away from targeting the Soviet Union. By 1968, under Communist rule in the U.S.S.R. and eastern Europe, antisemitism was emerging as a quasi-official state doctrine. "Anti-Zionism" provided the necessary rationalization for this new campaign. In 1968, an "ethno-nationalist Communist version of the myth of the Jew as the enemy of Poland" became openly manifest under Gomułka's rule.[64] Popular slogans like "Purge the Party of Zionists" (*Oczyścić Partię z Syjonistów*), or "Zionists represent Israel, not Poland" surfaced, alongside an official façade of "opposing antisemitism." The Government and Party hacks cynically substituted "Zionist" for "Jew" in their racist propaganda, though there were scarcely any Zionists left in post-Shoah Poland.

In defining who was a "Zionist," hard-core antisemites in the Communist regime did not shrink from utilizing biological criteria, recalling the rhetoric of Poland's pre-1939 ultra-nationalists who had relentlessly advocated the "ethnic cleansing" of Jews by forced emigration. Prime Minister Gomułka, in his notorious speech of 19 March 1968 to Party activists paid lip service to the possibility that there might be a few Polish patriots among the Jews but the great majority (defined as "cosmopolitans," "national nihilists," or else as "emotionally" tied to Israel) could have no place in Poland. Indeed, since July 1967 Gomułka had condemned anyone in Poland who dared to support "the Israeli aggressor" as belonging to "a fifth column" and as being a "threat" to national security. This was a theme widely disseminated on Communist State-controlled radio and television. "Zionists," in particular, were singled out for conspiring with the main external "enemies of Communist Poland"—the United States and West Germany. Zionist Jews supposedly constituted an antinational and anti-Communist group in the ruling Polish Workers Party, according to Mieczysław Moczar—at the time, Minister of the Interior, and the driving force of the 1968 anti-Jewish campaign. Others, like Andrzej Werblan (head of the Department of Science and Learning in the Party Central Committee) also favored excluding Jewish Communists on the grounds that they were imbued with a "bourgeois" and cosmopolitan ethos. Hence, they clearly lacked any national or proletarian roots. Werblan, like many in the Party, publicly blamed Jews for the errors of Stalinism in Poland. Their disproportionate influence "in certain organs of the power apparatus, in propaganda, and in the Foreign and Internal Affairs Ministries" had polluted Polish Communist thinking and alienated the Party from the Polish people.[65]

In Western Europe, a different kind of anti-Zionism was beginning to emerge around 1968, especially in the postwar New Left. Among students, intellectuals and disillusioned ex-Communists, a trend of identifying Israel with the sins of European colonialism became increasingly apparent.[66] The chorus found a lead tenor in the veteran ex-Trotskyist Isaac Deutscher, whose posthumously published essay in 1968 lashed out at

> that frenzy of belligerence, arrogance, and fanaticism of which the Israelis gave such startling displays as they rushed to Sinai and the Wailing Wall and to Jordan and the walls of Jericho.[67]

Deutscher's polemic on the Six Day War victory contained every known cliché about Israel as a "Western agent," a parasitic excrescence dependent on foreign aid and an outpost of "religious obscurantism and reaction." He asserted that the Jewish State was built on "the spirit of racial-talmudic exclusiveness and superiority."[68] Ignoring most of the pertinent facts, Deutscher squarely blamed Israeli "militarism" for the 1967 war, damning contemporary Jewish nationalism as that "of conquerors and oppressors." At the same time with breathtaking sophistry, he whitewashed an exclusivist, intolerant, radical Arab nationalism as being essentially anti-colonialist. The Israelis were dismissively caricatured as "the Prussians of the Middle East, swollen with "chauvinistic arrogance and contempt for other peoples," while the glaring backwardness and reactionary politics of the Arab world were treated with kid gloves.

Deutscher's special hatred was reserved for what he reviled as "Talmudic obscurantism" and "*hassidim* jumping for joy at the Wailing Wall. . . ." Nor did he fail to blame Israel for the vicious antisemitism in the Arab world even though this was a subject he deliberately chose to downplay. The Holocaust, too, was trivialized to the point of absurdity as a mere product of loathing for Jewish moneylenders and traders, which had been demagogically exploited by the Nazis. According to Deutscher: "The socialism of [the] fools gleefully watched Shylock led to the gas chamber."[69] Deutscher's final comments on the Jewish question were no less shallow and offensive. The Israelis in the Middle East, like the Jewish "usurers" of medieval times, yet again "arouse bitter emotions and hatreds in their neighbors"—themselves the victims of Western capitalism. They [the Jews] were to blame for appearing again "in the invidious role of agents" and as "protégés of neo-colonialism."[70] In a nutshell, the Jews were guilty for being hated! Incredibly, this tissue of baseless judgments and crude prejudices masquerading as prophetic insight, would soon attain a near-iconic status in New Left circles. So, too, did the equally partisan and jaundiced reflections of another ex-Communist, the American-Jewish muckraking journalist, I. F. Stone. Writing in August 1969, Stone bemoaned the "simplistic sophistry in the Zionist case." He rapidly glossed over the forced exodus of Jews from Arab lands after 1945 while at the same time accusing Israel of carrying out an "ethnic cleansing" of Arabs. Over forty years ago, Stone was already arguing that Israel was a racial and "exclusionist" State.[71] Ignoring the threat of Islamic Holy War, I. F. Stone concluded his overview with a characteristic piece of malevolent wit:

> That irascible Old Testament God of Vengeance is fully capable, if provoked, of turning the whole planet into a crematorium.[72]

During the past four decades, Jewish "critics" of Zion (especially on the Left) appear to be driven by an almost manic obsession with negating Israel's legitimacy and with defaming it as a monster of iniquity. They are not merely critics questioning the policies of the Jewish State but often bitter opponents of its *right to exist,* promoting efforts to boycott its institutions and bring about its demise.[73] Some, like the Anglo-Jewish academic Jacqueline Rose, even stigmatize Zionism as "a form of collective insanity"[74]; others (following the Soviet pattern) compulsively brand Israel as an "apartheid state," accuse it of systematic "ethnic cleansing" and brazenly compare it to Hitler's Third Reich. Israel is not only "bad for the Jewish people" but a threat to its safety and sanity, as well as provoking the "new" antisemitism.[75] Zionism is simply the latest form of messianic madness though one that is particularly violent, evil and dangerous. In this kind of discourse we are no longer engaged in any kind of rational argument since Zionism is *by definition* "delusional," defiled, and demonic.[76] Not surprisingly, then, Israel finds itself indicted as a uniquely horrendous and *criminal* State, the embodiment of the worst sins of European colonialism. In an equally extremist vein, the Canadian professor of philosophy, Michael Neumann, has accused Israel of "genocide" against the Palestinians and Diaspora Jewry of complicity in crimes worse than that of the German people in World War II. In response to charges that he was guilty of racist bigotry, Neumann declared that "it can be reasonable to be anti-Semitic"; indeed, he specifically accused Jews of pure racism for allegedly suggesting that "any shedding of Jewish blood is a world-shattering calamity. . . ."[77] He even claimed (without a shred of evidence) that Israelis were engaged in a "race war" against the Palestinians. Antisemites, it is worth remembering, have consistently charged the Jews with "racism." This helps to rationalize their own form of bigotry as "self-defense."

Jewish anti-Zionists from the Left increasingly provide a crucial alibi for those of their political persuasion who have transformed Israel-bashing into a fine art. One of their favorite ploys is to assert that Israel has irrevocably compromised Jewish ideals, turning the Jewish people into a nation of victimizers and oppressors. The recourse to Holocaust parallels has become de rigueur in this kind of literature. Children of Holocaust survivors, like Sara Roy or academics like Daniel Boyarin, are particularly agile in such maneuvers, whose main purpose is to redefine Diaspora Jewish identity *against* the Jewish State. In this way, Zionism can be denounced as a "heresy," a perversion and a betrayal of the Jewish prophetic tradition.[78] There can therefore be nothing positive about the Jewish State whose foundations are allegedly to be found in narrow particularism, exceptionalism, ethnicity, and chosenness; and whose practices are necessarily violent, sordid, and immoral. On these and other points Jewish anti-Zionist Leftists and the ultra-Orthodox enemies of Israel can and do, at times, come together in advocating the extinction of Israel. There are also those, like the Israeli saxophonist and anti-Zionist, Gilad Atzmon, who freely embrace the tropes of antisemitic rhetoric, even supporting the theory of a Jewish world conspiracy. This did not stop Atzmon from being enthusiastically promoted by the Trotskyist Socialist Workers Party in Great Britain.

The Trotskyists, it should be added, have a long history of virulent anti-Zionism, having for decades depicted Israel as a "militaristic," chauvinist settler-state—a watchdog for U.S. imperialism in the Middle East. For more than forty years they have been remorseless in branding the Jewish State as the supreme example of "world reaction," at times even exceeding Soviet propaganda in their vitriol. Trotskyists have been an ideological spearhead in the systematic defamation by the Western New Left of Zionism and Israel; and in promoting the malevolent myth of an imperialist and racist Jewish

State responsible for "ethnic cleansing" and "genocide" in Palestine.[79] For the new Leftists in the West, the Palestinians could do no wrong. They were a poor, stateless people of refugees fighting for a homeland denied to them by Zionist oppression. They were and remain paragons of resistance enjoying the halo of absolute victims. Israel, on the other hand, has assumed in the eyes of the radical Left the despised mantle of a conquering *Herrenvolk* exclusively to blame for Palestinian suffering. This New Left argumentation was scarcely different from official Communist rhetoric, except for its ultra-radicalism and violent negation of Israeli statehood. In the radical anti-Zionist dispensation, calls for the destruction of Israel—itself a racist demand—would become the indispensable prerequisite for the surrealist dream of a socialist revolution in the Middle East.[80]

Notes

1. Robert S. Wistrich, "Antisemitism as a 'Radical' Ideology in the 19th Century," *Jerusalem Quarterly,* no. 28 (Summer 1983): 83–94.

2. Richard S. Geehr, *Karl Lueger, Mayor of Fin-de-Siècle Vienna* (Detroit, 1990).

3. For this erroneous claim, see P. G. J. Pulzer, *Die Entstehung des politischen Antisemitismus in Deutschland und Österreich, 1867–1914* (Gütersloh, 1966).

4. Robert S. Wistrich, *The Jews of Vienna in the Age of Franz Joseph* (Oxford, 1989).

5. Brigitte Hamann, *Hitler's Vienna* (Oxford, 1999), 236–304.

6. Pierre-André Taguieff, *La Judéophobie des Modernes* (Paris, 2008), 136–208.

7. Jacques Hermone, *La Gauche, Israël et les Juifs* (Paris, 1970), 36–40.

8. Robert Michels, *Political Parties: A Sociological Study of the Oligarchical Tendencies of Modern Democracy* (New York, 1959; German ed., 1913), 260.

9. Werner T. Angress, "Juden im politischen Leben der Revolutionszeit," in *Deutsches Judentum im Krieg und Revolution 1916–1923,* edited by Werner E. Mosse and Arnold Paucker (Tübingen, 1971), 235–51.

10. Robert S. Wistrich, *Socialism and the Jewish Question in Germany and Austria 1880–1914* (Ph.D. diss., University of London, 1974) devotes more than 300 pages to the "Jewish Question" within the Austrian workers movement; see especially, pp. 502–738.

11. Victor Adler, "Unser Parteitag und die Presse," *Gleichheit,* 12 Jan. 1889, 2.

12. Victor Adler, "Christliche und jüdische Ausbeutung," 28 Feb. 1897, in *Aufsätze, Reden und Briefe* (Vienna, 1929), 10:110–18.

13. *Verhandlungen des sechsten österreichischen Sozialdemokratischen Parteitages* (Vienna, 1897), 87. The Congress was held in Vienna between 6 and 12 June 1897.

14. See Robert S. Wistrich, *Socialism and the Jews. The Dilemmas of Assimilation in Germany and Austria-Hungary* (London, 1982).

15. Robert S. Wistrich, *Revolutionary Jews from Marx to Trotsky* (London 1976), 110–11.

16. See "Der Zionistenkongress in Wien," *Arbeiter-Zeitung,* 4 Sept. 1913, 6–7.

17. Wistrich, *Revolutionary Jews*, 113–14. See also Julius Braunthal, "The Jewish Background of Victor and Friedrich Adler," *Leo Baeck Yearbook* 10 (1965): 266–76.

18. Bernstein Nachlass, *International Institute for Social History* (115 A, Amsterdam), B.10, for Huysmans's anecdote.

19. Theodor Lessing, *Der jüdische Selbsthass* (Berlin, 1930); Kurt Lewin, "Self-hatred among Jews," *Contemporary Jewish Record* 4, no. 3 (New York, 1941): 219–32; Jacob Golomb, *Nietzsche and Zion* (Ithaca, N.Y., 2004).

16. See Robert S. Wistrich, *Laboratory for World Destruction. Germans and Jews in Central Europe* (Lincoln, Neb., 2007), 304–24.

21. For a psychoanalysis of Marx, see Arnold Künzli, *Karl Marx. Eine Psychographie* (Vienna, 1966).

22. Robert S. Wistrich, "Antishemiut radicalit be-tsarfat ve-germania, 1840–1870," in *Israel and the Nations* [no editor] (Jerusalem: Historical Society of Israel, 1987). For a different approach, see Sander Gilman, *Jewish Self-Hatred: Anti-Semitism and the Hidden Language of the Jews* (Baltimore, 1986).

23. Robert S. Wistrich, "The Jews and Socialism," *Jewish Spectator* (June 1976): 13–21; idem, "Karl Kraus: Jewish Prophet or Renegade?" *European Judaism* 9, no. 2 (Summer 1975): 32–39; see also Paul Lawrence Rose, *Wagner. Race and Revolution* (London, 1992), 49–101, 177–84.

24. Robert S. Wistrich, *Laboratory for World Destruction*, 21–24.

25. For the Communist position, Edmund Silberner, *Kommunisten zur Judenfrage* (Opladen, 1983). On the Social Democratic perception, see Robert S. Wistrich, *Socialism and the Jews. The Dilemmas of Assimilation in Germany and Austria-Hungary* (London, 1982).

26. See Robert S. Wistrich, "Zionism and Its Jewish Assimilationist Critics (1897–1948)," *Jewish Social Studies* 4, no. 2 (Winter 1998): 59–111.

27. Thomas Haury, *Antisemitismus von Links. Kommunistische Ideologie, Nationalismus und Antizionismus in der DDR* (Hamburg, 2002).

28. Robert S Wistrich, *European Anti-Semitism Reinvents Itself* (New York: American Jewish Committee, 2005), 11–16, 21–23.

29. Gilles William Goldnadel, *Le Nouveau Bréviaire de la Haine: Antisémitisme et antisionisme* (Paris, 2001); Georges-Elia Sarfati, *L'Antisionisme: Israël/Palestine aux miroirs d'Occident* (Paris, 2002), 20–22, 38–39.

30. See Wistrich, *European Anti-Semitism*; Yossi Klein Halevi, "Hatreds Entwined," *Azure* 16 (Winter 2004): 25–31; Ron Rosenbaum, ed., *Those Who Forget the Past: The Question of Anti-Semitism* (New York, 2004).

31. Silberner, *Kommunisten,* 211–310.

32. See Lars Fischer, *The Socialist Response to Antisemitism in Imperial Germany* (Cambridge, 2007), who elaborates on a point I had made at least thirty years earlier, but does provide some additional examples.

33. See the final chapter in Bernard Lazare's 1894 study, *L'Antisémitisme. Son Histoire et Ses Causes*; and my introduction to the English translation, *Antisemitism. Its History and Causes* (Lincoln, Neb., 1995), *v–xx*.

34. Edouard Drumont, *La Libre Parole,* 10 Jan. 1895, 1.

35. *Berliner Volksblatt,* 7, 109 (13 May 1890). Engels's text was originally formulated as a letter sent to a Viennese correspondent Isidor Ehrenfreund on 21 Mar. 1890. See my discussion of Engels in *Socialism and the Jews,* 126–30.

36. See Fischer, *Socialist Response,* 64–81.

37. August Bebel, *Sozialdemokratie und Antisemitismus* (Berlin: Vorwärts, 1894). Reissued in 1906; and Robert S. Wistrich, *Socialism and the Jews,* 131–40 for a discussion of Bebel.

38. See Robert S. Wistrich, "The SPD and Antisemitism in the 1890s," *European Studies Review* 7, no. 2 (1977): 177–97.

39. See Robert S. Wistrich, "The Jewish Origins of Rosa Luxemburg," *Olam,* no. 3 (Winter 1977): 3–11. Her collected works were published in Berlin between 1970 and 1975; her *Gesammelte Briefe* appeared in 6 volumes, published by Dietz in Berlin between 1982 and 1993. See also Jack Jacobs, "Rosa Luxemburg. Den eigenen Weg gehen und die Leute reden lassen," in *Ketzer im Kommunismus,* edited by Theodor Bergmann and Mario Kessler (Hamburg: VSA, 2000), 22–35.

40. See Wistrich, *Socialism and the Jewish Question in Germany and Austria 1880–1914,* 381–99.

41. Silberner, *Kommunisten zur Judenfrage,* 286–92.

42. *Sopade* (Jan. 1936), quoted in Daniel J. Goldhagen, *Hitler's Willing Executioners. Ordinary Germans and the Holocaust* (New York, 1996), 107.

43. Silberner, *Kommunisten zur Judenfrage,* 290–91.

44. See Jeffrey Herf, *Divided Memory. The Nazi Past in the Two Germanies* (Cambridge, Mass, 1997), 106–61.

45. Ibid., 198–200.

46. See Yosef Govrin, "Paving a Path from Pankow to Jerusalem: GDR-Israel Relations 1989–1990," *Israel Journal of Foreign Affairs* 2, no. 3 (2008): 141–58.

47. Peter Brod, *Die Antizionismus und Israelpolitik der USSR. Voraussetzung und Entwicklung bis 1956* (Baden-Baden, 1980), 48–106.

48. See Robert S. Wistrich, "From Lenin to Today's Black Hundreds," *Midstream* (Mar. 1978): 4–12; idem, "The Anti-Zionist Masquerade," *Midstream* (Aug.–Sept. 1983): 8–17; idem, "The Soviet Union, Israel and the Western media," *Middle East Focus* (Spring–Summer 1988): 16–20.

49. Arkady Vaksberg, *Stalin against the Jews* (New York, 1994), 159–82 on the murder of Mikhoels.

50. Joshua Rubinstein and Vladimir P. Naumov, eds., *Stalin's Secret Pogrom* (New Haven, 2001), provides an important documentary record of the postwar Soviet inquisition of the Jewish Anti-Fascist Committee.

51. Chimen Abramsky, "Hitpatchut ha-Yachas kelapei Hayehudim be-ideologyia uvema'asei ha-Sovietim," in *Antishemiut be-brit ha-moatsot,* edited by Shmuel Ettinger (Tel Aviv, 1986), 72–79.

52. Rubinstein and Naumov, *Stalin's Secret Pogrom,* 33.

53. Ibid., 62.

54. Jonathan Brent and Vladimir P. Naumov, *Stalin's Last Crime. The Plot against the Jewish Doctors 1948–1953* (New York, 2003), 1–10.

55. Yakov Rapoport, *The Doctors' Plot of 1953: A Survivor's Memoir of Stalin's Last Act of Terror against Jews and Science* (Cambridge, Mass, 1991), 82–85.

56. Brent and Naumov, *Stalin's Last Crime,* 48–49.

57. Ibid., 253–57.

58. S. Levenberg, "Soviet Jewry: Some Problems and Perspectives" and C. Abramsky, "On the Birobidzhan Project, 1927–1959," in *The Jews in Soviet Russia since 1917,* edited by L. Kochan (Oxford, 1970), 36–37, 74.

59. Quoted by William Korey, "The Legal Position of Soviet Jewry: A Historical Inquiry," in ibid., 96.

60. Jack Miller, "Soviet Theory on the Jews," in ibid., 47.

61. Trofim Kichko, *Iudaizm bez prikras* (Judaism without embellishment) (Kiev: Ukrainian Academy of Sciences, 1963).

62. Robert S. Wistrich, "The New War against the Jews," *Commentary* (May 1985): 35–40.

63. See William Korey, *Russian Antisemitism, Pamyat, and the Demonology of Zionism* (Chur, Switzerland, 1995), 16–17; also the article by Yevgeny Yevseev on Zionism, *Komsomolskaya Pravda,* 4 Oct. 1967.

64. Quoted by Joanna Beata Michlic, *Poland's Threatening Other. The Image of the Jew from 1880 to the Present* (Lincoln, Neb., 2006), 242; see also Dariusz Stola, *Kampania antysyjonistyczna* (Warsaw, 2000).

65. See Adam Ciolkosz, "Anti-Zionism in Polish Communist Party Politics," in *The Left against Zion. Communism, Israel and the Middle East,* edited by Robert S. Wistrich (London, 1979), 145–47; Michlic, *Poland's Threatening Other,* 255.

66. Robert S. Wistrich, "The Anti-Zionist Masquerade," *Midstream* (Aug.–Sept. 1983): 6–16.

67. Deutscher's text is reproduced in Adam Schatz, ed., *Prophets Outcast* (New York, 2004), 168–87.

68. Deutscher, in ibid., 171.

69. Ibid., 185–86.

70. Ibid., 186.

71. I. F. Stone, "Holy War," in ibid., 19–209; first published in the *New York Review,* 3 Aug. 1969.

72. Ibid., 208.

73. Alvin H. Rosenfeld, *"Progressive" Jewish Thought and the New Antisemitism* (New York: American Jewish Committee, 2006).

74. Jacqueline Rose, *The Question of Zion* (Princeton, 2005), 17.

75. Ibid., 85, 154.

76. Rosenfeld, *"Progressive" Jewish Thought,* 10–11.

77. Michael Neumann, "What Is Anti-Semitism?" in *The Politics of Anti-Semitism,* edited by Alexander Cockburn and Jeffrey St. Clair (Oakland, Calif., 2003), 3–10.

78. Seth Farber, ed., *Radicals, Rabbis and Peacemakers: Conversations with Jewish Critics of Israel* (Monroe, Me., 2005), 15, 63.

79. See Robert S. Wistrich, *A Lethal Obsession. Anti-Semitism from Antiquity to the Global Jihad* (New York, 2010), 503.

80. Ibid.

CHAPTER 2

Karl Marx, Moses Hess, and Jewish Emancipation

The challenge which antisemitism has posed to the European Left cannot be understood without taking into account the extent to which socialist thought was tainted from its very origins with the heavy baggage of anti-Jewish stereotypes. This was especially evident in the case of France and Germany, where a form of radical and socialist Judeophobia had already developed in the 1830s and 1840s.[1] Though this hostility to Jews and Judaism often seemed anti-Christian, yet it was far from immune to the age-old "theological" and social animus of Christianity towards Judaism. In Germany, for example, residues of the violent diatribes against usury of Martin Luther (the great Protestant reformer and shaper of German culture) seeped into the latent Judeophobia of the Socialist and Communist movements.[2] Luther's view of the Jews as worldly agents of the Devil was certainly not part of the official socialist world-view; but his outbursts did help to promote the concept of *Verjudung* ("Judaization" or "Jewification") which became such a powerful myth in Germany—one that also affected the Left.[3] Moreover, Luther's incendiary calls in the 16th century to confiscate Jewish property, to institute harsh labor for young Jews, and to destroy Judaism itself, were never entirely forgotten in Germany. Though the German Left (unlike the Conservative Right or the National Socialists) could never openly identify with Luther's hysterical and murderous denunciations of Jewry, a paler echo of the demonic connotations which he had lent to the term *Jude* periodically appeared in its rhetoric.

By the mid-18th century, it is true that traditional Christian anti-Judaism was giving way to a new kind of secular antagonism towards the Jews. In France, it was the "enlightened" *philosophe* Voltaire who led the charge, branding the Jews as "an ignorant and barbarous people who have long united the most sordid avarice with the most detestable superstition. . . ." Voltaire unashamedly revived the classical pagan accusation that Jewry was constantly driven "by the most invincible hatred for every people by whom they are tolerated and enriched."[4] In 1793 the German philosopher Johann

Gottlieb Fichte—then in his Jacobin revolutionary phase—would go even further in constructing a new foundation for modern Jew-hatred. He declared that:

> in the bosom of almost all the nations of Europe there spreads a powerful state driven by hostile feelings that is continually at war with all the others, and that in certain places terribly oppresses the citizens. I speak of Jewry.[5]

In Fichte's radical Jacobin world-view *Das Judentum* was a "state within a state" which stood in contradiction to the new philosophical principles of freedom and morality. Judaism was deemed to be exclusivist, separatist, and indissolubly linked to the petty trading mentality "that enfeebles the body and closes the mind to every noble feeling."[6] This narrow "egoism" and misanthropy, supposedly embedded in the Jewish religion and national character, was soon to become a significant leitmotif in 19th-century German radical rhetoric. In discussing the question of civil rights for Jews, Fichte made a particularly macabre comment. He stated that he could see no alternative "other than that of some night cutting off their heads and attaching in their place others in which there is not a single Jewish idea." To ensure German self-protection, Fichte proposed "to conquer for them their promised land and pack them off there."[7]

Fichte, like other antisemitic German philosophers from the turn of the 19th century, used the term *Judentum* in a rather ambiguous, fluctuating way. It could mean Jews in an empirical sense and also serve as a metaphor for social evils that needed to be extirpated. "Judaism" simultaneously stood for a religious community, an ethnic group, a nation, and represented an abstract symbol for the mercantile or capitalist "spirit." This flexibility favored the kind of lurid imagery linking Jews with the all-devouring Moloch of Mammon that became increasingly prominent in socialist writings after 1840. The first German socialist Moses Hess (himself a Jew), writing in 1843, would even identify the "Jewish Jehovah—Moloch" and the Christian God with human sacrifice, capitalistic cannibalism, and social parasitism.[8] Though this proved to be a momentary aberration in the case of Hess, such terminology indicates the antisemitic potential of the new secular and revolutionary mythology already being embraced by a part of the German Left. It soon became a truism to regard the Israelite God as a manifestation of "Jewish" materialism with Christianity as its more refined offshoot. A prominent radical German Jewish journalist like Ludwig Börne had presented a slightly more sophisticated version of this critique as early as 1808. Börne considered the Jewish drive for trade and profit to be endemic, rooted in a perpetual need for intense activity. The Jews were a *Volk* (nation)

> whose southern origin endures still so pure in its blood and feeling, a race that is preoccupied more with fantasy than with reason. . .such a race must always be pushed to activity by its restless spirit.[9]

Börne anticipated Karl Marx in seeing Jews as being driven by their diseased egoism and frenzied obsession with money-making. For Börne, the eternal Jew (*der ewige Jude*) of Christian legend and newly revived by modern economic antisemitism, reflected a real Jewish proclivity for commerce and business *praxis*. No doubt Börne's identification of the business world with Jewishness (*Judentümlichkeit*)—defined as the money-demon—was one factor in endearing him to a visceral antisemite like Richard Wagner. At the same time, despite his own personal sensitivity to antisemitic persecution, Börne's assault on the "money-devil," Moloch and "Jewish" egoism undoubtedly fed the rising tide of "progressive" Jew-hatred. As Paul Rose put it,

> in the process of trying to rescue the Jews by stamping all capitalism as "Jewish," he made "Judaism" the archetypal metaphor for evil in modern life.[10]

Börne thereby bequeathed to Richard Wagner and also to his German socialist heirs (including Marx, Hess, and Franz Mehring) a distorted image of Judaism as the epitome of an alienated, dehumanized religion of Mammon.

Börne was a sarcastic, witty writer but he lacked the sympathy and humor of the poet Heinrich Heine, who had also gone through a similarly radical phase. In 1840 Heine had declared: "Money is the god of our time and Rothschild is his prophet." Like Börne, he did not spare Christians from his critique of Mammon and in his more doctrinaire moments, he shared the radical belief that social revolution would sweep away the modern economic forms of Jew-hatred. But Heine was far more alert to the dangers of the German Revolution, prophesying that once it arrived it would make the violent French upheavals of 1789 appear like a "harmless idyll." Heine foresaw that such a revolution would release the pagan Germanic instincts ("Thor with his colossal hammer") smashing the Gothic cathedral into fragments and bringing down unprecedented persecutions "on the heads of the poor Jews . . . ."[11] Unlike Marx and Börne, Heine had been moved since the early 1820s by the "spirit" of Jewish history and the mystery of Jewish survival. He was acutely sensitive to the fate of "this murdered people, this ghost-people" who through centuries of suffering "had preserved the treasures of the Hebrew Bible" in the darkness of their ghettoes.

By the late 1840s Heine had given up his youthful Hegelianism, the residues of Hellenic paganism and a somewhat arrogant self-deifying humanism. Revolutionary politics now seemed to him little more than a mad farce, producing only universal anarchy. Attacking his old Young Hegelian comrades he caustically remarked that their "cobweb Berlin dialectic" could not "kill a cat, much less a God. . . ."

> I recommend the Book of Daniel to the excellent Ruge as well as the rest of my still more deluded friends Messrs. Marx, Feuerbach, Daumer, Bruno Bauer. . .those godless self-gods.[12]

In his newly confessional mood, Heine now considered Judaism to be far more revolutionary than the visions of the Promethean German prophets of cataclysmic upheaval. The poet poignantly remarked: "Moses created a nation that was to defy the centuries—a great, eternal, holy people, the people of God, which could serve as the model for all humanity." Heine, the democrat, was no longer afraid to declare himself "a descendant of those martyrs of Israel who gave the world a God and a morality, and who fought and suffered on all the battlefields of thought."[13] This was the kind of sensibility conspicuously lacking in Karl Marx and other radicals committed to the "destruction" or disappearance of Judaism as the repulsive embodiment of soulless inhuman capitalism. They wrote as if universal human emancipation was being thwarted by "Jewish" money-worship. Their revolutionary message implied that human redemption could only be achieved through the elimination of a Judaic creed crassly reduced to petty huckstering and practical need.

Karl Marx (1818–1883), the co-founder of "scientific socialism" in Germany, was the heir of this Young Hegelian philosophical tradition. His intervention in the debate on German Jewish emancipation in the early 1840s came at a time when negligible political rights existed for the majority of citizens in the fragmented German states.[14] Moreover, he had to confront a Prussian Christian State which was unabashedly authoritarian in character, practiced censorship, and was far removed from the levels of secular debate that already prevailed in neighboring France. On the Jewish side, the debate also posed fundamental questions about collective self-definition, the status of Jews as a minority, and the historic role of Judaism in the context of emancipation and assimilation. Was Judaism compatible with the exercise of full equality of rights in a predominantly Christian State? Did a Jew have to renounce his Jewish identity in order to integrate into German society or to participate in the public affairs of the Prusso-Christian State? The different solutions proposed to these issues provoked a debate in the radical Hegelian camp not without significance for the subsequent development of German socialism.

Before examining these polemics we should briefly look at the evaluation of Judaism in modern German philosophy which provided basic premises for the internal debate among the Young Hegelians. Already in the writings of Immanuel Kant (1724–1804) one can find a hostile interpretation of Judaism denying it any authentic moral or even religious content.[15] Judaism was depicted by Kant as a particularistic, irrational, arbitrary, and misanthropic creed. A messianic, revealed religion, it stood in opposition to the Kantian emphasis on moral intentionality derived from the universal postulates of human reason. Kant believed (with some justification) that the Sinaitic revelation sought to definitively separate the Jews from other peoples and (more arbitrarily) that Mosaism was a form of juridical positivism which encouraged blind obedience to a despotic, divine will and the pedantic observance of ritual. A historical religion such as Judaism, based on a binding, external law, could only be an obstacle to human freedom and the development of rational ethics. It was irreconcilable with his humanist concept of philosophical reason and an inner-directed moral idealism derived from the tradition of Lutheran theology. Kant's erroneous idea that Judaism was concerned only with external behavior (an interpretation influenced by the writings of Jewish philosophers such as Spinoza and Moses Mendelssohn) and his insistence that it represented an obsolete tradition which had to be rejected, would be characteristic of much of the German philosophical tradition.[16]

Many of these themes were repeated in the writings of the towering figure of G. W. F. Hegel (1770–1831), whose dialectical philosophy expressed even greater antipathy to Judaism, especially in his early theological writings.[17] Hegel went beyond Kant in presenting the statutory nature of Judaism as a symbol of *spiritual self-estrangement*. Within early Hegelian thought, the Jew was described not only as alienated from himself, but also from God, from the Universe, and from other peoples. The Jews, lacking any concept of "self-consciousness" or a philosophy of the infinite spirit, were supposedly incapable of transcending their physical existence as a people or their absolute dependence on a "remote" God. The Hegelian concept of Judaism as a religion rooted in an all-pervasive legalistic externality which denied the unity of life and of the spirit was contrasted in highly unfavorable terms with the Hellenic ideal and with Protestant Christianity. Within Judaism there could be no inwardness or subjectivity, no union of God and the world, of man and God, or of the subjective and objective in a total dialectical process. Hegel's pantheistic monism with its misplaced transcendence of reality restated the traditional Christian view that Judaism was a *lower* form of revelation, but it did so in a novel dialectical form.[18] His philosophy of history presented Judaism as a stage in the universal, historical process (on the margins of the declining Oriental and the dawning Occidental culture) which involved a radical separation of God from the world of the senses.[19] According to this view, Judaic monotheism had stripped man and nature of their substance by subordinating them to an Absolute Will which did not descend into the world but remained an abstract essence. In the Hegelian schema, Judaism was sharply separated from Christianity and thus denied any influence over the development of the modern Western culture. It had completed its destiny in the Oriental world and could not therefore reappear or constitute a new factor in universal history. Though Hegel's system excluded Judaism from any positive consideration as a spiritual factor, he nonetheless opposed the Christian-Germanic student agitation against Jewish emancipation which had culminated in the antisemitic "Hep-Hep" riots of 1819. In his *Philosophy of Right* Hegel specifically argued that the modern State could *not* deny to the Jews their human and civil rights without contradicting its own rational basis.[20] In this respect Hegel was still a pupil of the eighteenth-century Enlightenment tradition of universalist rationality.

In the years following Hegel's death in 1831, his philosophy continued to exercise an immense influence in German universities, though his legacy was interpreted in a radically different sense by the Right and Left. The Young Hegelian school led by Bruno Bauer (1809–1882), a Protestant lecturer in theology at the University of Berlin since 1834, utilized his teachings in their struggle against religious orthodoxy and feudal reaction. Bauer had gradually evolved from an orthodox Hegelian position to the advocacy of radical, militant atheism which led to dismissal from his teaching post in 1842.[21] In the same year he first entered the debate over the "Jewish question," provoking an animated controversy by his pungent opposition to liberal advocates of Jewish emancipation.[22] Many of Bauer's ideas on Judaism were derived from Hegelian premises regarding the development of religion. Thus he accepted the assumption that Judaism was a lower level of revelation, lacking the element of self-consciousness in Christianity which had raised man to the level of God. His central thesis asserted that the Jews were an *unhistorical* people, and that their religion reflected a non-historical conception of life, wholly irreconcilable with personal liberty. This was a radical extension of Hegelian concepts. Bruno Bauer also attributed the static quality of the "Jewish spirit" to the Orient where (as Hegel had argued) man had yet to acquire consciousness of himself as a free and rational being.[23] The Jews clearly did not fit into the "progressive" version of the Hegelian philosophy of history. They had outlived their assigned role in history and their continued existence was perceived by the Young Hegelians as an affront to critical reason and modernity.

Bruno Bauer explicitly argued that Jews were a *fossilized* element whose very survival was possible only because they lived in a "chimerical" world, against the stream of time and the needs of historical evolution. The Jewish Law, he insisted, was the legal code of a completely *ahistorical* and "imaginary" people who did not participate in real life. The Talmud expressed this stubbornness of the Jewish spirit, its *arbitrary* and negative character—it was the "chimerical, illusory, mindless continuation" of Mosaism, "a collection of fragments and bits into which the old had disintegrated."[24] The Jewish Law lacked any reality because it was never implemented. It marked the end of Jewish history, the conscious desire to shut out the principle of creative evolution and change. "History demands an evolution of new phases, progress and transformations, the Jews always wish to remain the same, they fight therefore against the first law of history."[25] Jewish Law not only expressed the immutable, anti-historical essence of Jewry; it deliberately erected barriers between itself and the rest of humanity—thereby obstructing any rational, universal development. The Jewish Law, by hemming in the people with its petty restrictions, its "meaningless" rituals and ceremonies, reinforced the tenacity and stubbornness of the Jewish character, its egoism and exclusivity. The essence of Jewry lay in this illusory, national particularism, the fanatical clinging to chimerical privileges.[26] In its eyes no other people had a right to exist except as "slaves" of the Jews in a future messianic era. Illogical, inconsistent and totally submissive to the will of Jehovah, this [Jewish] nation was a "people without freedom," believing only in itself.

Bruno Bauer's theological and metaphysical theories eventually led to unmistakably antisemitic conclusions.[27] Against the advocates of Jewish emancipation he already argued in the early 1840s that the Jews "have deserved the oppression which they have suffered." This oppression was due to the tenacity with which they had maintained their uniqueness, their phantom identity. Incapable of integrating in the real world, of co-existing with other peoples, of establishing a natural, secular existence as a nation, or organizing an independent State, *the Jews were the cause of their own oppression*. "The Jews have been oppressed because they have first of all oppressed others and they went against the historical current."[28] Having excluded themselves by their attachment to their Law, their nationality, their language, and their denial of historical movement, they were not so much the victims of the Christian State but rather the *source* of its religious zeal and fanaticism. In branding Jews as "oppressors" and responsible for their own persecution, Bauer prophetically anticipated a central strand in contemporary antisemitic discourse on the Left. Even Bauer's rejection of Christianity also flowed naturally from his critique of Judaism. Christianity was as *exclusivist* as Judaism; it was the continuation on a higher plane of the same intolerant prejudice, the same hostility to nature, and the same repudiation of human reality. "Christianity is completed Judaism. Judaism is unachieved Christianity"—a formula that was to be repeated by both Ludwig Feuerbach and Marx.[29]

The Christian State, according to the Young Hegelian Bauer, when it excluded the Jews was only applying the narrow-minded, separatist principles it had imbibed from Judaism. It was simply perpetuating the essence of Judaism itself. The Christian State was founded on "privileges" that it had expanded and developed from its Jewish legacy.[30] Hence Christian hostility to Judaism was perfectly natural both in terms of the historical relationship between the two religions and with regard to their common exclusivist essence. Moreover, although Christians had not yet reached the highest stage of human self-consciousness, they had at least demonstrated a capacity for the scientific critique of religion. They had shown a sense of historical evolution, a willingness to fight for objective truth. The Jews on the other hand had contributed nothing to the arts or sciences. They had played no part, according to Bruno Bauer, in the development of the modern world.[31] The stultifying effect of Judaism as a religion had prevented any intercourse with the world except that necessitated by personal need. As long as Jews stayed as they were, enclosed in this non-historical conception of life, they had no claim to emancipation, since they had contributed nothing to the liberation of Germany. Indeed, to accept their claim under such conditions would simply reinforce the "privileges" of the Christian State to which Bauer was strongly opposed.[32]

Hence emancipation must be denied to the Jews unless they abandoned their Jewishness and particularist, exclusivist essence.[33] This would be more difficult for the Jew than the Christian, for he had not yet begun the process of freeing himself from religious prejudice. Moreover, the "parasitic" role of the Jews in bourgeois society was a further obstacle, for they had become agents of exploitation. In a passage that clearly impressed Karl Marx, Bruno Bauer remarked:

> As the gods of Epicurus live in the interstices of the world. . .so the Jews have established themselves outside the definite interests of the corporations, have nestled in the pores of civil society and taken advantage of the victims produced by the elements of insecurity in that society.[34]

Hence it was not correct that their degraded condition was due to persecution by the Christian State. For, as Bruno Bauer and Marx were to argue, Jewish usury and financial oppression existed even without political rights. Nevertheless, the economic argument was ultimately incidental to Bauer's case against emancipation. More fundamental was his assertion that the Christian State by its very nature was as incapable of granting universal human rights as was the Jew of receiving them. So long as there were no "citizens" in the absolutist State, the persistence of the ghetto was in harmony with general conditions. If no social classes in Germany were politically free, then what justification did the Jews have for demanding equality of rights? All civil and political castes as well as special privileges would first have to be abolished, before religious prejudice and separatism could vanish. Only in an *atheistic* State where there were no more Jews or Christians could emancipation become a human reality. Hence the suppression of the Christian State dialectically demanded the suppression of the Jews and Judaism.[35] Since Christianity itself was "completed Judaism," to abolish Judaism would greatly contribute to the emancipation of humanity.

Karl Marx, despite his rejection of Bauer's concept of political emancipation and human rights, absorbed much of his anti-Jewish venom while translating it into a *materialist* theory of Judaism. Though critical of the "abstract" and metaphysical aspects in Bauer's method, he shared the militant atheism of his former teacher and close friend.[36] He was appreciative of the fact that Bruno Bauer had posed "the question of Jewish emancipation in a new way." Marx altogether ignored the antisemitic implications of the text which he criticized. He felt that there was nothing much wrong with Bauer's "critique of the Jewish religion" or with his description of the *nature* of the Jew who had to be emancipated:

> He [Bauer] answers with a critique of the Jewish religion, he analyzes the *religious* opposition between Judaism and Christianity and he explains the essence of the Christian State, all this with dash,

perception, wit and thoroughness in a style as precise as it is pithy and trenchant.[37]

For Marx, as for Bauer and the Young Hegelian school in general, it was self-evident that the Jews had contributed nothing to historical development, except in a negative sense. The role of the Jew in history and his "essence" had remained unchanged. He was destined to vanish in the coming struggle for world liberation. Religion was an illusion, a separatist barrier in the fight for German emancipation.[38]

The Young Hegelians shared a common belief that Judaism was a major obstacle to this general process of emancipation even if they differed over their tactical approach to the problem of human rights. Without exception they rejected Jewish particularism as radically incompatible with the law of progress, and the Jewish religion as being the stationary remnant of a vanished historical mission. This assumption was as true for the Jewish Left Hegelians as it was for Bruno Bauer. All were agreed that Jews would have to strip off their "Jewish" essence if they were to participate as human beings in the coming redemption of man. This idea was as axiomatic as the radical Hegelian opposition to the Christian-Germanic State in Prussia.

The impact on Karl Marx of this left-wing Hegelianism can be observed not only in his borrowings from Bruno Bauer but also in his warm admiration for Ludwig Feuerbach (1804–1872), whom he hailed in his youth as "the true conqueror of the old philosophy." Since 1839 Feuerbach had been the pioneer of the humanistic critique of Hegelian dialectics, the philosopher whom both Marx and Engels acknowledged as the creator of a real theoretical revolution.[39] It was Feuerbach who had first exposed Hegelianism as the last refuge of theology. He did this in the name of an anthropological critique of religion which restored the primacy of *being* over thought. Feuerbach's *Essence of Christianity* (1841) and his *Preliminary Theses on the Reform of Philosophy* (1843) had an immensely liberating effect in Young Hegelian circles. Marx enthusiastically declared that "there is no other road to truth and freedom. . . . Feuerbach is the *purgatory* of our time."[40] Frederick Engels many years later added that Feuerbach had "placed materialism on the throne again." The Feuerbachian revolution turned philosophy upside-down by explaining the Hegelian alienated consciousness as the self-consciousness of real man and the world of religion as the product of this alienation. In his *Theses on Feuerbach* (1845) Marx acknowledged the achievement of Feuerbach "in dissolving the religious world into the worldly foundation" though he went beyond his predecessor in seeking the solution to self-alienation through revolutionary practice.[41] In his earlier writings, including the "Jewish Question," Marx was however a Feuerbachian in method and terminology. His conceptions of economic and political alienation followed the Feuerbachian model. His argument in "Zur Judenfrage" concerning the repossession by man of his own social forces and his theories of alienation in the 1844 Paris Manuscripts all show the influence of Feuerbach's humanism with its emphasis on the primacy of the sense-world, the finite, the empirical and the real. For the young Marx, as for Feuerbach, man was above all a "species being" (*Gattungswesen*) alienated from nature, his own life-activity and from other men by the egoism of civil society. Moses Hess, another enthusiastic disciple of Feuerbach, would work out a theory of philosophical communism before Marx, based on similar assumptions.

Feuerbach's *Essence of Christianity* contained an analysis of Judaism which shaped Marx's own terminology as much as his transformational criticism of Hegel. Like Bruno Bauer, Feuerbach held that Christianity was "spiritual Judaism"—in other words a more ethereal, purified version of the Jewish religion. It had freed its religious consciousness from "the limits of a particular, national interest," from the national egoism of the Jews.[42] Whereas the miracles of the Old Testament were concerned with the welfare of a particular nation, Christian miracles were about the welfare of all men. In the Hegelian tradition, Feuerbach favorably contrasted the Christian God of love with the punitive character of the Jewish Law, the Christian universal spirit with Jewish ethnocentrism. In the Kantian tradition, Feuerbach argued that there was no *moral law* in Judaism. As a religion it was based not on reason or ethics but solely on the Divine Commandments. The Jewish Law applied to a *national,* political community and was intended to encompass all worldly existence. Judaism was therefore the most extreme form of legalistic religion. "Israel is the most complete presentation of positivism in religion."[43] From these assumptions, Feuerbach drew his fundamentally negative conclusions about Jewish attitudes to nature and life which undoubtedly influenced Marx. Whereas heathen polytheism had encouraged the study and worship of nature, the Jews had *degraded* it to being a mere servant of divine will. While the arts and sciences had arisen out of a polytheistic world-view which accepted nature, the Jewish approach was narrowly practical and selfish. Philosophy and aesthetics were the product of heathen openness to life whereas "utilism" was the essential theory of Judaism.[44] Indeed, Feuerbach claimed (in all seriousness) that the whole of Judaism could ultimately be reduced to a gastronomic cult.[45] The only contact which the Jew had with nature was through the stomach. Eating was therefore the most solemn act in the Jewish religion.

This *worldliness* of the Jew, understood in the most narrow, utilitarian sense, was also reflected in the fundamental "dogma" of Judaism—the concept of Creation *ex nihilo*. The world had been created by magic fiat, by an arbitrary act of the divine will, in order to provide a rationale for divine, immutable laws that governed secular existence. This concept of creation was the dynamic principle of Judaism, the mirror of its essential egoism. "God is the ego of Israel which regards itself as the end and the aim, the lord of nature."[46] The God of Israel was concerned only with the well-being of his "chosen people," just as the Jew was preoccupied only with his own personal welfare. Hence, the practicality of the Jew, his *narrow-minded, utilitarian pursuit of material satisfaction* [my italics]. For Feuerbach, as for Karl Marx, Judaism symbolized a *philistine attitude to life*, a selfish drive for the satisfaction of *private* need, an atomistic view of the individual as an end in himself. In this Feuerbachian critique, one can see the genesis of Marx's image of the "worldly Jew" on which he was to build his antithesis to Bruno Bauer's "Sabbath Jew."

The stereotyped picture of Judaism as a *religion of egoism* was to survive Marx's break with the Left Hegelians in 1845. The economic role of the Jews in German society made it relatively easy for the young Marx to superimpose a materialist theory of Judaism on Young Hegelian "idealism," without critically analyzing its assumptions. This was even more true of Marxists after Marx, who had only a sketchy knowledge of Young Hegelianism and its philosophical background.[47] Little importance was attached by the end of the nineteenth century to those Hegelian influences on Marxism which had been so crucial in its first stages of elaboration. The one exception to this rule can be found in the writings of Franz Mehring, the first biographer of Marx and the leading historian of the German Social Democratic Party.

In 1902 Mehring brought out an edition of Marx's early works with an extended commentary that dealt with his analysis of the "Jewish Question."[48] Mehring favorably contrasted the dialectical "materialism" of Marx and Engels with the "idealism" of the Young Hegelians. Writers like Bruno Bauer, he claimed, had landed in the cul-de-sac of antisemitism and political reaction because they had ignored economic factors and maintained a purely "theological" approach to Judaism. On the other hand, Marx's materialist analysis had led him to connect the "Jewish question" to its socio-economic basis. According to Mehring, Bruno Bauer had "needed a scapegoat against which he could deflect the capitalist masses and he found it in the Jews."[49] In other words, for Bauer and the Young Hegelians, "antisemitism took the place of capitalism." Marxism, however, was supposedly immunized against this "bourgeois" diversion. This was, however, much too simplistic and historically misleading. Marx in 1844 was still a Left Hegelian who had not yet consummated his break with idealist philosophy. Nor had he worked out a consistent theory of historical materialism. He was still strongly influenced by Bruno Bauer, Feuerbach, Moses Hess and other Left Hegelians—not least in his analysis of the "Jewish Question."

Nevertheless, it is true that after 1845, following his final rupture with Bauer and the radical Hegelians, Marx moved in a diametrically opposed direction. In the late 1850s Bauer himself began an open collaboration with the Prussian conservatives. In 1863 he even published a radically anti-Jewish work, *Das Judentum in der Fremde,* which adopted an explicit racial theory. In this study, Bauer declared that Jewish emancipation was a priori impossible because of racial factors. (Moses Hess's *Rome and Jerusalem* published a year earlier also emphasized German racial antagonism to the Jews from an opposite standpoint.) Neither conversion nor inner spiritual emancipation could alter the ethnocentric Hebrew consciousness which underlay Jewish isolation and exclusivity. Bauer had fatefully introduced a new racial element into the German debate. Nevertheless there was a continuity between this virulently antisemitic work and his earlier view of 1843 (which he still maintained) that Judaism was centered on itself, unchanging and set apart from the historical process.[50] The German racial antisemites of the late 1870s and the early 1880s such as Wilhelm Marr and Eugen Dühring (who both came from the Left) could with some justification regard the Young Hegelian Bruno Bauer as their spiritual ancestor.[51]

It should be stressed that Marx's opposition to Bauer was unconcerned with the anti-Jewish content of his critique, focusing instead on his methodology and interpretation of human rights. Indeed, there is no evidence that Marx disagreed with Bauer's harsh observations about Jewish characteristics. Marx's socialist biographer, Franz Mehring, for example, defended Bruno Bauer's attack on German Jews. He specifically agreed with Bruno Bauer that German Jewry in the 1840s demanded emancipation, not so much to achieve civil equality but to reinforce their special status. According to Mehring, they had shown themselves "always ready to abandon liberal principles as soon as these contradicted a special Jewish interest."[52] It was typical of the Jews that they would "betray democracy and liberalism as soon as these contradicted their own domination."[53]

Karl Marx wrote *Zur Judenfrage* in 1843 before he had become a Marxist, yet it would exert considerable influence on the European socialist movement. On the one hand, he defended Jewish emancipation, but also undermined it by insisting that "the social emancipation of the Jew is the *emancipation of society from Judaism.*"[54] At the heart of the "Jewish Question," Marx perceived the contradiction between political and human emancipation, between man's existence as abstract citizen and the egoistic bourgeois in civil society, alienated from his species-essence as a social being.[55] The road to full emancipation must lead back to man himself, not as an isolated individual but as an integrated human being who has overcome all of the contradictions he experiences in everyday life.

The *solution* to the "Jewish Question" therefore demanded the resolution of the fundamental opposition between civil society and the political State. But since Marx identified Judaism with the worldly religion of money-worship (which underlay the atomism of society), it was self-evident that human emancipation would be impossible until the "Jewish essence" had been concretely *aufgehoben* (abolished). Thus, the young Marx supported Jewish emancipation only as a tactical political demand consistent with the principles of bourgeois society while simultaneously advocating its *liquidation* in the name of a higher social order. This dialectical paradigm which he bequeathed to the socialist movement encouraged a highly ambivalent stance toward the "Jewish Question." It was undoubtedly open to antisemitic interpretations. For the implication remained that "Judaism" was redundant in a post-capitalist society. Under socialism or Communism, there was no need for Jews as Jews to maintain their existence.

As part of his opposition to the Prusso-Christian State which "behaves in a political way towards religion and in a religious way towards politics,"[56] Marx did grudgingly support the campaign for Jewish emancipation. It had introduced a rational principle into a hypocritical order of things. Against Bruno Bauer who had emphasized "the *religious* opposition between Judaism and Christianity" and the impossibility of the *Christian* State granting human rights to the Jews, Marx reformulated the "Jewish Question" in purely *secular* terms.[57] Political emancipation did not necessitate the abandonment by the Jew of his religion, except in such politically backward societies as Prussia where "the dominance of religion is the religion of domination."[58] The Christian-Germanic polity was an *underdeveloped* State precisely because it declared the Christian religion to be its foundation. In more advanced societies such as the French and North American republics there was no connection between participation in the political community and the abolition of religion.

In answer to his Young Hegelian mentor, Bruno Bauer, Marx now affirmed: "In the same way as the state *evangelises,* when although a state, it adopts the attitude of a Christian towards the Jew, the Jew *acts politically* when, although a Jew, he demands civil rights."[59] Thus Marx did accept in principle that as a member of civil society the Jew was entitled to demand his civil and human rights. In that basic sense he was no antisemite. At the same time, Marx's critique, in the first part of his essay, of the *category* of political emancipation as contradictory and incomplete cast serious doubt on the value of this acceptance. For Marx interpreted the "so-called rights of man" merely as the "rights of egoistic man, separated from his fellow men and from the community." In other words, human rights were ultimately the expression of *inauthentic* existence within the framework of a society of atomized, antagonistic individuals. Jewish emancipation in this context was merely *an acknowledgment of the universal alienation embodied in the rights of man* [my italics] as a member of civil society—bound together only by private property, self-interest and egoistic needs. This was a very pale, lukewarm, and conditional defense of the fight for Jewish emancipation in Prussia.

In the second half of his essay, Marx developed the idea that only a radical emancipation *from* Judaism could overcome the self-estrangement of man which he had diagnosed at the heart of civil society: "Emancipation from *haggling* and from money, i.e., from practical, real Judaism, would be the same as the self-emancipation of our age."[60] Marx therefore called upon the Jew to abolish his *practical* nature," to turn against "the *supreme practical* expression of human self-alienation" and work for general human emancipation. He recognized in Judaism

> the presence of a universal and *contemporary anti-social* element whose historical evolution—eagerly nurtured by the Jews in its harmful aspects—has arrived at its present peak, a peak at which it will inevitably disintegrate.[61]

Quoting Bruno Bauer's assertion that "the Jew who is merely tolerated in Vienna, for example, determines the fate of the whole empire through the financial power he possesses,"[62] Marx concluded that the Jew had "already emancipated himself in a Jewish way."[63] Through his influence the whole world had become transformed into a vast Stock Exchange:

> *money* has become a world power and the practical Jewish spirit has become the practical spirit of the Christian peoples. The Jews have

> emancipated themselves in so far as the Christians have become Jews.[64]

Marx's terminology at this point was barely distinct from radical antisemitic rhetoric except in its greater dialectical sophistication and acrobatic use of Hegelian paradox. Even if one accepts that Marx used the term *Judentum* (Judaism) in a sense devoid of racial or religious content, in order to conceptually dramatize his vision of human self-alienation, such a total identification of the Jew with money-making could only reinforce traditional anti-Jewish stereotypes.[65] Marx's affirmation that "the god of the Jews has been secularized and become the god of the world. Exchange is the true god of the Jew,"[66] reeks of Jewish self-loathing. Moreover, his reduction of the Jewish religion to practical need, self-interest, and mere huckstering was an ugly and baseless libel.[67] He was followed by German sociologists like Werner Sombart in the early 20th century who sought to hold the Jews responsible for the entire development of modern financial capitalism—especially its less appealing features.[68] Sombart, at least, recognized some more positive features in the Jewish tradition of Talmudic learning, sobriety, discipline, and talent for abstract thought.

Marx's schema was void of any true empirical content. The characteristics of Judaism he had deduced from the nature of money itself as an "alien essence" which degrades nature and the species-relation itself, transforming even sex into a commercial object. The Jewish religion had clothed the world of self-interest with purely formal rites. The Bible and the Talmud were reduced by Marx to "the relationship of the world of self-interest to the laws that dominate it." Hebrew monotheism was contemptuously caricatured as "a polytheism that makes even the lavatory an object of divine law."[69] Marx, the offspring of generations of distinguished rabbis, was adamant that he had found "the secret of religion in the real Jew."[70] But in place of a genuine economic analysis of the Jews' position in modern society, the founder of Communism provided only a mythological portrait of the "Jewish spirit." His explanation came in the form of a dogmatic assertion: "*Judaism* could not develop further as a *religion,* could not develop further theoretically, because the world-view of practical need is by nature narrow-minded and rapidly exhausted."[71] Incapable itself of creating a new world, Judaism could attain "universal domination" only through Christianity which Marx presented as its "sublime thought," its refined and spiritual application. Baptised as a Lutheran at the age of six by his Jewish-born parents living in the predominantly Catholic Rhineland city of Trier, Marx did at least know something about Christianity. In contrast to Judaism, his opposition to it did not derive from crass ignorance.

Marx had described the "Christian egoism of eternal happiness" with considerable distaste for its hypocrisy. But ultimately, the Christian religion was much too ethereal to overcome "the material egoism of the Jew." Hence in the modern world Christianity had dissolved itself back into Judaism.[72] This enabled Jewry to achieve "practical domination over the Christian world," precisely in capitalist society where it had reached its highest level of economic development. On this point Marx shared the view of French utopian socialists such as Fourier and Proudhon as well as the anarchist Bakunin, who regarded Jewry as a parasitic social group. But Marx also made Judaism responsible for the commercialism of the Christian world as a whole. The French socialist identification of the Jewish merchant with *homo capitalisticus* found a more radical, totalistic formulation in Marx, one lacking in his predecessors.

It is, of course, true that in Marx we do not find the *racial* Judeophobia of contemporary German antisemites such as Wilhelm Marr and Eugen Dühring. There is no naturalistic or organicist imagery derived from the biological sciences. Marx still spoke of Judaism rather than "Semitism"; his concept of Jewish "parasitism" was social rather than racial. The Jews were not an alien *Volkskörper* (racial body) corroding the German national organism but the bearers of a commercial ethos that had infiltrated the Christian bourgeois world and obstructed the emancipation of humanity.

In Marx's revised critique of Judaism published in *The Holy Family* (1845), the tone somewhat softened. Having finally settled his accounts with the Young Hegelian Left, Marx felt able to approvingly quote a number of Jewish critics of Bruno Bauer who had challenged the latter's contradictory ideas on Jewish history and exposed his shallow understanding of human rights.[73] In particular, Marx singled out Gabriel Riesser (1806–1863), the most prominent leader of the movement for Jewish emancipation in Germany, agreeing with his caustic view that "Herr Bauer must have both Jews and Christians hanged in his critical State."[74] Bauer's assumption that atheism was a precondition for civil equality was based on purely speculative reasoning and betrayed a confused conception of the modern State. Marx again criticized Bauer for transforming the "Jewish question" into a critique of the Jewish religion, making it a "theological" rather than a social problem.[75] Jewish emancipation, he emphasized, could not be resolved by a critique of theology but only through transforming the structure of the modern State.[76] Nevertheless, Marx's reformulation of the problem still equated Judaism with the money system, even as he sarcastically acknowledged its compatibility with bourgeois society. "The Jew has all the more right to the recognition of his free humanity, as free civil society is thoroughly commercial and Jewish and the Jew is a necessary link in it."[77]

The Marxian model for a "solution" of the "Jewish Question" clearly contained highly ambiguous and hostile attitudes which it bequeathed to European socialism. On one side it echoed the radical secularism of the French Enlightenment which had undermined feudal privilege and the established church, creating a climate that favored Jewish emancipation. On the other hand, the attacks of French *philosophes* such as Voltaire on the Old Testament and the Jewish origins of Christianity influenced Marx as they did German radicals like Bruno Bauer, Wilhelm Marr, and Dühring, who would lay the groundwork for modern racial antisemitism. In 1844 Karl Marx stood at the crossroads of this intellectual development, still under the spell of the Young Hegelian philosophical tradition and its leading representatives, Bruno Bauer, Ludwig Feuerbach, and Moses Hess. Both "Zur Judenfrage" and *The Holy Family* remain transitional works on the road to mature Marxism. In neither study was there any specific mention of capitalism, the industrial proletariat, socialism or the class struggle. Not until the *German Ideology* of 1846 did Marx and Engels present a fully elaborated materialist interpretation of history. Nevertheless, Marx's earliest analyses of the "Jewish Question" remain part of the Marxist and Communist canon. This is all the more remarkable since they were so far removed from the *empirical* reality of Judaism, failing to provide any data on the socio-economic conditions of German Jewry in his own time.[78] Instead, the visionary prophet of full human emancipation fell back on a messianic call for the liberation of society from the sordid praxis of "Judaism"—a formula which recalled the most banal prejudices of the Christian bourgeois order he sought to overthrow.

Marx never repudiated the essays of his youth. In journalistic hackwork of the 1850s, such as his article on "The Russian Loan" (4 January 1856), one comes across invectives against Jewish bankers, characteristic of many nineteenth-century radicals and socialists. Thus, in drawing attention to the new Russian loan floated by the House of Stieglitz in St. Petersburg, Marx could sarcastically write:

> Thus we find every tyrant backed by a Jew, as is every Pope by a Jesuit. In truth, the cravings of oppressors would be hopeless and the practicability of war out of the question, if there were not an army of Jesuits to smother thought and a handful of Jews to ransack pockets.[79]

Marx observed that in addition to the big Jewish financiers such as the Rothschilds, the Raphaels, and the Koenigswarters, there was also a lower class of "loan-mongering Jews" involved in money-changing and negotiating bills. In Amsterdam they numbered not fewer than 35,000 and had their agents throughout the Netherlands and the surrounding German and French territories. Through their branch houses they found a market at home and abroad for these loans "which are a curse to the people, a ruin to the holders, and a danger to the government," but "a blessing to the houses of the children of Judah." Marx concluded his article by recalling that just as Christ had once driven the Jewish moneylenders from the temple, so now once again the loan-mongering Jews of Europe had enlisted on the side of tyranny—hence it was "timely and expedient to expose and stigmatize their organization." This observation was yet another nasty echo of classical Christian anti-Judaism.

There is also ample evidence of anti-Jewish prejudices in the Marx-Engels epistolary exchanges, which often reveal a distinct tendency to think in racial categories. (August Bebel and Eduard Bernstein in their 1913 edition of this correspondence felt obliged to censor many of the coarser vulgarisms.) A favoured target for such opprobrium was Ferdinand Lassalle, the chief political rival of Marx and Engels for control of the German workers' movement, whose successes appeared to have inflamed the anti-Jewish feelings of the co-founders of Communism. Marx's comments on the physiognomy of Lassalle in 1862 can only be described as a crudely *racist* outburst. "It is now perfectly clear to me," he confided in Engels,

> that, as the shape of his head and the growth of his hair indicate, he is descended from the negroes who joined in the flight of Moses from Egypt (unless his mother or grandmother on his father's side was crossed with a nigger). Now this union of Jewishness with Germanness on a negro basis was bound to produce an extraordinary hybrid. The importunity of the fellow is also niggerlike.[80]

Lassalle, a brilliant orator, dynamic organizer, and leading socialist intellectual, had himself become increasingly anti-Jewish during his university years in Berlin. Something of an exhibitionist with a penchant for the aristocratic lifestyle, he aroused envy and distrust in Marx. Engels had long warned his friend against Lassalle as a "real Jew from the Slav frontier," an opportunist and a social climber. He was no less vitriolic than Marx in his abuse, ridiculing Lassalle as "Jüdel Braun," "Ephraim Gescheit" and "Baron Itzig"—epithets that were unmistakeably antisemitic in their connotations. Similar remarks about Jews in the Marx-Engels correspondence, whether they were baptized or unbaptized, self-conscious or indifferent about their origins, reveal the same pattern of contempt. The frequency with which such expressions as "damned old Jew" (Engels on Leibel Choras) or a "real little Yid" (Engels on Leo Frankel in 1870) recur is significant precisely because they took place in intimate correspondence, as a spontaneous discharge of racist aggression.[81] These were certainly anti-Jewish remarks even though Marx and Engels never espoused race theories or a self-consciously anti-semitic world-view.[82] One of their prized targets for mockery was the "Communist Rabbi," Moses Hess—arguably the first philosophical exponent of Communism in Germany as well as being the founder of modern socialist Zionism. In 1862, Moses Hess himself commented on the prevalence of anti-Jewish prejudices in the German labour movement:

> My own personal experience not only among opponents but also among my own party comrades has borne out the fact that in every personal controversy they make use of this "Hep" weapon, which in Germany seldom fails to have its effect. I have decided to make this convenient weapon even more convenient for them by henceforth adopting my Old Testament name of *Moses,* and I only regret that my name is not *Itzig.*[83]

Hess's bitterness on this score did not prevent him playing an active role in the German workers' movement during the 1860s, nor from allying himself for a time with the meteoric career of Lassalle, the popular tribune and founder of German social democracy in 1863.[84] Lassalle came from a lower middle-class Jewish family in Breslau and for a time had briefly dreamed in the early 1840s of leading a struggle for Jewish national independence.[85] It is ironic that though Bismarck, the archetypal Prussian Junker, admired Lassalle as one of the most intelligent men he had ever met,[86] the socialist Engels should deride him as a "greasy Jew, disguised under brilliantine and flashy jewels," a pushy *parvenu* from the Eastern borders of Germany.[87] It would take Engels many years to free himself from such racist prejudices.

Friedrich Engels (1820–1895) came from a small-town Christian pietist background and, like Marx, he was notoriously prone to coarse over-generalizations about the national or group characteristics of individuals who aroused his irritation or antipathy.[88] One can scarcely say that the British, the Americans, the French, the Prussians, Hungarians, or Slavs come out significantly better than the Jews in his articles or correspondence. Moreover, his tirades against anarchists, priests, bureaucrats, militarists, royalists, Puritans, and bourgeois of every shape and size are at least as frequent as his outbursts about Jews.[89] As a young radical he had not displayed much interest in the debate over Jewish emancipation in Germany, though he did write to

Marx in March 1845 applauding his "polemics on the Jewish question" as "splendid" and predicted they would have an excellent effect.[90] In 1846 he also hailed an anonymous French antisemitic pamphlet against "Rothschild I, King of the Jews" as having "hit the nail on the head."[91]

It was during the revolutionary events of 1848–49 that a notable antipathy to East European Jews becomes more visible in Engels's utterances. During this period, in writings for the *Neue Rheinische Zeitung,* both Marx and Engels displayed a revolutionary Pan-Germanist contempt for the backward peasant peoples of Eastern Europe and the Balkans.[92] Engels in particular denied the capacity of Slavs to create a viable State or achieve national independence, dismissing them as "ethnic trash" destined for the rubbish bin of history. In contrast to the "revolutionary" Germans, Magyars, and Poles, Engels considered the Czechs and the South Slavs as "counter-revolutionary" tools of Russian and Pan-Slavist ambitions. They were "historyless peoples" (a concept later adopted by Otto Bauer) whose "mission" was simply to disappear in the *future revolutionary holocaust* that would sweep them away along with other "waste products" such as the Bretons, Basques, and Scottish Highlanders.[93] The Marx-Engels vision of historical progress in 1848–49 seemed to anticipate Darwinian principles of natural selection taken to their most radical conclusions. Reactionary classes and even whole peoples would have to disappear in order to make way for the more advanced, industrial nations that were called upon to realize the socialist revolution.

In this cataclysmic vision there was little room for the Jews of Eastern Europe, more especially those of Poland, whom Engels considered to be the epitome of "huckstering, sordidness and filth." The Polish Jews, this "dirtiest of all races," were castigated for their reactionary social role and rebuked as a Germanizing element which stood in the way of Polish national emancipation.[94] Though the prime object of Engels's ridicule was to flay the hypocrisy of the Prussian Junkers in claiming that the Polish Jews were "Germans," his mocking criticism of their anti-Polish attitudes had a distinctly antisemitic tinge.[95] Traces of this antipathy remained with Engels long after he had concluded that antisemitism was itself the reactionary product of backward cultures which no socialist could possibly condone. The designation "Polish Jew" in Engel's vocabulary usually referred to someone with a sharp eye for business, a tactless parvenu, or an opportunist with a strong propensity for swindling. As late as 1892, Engels would express such sentiments when confiding to Paul Lafargue, the French Marxist leader and husband of one of Marx's daughters:

> I begin to understand French antisemitism when I see how many Jews of Polish origin with German names intrude themselves everywhere to the point of arousing public opinion in the *ville lumière* of which the Parisian philistine is so proud and which he believes to be the supreme power in the universe.[96]

In spite of these lapses, there is solid evidence that in later years Engels opposed any *political* manifestation of anti-Jewish prejudice and tried hard to keep his tendency to sweeping generalizations in check on this issue.[97] Several factors contributed to this change which began in the late 1870s when antisemitism first emerged as a *modern* political ideology in Germany. The most important of these elements was the danger which the radical antisemitic movements were already posing to the German and Austrian Social Democratic labor movements. Engels, in his London exile, was kept informed of these developments by his closest German disciples, Eduard Bernstein, Karl Kautsky, and August Bebel. To this one should add Engels's growing admiration for the crucial role played by Jewish intellectuals in the workers' movement of Central Europe. True, he warned August Bebel in 1891 to keep a sharp eye on Jews who were flocking into the Social Democratic Party, since they were cleverer and more pushy than the average German philistines. Nevertheless Engels welcomed their growing participation in the labor movement.[98] In 1890 he reminded an Austrian Jewish correspondent of how much modern socialism owed to the devotion, self-sacrifice, and ability of individual Jews:

> To say nothing of Heine and Börne, Marx was of purest Jewish blood; Lassalle was a Jew. Many of our best people are Jews. My friend Victor Adler, who is present paying in prison for his devotion to the cause of the proletariat, Eduard Bernstein, editor of the London *Sozial-Demokrat,* Paul Singer, one of our best men in the Reichstag—people of whose friendship I am proud, are all Jews! Have I not been turned into a Jew myself by the "Gartenlaube"? And indeed if I had to choose, then better a Jew than "Herr von. . . "[99]

Engels was equally impressed by the rise of a Jewish proletariat in Eastern Europe, London, and New York which had been strongly influenced by socialist ideas and the militant class-struggle. It seems that like Eleanor Marx-Aveling (daughter of Karl Marx) he saw in the Jewish immigrant working class of London's East End a decisive rebuff to the argument that antisemitism was an anti-capitalist movement.[100] Karl Marx, it should be said, did not live to witness this change in his own family which might have mellowed his attitude towards the "Jewish Question." Nor did he show any awareness of growing Jewish national aspirations which were already making themselves felt before his death in 1883.

Yet it was one of Marx's closest comrades, Moses Hess, who would first give theoretical expression in distinctly socialist language to these hopes. In his classic work, *Rome and Jerusalem,* Moses Hess (1812–1875) presented an analysis of the "Jewish question" diametrically opposed to Marxian tradition. Judaism, he concluded, was not a superstructure of bourgeois society but one of the central elements in the spiritual development of humanity, destined to realize the earthly Kingdom of God. It was a historical religion impossible to detach from Jewish national history. Though the modern emancipated Jew, especially in Germany, had sought to abandon this national tradition, such efforts were doomed to failure, for the Jewish people could not organically assimilate. Emancipation could not therefore solve the Jewish problem. Nor did the Marxian theory of international class struggle have any relevance to the Jewish condition, since it denied the primary source of Judaism, its *national* consciousness. Hess insisted that neither emancipation, conversion, education, reform, nor the class struggle would solve a problem which was sui generis, resistant to the universal panaceas of the age. Only through the restoration of the ancient Jewish commonwealth in Zion would this last remaining "nationality question" receive its specific solution, consonant with the creative religious genius and messianic traditions of the Jewish people. The new Zion was to be based on Mosaic socialist principles, by which Hess meant not only economic justice but also a concept of national unity beyond the class struggle, egoism, hierarchy, and privilege. The auto-emancipation of the Jewish people was to be an essential prelude to the social regeneration of humanity.

These views expressed by Moses Hess in 1862 were the culmination of a long and painful process of overcoming the estrangement he had initially felt towards Judaism, the Jewish people, and its traditions. It is indeed an ironic fact that Hess, the outstanding secular thinker in the prehistory of the Zionist movement, should also have been an important influence on the intellectual development of the young Marx and Engels, whom he converted to communism. Hess's ideas had helped to shape Marx's own analysis of Judaism and his influence is indeed palpable in the *Economic and Philosophical Manuscripts* of 1844. Hess's essay "Über das Geldwesen" (On money) was probably written before Marx's "On the Jewish Question."[101] He was the first Young Hegelian to apply Feuerbach's critique of religion to the socio-economic sphere.[102] He drew the following analogy between theology and economics which was echoed in Marx's own concept of alienation. "What God is for the theoretic life, money is for the practical life . . . the alienated wealth of man, his pedlarized life activity."[103] As spiritually egoistic man externalized himself theoretically in God, so worldly man externalized himself materially in money. The modern commercial State based on money-worship was at bottom a "perverted world" which denied the species-essence of man as a cooperative producer. In this universal Stock Exchange which Moses Hess identified as the "Jewish-Christian pedlar world" (*Krämerwelt*), mutual estrangement had reached its climax. In other words, Hess's terminology at many points anticipates that of Marx, especially in his analysis of economic alienation. His passing remarks on Christianity ("the theory, the logic of egoism") and on the so-called blood mystique of Judaism were, if anything, even more extreme. Indeed, at least one nonsensical and hysterical sentence in this essay, in its antisemitic implications, exceeded anything in Marx. "The Jews, in the natural history of the social animal world, had the world-historic mission to bring out the predator in mankind. They have completed their task."[104] Hess concluded that only Communism could resolve the social conflicts created in modern society by such brutal, predatory instincts inherent in the logic of the free market.

Hess's ugly comment on Judaism in 1843 was an isolated reference. The bulk of his analysis was devoted to the evolution of man in nature and history. He made no attempt at any stage to construct a general theory linking Judaism or Christianity to the evils of modern society. Moreover, we know that the Damascus Affair of 1840 with its revival of the antisemitic Christian blood-libel accusation shocked him deeply. This was a common reaction among other radical Jews such as Heinrich Heine and the adolescent Ferdinand Lassalle, who was full of rage at the passivity of his fellow-Jews in the East.[105] Hess, too, was momentarily inspired by the atrocities against Jews in Damascus to affirm the need for Jewish national liberation. But he apparently suppressed his patriotic feelings for the sake of the proletarian cause. In *Rome and Jerusalem* he recalled his sentiments at the time:

> Then it dawned on me for the first time in the midst of my socialist activities, that I belong to an unfortunate, maligned, despised, and dispersed people—but one that the world has not succeeded in destroying. At that time, though I was still greatly estranged from Judaism, I wanted to cry out in anguish and express my Jewish patriotism, but this emotion was immediately stifled by the greater pain evoked in me by the suffering of the European proletariat.[106]

The Damascus Affair and a brutal personal insult which he experienced in 1840 at the hands of the German nationalist composer, Nikolas Becker, were early signs to Hess that in spite of its education and culture, Western Jewry would probably remain an anomaly among the European peoples.[107] Antisemitism, he would later conclude, was an enigma for patriotic German Jews only because they insisted on *denying* their own nationality. Hence they had failed to understand that German nationalism with its endemic racialist features was fundamentally incapable of assimilating "alien" groups. This unsparing analysis, published in 1862, condemning the new racist antisemitism, was to prove remarkably prescient.

Twenty-five years earlier, in his first book, *The Holy History of Mankind, by a Young Spinozist* (1837), followed by *The European Triarchy* (1841), Hess had opposed the separate existence of a Jewish people, arguing that its special role as a "ferment" among the nations was exhausted.[108] In the second work he went further, describing the Jews as a disembodied *phantom* people, incapable either of dying or being reborn. In typical Young Hegelian fashion he had suggested that Christianity was a higher stage of revelation than Judaism and that its universalism had rendered a specific Jewish mission superfluous. As for Jewish emancipation, Moses Hess publicly treated this as an issue that could not be isolated from the general struggle for human emancipation in Europe. What differentiated him from other German radicals during this period was not so much his specific analysis of events as the apocalyptic character of his communist faith—fundamentally activist rather than fatalist in spirit.

Moses Hess felt a deep inward attraction to the Jewish messianic idea of the "Kingdom of God" which he had reformulated in his first book in terms of Spinozist monism and the Hegelian philosophy of history. His messianic idea of the just society, pioneered by the Hebrew prophets, would find its modern consummation in a sweeping vision of the communist future based on the abolition of private property.[109] His utopian philosophical communism with its synthesis of French socialist doctrines (Fourier, Saint-Simon, Proudhon) and German idealism (Fichte, Schelling, Hegel) contained a strong impulse towards voluntarism and practical ethics. Hess's "philosophy of action" (*Philosophie der Tat*) introduced a new emphasis on "praxis" into early German socialism.[110] His revolutionary impatience (of which Marx and Engels were critical) was closely related to the messianic belief that the "Kingdom of God" must be realized here-and-now.[111] In spite of his collaboration with Marx, he could never fully identify with his materialist interpretation of history or accept the pivotal role of the class struggle. For

Hess, "ideas" were never mere superstructures, and ethical ideals such as fraternity, human solidarity, and love could not be reduced to their economic basis. A subjective, rather than a scientific impulse had initially drawn him to socialism—namely his feelings of compassion for the underprivileged and a truly visceral hatred of bourgeois egoism.[112] Hess's communism was envisaged more as the ultimate form of social altruism than as the "scientific" expression of the interests of the proletariat. He was always more of a believer in practical morality rather than in the immanent logic of the class struggle. In the *Communist Manifesto* (1848), Marx and Engels ridiculed such "true" socialism as a "robe of speculative cobwebs, embroidered with flowers of rhetoric, steeped in the dew of sickly sentiment."[113] Such sarcasm from the founders of "scientific socialism" was not surprising, but it was, nonetheless, an injustice to Moses Hess. For all his sentimentalism and lack of analytical rigor, he was gifted with a prophetic foresight that gave his social-revolutionary view of the "Jewish Question" an originality and vision lacking in some of his more illustrious contemporaries.

The "return to Judaism" of Moses Hess took place in the 1850s in his Parisian exile during which time he had devoted himself to scientific studies, in particular to anthropology. In France he experienced Jewish emancipation as a reality and discovered a degree of *social* integration much greater than in either Germany or Austria.[114] In France there was no contradiction between Jewish particularism and belief in the ultimate unity of mankind. French-Jewish intellectuals like Joseph Salvador (1796–1873) had already emphasized the historic continuity of the Jewish people—the unity of the spiritual and temporal, the national and universal within Judaism. Like the Jewish Saint-Simonian socialists, Salvador's Judeocentric vision of the New Jerusalem contained a strong belief in the universal mission of Israel, formulated in terms remarkably parallel to those of Moses Hess.[115] The foundation of the Alliance Israélite Universelle in Paris (1860) was a further example of Franco-Jewish efforts to harmonize the particularist tradition of Judaism with the universal French ideals of liberty, equality, and fraternity.[116] It was no accident that Hess's new insights into Judaism would find their first outlet in the 1860s in the *Archives Israélites*.

The importance of this French-Jewish milieu for Hess's rehabilitation of Judaism in a universalist rational synthesis has usually been underestimated. It may partly account for Hess's changed perspective on Jewish affairs. His Francophile attitudes were particularly prominent at the time when he wrote *Rome and Jerusalem*. Hess sharply contrasted the French capacity for assimilating alien races with the chauvinism, militarism, and racial intolerance of the Germans.[117] Since 1789 the French people had become in his eyes the torchbearers of progress, the "soldiers of modern civilization," the great agents of messianic change in Europe.[118] Even the plebiscitarian French dictator Napoleon III, in spite of his Caesarism, was seen by Hess as the best hope for liberating the oppressed nationalities of Europe.[119] Hess's Bonapartism (nourished by the Emperor's support for the Italian national liberation struggle against Austrian rule), and his belief in the French *mission émancipatrice,* convinced him that France "would help the Jews to found colonies which may extend from Suez to Jerusalem and from the banks of the Jordan to the coast of the Mediterranean."[120] Ernst Laharanne's book, *La Nouvelle Question d'Orient: Reconstitution de la Nation Juive* (1860), from which Hess quoted extensively in his own study, seemed to confirm this quasi-messianic confidence that France would become the protector of the Jews out of its own political and humanitarian motives. Laharanne, the private secretary of Napoleon III, was a French Catholic who firmly believed that the restoration of the Jewish State as "a living channel of communication between three continents" would be part of the answer to the unresolved Eastern question.

This faith of Moses Hess in the Bonapartist mission proved to be misplaced.[121] His insight into the awakening national movements in Europe was, however, deeper than that of Marx and Engels. Like Ferdinand Lassalle, Hess had become a "national" socialist by 1860 in the sense of affirming the inalienable right to national individuality along with ethnic and racial diversity. In *Rome and Jerusalem* there is a passage that seems to echo the Marxian polemic of 1848 against his own "true" socialism. Moses Hess, using similar imagery, now turns the tables on the anti-national "cosmopolitanism" of his German socialist critics:

> We are so saturated with the perfume of spiritual love and the chloroform of humanitarianism that we have become entirely unresponsive to the real misery that is caused by the antagonisms which still exist among the various members of the great human family.[122]

Moses Hess was firmly convinced by 1862 that the history of the nineteenth century would not be a history of class struggles as the *Communist Manifesto* had boldly predicted but rather a conflict of nationalities and races.

> The entire past history of humanity originally moved only in the context of race and class struggle. The race struggle is primary, the class struggle secondary. . . . Along with the cessation of race conflict,

> class conflict will also come to an end. Equality for all classes in society will necessarily follow the emancipation of the races.[123]

Hess, it should be noted, was probably the first socialist and Jewish thinker to take the new race doctrines and theory of "Aryanism" seriously.[124] Was he, then, a racist? From a contemporary standpoint his national socialism may seem suspect or even tainted by the repeated use of the term "race." Yet this would be to misread Hess's intentions and meaning. He totally rejected the Germanic chauvinist concept of a hierarchy of races. He opposed the Teutonic obsession with racial domination (*Rassenherrschaft*) which underlay the movement for national unity in Germany—recognizing its long-term consequences for Jewish integration in Germany.[125] In vain, Hess warned German Jewry that racial antisemitism was likely to triumph over the purely "theoretical internationalism" of the Germans.[126] Liberal and socialist assimilationism were therefore futile exercises in self-deception. "The beautiful phrases about humanity and enlightenment which he [the modern Jew] uses so freely to cloak his treason, his fear of being identified with his unfortunate brethren, will not ultimately protect him from the judgment of public opinion."[127] Hess added that the Jew might mask himself a thousand times over, change his name, religion, and character, travel through the world incognito, "yet every insult to the Jewish name would strike him harder than it would the honest man who admits his Jewish loyalties."[128] More than thirty years before Theodor Herzl's *Judenstaat,* Moses Hess foresaw that Jewish emancipation and assimilation in Europe was doomed to failure. In this respect his socialist "proto-Zionism" was certainly prophetic.

Hess's new emphasis on the primacy of race conflict sharpened his awareness of the destructive potential in the German-Jewish relationship. "The Germans hate the religion of the Jews less than they hate their peculiar noses."[129] He predicted that in the face of such race hatred, all strategies of self-denial would fail. In particular, Hess fiercely criticized the constant attempts of the German Jewish Reform movement to suck the marrow out of traditional Judaism, to deny its historical and national character. He deplored the arid rationalism of the liberal Reformers who, in their eagerness to imitate Christianity, were seeking to erase all sense of the historic continuity of Israel and its prophetic vocation. Their efforts, too, would be doomed, for "the Jewish race" was one of "the primary races of mankind" which had retained its integrity in spite of changing environments.

Hess firmly believed that Christianity was "a religion of death" whose historic mission would end with the current rebirth of the nations. Judaism, on the other hand, was peculiarly suited by its national *and* universalist character to usher in the coming messianic epoch.[130] In this newly emerging post-Christian era, heralded by the sight of a "regenerated Italian people" arising on the ruins of Rome, Judaism would again come into its own as the pattern and the *spiritual guide* for the civilized world. In the spirit of Herder, Mickiewicz, and Mazzini, Moses Hess declared that each nation would then become the people of God. The Jewish people, whose world religion was based on a unique national history, was destined to become the prototype for this future, since its teachings were also "the root of our whole contemporary universalist view of life." Hess thereby reversed the entire Hegelian Christological schema which he had accepted in his youth—a philosophy that had arrogantly downgraded Judaism to the lowest rung on the ladder of divine revelation. On the contrary, he was now convinced that the Jewish religion and its folk-genius would become the model for the future of humanity—heralded in the 1860s by contemporary European movements for national liberation inspired by similar ideals of fraternity and universal solidarity. The Hebrew prophets were the true bearers of this faith in a future messianic epoch, the belief that History, like Nature, was destined to achieve its harmonious perfection. Not for nothing was Jerusalem the symbol of the Jewish nation and also "the birthplace of the belief in the divine unity of life and of the hope for the ultimate brotherhood of all men."[131]

Moses Hess's recognition of the primal power of Jewish national feeling and his assertion of the creative vitality of religious messianism implied a complete and radical reversal of the Hegelian-Marxian conception of history. The materialist analysis of the "Jewish question" had equated Judaism with the egoism of bourgeois society and reduced Hebrew monotheism to vulgar practical need. In 1844 Marx had dismissed the "*chimerical* nationality of the Jew" as no more than "the nationality of the merchant, of the money-man in general."[132] Hess's response in 1862 was the passionate affirmation of Jewish national feeling. Nothing was more alien to Judaism than the "egoistic" Christian doctrine of the salvation of the individual. Within the Jewish religion, the individual could never be divorced from the family, the nation, humanity, organic or cosmic creation.[133] There was only one dogma in Judaism—*the belief in the divine unity of life*—expressed in the fusion of body and spirit, politics and religion, nation and individual. The divine law which governed the world of Nature and of History in prophetic Judaism was the complete *antithesis* of the "spiritualist egoism" of Christianity and the dogmatic materialism underlying Marxian socialism.[134] Biblical Judaism allowed no feudalism, no concept of social hierarchy, no chauvinistic nationalism, no caste spirit or privileged classes.[135] According to Hess, *the*

Mosaic code was socialist in its essence—with its institutions of the Sabbath, the fallow year, and the Jubilee totally negating the ethos of capitalist individualism based on private property.[136] The new Zion which Moses Hess advocated as a *socialist* commonwealth would implement rather than abolish these principles of Mosaism. The *earthly* Jerusalem would be founded on model egalitarian institutions. It would establish "Jewish societies of agriculture, industry and trade in accordance with Mosaic, socialist principles."[137] This could never be achieved in the Diaspora, where the Jews lacked a free soil of their own, without which social man "sinks to the status of a parasite, which feeds at the expense of others." Once freed from the curse of social parasitism and economic exploitation in the Diaspora, the Jews would eventually achieve their communal regeneration in a socialist Palestine rooted in Hebraic concepts.

There was little prospect, as Hess evidently realized, that more than a handful of German or Western Jews would respond to his call for the restoration of a Jewish socialist Commonwealth. In the 1850s and 1860s, the Jewish world, especially in Central Europe, was still dominated by the struggle for its emancipation and civil equality. The movement for religious reform even sought to banish the Hebrew language, national traditions, and the memory of Zion from the Jewish consciousness. In Russia and Eastern Europe conditions were more propitious but still not ripe for the acceptance of Jewish socialist nationalism. Moses Hess, it should be remembered, was writing before the pogroms of 1881, before the rise of political antisemitism in Central and Eastern Europe, and over thirty years before the rise of an organized Jewish labor movement. Inevitably his version of socialist Zionism was still-born. Not until 1901 would Theodor Herzl (five years after publishing his *Judenstaat*) first read *Rome and Jerusalem* to the end. He poignantly commented in his diary: "Everything that we have tried to do is already mentioned by him. . . . Since Spinoza, Judaism has produced no finer character than this forgotten and dim figure, Moses Hess."[138]

Nevertheless, though the bulk of his Jewish contemporaries (with the notable exception of the nationally-minded German-Jewish historian, Heinrich Graetz) completely rejected or ignored Hess's contribution, the main outlines of his prophecy were to be realized.[139] With great foresight, Hess realized that his messianic nationalism would achieve its resonance primarily among the Jewish masses of Eastern Europe and the Arab world—the "millions of our brethren who pray fervently every day to the God of our fathers for the restoration of the Jewish kingdom."[140] The living kernel of Judaism, "the sense of Jewish nationality" had been preserved in the ghettoes of Russia, Poland, and the Orient. This awareness allowed Hess to overcome his persistent feelings of hostility towards the rationalist Western Jews, whose assimilationist aspirations he came to despise. Significant in this respect was his positive evaluation of Hassidism as a popular religious movement among the East European Jewish masses which had—in his communitarian perspective—revived the spirit of biblical Judaism.[141] The existence of such pietistic folk movements confirmed in him the belief that the Jewish people was indeed capable of regeneration and of reviving the national ethos that had been eroded by the liberal individualism of the West.

Inevitably there were contradictions in Hess's view of Jewry which he was unable to escape. A positivist and secular thinker, he found himself driven by political and national considerations to defend the values of a Jewish Orthodox tradition that he did not personally observe. Unable to appeal to an organized Jewish proletariat, he tried vainly to interest Jewish capitalists in his enterprise. Though sharply opposed to racist Pan-Germanism, he fell back on a romantic belief in the Jewish "national spirit" and a dubious reliance on the primacy of race. A fervent supporter of European movements for national liberation, he could not foresee that the very success of Zionism might produce its own backlash in the form of Arab nationalism.[142]

There is no evidence that either Marx or Engels ever read his "Zionist book" and one can scarcely doubt that their reaction (if they had come across it) would have been wholly negative.[143] In the context of the 1860s, the fervent belief of Moses Hess in the Jewish national renaissance might have struck them as a mental aberration. In the middle of the liberal nineteenth century, as the German Communist Johann Philipp Becker scathingly reminded Hess, there was no basis for defending the concept of a Jewish people.[144] Nor, on the evidence of Jewish history since the dispersion, did the Jews seem obviously destined for restoring their ancient vocation of nationhood. Hess's Zionism *avant la lettre,* viewed from the standpoint of Marxist internationalism, seemed at best like the sentimental fantasy of a disappointed revolutionary.[145]

Moses Hess would remain a forgotten figure in the German workers' movement until the end of the nineteenth century. Yet, although his impact on contemporaries was minimal, his analysis of the Jewish condition was important in at least four respects. First, Hess was correct in sensing that Judaism was not a spent force in the modern world but a regenerative principle whose time was yet to come. His utopian socialist vision of *Gemeinschaft* (community) would be taken up again in a more extended form at the turn of the century by outstanding German-Jewish intellectuals like

Martin Buber and Gustav Landauer. Second, his prophecy of a Jewish socialist commonwealth in Zion anticipated major tenets of labor-Zionist ideology which would eventually lead to the founding of the State of Israel. In the writings of Syrkin, Ber Borochov, Aharon David Gordon, and Berl Katznelson one can find the continuation of Hess's emphasis on productive labor and cooperative settlement.[146] Third, Moses Hess perceived with remarkable clarity that Jewish assimilation was not viable in German society. His insight into the danger of German antisemitism *preceded* its emergence as a serious political force by almost twenty years. In this respect, Moses Hess was the prototype of those marginal, assimilated Jews such as Theodor Herzl, Max Nordau, and Bernard Lazare who (under the impact of the Dreyfus Affair) would subsequently come to understand that no dignified Jewish "self-dissolution" was either possible or desirable under conditions of racist xenophobia. Last, but not least, Moses Hess was a pioneer among his German socialist contemporaries in his capacity to synthesize proletarian internationalism with basic tenets of nationalist thought. Though lacking the analytical power of Karl Marx or the oratorical gifts of Ferdinand Lassalle, Moses Hess had the visionary faculty of the Hebrew prophets whom he so admired.

NOTES

1. See Robert S. Wistrich, "Karl Marx and the Jewish Question," *Soviet Jewish Affairs* 4 (1974): 53–60; idem, "The Marxist Critique of Judaism," *Patterns of Prejudice* 9, no. 4 (1975): 1–6; idem, "Karl Marx, the Enlightenment and Jewish Emancipation," *Jewish Frontier* (April 1979): 9–12; and idem, "Antishemiut radicalit be-tsarfat ve-germania, 1840–1870" (Radical antisemitism in France and Germany), in *Israel and the Nations: Essays Presented in Honor of Shmuel Ettinger* (Jerusalem: Historical Society of Israel, 1987), 157–84.

2. On Luther, see Heiko A. Oberman, *The Roots of Anti-Semitism in the Age of Renaissance and Reformation* (Philadelphia, 1984).

3. Steven Aschheim, "'The Jew Within': The Myth of 'Judaization' in Germany," in *The Jewish Response to German Culture,* edited by Jehuda Reinharz and Walter Schatzberg (Hanover, N.H., 1985), 212–41.

4. Voltaire, *A Philosophy Dictionary* (New York, 1932), entry on the "Jews."

5. On Fichte, see chapter 6 in Leon Poliakov, *La Causalité Diabolique* (Paris, 1980) and Paul Lawrence Rose, *German Question, Jewish Question. Revolutionary Antisemitism from Kant to Wagner* (Princeton, 1990), 119.

6. See Micha Brumlik, *Deutscher Geist und Judenhass* (Munich, 2002), 75–131.

7. Quoted by Rose, *German Question, Jewish Question,* 120.

8. Ibid., 49.

9. On Börne, see Orlando Figes, "Ludwig Börne and the Formation of a Radical Critique of Judaism," *Leo Baeck Yearbook* (hereafter, *LBIYB*) 29 (1984): 351–82. It should be mentioned that Börne converted to Christianity in 1818, at the age of 32.

10. Rose, *German Question, Jewish Question,* 149–52.

11. On Heine, see Siegfried Prawer, *Heine's Jewish Comedy* (Oxford, 1983).

12. This statement comes from Heine's preface to the new 1852 edition of his *History of Religion and Philosophy in Germany*. Quoted by Rose, *German Question, Jewish Question,* 166.

13. Ibid., 167.

14. Brumlik, *Deutscher Geist,* 280–320.

15. Immanuel Kant, *Religion within the Limits of Reason Alone* (New York, 1960), 116–17. Kant rather chillingly spoke of the "euthanasia" of Judaism, a way of saying that it was a dead religion or destined to die. See Léon Poliakov, *The History of Anti-Semitism,* vol. 3: *From Voltaire to Wagner* (London, 1975), 178–80. For the philosophical background, Nathan Rotenstreich, *The Recurring Pattern: Studies in Anti-Judaism in Modern Thought* (London, 1963), 23–47.

16. The sources for Kant's negative view of Judaism lay in Spinoza's *Tractatus Theologico-Politicus* and Mendelssohn's *Jerusalem* as well as in English Deism and German Protestant theology. Many emancipated Jews, from Solomon Maimon and Lazarus Bendavid to Hermann Cohen and Ernst Cassirer, were nonetheless admirers and disciples of Kant. He also exercised an influence on the Jewish Reform movement and its reaction against the legalistic and ritualistic character of Judaism.

17. Georg Wilhelm Friedrich Hegel, *Early Theological Writings,* translated by T. M. Knox (Chicago, 1948), 178–201, 224, 241, 285.

18. Rotenstreich, *Recurring Pattern,* 68, rightly points out that "Hegel considers Judaism as the antithesis of his own philosophy in so far as his own philosophy is nourished by a mystical pantheism."

19. G. W. F. Hegel, *Vorlesungen über die Philosophie der Weltgeschichte,* vol. 2: *Die Orientalische Welt* (Leipzig, 1924). See also Hans Liebeschutz, *Das Judentum in Deutschen Geschichtsbild von Hegel bis Max Weber* (Tübingen, 1967), 1–42.

20. Shlomo Avineri, "A Note on Hegel's View on Jewish Emancipation," *Jewish Social Studies* (April 1963), pp. 145-151.

21. See Zvi Rosen, *Bruno Bauer and Karl Marx: The Influence of Bruno Bauer on Marx's Thought* (The Hague, 1978).

22. Bruno Bauer, "Die Fähigkeit der heutigen Juden und Christen frei zu werden," in *Einundzwanzig Bogen aus dem Schweiz,* edited by G. Herwegh (Zurich and Winterthur, 1843), and the French translation in Plon, ed., *La Question Juive* (Paris, 1970),

collection 10/18, from which subsequent quotations are taken. A useful account of the debate provoked by Bauer can be found in by Nathan Rotenstreich, "For and Against Emancipation: The Bruno Bauer Controversy," *LBIYB*, 4 (1959): 3–36.

23. Bruno Bauer, *La Question Juive,* 71.

24. Ibid., 90–91.

25. Ibid., 64.

26. Ibid., 80.

27. See Zvi Rosen, "The Anti-Jewish Opinions of Bruno Bauer (1838–1843); Their Sources and Significance" (in Hebrew), *Zion* 33 (1968): 59–76.

28. Bauer, *La Question Juive,* 64–65.

29. Ibid., 111.

30. Ibid., 123.

31. Ibid., 103.

32. Ibid., 82.

33. See Robert S. Wistrich, *Socialism and the Jews. The Dilemmas of Assimilation in Germany and Austria-Hungary* (London, 1982), 18–23.

34. Wistrich, *Socialism and the Jews,* 20.

35. Ibid.

36. See David McLellan, *The Young Hegelians and Karl Marx* (London, 1969), 58–59, 77–78, who underlines Marx's debt to Bauer's critique of the Christian State. Georges Cottier, *L'Athéisme du jeune Marx et ses origins hégéliennes* (Paris, 1959), stresses the Hegelian influence.

37. Karl Marx, "On the Jewish Question," in *Early Writings* (London: Penguin Books: 1975), introduction by Lucio Colletti, 213.

38. See Eleanore Sterling, *Er ist wie Du: aus der Frühgeschichte des Antisemitismus in Deutschland, 1815–1850* (Munich, 1956), 110ff.

39. For Feuerbach's influence, see Robert Tucker, *Philosophy and Myth in Karl Marx* (Cambridge, 1961), 95–105; W. Schuffenhauer, *Feuerbach und der junge Marx* (Berlin, 1965); and McLellan, *Young Hegelians,* 85ff., 101ff.

40. *Marx-Engels Gesamtausgabe* (hereafter, *MEGA*) (Berlin and Moscow, 1927–1935), I, i(1), 175.

41. The theses are reprinted in Karl Marx, *Early Writings,* 421–23. Marx concludes his first thesis on Feuerbach by observing that "in *Das Wesen des Christentums,* he regards the theoretical attitude as the only human attitude, while practice is conceived and fixed only in its dirty-judaical manifestation. Hence, he does not grasp the significance of 'revolutionary,' of 'practical-critical,' activity."

42. Ludwig Feuerbach, *Essence of Christianity,* translated by George Eliot (New York, 1957), 120.

43. Ibid., 330–31.

44. Ibid., 113–14.

45. Ibid., 114.

46. Ibid., 119.

47. See David McLellan, *Marx before Marxism* (London, 1970), 266–69.

48. Franz Mehring, ed., *Aus dem literarischen Nachlass von Karl Marx und Friedrich Engels 1841–50* (Stuttgart, 1902), 1: 352–56.

49. Franz Mehring, "Drillinge," *Die Neue Zeit* 2 (1893–1894): 581.

50. Nathan Rotenstreich, "For and Against Emancipation," 35–36.

51. See Ernst Barnikol, ed., *Bruno Bauer, Studien und Materialen* (Assen, 1972), 427ff., for his role as a pioneer of racial antisemitism in Germany; and Wistrich, *Socialism and the Jews,* 22–24.

52. Franz Mehring, *Karl Marx: Geschichte seines Lebens,* 4th ed. (Leipzig, 1923), 94.

53. Mehring, *Aus dem literarischen Nachlass,* 1: 354–55.

54. Karl Marx, "On the Jewish Question," 341.

55. See Robert S. Wistrich, "Karl Marx and the Jewish Question," *Soviet Jewish Affairs* 4, no. 1 (1974): 53–59; Dietmar Scholz, "Politische und menschliche Emanzipation: Karl Marx's Schrift "Zur Judenfrage" aus dem Jahre 1844," *Geschichte in Wissenschaft und Unterricht* 18(1) (1967): 1–16, for a summary of what Marx understood by "human emancipation."

56. Marx, "On the Jewish Question," 223. For Marx, this meant that the State demeaned both political forms and religion itself "to a mere appearance."

57. In March 1843 he wrote to Ruge that "we must riddle the Christian State with as many holes as possible and smuggle the rational in, as far as we can." This was the argument he gave for supporting a petition for Jewish civil rights. *MEGA,* 1, 308. Also note Marx's comment: "We do not turn secular questions into theological questions. We turn theological questions into secular questions," ibid., p. 217.

58. Ibid., 224.

59. Ibid., 226–27.

60. Ibid., 236.

61. Ibid., 237.

62. The original quote came from Bruno Bauer, *Die Judenfrage,* 114. Marx reproduced it in full (ibid., p. 237) and stressed that Jewish financial power in Vienna was "not an isolated fact."

63. Ibid., 237.

64. Ibid. At this point, Marx goes off into a digression designed to show that the commercialization of Christianity in the United States proved "the practical domination of Judaism over the Christian world."

65. David McLellan, *Marx before Marxism,* 184, regrettably trivialized the subject when he calls Marx's use of the term *Judentum* "an extended pun at Bauer's expense."

66. Marx, "On the Jewish Question," 239.

67. Richard Schacht, *Alienation* (London, 1971), 110. See also Robert Misrahi, *Marx et la Question Juive* (Paris, 1972).

68. See Freddy Raphael, *Judaïsme et capitalisme. Essai sur la controverse entre Max Weber et Werner Sombart* (Paris, 1982); and Joseph Gabel, *Réflexions sur l'Avenir des Juifs* (Paris, 1987), 82–86, 180–85.

69. Marx, "On the Jewish Question," 238–39.

70. Ibid., 236. "Let us not look for the Jews' secret in his religion; rather let us look for the secret of religion in the real Jew."

71. Ibid., 230.

72. Ibid. Marx's assertion that "the Christian was from the very beginning the theorizing Jew" and that "the Jew is therefore the practical Christian" echoed similar formulations made by Bruno Bauer and Feuerbach. Nevertheless, the tone was sharper and more hostile.

73. Karl Marx, "Die Judenfrage," no. 2 in Mehring, *Aus dem literarischen Nachlass,* 1: 197–202.

74. Ibid., 197.

75. Marx, "Die Judenfrage," no. 3, ibid., 217.

76. Ibid., 215–16. Marx emphasizes more strongly in this revised version of his earlier essay that those nations which have failed to emancipate the Jews are politically backward.

77. Ibid., 219.

78. Wistrich, *Socialism and the Jews,* 30–31.

79. Karl Marx, "The Russian loan," *New York Daily Tribune,* 4 Jan. 1856, reprinted in idem, *The Eastern Question,* edited by Eleanor Marx and Eduard Aveling (1897; new ed. London, 1969), 600–6. See also Shlomo Avineri, *Karl Marx on Colonialism and Modernization* (New York, 1968), 134–43.

80. Marx to Engels, 30 July 1862, *MEGA,* 3, 3:. 82–84. For a more just analysis of Lassalle's personality and historical importance, see Shlomo Barer, *The Doctors of Revolution* (London, 2000), 1120–25.

81. Engels to Marx, 7 Mar. 1856, *MEGA*, 3, 2: 122; also Engels to Marx, 11 Oct. 1867, *MEGA,* 3, 3: 432; ibid., 4: 52; Engels to Marx, 6 May 1868, 4: 305; Engels to Marx, 15 Apr. 1870.

82. Robert S. Wistrich, "Marxist 'Racism'?," *Encounter* (Nov. 1975): 94–96.

83. Moses Hess, *Rom und Jerusalem: Die letzte Nationalitätenfrage* (Tel Aviv, 1935), 56.

84. See Robert S. Wistrich, "Ferdinand Lassalle: The Gladiator," *European Judaism* 10, no. 1 (Winter 1975–1976): 15–23.

85. Eduard Rosenbaum, "Ferdinand Lassalle: A Historiographical Meditation," *LBIYB* 9 (1964): 122–30.

86. Bertrand Russell, *German Social Democracy* (London, 1965), 61–62.

87. Engels to Marx, 7 Mar. 1856, in *Engels: Selected Writings,* edited by W. O. Henderson (London, 1967), 129–30.

88. On Engels's Rhineland family milieu, see Helmut Hirsch, "Friedrich Engels und seine Heimat," *Freiheitsliebende Rheinländer: Neue Beiträge zur deutschen Sozialgeshichte* (Düsseldorf and Vienna, 1977), 7–49.

89. Ibid., 31.

90. Engels to Marx, 17 Mar. 1845, *MEGA*, 3, 1:19.

91. Ibid., 6: 341. The pamphlet in question was by Georges-Marie Mathieu-Dairnvaell, *Historie édifiante et curieuse de Rothschild Ier, Roi des Juifs, par Satan* 5th ed. (Paris, 1846); see also Edmund Silberner, "Friedrich Engels and the Jews," *Jewish Social Studies* 11 (1949): 323ff.

92. P. W. Blackstock and B. F. Hoselitz, *Marx/Engels: The Russian Menace to Europe* (New York, 1952), 59–59, 247.

93. For a critique of this attitude, see the remarks by George Watson, "Race and the Socialists: On the Progressive Principle of Revolutionary Extermination," *Encounter* (Nov. 1976): 15–23.

94. *MEGA*, 1, 7:29, 165, 176, 291. Engels disapproved of the Jews in Posen as a Germanizing element. See *Neue Rheinische Zeitung* (henceforth *NRZ*), 11 July and 9 Aug. 1848. The reference to this "dirtiest of all races" is in the *NRZ*, 29 Apr. 1849. For antisemitic commentaries on the role of Jews in the Viennese Revolution of 1848, see *NRZ*, 22 Feb. 1849.

95. Friedrich Engels, "Die Polendebatte in Frankfurt," *NRZ*, no. 91, Sept. 1848, 1, in *MEGA*, 1, 7: 331. "So weit ein polnischer Jude deutsch kauderwelscht, auf Wucher leiht, Münz und Gewicht verfälscht, so weit reicht das Vaterland des Herrn Lichnowski."

96. Engels to Paul Lafargue, 22 July 1892, in Friedrich Engels, Paul and Laura Lafargue, *Corréspondance,* vol. 3: *1891–5* (Paris, 1959), 197.

97. Apart from Engels's own correspondence, there is his reported remark to Abraham Cahan, the prominent American-Jewish socialist: "Do you think that I can't read *Lashon Ha-Qodesh*? Not for nothing do the capitalist press call me a Jew," in A. Cahan, *Blätter aus meinen Leben* (New York, 1926), 3: 264.

98. Engels to Bebel, 1 Dec. 1891, *August Bebels Briefwechsel mit Friedrich Engels,* edited by W. Blumenberg (The Hague, 1965), 487.

99. This letter written on 19 April 1890 to a Viennese correspondent, Isidor Ehrenfreund, is reproduced in Victor Adler, *Aufsätze, Reden und Briefe* (Vienna, 1929), 1: 6–8; first published by the Viennese *Arbeiterzeitung,* 9 May 1890.

100. It is worth noting that Engels wrote to Sorge on 9 August 1891 that he was unhappy with the English dockers' protest at the immigration of foreign paupers, i.e., Russian Jews. On the Jewish immigrant working class in London, see William J. Fishman, *East End Jewish Radicals, 1875–1914* (London, 1975); on Eleanor Marx-Aveling, there is the biography by Chusichi Tsuzuki, *The Life of Eleanor Marx 1855–98: A Socialist Tragedy* (Oxford, 1967), and the study by Yvonne Kapp, *Eleanor Marx: Family Life 1855–83* (London, 1972). See also Edmund Silberner, "Eleanor Marx: Ein Beitrag zu ihrer Biographie und zum Problem der jüdischen Identität," *Jahrbuch des Instituts für Deutsche Geschichte* (1977): 259–95.

101. Edmund Silberner, *Moses Hess: Geschichte seines Lebens* (Leiden, 1966), 192, argues that Hess's essay "On Money" profoundly influenced the young Marx. Julius Carlebach, "The problem of Moses Hess's influence on the young Marx," *LBIYB* 18 (1973): 27–39, on the other hand, rejects this view, suggesting that the gap between the two was already wide and their arguments fundamentally different. He accepts, however, that Hess was indeed Marx's precursor in the transition from humanism to socialism.

102. Hess's essay was first published in the *Rheinische Jahrbücher zur gesellschaftlichen Reform* (Darmstadt, 1845). It has been reproduced in T. Zlocisti, ed., *Moses Hess: Sozialistische Aufsätze 1841–7* (Berlin, 1921), and in *Moses Hess: Philosophische und Sozialistische Schriften 1837–1850*, ed. Auguste Cornu and Wolfgang Mönke (Berlin, 1961).

103. Moses Hess, *Philosophische und Sozialistische Schriften,* 334f.

104. Ibid., 345.

105. See Paul Lindau, ed., *Ferdinand Lassalles Tagebuch* (Breslau, 1891), 2 Feb. 1840, pp. 85–86, 160–61, 180–81. For the impact of the Damascus Affair on Hess, see *Rom und Jerusalem,* 35–37.

106. Ibid., 35.

107. Ibid., 40.

108. August Cornu, *Moses Hess,* 19, called this early work the "first exposition of a socialist theory in Germany." See also Moses Hess, *Die europäische Triarchie* (Leipzig, 1841), 138–40. Hess argued that the treatment of Jews by the State should be considered a barometer of intellectual freedom.

109. Like Feuerbach, Hess assumed that the positive ideal of the new society would be based on the principle of love. His socialist interpretation of Feuerbach's humanist anthropology proposed the unity of the species through the overcoming of egoism.

110. Horst Lademacher, "Die politische und soziale Theorie bei Moses Hess," *Archiv für Kulturgeschichte* 42 (2) (Cologne and Graz, 1960): 194–266, sees in Hess's voluntarism, his Fichtean emphasis on the deed, and his desire to overcome this dichotomy, the central feature of his outlook.

111. Moses Hess, "Jugement dernier du vieux monde social," is a good example of his revolutionary utopianism. It was reprinted by Eduard Bernstein, ed., *Dokumente des Sozialismus,* vol. 1 (Berlin, 1902–1905). See Bruno Frei, *Im Schatten von Karl Marx. Moses Hess—hundert Jahre nach seinem Tod* (Vienna, 1977), 51–84.

112. Isaiah Berlin, *The Life and Opinions of Moses Hess* (Cambridge, 1959), 11–15; see also Shlomo Avineri, *Moses Hess: Prophet of Communism and Zionism* (New York, 1985).

113. Karl Marx and Frederick Engels, "Manifesto of the Communist Party," *Selected Works* (Moscow, 1962), 1: 59.

114. On this point, see Patrick Girard, *Les Juifs de France de 1789 à 1860: de l'émancipation à l'égalité* (Paris, 1976).

115. See J. Salvador, *Paris, Rome, Jerusalem ou la question religieuse au XIXe Siècle,* 2 vols. (Paris, 1860); he is mentioned by Hess in *Rom und Jerusalem,* 78–79.

116. Gérard Israel, "The Adventure of the Alliance Israélite Universelle," *Wiener Library Bulletin* 27, new series nos. 30–31 (1973–1974): 49–58. See also Michael Graetz, *Haperipheria hayita La-Mercaz* (From periphery to center) (Jerusalem, 1982). This pioneering study examined chapters in the history of 19th-century French Jewry from Saint-Simon to the founding of the Alliance. It includes some material on Moses Hess.

117. Hess, *Rom und Jerusalem*, 22–23, 39, 85, 131–32, 199–200, 206.

118. Ibid., 42, 131–32.

119. For an analysis of Hess's "Red Bonapartism," see Shlomo Na'aman, "Moses Hess in der Deutschen Arbeiterbewegung," *Jahrbuch des Instituts für deutsche Geschichte* (Tel Aviv) (1976): 247–58.

120. Hess, *Rom und Jerusalem,* 114–23.

121. Moses Hess, *La haute Finance et l'Empire* (Paris, 1869); in this book, Hess renounced his Bonapartist illusions.

122. Hess, *Rom und Jerusalem,* 85.

123. Ibid., 199.

124. Ibid., 149–51, 238, for Hess's view of the opposition between "Aryans" and "Semites." Alain Boyer, "Du socialisme vrai au socialisme sioniste: l'itinéraire d'un prophète: Moïse Hess," *Mouvement social* 95 (Apr.–June 1976): 38–39, suggests that Hess was a racial Darwinist *avant la lettre*. He points to the influence of Ernst Renan and Augustin Thierry and the vogue which racial theories began to enjoy in France during the 1850s.

125. Hess, *Rom und Jerusalem,* 24.

126. Ibid.

127. Ibid., 40.

128. Ibid., 25.

129. Ibid.

130. Ibid., 42.

131. Ibid., 12.

132. Marx, "On the Jewish Question," 239.

133. Hess, *Rom und Jerusalem,* 16.

134. Ibid., 49.

135. "Hess an die Redaktion der Zeitschrift "Ben Chananja," 22 August–5 September 1862," in *Moses Hess Briefwechsel,* edited by Edmund Silberner (Leiden, 1959), 403.

136. Ibid. See also Shlomo Avineri, "Socialism and Nationalism in Moses Hess," *Midstream* (Apr. 1976), 41; and Jonathan Frankel, *Prophecy and Politics. Socialism, Nationalism and the Russian Jews 1862–1917* (Cambridge, 1981), 6–48.

137. Hess, *Rom und Jerusalem,* 135.

138. *Theodor Herzls Tagebücher,* 2 May 1901 (Berlin, 1923), 2: 599.

139. For Graetz's considerable influence on Hess's Jewish nationalism, see Reuven Michael, "Graetz und Hess," *LBIYB* 9 (1964): 91–121; and "Heinrich Graetz. Unveröffentliche Briefe an Moses Hess: 1861–1872," Instituto Giangiacomo Feltrinelli, Milan, *Annali* 4 (1961).

140. Hess, *Rom und Jerusalem,* 42.

141. Ibid., 219–21.

142. Alain Boyer, "Du socialisme vrai," 48–49 sees Hess's project for the colonization of Palestine as an unconscious "colonialism" and even links it to his lack of sympathy for the Arabs of Algeria in the 1860s, in their opposition to French occupation. This argument seems to me exaggerated.

143. Edmund Silberner, *Sozialisten zur Judenfrage* (Berlin, 1962), 135–36, speculated that Marx probably read Hess's work but there is no evidence of his reaction. The German socialist Carl Hirsch, on the other hand, was astonished to discover that his friend Hess had indeed been a Jewish patriot, unbeknown to him. See Silberner, *Moses Hess,* 635.

144. Johann Philipp Becker, "Warnung für Warnung," *Nordstern,* 16 Sept. 1865, 2, quoted in Silberner, *Moses Hess,* 197. The only other German socialist to comment (equally unfavorably) on Hess's work was Bernhard Becker, *Der Missbrauch der Nationalitätenlehre* (Brunswick, 1873), 129.

145. Bruno Frei, *Im Schatten von Karl Marx,* emphasizes the constant oscillations in Hess's thought between materialism and idealism, socialism and religion, Marx and

the prophets. Shlomo Na'aman, "Moses Hess: Zwischen Messianismus und Emanzipation," *Juden und Jüdische Aspekte in der Deutschen Arbeiterbewegung* 2 (Dec. 1976): 15–44, regards messianism as the unifying factor in Hess's multiple allegiances.

146. See for example Nachman Syrkin, "Moses Hess: The Founder of Socialist Judaism," in *Nachman Syrkin: Socialist Zionist: A Biographical Memoir and Selected Essays,* edited by Marie Syrkin (New York, 1961), 306–15.

CHAPTER 3

German Social Democrats on the *Völkisch* Movement

In the 1880s the German Social-Democratic Party (SPD) for the first time in its history had to confront a noisy, antisemitic agitation, led by the Protestant court preacher Adolf Stöcker in Berlin. The so-called Berlin movement transformed the "Jewish Question" into an issue of German electoral politics. It was instigated after Stöcker had failed in his initial attempts to win the Berlin workers for German Chancellor Otto von Bismarck's social legislation. Stöcker's Christian-Social movement emerged at a time when the antisocialist laws had driven the SPD underground and deprived the working class of any meaningful political freedom. Troubled by proletarian indifference and hostility to the newly united German fatherland, the monarchical State and Lutheran Christianity, Stöcker tried to mobilize the discontent of the petty-bourgeois masses (*Kleinbürgertum*) against the recently emancipated Jews. The SPD had every reason in the early 1880s to oppose this crusade, which they identified with Bismarck's authoritarian efforts to root out social democracy by Prussian strong-arm methods. While Stöcker denounced the "atheistic," materialistic, and unpatriotic SPD, the socialists in their turn vehemently opposed a demagogue whom they regarded as the "spiritual gendarme" of Bismarck.[1] Resistance to the Jew-bait thus became part of the broader working-class defiance of the Bismarckian regime and its witchhunt against German Social Democracy. The SPD campaign against Stöcker was essentially an act of self-defense in the face of what they saw as a repressive clerical-authoritarian State.

By the 1890s, however, the situation had changed. The Protestant "Christian socialism" of Stöcker with its echoes of Luther's tirades against the Jews, had given way to a new anti-Christian, radical-populist brand of agitation. The strongholds of the antisemitic movement were no longer in Berlin and other big cities, but in the provinces, among the peasantry and the rural *Mittelstand*. The new demagogues of antisemitism like Otto Böckel, Hermann Ahlwardt, and Theodor Fritsch spoke the language of blood and race, and evoked the virtues of the Germanic *Volk*. They had no interest in the ideology of the Christian State. Their propaganda was directed against the ruling Prusso-German establishment instead of being orchestrated from above as in the early 1880s. Fin-de-siècle German populism was anti-capitalist and anti-Junker as well as being antisemitic in orientation.

This new democratic trend in *völkisch* antisemitism presented the SPD with an awkward tactical dilemma, heightened by its own internal evolution since the 1880s. With the end of the anti-socialist laws in 1890, the Social Democrats had emerged as a powerful factor in State and society, strengthened by their experience of governmental repression. Their gradual integration into the German political system encouraged an increasingly reformist "praxis": at the same time, the SPD still espoused a revolutionary Marxism in questions of theory, stubbornly clinging to its utopian belief in the imminent demise of capitalist society. This belief was interpreted in a peculiarly mechanistic and determinist manner—far removed from the idealism which had animated the party in an earlier phase of its history.

Antisemitism was one of the more important political phenomena of the 1890s which needed to be fitted into the general perspective of Marxian doctrine as interpreted by SPD leaders after the Erfurt Congress of 1891. The German Marxist consensus regarded it as "reactionary degeneration" of feudal "socialism," following the definition given by Frederick Engels in a well-known article published in the Viennese *Arbeiter-Zeitung* in May 1890. Engels had unequivocally pinpointed the *reactionary* features of antisemitism, which he deduced from its social basis in the *Mittelstand*—those intermediate strata between the bourgeoisie and proletariat, which according to Marxian theory, were doomed to disappear. The SPD accepted Engels's viewpoint but gave it a fatalistic interpretation which further reinforced the trend towards passively waiting on events that would characterize party policy in the 1890s. Instead of considering antisemitism as a direct threat to social democracy (as it had a decade earlier), it now saw the movement as preparing the road for socialism itself. The campaign against the Jews was expected to awaken the lethargic lower middle-class strata of German society to a more "progressive" standpoint.

According to Marx and Engels, modern capitalist society would inevitably polarize into two great camps—the bourgeoisie and the proletariat. The *Mittelstand,* so it was assumed, would be driven by economic adversity into the proletarian camp, accelerating the coming crisis of capitalism. This theory of class polarization corresponded well with the general mood of socialist thinking at the time. It also offered a useful framework for explaining the "revolutionary" as well as the more reactionary features of the antisemitic agitation. At the same time an answer had to be found for Social Democrats faced with a growing challenge from *völkisch* Jew-baiters in German provinces like Hesse and Saxony. Already at the SPD Party Congress of 1890 in Halle, the Marburg delegations had asked the party executive for more assistance in countering the propaganda of the Hessian antisemitic leader Otto Böckel.[2] The Hessian "peasant king" had shown how antisemitism could help to mobilize the rural masses, in a region where social democracy had not yet gained a significant foothold. The Marburg delegates declared:

> We in Hesse are convinced that something must be done for the rural population, if we are not to fall back in some districts before Böckel's agitation.[3]

August Bebel, the principal SPD leader in the 1890s, was well aware that the antisemites were making progress across Germany. In Saxony and Hesse the rural *Mittelstand* were particularly susceptible to antisemitic appeals, directed not only against Jews, but also against the landowning Junker aristocracy. Hermann Ahlwardt in Pomerania epitomized this newer brand of anti-Christian and anti-conservative *Radauantisemitismus* (hooligan antisemitism) which was threatening to undermine Junker hegemony in agrarian Germany. Ahlwardt's election in the Conservative stronghold of Friedeberg-Arnswalde on 24 November 1892, was one of the high points of the *völkisch* movement. Antisemites in the 1893 Reichstag elections received 263,000 votes, a fivefold increase over their results a few years earlier. This increase in support coincided with a disastrous slump in the number of Liberal Progressive deputies from 67 to 37. There were now 16 antisemitic deputies in the German Parliament. Moreover, on 8 December 1892, the Conservatives adopted for the first time an openly antisemitic plank in their Tivoli program, in order to stem the *völkisch* tide which was moving against them.

August Bebel, Wilhelm Liebknecht, and other German socialist leaders followed these political developments between 1890 and 1893 with close attention. In a letter to Engels on 24 June 1892, Bebel stressed the anti-capitalist character of *Mittelstand* antisemitism:

> They [the lower middle classes] feel oppressed by the power of capital and since the Jews appear to personify the latter in its most pronounced form, their hatred turns especially against Jewry. Since racial and religious antipathy also play a part this is all the easier for the Jew-baiters to bring out.[4]

Bebel attributed the success of antisemitic agitation to the migration of Jews from the Eastern provinces and to their monopoly in the marketing of agricultural products.

> When one observes how the Jews immigrate here in droves from the Eastern provinces it is understandable that the [antisemitic] agitation should find such a fertile soil. With their persistence and industry they [the Jews] gradually take control of the whole cattle-trade and commerce in agricultural products which is almost exclusively in Jewish hands in Hesse, Baden, and Franconia etc. The [antisemitic] movement destroys the established parties, and that is its advantage for us.[5]

From the tactical standpoint, Bebel hoped that the antisemites would help to break up the conservative-liberal monopoly in politics. This was an electoral consideration which had not previously been so dominant in German socialist thinking. It reflected a certain immobilism in party strategy since the lifting of the anti-socialist laws in 1890. But it also corresponded to the real possibility that Social democracy could reach out to a broader mass of voters. In an interview with the Austrian writer Hermann Bahr in 1893, Bebel was optimistic that antisemitism would eventually play into socialist hands. It was an "internal conflict" within the ruling class, foreshadowing the imminent collapse of capitalism.

> It is all right with us if the members of the ruling classes wage war among themselves, if all confidence is shattered and a revulsion against this whole social order grows. We calmly watch and wait.[6]

This deterministic viewpoint was fully in line with the general Marxian perspective, which Bebel had delineated at the Erfurt Party Congress of 1891. Capitalism was rushing blindly towards its demise, like the hero of a classical tragedy driven to his doom by the fates. "Bourgeois society is contributing so powerfully to its own destruction, that we only need to wait for the moment when we can pick up the power which has fallen out of its hands."[7]

The fatalistic interpretation of Marxism which mesmerized the SPD as a whole in the 1890s found classic expression in a resolution on antisemitism that Bebel presented for approval at the 1893 Party Congress.

> Antisemitism arises from the depression of certain middle-class strata which find themselves oppressed by the development of capitalism and which are destined as a result of these trends to economically decline. These groups however misinterpret the real

> causes of their situation and instead of fighting the capitalist system, they direct their resentment against surface phenomena which threaten them most in the competitive struggle: namely against the Jewish exploiters.[8]

This was a classic Marxian mantra regarding the socio-economic roots of antisemitism. Its main thrust was to underline the *partial* character of the antisemitic protest against capitalist society. Antisemitism was a one-sided attack on Jewish exploitation, a symptom of the "false consciousness" of the *Mittelstand.* Such an interpretation of antisemitism encouraged a passive attitude since it assumed that there could be no amelioration of the situation without the overthrow of capitalism. Any militant struggle against antisemitism would be shelved in favor of the "wait and see" opportunism which characterized the SPD in the 1890s. Behind the long-term "optimism" of official ideology, a short-term pessimism with regard to the "Jewish Question" was also becoming apparent. This comes out more clearly in Bebel's private observations to Engels, in a letter of June 1893. He explained that the German Social Democrats could do little to persuade peasants and craftsmen that capitalism was the real cause of their misery.

> I heard artisans say: you frankly admit that you cannot help us; but we do not want to go under, and so we vote for the antisemites. . .similarly with the small peasants. One can try and prove to them in razor-sharp fashion that it is all a swindle, they will cling to their view. . . .[9]

August Bebel fully shared Engels's view that antisemitism was ultimately a *reactionary* movement. But he was forced to confront the practical implications of its growing efficacy. He concluded that nothing could be expected of social strata who were ready to clasp at any straw to save themselves from economic ruin. At the same time he had few illusions about the narrow-minded stupidity and endemic Judeophobia within German society.

> I was astonished at the deep, fanatical hatred of the Jews among merchants and craftsmen. At the present time the most unenviable man is the Jewish traveling salesman: he is frequently treated like a dog; there are even firms in Saxony which display the sign: entrance forbidden to beggars, dogs and Jews.[10]

Bebel explained this hatred by the role Jews played in the German economy. He concluded that this was truly detrimental to a significant part of the commercial and artisan class. Bitter experience would gradually teach these strata that their misery was not a direct consequence of Jewish exploitation and that Christian usurers would act in the same way.[11] But only after the failure of antisemitism could the Social democrats hope to win support among the German peasants and artisans: "Once antisemitism and conservatism both prove powerless to save them, then we can hope to make some ground and win support, not before."[12]

At the 1893 Party Congress in Cologne, Bebel nonetheless opposed the view of some delegates that the SPD should avoid specifically opposing antisemitism since "it contained a whole string of revolutionary elements. . . ."[13] These delegates went too far for Bebel's taste, in suggesting that the SPD should keep all options on the table in its response to the *völkisch* challenge.

Bebel's speech to the party delegates deserves close attention, since it was the most important *programmatic* statement of the SPD on the "Jewish question" before 1914. He began by emphasizing that popular Jew-hatred was an age-old manifestation, rooted in racial and religious prejudice. Modern political antisemitism had added a new dimension by arguing that the Jews were a separate and distinct *race,* whose characteristics were harmful for every people among whom they lived. Bebel acknowledged a certain validity to this *völkisch* thesis[14]:

> We are dealing with two races [Germans and Jews] who in their character and their whole being are fundamentally different and whose difference has been maintained for 2,000 years until the present day.[15]

Indeed, Bebel was insistent that the Jews had indeed preserved their "racial" characteristics, which (historically speaking) could be considered as a remarkable achievement:

> I admit that I cannot suppress a certain admiration for a race, which despite all these dreadful persecutions, still continues in its own way to develop and independently maintain its existence.[16]

Bebel further observed that the Jews had inherited a "Semitic" disposition to trade and commerce, also found among the Phoenicians and Carthaginians in the ancient world. This "commercial spirit" was highly developed amongst the Jews, but Bebel refused to draw openly antisemitic conclusions from this assumption. Thus far, the SPD leader seemed to have internalized all the prevailing *völkisch* and antisemitic stereotypes concerning Jewish "racial" traits. The main difference was Bebel's insistence that Christians were responsible for this "racial" division, since they had forbidden Jews to own land, to work with their hands, or to exercise a craft. They had also forced the

Jews into ghettos where they developed those commercial skills and "huckster" mentality depicted by the young Marx.

Bebel did not unequivocally repudiate the unflattering Marxian portrait of the huckstering Jew. On the contrary, he claimed: "Undoubtedly what is called huckstering characterizes one part of Jewry."[17] He even echoed the Marxian phrase that money was the "secular God of the Jews," and accepted that one could equate Judaism and capitalism: "Our whole society is huckstering and striving to make money and therefore a judaized society."[18] This reference to the *Verjudung* (judaization) of bourgeois society was a common link between socialists and antisemites.

Bebel did try to put some flesh and blood on these Marxian abstractions by relating them to the Jewish economic role in German regions like Hesse, Thuringia, Baden, Wurttemberg, Bavaria, and Alsace-Lorraine. The Jews, he claimed, had achieved a monopolistic position as middlemen in buying and selling agricultural products to the peasantry. They were, for the most part, usurers in these regions. *Völkisch* antisemitism had taken advantage of this popular identification of Jew and money-lender in the peasant mind: "Everywhere the Jew confronts the peasant as buyer and seller; for the peasant the Jew is the capitalist. . . . Jew and capitalist are for him [the peasant] identical concepts."[19] Bebel appeared to be playing the [amateur] sociologist here, writing with so-called clinical detachment. His remarks could also be construed as going a long way towards acceptance of antisemitic clichés in their racial and socio-economic dimensions. The same is true of his explanation for the anti-capitalist character of the Böckel-Ahlwardt agitation on the land. In urban areas, according to Bebel, the Jews had also achieved a dominant position in industries like shoemaking, clothing, and tailoring. Their "huckstering" stemmed from a peculiar flair for creating wealth out of extremely modest beginnings. By "huckstering" Bebel made it plain that he understood "trade for a small profit, trafficking in those things which other people keep clear of, which seem insignificant, without value or even contemptible."[20] Again, the ambivalence is striking—mixing pejorative language with a tinge of admiration for Jewish business enterprise.

Bebel interpreted the existence of Jewish "characteristics" in the Marxist, rather than the purely racial sense, but the lines were blurred. He did not directly condemn the Jews for corrupting the Germans with their "huckster" mentality and he was fully aware of Christian business envy and resentment at unwelcome economic competition: "The fact that the Jews are unusually strongly represented in commerce and generally superior in this area to so-called Christians has called forth hostility and envy against them."[21] This emphasis on Jewish business skill as a product of Christian persecution, and on antisemitism as an expression of economic rivalry, to some extent neutralized the damage done by his playing with racial stereotypes. Moreover, he did stress that Jews were members of an *oppressed* race. In this respect his position was more balanced than that of Marx or many Jewish party members. He believed, moreover, that the "peculiar characteristics" of the Jews would fade with the collapse of bourgeois society.[22] Unlike Marx, he pointed out that the antisemites also attacked those Jewish *virtues* which had flourished under capitalism. Bebel portrayed Jewish students, for example, as being models of sobriety and industriousness compared to their rowdy, beer-drinking Germanic counterparts.

> The generally known fact that the Jews are noted for their unusual assiduity, persistence and frequently for their sobriety (Schoenlank: Oho!)—Yes, Comrade Schoenlank (laughter), makes them even more hated by their adversaries.[23]

What did Bebel think, however, about the program of the German antisemitic parties in the early 1890s? The SPD leader conceded that there were some positive features in the antisemitic program, with quasi-revolutionary and reactionary demands uneasily mixed together. Thus the populist antisemites called for universal suffrage, a progressive income tax, nationalization of certain industries, and the liquidation of peasant debts. On the other hand they also favored restoring the professional guilds, strengthening the military and naval program, protecting the "Christian" character of schools, and eliminating Jewish department stores, peddling and bazaars. Bebel believed that such a program was essentially demagogic. The antisemites had nothing to offer the artisan and peasant, except anti-capitalist rhetoric directed solely against the Jews. Marxists should not seek to compete with this wild talk, but rather explain to the rural masses: "We have no panacea which in the long-run will save you as artisans, small farmers, small traders, within the existing framework of society."[24] Nothing would be more foolhardy and immoral for a Marxist than to offer palliatives designed to counter antisemitic appeals: "A Social-democrat ought not to hazard anything of the kind; he would be swept with a broom out of the meeting by his own party comrades."[25]

Bebel clearly followed the advice of Friedrich Engels on this point, adding the full weight of his authority as the SPD leader against any temptation to flirt with antisemitism on the agrarian question.[26] The resolution which he proposed to the Party Congress in 1893 summed up these points in a dialectical perspective which would completely unravel 40 years later with the victory of Nazism.

> Social-democracy fights antisemitism as a movement which is directed against the natural development of society but which, despite its reactionary character and against its will, ultimately must become revolutionary. This is bound to happen because the petty-bourgeois and small peasant strata, which are being whipped up by antisemitism against the Jewish capitalists, will finally realize that not merely the Jewish capitalist, but the capitalist class as a whole is its enemy. Hence only the fulfillment of socialism can free them from their poverty.[27]

The fatal flaw in this Marxist approach lay in its economic determinism—the assumption that capitalism *must* lead to socialism with the certainty of a "law of nature." Only in that context could one argue that antisemitism was working in favor of revolution. Moreover, the idea that attacking "Jewish" capitalism was at the core of the antisemitic program was in itself grossly simplistic. Not all delegates were satisfied with Bebel's prognosis, but the critique mostly came from the moderate revisionist quarter, which regarded official Marxist policy on the agrarian question as misguided. Simon Katzenstein, a socialist Jew from Hesse, opposed the publication of Bebel's speech as a brochure: "because that would give it an official Party character, which should not happen."[28]

The SPD leadership, whatever it ambiguities and failings, undoubtedly despised the antisemitic movement. This was evident from the Reichstag speech of Wilhelm Liebknecht on 30 November 1893. A veteran leader of the Party for over thirty years, Liebknecht vehemently denounced the assertion that antisemitism was an international cultural movement. Liebknecht claimed that antisemitism was, above all, the product of backward *political* conditions in Germany:

> First of all, antisemitism is not a cultural movement and secondly the movement which it represents does not exist in other civilized countries. . .the movement is restricted to Germany and it has become possible here only because of the unhealthy political conditions which prevail in our country. Though I do not at all deny the economic basis of antisemitism.[29]

Liebknecht dismissed the antisemites as "Luddites," who blindly struck out against modern machine-technology in the mistaken belief that it was responsible for their economic ruin. These enemies of progress had failed to grasp that behind large-scale agriculture and modern industry stood the productive forces of the capitalist system. Liebknecht contrasted the *futurist* orientation of modern socialism with the backward-looking utopia of the antisemites. The latter longed for a tribalistic society based on organic community and the ties of blood and race. Socialists, on the other hand, while recognizing the social evils of capitalism, accepted it as a necessary transition to a *higher* form of society. Marxists welcomed the full blossoming of productive forces under capitalism as an indispensable precondition of socialism. On the other hand, by seeking to eliminate the *modernizing* elements of capitalism, antisemites were engaged in a hopeless project to turn back the clock. Their attempts to revive consumer and credit associations in order to save the declining artisan and peasant class were doomed to failure. The agitation against *Jewish* capital, Liebknecht maintained, was irrelevant and obtuse in a broader comparative perspective:

> Look at England, at America! Jewish capital has never played a role there, a Rothschild cannot play a part, because bourgeois society has developed on too gigantic and grand a scale. If you ask in England about the peasant class, people will laugh at you! For generations there have been no more peasants in England—they were wiped out by big capital, by big capitalist concerns, which are almost exclusively in Christian hands.[30]

In England and America, the model examples of modern capitalist development, the exploiting class of entrepreneurs consisted almost exclusively of non-Jews. In America, where the farmers faced a crisis in the 1890s similar to that of the German peasantry, their exploiters were Gentiles; they were "just as Germanic as our own antisemitic gentlemen, and at least as Christian. For the English and American capitalist conscientiously goes twice every Sunday to church."[31]

Wilhelm Liebknecht pointed out that in Germany it was the Prussian Junkers (who cynically addressed peasants as "fellow farmers"), and not the Jews, who were directly responsible for the misery on the land: "Look at the lists of those who have driven off the peasants in Prussia, particularly in the eastern provinces! How many Junkers do you find, and how many Jews are there!"[32] The German Marxists had repeatedly explained that there was no solution for the peasantry under the capitalist system which was their real enemy.

> We have told the peasants: you cannot be saved in our present society; it is not the Jews, as the antisemitic gentlemen who

appeal to your prejudices and stupidity tell you. . .but the present social system, it is capitalism, which is your enemy. . . .[33]

As chief editor of *Vorwärts* in Berlin, Liebknecht followed a similar political line in dealing with antisemitism. This position was in no sense "philosemitic." The central SPD newspaper was ready to quote Karl Marx to the effect that the "emancipation of the Jews was the *emancipation of society from Judaism.*"[34] The interpretation which *Vorwärts* put on Marx's essay of 1844, nearly fifty years later, was somewhat confused but ostensibly well-intentioned. Thus an editorial of 9 December 1893 answered Adolf Stöcker's charge that the Jews had corrupted Germany with their huckstering mentality, by offering a re-edited version of Marx.

> Our solution consists in saying, that the so-called "Jewish spirit" is the spirit of capitalism. Certainly not every Jew is a capitalist but every capitalist is a Jew—and therefore the emancipation of the Jews and the rest of mankind coincides with the emancipation of humanity from Jewish—and other capitalism. . . . *Probatum est!*[35]

What *Vorwärts* wished to say by means of this tortuous jargon, was that Marxism was even-handed when it came to Jewish and Christian capital. For socialists, it was ultimately irrelevant whether bankers or capitalists were called Bleichröder or Hansemann, Rothschild or Stamm, Bamberger or Kardorff. *Vorwärts* categorically rejected the antisemitic assertion that social democracy "is to be credited with a special partiality for Jewry! It is true that social democracy is not antisemitic, but it also goes in for no philosemitism."[36] The Jewish big bourgeoisie (*Grossbürgertum*) was a legitimate target in its political propaganda: "Whether it be on the stock exchange, in big business, in commerce, in politics or in literature, capitalist Jewry is no more attractive to us than uncircumcised big capital and its representatives."[37]

For the SPD it was self-evident that the prominence of big Jewish capitalists and entrepreneurs was fully in accordance with the logic of the capitalist system.

> Although it is certain that upper-middle class Jewry, thanks to its entire historical development, has known how to bring the technique of exploitation to a peak of perfection—that it has cultivated and refined its financial skills—it is equally evident that the Jew-capitalists are what they are as a result of our mode of production.[38]

The exclusive antisemitic focus on Jewish capital produced an optical illusion. By looking only at the surface of society, where Jewish entrepreneurs *appeared* to be the most mobile and dynamic element in the German capitalist class, a false impression was created.

> It is an indisputable fact, historically speaking, that the Jewish magnates of capital emerge on the canvas of the bourgeoisie in the most lurid relief. Loving gaudy and strong effects, mobile and equipped with an astonishing social ubiquity, they float everywhere, like cork, on the surface of society—attracting attention to themselves. This encourages an outmoded manner of understanding things which sees only the part instead of the whole, the Jew rather than the wealthy upstart.[39]

In the Marxian analysis, antisemites mistook what was a temporary and accidental phenomenon—the prominence of Jewish capitalists—as a true reflection of underlying social development. The role of Jewish financiers was only a *symptom* and an effect, rather than the cause of capitalist expansion. From this standpoint, *Vorwärts* could brush aside the narrow-minded ignorance of antisemitic deputies like Stöcker, Otto Böckel, Werner, and Zimmermann, who only attacked unproductive "Jewish" capital. Such rhetoric was in Bebel's phrase the "socialism of fools" ("Sozialismus des dummen Kerls")—the last illusion of the petty-bourgeoisie. (Originally this disparaging term had been coined by Ferdinand Kronawetter, an Austrian radical-democrat, during his campaign against the Viennese antisemites in the mid-1880s.) The declining *Mittelstand* would inevitably be crushed under the streamroller of capitalism and sink like a stone into the proletariat. As *Vorwärts* optimistically put it in June 1891: "The discontented, the oppressed, the antisemitic mass will have to follow us, because conditions are driving them to our banner."[40]

Vorwärts in the early 1890s unquestionably regarded the antisemitic movement, for all its one-sided and wild rhetoric, as a promising development. But as an editorial in December 1892 noted, there was another historical irony behind the *völkisch* Jew-bait. The Jews, despite the persecution which they had endured throughout the Middle Ages, had emerged as pace-makers of the modern bourgeoisie. Forcibly prevented from owning land or exercising a craft, they had gained great experience in dealing with money and could finally take their revenge on their erstwhile persecutors. Indeed, they were the masters now:

> Behold, the oppressed [the Jews] have become the lords of this world, a powerful part of the dominant bourgeoisie, impregnated with the same spirit. The irony of history has turned everything upside down and punishment has brought its reward. It has made servants out of the persecutors and masters out of the persecuted.[41]

Nothing should have illustrated more clearly the folly of antisemitic persecution than this reversal of roles, whereby the Jews had emerged in the forefront of the capitalist avant-garde. Neither Bismarck, the Prussian Junkers, nor the Protestant clergy had learnt the lesson. In the early 1880s they had instigated a conservative clerical Jew-bait. The signal had been given from above—"Cherchez le Juif"—but it had backfired on its promoters.[42] The Frankenstein monster of antisemitism, created by the reactionary Junkers, was beginning to take its toll on those who invented it.[43] Medieval persecution which centuries later ensured Jewish financial supremacy, now threatened the ruling class itself, ever since populist demagogues like Böckel and Ahlwardt had discovered capitalist corruption in high places.[44] *Vorwärts* saw no reason not to welcome the sympathy which Ahlwardt's agitation had aroused in the German masses. The most likely consequence would be to further the decline of the bourgeois parties—a consummation devoutly to be wished.[45]

Ahlwardt's *völkisch* antismitism was therefore performing a useful and even therapeutic function. It was undermining both the Conservative and liberal parties, and awakening mass frustrations. Despite his monumental clumsiness, Ahlwardt had held the German Parliament in thrall for two full days with his insinuations of financial scandal.

> The stupid, blind rogue aims at the Jews, and he strikes capitalism instead, and through it the prevailing form of State and social order; hence the feverish excitement of the Reichstag, which would otherwise be completely inexplicable.[46]

The Social democrats viewed this exposure of ruling-class corruption as a useful confirmation of their own strictures against capitalism. *Vorwärts* was convinced by the Reichstag election results of 1893 that the social and political order was indeed close to collapse. The antisemites on the Right and the socialists on the left would be the main beneficiaries of a decline in the strength of the bourgeois parties. In June 1893, a *Vorwärts* editorial analyzed the successes of the antisemites in Hesse and Saxony. It rejected the despairing view of the German liberal historian, Theodor Mommsen, that antisemitism was an incurable plague of the human spirit "which incomprehensibly and destructively follows its course through Europe as did once the Black Death in the Middle Ages."[47]

Vorwärts did not share this pessimism and insisted that *economic* causes were paramount in the contemporary agitation against the Jews. It also noted that the radical populist movement under the Hessian peasants' leader, Otto Böckel, had broken away from Conservative tutelage and rejected the foundations of Christianity.[48] Böckel treated both the Old and New Testaments as a "Jewish machination." *Vorwärts* by no means underestimated Böckel's talents as an educated demagogue with a doctoral degree in languages and literature. An expert on local folk customs, songs and legends which he assiduously collected (Böckel had been assistant librarian at the University of Marburg), he knew how to assume the guise of a simple farmer in his passionate appeals to the Hessian peasantry. His proto-Nazi agrarian populism idealized peasants as the backbone of the German nation, the repository of its "racial" purity and of "Germanic" virtues such as hard work, loyalty, and strong character. This *Blut und Boden* (blood and soil) ideology drew much of its strength from the negative effects of liberal economic reforms in the Second Reich, rampant anti-Prussianism (Hesse had been forcibly annexed after it fought on the Austrian side against Prussia in 1866) as well as the Jewish emancipation of 1870–71. Böckel was fully aware of peasant resentment at the important role of Jews as dynamic entrepreneurial newcomers to the region. He skilfully rode the wave of reaction against the prominence of Jewish middlemen in the cattle and grain trade, in the real estate business and in providing credit to local farmers. It was relatively easy to blame Jewish speculators for manipulating mortgage and credit rates or for raising land values beyond the reach of most peasants. At the same time, Böckel also attacked the hated Prussian Junker landowners for feathering their own nests and protecting Jewish "usurers," even as they hypocritically claimed to sympathize with the peasantry. Böckel's antisemitism was to a certain extent anti-establishment, as well as being anti-cosmopolitan and antimodernist, building on the traditional hostility in the countryside to the Jews as "blood-enemies of Christ" and as representatives of urban market forces. "Jewish" free enterprise, Böckel claimed, was destroying the healthy "racial instincts" of the *Volk*. It symbolized something alien and remote—the sinful metropolis of Berlin—where Jewish influence guided the stock exchange, the liberal press, atheistic trends and revolutionary subversion.

The Social Democrats placed special emphasis on the threat of economic ruin, which was driving much of the rural population to look upon the *völkisch* antisemites as their last hope. Böckel appeared to the agrarian masses as the enemy of a corrupt ruling class, and its Jewish allies. This was an easy argument to follow, especially for those ready to clasp at any straw. It also explained the appeal of Hermann Ahlwardt, a schoolteacher (later unmasked as an embezzling crook) who ran for a Saxon seat in the Reichstag in 1892 on an anti-Junker, antisemitic program. *Vorwärts,* as yet unaware of Ahlwardt's own corrupt practices, rationalized his popularity as follows:

> The Jews appear on account of their business skills as rogues, as a corrupting clique to the coarse peasants and artisans. Ahlwardt had the courage to uncover the damage caused by this corruption and to pursue it into the ruing circles. Ahlwardt is the enemy of corruption and of the rich, Jew and Christian alike. He is the friend of the poor—that is the popular logic which has carried him to his Reichstag seat.[49]

Ahlwardt's vicious antisemitism helped him gain a landslide victory in the 1893 elections in Saxony, where there were virtually no "Semites." As *Vorwärts* noted, Jews represented no more than 0.2 percent of the population. Yet it was in this region that the German antisemites won nearly half of all their Reichstag seats in 1893. *Vorwärts* logically concluded that antisemitism was more of a protest vote against Junker Conservatives by the economically threatened *Mittelstand* than a specific response to Jewish activities.

> The success of the Böckelite antisemites was not due to their antisemitism. Rather they were able to drum together 90,000 votes almost exclusively at the expense of the Conservatives—they convinced people that the Conservatives represented the exploiting elite, but that they were the real representatives of the starving *Mittelstand.*[50]

This was a reasonable interpretation of the antisemitic vote, and it also reflected socialist satisfaction at the discomfiture of the German conservatives. Less convincing was the confidence expressed by *Vorwärts* that the rural masses would eventually reject Böckel and Ahlwardt in favor of the SPD. On 26 June 1893 the central organ of the German socialist party declared: "It is only logical that the antisemites have taken over the leadership of the bourgeois camp, in the struggle of capitalism against socialism."[51] It was in this sense that *Vorwärts* could describe antisemitism as "cultural manure" for socialism. It simultaneously represented the apogee of capitalist barbarism and pointed the way to the coming social revolution. On 28 June 1893 *Vorwärts* suggested a new metaphor. It described German capitalism as a candle burning at both ends of a fire lit by socialists and antisemites. In this crisis, every palliative invented by capitalist society simply speeded up the process of disintegration. This was especially true of antisemitism—"the last refuge of a desperate bourgeois society."[52]

Vorwärts optimistically predicted that the Prussian Junkers would be worst hit by the antisemitic deluge, while Social Democrats could stand on the sideline and eventually reap the harvest. "The Hep-Hep concerns itself today with Junker and Jew and the reactionary gentlemen will experience still more remarkable things from their pampered foster-child."[53] This neutral position adopted by *Vorwärts* was a far cry from the militant opposition by socialists to the Christian-social Jew-baiting of Adolf Stöcker's Belin movement during the early 1880s. The influence of Bebel and Liebknecht nonetheless prevented any opportunist efforts to ride the crest of the antisemitic wave. On 21 July 1893 *Vorwärts* repudiated any suggestion of collaboration with the antisemitic parties, stressing that the economic crisis of the *Mittelstand* had nothing to do with the Jews. "Apart from Hesse and a few other regions, even the most brazen and mendacious demagogue can no longer connect the Jews with the decline of the peasant and the artisanal class."[54] *Vorwärts* also pointed out that there was no ideological common ground between socialism and antisemitism. "We repudiate the disgusting handshake proffered by antisemitism with contempt. Neither the Social-democratic Party nor socialism itself has anything in common with it."[55]

According to the official German Marxist position, populist anticapitalism was not the same as socialism—a movement which looked to the future and the fundamental restructuring of capitalist society.[56] Antisemitism, wrote *Vorwärts,* was at best "a backward-looking, distorted and twisted version of socialism."[57] Marxist Socialists could never go along with the credit utopias or guild fantasies of the followers of Böckel or Ahlwardt. To restore the guilds and other features of medieval corporatism was a doomed exercise. Antisemitic votes had indeed risen from 56,900 in 1890 to 400,000 in 1893—about 5% of the electorate. The antisemitic parties now had sixteen Reichstag seats. More importantly, the 20% of the German electorate who voted for the powerful Conservative Party (which in 1892 had officially adopted an anti-Jewish platform) were, in effect, supporting antisemitism. Nevertheless, *Vorwärts* did not think this movement had any future. It respected Böckel for having "a good knowledge of rural conditions" and as a skilful organizer able to mobilize the agrarian masses.[58] But despite his oratorical powers and knowledge of local conditions, his producer and consumer associations had done nothing to improve the conditions of the peasantry. The *practical incompetence* of the antisemites encouraged *Vorwärts* in the view that it would not be long before Social democracy began to advance in rural areas and to convince the peasants that their place was not with the landowner class.[59] *Vorwärts* was confident that the Hessian peasantry would soon join the socialist struggle against Prussian militarism, bureaucracy and modern capitalism. It was the task of Social Democrats to accelerate the growth of political consciousness in the rural masses. "And here Antisemitism has prepared the way. It has performed what should have been the task of bourgeois democracy. . . ."[60]

Vorwärts derived a certain *Schadenfreude* from the local antisemitic triumphs, emphasizing the consternation that Ahlwardt's plebeian Jew-baiting had caused in the conservative camp. The resultant antisemitic program of the Conservative party convinced *Vorwärts* that the Prussian Junkers had lost their reason.[61] This claim greatly underestimated the shrewdness of the Conservative party and its even more antisemitic extra-parliamentary organization, the *Bund der Landwirte* (Agrarian League). The Conservatives adopted a party platform in 1892 to "do battle against the many-sided aggressive, decomposing and arrogant Jewish influence on the life of our people." Henceforth, it presented Jews as the "uncompromising opponents of Conservative principles," as the avant-garde of liberalism and Social Democracy. This was hardly a matter for general rejoicing or to be dismissed as a mere act of despair. On the contrary, antisemitism had gained considerably in prestige and legitimacy once it was adopted by a leading party of the Second Reich, close to the throne and holding many key positions in the Hohenzollern monarchical State. Even the anti-establishment populist antisemites were ecstatic at this success though in succeeding years they would, ironically enough, be weakened as a result of the annexation of their program by the much more influential Conservative Right. Antisemitism, as a consequence, had become *more* rather than less entrenched in German society—especially among the military, academic, and upper class elites. Only the somewhat weakened liberal "Progressives" remained as potential allies for Jews and Social Democrats.

The sincere efforts of "Progressive" deputies in the Reichstag to discredit Hermann Ahlwardt offered the SPD press more targets for its contemptuous scorn.[62] Liberals who called for the public prosecution of antisemites were accused of committing hara-kiri on their own principles and denying freedom of speech. It was with half an eye on the embarrassment of the bourgeois parties that *Vorwärts,* on 17 June 1893, declared: "The progress of antisemitism is therefore not at all unwelcome to us. On the contrary, we know that we can only reap success from it.[63]

This was a decidedly myopic standpoint, exuding simplistic assumptions, political opportunism and expediency. There was no real evidence that antisemitism was the movement of moribund social classes, heralding the coming disintegration of bourgeois society. Nor was it true that the "socialism of fools" was the hare-brained program of half-educated Jew-baiters. This dismissive assessment ignored, for example, the penetration of antisemitic ideas among German intellectuals, academics and students. It failed to anticipate the integrative role that antisemitism would play in times of crisis, bringing together forces from the lower depths of society and fusing them with anti-democratic trends in the establishment. It grossly underestimated the nationalist appeal of antisemitism in fin-de-siècle Europe.

One of the few exceptions to this scornful hubris was Karl Kautsky, the leading theoretician of Marxist orthodoxy in the SPD.[64] Editor of the influential socialist journal, *Die Neue Zeit,* executor of Marx's literary estate, and co-drafter of the SPD's 1891 Erfurt Party Program, Kautsky was an authority who could not be ignored. He wrote extensively on antisemitism and exhibited considerable sympathy for the Jewish plight. Perhaps because of this and the fact that his paternal grandfather had owned a house in the Jewish quarter of Prague, many commentators wrongly assumed (until the present day) that Kautsky was Jewish. Curiously enough, during his childhood in Vienna in the 1860s, he had indeed been victimized precisely because of this suspicion.[65] At the Viennese Academic Gymnasium, some of his closest friends were in fact Jews. In 1880 an article on the "Jewish Question" submitted by Kautsky to the *Jahrbuch für Sozialwissenschaft und Sozialpolitik* (edited by a leading patron of the SPD), was even rejected for displaying "too good an opinion of the Jews." The editor, Karl Höchberg, a wealthy socialist Jew racked by self-loathing, reproached Kautsky for his *overly positive view* of the "Jewish character."[66]

Kautsky joined the Austrian socialist ranks in 1875 but moved to Imperial Germany a few years later, coming under the spell of Engels and his close friend Eduard Bernstein. This influence is also felt in his writings on the "Jewish question" which avoided any mention of Marx's *Zur Judenfrage,* though he certainly had read the text.[67] Towards the end of 1883 Kautsky sharply condemned the reactionary character of antisemitism, especially in Hungary, which he interpreted as the "death spasm" of a declining social order. In December 1884, writing from Vienna, he warned Engels that Austrian antisemitism (more "oppositional and democratic") had become an enemy of "colossal dimensions" to the workers movement.[68] In 1885 Kautsky returned to the subject, arguing that antisemitism was especially prevalent in declining social classes and areas where Jews were still nationally separated from the rest of the population.[69] The movement was thoroughly "reactionary" even when it claimed to oppose big capital and aped socialist rhetoric. Antisemitism, Kautsky insisted, was not "misunderstood socialism, but misunderstood feudalism." This article suggested a more unequivocal opposition to antisemitism than was generally adopted by the SPD in the 1890s. It was more in line with the views of Engels and Bernstein, both of them then in English exile.[70]

In 1890, Kautsky developed his ideas a stage further, noting that antisemitic ideology proclaimed itself to be based on "natural" laws and the assumption of an "eternal" antagonism between races.[71] Kautsky, unlike Bebel, sharply rejected the idea of inherited racial characteristics. However, he did recognize that antisemitism was a deeply-rooted problem that had existed since Antiquity. It had been caused and also exacerbated by the fact that the Jew had been overwhelmingly an urban man (*Stadtmensch*) for nearly 2,000 years. According to Kautsky, "the unbridgeable racial opposition between the 'Aryan' and the 'Semite' is, in truth, only the opposition between the peasant and the city dweller driven to the extreme by special circumstances."[72] However, class stratification within the Jewish people was already significantly diminishing the number of distinct Jewish characteristics. Nonetheless, Kautsky did not expect antisemitism to swiftly dissolve in modern society, as long as the petty-bourgeois and peasant strata maintained their economic existence. In this respect, he shared the analysis of Engels and Bebel but (probably because of his Austrian background) he remained far more conscious of the power of *national* and *religious* differences. Indeed, in a letter of 1895 to Emma Adler (wife of the Austrian Social Democratic leader, Victor Adler), Kautsky was openly critical of the SPD's complacency and dismissive attitude to the antisemites as if they were a *quantité négligeable*. With one eye on the seemingly irresistible rise of Austrian antisemitism he wrote: "As an element of decomposition, and nullification of the stability of what exists, antisemitism in my opinion has great significance."[73]

The importance Karl Kautsky attached to opposing the Jew-baiters may explain why he was the most supportive of all the German Marxists in defending the intervention in 1898 of Jean Jaurès (leader of the French socialists) on behalf of Captain Alfred Dreyfus. Dreyfus was a French artillery officer of Jewish origin, falsely accused and sentenced to life imprisonment for selling military secrets to the Germans. Kautsky rejected the widespread view among many Marxists in France and Germany that the working class should *not* take sides in such an "internecine conflict between bourgeois cliques," even if it was a matter of defending fundamental human rights. Unlike Wilhelm Liebknecht, he was convinced that the Dreyfus Affair was an issue of great political import, in which opposition to the antisemites was a matter of Socialist principle rather than a "deviation" from the class struggle.[74] Indeed, Kautsky publicly praised the activist stance of Jaurès both in the German socialist press and in a note published in *La Petite République* in July 1899. He declared his "deep admiration" for Jaurès's "noble work" in defending Dreyfus in the name of French socialism. It would have been destructive for a "party of social regeneration" to "remain indifferent" and irresolute in a question that so fundamentally related to militarism and the rule of law. "I can think of no more disastrous position for a fighting class," Kautsky added, "than to persist in a position of neutrality in a crisis which stirs the whole nation."[75]

Kautsky also took a resolute stand against the violent antisemitism that exploded in periodic waves of pogroms throughout the Russian Empire. He understood that the social causes of antisemitism in Tsarist Russia were very different from those in Western Europe. The problem in Russia and Eastern Europe was not at all one of declining social strata, economic competition within the *Mittelstand,* or rivalries among the intelligentsia. Antisemitism in autocratic Holy Russia was not primarily a popular backlash against Jewish wealth. Furthermore, the issue of Jewish assimilation and racism was wholly marginal to understanding the pogroms that had occurred in the Russian Empire. In comparison with their German co-religionists, Russian Jews were complete outsiders and "aliens." Kautsky tended to agree with SPD leader Bebel, that Imperial Germany—still a *Rechtstaat* (a State based on law)—would never become the scene of barbarous pogroms on the Russian model. But he recognized more clearly than his party comrades, the urgent need to refute the racist doctrines so popular in the Second German Reich at the turn of the 20th century.[76] For most Marxists, race was presumed to be irrelevant, class war everything. Kautsky, however, was already aware by 1914 that millions of Germans had been contaminated by racial ideology. Hence the need to demonstrate that there were no fixed racial traits.[77] Karl Kautsky nonetheless erred in assuming that racist Jew-baiting was simply a means to distract ordinary citizens from the "real" issues of economic inequalities and social injustice. Like other Marxists of his era, he also failed to grasp the potential power of European antisemitism and racism or the extent to which it was already embedded in German society. The "socialism of fools" did *not* become the herald of Social Democracy. Four decades later with the victory of Hitler, antisemitism proved to be the harbinger of destruction for the Jews as well as a huge political disaster for the Left.

NOTES

1. Robert S. Wistrich, "German Social Democrats and the Berlin Movement," *Internationale Wissenschaftliche Korrespondenz zur Geschichte der Deutschen Arbeiterbewegung* 4 (1976): 433–43; and Enzo Traverso, *Marxisten und die jüdische Frage* (Mainz, 1995).

2. *Protokoll über die Verhandlungen des Parteitages der Sozialdemokratischen Partei Deutschlands, Halle 1890* (Berlin, 1890) (hereafter, *Protokoll*), 270–71: "in view of the gains made in ever wider circles by the antisemitic movement and the objectionable methods used by the antisemites, especially in their struggle against social democracy. . . ."

3. Ibid., 48.

4. *August Bebel's Briefwechsel mit Friedrich Engels,* edited by W. Blumenberg (The Hague, 1965). (hereafter, *August Bebel's Briefwechsel*), 549: Bebel to Engels, 24 June 1892.

5. Ibid.

6. Hermann Bahr, *Der Antisemitismus. Ein Internationales Interview* (Berlin, 1894), 25.

7. *Protokoll,* Erfurt 14–20 October 1891 (Berlin, 1891), 172.

8. August Bebel, "Sozialdemokratie und Antisemitismus," *Protokoll,* Cologne, 22–29 October 1893 (Berlin, 1893), 224. Bebel's speech at the 1893 Congress was republished in 1906 by the official SPD publishing press in Berlin.

9. *August Bebel's Briefwechsel,* 697, Bebel to Engels, 25 June 1893.

10. Ibid.

11. Ibid.

12. Ibid.

13. *Protokoll,* Cologne 1893, 104. This remark was made by the delegate representing Berlin's fourth district, Heymann.

14. Bebel had a certain propensity for believing in "racial" characteristics which was common at the time. See his remarks to Hermann Bahr, in Bahr, *Der Antisemitismus,* 23: "The Germans easily recognize the Jew and therefore regard him as an alien, as the race question still plays a great role, especially for the uneducated."

15. *Protokoll,* Cologne, 1893, 227.

16. Ibid.

17. Ibid., 230.

18. Ibid.

19. Ibid., 231.

20. Ibid., 230.

21. Ibid.

22. Ibid., 230: "With the fall of bourgeois society the peculiar nature of the Jew will disappear."

23. Ibid., 234. This intervention by Bruno Schoenlank—a convert to Christianity—probably reflected his surprise at such a philosemitic comment. Schoenlank, it should be said, was no friend of the Jews.

24. Ibid., 231.

25. Ibid.

26. Cf. *August Bebel's Briefwechsel,* 562, Bebel to Engels, 9 July 1892: "I see that the latest issue of the *Socialiste* has published an article by you on antisemitism just when I needed it."

27. *Protokoll,* 224.

28. Ibid., 237.

29. Wilhelm Liebknecht, *Stenographische Berichte über die Verhandlungen des Reichstags,* 30 Nov. 1893, 180ff.

30. Ibid.

31. Ibid.

32. Ibid.

33. Ibid.

34. "Zu viel des Eifers," *Vorwärts,* 24 Mar. 1893, 1.

35. "Decadence," *Vorwärts,* 9 Dec. 1893.

36. *Vorwärts,* 5 June 1891.

37. Ibid.

38. Ibid.

39. Ibid., 2.

40. Ibid.

41. "Cherchez le Juif," *Vorwärts,* 8 Dec. 1892, 1.

42. Ibid.

43. Ibid.

44 Ibid.

45. "Zu viel des Eifers," *Vorwärts,* 24 Mar. 1893, 1.

46. Ibid.

47. "Die Böckelei und Ahlwardtserei," *Vorwärts,* 21 June 1893, 1. For Mommsen's anti-antisemitic views, see Bahr, *Der Antisemitismus,* 28ff: "Canaille remains canaille, and antisemitism is the conviction of the mob. It is a horrible epidemic, like

cholera—one can neither explain nor cure it. One must patiently wait, until the poison has consumed itself and lost its force."

48. Ibid. On Böckel, see John Weiss, *Ideology of Death. Why the Holocaust Happened in Germany* (Chicago, 1996), 99–103, 114–19.

49. *Vorwärts,* 21 June 1893, 1.

50. Ibid. Also *Vorwärts,* 12 Sept. 1893, 3; and "Die bösen Antisemiten," 1 Oct. 1893, 3.

51. *Vorwärts* 26 June 1893.

52. "Die Wahlen," *Vorwärts,* 28 June 1893, 1.

53. "Die Sozialdemokratie und die letzte Wahl" (III), *Vorwärts,* 21 July 1893.

54. Ibid.

55. Ibid.

56. Ibid. This formulation, like a number of others in the editorials of *Vorwärts,* suggests Liebknecht as the likeliest author.

57. Ibid.

58. "Die Hessische Bauernbewegung," *Vorwärts,* 29 Aug. 1893, 1.

59. Ibid.

60. Ibid.

61. "Regierung und Plutokratie," *Vorwärts,* 12 July 1892, The Tivoli antisemitic program of the Conservative Party was overconfidently described in the German sociaist press as a last desperate attempt by the Prussian Junker class to salvage a lost cause.

62. "Das Mene Tekel des Deutschfreisinns," *Vorwärts,* 26 June 1892; and *Vorwärts,* 31 Mar. 1893 and 6 Apr. 1893.

63. "Die Wahl," *Vorwärts,* 17 June 1893.

64. See Robert S. Wistrich, *Socialism and the Jews. The Dilemmas of Assimilation in Germany and Austria-Hungary* (London, 1982) for an extensive discussion.

65. K. Kautsky, *Erinnerungen und Erörterungen,* edited by Benedikt Kautsky (The Hague, 1960), 105.

66. Ibid., 421–22. On Karl Höchberg, see Robert S. Wistrich, *Socialism and the Jewish Question in Germany and Austria (1880–1914)* (Ph.D. diss., University College, London, 1974).

67. Robert Wistrich, "Karl Marx, German Socialists and the Jewish Question, 1880–1914," *Soviet Jewish Affairs* 3, no. 1 (1973): 92–93.

68. Kautsky to Engels, 22 Dec. 1884 in *Friedrich Engels' Briefwechsel mit Karl Kautsky* (Vienna, 1954), edited by Benedikt Kautsky.

69. C[arolus] Kautsky, "Der Antisemitismus," *Oesterreichischer Arbeiter-Kalender für das Jahr 1885,* 100–4.

70. See Jack Jacobs, *On Socialists and "the Jewish Question" after Marx* (New York, 1992), 12–13. Jacobs overstates the case when he argues that Kautsky's 1885 article was "the first open attack on the antisemitic political movements that could be definitely attributed to a major Marxist theoretician."

71. K. Kautsky, "Das Judenthum," *Die Neue Zeit* (hereafter, *NZ*) 8 (1890): 23–27. The article was written under the pseudonym "S."

72. Ibid., 27.

73. Kautsky to Emma Adler, 22 Apr. 1895, in *Victor Adler. Briefwechsel mit August Bebel und Karl Kautsky,* edited by Friedrich Adler (Vienna, 1954), 175. The letter was written at a time when the Austrian antisemites under Dr. Karl Lueger had already emerged as the strongest political party in Vienna. See Robert S. Wistrich, *The Jews of Vienna in the Age of Franz Joseph* (Oxford, 1989), 205–37.

74. Harvey Goldberg, "Jean Jaurès and the Jewish Question: The Evolution of a Position," *Jewish Social Studies* 20, no. 2 (Apr. 1958): 68; Robert S. Wistrich, *Socialism and the Jewish Question,* 387–88 for the nuanced position taken by Rosa Luxemburg. Kautsky published her analyses of "Die sozialistische Krise in Frankreich" in *Die Neue Zeit* 1 (1900–1901): 495–99, 516–25, 548–58, 619–31, 676–88.

75. "Un Mot de Kautsky," *La Petite République,* 850 (24 July 1899): 1; also Kautsky's article, "Jaurès Taktik und die deutsche Sozialdemokratie," *Vorwärts,* 172 (26 July 1899): 3.

76. Karl Kautsky, *Rasse und Judentum* (Stuttgart, 1914). See my discussion of this work in my dissertation *Socialism and the Jewish Question,* 321–28.

77. See Robert S. Wistrich, "The SPD and Antisemitism in the 1890s," *European Studies Review* 7 (1977): 177–97. For the issue of anti-Jewish racism in German society on the eve of the First World War, see Klaus Fischer, *The History of an Obsession. German Judeophobia and the Holocaust* (London, 1998), 81–118; and Reiner Zilkenat, "Historisches zum Antisemitismus in Deutschland,"in *Neues vom Antisemitismus: Zustände in Deutschland,* edited by Horst Helas et al (Berlin, 2008), 13–44.

CHAPTER 4

The "Jewish Question" from Engels to Bernstein

In May 1890 extracts from a private letter written by Friedrich Engels to an Austrian correspondent, Isidor Ehrenfreund, were published with his consent in the Viennese *Arbeiterzeitung*. The observations made by Engels in this letter contain one of the more unequivocal repudiations of antisemitism to be found in modern socialist journalism.[1] The German and Austrian labor leadership enjoyed close relations with Marx's comrade-in-arms, and were undoubtedly influenced by the arguments he put forward. In contrast to Marx's own formulations of 1844, the approach of the mature Engels seemed more congenial to a generation of socialists brought up on "scientific" Darwinism rather than Hegelian dialectics. Moreover, Engels was dealing with the *Judenfrage* as it existed in 1890, not with the debate on Jewish emancipation which had originally provoked Marx's essay. Engels had come a long way since his own deprecating remarks about Jews before the rise of an organized antisemitic movement in Berlin. Indeed, along with Karl Kautsky, he was the first Marxist theorist to stamp the new Jew-hatred so decisively as the ideology of declining social classes seeking to turn back the wheel of history:

> In Prussia, it is the small nobility, the *Junkers* with an income of 10,000 marks, who spend 20,000 and therefore fall into the hands of the usurers, who foment antisemitism; and in both Prussia and Austria it is the petty-bourgeois sinking into ruin through the competition of large-scale capitalism, the craftsman and small shopkeeper who join the chorus and scream in unison with them. But in so far as *capital* destroys *these* classes of society, which are reactionary through and through, then it is fulfilling its mission and does a good job whether it is Semitic or Aryan, circumcised or baptized; it helps the backward Prussians and Austrians advance until at last they reach the modern standpoint, where all the old social differences are resolved into the one great contradiction between capital and wage-labor. Only where this is

> not yet the case, where there is as yet no strong capitalist class and therefore also no strong wage-earning class, where capital, being still too weak to control the whole national production, has the Stock Exchange as the main scene of its activity, and where production is still in the hands of peasants, land-owners, handicraftsmen and similar classes surviving from the Middle Ages—only here is capital predominantly Jewish and only here is antisemitism to be found.
>
> In the whole of North America, with its millionaires whose riches can hardly be expressed in our miserable marks, guilders or francs, there is *not a single* Jew among these millionaires, and the Rothschilds are real beggars compared with these Americans. Even here in England, Rothschild is a man of modest means compared, for instance, with the Duke of Westminster. Even with us on the Rhine where, with the help of the French, we chased the nobility out of the country ninety-five years ago and created a modern industry for ourselves, where are the Jews?
>
> Antisemitism, therefore, is nothing but the reaction of the medieval, decadent strata of society against modern society, which essentially consists of wage-earners and capitalists; under a mask of apparent socialism it therefore only serves reactionary ends; it is a variety of feudal socialism and with that we can have nothing to do. If it is possible in a country, that is a sign that there is not yet enough capital in that country. Capital and wage-labor are today inseparable. The stronger the capital the stronger also the wage-earning class and the nearer therefore the end of capitalist domination. To us Germans, therefore, among whom I include the Viennese, I wish a rapid development of capitalist economy and in no wise that it should sink into stagnation.[2]

This text has been quoted at such length because it so neatly crystallizes the *theoretical* premises underlying the fin-de-siècle Marxist class analysis of antisemitism. The basic assumption developed by Engels (and followed by Bebel and Kautsky) presented antisemitism as an economically determined and transitional phenomenon afflicting those classes threatened with extinction by modern capitalism. It took root, according to Engels, primarily in those countries where "reactionary social strata" inherited from the Middle Ages had not yet been wiped out. It was most frequently present wherever capitalist society had not yet polarized into the two great classes of bourgeoisie and proletariat; or where Jewish capital played a conspicuous role in capitalist modernization. According to this theory the rapid development of modern capitalism in Central and Eastern Europe would eventually eliminate its social basis. As a brief sociological portrait of anti-Jewish sentiment in late-19th-century Central Europe, this dialectical view had some merit and corresponded to some observable socio-economic trends. Nevertheless it proved to be deeply flawed as a prognosis for the future. Within only a few years of Engels's analysis, the general validity of the theory was being undermined by the paroxysm of antisemitic hysteria in France which grew out of the Dreyfus Affair. This reached heights that were not equaled elsewhere in Europe at that historic moment. Yet in 1890 Engels had dismissed the French antisemite, Edouard Drumont, as a "one-day sensation" and mistakenly predicted that "he will have to declare that he is as much against Christian as Jewish capital." At the time, the French Republic was the most politically modern and civilized nation on the Old Continent, the cradle of human rights and the fountainhead of European Jewish emancipation. One could hardly depict the emergence of mass antisemitism during the Dreyfus Affair as the by-product of a "backward culture."[3]

Nor did Engels and his disciples foresee that the "Jewish question" would become such a potent factor in Germany, despite its rapid industrial modernization and the rise of a highly organized monopolistic capitalism around 1900. After 1918, antisemitism in Central Europe became even more intense despite the progress of modern technology and the sharpening of the class struggle. Even a revolutionary Bolshevik like Leon Trotsky had to concede by 1937 that antisemitism would not disappear in "quasi-automatic fashion" as European Marxists had once believed. On the contrary—to quote Trotsky himself—decaying monopoly capitalism "everywhere swung over to an exacerbated nationalism" and "the Jewish question has loomed largest in the most highly developed capitalist country of Europe, in Germany."[4] The rise of Hitler had exposed the hollowness of a purely "materialist" interpretation of the "Jewish Question." Conventional Marxist analyses could make no sense of Nazi racism or explain the far greater impact of antisemitism in the Third Reich as compared to the much less economically developed Fascist Italy. Nor did economic determinism offer any explanation for the persistence of antisemitism in the countries of Soviet Russia and post-1945 Eastern Europe which claimed to have abolished both feudalism and the capitalist mode of production.

Engels simplistically assumed that antisemitism was, above all, an economic phenomenon linked to objective processes in the development of capitalism. Such an interpretation ignored the long history of anti-Jewish prejudice in pre-capitalist societies, including its religious, cultural, and socio-psychological roots. Moreover, it looked at the Jews solely as members of a class, not as a religious community, let alone as an ethnic group or a nation. Even at the level of class analysis, the assumptions as well as the prognoses were seriously mistaken. The *Mittelstand* (lower middle class) which Marxist analysis had condemned to extinction would demonstrate an altogether unexpected vitality. The polarization of capitalist society into the two great antagonistic camps of bourgeoisie and proletariat (a cornerstone of Marxian theory) simply did not take place. Moreover, it was never convincingly explained why those "obsolete" groups attracted to antisemitism would "inevitably" turn to socialism as the solution for their problems. Engels, like other German, Austrian, and French socialists, was far too optimistic on this score. His theory implied that antisemitism and the social classes which supported it, were on the way out and could exercise no future role in German or European politics. Marxists, it would appear, had imbibed the liberal faith in progress to a point where they were incapable of perceiving the irrational power which doctrines of cultural despair, racism, and religious intolerance could still exercise over the masses.

In the early 1890s, it should be recalled, Engels, Bebel, Liebknecht, and most leading German Marxists were convinced that private ownership of property was doomed by modern economic development. Hence, no concessions to the urban petty-bourgeoisie or the peasantry were considered necessary. Modern capitalism, so they believed, would collapse through the sheer weight of its own contradictions. Engels, in particular, was adamant that the labor movements in France and Germany should make no promises to salvage small peasant property or protect the interests of the lower middle class. Perceiving the connection between the agrarian question and the anti-semitic movement, Engels wrote:

> If these peasants want a guarantee for the continuance of their businesses, we absolutely cannot offer it to them. Their place is with the antisemites, the Farmers' Unions and similar parties who take pleasure in promising everything and keeping to nothing.[5]

The noisy demagoguery of the antisemities was utilized by Engels as a warning against the danger of compromising on "reformist" lines with the peasantry—"these people belong to the antisemites, let them go there." A Marxist proletarian party had no interest in competing with the *Mittelstand* parties for the favor of social groups that would inevitably be wiped out by the process of capitalist concentration in agriculture. Precisely the same reasoning applied to the master artisans. Already in the *Communist Manifesto* of 1848, Marx and Engels had written:

> The lower middle class, the small manufacturer, the shopkeeper, the artisan, the peasant, all these fight against the bourgeoisie, to save from extinction their existence as fractions of the middle class. They are therefore not revolutionary, but conservative. Indeed, they are reactionary, for they try to roll back the wheel of history.[6]

Nearly half a century later, Engels must have seen the adoption of antisemitism by precisely these social classes as a striking confirmation of the *Manifesto*. The dogma concerning the intrinsically "reactionary character" of the lower middle classes also served another function—to discredit the moderate reformist wing of German Social Democracy (SPD) under Georg von Vollmar and the Bavarian socialists. Much to the horror of Engels, they advocated a new agrarian policy aimed at winning over sections of the peasantry, a strategy that seemed to admirably fit Bavarian social conditions.

Engels had little time for this Bavarian particularism which he regarded in the same unfavorable light as any tactical concessions to the antisemites. It was a threat to the core principles of a self-styled revolutionary proletarian movement.[7] In his well-known article on the peasant question in France and Germany published in the *Neue Zeit* (1894–5), Engels underlined his earlier warnings.

> Hence we can render no worse service not only to the party, but also the small peasants themselves, than even to awaken the illusion through promises that we intended the lasting preservation of parceled-out property. That would entail directly blocking for the peasants the road to their liberation and would degrade the party to the level of street-corner antisemitism. On the contrary, it is the duty of our Party to make clear, again and again, to the peasants, the absolute hopelessness of their situation, as long as capitalism rules.[8]

Engels's view of the agrarian question and the way he linked it with the issue of antisemitism was largely accepted by Bebel, Liebknecht, and Kautsky.[9] They all shared his concern with maintaining the character of the SPD as an orthodox Marxist party and rejected any concessions to peasants, artisans, and small businessmen "within the framework of existing society." They were all convinced that the *Mittelstand* was doomed to undergo rapid proletarization and that this was a necessary feature of the transition from capitalism to socialism. The notion that antisemitism might herald the emergence of a third force in German politics, that it might be the prelude to a "fascist" mobilization of masses, was not a possibility that anyone could envisage at the end of the nineteenth century.

After Marx's death in 1883, Engels's closest collaborator during his London exile would be Eduard Bernstein, later to be known as the founder of "revisionist" Marxism. Bernstein sought to combine Kantian ethics and humanist ideals with Marx's materialism—a trend shared by a number of other Jewish intellectuals in the labor ranks like Karl Höchberg, Hugo Haase, Ludwig Frank, Kurt Eisner, and Max Adler. This tradition went hand in hand with the abhorrence of Prussian militarism, opposition to the cult of working class revolutionary violence, and dislike of exaggerated class hatred. Bernstein's emphasis on critical rationalism and political moderation provided a striking contrast to the prevailing Marxian orthodoxy of the SPD. Before Engels's death in 1895, these signs of dissidence were not yet transparent. However, Bernstein's distaste for utopian and ultra-radical slogans was in evidence well before the emergence of his Marxian "revisionism" which advocated social reform rather than violent revolution. From his years of exile in London and his contact with the British Fabians, Bernstein had come to believe in the value of piecemeal improvements and parliamentary legislation. He also recognized the resilience of capitalism and the vital importance of trade unions.

Bernstein's social-democratic project with its commitment to a legal, *evolutionary* path towards socialism and the principle of a democratic polity established by *constitutional* means was seen as "heresy" by many orthodox German Marxists still wedded to a fundamentalist view of class struggle. He had never been attracted by catastrophist visions of Marxism and the credo of ultimate redemption in a classless society. Not surprisingly, there is no place for him in Isaac Deutscher's pantheon of universalist "non-Jewish Jews," such as Marx, Rosa Luxemburg, or Trotsky, with their "dialectically dramatic vision of the world and its class-struggles."[10] Yet in his own quiet, modest, unassuming way Bernstein, by the late 1890s, was laying a time-bomb under the hallowed truths of Marxist orthodoxy. From a Jewish perspective, too, he stands out as a maverick among the leading German Jewish socialists of his generation, in his refusal to expunge, deny, or repudiate his Jewishness. Unlike Marx, Lassalle and many of their Jewish (and non-Jewish) disciples he rejected any simplistic identification of Jews with capitalism. One cannot find in his writings any residue of the *Schacher* (huckster) stereotype popularized by the young Karl Marx in his *Zur Judenfrage,* or of that hostility to the "obscurantist backwardness" of the ghetto so visible in Karl Kautsky's *Rasse und Judentum*. In contrast to most of his fellow Marxists, Eduard Bernstein never called on his co-religionists to abandon their Jewish affiliations in order to become "humanly emancipated" or to benefit from progress and enlightenment. Nevertheless, he firmly opposed any manifestations of Jewish separatism or isolationism.

Part of the explanation for Bernstein's moderation may lie in his family background with its relatively smooth assimilation to the German Protestant environment. A locomotive driver by occupation, Bernstein's father had been a loyal, patriotic, assimilated German. His liberal attitude to Christianity was characteristic of the family, which celebrated Christmas according to German traditions.[11] They nonetheless remained faithful to their Jewish origins and were members of the reform community in Berlin. Bernstein recalled that his parents, his elder sisters, and later himself, preferred the "dogma and ritual-free Judaism of the Reform community to the two great Christian denominations. . . ." Reform Judaism, free from "confessional narrow-mindedness," was in Germany, at least, a movement of adaptation and response to emancipation. It embraced a critical, scientific approach to the sources of Judaism and the belief that organic change was the core characteristic of Jewish history. Reform Judaism also held that the Jews were no longer a nation and their messianic hope should henceforth be expressed in universal terms. In other words, liberal Judaism was an important modality of assimilation to the German environment. As Eduard Bernstein observed in his memoirs, the Reform Judaism of his parents abhorred any form of separatism. German Jewish reformers sharply repudiated any notion of a nationally-distinct Jewish identity.[12]

Perhaps the most significant example of enlightened liberalism in his family was the career of his celebrated uncle, Aron Bernstein. A number of traits link uncle and nephew—journalistic talent, critical judgment, a passion for science, an instinct for moderation,and a marked sensitivity to antisemitism. The son of a rabbi, Aron Bernstein had been educated at a rabbinical seminary and subsequently became one of the founders of the Jewish reform movement in Germany as well as a close friend of the great Jewish scholar, Leopold Zunz, pioneer of the *Wissenschaft des Judentums*. Aron Bernstein was well-known in the Jewish world as the author of popular stories about Jewish life in the *shtetl* such as "Vögele der Maggid," which created a new literary genre. But he was also a militant liberal reformer of the 1848 generation in German politics (he wrote an important history of the 1848 revolution) and a leading advocate of the radical ideas of Schulze-

Delitzsch. In view of this family background, it is hardly surprising that Eduard Bernstein's socialism should contain a strong residue of liberalism. But family background was by no means a factor that inevitably led to political identification with the labor movement in Germany. Nor did "liberal" attitudes preclude a tinge of antismitic feeling in the politics of the young Bernstein. He strongly disliked certain sections of the Jewish community, which in his words had "pushed itself forward in Germany in a way which even repelled many Jews such as myself."[13] Around 1873, during the feverish stock market speculation that followed the Franco-Prussian War, Bernstein even became a disciple of Eugen Dühring—later one of the most zealous racial antisemites in Germany. Though Dühring had made several ugly polemical attacks on the "Jewish Social Democrats," Marx and Lassalle, this evidently did not yet disturb Bernstein enough to turn against his mentor.

In 1881, Bernstein became editor of *Der Sozialdemokrat,* the newspaper produced in Zürich which was to play such an important role in the German labor movement under the anti-socialist laws. The paper was by no means free of anti-Jewish nuances during the Russian pogroms of 1881.[14] But it did faithfully reflect militant working class resistance inside the newly unified German Reich to the antisemitism of Adolf Stöcker's Berlin movement. Bernstein, in a letter to Friedrich Engels in September 1882, attributed this strong resistance to the class consciousness of the Berlin workers. He also observed that there would have been stronger attraction to Christian socialism were it not for German working class loathing for organized religion.[15] Moreover, opposition to Stöcker expressed proletarian defiance of the hated Bismarckian repression.[16] *Der Sozialdemokrat* favorably contrasted the willingness of the Berlin workers to risk expulsion and unemployment in protesting against the Jew-baiting with the indifference of German liberals and middle class Jews to the anti-socialist persecution. Liberals and Jews had not found a word of condemnation when Bismarck's persecution of the labor movement began in 1878. Workers, on the other hand, had been ready to "uphold the rights of man for those who helped and still help to outlaw and persecute us."[17]

Bernstein's critical attitude to the official Jewish community did not, however, paralyze his awareness of the dangerous potential manifested by the German antisemitic movement. In a letter to Engels he wrote in July 1881:

> In Berlin alone, apart from the conservative and Catholic press, there are no less than seven of these newspapers and their numbers increase every day in the provinces. . . . The entire civil service, including the judiciary and the teaching profession, the

> petty bourgeoisie and the peasantry sympathize with antisemitism, the former in bad faith, the latter *bona fide*.[18]

In another letter to Engels, Bernstein continued to emphasize the broad social base of the antisemitic movement, noting that

> the Jew-baiting falls on a very receptive terrain as far as the peasantry, the artisans, officials and teachers etc. are concerned. I think, therefore, it would be a great mistake if we were to treat the antisemitic movement simply as a political-religious movement. In Dresden, at any rate, this has scarcely proved to be tenable. Furthermore, there is no reason to do that, since precisely in social terms we can point with satisfaction to socialism as the only solution to the conflicts of contemporary society.[19]

Bernstein's assessment of the antisemitic movement was in many respects accurate. Unlike Engels, he did not write it off as a transient historic phenomenon. Moreover, as a Jew, he was becoming increasingly sensitive to manifestations of anti-Jewish prejudice *within* the German labor movement, though this was never licensed as official party policy. For example, Bernstein was acutely aware of the fact that many prominent Jews in the German labor movement beginning with Marx and Lassalle (and including such personal friends as Karl Höchberg, Paul Singer, and Max Kayser), had internalized anti-Jewish prejudices, or else felt obliged to take account of them. Commenting on Paul Singer's reluctance to support an alliance with the liberal "progressives" against Adolf Stöcker, he noted in another letter to Engels:

> There is [in this position] a conflict with his feelings, since I have observed that it is antisemitism, especially among our "educated people" (*Gebildeten*) which very much disturbs him. Out of exaggerated conscientiousness, he believes that he must play the antisemite and State socialist.[20]

Singer, it should be noted, was the highly influential head of the SPD parliamentary fraction and a very successful businessman who had given his personal fortune for the workers' cause. Similarly, in a sarcastic comment to Engels in September 1884, regarding the initiative of a Jewish socialist in supporting antisemitic agitation for a stock exchange tax, Bernstein remarked that "at the same time he can perform an act of 'heroic circumcision' since like most Jews in the Party, he feels obliged to take account of antisemitism. That is, for example, the case with [Max] Kayser, [Karl] Höchberg, Singer and many others."[21]

A decade later a number of leading Jews in the SPD would propose that the party should remain neutral with regard to the antisemitic agitation, so as to avoid the charge of being a *Judenschutzgruppe* (a Jewish protective guard). Bernstein promptly reproached those who "are the most frequently on hand with declarations against 'philo-semitism'—namely comrades of Jewish descent, who, precisely because of their origins, consider it their special duty to keep the party free of any suspicion of favoring Jewish interests."[22]

Bernstein's ironic comments on internalized Jewish antisemitism in his own party were unusual. He also opposed the prevalent tendency in the labor movement to equate anti- and philosemitism as if they were parallel or equivalent phenomena. He was especially critical of the pervasive Marxist definition of "philosemitism" (popularized by Franz Mehring) which equated it with "sycophancy before capitalist, monied Jewry, support for Jewish chauvinism and glossing over Jewish injustices."[23] Bernstein shrewdly argued that such a standpoint would tend to identify socialists with the antisemitic cause. He was also doubtful about the official SPD line on *völkisch* antisemitism in the 1890s which argued that it would eventually lead the declining *Mittelstand* into the Socialist camp. Nevertheless, at least until 1894, Bernstein clearly upheld the Marxist thesis that antisemitism was ultimately a product of the false consciousness of the lower middle class. In that same year, he wrote in the *Neue Zeit*: "Among the masses of the people antisemitism will find followers only among those who have not yet been enlightened by social democracy and where—as in the case of small peasants, artisans and businessmen—a falsely perceived self-interest blurs the view."

At the same time, Bernstein emphasized that the emancipation of German Jewry removed "any excuse for isolation, for a special Jewish solidarity against non-Jews, for a tribal or racial morality in intercourse with non-Jews. . .and where anything of that kind exists, it must be fought against as energetically as possible."[24] He also recognized that modern racial antisemitism "directed itself precisely against Jews who were assimilating themselves." But his faith in Socialism still prevailed over any nagging doubts. If Jewish emancipation had occurred in an era "when the bourgeoisie still believed in itself, only a rising [socialist] society can complete it."[25] Bernstein did not, however, believe that one could defer the "solution" of the Jewish problem to the distant utopia of a classless society. He could see little value in the formula of Karl Kautsky, predicting the dialectical self-dissolution of Judaism. Moreover, the pogroms in Russia, Romania, and Algeria, the election of the Christian-Social Judeophobe Karl Lueger as

Mayor of Vienna in 1897, the virulent plebeian antisemitism in Germany, the Dreyfus Affair in France, and the anti-alien agitation in Great Britain could not be dismissed as transitory phenomena, except by those irreparably blinded by dogma or wishful thinking. In these circumstances, Bernstein, writing in 1898, reminded the English socialist, E. Belfort Bax, "that under present circumstances, it is a categorical imperative for me to be a 'philosemite' in the face of all antisemitism."[26]

This statement suggests the growing concern that Bernstein felt for the fate of the Jews as a group. An interesting pointer to this change of heart can be found in his obituary of Eleanor Marx-Aveling, also written in 1898 for the *Neue Zeit*. Bernstein had often accompanied the fiery daughter of Karl Marx on her visits to London's East End and her Jewish identification clearly made a deep impression on him. In his obituary notice he wrote:

> A striking characteristic of Eleanor Marx was her strong sympathy for the Jews. At any opportunity she would affirm her descent [*Abstammung*] with a certain defiance: how often I heard her assert with pride from the platform to the crowd below: "I am a Jewess"—though she was not religious and had no contact with the official representatives of Jewry. . . . All the more she felt attracted with even greater empathy to the Jewish proletarians of the East End.[27]

Eduard Bernstein was fully aware of the contrast between Eleanor Marx's "philosemitism" (she was sickened by the neutrality of the French socialists at the outset of the Dreyfus Affair) and the hostile attitude to Jews exhibited by her own father. He summed up Eleanor Marx's moral stance on the Jewish issue in terms which echoed his own developing position.

> She did not allow herself to be led astray by her deep-rooted proletarian class feeling whenever the Jew was oppressed as a Jew, but declared herself for the oppressed, irrespective of class-affiliation. This determined her attitude in the Dreyfus trial and towards [Emile] Zola.[28]

A concrete example of Bernstein's increasingly robust response to the persecution of his coreligionists, particularly in Eastern Europe, came in his maiden speech as a Reichstag deputy in 1903. He dwelt extensively on the plight of Jews in Romania, demanding that the German government intervene as a guarantor of Jewish civil rights and condemn the treatment of Jews by the Romanian authorities.[29] Bernstein's evident concern with the condition of East European Jewry also made him more sympathetic to the humanitarian goals of the Zionist movement, though before 1914 he generally opposed the ideology of Jewish nationalism. The shift was nonetheless visible as early as 1903 with the news of the Kishinev massacre followed by the Russian pogroms of 1905. Bernstein's close collaboration with the *Sozialistische Monatshefte* (the leading theoretical organ of the "revisionists" in Germany) was another factor. The editor of the revisionist flagship, Joseph Bloch, was a passionate Zionist who did a great deal to familiarize German socialists with the general crisis driving millions of poverty-stricken *Ostjuden* to a mass exodus from Russia and Eastern Europe.[30]

As early as August 1902, there were signs that the Zionist movement also believed Bernstein might be won over to their cause. Writing to his future wife, Vera, the young Russian Zionist leader, Chaim Weizmann, observed that Bernstein "is on the road to Zionism[31]:

> I had a long talk with Bernstein (the famous one) and his daughter in Berlin. I took him to task for taking up the Armenian cause. He declared: "Wenn ich jüdisches Gefühl hätte, ich ware Zionist. Vielleicht kommt es." [If I had any Jewish feeling, I should be a Zionist. Perhaps it will come to pass.][32]

There are further indications that other Zionist representatives in Germany believed that Bernstein might identify with their aims. One example was the effort by the German Zionist, Arthur Meyerowitz, to enlist his support to gain access to the papers and archives of Moses Hess. The resulting dispute over the Hess archive led Karl Kautsky to make a sardonic comment to Julius Motteler on the prospect of Bernstein's "conversion" to Zionism. "Nothing would be nicer than if Bernstein were to turn to Zionism, and if I could be of assistance, I should be happy to do so. The Zionists need a prophet, Bernstein needs believers in his prophecies and we do not need him. So all concerned would benefit. [Theodor] Herzl and Nordau should be informed about this new reinforcement."[33] Kautsky's irony was not quite as benign as it sounds. As the guardian of German Marxist orthodoxy, Kautsky sharply opposed all forms of Zionism as well as Bernstein's revisionist "heresy." Not for nothing did the Russian Bolsheviks (including Lenin) regard Kautsky as the Pope of Marxism until the First World War.

Bernstein's published writings before 1914 nonetheless indicate that concern for the fate of his oppressed coreligionists did not bring him to support Zionism and Jewish nationalism. In 1914, in a long article for Kautsky's *Neue Zeit,* he was particularly critical of the Jewish nationalists in Palestine. They had attacked the *Hilfsverein deutscher Juden* (a philanthropic organization of German Jewry) and its director, Dr. Paul Nathan, for sponsoring German cultural "imperialism" at the expense of Hebrew education in the Holy Land. Paul Nathan (a convinced assimilationist and supporter of the German Social Democrats) was also a personal friend of Bernstein, who publicly deplored the abuse heaped on him in Palestine. While recognizing that Zionism thrived on despair at the endemic antisemitism in German universities, in the bureaucracy, and army, Bernstein nevertheless concluded his article by describing it as "a kind of intoxication which acts like an epidemic. It [Zionism] may, and presumably will, also pass away like one. But not overnight. For, in the last resort, it is only part of the great wave of nationalistic reaction which has overflowed the bourgeois world and seeks to invade the socialist world as well."[34]

It was the cataclysm of the First World War which awakened Bernstein not so much to Zionism as to a Jewish "world mission which no other national community had to fulfill to such a lofty and extensive degree. . . ."[35] In his wartime pamphlet *Von den Aufgaben der Juden im Weltkriege* (1917) Bernstein described the Jews as "a connecting link between the peoples of the civilized world."[36] Their vocation as *Lehrer der Völker* (teachers of the nations) and as a mediators among the warring peoples must be to influence humanity toward a "cosmopolitan" view of international affairs.[37] Bernstein sharply condemned the "distortions of the national idea" and in particular the Jewish "assimilationist" form of super-nationalism—the total identification among some of his coreligionists with the aims of Pan-German imperialism. Bernstein's long-standing dislike of ostentatious flag-waving revived with full force, especially when he saw Jews attempting to outdo their fellow Germans in uncritical support for German militarist objectives.

Bernstein's attitude towards Zionism in *Von den Aufgaben* was more complex. On one level, the non-identification seems explicit enough. "I am no Zionist, I feel myself too German, to become one."[38] Equally unequivocal was his disapproval of any form of Jewish *Stammespatriotismus* (tribal patriotism) or manifestations of Zionist "chauvinism," which he considered as particularly regressive for Western Jewry. Yet this is only one facet of the problem. Against this there is the fact that Bernstein for the first time openly expressed admiration for the idealistic élan and creative vitality of the Zionist movement. He singled out for praise Zionist contributions to the enlightenment of the Jewish masses in the Russian Pale of Settlement. His modification of earlier assumptions is also apparent from an unpublished manuscript in the Bernstein archives located in Amsterdam. The draft was written in 1916–17, and entitled *Die demokratische Staatsidee und die Jüdisch-nationale Bewegung*. Bernstein concludes that the early socialists (including Marx and Engels) who opposed the preservation and renewal of small nationalities as "reactionary," were wrong. The progressive development of humanity did not depend on centralization or the accelerated absorption of smaller, more backward nations into larger units. Every people had an *inalienable* right to determine freely their own destiny. Ethnic minorities also had the right to national autonomy, along the lines first suggested by Karl Renner and the Austro-Marxist school. Bernstein clearly believed that this axiom ought to apply to the Jewish "nationality" in Eastern Europe and he did not exclude its extension to the Zionist settlements in Palestine. "If this [idea] finds general approval, then the Jewish national movement would appear as reconcilable with the most advanced form of the democratic idea and in line with its development."[39]

Further confirmation that Bernstein was more prepared to lend a sympathetic ear to Zionist entreaties is provided in a memoir by Salman Rubaschow (Shazar), subsequently President of the State of Israel. During the First World War, Shazar was the Poale-Zion representative in Berlin. In a manuscript preserved in the Amsterdam Archive, he emphasized that Bernstein's Jewish identity had an authentic quality, which made him more receptive than other European socialist leaders to the aims of Poale-Zion. Shazar wrote that while he did find political support among Gentile socialists, the sense "of belonging through the generations" and of "instinctive recognition" was more manifest in Bernstein.[40] This instinct was apparent in his unbending opposition to antisemitism during the Weimar years. It should be added that Bernstein's gradualist, evolutionary socialism also made a considerable impression on the Zionist socialist pioneers in Palestine. The father of Marxist "revisionism" was highly esteemed by top trade union leaders like Berl Katznelson, one of the outstanding labor organizers of Palestinian Jewish Zionism. There was an obvious affinity between the Zionist mode of constructivist socialism, with its emphasis on voluntarism, democracy, and mutual aid, and the ideas pioneered by Bernstein two decades earlier. A grateful telegram from the Palestinian Poale-Zion (dated 18 July 1928) addressed to Eduard Bernstein, described him without reserve as the "teacher of the international proletariat" and a "true friend of the Jewish worker in Palestine."[41]

Similarly, in the 1920s, Bernstein (along with many other leaders of the Socialist International) is on record as warmly praising the efforts of the Zionist pioneers in Palestine to establish a "free human community" rooted in their own soil. Many democratic European Socialists, including Bernstein, Léon Blum, and Emil Vandervelde, were struck by the boldness with which early Zionists practiced their experimental cooperative socialism. Berl Katznelson reports in his memoirs that Bernstein even considered the 1920 program of the Histadrut as a model of what a free workers' commonwealth should resemble.[42] On several occasions the veteran German socialist would defend the pioneering achievements of Jewish cooperative labor in Palestine against the anti-Zionist polemics of Karl Kautsky. But though Bernstein welcomed the admission of Poale-Zion to the Socialist International in 1919 and though he served (together with Vandervelde, Blum, and Arthur Henderson) on the International Committee for a Workers Palestine established in 1928, he was never committed to Zionist ideology per se. His change of attitude was determined more by humanitarian considerations and the resurgence of violent German antisemitism in the early years of the Weimar Republic. The organized xenophobic campaign against the *Ostjuden* in the 1920s convinced him that a Jewish National Home in Palestine was a pressing need of the hour. This did not, however, mean that he had abandoned the pacifist, ethical, and humanitarian core of his socialist beliefs.

In his concept of the "mediating vocation of Jews" Eduard Bernstein's relationship to Jewry probably found its most characteristic expression. The Jews, he had argued in 1916, were no longer "guests" or "strangers" among the nations but *Mitbürger* (co-citizens) in every sphere of cultural, economic, and public life. This process of *Einbürgerung* (naturalization) did not stand in contradiction to cosmopolitanism. "Cosmopolitan sentiment is not identical with anti-national or anti-patriotic conviction. It is compatible with recognition of individual nations as legitimate members of the great organism of civilized mankind, with their own needs and interests."[43] Bernstein was adamant that Jews must feel free to criticize and oppose the "excesses of the nationalist spirit," that they should not join the chorus of super-patriots because their integration might then be called into question. To this end, he even argued that it was the moral obligation of Jews to transcend their "tribal" interests and patriotic attachments to the warring belligerent nations.[44] In the hour of world crisis, the Jewish people needed to remember the Biblical injunction, that they had once been slaves in Egypt and recall their mission to secure peace among the nations: "at all times to emphasize what binds the peoples and in times of conflict to plead for the voices of reason through measured judgment. . .to act as mediators among the nations." This was the central task of world Jewry precisely because Jews were "guests" among the nations"—with a history and a status that should preserve them from all the transgressions and excesses of nationalism."[45] The categorical imperative of Jewish history was to "oppose everything which divides the nations and sows hatred among them."[46] Eduard Bernstein's attitude to the Jews thus came to express a particular form of "moral consciousness of duty," animated by feelings of "solidarity with the great family of nations." It was an intriguing synthesis of the Jewish cultural heritage with neo-Kantian German philosophy and the socialist vision of human brotherhood. At the end of his long life, a minimalist form of Zionism also found its place in his eclectic vision. Tragically, less than a year after his death, the last vestiges of German-Jewish humanism would be swept away by Hitler's hordes.

Notes

1. Isidor Ehrenfreund, a Viennese bank employee and Jewish sympathizer with the labor movement, wrote to Engels on 21 March 1890 asking for his opinion concerning antisemitism; see *Marx-Engels Werke* (*MEW*) (East Berlin, 1963), 22: 570. The text of Engels's reply was first published on 9 May 1890 in the *Arbeiterzeitung* (Vienna); four days later in the *Berliner Volksblatt* and in *Der Sozialdemokrat,* 7 June 1890; it is reproduced in Victor Adler, *Aufsätze, Reden und Briefe* (Vienna, 1929), 1: 6ff.

2. Ibid.

3. French antisemitism in the nineteenth century had a decidedly left-wing flavor. See Edmund Silberner, "French Socialism and the Jewish Question 1865–1914," *Historia Judaica,* 16 Apr. 1954; George Lichtheim, "Socialism and the Jews," *Dissent* (July–Aug. 1968): 314–42; and Robert S. Wistrich, "French Socialism and the Dreyfus Affair," *Wiener Library Bulletin* 18, New Series nos. 35–36 (1975): 9–20.

4. Leon Trotsky, *On the Jewish Question* (New York, 1970), 20. For an earlier analysis of Trotsky's views, see Robert S. Wistrich, *Revolutionary Jews from Marx to Trotsky* (London, 1976), 109–207.

5. Friedrich Engels, "Die Bauernfrage in Frankreich und Deutschland," *Neue Zeit* 1 (1894–1895): 303; also in *MEW,* 39: 502.

6. Karl Marx and Friedrich Engels, "Manifesto of the Communist Party," *Selected Works* (Moscow, 1962), 1: 44.

7. Georg von Vollmar's agrarian program was a forerunner of the revisionist critique of Marxist orthodoxy in the SPD. There is no evidence that he was antisemitic. However, in a letter to Wilhelm Liebknecht on 24 November 1894, Engels remarked, "The man may be an antisemite, a bourgeois democrat, a Bavarian particularist or whatever, but a Social Democrat?" *MEW,* 39: 330.

8. Friedrich Engels, "Die Bauernfrage," 303.

9. Karl Kautsky, "Der Breslauer Parteitag und die Agrarfrage," *Neue Zeit* 1 1895–1896): 113.

10 Isaac Deutscher, *The Non-Jewish Jew and Other Essays* (London, 1968); Robert S. Wistrich, *Revolutionary Jews from Marx to Trotsky* (London, 1976).

11. Eduard Bernstein, "Herkunft und Eltern," Bernstein-Nachlaß, International Institute of Social History, Amsterdam, A.57.

12. Eduard Bernstein, *Von 1850 bis 1872. Kindheit und Jugendjahre* (Berlin, 1926), 40–41.

13. Eduard Bernstein, *Entwicklungsgang eines Sozialisten* (Leipzig, 1930), 8.

14. Robert S. Wistrich, "German Social Democracy and the Berlin Movement," *Internationale Wissenschaftliche Korrespondenz* 4 (Dec. 1976): 433–42.

15. Bernstein to Engels, 1 Sept. 1882, *Eduard Bernsteins Briefwechsel mit Friedrich Engels* (*Bernstein-Engels*), edited by Helmut Hirsch (Assen, 1970), 123.

16. Eduard Bernstein, *Geschichte der Berliner Arbeiterbewegung* (Berlin, 1907–1910), 2: 164.

17. *Der Sozialdemokrat,* 6 Feb. 1881.

18. *Bernstein-Engels,* 23 July 1881, 28.

19. *Bernstein-Engels,* 9 Sept. 1881, 37.

20. *Bernstein-Engels,* 18 Aug. 1884, 293.

21. *Bernstein-Engels,* 24 Sept. 1884, 299.

22. E. Bernstein, "Das Schlagwort und der Antisemitismus," *Die Neue Zeit* 2 (1893–1894): 233–34.

23. Ibid., 233.

24. Ibid., 236–37.

25. E. Bernstein, "Der Antisemitismus im Lichte der modernen Wissenschaft" (review), *Die Neue Zeit* 2 (1893–1894): 407.

26 *Die Neue Zeit* 2 (1897–1898): 232.

27. E. Bernstein, "Eleanor Marx," *Die Neue Zeit* 2 (1897–1898): 122. See Edmund Silberner, "Eleanor Marx und die jüdische Identität," in *Jahrbuch des Instituts für Deutsche Geshichte* 6 (1977): 259–96.

28. Bernstein, "Eleanor Marx."

29. *Stenographische Berichte über die Verhandlungen des Reichstags. X. Legislaturperiode, II. Session 1900/03*, Mar. 10–Apr. 30, 10: 8756–59.

30. See Robert S. Wistrich, "German Social Democracy and the Problem of Jewish Nationalism 1897–1917," *Leo Baeck Institute Yearbook* (1976): 109–42; Charles Bloch, "Der Kampf Joseph Blochs und die 'Sozialistischen Monatshefte' in der Weimarer Republik," in *Jahrbuch des Instituts für Deutsche Geschichte* 3 (Tel Aviv, 1974): 257–87.

31. Chaim Weizmann, letter dated 29 Aug. 1902 (original in Russian), *Letters and Papers of Chaim Weizmann* (Oxford 1968), 389.

32 Ibid.

33 Kautsky to Motteler, 9 Nov. 1903, Motteler-Nachlaß, 2222/I, International Institute of Social History.

34. E. Bernstein, "Der Schulstreit in Palästina," *Die Neue Zeit* 1 (1913–14): 752.

35. E. Bernstein, "Vom Mittlerberuf der Juden," *Neue Jüdische Monatshefte,* no. 14 (1917): 398.

36. E. Bernstein, *Von den Aufgaben der Juden im Weltkriege* (Berlin, 1917), 24.

37. E. Bernstein, "Vom Mittlerberuf," 399.

38. Ibid., 32.

39. Bernstein-Nachlaß, A.144, French copy of the German original.

40. Salman Rubaschow, Bernstein-Nachlaß, A.23, p. 7.

41. Bernstein-Nachlaß, D.545.

42. Berl Katznelson, *K'tavim* (Tel Aviv, 1954), 11: 201.

43. E. Bernstein, "Vom Mittlerberuf," 399.

44. E. Bernstein, *Von den Aufgaben,* 24.

45. E. Bernstein, "Vom Mittlerberuf," 399.

46. Robert S. Wistrich, "Eduard Bernstein's Einstellung zur Judenfrage," in *Juden und deutsche Arbeiterbewegung bis 1933,* edited by Ludiger Heid and Arnold Paucker (Tübingen, 1992), 79–90.

CHAPTER 5

Anti-Capitalism or Antisemitism? The Enigma of Franz Mehring

The Marxist labor movement in Wilhelminian Germany viewed the "Jewish Question" as an inseparable aspect of the crisis of modern bourgeois society. It also recognized that Jewish emancipation had been brought about by capitalism but considered that the process could only be completed in a new, classless society. By the end of the 1870s it was already evident that liberalism was on the defensive in Germany and one of the symptoms of its fading hegemony was the deflection of social tensions against the Jewish minority.[1] Discontented groups in German society who opposed the liberal status quo now began to focus their offensive against the Jews who were depicted as a domineering and privileged clique. This led to the formation of a number of antisemitic political parties who achieved temporary electoral successes in the early 1890s, only to subside again in the first decade of the twentieth century.[2] At the same time, it has been widely claimed that the German Social Democratic Party (SPD)—which had many Jewish intellectuals in its top ranks—was more resistant than any other political party to the impact of antisemitism in Wilhelminian Germany.[3] The evidence for and against this assumption has been documented by me elsewhere and it is mixed.[4] However, a detailed examination such as I have carried out in this book, reveals that the German labor movement adopted a more equivocal attitude towards Jews than is widely believed.

A case-study of one of the leading publicists of the German labor movement, the revolutionary socialist and widely admired historian Franz Mehring, is particularly illuminating in this respect. No other German socialist wrote as extensively on the "Jewish Question" in this period. Hence an examination of Mehring's writings on this topic can tell us a great deal about the tactical and ideological dilemmas which confronted the labor movement with the emergence of *völkisch* antisemitism in the 1890s. More than any of his contemporaries in the German workers' movement, Mehring exhibited attitudes which illustrate the difficulty in clearly demarcating the Marxist from the antisemitic critique of liberal capitalism. In particular, he insisted on regarding so-called philosemitism as a more dangerous threat than antisemitism to the labor movement.

Franz Mehring was born in to a middle-class Pomeranian family in 1846. Nothing in his early journalistic career suggested that many years later he would, together with Rosa Luxemburg and Karl Liebknecht, become one of the co-founders of the German Communist Party. His road to Marxism followed a long and painful detour which necessitated a sharp break with his class, culture, and family background. He had gone through a militant anti-socialist phase—one in which he had written antisemitically-tinged articles for the *Saale-Zeitung* which even led to calls for a boycott of the paper by Jewish advertisers and subscribers—something of which he was actually proud rather than apologetic. Mehring combined a rebellious and artistic temperament with a chivalrous sympathy for the oppressed masses. More than any other German socialist he sought to transmit the heritage of German classical philosophy, poetry, and drama to the proletariat. In the words of Rosa Luxemburg, who hailed him on his seventieth birthday as "the representative of authentic intellectual culture in all its brilliance," Mehring had taught the German workers "through every line from your wonderful pen, that Socialism is not merely a knife-and-fork question, but a civilizing movement, a great and proud world-view."[5] Nevertheless, Mehring did not finally commit himself to the labor movement until 1890, when at the age of forty-four he became the Berlin correspondent of the Marxist review, *Die Neue Zeit*. By this time his views on the Jews in Germany had definitively crystallized. If, therefore, his writings after 1890 clearly reflect the ideological prism of historical materialism and the German socialist consensus, they also express pre-Marxist attitudes which had taken shape at least a decade earlier.

Franz Mehring first encountered the "Jewish Question" in Berlin at the end of the 1870s. As an independent young journalist in his early thirties he witnessed at first hand the rise of a new literary antisemitism. The embittered social climate which gave rise to this trend also produced some convergence between conservative and radical critiques of the dominant liberal-capitalist order. Conservative publicists like Rudolf Meyer and Hermann Wagener as well as *Kathedersozialisten* (Socialists of the Chair) such as Gustav Schmoller, Lujo Brentano, and Adolph Wagner sharply attacked the laissez-faire ethos of German liberalism.[6] Christian social agitators like Adolf Stöcker joined in this assault from the Right, while espousing the principles of a vaguely defined Prusso-Christian socialism. On the Left, socialists like Eugen Dühring and the neo-Lassalleans led by Wilhelm Hasselman were no less severe in their critique of "Manchesterism."[7] Not all the opponents of free-trade liberalism were antisemites. But the prominence of Jewish names among the entrepreneurs, stockbrokers, and money-changers implicated in the *Gründungsschwindel* (promoters' swindle) of the early 1870s, inevitably led to unfavorable comment. Petty-bourgeois pamphleteers of radical tendencies like Otto Glagau and Wilhelm Marr made Jewish participation in the swindles the starting-point of an antisemitic indictment of the new Bismarckian *Reich.*[8] They presented their campaign as an *Abwehrkampf* (defensive struggle) to defend the interests of the "little man" against the domination of a Jewish financial clique which had succeeded in gaining control of German society.

Mehring who had become personally embroiled in 1876 with the proprietor of the liberal *Frankfurter Zeitung,* Leopold Sonnemann, himself of Jewish origin, was undoubtedly influenced by this current of anti-capitalist antisemitism. It had even infiltrated into the German labor movement where the Lassalleans openly attacked the "Marxist" Eisenachers as *Judenknechte* (Jewish lackeys) for their alliance with Sonnemann and other liberal democrats.[9] Mehring shared the antipathy of the Lassalleans towards "Jewish liberalism" and specifically accused Sonnemann of having accepted bribes and of involvement in the feverish speculation of the early 1870s. His accusations were not supported by the Social Democratic leaders, Bebel and Liebknecht, which led to a rift between the young Mehring and the labor movement that took years to heal. Much of the subsequent suspicion and distrust of labor leaders towards Mehring relates back to this period. Equally it is in the Sonnemann Affair that one can find the origins of Mehring's intransigent hostility to what he scathingly called the "Frankfurt stock-exchange democracy."[10]

The anti-Jewish strand in Mehring's writings was not unconnected with his early Lassallean sympathies and with his hatred for what he called the cringing servility, philistinism and cowardice of the German bourgeoisie. Though he did not share the admiration of the Lassalleans for Bismarck's *Realpolitik* he echoed their contempt for the middle classes and for Jews. Indeed his favorable treatment of the Lassallean contribution to German Social Democracy remains a distinctive feature of Mehring's writing that was periodically subjected to criticism in orthodox communist historiography.[11] Nevertheless, this did not prevent Mehring from being widely cited in East German, Polish, and Russian Communist literature as an exemplary exponent of historical materialism.[12] Needless to say, this same literature did not discuss the problematic aspects of his position on the "Jewish Question."

Mehring's ambivalence was already apparent in 1881, a decade before he had become a leading pillar of philosophical and historical materialism. Writing in the *Weser-Zeitung,* Mehring blamed the anti-Jewish riots in his native Pomerania on the "philosemitic" *Hetze* (incitement) of the liberal press in Berlin.[13] By its mania for denunciation and its desire to stifle any criticism of Jews, it had allegedly provoked an antisemitic climate of opinion. The most insignificant street brawl or casual remark was being inflated into a threat against the established order. Mehring not only considered that the Berlin press was dominated by Jewish interests but that its intolerance and paranoia was a major factor in provoking the anti-Jewish backlash. In a pamphlet published in 1882 he claimed that the situation in the Eastern provinces of Germany had been blown up out of all proportion.

> As for the anti-Semitic riots, it so happens I was visiting my Pomerania home when they took place. I looked into the matter carefully and can only say that the reporting of them was in part wholly fabricated, and that in more than one small town, the trouble started solely because of the fuss made over the affair.[14]

Mehring may have been partially correct about this but he was too shrewd an observer not to realize that the *Judenfrage* in Germany was created and manipulated by powerful interest-groups enjoying a broad-based popular support. In 1882 he devoted twelve pages to this theme as part of a hard-hitting tract for the times directed against the Christian-Social leader Adolf Stöcker.[15] Mehring made a clear distinction between the inflammatory exploitation of racial and religious prejudice by ambitious agitators like Stöcker and the seemingly calm, dispassionate analysis of the Jewish question by historians like Heinrich von Treitschke. What was unacceptable in Stöcker's approach was his open appeal to the passions of the mob, his deliberate "unleashing of the beast" which could only exacerbate a complex problem. When the Protestant Court-preacher declared that modern Jewry was "a nation within a nation, a State within a State," "a tribal entity and an alien race," it was clear to his lower-middle-class audience that Stöcker was questioning the premises of Jewish emancipation.[16] Their enthusiasm was not so much a response to Stoecker's theological interpretation of the *Judenfrage* as a "socio-ethical problem" but to his unleashing of what Mehring called "the three most potent sources of hatred known in history: a religious, a racial, and a class conflict."[17]

What the pre-Marxist Mehring found so "unspeakably depressing" in Stöcker's demagogic approach were the long-term consequences it might have on the Jewish minority and on German society as a whole. The "Jewish

Question" was already peculiarly difficult in Germany because, as Mehring put it, "the fusion of the Germanic and Semitic elements has not yet proceeded far enough and at the same time too far."[18] The fanaticism of Stöcker and his followers could therefore only act as a further obstacle to the integration of the Jews in German society. With considerable sensitivity and insight, Mehring glimpsed into the abyss and saw perhaps further than he knew. "No man of feeling," he wrote, "can think without the deepest pangs of those many honorable and high-minded fellow citizens who, hurt to the quick, must become obsessed by the devilish thought that their life and work among the German people, the best and deepest part of their earthly existence, is after all nothing but a snare and a delusion."[19]

This was the only occasion on which Mehring seriously took into account the impact of German antisemitism on the Jews themselves. However, his harsh judgment on Stöcker in 1882 was to change significantly a decade later, when he depicted the *Hofprediger* (Court preacher) as more akin to a "second Luther" who had lacked "the revolutionary period in his life," than to a miserable demagogue.[20] But even in 1882 it was evident that Mehring's critical assessment of Stöcker's Berlin movement was not based on any real sympathy for German Jewry. This is clear from his far-reaching identification with Heinrich von Treitschke's strictures against Jewish behavior. Mehring had no doubt that the Jews were the main cause for the emergence of German antisemitism.[21] Like the Berlin professor of history, he felt strongly about what he called the "alien, unpleasant, or at least unaccustomed features" of Jewish Berliners in the 1870s. The *Judenfrage,* he claimed, was largely a consequence of "Jewish vulgarities and ill-manners"; the tactless and ignorant criticism of the Christian churches by the "Jewish" press during the so-called *Kulturkampf* (culture war); and the stock market swindles of the new Reich brought about by the "more mischievous elements of Berlin Jewry." Each day, Mehring concluded, "produced new evidence of that strange lack of truthfulness which Schopenhauer rightly or wrongly attributes to the Jewish people."[22] Schopenhauer's metaphysical, revolutionary anti-semitism was, it should be stressed, among *the* most virulent examples of German philosophical Jew-hatred in the 19th century—a point obscured by Mehring's remarks.

Comments like those of Treitschke, Schopenhauer, or Mehring himself effectively shifted the responsibility for antisemitism back to the Jews. Even as a Marxist historian, Mehring many years later made it clear that he regarded the antisemitism of the late 1870s as a *natural* reaction to the parvenu tactlessness of *Das Geldjudentum*:

> monied Jewry had given itself airs which inevitably made it a center of unpleasant attention; the Judaization of public life (*die Vermauschelung des öffentlichen Lebens*), especially in Berlin, had reached proportions such as to make the most uninhibited enthusiasts of Nathan the Wise uncomfortable.[23]

In his pre-Marxist phase Mehring had not ignored the historical forces which contributed to exacerbating the "Jewish Question" in German society. He still recognized that the Jews, through no fault of their own, had been forced "into an unnaturally narrow channel" which had bottled up their energies. As members of a "gifted, shrewd, tenacious race," they had inundated German society as soon as the artificially constructed dykes of the ghetto had been removed. The tone of this analysis, behind the mask of scientific objectivity, was sharply disapproving.

Hence it is not surprising to find that Mehring, like the more conservative Treitschke, strongly attacked the German liberals for ignoring the "historical fact of Judaism" and the negative effects of Jewish emancipation. At the same time he was openly contemptuous of those critics who accused Heinrich von Treitschke of antisemitism when he had simply ventilated the "deep animosity against the Jewish character" felt in all cultivated circles of Berlin society.[24] Mehring even claimed that the aim of the liberals was to suppress free speech when it came to the "Jewish Question." This, he charged, was a "wretched attempt at intellectual terrorism" designed by bourgeois liberals to procure for the Jews an unjustified immunity from criticism.

> It is an ironic fact that one may publicly speak and write about God and the world, about Church and State, about everything between heaven and earth—except the contemporary effects of Jewish emancipation, or rather its bad effects. For enthusiastic praise of its good effects is considered the highest flower of "liberalism" in certain circles. Some of these people seem to believe in good faith that, once Jewish civil emancipation has been written into our laws, the historical concept and the historical fact of Judaism had thereby ceased to exist and that it would be a grave mistake to revive them.[25]

What Mehring most admired in Treitschke's exposition was the fact that he had broken through the curtain of silence and made explicit what lay dormant in the hearts of most educated Germans. This was his "great and unforgettable service" performed with "courage," "manly frankness," and "scientific seriousness," according to Mehring. This verdict altogether ignored the fact that the renowned historian, no less than Adolf Stöcker, had unmistakably branded the Jews as an "alien" element in the Christian-Germanic State.[26] It passed over the even more disturbing implication that antisemitism had for the first time in Imperial Germany received the halo of *academic respectability,* once one of the most famous of contemporary Prussian academics could publicly declare that "the Jews are our misfortune." Among the younger generation of the educated middle classes (to which Mehring himself belonged) Treitschke's "scientific" approach inevitably enjoyed far greater prestige than the noisy agitation of Stöcker or the openly racist Judeophobia of Marr and Dühring. Treitschke was an undisputed authority in the field of modern German history. As a nationalist he demanded that the Jews totally surrender their historic identity and group cohesion in order to become completely absorbed by the German majority. Although Mehring did not share Treitschke's views on other issues (such as his antipathy to materialism, atheism, or enlightenment) he did approve of his sharply critical reprobation of German Jewry.[27] Hence, only those critics of the Berlin professor such as the philosopher Hermann Cohen (described by Mehring as a serious, "high-minded" and patriotic Jew) who sought the complete integration of the Jewish minority into German society, were given a respectful hearing.[28] The remainder were mostly accused of "disgusting vilification" or intolerance of any criticism that threatened their privileges.

Already in 1882 it was characteristic of Mehring that he distinguished sharply between assimilated Jewish writers, scholars, and revolutionaries and the Jewish community as a whole. To the former he was often bound by ties of friendship and mutual esteem. The latter he identified with *Judentum* (Jewry)—exploiting in a fashion reminiscent of the young Marx—the additional connotations of Judaism and commerce. In his pamphlet against Stöcker, he had suggested that Jewry emerged as a conquering force in German society, thanks to its money-power, "the mightiest weapon of our time." Increasingly, Mehring came to equate *Judentum* not only with unsavory swindling, or unscrupulous stock-exchange dealing, but with the material and intellectual pretentiousness of the *nouveaux riches* in German society. Through the elastic use of this term Mehring could express his evident aversion to the vulgarity and philistinism of the German bourgeoisie which had adopted the mercenary values of "monied Jews."

A characteristic feature of Mehring's antipathy to "Judaism" was his preoccupation with the crudity of much modern journalism and his resentment at its subordination to purely commercial criteria. Mehring was never a *Sprachmystiker* (language mystic) like Karl Kraus in Vienna, but he was no less concerned with the corruption of the mainstream press by business interests and their responsibility for the "cretinization of the masses."[29] It was not for nothing that Mehring initially respected Maximilian Harden, the Jewish-born editor of *Die Zukunft,* a self-appointed "Censor Germaniae" who conducted a relentless guerrilla war against the modern press.[30] At the same time it was probably significant that Harden, like Kraus, was an antisemitic Jew who sharply attacked the influence of his co-religionists in the liberal press while indulging in the aesthetic idolization of such radiant Germanic figures as Bismarck.[31] Their masochistic self-hatred notwithstanding, satirists like Harden or Kraus were infinitely wittier and more penetrating in their criticism than the antisemites who blamed all the evils of modern urban civilization on the *Judenpresse*. Mehring, although he personally came to loathe Harden, nonetheless shared his standpoint of strong opposition to liberal "philosemitism."

No doubt one factor in this vendetta against German liberalism was Mehring's removal in 1886 from his post as editor of the *Berliner Volkszeitung* as a result of intervention by a Jewish millionaire and co-proprietor of the rival *Berliner Tageblatt,* Emil Cohn. Mehring's protest against the application of the anti-socialist laws (which landed him in difficulties with the authorities and threatened the continuation of the newspaper) had contributed to his resignation. A second factor was his crusade against Paul Lindau, an influential German Jewish theater critic whose unscrupulous behavior towards an actress he had ruined aroused Mehring's anger.[32] Mehring, who detested Jews like Leopold Sonnemann (proprietor of the *Frankfurter Zeitung*), Cohn, or Lindau also regarded the role played by prominent Jewish press magnates such as Rudolf Mosse and his chief editor on the *Berliner Tageblatt,* Artur Levysohn, as being socially harmful. In his eyes their influence indicated to what extent the popular press had become an appendage of commercial advertising, financial interests and "stock-exchange democracy."[33] In this respect, Mehring's attitudes were virtually indistinguishable from the more refined versions of antisemitism associated with a whole trend of conservative cultural criticism. Mehring's sophisticated intellectual tastes did not, however, make his transition from the bourgeois to the proletarian camp any easier. Nor were his harsh earlier criticisms of the labor movement readily forgotten.[34]

For many of his new comrades, Mehring was not only a "homeless" outsider (*Heimatloser*) but a "psychological riddle," whose hypersensitivity and capacity for irrational feuds made close personal contact difficult. In a letter to Engels in March 1892, the German party leader August Bebel touched on some of the traits which had made Mehring an isolated figure in the labor movement.[35] They included his aloofness, prickly character, suspiciousness, and the widespread fear that he noted down everything that he heard for possible use.[36] Nevertheless, his polemical talents were so highly regarded by Karl Kautsky, editor of the *Neue Zeit,* that he was almost immediately appointed its Berlin correspondent in 1891. This would give him an excellent vantage point from which to report on the mushrooming antisemitic movement in Wilhelminian Germany. No other contributor to the review was so frequently to make the *Judenfrage* his starting point for a general critique of capitalism. None so consistently took the essay of the young Marx (written in 1844) on the same theme, as his model and inspiration.[37] None was so adamant that Marx's views were "completely applicable to German society in the 1890s."

Mehring's admiration for this essay is certainly one touchstone in attempting to assess the anti-Jewish element in his writings. Marx's *Zur Judenfrage* provided a seemingly unbreakable retrospective alibi for his own (pre-Marxist) negative judgment on Jews and Judaism. If the founder of "scientific" socialism had virtually equated *Judentum* and *Kapitalismus,* then this offered a perfect ideological justification for the longstanding emotional resentment of Mehring. There was no doubt that Marx's opinions were acceptable to antisemites and that Socialists with antisemitic inclinations like Wilhelm Hasselmann had long ago accepted his verdict.[38] At the same time the essay offered what Mehring once called an "Olympian" perspective from which to view the "Jewish question" as a symptom of the death-agony of capitalist society.

> Today, a single look at the anti-philosemitic war enables one to grasp all the depth of these sentences. From this secure bulwark of knowledge one may watch with a calm smile how the furious fighters in both camps storm against and beat each other.[39]

Mehring not only considered that Marx's analysis was completely valid fifty years later but he made every effort to popularize it in the working-class milieu.[40] This was in significant contrast to other leading German socialists like Kautsky, Bernstein, Bebel, and Wilhelm Liebknecht, who rarely mentioned *Zur Judenfrage* or else tried to moderate its sharp edges.[41] Even Frederick Engels refrained from trying to adapt Marx's terminology to the post-emancipation "Jewish Question" and warned the labor movement against any flirtation with anti-capitalist antisemitism.[42] This prudence of German labor leaders with regard to the essay of the young Marx may partly explain why Mehring sought so insistently to free the founder of scientific socialism from any taint of antisemitism. Without reinterpretation the essay would be more difficult to use in a political movement dedicated to eliminating all forms of racial, religious and class discrimination. Moreover, one might surmise that Mehring's own alibi for maintaining the anti-Jewish tone in some of his writings would disappear.

It was easier for Mehring to engage in this apologetic operation precisely because he was a historian with philosophical interests, well equipped to place Marx's intellectual development in its social and historical context. This was the case in his introduction written for a Polish edition of *Zur Judenfrage* (published by the Polish Socialist Party in 1896) where he asserted: "Marx has nothing in common with antisemitism. He not only says this but also proves how the Jew has an unassailable claim to political emancipation and to the enjoyment of general human rights."[43] Similarly in another commentary on the essay in 1902, Mehring sought to explain the profundity of Marx's analysis in relating Jewish political emancipation to the development of capitalism. The Jews were entitled to civil equality because it was part of the rights and freedoms guaranteed to the individual in modern bourgeois society. But as Marx had argued, the *social* essence of Judaism already permeated the ethos of commercial capitalism. In other words bourgeois society was already "judaized" (*verjudet*). In this context the issue was not political emancipation (reduced to the expression of human self-alienation, egoism and materialism) but the emancipation of the Jews *from* capitalism and of society from *Judentum*.[44] "Beseitigt den Schacher, und ihr seid den Juden los" (Remove huckstering and you will be rid of the Jews), as Mehring bluntly put it in an article of 1894, that evoked the Young Hegelian roots of Marxism.[45]

On the philosophical level, Mehring tried to emphasize the difference between the "idealism" of the Young Hegelians and the "materialism" of Marx and Engels, as being crucial to their subsequent political development. With regard to the "Jewish Question," Bruno Bauer's perspective had remained purely theological and was predicated on an elitist disdain for the masses. Hence his subsequent decline into racial chauvinism and his collaboration with Hermann Wagener (the ideologist of the East Elbian Junkers) was no surprise to Mehring.[46] Marx, on the other hand, had taken "the decisive step by bringing the religious question down to its secular basis" and demonstrating "why civil society perpetually creates the Jew from its own entrails. . . ."[47] Mehring did not question the ambiguity of Marx's references to Jewish money-power (*Geldmacht*) or his chilling call for the ultimate "disappearance" of Jewry in a new socialist order. Instead, he shifted the issue to advocating a general human transformation in which society itself needed to transcend its own "Jewishness."[48]

More disturbing still, Mehring believed that the German masses hated the Jews with good reason—for the "murderous role" that Jewish usury had allegedly played under the feudal system in exploiting the peasantry. He even agreed with the Young Hegelian Bruno Bauer that German Jewry had demanded emancipation in the 1840s, not in order to achieve civil equality but primarily to reinforce their special economic status. According to Mehring, they had shown themselves "always ready to abandon liberal principles as soon as these contradicted a special Jewish interest."[49] It was a characteristic of Jews that they would "betray democracy and liberalism as soon as it obstructed their own domination."[50] Mehring went still further in a passage which betrays a deep-rooted antipathy to Jewry beneath the Marxist veneer.

> We have lived through enough examples during the last fifty years and still experience it every day, that Jewish fellow-citizens, whom we have even admired as unshakable flagbearers of bourgeois democracy, become corrupt reactionaries if the result of civil legislation harms any specifically Jewish interest. This phenomenon is as old as the participation of Jewry in political struggles and precisely this provoked Bruno Bauer's works on the Jewish question.[51]

Once again Mehring implied that liberalism and democracy were merely a camouflage which "Jewish" interests deserted if it no longer suited their purposes. The image of the Jew conveyed in such passages was that of the *Schutzjude* (protected Jew) who seeks double privileges, the gratification of enjoying wealth and a special claim to protection *because* he is a Jew.[52] His preoccupation with exposing this maneuver doubtless explains why Franz Mehring devoted so much energy to denouncing the hypocrisy of liberal newspapers in the face of antisemitism. He was particularly severe on Rudolf Mosse and his colleagues who

> defend in Judaism the possibility and the presuppositions of huckstering on which the glamour of the capitalist world stands: hence they happily close both eyes when a Jew is crushed because his Judaism obstructs capitalism in some way, but equally they raise a wail of lamentation if an anti-capitalist movement comes too near a Jew on account of his Judaism.[53]

The word-play and the bitter, sarcastic tone are themselves reminiscent of the young Marx, whose analysis was interpreted by Mehring to mean that no socialist could be "philosemitic" without betraying his class principles.[54] In order to avoid any confusion, Mehring stressed that there was nothing in common between contemporary liberal-capitalist philosemitism and the *Judenfreundschaft* (friendliness to Jews) of eighteenth-century *philosophes* like Lessing.[55] The Lessing legend of the fin-de-siecle German bourgeoisie had been fabricated to serve venal capitalist interests and to counter the claim that all great Germans from Luther to Bismarck had been antisemites. In fact, Lessing's defense of Jews was no different from his attitude to other persecuted and oppressed groups and he had never ignored the "shadowy sides of the Jewish character."[56] It was therefore as mistaken to see in Lessing's play, *Nathan der Weise* (Nathan the wise), a eulogy of the Jew as to imagine that it was intended to downgrade Christianity.[57] Moreover, the social situation in Imperial Germany at the end of the 19th century precluded any comparison with the position taken up by Lessing more than a century earlier.

In Mehring's terminology, in the 1890s "philosemitism" became identical with the apologetic defense of rich Jews and the dishonest whitewashing of capitalistic injustices. Hence he considered "artificially bred philosemitism" as more repugnant and also more dangerous to the German labor movement than the "spontaneous Jew-hatred of primitive peasants and half-educated artisans."[58] The most representative figure of "artificial" philosemitism was the non-Jewish leader of the German liberal *Freisinn* (free-thinking) party, Eugen Richter—"no more a glaring satire of Lessing, than is Herr Stöcker of Karl Marx."[59] By the early 1890s Mehring had come to regard Stöcker as "a model of truthfulness in comparison with Eugen Richter."[60] Philosemitism, in terms of Marxist class analysis, represented the worst form of *Schacherpolitik* (political huckstering), a solidly entrenched front of wealth and privilege—"the last ideological disguise of exploiting capitalism."[61] It was the task of the socialist press to ruthlessly expose this liberal hypocrisy. Seen in this context it is not surprising that an anti-liberal Marxist like Mehring could consider "philosemitism" as much more of a threat than the hysterical, but impotent rhetoric of noisy, semi-literate Jew-baiters. "In considering the brutalities which antisemitism with words rather than deeds commits against the Jews, one should not overlook the brutalities which philosemitism with deeds rather than words is committing against everyone, be he Jew or Turk, Christian or pagan, who opposes capitalism."[62]

Such was Mehring's obsession with the iniquities of "philosemitism" that he even accused those Germans who had taken up a public collection for the Jewish butcher, Buschhoff (accused of ritual murder in Xanten, 1891), of humbug and cheap publicity-seeking "at the expense of human misery."[63] In his commentary on the episode Mehring appeared more concerned with mocking the "idiotic fanaticism" of Buschhoff's liberal defenders than with the barbaric superstitions of the antisemites. It is not surprising, therefore, that some colleagues of Mehring in the SPD, notably Eduard Bernstein, challenged his one-sided emphasis on the philosemitic specter threatening the labor movement. In an essay published in the *Neue Zeit* in 1894 Bernstein pointed out that it had become difficult to differentiate between the use of the term "philosemitism" by socialists or by antisemites. Both misleadingly equated it with sycophantic subservience to capitalist interests.[64] There was a danger that as a result antisemitism might come to be regarded as the "lesser evil" by the labor movement (a position implicit in Mehring's writings despite his denials).

Mehring's reply to Bernstein's criticisms disclaimed any desire to minimize the importance of antisemitism, if only because its progress would ultimately benefit Social Democracy. But it was inconceivable, he insisted, that a Marxist proletarian party could support the "brutal capitalistic interests, politically organized in the Freisinn [Liberal] party" against the antisemites. Did not the Jew-baiters "in their way also represent a social rebellion"?[65] There could be only one effective alternative to such protest—namely the revolutionary faith of the German labor movement in the inevitable victory of socialism.[66] Mehring usually presented his analyses of the Jewish question within this semi-apocalyptic framework. Both philo- and antisemites ultimately represented two poles of a moribund society engaged in a sham battle which was little more than a vulgar if "particularly instructive" parody of the class struggle.[67] In the accelerating social process of decomposition, the feverish war between philo- and antisemites played an unusually "ugly and repulsive role" but one well worth analyzing. Their grotesque skirmishes, however superficial, would prove to be "a powerful midwife to accelerate the birth of a new society."[68]

This analysis was reflected in many statements that appeared in the German socialist press during the 1890s. For example, in an editorial of 26 June 1893, *Vorwärts,* the central organ of the SPD, described antisemitism as the "cultural manure for socialism in the truest sense of the word."[69] Party newspapers rejoiced over antisemitic successes in the 1893 elections as they appeared to strike a blow at the capitalist parties and herald the imminent triumph of socialism.[70] Heinrich Braun, himself a converted Austrian Jew and editor of the *Archiv für soziale Gesetzgebung und Statistik,* wrote in 1893 that antisemitism was "the seed of Social Democracy," a view shared by most party ideologists and leaders. Braun asserted that through its brutal demagogy, antisemitism was overcoming the "rural idiocy" of the peasants and other backward strata in Germany. "Its rapid growth is not unlike that of Social Democracy. . .there can be no doubt that in antisemitism we are faced with a strong social movement and that together with the attacks upon Jewry, a radical anti-capitalist trend of a general kind is more and more openly and consciously seeking to affirm itself."[71] Braun, like Mehring and other central European Marxist theorists, was convinced that antisemitism was essentially an *anti-capitalist* movement which would be tactically useful for Social Democracy. This popular assessment did not prevent Mehring from mocking Braun (in his private correspondence) as an "exploitative Viennese merchant-Jew"—resourceful, enterprising and tenacious—who needed careful watching!

By the early 1890s Mehring had revised his assessment of antisemitic demagogues like Adolf Stöcker, whom he had pitilessly exposed a decade earlier as an ambitious charlatan and megalomaniac. In 1893, Stöcker would even be described by Franz Mehring as a man of "native wit, with the gift of ready repartee, quickness of thought, and indestructible good humor."[72] The *Hofprediger* was increasingly depicted as a "bold and God-fearing man" destroyed by liberal wickedness and the ungrateful "howling mob of his own followers." It might be true that Stöcker had always tended to light-headedness on points of fact, but "it was this aspect of his character," Mehring complained, "that was exploited to the utmost by the hired scribblers of monied Jewry to present Stöcker as a scarecrow of mendacity. His admirers came much closer to the truth when celebrating him as a 'second Luther.'"[73]

Through the new-found prism of historical materialism, even Stöcker's antisemitism could be characterized as exhibiting a truly "proletarian" instinct by Mehring. Nevertheless Stöcker lacked the typically populist, anti-clerical appeal of Böckel and Ahlwardt. Fin-de-siècle *völkisch* demagogues who had taken on the mantle of the fading Court preacher, turned out to be more effective in mobilizing support from the growing phalanx of impoverished peasants, shopkeepers, and artisans. They tended to identify capitalism with Jewish money-lenders, cattle-dealers, and middlemen.[74] In 1892 the populist antisemite Hermann Ahlwardt temporarily succeeded in obtaining a Reichstag seat by exploiting such perceptions. He defeated the Conservative Party candidate in the rural district of Arnswalde-Friedeberg, east of Berlin, with a plebeian campaign which branded Jews, Junkers, and clerics as "enemies of the people." Mehring saw in this crude agitation a genuine protest movement against the establishment, a powerful blow struck at big business, anonymous exploitation, and remote control from Berlin.[75] The *völkisch* Jew-baiters expressed the spontaneous, blind fury of oppressed strata in German society enraged at financial corruption in general and the domination of oligarchical capitalist cliques in particular. Sometimes, as in Ahlwardt's hysterical pamphlet, *Judenflinten* (which accused the liberal Jewish industrialist Ludwig Loewe of deliberately supplying the German army with defective rifles on the orders of the Parisian Alliance Israélite Universelle) the antisemites were a long way off the mark. But Mehring saw no need to moralize about their failings, since as long as financial corruption existed—"the Ahlwardt type remains a Siegfried against whom the capitalist world vainly seeks the place where he can be struck down by a deadly spear."[76]

Ahlwardt and his followers had, at least, the merit of revealing that antisemitism was a two-edged sword for the Junker ruling class. In the long run it would help to sweep away the dominant elites along with all the other junk and débris of bourgeois society. "In Berlin," Mehring observed, "it has taken half a man's lifetime for pampered and adored antisemitism to become a fire that all the extinguishers of society and state can no longer put out."[77] From a Marxist perspective one could only welcome the fact that the antisemitic movement was proving such an acute embarrassment to its original sponsors, the Junker and capitalist establishment. In this respect, at least, Mehring's interpretation of antisemitism was fully in line with the prevailing trends in the German, Austrian, and French labor movements of the 19th century. But when taken in conjunction with his treatment of "philosemitism," it becomes clearer that Mehring's selectivity did betray a highly subjective bias. Particularly revealing in this respect were his comments on the Jewish backgrounds of Karl Marx and Ferdinand Lassalle, the founding fathers of the German labor movement, who were also Mehring's main intellectual and political guides. Although Mehring noted that the adolescent Lassalle at one time dreamed of leading the Jews to their independence[78] he felt little empathy for his Jewishness, emphasizing instead the "civilizing" influence of German culture upon his hero. Mehring reduced Lassalle's "Jewishness" to a remnant of the tradition of medieval usury. "In so far as Lassalle turned away from huckstering he also removed himself from Jewry: the fluent knowledge and preoccupation with the German classics had opened his eyes to the spiritual resources of modern culture."[79]

Elsewhere Mehring spoke of the unfavorable influence which the Russo-Polish [*sic*] family milieu had exercised on Lassalle's character, though his birthplace was in fact in Breslau.[80] Mehring claimed that Lassalle's parents "belonged to East European Jewry, which was still deeply stuck in huckstering and usury."[81] In fact, this was quite misleading since Lassalle's father belonged to the reform community in Breslau and was a supporter of Abraham Geiger's efforts to synthesize Judaism with the most "progressive" achievements of modern European culture. A similarly "enlightened" bias can be found in Mehring's book on Karl Marx, perhaps the first serious biography in the field. Typically, he had nothing of note to report about the truly remarkable rabbinical ancestry of Karl Marx. Indeed, Mehring devoted only a few pages to the Jewish background of the founder of Communism, yet they reveal much about his own preconceptions concerning Judaism. In the first place he felt obliged to emphasize that Karl Marx's father, Heinrich, did not convert to Lutheranism for opportunistic reasons, but purely out of conviction. For Mehring, it was self-evident that as a follower of Rousseau and Voltaire, Heinrich Marx could not be expected to feel anything in common with the synagogue. This overlooked the fact that Marx's own father had interacted with the Jewish community before his conversion. Mehring's antipathy towards the Jews of the Rhineland whom he accused of "murderous exploitation" of the local peasants was another sign of his bias.

According to Mehring, German Jewry in the 1820s was still languishing in "the depths of medieval barbarism."[82] In spite of the solitary efforts of Moses Mendelssohn they had not participated in the great cultural achievements of the German enlightenment. In this social context, the renunciation of Judaism was a "progressive" step, an act of *human* emancipation. The conversion to Christianity of other "free spirits" like Heinrich Heine, Ludwig Börne, and Eduard Gans were also signs of "civilized progress."[83] Missing altogether from Mehring's account was any mention of the reactionary political pressures to conform, instigated by the Prusso-Christian State in the aftermath of the Napoleonic wars. Prussian rule left little alternative to Rhineland Jews like Heinrich Marx who wished to practice their legal profession. Nor did Mehring mention that "free spirits" like Heine and Börne bitterly regretted their "conversion," or that Karl Marx's Jewish self-loathing was almost certainly related to his delicate position as a convert.

In his eagerness to *dejudaize* Marx's background, Mehring emphasized the "authentically German" quality of the letters from Heinrich Marx to his son Karl, which betrayed not a trace of "Jewish mannerisms or incivility."[84] Heinrich Marx had already been liberated "from all Jewish prejudices" by his humanistic culture which he transmitted to his gifted son as a "most valuable heritage."[85] After this extended apologia with its implied contempt for Jewish backwardness, it was self-evident that any civilized "progressive" would wish, at the first opportunity, to free themselves from the national, religious, and economic characteristics of Jewry. Mehring could eulogize radical Jews like Heine, Börne, Gans, Marx or Lassalle but only by condemning those co-religionists who remained within the Jewish fold. The former were admired as fighters for humanity while the latter were dismissed as ethnic obscurantists or denounced as parvenu "monied Jews." This has remained a dominant perception in many left-wing circles until the present day.

Franz Mehring, like Karl Marx, insisted (not without reason) that Jewish emancipation was a consequence of social development. But he also considered that the Jews, as a result of their history, had become prime representatives of excessive money-power and hence "an anti-social element." Mehring strenuously denied that this position was antisemitic. In a polemic in 1910 defending his left-wing comrade Rosa Luxemburg against the accusations of Polish antisemites, he insisted that Marxism had adopted a standpoint towards the Jews which was "completely free of prejudice." In Mehring's interpretation, the Marxist attitude was "equally far removed from anti- as it was from philosemitism."[86] This claim should be regarded with considerable skepticism. Like Marx himself, Mehring gave philosophical and historical respectability to long-standing stereotypical folk-images about Jews which had come to permeate Western Christian culture. Moreover, he tended to regard German Jewry not as an oppressed group but rather as the embodiment of the worst features of capitalist behavior. From the young Marx to Mehring (and beyond), this anti-Jewish stereotype had continued to haunt the socialist movement like a ghostly specter.[87]

Notes

1. Reinhard Rürup, "Emanzipation und Krise. Zur Geschichte der 'Judenfrage' in Deutschland vor 1890," in *Juden im Wilhelminischen Deutschland 1890–1914. Ein Sammelband,* edited by Werner E. Mosse and Arnold Paucker (Tübingen 1976), 1–56; Hans Rosenberg, *Grosse Depression und Bismarckzeit* (Berlin, 1967), 88–117.

2. See Richard S. Levy, *The Downfall of the Anti-Semitic Political Parties in Imperial Germany* (New Haven, 1975).

3. See, for example, Robert Michels, *Political Parties,* 2nd English ed., translated by Eden and Cedar Paul (1913; New York, 1959), 262. The first German edition, a sociological classic, appeared in 1913. Michels claimed that "the consciousness of all that the party owes to Jewish intellectuals" was as important in its resistance to antisemitism as any "theoretical socialist aversion for 'nationalism' and racial

prejudices." Eduard Bernstein, writing in a Dutch socialist periodical, was more emphatic. "In the German Social Democratic Party an outspoken antisemite is an impossibility. One can find some anti-Jewish sentiment here and there in the party or the socialist trade unions but this does not influence the distribution of positions or privileges." See Eduard Bernstein, "De Joden in De Duitsche Sociaal-Demokratie," *De Socialistische Gids* 6, no. 11 (Nov 1921): 984.

4. For a detailed discussion, see Robert S. Wistrich, *Socialism and the Jewish Question in Germany and Austria 1880–1914* (Ph.D. diss., University of London, 1974); also Mario Kessler, ed., *Arbeiterbewegung und Antisemitismus* (Bonn, 1993).

5. Quoted from Rudolf Lindau, *Franz Mehring zu seinem 100. Geburtstag am 27.Februar* (East Berlin, 1946), 11; see also Clara Zetkin, *Rosa Luxemburg. Karl Liebknecht. Franz Mehring. Den Führern des Spartakusbundes und Gründern der Kommunistischen Partei Deutschlands* (Moscow, 1934), 64.

6. See in particular Rudolf Meyer, *Politische Gründer und die Korruption in Deutschland* (Leipzig, 1877), a work which Mehring much admired. Fritz Stern, "Money, Morals and the Pillars of Bismarck's Society," *Central European Affairs* 3 (1970): 49–72.

7. See Franz Mehring, *Geschichte der deutschen Sozialdemokratie,* 2nd ed. (Stuttgart, 1921), 3: 14, 70, 86; also Eduard Bernstein, *Sozialdemokratische Lehrjahre* (Berlin, 1928), 26.

8. Otto Glagau, *Der Börsen und Gründungsschwindel in Berlin* (Leipzig, 1876).

9. See Bernstein, *Sozialdemokratische Lehrjahre,* 26.

10. Thomas Höhle, *Franz Mehring. Sein Weg zum Marxismus 1869–91* (East Berlin, 1956), 109, 113, 119. Also Franz Mehring, "Über Geschäfts- und Prinzipblätter," *Die Neue Zeit* 1 (1892–1893): 329 ff., where he wrote that the Frankfurt *Börsendemokratie* was among "the most effective levers of antisemitism."

11. See the standard biographies by Höhle, *Franz Mehring;* and Josef Schleifstein, *Franz Mehring. Sein Marxistisches Schaffen 1891–1919* (East Berlin, 1959), which faithfully reflect the communist standpoint. Also Walter Kampmann, "Franz Mehring als Vertreter des Historischen Materialismus," *Veröffentlichungen des Osteuropa-Institutes* 29 (Munich, 1966): 150–52.

12. See Annelies Laschitza, "Franz Mehring. Ein Lehrmeister der marxistischen Biographie," and Hans Jürgen Friederici, "Historiker, Journalist, Revolutionär. Franz Mehring," in *Beiträge zur Geschichte der Arbeiterbewegung* 18, no. 1 (1976): 58–69, 120–29.

13. Significantly, Mehring's watchword at this time was "Weder Judenhetze, noch Judenherrschaft." See Franz Mehring, *Kapital und Presse Ein Nachspiel zum Falle Lindau* (Berlin, 1891), 83–84.

14. Franz Mehring, *Herr Hofprediger Stöcker der Socialpolitiker. Eine Streitschrift* (Bremen, 1882), 67.

15. Ibid., 64–76.

16. Adolf Stöcker, *Christian-Sozial. Reden und Aufsätze* (Bielefeld-Leipzig, 1885), 151. See also Peter Pulzer, *The Rise and Fall of Political Anti-Semitism in Germany and Austria,* revised ed. (London, 1988).

17. Franz Mehring, *Herr Hofprediger Stöcker,* 69.

18. Ibid.

19. Ibid., 75–76.

20. Franz Mehring, "Das Ende eines Demagogen," *Die Neue Zeit* 2 (1892–1893): 545.

21. On the controversy over Treitschke and the Jewish reactions, see Hans Liebeschütz, "Treitschke and Mommsen on Jewry and Judaism," in *Leo Baeck Institute Year Book* (hereafter *LBIYB*) 7 (1962): 153–82; Wanda Kampmann, *Deutsche und Juden* (Heidelberg, 1963), 265–79; Michael A. Meyer, "Great Debate on Antisemitism. Jewish Reactions to New Hostility in Germany 1897–1881," in *LBIYB* 11 (1966): 137–70; Hans Liebeschütz, *Das Judentum im deutschen Geschichtsbild von Hegel bis Max Weber* (Schriftenreihe wissenschaftlicher Abhandlungen des Leo Baeck Instituts 17) (Tübingen, 1967): 212–19; and Ismar Schorsch, *Jewish Reactions to German Anti-Semitism 1870–1914* (New York, 1972).

22. Franz Mehring, *Herr Hofprediger Stöcker,* 64–65; on Schopenhauer's antisemitism, see Paul Lawrence Rose, *Wagner. Race and Revolution* (London, 1992), 92ff.

23. Franz Mehring, *Geschichte der deutschen Sozialdemokratie* (Stuttgart, 1913), 4: 96.

24. Walter Boehlich, ed., *Der Berliner Antisemitismusstreit* (Frankfurt a.M., 1965), which includes Treitschke's original articles in the *Preussische Jahrbücher* (Nov./ Dec. 1879, Jan. and Dec. 1880, Jan. 1881), and replies by Heinrich Graetz, Harry Bresslau, Hermann Cohen, Ludwig Bamberger, and Theodor Mommsen.

25. Franz Mehring, *Herr Hofprediger Stöcker,* 66.

26. See especially Heinrich von Treitschke, "Unsere Aussichten," *Preussische Jahrbücher* (Nov. 1879), reproduced in Boehlich, *Der Berliner Antisemitismusstreit,* 11, where he calls the antisemitic agitation a natural reaction "des germanischen Volksgefühls gegen ein fremdes Element, das in unserem Leben einen allzu breiten Raum eingenommen hat" ([and expression of] Germanic popular feeling against an alien element which has assumed an all-too-wide dimension in our life).

27. For Mehring's socialist appraisal of the great Prussian historian, see "Heinrich von Treitschke," *Die Neue Zeit* 14, 2 (1896) 193ff.; see also Detlev Claussen, *Vom Judenhass zum Antisemitismus* (Darmstadt, 1987).

28. Hermann Cohen, *Ein Bekenntnis in der Judenfrage* (Berlin 1880) is reproduced in Boehlich, *Der Berliner Antisemitismusstreit,* 124-79. For a discussion of Cohen, see Uriel Tal, *Christians and Jews in the "Second Reich" (1870-1914)* (in Hebrew) (Jerusalem, 1969), 33–36, 141–48; English ed., *Christians and Jews in Germany. Religion, Politics, and Ideology in the Second Reich, 1870–1914* (London, 1975).

29. See Franz Mehring, *Kapital und Presse*. On Karl Kraus, see Wilma Abbeles Iggers, *Karl Kraus. A Viennese Critic of the Twentieth Century* (The Hague, 1967); and Robert S. Wistrich, "Karl Kraus: Jewish Prophet or Renegade?," *European Judaism* 9, no. 2 (Summer 1975): 32–38; and idem, *Laboratory for World Destruction. Germans and Jews in Central Europe* (Lincoln, Neb., 2007), 304–24.

30. Mehring played for a time with the idea of regular collaboration with Harden. See Ursula Ratz, "Aus Franz Mehrings marxistischer Frühzeit." (Ein Briefwechsel Franz Mehrings mit Lujo Brentano 1891–93), *Internationale Wissenschaftliche Korrespondenz zur Geschichte der deutschen Arbeiterbewegung,* no. 19/20 (Dec. 1973): 40.

31. Erich Gottgetreu, "Maximilian Harden: Ways and Errors of a Publicist," in *LBIYB* 7 (1962): 205–46. For the relations between Mehring and Harden, see Lars Fischer, *The Socialist Response to Antisemitism in Imperial Germany* (Cambridge, 2007), 105–8. On Karl Kraus, see Paul Reitter, *The Anti-Journalist. Karl Kraus and Jewish Self-Fashioning in Fin-de-siècle Europe* (Chicago, 2008).

32. Franz Mehring, *Kapital und Presse*.

33. On these points see the articles by Ernst Kahn, "The *Frankfurter Zeitung*," *LBIYB* 2 (1957): 228–35; and Werner E. Mosse, "Rudolf Mosse and the House of Mosse 1867–1920," *LBIYB* 4 (1959): 237–59, which provide a valuable corrective to this simplistic view.

34. See Karl Kautsky, "Franz Mehring," *Die Neue Zeit* 1 (1903–1904): 103ff.

35. Bebel to Engels, 20 Mar. 1892, in *August Bebel. Briefwechsel mit Friedrich Engels,* edited by Werner Blumenberg (The Hague, 1965), 527.

36. Ibid.

37. See in particular his introduction to Marx's essay in Franz Mehring, ed., *Aus dem literarischen Nachlass von Karl Marx, Friedrich Engels und Ferdinand Lassalle* (Stuttgart, 1902), 1: 356: "Any commentary would only weaken this fundamental investigation: its few pages outweigh the mountain of the literature on the Jewish question which has since appeared."

38. See Eduard Bernstein, "Die Joden in De Duitsche Sociaal-Democratie," 970; Robert S. Wistrich, *Revolutionary Jews from Marx to Trotsky* (London, 1976).

39. Franz Mehring, "Kapitalistische Agonie," *Die Neue Zeit* 2 (1891–1892), 548; Julius Carlebach, *Karl Marx and the Radical Critique of Judaism* (London, 1978).

40. See note 37 and his commentary in Franz Mehring, *Karl Marx. Geschichte seines Lebens,* 4th ed (Leipzig, 1923), 71–78.

41. On this point see Robert S. Wistrich, "Karl Marx, German Socialists and the Jewish Question 1880–1914," *Soviet Jewish Affairs* 3, no. 1 (1973): 92–97. Lars Fischer, *Socialist Response to Antisemitism,* 60 takes issue with this statement without providing any compelling evidence to the contrary.

42. Friedrich Engels, "Über den Antisemitismus," *Arbeiter-Zeitung* (Vienna), 19 May 1890.

43. The introduction, obviously translated from the German, prefaced a pamphlet entitled Karol Marks, *W Kwestyi żydowskiej,* Biblioteka politycznospołeczna, t. IV (London, 1896), xxvi. It was published by the nationalist-minded PPS (Polish Socialist Party) through its Overseas Union.

44. For an extended analysis of this dialectical paradox see chapter 1 of Wistrich, *Revolutionary Jews from Marx to Trotsky,* 30–38.

45. Franz Mehring, "Drillinge," *Die Neue Zeit* 2 (1904): 582.

46. On Bauer, see Nathan Rotenstreich, "For and Against Emancipation. The Bruno Bauer Controversy," in *LBIYB* 4 (1959): 3–36; Zvi Rosen, "The Anti-Jewish Opinions of Bruno Bauer (1838–1843). Their Sources and Significance" (in Hebrew) *Zion* 33 (1968): 59–76; Ernst Barnikol ed., *Bruno Bauer. Studien und Materialien* (Assen, 1972); Franz Mehring, "Geschichte der deutschen Sozialdemokratie," in *Gesammelte Werke,* 2nd ed. (Berlin, 1976), 1–15.

47. Mehring, "Drillinge," 581; see also Fischer, *Socialist Response to Antisemitism,* 62–63.

48. Mehring, "Drillinge," 582.

49. Mehring, *Karl Marx. Geschichte seines Lebens,* 94.

50. Mehring, *Aus dem literarischen Nachlass,* 1: 354–55.

51. Ibid.

52. See the perceptive comments by Paul Massing, *Rehearsal for Destruction. A Study of Political Anti-Semitism in Imperial Germany*(New York, 1959), 187.

53. Franz Mehring, "Kapitalistische Agonie," *Die Neue Zeit* 2 (1891–1892): 546.

54. Franz Mehring, "Anti- und Philosemitisches," *Die Neue Zeit* 2 (1890–1891): 587.

55. Franz Mehring, *Die Lessing-Legende* (Stuttgart, 1893), 7. This study, highly thought of by Engels, was a pioneer effort to apply historical materialism to the domain of literary criticism.

56. Franz Mehring, *Aufsätze zur deutschen Literaturgeschichte* (Leipzig, 1960), 76.

57. Ibid.

58. Franz Mehring, *Geschichte der deutschen Sozialdemokratie* (East Berlin, 1960), 2: 451.

59. "Aber Herr Stöcker ist keine grellere Satire auf Karl Marx als Herr Eugen [Richter] eine grille Satire auf Lessing ist." Mehring, "Anti- und Philosemitisches," *Die Neue Zeit* (1890–1891): 587.

60. Franz Mehring, *Geschichte der deutschen Sozialdemokratie* (Stuttgart, 1913), 4: 131.

61. Franz Mehring, "Das erste Wahlergebnis," *Die Neue Zeit* 2 (1892–1893): 389: "Diesen Philosemitismus, der nichts als die letzte ideologische Verkleidung des ausbeuterischen Kapitalismus darstellt, rücksichtslos zu brandmarken, ist doch wohl recht eigentlich die Aufgabe der sozialistischen Presse. . . ."

62. Mehring, "Anti- und Philosemitisches," 487.

63. Mehring, "Kapitalistische Agonie."

64. Eduard Bernstein, "Das Schlagwort und der Antisemitismus," *Die Neue Zeit* 2 (1893–1894): 233. For a somewhat unfairly critical discussion of Bernstein's views, see Fischer, *Socialist Response to Antisemitism,* 173–208; see also Jack Jacobs, *On Socialists and "the Jewish Question" after Marx* (New York, 1992).

65. Mehring, "Das erste Wahlergebnis," 389.

66. Ibid.

67. Mehring, "Kapitalistische Agonie," 546.

68. Ibid.

69. *Vorwärts,* 26 June 1893. For a detailed examination of this trend, see Robert S. Wistrich, "The SPD and Antisemitism in the 1890s," *European Studies Review* 7 (1977): 177–97.

70. Wistrich, *Socialism and the Jewish Question,* 223–31.

71. Heinrich Braun, "Zur Lage der deutschen Sozialdemokratie," *Archiv für Soziale Gesetzbegung und Statistik* (1893): 513–14. Braun was the brother-in-law of Victor Adler, leader of the Austrian socialist party. He played an important role in the "revisionist" wing of German Social Democracy. At one time on friendly terms with Mehring, their relations soon soured. See Ratz, "Aus Franz Mehrings marxistischer Frühzeit," 37. After Braun's criticisms of his *Lessing-Legende,* Mehring confided in Kautsky: (1 Oct. 1893, *Kautsky Nachlass,* I.I.S.H. Amsterdam) "und läuft mir dieser 'talentvolle' Geschäftsjude nochmals über den Weg, dann gnade ihm Gott!"

72. Franz Mehring, "Das Ende eines Demagogen," 545.

73. Ibid.

74. Franz Mehring, *Geschichte der deutschen Sozialdemokratie,* (1913), 4: 96.

75. Franz Mehring, "Sauve qui peut!," *Die Neue Zeit* (1892–1893): 161–64.

76. Franz Mehring, "Sic vos, non vobis," *Die Neue Zeit* (1892–1893): 361.

77. Ibid., 363: "In Berlin hat es ein halbes Menschenalter gewährt, bis der gehätschelte und geliebkoste Antisemitismus zu einem Brande geworden ist, den alle Spritzen von Gesellschaft und Staat nicht mehr löschen können."

78. Franz Mehring, *Zur deutschen Geschichte* (Berlin, 1931), 186.

79. Ibid.

80. Ibid., 207.

81. Ibid., 186; see also Eduard Rosenbaum, "Ferdinand Lassalle. A Historiographical Meditation," in *LBIYB* 9 (1964): 122–30; and chapter 2 of Wistrich, *Revolutionary Jews,* 46–58.

82. Franz Mehring, *Zur deutschen Geschichte,* 148.

83. Franz Mehring, *Karl Marx,* 25.

84. Ibid., 26.

85. Ibid.

86. Franz Mehring's intervention on behalf of Rosa Luxemburg occurred after the Polish antisemite Andrzej Niemojewski had attacked her Polish Social Democrats (the SDKPiL) as anti-national and "judaized" and further claimed that Western socialists from Marx to Kautsky (and Mehring) were all antisemites. On the background to this affair see Wistrich, *Revolutionary Jews from Marx to Trotsky,* 83–90; and Georges Haupt and P. Korzec, "Les socialistes et la campagne anti-Semite en Pologne en 1910: un episode inédit," *Revue du Nord* (Université de Lille, No. 225) 57 (Apr.–June 1975): 185–94. Mehring's reply concentrated mainly on the historical background to Marx's essay and denied that it had anything in common with the standpoint of Niemojewski. It appeared as an open letter in *Młot,* no. 12 (12 Nov. 1910), a socio-political review in Warsaw which was the official organ of the SDKPiL. Apart from Rosa Luxemburg, the contributors to this review (which I studied carefully in the Polish original) included Karl Radek, Leo Jogiches, and Adolf Warski, the first three being Polish-Jewish revolutionaries who were also very active in the German labor movement.

87. Joseph Gabel, *Réflexions sur l'Avenir des Juifs* (Paris, 1987), 61–85, 170–74.

CHAPTER 6

Socialists and Antisemites in Europe before 1914

The relationship between Socialism and antisemitism is a rather obscure chapter in European history which only began to attract the attention of historians in the aftermath of the Second World War. Perhaps the first systematic attempt by a historian to investigate the attitudes of Social Democracy in Central Europe to the phenomenon of antisemitism was made by Paul Massing in his book *Rehearsal for Destruction*. Massing, himself an exiled (non-Jewish) Social Democrat forced to flee from Nazi Germany, came to the conclusion that:

> the socialists never wavered in their stand against all attempts to deprive Jews of their civil rights. They treated with contempt the antisemitic agitators and the groups behind them. They never gave in to the temptation—considerable at times—to gain followers by making concessions to anti-Jewish prejudice.[1]

Massing's thesis, based exclusively on the analysis of positions adopted by the German labor movement before 1914, argued that the Social Democrats were the most consistent champions of equal rights for the Jewish minority in Imperial Germany and that they became immunized during this period against antisemitic tendencies. Indeed, Massing claimed that not only did the German Social Democrats consistently battle against antisemitism, they were also the first theoreticians to provide a coherent sociological analysis of the phenomenon. He pointed out that they correctly perceived the special attraction of antisemitism for the decaying *Mittelstand,* for the small peasantry, a section of the Junker aristocracy, and the semi-proletarianized intelligentsia.

The antisemitism of these social groups, adversely affected by industrialization and modernization, was, according to the German Socialists, the product of their mistaken view of the role played by Jews in the capitalist economy. Once these declining social strata came to grasp the real nature of their misery and to realize that the allegedly exploitative role of the Jews was a temporary, historically-conditioned phenomenon, they would gravitate towards Social Democracy. The "Jewish Question," according to this view (pioneered by Friedrich Engels and August Bebel), was an incidental by-product of the class struggle in modern bourgeois society. It would be resolved by the victory of Socialism which was opposed in both theory and practice to all forms of antisemitism. Massing's account of the position adopted by the German Social Democrats was in broad terms accepted by many later historians—Marxist and non-Marxist alike. Indeed, modern Communist historiography invariably stretched this line of argument to claim that Socialism, in general, is by its very nature immune to antisemitism.[2]

The Communist position, echoed on this point by Trotskyist and New Left historiography in the West, defines antisemitism in purely instrumental class terms as:

> one of the most brutal weapons, which the exploiting classes utilise to stabilise and extend their position of power (*Machtposition*).[3]

Since capitalism and its exploiting classes are held to be responsible for the existence of a "Jewish Question" and for aggravating antisemitism, it is a self-evident truth for many Marxists that Socialism—as part of the solution to the problem—must be a priori immune to anti-Jewish prejudice.[4] We find another influential variation on the Marxist position in Jean-Paul Sartre's sweeping assertion that there are "hardly any anti-Semites among the workers," because "the workman sees society as the product of real forces acting in accordance with rigorous laws."[5] Sartre's assumption, like that of many Marxists, was that the socio-economic conditions of the working class and the way its individual members supposedly view the world (through the prism of historical materialism) preclude the proletariat from adopting antisemitic attitudes. Independent sociological investigations such as the study by James Robb of the British working class in East London have, in fact, long ago shown this thesis to be empirically false.[6] Yet many socialists have found it difficult to abandon.

More surprising, perhaps, is the readiness of some liberal historians to credit the idea of an inborn immunity of the labor movement to antisemitism. A typical variant of this argument was presented by Peter Pulzer, who suggested that because Social Democracy had been concerned traditionally with universal emancipation, with spreading education, combating poverty, tyranny, and evil, it was inevitably opposed to the antisemitic creed which "set forth the primacy of the national and the integral over the universal."[7] In more recent memory, this assumption that Socialism with its universalist, emancipatory ideals is somehow irreconcilable with an antisemitic "world-view" has been clearly disproved by developments in contemporary history.

Already, the anti-Jewish motifs in the "anti-cosmopolitan" campaigns that occurred in the Socialist countries,beginning with the Soviet Union (1948–1953) and Eastern Europe, began to shake the confidence of independent-minded liberal and Marxist scholars. The so-called anti-Zionist crusades directed against Jews in post-Stalinist Russia, in Communist Poland and in Czechoslovakia (1968–1970), and the militant antisemitic type of anti-Israelism manifested by sections of the Western old and new Left, have further called into question long-held assumptions about the relation of socialism to antisemitism. This and other factors led even some modern German historians on the Left to reassess, a little more critically, the record of the Social Democrats towards the "Jewish Question." Reinhard Rürup acknowledged years ago that the pre-1914 Socialists seriously under-estimated the strength of antisemitism and that a negative image of Jews was quite widespread among the working classes of Central Europe. Official Party opposition to political antisemitism, he admitted, was not necessarily incompatible with anti-Jewish resentment and prejudice among many rank-and-file socialists, though he tended to play down the significance of the latter phenomenon.[8]

Another study of German Social Democracy, written in 1978 from a Socialist viewpoint, revealed that while the party-political press and most of its major leaders did indeed oppose antisemitism, their struggle was not carried over successfully into the cultural sphere. In popular working-class literature, in caricatures, *feuilletons,* anecdotes, verses, short stories, and serial novels, traditional antisemitic stereotypes continued to flourish unchecked. Though derivative in other respects, this study by Rosemarie Leuschen-Seppel broke some new ground, showing that the Social Democratic subculture in Imperial Germany, in its vocabular, images, and associations remained as tainted with anti-Jewish values and modes of thought as the dominant bourgeois German culture.[9] The glaring gap between the political and cultural work of the Social Democrats meant, therefore, that conventional prejudices against Jews remained largely unaffected by the official opposition of the leadership in the German labor movement to antisemitism. Nevertheless, while more differentiated than Massing's original thesis, both Leuschen-Seppel and Rürup basically reiterated the standard contention that Social Democracy as an emancipatory movement was uncompromisingly opposed to political antisemitism.

A diametrically contrary theory had been propounded as far back as 1955 by the Israeli scholar Edmund Silberner who wrote that modern Socialism in general is characterized by a "long-standing antisemitic tradition," so much so that "Socialist antisemitism" can be classified as a specific brand of modern antisemitism.[10] Silberner's study was the first seriously documented interpretation of the antisemitic tradition in modern socialism and drew on a broad range of sources in various European languages. Silberner claimed that there was a consistent anti-Jewish mode of thought characteristic of European socialist ideologues and political leaders. He regarded the youthful essay of Karl Marx, *Zur Judenfrage,* written in 1844, as "the source" of this endemic antisemitism. Silberner's work was, however, attacked even by those who relied on his documentation, for quoting selectively and out of context. Critics argued that Marx's position had to be analyzed in the framework of his overall thought at the time. Moreover, his articles of 1844 purportedly had little effect on the future development of German or Russian Social Democracy. Similarly, it was argued that anti-Jewish remarks made by other socialist politicians, ideologues or writers did not necessarily constitute a structural phenomenon called "socialist antisemitism" that could be differentiated from bourgeois antisemitism.

Silberner's simple definition of antisemitism as a "hostile" or "unfriendly" attitude to Jews was regarded, with some justification, as far too sweeping and methodologically inadequate. According to such a definition (or lack of definition) only very small, marginal groups in European society could be considered as non-antisemitic. Insofar as Silberner's critics did acknowledge a partial validity to his thesis they have generally confined it to the early (pre-Marxist) Socialist movement. The simplistic identification of Jews with capitalism by early socialists was characterized as part of the birth-pains of the labor movement which in its mature phase could and did dispense with such "primitive" antisemitic stereotypes. Our own research, conducted over four decades, shows that the evidence does not warrant this apologetic interpretation.

A useful extension of Silberner's thesis first appeared in 1968 with George Lichtheim's seminal article on "Socialism and the Jews," which analyzed the anti-Jewish current in the European labor movement before 1914 as being "rooted in a complex of attitudes going back to the French Revolution and its impact upon traditional society." Lichtheim, while drawing extensively on Silberner's source material, shifted the focus of attention to "the complex process whereby European socialism in general, and French socialism in particular, shed its anti-Semitic aspects."[11] He considered the intertwining of anti-capitalist and anti-Jewish themes in 19th-century Socialist literature to be a consequence of the French Revolution, which had simultaneously unshackled the Jews and the market economy. Antipathy to Jewish emancipation and bourgeois liberalism was not, therefore, accidental among the early Socialists. The followers of Charles Fourier, for example, advocated a return to communitarian values and were hostile to the economic individualism of modern capitalist society, exemplified for them by Jewish high finance (*la haute banque*). Because he focused on French rather than German Socialists, Lichtheim's analysis tended to reinforce Silberner's thesis, although on a philosophical rather than historical level. At the same time it also appealed to some Marxist critics by arguing that:

> anti-Semitism could and did become an element of the *primitive* system of ideas in which the anti-capitalist reaction of the 1830s and 1840s at first presented itself."[12]

Lichtheim followed Silberner in characterizing the French Socialists, Alphonse Toussenel (1803–1885), Pierre Leroux (1797–1871), Pierre Joseph Proudhon (1809–1865) and Auguste Blanqui (1809–1881) as "antisemites" who saw in the Jews the incarnation of the spirit of Mammon, the inventors of the banking system, and the representatives of a new industrial feudalism. However, he also pointed to the streak of primitive barbarism, the hostility to "civility" and urban civilization which, in his view, linked the Russian revolutionary anarchist Bakunin with Proudhon and lay behind the visceral antisemitism of both men. Lichtheim did not deny that socialist Judeophobia in France continued to be a factor throughout the 19th century, but suggested that the Marxist "internationalist" wing of the labor movement gradually prevailed over the tradition of French "antisemitic" Socialism, whether Fourierist, Blanquist, or Proudhonist.

During the Dreyfus Affair (1894–1906), the national socialist antisemitism of the French Left was allegedly vanquished by a republican, universalist, non-antisemitic Socialism represented by Jean Jaurès. One problem with this thesis is that the anti-Dreyfusard and antisemitic type of national "socialism" did not disappear in France in the twentieth century and was indeed to enjoy a kind of belated revival under the Vichy regime (1940–1944). Moreover, the anarcho-syndicalists, beginning with Georges Sorel at the turn of the 20th century, continued to employ the standard vocabulary of antisemitism and this provided one of the primary roots for *rapprochement* on the eve of the 1914 war with the integral nationalists of *Action Française*. The extreme Left and the nationalist Right found common ground in France after the Dreyfus Affair in their hatred of Jewish finance, Jewish intellectualism, liberal republican democracy, and bourgeois parliamentarianism. The Proudhonist tradition of national socialism was revived in France, by both Left and Right, as demonstrated by Zeev Sternhell—providing one of the major ideological roots of modern fascism during *La Belle Epoque*.[13] Earlier research by the American historian George L. Mosse had also demonstrated that the French Right managed to influence the working classes with national "socialist," xenophobic, and racist-antisemitic ideas before 1914.[14] This further undermined the simplistic notion that the industrial proletariat was immune to what Marxists usually classify as "reactionary bourgeois ideologies" like antisemitism.

Historical research focused on France has tended, therefore, to indicate that some of the principal themes of 20th-century antisemitism derived from a cross-fertilization of concepts between Left and Right. They resulted from the fusion of socialist, nationalist, and conservative ideology which eventually constituted a major component in interwar fascism. *L'idéologie française* (Paris, 1981), a polemical work by Bernard-Henri Lévy, argued indeed that just as Germany was originally the fatherland of Marxism, so France was and remains the classic land of fascism and "national" socialism. The tradition of socialist antisemitism could be looked at and analyzed from this viewpoint as a component part of the dominant "French ideology," centered on the formula "France for the French" invented by such fin-de-siècle nationalist thinkers as Edouard Drumont and Maurice Barrès. Antisemitism, seen from this perspective, might best be understood as the single most effective integrationist ideology to have transcended the Left-Right schism in French society.

Biographies dealing more narrowly with Marx and his writing on the "Jewish Question," long ago began to challenge the conventional wisdom that Marxism was an internationalist ideology impervious to antisemitism. The political philosopher, Robert Misrahi, in his *Marx et la question juive* (Paris, 1972) showed, for example, that *structural* antisemitism was indeed rooted in the mode of thought of the young Marx. But he argued that this was an archaic pattern of prejudice, a victory of passion over reason, a manifestation of opportunism and subjective choice, rather than a sociological or political necessity for the labor movement. Others, including the present author more than thirty-five years ago, suggested that in the case of Marx and many of his disciples in the Socialist movement, anti-Jewish stereotypes had been internalized through the impact of the Christian environment and nationalist context in which they operated.[15]

There are also historians who, on the basis of their correspondence and journalistic articles, have charged both Marx and Engels with antisemitic and racist tendencies.[16] They stress the extent to which Marx's antisemitism was in the past played down and even ignored "in some popular socialist accounts of Marx's career published in the West and intended for radical and socialist consumption."[17] In the 1970s, a well-researched study by Julius Carlebach reexamined the claim that Marx was the *fons et origo* of Socialist antisemitism, as well as reviewing some of the subsequent polemical literature on the subject. Carlebach pointed out that the young Marx was indeed aggressively hostile to Jews and Judaism, but suggested that once his conception of historical materialism had matured, his attitude became more balanced. In Marx's final period, Jews "ceased to be of interest or consequence" to the author of *Das Kapital.*[18] Carlebach accepted that the second half of the young Marx's essay "must be regarded as an anti-Semitic document," one which gave an aura of social and philosophical respectability to popular stereotypes. But Carlebach's book did not tackle the crucial question as to how far and in what ways Marx's opinions on the Jews influenced the European labor movement.

This has indeed been a principal theme of my own research, which not only traces Marx's ideological influence, but demonstrates the multiple causes and consequences of antisemitism in the labor movement. They include retarded economic development in Central and Eastern Europe, the Christian cultural inheritance, the fragility of political liberalism outside Western Europe and North America, the intensity of national conflicts and the quality of leadership and class consciousness within the proletariat itself.[19] Without taking this multiplicity of factors into account within the broad context of late 19th- and early 20th-century European society, culture, and politics, one cannot hope to disentangle the complex relationship between Socialism and antisemitism. In my view, the period between 1830 and 1900, was crucially important in the crystallization of anti-Jewish stereotypes (some inherited from the Middle Ages and others of more recent origin) among radical ideologues of the Left.[20]

Before the late 1880s the existing labor movements in Europe had not yet evolved into distinctive mass parties of industrial workers with a fully developed class-consciousness, an independent subculture, or a unified political ideology. Marxism had not yet been endorsed as the dominant world-view of any single European labor movement, though after 1880 it began to consolidate its grip in Imperial Germany, in the wake of Bismarck's anti-Socialist laws. Antisemitism itself also started to crystallize in the form of organized political parties during this same decade as a mass movement in Germany, Austria, Hungary, and France.

It had evolved from ideological antisemitism and the radical critique of Judaism pioneered in France and Germany during the 1840s. It was this earlier period that saw the emergence of the "Jewish Question" and an extensive debate on emancipation, centered mainly in Germany.[21] It was in Young Hegelian circles—that section of the nascent radical German intelligentsia which opposed the established institutions in the Prusso-Christian state—that one can first observe the transition from traditional anti-Judaism to a secular, "scientific" form of Jew-hatred.[22]

Modern racial antisemitism in Germany, like Marxism itself, grew out of this *secular* anti-Judaism expressed in the writings of such philosophical radicals as Bruno Bauer, Ludwig Feuerbach, Friedrich Daumer, Friedrich Wilhelm Ghillany, Richard Wagner, and Wilhelm Marr during the 1840s. The Young Hegelians built on the post-Christian (and anti-Christian) tradition of 18th-century French Enlightenment *philosophes* such as Voltaire and d'Holbach whose rationalist attack on the Old Testament held Jewry and Judaism responsible for the "barbarism," fanaticism, and intolerant obscurantism which the Catholic Church had inflicted on the world.[23] From Voltaire and the Baron d'Holbach through to Bruno Bauer and Karl Marx, Judaism was attacked as the root of Christianity and as a symbol of human self-alienation. The early French and German radicals bequeathed to the European labor movement not only their rationalist anti-clericalism, but a "scientific" negation of Judaism as a fossilized religion, tradition, and way of life, as well as a hostile view of Jewry as an anti-social element. The leader of the Left Hegelians, Bruno Bauer, in his *Die Judenfrage* (1843), had depicted Jews as an ahistorical people whose stubborn particularism conflicted with the law of progress. The Jewish "essence" was presented as unchanging, separatist, bound to an illusory Mosaic law which excluded Jews from participating in the real life of nations and made it impossible for the Christian state to grant them emancipation.[24]

Twenty years later, Bruno Bauer was to emerge as one of the founders of the new antisemitism in Germany, arguing that Jews were racially incompatible with the German *Volk*.[25] Bauer, as in 1843, continued to emphasize the unchanging character of the Jewish Law and the *isolationism* of the Jewish people; only now these characteristics were attributed to blood and race, which could not be eliminated by conversion to Christianity or total assimilation. Karl Marx's polemic against Bauer in 1844 significantly did not take issue with the anti-Jewish elements in his ex-mentor's writings. Indeed

Marx emphasized that Bauer's critique of the Jewish religion, of "the religious opposition between Judaism and Christianity" and of the Christian State had been carried out with profundity, "in a style which is as precise as it is pithy and vigorous."[26]

Marx's assault on Jewry was even more radical:

> Let us consider the real Jews, not the *Sabbath Jew,* whom Bauer considers, but the *everyday Jew*. Let us not seek the secret of the Jew in his religion, but let us seek the secret of his religion in the real Jew. What is the profane basis of Judaism? *Practical* need, *self-interest*. What is the worldly cult of the Jew? *Huckstering*. What is his worldly god? *Money*. Very well: then in emancipating itself from *huckstering* and *money*, and thus from real and practical Judaism, our age would emancipate itself.
>
> An organization of society which would abolish the preconditions and thus the very possibility of huckstering, would make the Jews impossible. . . . In the final analysis, the *emancipation* of the Jews is the emancipation of mankind from *Judaism*.[27]

In these and other passages, Marx *goes beyond* Bruno Bauer and indicates that there will be no place for the Jew or Judaism in the truly liberated, human society that will one day exist under Communism. The Jew through whom "money has become a world power," who has "judaized" bourgeois society and "the practical spirit of the Christian nations," is for Marx the embodiment of egoism, commercialism and the capitalist spirit:

> The god of the Jews has been secularized and has become the god of this world. The bill of exchange is the real god of the Jew.[28]

Marx's "solution" for the "Jewish Question" was generally acceptable to the labor movement especially in Germany, Russia, and Austria-Hungary. The assumption was that the overthrow of capitalism would remove "the *empirical* essence of Judaism" or the sway of material self-interest and the alienation of man from man. It would, therefore, make impossible the "Jew" understood as a symbol of capitalism. "The *social* emancipation of the Jew is the *emancipation of society from Judaism*."[29]

Undoubtedly, Socialists with antisemitic inclinations could and did interpret this identifying of Judaism with the practice of buying and selling in an anti-Jewish way. Such Socialists or Communists were, of course, impervious to the fact that Marx's concept of the capitalist Jew applied (if at all) only to a minority of Jews in Western Europe. It was largely irrlevant to the majority of world Jewry who lived in the small towns or urban ghettos of tsarist Russia and Poland. Furthermore, the essay was itself accompanied by many highly uncomplimentary anti-Jewish remarks which appear in the Marx-Engels correspondence. In many cases, Marx would add to the proper name of a Jew such expressions as "der Jud," or "der verfluchte Jude" (the cursed Jew) while both he and Engels referred to their socialist rival Ferdinard Lassalle (himself a self-hating Jew) as "Baron Itzig," Jüdel Braun" or "Ephraim Gescheit"—all derogatory, antisemitic epithets widely used in Germany at that time. Moses Hess, an associate of Marx, Engels, and Lassalle in the German Socialist movement, would comment on his own party comrades in 1862:

> that in every personal controversy they make use of this [antisemitic] "hep" weapon, which in Germany seldom fails to have its effect.[30]

It was not only in private letters to Engels that Marx engaged in antisemitic outbursts. He savagely attacked Jewish financiers—Königswarter, Raphael, Stern, Rothschild, Mendelssohn, Bleichröder, Fould, and many others—for cooperating in raising loans for the Russian government to finance the Crimean War.

Marx went on to lash out at the "loan-mongering Jews" of Amsterdam,

> Many of whom are engaged in this gambling and jobbing of securities. . . . Here and there and everywhere that a little capital courts investment, there is ever one of these little Jews ready to make a little suggestion or place a little bit of a loan.[31]

Marx concluded his article by recalling: "that 1855 years ago Christ drove the Jewish money-changers out of the temple," and that once again the money-changers of our age enlisted on the side of tyranny "happen chiefly to be Jews."

There is no small irony in the fact that Marx, who so clearly repressed his own rabbinical background, should himself have been attacked as a Jew and the political movement which he led stigmatized as a "Jewish conspiracy" by Socialist and anarchist rivals such as the Frenchman Proudhon, the Russian Bakunin, and the German Eugen Dühring. Proudhon's celebrated quarrel with Marx was one factor which led the most influential thinker in the early French labor movement of the 19th century to observe in December 1847:

> Jews—Write an article against this race which poisons everything, by meddling everywhere without ever joining itself to another people—Demand their expulsion from France, with the exception of individuals married to Frenchwomen—Abolish the

> synagogues; don't admit them to any kind of unemployment; pursue finally the abolition of this cult.
>
> It is not for nothing that the Christians call them deicides. The Jew is the enemy of the human race. One must send this race back to Asia or exterminate it.
>
> H. Heine, A. Weil, and others are nothing but secret spies; Rothschild, Crémieux, Marx, Fould—malignant beings, bilious, envious, acrid, etc., etc., who hate us. By fire or fusion, or by expulsion, the Jew must disappear. . . .[32]

These savage remarks whose extreme antisemitism presaged that of the German Nazis, were confined to Proudhon's diary. But in his published work, Proudhon showed that his very personal hatred for Marx did not prevent him from sharing the latter's view on the "parasitic" role of the Jews and expressing this antipathy in unequivocally racist language.

> The Jew is by temperament an anti-producer, neither a farmer, nor an industrialist, nor even a true merchant. He is an intermediary, always fraudulent and parasitic, who operates in trade as in philosophy, by means of falsification, counterfeiting and horse-trading. He knows but the rise and fall of prices, the risks of transportation, the incertitudes of crops, the hazards of demand and supply. His policy in economics has always been entirely negative, entirely usurious. It is the evil principle, Satan, Ahriman incarnated in the race of Shem, which has already been twice exterminated by the Greeks and by the Romans, the first time at Tyre, the second time at Carthage.[33]

Bakunin and his followers, along with the Proudhonists, represented the chief opponents of Marx in the period of the First International (1864–1871), and they were no less antisemitic. The founder of Russian anarchism demonized the Jews as

> an exploiting sect, a bloodsucking people, a unique devouring parasite, tightly and intimately organized. . .cutting across all the differences in political opinion.[34]

In a passage dating from the end of 1871, Bakunin even asserted that Marx and the Rothschilds were linked by secret sympathies—the classic "Jewish conspiracy" thesis which was so effectively used by National Socialist propaganda during the twentieth century. Here is Bakunin's stunning revelation:

> This may seem strange. What can there be in common between communism and high finance? The communism of Marx wants a

> mighty centralization by the State, and where this exists there must nowadays inevitably be a Central State bank, and where such a bank exists, the parasitical Jewish nation, which speculates on the labor of the people, will always find a means to sustain itself.[35]

Bakunin's rabid antisemitism was shared by a number of Russian revolutionary populists who later defended the pogroms of 1881 in Russia as a rising of the masses against the "Jewish Tsar," the nobility and the Jewish "exploiters." Typical of their prejudices was the reaction of the Ukrainian revolutionary, Yantsin, who wrote an angry letter in 1876 to the exiled Russian populist leaders Lavrov, Smirnov, and their circle in London protesting against the efforts of Aron Liberman, the first Hebrew Socialist, to integrate the struggle of the Jewish masses with the Russian revolutionary movement. Rejecting the idea of class divisions among the Russian Jews, the Ukrainian Socialist claimed that:

> the weight of their [the Jews'] exploitation is great and their harmfulness unlimited.... If we find it possible to preach revolution, and only revolution against the nobles, how can we defend the Jews? ... We cannot have any faith in the laughable Yiddish International nor in the sympathies of the Yids for the Revolution.[36]

Another leading Ukrainian Socialist, Serge Podolinsky, declared in June 1876 that "in my view Yidophobia is as indispensable for every Russian socialist as is hatred of the bourgeoisie."[37] Podolinsky explicitly denied:

> even the possibility of the existence in Russia (not only in the Ukraine) of socialist *Zhidy* [derogative term meaning "Yid"] being completely sincere in their behavior as a socialist should be.[38]

The antisemitic prejudices of the Russian and Ukrainian Social Revolutionaries of this generation, active in the 1870s and early 1880s, were themselves shared by many Jews who had rebelled against their traditional Jewish heritage, were alienated from the Jewish collectivity, and had adopted Russian culture. Vladimir Iokhelson, a friend of Aron Liberman and one of these socialist Jews, explained their complete indifference to all things Jewish and their willingness to refer to Jews as kikes (*zhidy*) as a result of:

> our estrangement from the culture of the Russian Jews and. . .our negative assessment of their religious and bourgeois leaders. Regarding the Jewish lower classes we thought that the liberation

> of the whole of Russia would bring along the liberation of all nations living there. . . . One has to admit that Russian literature has instilled in us a view that Jewry was not a nation but a parasite class.[39]

The efforts of these Jewish radicals in the 1870s to "go to the people," to the Russian *moujiks* (peasants) in an attempt to identify themselves socially with the peasantry, failed miserably. They did not succeed in overcoming peasant hostility or the radical antisemitism prevalent in the Populist movement and as a result some, like Aron Liberman, acquired a renewed interest in the liberation of the Jewish people. The pogroms of 1881 and the indifferent, or even supportive, attitude of the Russian revolutionaries towards them shocked the Jewish radicals. On 30 August 1881 the executive committee of the revolutionary terrorist organization of Narodnaya Volya (The people's will) issued a proclamation to the Ukrainian people which vindicated the pogroms in Bakuninist style as a popular, anti-capitalist movement.

> The damned police beat you, the landowners devour you, the kikes, the dirty Judases, rob you. People in the Ukraine suffer most of all from the kikes. Who has seized the land, the woodlands, the taverns? The kikes. Whom does the peasant beg with tears in his eyes to let him near his own land? The kikes. Wherever you look, whatever you touch, everywhere the kikes. The kike curses the peasant, cheats him, drinks his blood. The kike makes life unbearable.[40]

This antisemitic attitude of the populist revolutionaries prompted Paul Axelrod, a leading socialist Jew and one of the founders of the first Russian Social Democratic organization (Liberation of Labor) and later of the Menshevik wing of the labor movement, to write a pamphlet describing the disillusion of young Jewish radicals. Axelrod admitted that the greatest disappointment of all for the Jewish student youth came:

> when they realized that the socialist-minded Russian students sympathized with the crusade against the Jewish masses and, worse yet, exhibited their antisemitic feelings toward their Jewish fellow-revolutionaries.[41]

The pogroms made a sizeable part of the Jewish socialist intelligentsia in Russia feel that they had made a mistake in forsaking the Jewish masses in the name of cosmopolitanism. For the first time they understood that the majority of Russian society, including the radical elements,

> considered all Jews—a pious Jewish worker, a petit bourgeois, a moneylender, an assimilated lawyer, a socialist prepared for prison or deportation—as kikes, harmful to Russia, whom Russia should get rid of by any and all means.

Nor was there any basis for believing in the indigenous laboring masses, for

> they lacked not only cosmopolitan feelings and ideas, but were wanting even in the idea of class solidarity among the poorer classes of Russia's nationalities.[42]

In this period, before the rise of an organized, class-conscious labor movement, socialism was easily reconcilable in Russia (as in Western and Central Europe) with antisemitic stereotypes. Moreover, it actively encouraged a negative view of the Jews as a *parasitic* element in the agrarian economy. The Russian Socialist-Revolutionary and Yiddishist, Chaim Zhitlovsky, recalled in his memoirs that his first encounter with socialist ideas in Russia forced him to conclude that Jews were, in the main, "parasites"; that as merchants, storekeepers, bankers, manufacturers, landowners, they were "exploiters, living. . .on the body of the laboring people, sucking their lifeblood, and condemning them to eternal poverty and enslavement." Zhitlovsky did not actually say that the new socialist ideology directly promoted antisemitism, "but if I would then have asked 'Are you for us or against us,' the answer definitely could not have been 'for you.'" Zhitlovsky explained that: "Socialism was a stream of ideas containing elements inimical to Jewish existence in the Diaspora" and that "between my Judeophilia and this socialism which regarded the whole Jewish people as a multitude of parasites yawned a chasm which I had to vault."[43]

Zhitlovsky's embrace of a socialism which had a pronounced Russian populist, agrarian-socialist character, made him reject with contempt all "philosemitism" as "justifying Jewish merchantry."

> Wherever I turned my eyes to ordinary, day-to-day Jewish life, I saw only one thing, that which the antisemites were agitating about: the injurious effect of Jewish merchantry on Russian peasantry. No matter how I felt, from a socialist point of view, I had to pass a death sentence not only on individual Jews but on the entire *Jewish* existence of individual Jews.[44]

However, by 1884, like many of his generation in Russia, the young Zhitlovsky had come to the conclusion that assimilation was bankrupt. For the rest of his active life he would seek to find ways to reconcile his Socialist ideas with Jewish nationalism and the problems of Jewish life. At the same time, by the late 1880s the growing influence of Marxism and Western-style "Social Democracy" in the Russian labor movement, along with the emergence of an industrial proletariat, encouraged Jews to join the revolutionary ranks in greater numbers. This, in turn, contributed to a diminution of the earlier antisemitic tendencies—a trend similar to that in the German labor movement.

The German workers' movement in its early phase before 1880 had undoubtedly made tactical concessions to prevailing antisemitic sentiments in German society. This was especially true of the Allgemeiner Deutscher Arbeiter-Verein (ADAV) founded by the fiery Ferdinand Lassalle in 1863, the year before his death. At this time the workers' party was still primarily a movement of artisans. Not until the 1880s and 1890s would the industrial proletariat take over as the dominant social force in the ranks of the Social Democratic Party and the trade unions. Among German artisans, who feared proletarianization and social decline, the tendency to equate Jews with modern capitalism had long been evident. In the 1860s there were antisemitic overtones evident from time to time in the German Socialist press, which blamed Jewish usurers for the plight of the artisans. But the main focus of antisemitic agitation in the ADAV was directed against the Jewish intelligentsia, the "Press Jews." This built on a tradition first created by Lassalle himself who had sometimes used antisemitic arguments in his polemics against the liberal-bourgeois press.[45]

Lassalle's successor as head of the ADAV, Johann Baptist von Schweitzer, also used antisemitic jargon in his attacks on Jewish capitalists like Leopold Sonnemann who were sympathetic to the workers and sought to develop a social-liberal program. On the other hand, the fact that Lassalle himself (like Marx) was a Jew probably tended to inhibit antisemitic rhetoric and propaganda. It did, at least, indicate that not all Jews sided with the bourgeoisie and that some of them had indeed embraced the cause of the German working class, providing it with outstanding leaders and men of science. However, there were relatively few Jews in the ADAV after 1870 unlike the Sozialdemokratische Arbeiterpartei (SDAP), the "Marxist" wing of the German labor movement. This was perhaps a reflection of the antisemitic tendencies in the Lassallean organization. The conflict between the two socialist organizations encouraged the ADAV to use anti-Jewish rhetoric as a weapon against the rival SDAP which was depicted as a "party of intellectuals" and as agents of the bourgeoisie. The editor of the *Neuer Social-Demokrat* (the main press organ of the ADAV), Wilhelm Hasselmann, was particularly aggressive in his attacks on the "Press Jews" as the greatest danger to the workers' movement. This anti-intellectual type of antisemitism was also shared by another leading neo-Lassallean agitator, Tölcke, and the new President of the movement, Hasenclever, who in 1872 wrote in the *Neuer Social-Demokrat*:

> [O]nly in Lassalle's organization, only in the *Allgemeiner Deutscher Arbeiter-Verein* can workers find the fulfillment of their aspirations, where all other organizations, spawned by the overheated imagination of arrogant Jew-boys and other mischief-makers, are falling apart. . . .[46]

Tölcke denounced efforts to unite the two workers' parties as being inspired by "boundless, typically Jewish arrogance" and he accused "Jewish speculators" of being behind the rival SDAP labor movement. The origins of Jewish members of the Marxist SDAP, like Eduard Bernstein, were stigmatized ("that honest-to-God little Jew") and the organ of the SDAP, *Volksstaat,* was dismissed as a "Jewish rag."[47] Agitators of the ADAV in the Berlin area did not hesitate to exploit the primitive antisemitic prejudices nourished by the post-1871 speculative boom and stock-market crash. Some, like the joiner Carl Finn, eventually joined the antisemitic Berlin movement of the 1880s. As members of the ADAV, Finn and other agitators characterized their Socialist opponents as *Mühlendammer* (after the Berlin district of Mühlendamm where Jewish retail shops and second-hand clothes dealers were concentrated)—claiming they behaved with all the "pushiness," deceit and low cunning of Jewish traders. Wilhelm Hasselmann went furthest in the demagogic use of antisemitism, distinguishing between Judaism as a "religious sect" and Jewry as a tribe of "worldly jobbers." Hasselmann claimed that:

> we shall never object to the paring of the flesh in the Judaic rite of circumcision, while strenuously opposing the Jewish habit of the paring of ducats.[48]

In election speeches Hasselmann encouraged farmers to believe that "the Jew" was responsible for their economic plight and in his journalistic articles he tried to prove with quotations from Marx, Lassalle, and Heine (all radical Jews) "that the Jews are the embodiment of egoism and that for centuries past they have been burrowing, haggling and deceiving." Hence it was necessary not only to exterminate the (Jewish) "press bandits," but to "lead the Jews altogether, with a few exceptions, not through, but into, the Red Sea." Hasselmann's macabre solution was as chillingly proto-genocidal as anything in Proudhon or Bakunin.

> Egoism must be exterminated, and for those who will not renounce it, death by drowning would only mean liberation from the bondage of devilish egoism.[49]

Although bitterly anti-Marxist (he denounced the "Marxist" SDAP as controlled by "Jewish wire-pullers") Hasselmann nonetheless invoked Karl Marx's 1844 essay on the Jews to support his theses. Indeed, he was the first German socialist to reprint the essay, claiming that Marx, and with him,

> all other clear-headed Socialists look upon the Jewish tribe as the nucleus of bourgeois society [*Bourgeoisgesellschaft*] and as the enemy of the workers' causes, bound to perish when the hour has come for the emancipation of the proletariat.[50]

Hasselmann clearly used Marx's "On the Jewish Question" for antisemitic purposes but went beyond the radical critique of Judaism (fashioned by the Young Hegelians in the 1840s) and the concept of Jewish money-worship developed by Marx. In an article entitled *Der Jüdische Stamm* (The Jewish tribe) published on 6 November 1872, Hasselmann abandoned any pretense at an objective analysis of class society and denounced the "naked selfishness" of the Jews as a "congenital defect of that tribe" which had "a pernicious effect on all nations and all states." "The Jewish tribe," Hasselmann concluded, "is exploitation of the workers personified"—it is *the* enemy of the proletariat. This crude type of antisemitism with its naturalistic imagery of the Jews as an alien *Volkskörper* corroding the national organism was exactly parallel to and in effect preceded that which developed in Germany after 1880 in the racist writings of Wilhelm Marr, Otto Glagau, and Eugen Dühring. All of them were radical writers and journalists with a quasi-socialist background. In the climate of social aggression engendered by the stock-market crash and the assault on Manchester liberalism in the 1870s, this type of antisemitism (distinctly "leftist" in flavor) flourished. Otto Glagau, the pamphleteer whose best-selling book on the stock exchange "swindlers" had been published in 1876, had, like Hasselmann, identified the social with the "Jewish" question, *homo capitalisticus* with the iniquities of Jewish merchants and bankers. He consciously appealed to the embittered artisans and small businessmen who had been badly hit by the crash, declaring that the "Semites" aimed at imposing their tribal racial domination over German Christians through the banks, the stock exchange, the liberal parties, and the State.

The message of Wilhelm Marr was similarly tinged with democratic radicalism. His hatred of Jews, like that of his contemporaries who had come from the radical republican Left, owed nothing to Christian theology. A veteran revolutionary of 1848, Marr explicitly rejected the notion of "religious hatred," just as did Socialist antisemites of the Hasselmann/Dühring variety. He was violently anti-clerical, as anti-Catholic as he was anti-Jewish. Like Voltaire, Feuerbach, Bruno Bauer, Daumer, and other radical Hegelians of the 1840s, Marr convinced himself that Judeo-Christian monotheism was "a malady of human consciousness," the root of all tyranny and evil. Like Dühring and the French Socialist disciples of another violently anti-clerical atheist, Auguste Blanqui, the tenacious Wilhelm Marr saw the struggle against "Semitism" as a racial struggle against Judaism and Christianity, which had to be superimposed on the class-struggle over which it took precedence.[51]

Dühring, the academic socialist who exercised considerable influence on the German labor movement in the mid-1870s (significant enough to oblige Engels to devote an entire book to demolishing his theories), took Marr's racial-biological antisemitism even further. By 1881 he was calling for a compulsory Jewish return to the ghetto and a war of liberation of the modern "Aryan" peoples against the Judeo-Christian "yoke" of the Old and New Testaments. Christianity was part of the problem rather than the solution. It was a product of the "Asiatic" legacy of Semitism to the West which had to be stripped off if the Germanic peoples were ever to emancipate themselves. Both Dühring and Marr insisted, like the socialist antisemites, that the Jews were not merely a religious group but a tribal-racial community (*Stamm*) whose characteristics were incompatible with the German people—a view already put forward in the early 1860s by Bruno Bauer.

Such ideological confusion allowed radical antisemitism to masquerade as an acceptable form of "socialism" in some sections of the labor movement. Nevertheless, the efforts of Hasselmann, Dühring, and others did not ultimately succeed in persuading the rank-and-file that Jewish capital was the prime enemy of the German working class. The "Jew" as anti-symbol ultimately proved insufficient as a rallying-point for the frustrations and animosities of the German proletariat. By 1880 both Hasselmann and Dühring had left the labor movement which began to firmly oppose the efforts of the Protestant court preacher Adolf Stöcker to win over the industrial workers to his antisemitic Christian-Social Party in Berlin.[52]

Dühring's influence over the Berlin Social Democrats, which had reached its peak between 1874 and 1877, declined for reasons largely unconnected with his antisemitism. Neither Eduard Bernstein nor August Bebel, who had been among his early disciples, dealt with or opposed his antisemitic remarks (directed inter alia against Marx and Lassalle) nor did the Jews in the Party—nearly all of them highly reticent about their origins. Only Engels mentioned the problem of antisemitism in passing in his *Anti-Dühring* (1878) describing Dühring's hatred of the Jews as "if not specially Prussian, at any rate a specifically East Elbian," characteristic of the Junkers (landed gentry) and a Conservative weapon against the working class.

The change in attitude of Engels (whose correspondence with Marx shows that he partly shared the latter's anti-Jewish prejudices) appears to have had a political motivation. It was clearly a reaction to the anti-Socialist laws of 1878 and to the efforts of Bismarck's spiritual *gendarme* in Berlin, the court preacher Adolf Stöcker, to win the workers over to "Governmental Socialism" and to channel their frustrations against the Jews. It was the danger of the Stöcker agitation to their own survival as an independent labor movement, rather than sympathy for the Jews which ensured the opposition of the workers' leaders to the Protestant court preacher and his antisemitic crusade. Hence in the 1880s the battle against political antisemitism became part of the socialist struggle against the Conservative ruling classes in Germany. But the battle to immunize their own supporters against antisemitic slogans did not alter negative stereotypes of German Jewry as belonging to the exploiting classes, nor did it eliminate altogether the antisemitic vocabulary of an earlier era. But it did hold in check open expressions of *political* hostility to the Jews after 1880.

The situation was very different in France, the cradle of European Socialism, where left-wing antisemitism had its oldest tradition. The Socialists of the 1830s and 1840s reacted to what they regarded as the consequences of the Jewish emancipation (which had occurred forty years earlier) as part of the thrust of the victorious French bourgeoisie towards establishing a modern economy, based on free trade, social mobility, and economic individualism. Fourier had already denounced the emancipation of the Jews as among the most "shocking actions" of the great French Revolution—

> doubly impolitic in that it opens the door to parasites and unproductive people, all of whom are devoted to trade and not to agriculture. An enlightened policy would have excluded these people as a social contagion.[53]

Fourier's abuse of Jews as "parasites," "merchants," and usurers"—a race which "had achieved nothing in art and science" and who "are distinguished only by a record of crime and brutality" was echoed by his followers. It was further intensified by the rivalry between his school and the Saint-Simonian movement in France. The "philosemitism" and sympathy with Jewish messianism of the Saint-Simonians was well-known, as was their affirmation of the Industrial Revolution.[54] The Fourierists, on the other hand, were implacably hostile to the progress of commercial-industrial civilization, to the banking and capitalist system, denouncing Jewish financiers with the same fervor that the Saint-Simonians had extolled their civilizing mission. Fourier's disciple, Alphonse Toussenel, sharply expressed this populist hatred of capitalism in his *Les Juifs, Rois de l'Époque*—which was the Bible of French antisemitism until the appearance of Edouard Drumont's even more scurrilous *La France Juive* forty years later. This best-selling work, according to Drumont, had been consciously influenced by his socialist predecessor. From the outset, Toussenel defined

> by the despised name of Jew every dealer in money, every unproductive parasite living off the work of someone else. Jew, usurer, money-dealer—all are synonymous to me.[55]

For Toussenel, like the Christian Socialist, Pierre Leroux, the "Jewish spirit" was identical with capitalism and money-worship. As Leroux put it in 1846, "*l'esprit juif*" was a synonym for "the mentality of gain, of profit, of exploitation, the mentality of banking."[56] This updating of the medieval Christian image of the Jew as moneylender to fit the new social realities of early industrial capitalism in France (which developed under the auspices of the "Bourgeois Monarchy" of Louis Philippe between 1830 and 1848) was especially popular in socialist circles. However, in Toussenel's lexicon, the term "Jew" was stretched to cover every form of capitalism, irrespective of nationality or religious denomination. It was especially used as a weapon against the French Jews and the *bourgeoisie protestante* (the Protestant bourgeois oligarchy), who together with the Rothschilds and their associates, dominated French banking and government. In addition to denouncing Jewish-Protestant influence, Toussenel's antisemitic vocabulary had a strong Anglophobic edge—a theme echoed by Proudhon in 1847 who wrote in his diary: "the hatred of the Jew, as that of the English, must be an article of our political faith."[57]

Victorian England of the 1840s and 1850s, it must be remembered, was regarded by French Socialists with particular venom. It was not just the hereditary enemy (this element of nationalist rhetoric continued throughout the century), but the cradle of modern industrialism and commercial imperialism, responsible for the "pernicious" doctrines of classical economics, unrestrained liberal individualism and Malthusianism. For some French leftists (children of a Catholic agrarian culture and powerfully influenced by the revolutionary nationalism of 1789), Protestant Britain and especially the Bible-fearing, "rapacious" English (the "nation of shop-keepers" in Napoleon's famous phrase) went hand in hand with Judeophobia. Toussenel, like the integral right-wing nationalists of Action Française at the beginning of the 20th century, saw the root of the modern exploitative ethic in the Judaic teaching absorbed by the Protestant nations, especially Great Britain, the United States, the Netherlands, and Switzerland.

> Who says Jew also means Protestant, and it is inevitable that the Englishman, the Dutchman and the Genevan who learn to read the will of God in the same book as the Jew [the Bible], profess the same contempt as the Jew for the laws of equity and the rights of the workers.

Unlike the Englishman, "the Jew" represented, however, an *internal* enemy who had successfully seized control of France and inaugurated the reign of a new industrial feudalism:

> The French people, supposedly emancipated by the revolution of '89 from the yoke of the feudal nobility, has only changed masters.

By obtaining a monopoly control over the banks and railways, the cosmopolitan Jewish financiers like Rothschild, Fould, and Péreire had become "the kings of the epoch." Under their sway

> Europe is entailed to the domination of Israel. This universal domination, of which so many conquerors have dreamed, the Jews have in their hands.[58]

Toussenel's antisemitic socialist vocabulary, his image of the Jews as "a nation within the French nation," as a conquering cosmopolitan tribe, and a deicidal race especially hostile to Catholicism, exercised a great influence on late-19th-century antisemitism. Edouard Drumont openly admitted:

> my sole ambition after long literary labour would be that my book might take its place beside his [Toussenel's work] in the libraries of those who would understand the causes which have brought ruin and shame to our country.[59]

Toussenel, it might be argued, was an antisemite who happened also to be a Socialist, but that did not lead to disapproval from the French Left. We have already cited Proudhon, but not his remark in the summer of 1847 under the heading "Work to be done" that, with regard to the Jews, "what the people of the middle ages hated by instinct, I hate upon reflection, and irrevocably." The only solution Proudhon could see was, as he put it, to accomplish the wish of Voltaire—"I hate this nation. . .it must be sent back to Jerusalem."[60] Such antisemitically motivated "Zionism" would later be echoed by Dühring, Marr, and the Hungarian antisemite von Istoczy.

It is curious that an atheist anticlerical like Proudhon could blame the Jews for not following Jesus and yet deny the Jewish ancestry of the founder of Christianity. Proudhon insisted on the "Aryan" origins of monotheism—one of several indications that in the 1860s the myth of "Aryan" superiority over the "Semites" had begun to infiltrate French socialist circles. It was, however, the followers of the revolutionary insurrectionist and militant atheist, Louis Auguste Blanqui, who first systematically developed this racial type of antisemitism in the French labor movement. It was they who would popularize the doctrines invented in France in the 1850s by Count Gobineau and Ernest Renan.

Blanqui himself was a radical antisemite in the 18th-century rationalist tradition of Voltaire and Baron d'Holbach. His primary target was the Catholic Church and he regarded Christianity as the most ferocious of the "terrible monotheistic sects" whose function was to reduce the people to a mass of docile beasts in the hands of clerics, capitalists, and aristocrats. The watchword of Blanqui and his followers, *Ni Dieu, Ni Maître,* expressed the central role of the war against all religion and authority in their socialist ideology—especially the destruction of Judeo-Christian monotheism. At the same time, Blanqui and his chief lieutenant Gutave Tridon, who wrote *Du Molochisme juif* in 1868 (it was first published only in 1884), soaked up the new racialism, expressing the hatred of "Semitism," which became fashionable at the end of the Second Empire. Tridon presented the Semites as the "evil genius of the world" who worshipped a perverse, sadistic God, practiced cannibalism, ritual murder, and human sacrifice. Jewish Moloch-worship with its alleged blood-lusts (this myth had been developed in the 1840s by the Young Hegelians in Germany like Daumer, Ghillany, Bruno Bauer, and even Moses Hess) was, according to the Blanquists, the root of Christian sacrifice. The modern Moloch was the lust for profit of modern capitalism. Tridon, like Blanqui and Proudhon, regarded the Jews as the nation par excellence of rapacious "swindlers" and "Shylocks." The origins of exploitation in the contemporary era went back to the Bible and the covenant by which Israel had been given universal domination over the nations. The Jews were the archetype of "Semitism" (the "shadow in the picture of civilization")—whom the liberal French scholar Ernest Renan had already "proved" to be inferior to the Aryans in culture and creativity. It was, therefore, the task of revolutionary Socialists "to fight the Semitic spirit and ideas" in the name of the "Indo-Aryan race."[61]

The *racist* antisemitism of the Blanquists was much appreciated by Edouard Drumont who had recognized, among French socialists in the 1880s some of his most important precursors. "Of all the revolutionaries," he wrote in *La Fin d'un Monde* (1889), "only the Blanquists have had the courage to refer to the Aryan race and to proclaim that race's superiority." It was no accident that during the Dreyfus Affair, the nationalist wing of the Blanquist party adopted an extreme anti-Dreyfusard and antisemitic position, branding French Jews as "Prussians from within." They were the prime agents of the enemy across the Rhine and of an international capitalist conspiracy against the French working class.

In France there was no immediate turning point in Socialist attitudes to the "Jewish Question" after 1880, similar to that which occurred in Germany or tsarist Russia. The continuity in left-wing antisemitism was maintained and not challenged until the Dreyfus Affair clearly demonstrated that Jew-hatred could become a powerful political weapon of the French Right, the Church and the Army in its struggle against the Republic. Hence it became politically dangerous to the working class. In the 1880s and 1890s, however, socialist antisemitism seemed more respectable than previously in France. This was partly the result of the crash of the Catholic bank, Union Générale, in 1882 (widely attributed to the machinations of the Rothschilds) and a series of financial scandals culminating in the Panama Affair of 1893 in which a number of German-Jewish financiers were involved. Even the mainstream socialist theoretical journal, *Revue Socialiste,* edited by Benoît Malon, adopted an antisemitic line in the 1880s (Malon had been influenced by Proudhon and Bakunin in his earlier years)—publishing, for example, a series of articles entitled "Aryens et Sémites" from 1887–1889. Their author, an ex-Communard and Blanquist, Albert Regnard (1832–1903), claimed that capitalism was mainly "a Jewish creation" whereas Socialism "is a Franco-German creation, Aryan in the fullest sense of the term."[62]

Regnard, drawing heavily on the ideas of Gobineau, Renan, and various racist authors, sought to prove "Aryan" (which included the Graeco-Roman, Indian, Persian cultures) superiority over the nomadic, sterile, materialistic "Semitic" race. Though scarcely different from the antisemitic stereotypes in *La France Juive,* Regnard's "scholarly and superb study," which breathed the spirit of genuine "Aryanism," was welcomed by Malon, who had recently introduced his friend Drumont to Parisian workingmen. Moreover, Malon threw open the columns of *Revue Socialiste* to Auguste Chirac, another socialist antisemite who sought to adapt Toussenel's lexicon to the conditions of the Third Republic. Chirac's attacks on the *féodalité financière* used the same sweeping definition of *la juiverie* (Jewry in a pejorative collective sense) which claimed to embrace capitalists of all denominations—Jewish, Protestant and Catholic. However, it was apparent to all that Chirac's "Kings of the Republic" were primarily Jewish international financiers engaged in shady deals who were ruining France as well as undermining other European states.[63]

The rise of the chauvinist wave of revanchism associated with General Boulanger in 1886 favored a new coalition of Conservative, Catholic, nationalist, and socialist elements, leading for the first time in France to the use of antisemitism as an electoral weapon. It was on the back of this Boulangist hysteria that demagogic populist politicians and journalists like Edouard Drumont, Maurice Barrès, Henri Rochefort, and the Marquis de Morès now developed a national-socialist ideology in which antisemitism was a central element. They blamed *la haute banque juive* (the Rothschilds above all) for working class misery and argued that the expropriation of Jewish fortunes would be a revolutionary act of liberation. In his *Le Testament d'un anti-Semite* (1890), Drumont even predicted that the day would come when "a man of the people," "a Socialist leader" independent of the "synagogue" would take up his campaign and rally the *déclassés*—the oppressed, the disinherited and uprooted of all classes—around his national-social-antisemitic banner. This was an uncanny anticipation of German National Socialism *avant la lettre*.

The Boulangist deputy, Maurice Barrès adopted a similar line in the 1890s, as did other French antisemitic leaders like the Marquis de Morès and Jules Guérin who embellished their populist demagogy with "socialist" rhetoric designed to attract the workers. It was Guérin, for example, who coined the phrase: "Plus on est loin des juifs, plus on est près du peuple" and defined antisemitism as "a precise and formal claim of national labour against Jewish speculation." Antisemitic "socialists" of this type, like the socialist antisemites who preceded them, regarded the "Jew" as the embodiment of capital and as the enemy of the worker. During the Dreyfus Affair, however, they went even further and attacked the leaders of the Socialist movement as mercenaries of Rothschild and the "Jewish system." By supporting the bourgeois Republic dominated as it was by Jews, Protestants, freemasons, liberal cosmopolitans, and the yoke of finance capital, they had reduced the French workers to becoming "slaves of the Jew."

The refusal to participate in the rehabilitation of Captain Dreyfus became, for the antisemitic section of the French Left, part of their general struggle against the organized "Jewish syndicate" which they believed was out to ruin France for its own profit. Even the official Marxist Left led by Jules Guesde and the mainstream pro-republican Socialists who followed Jaurès, believed for a time that the agitation on behalf of Dreyfus's release was nothing but an attempt by the Jewish financial bourgeoisie to regain its hegemonic position. It was only Emile Zola's forceful intervention on behalf of Dreyfus and against the military clique that first split this consensus of the parliamentary Socialist group. The "moderates" argued that Dreyfus's cause was unpopular and that intervention on his behalf was electorally imprudent; Jaurès, Guesde, and Vaillant (leader of the Blanquist-Marxist wing of the labor movement) were converted to a more positive view, but the manifesto they composed on 19 January 1898 still claimed that "the Jewish capitalists, after all the scandals which have discredited them, needed to rehabilitate themselves" and "to wash out the stains of Israel."

French Socialists, like their German, Austrian, and Polish comrades, when accused of being lukewarm or indifferent to the danger of antisemitism, invariably replied that antisemites were "incipient Socialists." Even the cry of "Death to the Jews," which was sweeping France in early 1898, was initially shrugged off as if it was a marginal item of the proletarian revolution. The Dreyfus case did, however, lead some French Socialists and anarchists to reject antisemitic chauvinism and to use the Affair as a means to rally the workers against their traditional enemies, the Army and the Church. Not a few, who had flirted with an antisemitically-tinged socialism before 1900, would change their spots once they understood that Judeophobia was a powerful weapon in the hands of the counter-revolutionary Right.

Although the Marxist Parti Ouvrier Français declared its neutrality in the Affair, the more liberal wing of French Socialism led by Jean Jaurès came to see in antisemitism a political danger to the labor movement no less grave than militarism, clericalism, and extreme nationalist hysteria. The emergence of a "Dreyfusard" Socialism ready to defend the Republic did not, however, eliminate left-wing antisemitic stereotypes in France—especially among syndicalist intellectuals like Georges Sorel, Edouard Berth, and Robert Louzon. They greeted the victory of the Dreyfusard forces as a triumph for "the Jewish party" over its Catholic rivals. Some syndicalists like Emile Janvion and Emile Pataud even claimed that the Jews, through their alleged control of high finance and freemasonry, had infiltrated and neutralized the labor movement. Together they sponsored a mass meeting in Paris in April

1911 which was advertised as "a great anti-Jewish and anti-Masonic demonstration."[64]

The antisemitic syndicalists who claimed that socialist internationalism only benefited the "kikes" at the expense of honest French workers, clearly had some popular support. Their campaign against capitalism, philosemitism, Jewish immigrant workers, and also against the "Dreyfusard" Socialists led by Jaurès, was enthusiastically welcomed by the integral nationalists. The most important of the syndicalist intellectuals in France, Georges Sorel, who in 1898 had been a Dreyfusard, went in a virulently antisemitic direction, turning his back on bourgeois democracy and denouncing Jaurès's moderate, parliamentary Socialism. Sorel's concern for the national tradition, his obsession with myth, his hatred of liberalism and "class collaboration"—above all, his cult of heroic irrationalism—undoubtedly influenced his turn to antisemitism. Between 1908 and 1914 he was one of the driving forces of the Cercle Proudhon which attacked democracy as a "Jewish" invention that had substituted "the laws of gold for the laws of blood." Like the integral nationalists and monarchists of Action Française, the anarcho-syndicalist Sorel blamed Jews for the decomposition of traditional European culture, linking them to the nefarious impact of liberalism, capitalism, and rationalism. A specifically socialist variant of antisemitism continued, therefore, to exist within the French labor movement and on its intellectual fringes before 1914. The evidence suggests, however, that the crisis provoked by the Dreyfus Affair did weaken its grip, at least among those in the labor movement who came to see in antisemitism a direct threat to republican democracy. Only in the late 1930s would left-wing antisemitism revive in France in the wake of pacifist trends and the desire to avoid any confrontation with Nazi Germany.

Socialist antisemitism also had significant presence in liberal England, described in 1900 by Theodor Herzl as "the one spot left throughout the whole world in which God's ancient people are not detested and despised." Although Great Britain appeared to many Jews as an island of tolerance and sanity compared to the rampant antisemitism that had spread across the European continent, it was by no means free of the anti-Jewish virus. Indeed, British Socialists played a not insignificant part in fueling it. The marked increase in alien Jews, mainly from Russia and Poland, who had fled persecution in Eastern Europe and arrived in England in the 1880s and 1890s increasingly provoked fears of the indigenous proletariat for their jobs. This was especially true in the East End of London where most new immigrants were concentrated and the problem of social pauperism was already acute. It was not too difficult for political agitators to fan the irrational hatreds and prejudices of the slum dwellers against "destitute aliens" (a codeword for Russian Jews); claiming that they were driving British workmen out of the labor market, lowering the moral tone of their neighborhoods, reducing wages, and encouraging nihilist violence.[65]

Radical and trade-union leaders, no less than Conservatives and imperialists, saw the vote-catching potential of *anti-alienism* and calls for the restriction of foreign immigration. Virtually all the big British unions, from the dockers to the miners, engineers, carpenters, shoemakers, and tailors favored restriction of immigration. Trade-union leader John Hodge, presiding over a session of the twenty-fifth Trades Union Congress (TUC) at Glasgow (September 1892), condemned the "enormous immigration of destitute aliens" who "take work at any price," so that "the tailoring and kindred trades have been practically ruined." The TUC passed, not for the last time, a resolution calling for government legislation to stop the entry of pauper aliens. The fact that immigrants' trades were mostly sweated trades, that the Yiddish-speaking Jews kept to themselves, and that they were more socially mobile than working-class Gentiles, added to tension in a period of economic stress and unemployment. The Socialist Beatrice Webb, who observed the Jews of Whitechapel in the late 1880s, even claimed that they were altogether indifferent to class solidarity and professional ethics, that they had no desire for trade-union organization and undercut the wages of their fellow-workers. They were solely concerned with preserving themselves and their families, motivated by the love of profit and unmoved by sentiment or moral considerations. The Jewish immigrant, according to Beatrice Webb, "seems to justify by his existence those strange assumptions which figure in the political economy of Ricardo—an always enlightened selfishness, seeking employment or profit with an absolute mobility of body and mind. . . ."[66]

Alien Jews were constantly being accused, by representatives of such British trades as the tailors and the bakers and confectioners, of malpractice, of monopolizing local trade, of depressing business, and by other trade-union leaders of blacklegging (strike-breaking). In 1894 and 1895 the TUC repeated its resolutions against the admission of "pauper aliens." In the East End, anti-alienist sentiment was spreading in spite of genuine public distaste (expressed in Parliament and the press) for Russian-style pogroms or for the semi-hysterical antisemitism in France at the time of the Dreyfus Affair.

Most of the British working-class reaction was probably more xenophobic than antisemitic, an outgrowth of economic conflict and traditional native insularity. Antisemitism as an ideology was indeed officially condemned by many in the British Socialist movement as being in conflict with their civic norms of tolerance and internationalist ideals of brotherhood. Nevertheless, there was an indigenous English radical Judeophobic tradition which had manifested itself in the writings of William Cobbett during the early 19th century. Cobbett regarded the term Jew as synonymous with cheat, sharper, or rogue. There was also a growing economic antisemitism in socialist circles directed at the rich Jews of Hampstead, Bayswater, and the West End, and those prominent in international finance.[67] Beyond that, there were "progressive" English intellectuals like H. G. Wells, whose Edwardian-era novels link alien or monied Jews to the organic decline of England. They represent the acquisitive instinct at its worst and a parasitic plutocracy which was ruining the country. The Marconi Affair sharpened this antipathy. After World War I, Wells would display a particularly sharp animus towards Hebraic separatism, the biblical idea of the "Chosen People," and the irrepressible "national egotism" of Jewry. At the same time, Wells was also opposed to the more delusional forms of fascist antisemitism based on conspiracy theory, and expressed some admiration for universalist-minded Jews who shared his futurist ideals.

Socialist antisemitism first exploded in England during the Boer War (1899–1902), the most controversial conflict in British imperial history. The radical anti-war movement exploited the Jewish origins of prominent financiers in South Africa to influence public opinion and discredit the Conservative government. "Jewish finance" came to symbolize in the eyes of the radical Left everything shady and disreputable about the South African war. Jewish entrepreneurs like Barney Barnato, the Hamburg-born Alfred Beit, Lionel Phillips, the Albu brothers, and others with banking and business connections who had become millionaires through the discovery of diamonds and then of gold, symbolized a *nouveau riche* class of cosmopolitan financiers. They were now blamed for the imperialist machinations that had drawn Britain into the South African war. The anti-war British Left seized on an allegedly monolithic Jewish conspiracy even though many of the "Jewish" magnates had only marginal ties with Judaism, were frequently in conflict with each other and pursued individual or class rather than specifically Jewish communal interests. In this approach the Labour Left was much influenced by the liberal British economist John A. Hobson and his articles on the South African War. For Hobson, it was a small clique of international financiers, "chiefly German in origin and Jewish in race" who had plunged the British Empire into a disastrous war. They had achieved an alarming monopoly of economic power, controlling politics and legislation through bribery and other illicit means of persuasion. According to Hobson, writing in 1900, the Jews had succeeded in adding "the business of politics" to their many other businesses. The antisemitic tone of Hobson's work undoubtedly influenced many leftists in Britain, especially in Independent Labour Party circles and in the Marxist clique around Henry Hyndman.

The chief organ of the Social Democratic Federation (SDF), *Justice,* edited by Hyndman, was central to a vicious campaign against "Jewish plutocracy" which it saw as the soul of a sinister "Gold international." Hyndman and his followers had repeatedly identified "Judaism" with the corrupt domination of money during the 1880s and sympathized with the openly antisemitic campaign that developed in France during the Panama Scandal. In 1893 Hyndman had even described Jewish newspaper magnates in Britain as "poisoners of the wells of public information" and protested that "capitalist Jews of the baser sort are already influential in both our political parties."[68]

It was however the nexus between international Jewry and late-19th-century British imperialism, especially in Egypt and South Africa, which mainly preoccupied Hyndman and like-minded radicals. In a virulently hostile essay entitled "Imperialist Judaism in South Africa," he charged that Beit, Barnato, and their fellow-Jews were planning "an Anglo-Hebraic Empire stretching from Egypt to Cape Colony and from Beira to Sierra Leone."[69] Hyndman, Harry Quelch, and other left-wing radicals blamed the outbreak of the South African war on the "Jew-jingo" gang and the "Jew press," which had supposedly brainwashed the British public into supporting "piratical imperialism in the Transvaal and elsewhere." The Jewish financiers personified in Socialist eyes "that gold international which today dominates the Government and jingo press of all countries." *Justice* consistently referred to the South African war as the "Jew war in the Transvaal" engineered by a "Jew clique" around Joseph Chamberlain and Arthur Balfour, a war in which it was "us common Englishmen [who] shall have to pay. . .in blood."[70]

The blatant Judeophobia of Hyndman and his colleagues aroused some criticism in the columns of *Justice,* especially among Jewish members of the SDF. In a letter to the editor on 21 October 1899, Theodore Rothstein wrote:

> in Hyndman and in you [Harry Quelch] the Socialist movement of this country has two leaders ready—in theory, at least—to go hand in hand with Lueger [leader of the Austrian antisemites], Stoecker, Drumont and others. . . . [*Justice*] is preaching from its pulpit rank anti-Semitism. Is it not a strange and sad spectacle? . . . Referring recently to the part which you imagine Jew-capitalism had been playing all along in the Transvaal

> business, you express yourselves to the effect that you would not be surprised if an anti-Semitic movement were to arise in this country, as it did on the Continent. Nor should I, I may tell you candidly, were I sure of the wide influence of *Justice*; that very sentence is enough to have an anti-Semitic effect on the mind. . . .

Rothstein went on to ask how Jewish Socialists could combat the rise of Herzlian Zionism in the face of such left-wing antisemitism. How they could expect that Jew-hatred would disappear in a socialist society, given the hostile line that *Justice* had taken on "the subject of Jew-capitalism"? Other critics also objected to the race prejudice that Hyndman and his followers had "imbibed with their mother's milk" and to their "unsocialist attack on Jews" and after 1900 the overtly antisemitic campaign in *Justice* was somewhat moderated. One factor in this was the realization that such rhetoric damaged Socialist prospects of organizing the largely Jewish proletariat in such impoverished areas of London's East End as Tower Hamlets. At heart, however, Hyndman, Quelch, and their colleagues continued to believe in the "Jewish conspiracy," in a secret cabal that dominated the press and the stock exchanges of the world and was responsible for the imperialist plot to seize the gold-rich Boer lands in the Transvaal in order to enrich world Jewry.

The less ideologically-orientated *Reynolds News,* which saw itself as the guardian of the British working class, was no less hostile to the Jews, whether they were rich capitalists or poor foreign immigrants. It focused its attacks against the financiers, mostly "of German Jewish origins," or on the danger to British labor from impoverished Jewish aliens and on the "racial solidarity" of the Jews:

> who, by refusing to intermarry with the people among whom they dwell, and by their ever growing control of the money markets and Press of all civilized states, may probably establish. . .a dominancy which will keep the entire world in subjection.[71]

The Jews were presented as a strange Asian people, as being only nominally English, and as a "secret order established in the heart of every nation" in which each branch supported the other internationally—classic arguments of continental antisemitism. These outpourings of the popular press were echoed even by the most prominent British Labour leaders of the era, Keir Hardie and John Burns. They all shared the view, expressed by Hardie, that:

> modern imperialism is really run by half a dozen financial houses, many of them Jewish, to whom politics is a counter in the game of buying and selling securities.[72]

The anti-war movement in Britain as a whole was all-too-easily sucked into the conspiratorial view that the British government was itself in the hands of Jewish capitalists and "foreign financiers." The campaign rapidly escalated into a truly repulsive antisemitic terminology which characterized all Jews as "bloodsuckers" and corrupt vampires preying on innocent victims. John Burns, the Labour MP for Battersea, considered an outstanding leader of the labor movement in Britain, fully subscribed to the mythic vision of a Jewish conspiracy. In a speech in the House of Commons on 6 February 1900 he declared:

> Wherever we go in this matter we find the same thing. Wherever we examine, there is the financial Jew, operating, directing, inspiring the agonies that have led to this war. They were supreme at the South African Committee in 1897. I thought I had landed myself in a synagogue when I went to hear the trial of the Johannesburg prisoners before the Chief Justice. . . . The trail of the financial serpent is over this war from beginning to end.[73]

Burns's public rhetoric against the war resembled the antisemitic "socialism" rampant in France during the Dreyfus Affair, and his diaries reveal that he regarded all Jews, rich and poor, capitalist and proletarian, native and alien, with a similar hatred and contempt. The allegations of a "Jewish plot" spread by Burns and also to be found in the pamphlet literature put out by the anti-war leagues were generally accepted by the trade-union elite. In September 1900, the TUC passed a resolution condemning the war as designed "to secure the gold fields of South Africa for cosmopolitan Jews most of whom had no patriotism and no country."[74]

However, the British working class as a whole tended to support the South African war or else was indifferent to the issue, so that no systematic Jew-baiting on continental lines developed in Great Britain, though "anti-alien" agitation continued to be a central public issue. Even the crusading zeal of John Hobson, who relentlessly attacked "Jew power" in South Africa and denounced the manipulation of British foreign policy by a secret "racial confederacy," failed to mobilize public opinion. The image of a sinister Jewish elite seeking world domination proved to be more successful on the Continent where, ironically, it became linked with the Anglophobia that swept France and Germany in 1900 in the wake of the Boer War. Thus the alleged "robbery committed by international Jewry" was invariably linked by continental antisemites (especially on the Right) with British imperialist piracy against the "plucky Boers" fighting for self-determination.

In Germany and tsarist Russia antisemitic conspiracy theories at the beginning of the twentieth century had become the staple diet of the Radical Right. They were notably less common in the labor movement after the early 1880s. With a few exceptions, the German Social Democrats, who were steadily increasing their strength in electoral terms, resisted antisemitism as the "socialism of fools" in the classic phrase of their leader, August Bebel. There were, nonetheless, periodic attacks on Jews, mainly by right-wing Socialists like Wolfgang Heine (who resented the influence in the German Party of Russian- and Polish-born revolutionaries such as Rosa Luxemburg) or by Richard Calwer who wrote in 1894:

> For every good Jewish writer there will be found at least half a dozen who are altogether worthless, but who possess an extraordinary power of self-assertion and an inexhaustible flow of words, but no real understanding of socialism.[75]

But such barbs were far milder than the noxious hatred of Jewish socialist intellectuals expressed twenty years earlier by German left-wingers like Dühring and Hasselmann. More widespread was the Socialist ambivalence towards Jews that derived from the long-standing anti-liberalism in the party and expressed itself in a bizarre campaign against philosemitism in the 1890s. The main exponent of this line of thought was Franz Mehring, a highly regarded journalist and leading Marxist historian on the left wing of the German Social Democratic Party (SPD), whose views on the "Jewish Question" were strongly influenced by Karl Marx. Mehring denounced liberal philosemitism as a defense of capitalist privileges, as a hypocritical whitewash of rich Jews, while partly justifying German antisemitism in the 1890s as a movement of the downtrodden exploited peasantry and lower middle class.[76]

He firmly believed that the defense of capitalist Jews was a much greater crime or danger to the labor movement than antisemitism, which he saw as a primitive form of anti-capitalism. Mehring reinterpreted Marx's attack on "Judaism" in this spirit.[77] His hostility to *Geldjuden* and the anti-Jewish stereotypes he derived from Marx were prevalent and widely shared in the German labor movement, even by labor leaders like August Bebel who strongly opposed political antisemitism. In his speech to the SPD Party Congress in 1893 Bebel, quoting Fourier and Marx, even linked the Jewish preference for commerce to acquired racial characteristics. It was in his view "indisputable that the spirit of commerce—as Fourier calls it. . .is developed to a high degree in the Semitic race." Bebel insisted that "our whole society is based on haggling and money-making and therefore a Judaized society (*verjudete Gesellschaft*)," but that the "peculiar essence of the Jews" would disappear with the abolition of bourgeois society.[78]

In contrast to Marx and Mehring, Bebel, however, did emphasize that the Jews were an *oppressed* race and that the social role of Judaism was a result of Christian persecution and medieval legislation. Together with other leading German Marxist theoreticians like Engels and Kautsky, his negative stereotype of the social role of some Jews was partly balanced by recognition that there was a growing Jewish proletariat and labor movement in Eastern Europe.[79] Bebel held the view, first articulated by Engels, that antisemitism was the product of backward semi-feudal societies and declining social classes threatened by capitalism with which the German labor movement should have nothing to do. Like Kautsky, he also recognized that "the Jews have become an eminently revolutionary factor," even if Judaism itself was derisively treated as an obscurantist relic of the Middle Ages. In accordance with this questionable credo, German Socialists looked forward to the disappearance of corporate Judaism as an obstacle to human progress. But increasingly they welcomed the participation of Jews as individuals in the revolutionary movement across Europe as a whole.

A similar attitude of hostility to Judaism combined with appreciation of "progressive" Jewish revolutionaries developed in the Russian Marxist parties after the 1890s. The impact of Marxist theory and the growth of an industrial proletariat in tsarist Russia, together with the barbarous use of pogromist antisemitism by the autocratic Russian government, influenced the Russian Social Democrats to instigate a campaign against the deeply-rooted Judeophobia of the peasant masses. The revolutionary movement in Russia, swelled by the presence of many Jews driven into its arms by persecution and oppression, increasingly emerged as a defender of Jewish civil rights. Nevertheless, it did not always succeed in preventing Russian and Ukrainian workers from participating in pogroms, as happened in 1905.

The different factions in Russian Social Democracy, while opposed to antisemitism, fought equally hard against Zionism and the national "separatism" of the Bund, the leading Jewish Social Democratic organization in tsarist Russia and Poland. Basing themselves in part on the orthodox Marxist theories of Karl Kautsky, Russian Social Democrats (whether Bolshevik or Menshevik), denied that Jews constituted a nation. Instead, they were classified as a "caste" which continued to exist only because of the artificial segregation of the Pale of Settlement and the reactionary policies of the tsarist government. This was the position of Lenin, Trotsky, Stalin, Martov, and other Russian Marxist leaders—all of whom branded antisemitism as an extreme form of political reaction, diverting the hatred of workers and peasants away from their exploiters towards the Jewish minority. This anti-antisemitism went hand-in-hand with the rejection of demands for national autonomy for the five million Russian Jews in the Tsarist Empire. In their polemics against the Jewish labor movement, the Russian Marxists consistently denounced the advocacy by the Bund of federalism, non-territorial cultural autonomy, and claims to be "the sole representative of the Jewish proletariat" as bourgeois nationalism.[80] Plekhanov, the founder of Russian Marxism, was especially contemptuous of the Jewish Socialist Bund and his opinions were antisemitically tinged. According to Lenin's notes:

> He declared straight out that this is not a Social Democratic organization, but simply an organization of exploitation—to exploit the Russians. He felt that our goal is to kick the Bund out of the Party, that the Jews are all chauvinists and nationalists, that a Russian [*ruskaia*] party must be Russian and not "give itself into captivity to the tribe of Gad," etc. . . .[81]

Lenin's own polemics against the Bund were also extremely harsh but focused specifically against Jewish organizational separatism and national assertiveness. In 1903 he declared that "the idea of a separate Jewish people is politically reactionary and scientifically untenable." Indeed, in Lenin's view the notion of an independent Jewish culture was rejected out of hand. "Jewish national culture is the slogan of the rabbis and the bourgeoisie, the slogan of our enemies." At the same time, however, Lenin identified himself with the "progressive" elements among Jews in the Western world and warmly praised the contributions of Jewish revolutionaries to the Social Democratic movement. There was a more sympathetic tone to his position than that exhibited by Joseph Stalin, whose *Marxism and the National Question* (1913) also dealt extensively with the Bund and the "Jewish Question." Stalin perceived only the negative sides of Jewish culture and stressed the desire of the Bund to isolate itself from everything non-Jewish, calling it a nationalist *betrayal* of Marxism. The defense of Yiddish, Jewish hospitals, schools, and traditional holidays were seen as isolationist and regressive. The Jews could not, in any case, legitimately claim national rights since they were in Stalin's opinion, a *nebulous,* amorphous entity, lacking all the attributes of nationality. They had no common language, territory, economic life, or a community of culture. In other words, for Stalin the Jews were no more than a "paper nation" with no basis in this-worldly reality. They represented something mystical and intangible. Living dispersed in different parts of the world, never seeing one another or acting together in war or peace, how could they possibly be a true nation? Moreover, they had no "stable stratum connected to the soil"—whether in Russia or abroad. Divorced from the land and the peasantry, their national demands should be ignored.

Stalin's position was still within the tradition of doctrinal Marxist orthodoxy though tinged, even before 1914, with a Russian nationalism that was hyper-centralist and intolerant of minorities. Writing to his Bolshevik comrades in Baku during the 1907 London Congress of the Russian Social Democratic Party, Stalin had been unfavorably struck by the high percentage of Jews in the rival Menshevik faction. He felt compelled to record that

> one of the Bolsheviks. . .jestingly remarked that the Mensheviks were a Jewish faction while the Bolsheviks were *truly Russian* [my emphasis] and hence it would not be amiss for us Bolsheviks to instigate a pogrom in the party.[82]

The "jest" was made at a time when Russian antisemitism was at the peak of its prewar violence. The Black Hundred counterrevolutionaries had carried out many pogroms in the previous two years, about which Stalin had nothing to say. The fact that he could even jokingly contemplate "a pogrom in the party" during a period when the "non-existent" Jewish "paper nation" was being persecuted, humiliated, and murdered, speaks for itself. Nevertheless, Stalin (the "marvellous Georgian" as Lenin called him in 1913) managed to conceal his own antisemitism for approximately thirty years after writing his first essay on the "National Question." It was a remarkable feat of dissimulation.

The Austrian Social Democrats, who like the Russian party operated in a multi-national Imperial framework, were no less opposed to Jewish national autonomy, even though they had accepted it for other smaller peoples in the Habsburg Monarchy. Their chief theoretician, Otto Bauer (a Marxist Jew estranged from Judaism and Jewish culture) argued that "the Jewish workers should not demand national autonomy," because the Jews were a nation without a future, whose assimilation was historically inevitable. Even if one accepts that Otto Bauer was personally devoid of antisemitic prejudice, it is remarkable that he would deny to Jews what the Austro-Marxists accepted as valid for Germans, Poles, Czechs, South Slavs, and other smaller nationalities in Austria-Hungary—the right to develop their language, national individuality, independent schools, and culture.[83] After all there were over two million Jews in the Habsburg Empire—many of whom were asking for recognition as a "nationality" after 1900.

Otto Bauer's terminology was derived from Marx, making the untenable assumption that Judaism and Christianity were mere superstructures on a capitalist, economic basis and that the Jews were a "non-historical nation." Like other Austrian Democrats and their Polish allies in Galicia, Otto Bauer's disqualification of East European Jewry as a national entity had a self-evident political purpose—to weaken Jewish nationalism while strengthening the orientation of *Ostjuden* to the proletarian class-struggle. He patronisingly dismissed the Jewish masses (especially in Galicia) as backward, under the sway of clerical obscurantism and heirs of a petrified tradition which represented the antithesis of a Marxist approach to the "Jewish Question." His attitude reflected the ethnic death-wish displayed by many assimilated Jewish leaders of the Austrian Social Democratic Party, founded and guided for nearly thirty years by a converted Jew, Victor Adler, who in his youth had been an enthusiastic pan-German.[84]

Especially significant is the fact that the socialist antisemitism which developed in Austria during these years was more deep-rooted and persistent than elsewhere in Europe, though distinct from the antisemitic mass movements led by the pan-German Georg von Schönerer and the Catholic populist Karl Lueger before 1914.[85] Antisemitism had first infiltrated the Austrian labor movement in the period of "anarchist" confusion during the early 1880s—at a time when the antisemitic movement was more "oppositional," more "democratic" and radical in Austria than in Germany. In 1884 Karl Kautsky had written to Engels from Vienna and emphasized the danger:

> [I]t has been proved that a part of the anarchist leaders are in the pay of the antisemites. The latter are becoming significant in Austria; thanks to anarchist muddleheadedness the workers fall to them and we have trouble in keeping our own people from fraternizing with the antisemites.[86]

The petit-bourgeois, artisan background of the Austrian working class and the influence of German nationalism on some of its leaders like Victor Adler, Engelbert Pernerstorfer, and Heinrich Braun ensured that an antisemitic undercurrent would remain entrenched in the labor movement. The strength of clerical and nationalist antisemitism as mass movements in Austria—especially the electoral successes of the Christian Social Party led by Karl Lueger in the 1890s—drove the Socialists further on the defensive. Though they rejected an exclusive struggle against "Jewish" capitalism, the Social Democrats shared the unrelenting hostility of the antisemitic parties to Austro-liberalism. Liberalism (with its strongly Jewish coloring in Austria) was still regarded by many Socialists as the prime enemy of the labor movement. The so-called *Judenpresse* (which included such influential liberal newspapers as the *Neue Freie Presse*) was often presented by the socialists as far more dangerous than the antisemitic press. Moreover, the leaders of the Social Democrats realized that, given the electoral popularity of antisemitism in Austria, there was nothing much to be gained politically by defending Jews. On the contrary, such a defense would only play into the hands of the antisemites who, in any case, had branded Austrian Social Democracy as a "Jewish protective guard" because of its high percentage of Jewish-born leaders.

Thus in Austria the Socialists took a more opportunist position than in Imperial Germany, not infrequently exploiting Judeophobic nuances in their attacks on liberalism and even branding their Christian-Social rivals as "agents of Jewish capital."[87] Efforts at Jewish self-defense were stigmatized as an attempt to justify the financial power of the Rothschilds, the Jewish capitalists, and the liberal press. The "struggle against antisemitism" was caricatured as an egoistic mask for preserving Jewish-Liberal privileges. At the same time, Austrian Socialists defended the antisemitic movement as a "persecuted" party of the masses. If that were not enough, Jewish nationalism was frequently ridiculed by the Socialists (especially those of Jewish origin) as a clerical, reactionary "return to the ghetto."

At the 1897 Austrian Social Democratic Party Congress there were also voices protesting that too many bourgeois Jews were entering the workers' movement. Victor Adler himself preferred to put up "Christian" candidates in the elections and, if possible, to restrict the number of Jewish intellectuals—a policy of *numerus clausus* that remained informal and failed to prevent the Party from being dominated largely by Jews. Nevertheless, the Jewish leaders of the Austrian Social Democrats went to great lengths to dissociate themselves from capitalist Jewry and even to justify antisemitism. Typical of this stance was the attitude of Friedrich Austerlitz, editor of the central Party newspaper, *Arbeiterzeitung,* who wrote that before Lueger came to power in Vienna in 1897 there had been "a conspiracy in favor of the Jews." Nothing, according to Austerlitz, "so promoted Viennese antisemitism as the fact that for a long time the Viennese press has been controlled by the Jews."[88] The Polish Socialists, like their colleagues in Vienna, also rationalized the antisemitic pogroms in Galicia during the summer of 1898 as an understandable reaction of oppressed Polish peasants against Jewish middlemen and usurers.[89] The leader of the Russian Poale Zion, Ber Borochov, who lived for several years in Vienna at the beginning of the 20th century, bitingly summed up the attitude of the pan-Austrian Social Democratic Party to the "Jewish Question" around 1910:

> [T]heir own newspapers never deem it necessary to oppose antisemitism unequivocally. Its manifestations in everyday life, in the press and in the trade unions, are tolerated by the Social Democrats. They generally tend either to dismiss the Jewish Question and to pass it over in silence, or to ridicule it with antisemitic jokes.[90]

The Austrian Social Democrats, like their colleagues in the labor movements of Germany, Russia, Poland, France, Belgium, and Great Britain, denied, of course, that they were antisemitic or that they tolerated anti-Jewish utterances. They did, however, sometimes admit, as Otto Bauer put it in 1910, that "Marx's essay on the Jewish Question already differentiated us sharply from liberal philosemitism." Equally they were at pains to emphasize that Social Democracy was not "a Jewish protective guard." Officially, the Socialist position remained one of neutrality—neither for nor against the Jews. As the Second Congress of the Socialist International held in Brussels (1891) phrased it, both "anti- and philosemitic outbursts" (!) were to be condemned "as one of the means by which the capitalist class and reactionary governments seek to divert the Socialist movement and divide the workers." This was clearly an obfuscation, since the Socialist International had been asked (by the American Jewish delegate, Abraham Cahan) to unequivocally condemn the violent antisemitic persecution in tsarist Russia. Instead, under the influence of French and Belgian Socialists (supported by two leaders of Jewish origin, Victor Adler and Paul Singer, the prominent SPD deputy) it had equally *condemned* "philosemitism," as if Jews were organizing pogroms against Gentiles![91]

The equivocacy of the Socialist International reflected a much deeper ambiguity and a tradition of hostility, indifference and contempt. Socialists throughout Europe were evidently reluctant to distinguish between anti-capitalism and antisemitism. They had frequently lent their support to a leftist variety of Judeophobia that equated capitalist and "Jew." Many European Socialists believed, moreover, that antisemitism could serve to advance the cause of Socialism. Even the German Social Democrats flirted with the proposition that Jew-baiting was ultimately beneficial to the revolutionary cause, because it was accelerating the disintegration of bourgeois society. As the veteran Social Democratic leader, Wilhelm Liebknecht, summed it up in 1893: "Yes, the antisemites plough and sow, and we Social Democrats will reap. Their successes are therefore not at all unwelcome to us."[92] This opportunist stance was no less common in France and Austria-Hungary. It revealed the reluctance of many Socialists to risk openly combating the antisemitic wave at its height.

The European Left signally failed in its dubious endeavor to channel the discontent of the petty bourgeois masses into a Socialist direction. Far from immunizing the workers against Judeophobic prejudices, such a strategy unwittingly reinforced the potency of racist antisemitism.[93] As we have seen, even Social Democrats, who persistently defended Jewish equality whenever it was directly threatened by antisemites, were not immune to this opportunist tendency. Moreover, they consistently underestimated the potency of antisemitism, assuming that it was doomed to disappear along with the declining *Mittelstand.* In practice, almost the reverse trend would take place. Far from disappearing, an enraged lower middle class along with other disillusioned sectors of European society after 1918 would embrace antisemitism in the broader and more dynamic framework of fascist regimes that would destroy the labor movements in their path.

Notes

1. Paul W. Massing, *Rehearsal for Destruction. A Study of Political Antisemitism in Imperial Germany* (New York, 1949), 151.

2. Walter Mohrmann, *Antisemitismusideologie und Geschichte im Kaiserreich und in der Weimarer Republik* (East Berlin, 1972).

3. Ibid., 11; see also I. Rennap, *Anti-Semitism and the Jewish Question* (London, 1942). Rennap was a British Communist of Jewish background.

4. Abram Leon, *The Jewish Question. A Marxist Interpretation* (New York, 1970), 275ff.

5. Jean-Paul Sartre, *Anti-Semite and Jew* (New York, 1973), 35–36.

6. James Robb, *Working-Class Anti-Semite. A Psychological Study in a London Borough* (London, 1954).

7. Peter G. J. Pulzer, *The Rise of Political Anti-Semitism in Germany and Austria*, 2nd rev. ed. (London, 1988), 252.

8. Reinhard Rürup, "Sozialismus und Antisemitismus in Deutschland vor 1914," in *Juden und Jüdische Aspekte in der Deutschen Arbeiterbewegung 1848–1918,* edited by Walter Grab (Tel Aviv, 1976), 203–27.

9. Rosemarie Leuschen-Seppel, *Sozialdemokratie und Antisemitismus im Kaiserreich* (Bonn, 1978), 231–79.

10. Edmund Silberner, "The Anti-Semitic Tradition in Modern Socialism," Inaugural lecture, Hebrew University, 4 Jan. 1953; idem, *Ha-Sotsialism ha-maravi ve-*

shelelat ha-yehudim (Jerusalem 1955). Silberner reiterated his earlier thesis in *Kommunisten zur Judenfrage* (Opladen 1983), adding some new material on Polish and German Communism.

11. George Lichtheim, "Socialism and the Jews," *Dissent* (July-Aug. 1968): 314.

12. Ibid., 319.

13. Zeev Sternhell, *La Droite Révolutionnaire 1885–1914. Les Origines Françaises du Fascisme* (Paris 1978), 177–214; see also idem, *Ni Droite ni Gauche. L'idéologie fasciste en France* (Paris, 1983).

14. George L. Mosse, "The French Right and the Working Classes. Les Jaunes," *Journal of Contemporary History* 7, nos. 3–4 (July-Oct. 1972); Sternhell, *La Droite Révolutionnaire,* 245–316.

15. Robert S. Wistrich, *Revolutionary Jews from Marx to Trotsky* (London, 1976).

16. W. H. Chaloner and W. O. Henderson, "Marx/Engels and Racism," *Encounter* 45, no. 1 (July 1975): 18–23.

17. Ibid., 22.

18. Julius Carlebach, *Karl Marx and the Radical Critique of Judaism* (London, 1978), 357; see also Shlomo Barer, *The Doctors of Revolution* (London, 2000), 828–73.

19. Robert S. Wistrich, *Socialism and the Jews. The Dilemmas of Assimilation in Germany and Austria-Hungary* (London, 1982).

20. See idem, "Radical Antisemitism in France and Germany," in *Israel and the Nations. Essays presented in Honor of Shmuel Ettinger* (in Hebrew) (Jerusalem, 1978), 157–84, which discusses the years between 1840 and the mid-1870s.

21. Jacob Toury, "The Jewish Question—A Semantic Approach," in *Leo Baeck Institute Year Book* (hereafter *LBIYB*) 11 (1966): 85–106.

22. Shmuel Ettinger, "Biqoret hadat ha-yehudit shel ha-Hegelianim ha-Tsairim," in *Ha'antishemiut ba-et ha-hadasha* (Tel Aviv, 1978); see also Wistrich, "Radical Antisemitism in France and Germany," 157ff.

23. Arthur Hertzberg, *The French Enlightenment and the Jews* (New York, 1968).

24. Zvi Rosen, "The Anti-Jewish Opinions of Bruno Bauer (1838–1843)" (in Hebrew), *Zion*, 33 (1968): 59–76.

25. Bruno Bauer, *Das Judentum in der Fremde* (Berlin, 1863); see also Paul Lawrence Rose, *German Revolutionary Antisemitism from Kant to Wagner* (Princeton, N.J., 1990), 273–78.

26. Karl Marx, "On Bruno Bauer's *The Jewish Question,*" in *Karl Marx. Early Writings,* edited and translated by T. B. Bottomore (New York, 1964), 1–40.

27. Ibid.

28. Ibid.

29. Ibid.

30. Moses Hess, "Sechster Brief," in idem, *Rom und Jerusalem, die letzte Nationalitätsfrage* (Leipzig, 1862), 47.

31. The article, which originally appeared in the *New York Tribune*, 4 Jan. 1856, was reprinted in Karl Marx, *The Eastern Question* (1897; new ed., 1969), 600–6. It is quoted in Chaloner and Henderson, "Marx/Engels and Racism."

32. *Notebooks of P. J. Proudhon* (Paris, 1960–1961), 2: 337–38.

33. Pierre Joseph Proudhon, *Césarisme et Christianisme* (Paris, 1883). This was first published eighteen years after Proudhon's death and is quoted in Lichtheim, "Socialism and the Jews," 322.

34. A. Lehning, A. J. C. Rüter and P. Scheibert, eds., *Bakunin-Archiv* (Leiden, 1963), vol. 1, Part 2, 124–26.

35. "Rapports personnels avec Marx," in Bakunin, *Oeuvres,* 3: 209–99; quoted in Lichtheim, "Socialism and the Jews," 338.

36. Quoted in Jonathan Frankel, *Prophecy and Politics. Socialism, Nationalism, and the Russian Jews, 1862–1917* (Cambridge, 1981), 34.

37. Ibid., 567.

38. Boris Sapir, "Jewish Socialists around *Vpered,*" *International Review of Social History* (1965): 369.

39. Ibid., 383; see also Erich Haberer, *Jews and Revolution in Nineteenth-Century Russia* (Cambridge, 1995).

40. Quoted in Lucy S. Dawidowicz, *The Golden Tradition. Jewish Life and Thought in Eastern Europe* (London, 1967), 406.

41. Ibid., 410.

42. Ibid.

43. Ibid., 415.

44. Ibid., 418; see also Yuri Slezkine, *The Jewish Century* (Oxford, 2004).

45. Wistrich, *Revolutionary Jews,* chap. 2.

46. *Neuer Social-Demokrat,* 18 Sept. 1872; on Wilhelm Hasenclever see Shlomo Na'aman, "Social Democracy on the Ambiguous Ground between Antipathy and Antisemitism—The Example of Wilhelm Hasenclever," in *LBIYB* 36 (1991):. 229–40.

47. *Neuer Social-Demokrat,* 22 Jan. 1873.

48. Quoted in Arno Herzig, "The Role of Antisemitism in the Early Years of the German Workers' Movement," in *LBIYB* 26 (1981): 253.

49. *Neuer Social-Demokrat,* 3 Nov. 1872; Herzig, "Role of Antisemitism," 252.

50. *Neuer Social-Demokrat,* 20 Sept. 1872, 8 Nov. 1872.

51. For a discussion of the concept of anti-Christian antisemitism, see Uriel Tal, *Christians and Jews in Germany. Religion, Politics and Ideology in the Second Reich, 1870–1914* (Cornell, 1974).

52. Robert S. Wistrich, "German Social Democracy and the Berlin Movement," *Internationale Wissenschaftliche Korrespondenz* (Dec. 1976): 323–33.

53. Quoted in Edmund Silberner, "Charles Fourier on the Jewish Question," *Jewish Social Studies* 8, no. 4 (Oct. 1946): 245–66.

54. See Michel Dreyfus, *L'Antisémitisme à Gauche* (Paris, 2009), 24–5.

55. Alphonse Toussenel, *Les Juifs, Rois de l'Époque. Histoire de la Féodalité financière* (Paris, 1845, 1847).

56. Pierre Leroux, "Les juifs, rois de l'époque," *Revue Sociale* (Jan. 1846); quoted in Victor M. Glasberg, "Intent and Consequences. The 'Jewish Question' in the French Socialist Movement of the Late Nineteenth Century," *Jewish Social Studies* 26, no. 1 (Jan. 1974): 61–71.

57. *Notebooks of P. J. Proudhon,* 2: 337–38.

58. Toussenel, *Les Juifs, Rois de l'Époque*; Lichtheim, "Socialism and the Jews," 320.

59. Edouard Drumont, *La France Juive* (Paris, 1886).

60. *Notebooks of P. J. Proudhon,* 2: 150.

61. Gustave Tridon, *Du Molochisme juif* (Paris, 1884), 5.

62. Edmund Silberner, "French Socialism and the Jewish Question 1865–1914," *Historia Judaica* 16 (Apr. 1954): 6–7; see also Dreyfus, *L'Antisémitisme à Gauche,* 41–2, 57–61.

63. Auguste Chirac, *Les Rois de la République* (Paris, 1888).

64. Edmund Silberner, "Anti-Jewish Trends in French-Revolutionary Syndicalism," *Jewish Social Studies* 15, nos. 3–4 (1953); see also Dreyfus, *L'Antisémitisme à Gauche,* 110–11.

65. William J. Fishman, *East End Jewish Radicals 1875–1914* (London, 1975), 61–96; and idem, *East End 1888* (London, 1988), 280–302.

66. Fishman, *East End Jewish Radicals,* 82.

67. John A. Garrard, *The English and Immigration. A Comparative Study of the Jewish Influx (1880–1910)* (London, 1971); see also Anthony Julius, *Trials of the Diaspora. A History of Anti-Semitism in England* (Oxford, 2010), 401–2 on Cobbett.

68. *Justice,* 21 Jan. 1893; see also Julius, *Trials of the Diaspora,* 268–76..

69. *Justice,* 25 Apr. 1896.

70. *Justice,* 7 Oct. 1899.

71. *Reynolds News,* 12 Nov.1899.

72. *Labour Leader,* 24 Feb. 1900.

73. Quoted in Claire Hirshfield, "The British Left and the 'Jewish Conspiracy.' A Case Study of Modern Antisemitism," *Jewish Social Studies* 43, no. 2 (Spring 1981): 105.

74. Ibid., 106–7.

75. Richard Calwer, *Das Kommunistische Manifest und die heutige Sozialdemokratie* (Braunschweig, 1894), 41.

76. See Robert S. Wistrich, "Anti-Capitalism or Antisemitism? The Case of Franz Mehring," in *LBIYB* 22 (1977): 35–54.

77. Idem, "Karl Marx, German Socialists and the Jewish Question, 1880–1914," *Soviet Jewish Affairs* 3, no. 1 (1973): 92–97.

78. Ibid., 95.

79. See Nathan Weinstock, *Le Pain de Misère. Histoire du Mouvement ouvrier juif en Europe,* 2 vols. (Paris, 1984).

80. John Mill, *Pionirn un Boyer,* 2 vols. (New York 1946–1949); see also Henry J. Tobias, *The Jewish Bund in Russia from Its Origins to 1905* (Stanford, 1972); Nora Levin, *Jewish Socialist Movements 1871–1917* (London, 1978), 109–12; and Jonathan Frankel, *Prophecy and Politics,* 171–257.

81. Quoted in Frankel, *Prophecy and Politics,* 229.

82. J. V. Stalin, "Londonskii Syezd Rossiskoi Sotzial-Demokraticheskoi Rabochei Partii," in *Sochineniya,* vol. 2 (*1907–1913*) (Moscow, 1949), 50–51; see also Arkady Vaksberg, *Stalin against the Jews* (New York, 1995), 5–61.

83. Wistrich, *Socialism and the Jews,* 335–43.

84. Ibid., 240ff.

85. On the Lueger movement, see the detailed study by John Boyer, *Political Radicalism in Late Imperial Vienna. Origins of the Christian Social Movement 1848–1897* (Chicago, 1981); also Robert S. Wistrich, *The Jews of Vienna in the Age of Franz Joseph* (Oxford, 1989).

86. Karl Kautsky to Friedrich Engels, 23 June 1884, in *Friedrich Engels' Briefwechsel mit Karl Kautsky,* edited by Benedikt Kautsky (Vienna 1955), 125.

87. Robert S. Wistrich, "Socialism and Antisemitism in Austria before 1914," *Jewish Social Studies* 37, nos. 3–4 (Summer–Fall 1975): 323–33.

88. Ibid., 330.

89. Robert S. Wistrich, "Austrian Social Democracy and the Problem of Galician Jewry 1890–1914," *LBIYB* 26 (1981): 107–9.

90. Ber Borochov, *Ketavim* (Tel Aviv, 1955–1966), 3: 121. On Borochov, see Mitchell Cohen, ed., *Class Struggle and the Jewish Nation. Selected Essays in Marxist Zionism* (New Brunswick, N.J., 1984).

91. James Joll, *The Second International* (London, 1955), 68.

92. Wistrich, *Socialism and the Jews,* 115.

93. Idem, "Social Democracy, the Jews, and Antisemitism in Fin-de-Siècle Vienna," in *Living with Antisemitism. Modern Jewish Responses,* edited by Jehuda Reinharz (Hanover, 1987), 193–209.

PART II

Nationalism and Internationalism

CHAPTER 7

Bernard Lazare: Anarchist, Dreyfusard, and Revolutionary Jew

There are few intellectual journeys in modern Jewish history more unusual and illuminating than the path traversed by Bernard Lazare, the prophet of the Dreyfus Affair. A revolutionary anarchist and a deeply sincere internationalist, he came to embrace a radical form of nationalist particularism which remains altogether distinct in the history of socialism and also of Zionism.[1] Nothing in his social or family background seemed to predestine him to become the "Prophet of Israel" whose crusade for Dreyfus helped to redeem the honor of French Jewry. But his metamorphosis from self-hating Jew to tribune of his people offers the observer a unique vantage-point from which to study the identity conflicts of an authentic Jewish revolutionary. Lazare Marcus Bernard was born in 1865 in the ancient French city of Nîmes in the Languedoc. Like a number of other provincial towns in the South, Nîmes had a small, cohesive, practicing Jewish community which could trace its French roots back over many generations. In the Middle Ages Provençe had been a center of Hebrew learning, and the Jews had lived peacefully for centuries with their neighbors, under special papal protection. By the time of the Third Republic traditional Jewish customs had, however, lost much of their original meaning and significance, though they were still observed. This was the case with Lazare's parents, Jonas Bernard and Douce Noémi Rouget, who celebrated the Passover and other festivals at home without transmitting any specifically Jewish education to their four sons.[2] The children learned their Bar-mitzvah recital by rote, without really understanding it. They were already integrated thoroughly into French culture and society; Fernand became a colonel in the French Army, Armand a doctor, Edmond a picture frame dealer, and the family had great hopes that Bernard Lazare might become a lawyer. But the ambitions of the young Lazare were first and foremost literary, and in 1886 he left his home town for the bright lights of Paris.

At first Lazare studied palaeography and history at the Sorbonne, but with the help of his cousin Georges Michel (Ephraïm Mikhaël), he was soon introduced into the bohemian, avant-garde circles of Parisian literary life. Both Mikhaël and Lazare Bernard were strongly attracted by the Symbolist movement whose high-priest was the poet Mallarmé, and their joint literary début, *La Fiancée de Corinthe,* reflected this influence. By the early 1890s Bernard Lazare (this was the pen-name he henceforth adopted) had become a leading literary critic of the Symbolist group, respected for his fearless and sometimes harsh judgment on his contemporaries. His conception of the writer's role already reflected both the passionate, fighting nature of his temperament and his profound conviction that literature had to serve the cause of social justice.[3] This belief, allied to Lazare's involvement with the Symbolists, led him to embrace anarchism as the universal hope of the future. From 1892, when he became director of the symbolist review, *Entretiens politiques et littéraires,* Lazare increasingly began to interpret art as a form of social action, whose mission was to oppose all authority and dogma and help prepare the revolution from below. It was also in the *Entretiens* that Bernard Lazare contributed his first two articles on the "Jewish Question," a subject which he had as yet not studied in any depth. These two articles, which appeared in September–October 1890, manifested a radical Jewish self-hatred which makes Lazare's subsequent Dreyfusard odyssey and conversion to Zionism all the more remarkable. They had been sparked by the noisy antisemitic campaign which Edouard Drumont and the Marquis de Morès had triggered in Paris. The Bible of this new political movement was Drumont's scurrilous best-seller, *La France Juive,* which had enjoyed a sensational vogue since its publication in 1886. Drumont traced the decline of France since the great Revolution of 1789 to "the Jewish Conquest" (*la conquête juive*)—the ability of a small but cohesive minority to seize control of French institutions, politics, economy, and culture.[4] Drumont openly called for the expulsion of the Jews from France, under the watchword of *La France aux Français* (France for the French). Racism, xenophobia and populist anticapitalism would soon turn Drumont into the new "Pope" of French antisemitism.[5]

Lazare's two articles of 1890 offered an unexpected confirmation of Drumont's contentions, even if his motivations and intentions were fundamentally different. The young Lazare shared with Drumont a vehement hatred of the "Jew" as an alien, a rich capitalist, and a venal agent of corruption. His outlook was nonetheless predicated on a sharp differentiation between *Juifs* (Jews) and *Israélites* (Israelites), whom he depicted as two altogether different categories of being. He unreservedly applied all of Drumont's strictures to the *Juifs*—foreign "Jews," whether rich or poor, whom he designated as depraved and corrupt creatures, wanderers without a home, a herd of cosmopolitan Bedouin who would contaminate everyone and everything with which they came into contact. They were mean, narrow-minded, sly and unscrupulous, owing their allegiance only to the "Golden Calf." Their philosophy of life was based on the sectarianism of the Talmud. It had nothing in common with cultivated French Israelites (like himself), who had absorbed the blessings of Latin civilization. The Israélites of France were honest, upright, decent people, indistinguishable from their compatriots. They could be counted upon to support Drumont as long as he confined himself to attacking the *Juifs*.[6]

Lazare's second article, entitled "La Solidarité juive," focused its attack on the French philanthropic organization, the Alliance Israélite Universelle, which had been set up by Adolphe Crémieux in 1860 to give succor and aid to oppressed Jews all over the world. It had been violently attacked by Drumont in *La France Juive* as the central Paris-based headquarters of a secret conspiracy to achieve Jewish world domination. Lazare joined in this attack, though from a different standpoint. The Alliance was in his view guilty of the unpardonable error of trying to protect the persecuted Jews in Algeria, in Russia, Eastern Europe, and the Balkans. The doors of France had been opened as a result to a flood of coarse, uncultivated, money-grubbing nomads.[7] They had "swarmed down on our country like locusts," inevitably breeding the antisemitic backlash with which the young Lazare partially identified himself.[8] "Thanks to these hordes with whom we are confused, it is forgotten that we have lived in France for nearly two thousand years, like the Franks who invaded this country. . . ."[9]

With all the arrogance of the assimilated *Israélite* proud of his bi-millennial roots on French soil, Bernard Lazare somewhat callously declared: "We have nothing in common with those who are constantly being thrown in our face, and we should abandon them."[10] He advised his fellow-Israelites to "halt, to dam up if they can, the perpetual immigration of these predatory, vulgar and dirty Tartars who come to feed unduly on a country which is not their own."[11] These impoverished *Ostjuden* (Eastern Jews) threatened the integration and identity of the French Israelites. As rootless *Juifs* from Russia and Central Europe, imbued with "Talmudism" and the ghetto mentality, their misery and suffering would transform a free country into a pigsty. With almost sadistic wrath and contempt, the young Lazare could write:

> Russian usurers, Galician tavern-keepers and money-lenders, second-hand pedlars from Prague, Polish horse-dealers, money-merchants from Frankfurt, what do they mean to me, a French

> Israelite? In the name of what supposed fraternity should I care about measures taken by the Tsar against subjects who appear to him as harmful?[12]

The anarchist revolutionary who would later devote himself so selflessly to the cause of Jewish brotherhood and liberty could, in 1890, only advise his fellow French "Israelites" to kick the alien "lepers" out from their midst.

By the early 1890s Bernard Lazare was already a well-known critic and literary anarchist committed to the cause of social revolution. His writing on social problems was characterized by unusual vehemence, a marked capacity for hatred, and the classic anarchist loathing for authority. The milieu in which he moved was thoroughly infiltrated with antisemitism, which in 19th-century France had long been a feature of the Left. Hatred of the Rothschild "dynasty" was almost obligatory in socialist and anarchist circles. Even fin-de-siècle nationalist antisemites like Drumont, Rochefort, and Maurice Barrès by using a populist, anti-capitalist phraseology had achieved a certain respectability in left-wing circles.[13] Hence there was nothing especially surprising in the fact that a young Jew, ignorant of his tradition and history, should identify with the commonplace antisemitic stereotypes of the time. What was nevertheless to distinguish Lazare from so many other revolutionary Jews was his restless search for more authentic personal identity and his questioning mind. His Jewish antisemitism had flared up at a time when socialism and Judeophobia did not seem so incompatible. But the campaign unleashed by Drumont soon began to outgrow its original left-wing orientation, attacking not only Jewish bankers and foreign immigrants but also assimilated Jews in all walks of life.

This development prompted Bernard Lazare to undertake a remarkable, wide-ranging and deeply problematic study entitled *L'Antisemitisme, son histoire et ses causes* (1894). The early sections of this book first appeared as review articles in 1891 and 1892, and they seem to reflect the earlier anti-Jewish prejudices of the author. Lazare evidently believed that "the Jews were themselves, in part, at least, the cause of their own ills."[14] Though they did not determine the particular character of antisemitism in any time or place, they were the one constant factor in its development. It was the "unsocial" character of the Jew, rooted in his religion with its strict and precise ritual and his tenacious patriotism which was ultimately responsible for antisemitism.[15] The Jews had everywhere remained part of a long, unbroken chain of tradition, a nationality of the confessional type, refusing to merge with their neighbors.[16] Lazare agreed with Drumont that this had turned them into a "state within the State." Before the Dreyfus case began in

October 1894, Lazare still disapproved strongly of Jewish particularism. The Jews, indoctrinated by the Talmud and convinced of their own superiority to other nations, had remained refractory to all attempts at assimilating them.[17] Jew-hatred was primarily a reaction of the Gentile nations to this obdurate survival of an alien minority in their midst. If, until the 17th century, its causes had been primarily religious, in modern times it had assumed a new colouring—whether socio-economic, nationalist, or racist.

Lazare fundamentally disagreed with Drumont, however, over his assertion that the Jews could *never* assimilate. The antisemites, he argued, were caught in a "perpetual and fundamental contradiction," once they had embraced the pseudo-scientific doctrine of racial exclusivism. Their reliance on false analogies from biology and anthropology had turned antisemitism into a self fulfilling prophecy:

> Antisemitism was born in modern societies because the Jew did not assimilate, did not cease to be a people, but when anti-Semitism had ascertained that the Jews were not assimilated, it violently reproached them for it, and at the same time whenever possible, it took all necessary steps to prevent their future assimilation.[18]

In his chapter on modern antisemitism, Lazare began to abandon the neutral tone of his earlier discussion and to take issue with Drumont's ideas, and those of his counterparts elsewhere in Europe. Nevertheless, a certain parallelism is still discernible in his argument—relying as it did on the assumption that the Jews had themselves always been an exclusive and separate people. In his treatment of the post-emancipation period of Jewish history the influence of Drumont is also apparent, though Lazare was clearly critical of antisemitism as a racial or "scientific" doctrine. Thus Lazare insisted that in the period following the French Revolution the Jews had become a valuable ally of the European bourgeoisie. "As conquerors, not as guests, they came into modern societies. They were like a penned-in flock; suddenly the barriers fell and they rushed upon the field opened to them."[19] No wonder that French antisemites from Drumont and Charles Maurras to Xavier Vallat or (for that matter) left-wing Holocaust deniers in France today, enjoy quoting selective passages, especially from Lazare's earlier work.

The industrialization of Europe was depicted by Lazare in quasi-antisemitic language as a kind of "Jewish conquest," whereby a race of greedy moneylenders and merchant-capitalists with a marvelous power of adaptation had seized their opportunity. Within two generations they had emerged in the forefront of European society as financiers, industrialists, *littérateurs*, politicians, and revolutionaries.

> The Jews, it may be said, are situated at the poles of contemporary society. They are found among the representatives of industrial and financial capitalism, and among those who have vehemently protested against capital. Rothschild is the antithesis of Marx and Lasalle.[20]

The young Lazare was very close to embracing the thesis espoused in 1869 by the French Catholic antisemite Gougenot des Mousseaux, that the Jews were "breeders of revolutions."[21] The difference was rather one of evaluating the results of this phenomenon. Many French Catholics, as well as conservative and nationalist circles feared the Jew as a subversive and destructive element in traditional society. Lazare, on the other hand, as a revolutionary anarchist took pride in Jewish radicalism, which, he believed, had an ancient biblical lineage. It was the very essence of the "Hebrew spirit" that had driven many of his emancipated coreligionists to embrace radical causes, just as their distant forefathers had fathered prophetism, messianism, and early Christianity. The Jews had always been restless malcontents, seeking immediate satisfaction rather than remote promises of eternal salvation.[22] This pattern had been set by the ancient Hebrews from Abraham to Moses and Isaiah, who demanded justice from Yahweh along with reciprocity and the fulfillment of mutual obligations. "The man whom the Jew lauds is not a saint, not a resignee: it is the just man. The charitable man does not exist for the people of Judah; in Israel there can be no question of charity, but only of justice."[23]

The poor and humble (the *ebionim*) of ancient Israel possessed a concrete ideal of social justice. They dreamed of the day when the wicked would be hurled into oblivion. Justice was not something to be realized beyond the grave, but was to be achieved in *this* life. Moreover, the Israelites had never acknowledged any human authority beside Yahweh. They were driven by a fanatical preoccupation with equality, based on the idea that all of Yahweh's children were entitled to an equal share of his joys and blessings.[24] It was this notion which had inspired the "communistic" precepts of Leviticus, Exodus, and Numbers, and the sayings of the Hebrew prophets. The centuries of bondage, humiliation, and martyrdom which the Jewish people had undergone in exile reinforced rather than destroyed their invincible belief in the future coming of the Messiah. Bernard Lazare saw the modern Jewish revolutionary as "the child of biblical and prophetic tradition, that same tradition which animated the fanatic Anabaptists of Germany in the sixteenth century and the Puritan warriors of Cromwell."[25] In Karl Marx he perceived the "powerful logic of the ancient rabbis," and in Ferdinand Lassalle "the passionate thirst for liberty of the ancient Hebrew rebels."[26] Those who had joined the ranks of the Revolution did not, despite their atheism, cease to be Jews.

> But as a general rule, the Jew, even the extreme Jewish radical, cannot help retaining his Jewish characteristics, and though he may have abandoned all religion and all faith, he has none the less been subjected to the national influence acting through heredity and early education.[27]

In other words, for Bernard Lazare, the Jewish revolutionary was not the destructive solvent of antisemitic fantasy, bringing disorder and catastrophe, but a fighter for freedom, seeking to realize the ancient Hebrew dream of a terrestrial paradise. It was the Jewish ancestry of Marx, Börne, Heine, and Lassalle that had made them rebels, agitators and controversialists with a unique gift for critical sarcasm and invective. There was some truth in this analysis, but his conclusion was nonetheless phrased in terms that French antisemites could readily seize upon.

> The emancipated Jew, being no longer bound by the faith of his ancestors, and owing no ties to the old forms of society in the midst of which he had lived as an outcast, has become in modern nations a veritable ferment of revolutions.[28]

What then was Lazare's solution to the antisemitism whose history and causes he had been the first to trace from antiquity to modern times? Where did his prognoses fundamentally differ from those of Drumont and the French antisemites? The conclusion to his book sounded, in effect, a curiously optimistic note seemingly at odds with his vision of persistent and ubiquitous antisemitism. His revolutionary perspective led Lazare to believe that both Judaism and antisemitism were on the verge of dissolution. The "Talmudic spirit" which had preserved the East European Jews as ghetto creatures was rapidly disappearing among their emancipated occidental brethren who were abandoning "their ancient prejudices, their peculiar modes of worship, the observance of their special laws."[29] The enlightened Jew "who professes at most a sort of ceremonial deism" was ripe for Western rationalism. For the free-thinking, anti-clerical Lazare, this was the sine qua non of successful assimilation. At the same time, he was convinced that the spirit of national egotism was also on the wane. A new era of internationalism was emerging, which would sweep away the "hatred of the alien" which lay at the root of anti-Judaism. The antisemites in France, Germany, and Austria were unconsciously preparing the road to socialism with their anti-capitalist populist demagogy. The antisemitic movement, in its origins, fundamentally reactionary, was now serving the cause of Revolution against its own wishes.

> Anti-Semitism stirs up the middle class, the petty-bourgeois and sometimes the peasant against the Jewish capitalists, but in doing so it leads them gently towards socialism, prepares them for anarchy, drives them to hate all capitalists and more than that, capital in the abstract.[30]

Socialism would inevitably triumph over antisemitism—"one of the last, though most long-lived, manifestations of that old spirit of reaction and narrow conservatism."[31] This was exactly the prognosis made by the Marxist Social Democrats in France and Germany whom Lazare generally despised.[32]

The Dreyfus Affair which broke out only a few months after the publication of Lazare's study proved his predictions to have been completely misplaced. It forced him to recognize that antisemitism, far from disappearing or preparing the road to revolution, was gaining ground every day. The arrest of a Jewish officer in the French Army on the charge of high treason had given a new lease of life to Drumont's *Libre Parole* and other organs of antisemitic opinion. Lazare's relations with Drumont, which up to this point had been cordial (in spite of their growing divergence of view) now rapidly deteriorated.[33] In January 1895 Drumont still felt able to lavish praise on Lazare's study of antisemitism, as being "dominated from beginning to end by a fine effort at impartiality" and a determination "not to yield to the impulses of the race."[34] Even in October 1895, he would publish Bernard Lazare's letter in *Libre Parole,* in which he agreed to help adjudicate a competition designed to find the best solution to the "Jewish peril." Lazare was prepared to sit on the jury, assuring Drumont of his "absolute impartiality," and quixotically stating in advance that "the only logical solution to the problem seems to me a massacre. . . ."[35] By the time the first meeting of the jury occurred the two men were sworn enemies, and after a number of insults a duel took place in which neither was injured.

The extraordinary metamorphosis through which Bernard Lazare emerged as the leading Jewish defender of Dreyfus and the bitterest enemy of the antisemites began in November 1894, during the first Dreyfus trial. At that time, Lazare still had no obvious reason to doubt the verdict. However, he was undoubtedly shaken by the way in which the treason trial had been immediately exploited to whip up a frenzied xenophobic crusade in France. In an article of November 1894, Lazare gave vivid expression to his anxiety at the new "anti-Semitic state of mind" which had flared up everywhere in French society. Even the most assimilated French "Israelite," Lazare shrewdly observed, now discovered that he was after all only a pariah, living in a new ghetto surrounded by an impenetrable wall of suspicion. "This animosity is hidden, and yet the intelligent Jew can perceive it; he has the impression of a wall that his adversaries have built between himself and those in whose midst he lives."[36] This latent hatred was more shocking for the sensitive, educated Jew than the physical ghetto in which his non-assimilated brethren in Eastern Europe and North Africa still vegetated. It awakened for the first time in Bernard Lazare an understanding of the ambiguity of emancipation and the pariah quality of Jewish existence. Henceforth his activity became one prodigious and often misunderstood effort to bring into the light the psychological servitude which afflicted French Jews, and to give political expression to the Jewish people as an oppressed nation of outcasts.

Even in civilized France, the land of the Revolution and the Rights of Man, the Dreyfus Affair had prompted Jews to discover the precarious and uncertain character of their citizenship. At the same time, Lazare also became aware that his anarchist and socialist comrades had the same distorted perception of his co-religionists as he himself had once shared. It was now clear to him that Jews could not passively wait until they were stripped of all their rights in the hope that one day the social revolution might deliver them. In a small pamphlet entitled *Antisémitisme et Révolution* (March 1895), which featured an imaginary discussion between two simple French workers, Lazare for the first time unmasked the pseudo-socialist, demagogic character of Drumont's propaganda. He emphasized that antisemitism was essentially an internecine conflict between Christian and Jewish capitalists, in which the Catholic bourgeoisie sought to supplant their "Semitic" rivals. This was also the classic argument of leading French Marxists like Jules Guesde. Lazare added that the Jews in Russia, Eastern Europe, and North Africa constituted the most miserable and disinherited proletariat in the world. "In Russia, Galicia, Rumania and Turkey, in London and New York, even in some areas of Paris, their poverty is dreadful."[37]

The next stage in Lazare's evolution was a bold press campaign in the radical periodical *Le Voltaire* against Drumont's racist teachings, originally provoked by reading Émile Zola's article "Pour les Juifs" in *Le Figaro* (16 May 1896). In a series of polemics later published as a pamphlet entitled *Contre L'Antisémitisme* Lazare took sharp issue with Drumont's assertion that antisemitism was a form of class-struggle directed against capitalism and Jewish finance. Decisively rejecting his earlier view that the antisemites were smoothing the road to socialism, Lazare frankly admitted that "I was very naïve at that time."[38] The only beneficiaries of Drumont's anti-Jewish crusade would be the Christian capitalists. Antisemitism was in reality a safety valve for capitalism rather than a movement against the status quo. Moreover, it threatened the basic Rights of Man, seeking to deprive all Jews of their freedom in order to restore the medieval ghetto. "It is not only the Jewish banker who is being condemned but the Jewish tradesman, the Jewish lawyer, the Jew in medicine, in the army, in the arts, letters and sciences."[39] Behind this campaign stood the efforts of the Catholic Church to reassert its authority and to undermine the principles of the French Republic. The war against the Jew was a necessary prelude to the future battle to be waged against the Protestants, free-thinkers, anti-clericals, republicans, anarchists, and socialists. By the summer of 1896 it was clear to Bernard Lazare that antisemitism aimed to destroy the fundamental values of the French revolutionary tradition by reversing the edict of emancipation and abrogating the Rights of Man. It attacked Jews irrespective of their social class, as the Dreyfus Affair would soon illustrate in all its macabre detail.

Bernard Lazare had at first scorned the suggestion of his Gentile publisher Stock that he look into the Dreyfus case, using arguments similar to those put forward by his anarchist colleagues. Dreyfus was, after all, a wealthy bourgeois, a Jewish officer—his rich family would hardly need the help of a troublesome anarchist opposed to all forms of militarism. However, by the time Mathieu Dreyfus (brother of the accused) approached him in February 1895 Lazare already had serious doubts concerning the legality of the original trial. His indignation and wrath were aroused by the suspicion that evidence had been forged. Dreyfus, he came to believe, had been the victim of a carefully orchestrated conspiracy. With great tenacity he began to seek out documents, to reexamine testimony, to consult handwriting experts and expose contradictions in the official case against Dreyfus. The result of his investigations was the publication in Brussels on 6 November 1896 of the first pamphlet in the Dreyfusard campaign—*Une erreur judiciaire: la vérité sur l'affaire Dreyfus*. Three thousand copies of the pamphlet were sent out to influential personalities in the French press, parliament, and public life. Lazare argued that Dreyfus's guilt had never been satisfactorily demonstrated, and that illegal methods had been used to secure his conviction. He pointed out that the French General Staff had brought extraordinary pressures to bear on the judges, taking advantage of a general climate of hatred and suspicion. Lazare also left little doubt that antisemitism had played a substantial role in the case. "Did I not say that Captain Dreyfus belonged to a class of pariahs? He is a soldier, but he is a Jew, and it is as a Jew above all that he was prosecuted."[40]

Reaction to Lazare's pamphlet among his anarchist comrades and even future Dreyfusards such as Clemenceau and the socialist leader, Jean Jaurès was decidedly cool and even hostile in tone. The main socialist paper *La Petite République,* like the rest of the left-wing press, simply did not believe that a wealthy officer could be falsely convicted by members of his own class. The French Marxist militant Alexandre Zévaès even challenged Lazare's personal integrity, describing him as "the distinguished representative of anarchist *high life,* who is at the same time one of the most faithful admirers of His Majesty Rothschild."[41] Sarcastically he dismissed his pamphlet as a "cynical, personal advertisement rather than a sincere attempt to rehabilitate an innocent man."[42] This cruel comment was of course grotesquely wide of the mark, but it did reflect the persistent socialist obsession with the power of Jewish bankers. The myth of Rothschild and belief in an all-powerful clique of cosmopolitan Jewish bankers was one of the main reasons why the French Left proved so hesitant in taking a stand for Dreyfus, whose cause never won broad popular support among the socialists.[43]

The tenacity of left-wing antisemitism meant that Lazare found himself very isolated within his own political camp during the early days of the Dreyfus Affair. Among the first Dreyfusards were passionate defenders of truth like Colonel Picquart and the lawyer Fernand Labori (neither of them free of anti-Jewish prejudice), the senator from Alsace, Scheurer-Kestner; the liberal Jewish politician, Joseph Reinach; the Jacobin radical Georges Clemenceau, as well as a handful of socialists like Jean Allemane and the librarian of the École Normale Supérieure, Lucien Herr. In the summer of 1897 it was Herr who convinced the socialist tribune Jean Jaurès and the young Léon Blum of Dreyfus's innocence. At the beginning of 1898 the Dreyfusards were inspired primarily by Emile Zola's stirring *J'Accuse,* by a small group of students and intellectuals at the Sorbonne and École Normale, and by the adhesion of Jaurès. But Lazare's earlier campaign for Dreyfus remained qualitatively different. Indeed, it was unique of its kind in France. In Lazare's fevered imagination, the prisoner on Devil's Island rapidly became a symbol of Jewish martyrdom throughout the centuries, of the tragedy which had befallen a dispersed and disinherited race. "He has been for me the tragic image of the Algerian Jews, beaten and pillaged, the unhappy immigrants dying of hunger in the ghettoes of New York or of London."[44]

It was in many way an extraordinary paradox that the misfortune of a rich Alsatian officer should have been the detonator for Bernard Lazare's voyage of Jewish self-discovery. In an open letter published in *L'Aurore* on 7 June 1899 Lazare made it clear, however, that he did not want either his personal role or that of the "Jewish Question" to be subsumed or swallowed by the universalist ideology of the Rights of Man.

> I want it to be said that it was a Jew who first stood up for the Jewish martyr. . .a Jew who knew to what an outcast, disinherited, ill-starred people he belonged, and drew from this consciousness the will to fight for justice and truth.[45]

Bernard Lazare was perhaps the first French Jew to fully comprehend that his origins had a *political* significance, and that to deny them would make any effective struggle against antisemitism impossible. Certainly, there were a few French Israelites, beginning with the Chief Rabbi Zadoc Kahn, who played an active role behind the scenes, in organizing the Jewish response to antisemitism.[46] Others, like Isaïe Levaillant, Salomon Reinach, and the members of a secret Jewish defense committee during the Affair, also played their part. Above all, there was Joseph Reinach, a republican disciple of Léon Gambetta and the future historian of the Affair, whose militant defence of Dreyfus made him a symbol of the "Jewish Syndicate" in the eyes of anti-Dreyfusards and antisemites. Lazare's position was different, nonetheless, since he was a revolutionary outsider who did not identify with the republican establishment or the organized Jewish community. Moreover, he was firmly convinced by 1897 that the politics of assimilation had truly been a disaster in France. This belief led him between 1897 and 1899 to formulate what was perhaps the most profound critique by any left-wing revolutionary or Western Jew of the dominant assimilationist ideology. Like Theodor Herzl, the translation of whose famous pamphlet, *Der Judenstaat* (1896), into French had been arranged through his mediation, Lazare realized that emancipation had not resolved, but on the contrary, even aggravated the Jewish problem. Assimilation—this "spurious doctrine" (*doctrine bâtarde*), as Lazare derisively called it—far from ensuring the security and prosperity of the Jews, had radically undermined the foundations of their existence.[47] It had left them powerless and incapable of self-defense as soon as they became the focal-point of antisemitic hatred. Assimilation had thoroughly corrupted the elite of French Jewry, destroying the natural sentiment of solidarity with their less fortunate brethren. It had *de-judaized* the community, eroding traditional virtues and substituting the modern vices of mercenary egoism and callous indifference.[48]

Lazare accused the rich Jews, concerned above all to safeguard their social status and privileges, of having abandoned the masses of their impoverished co-religionists to the antisemites. The last tenuous link which still remained between them and the poor Jews was organized philanthropy, but it merely served to perpetuate a rigid class system within the Jewish community. The real problem, therefore, was not so much antisemitism as the demoralization of an oppressed "nation of pariahs" by their own leaders. What was necessary was a complete transformation of Jewish life from the bottom upward—to initiate a movement of the Jewish masses that would establish control of its own destiny from a decadent and bankrupt communal leadership. It is in this idiosyncratic sense that Lazare's conversion to a social-revolutionary brand of Zionism must be understood, and it was precisely this perspective which would always make him an outsider within the French Jewish community.

In a lecture given in March 1897 to the Association of Russian-Jewish Students in Paris, Bernard Lazare first expounded his *national* solution to the Jewish problem. He explained that Jewish nationalism did not contradict but would rather complete the emancipation granted by the French Revolution of 1789. The latter had failed because it insisted on *denationalizing* the Jews, thereby reducing them to a state of psychological inferiority. Emancipation had merely made "a conscious pariah out of an unconscious pariah."[49] Instead of heralding the end of Jewish misery, it had created a new wave of persecution, and engendered a process of demoralization within the Jewish community. For example, the French Jews as a community had (according to Lazare) passively acquiesced in the campaign against Dreyfus, thereby becoming accomplices and agents of antisemitism. The Algerian Jews who had been granted full citizenship by decree of the French Jewish lawyer, Adolphe Crémieux (then head of the Ministry of Justice) in 1871, had not only been chased from their workshops and factories, but even their right to exist was being challenged.[50] In French Algeria during the Dreyfus Affair, the antisemites were in the ascendant. They had been carried to power in the capital city in 1898 by an ugly nationalist wave led by the young Italian-born student Max Régis. This populist upsurge had been accompanied by a barrage of antisemitic intimidation, violence, boycotts, and open discrimination much more extreme than in France itself.[51]

What then could Western emancipation have to offer to the mass of his non-assimilated brethren in Russia, Romania, Eastern Europe, and North Africa? Lazare's thesis argued that it would remain ineffectual until there was a rebirth of the ancient Hebrew nation. Only Jewish libertarian nationalism could free the Jewish proletariat from the pressures of antisemitism.

Freedom, in any event, would never be complete, if it were granted as a gift from above or preserved for the individual alone without a collective will to assert national identity. "Nationalism is for me the expression of collective liberty and the condition of individual liberty."[52] The Jews would have to fight for their collective rights. Nationalism, at least, offered them a chance of success. This was not a call to reconquer Judea. Lazare's nationalism was *not* territorial or exclusivist. It was profoundly internationalist in its support for all oppressed minorities.[53] "For a Jew," he insisted, "the word nationalism should mean freedom." Lazare sought to find allies for the Jews among other oppressed groups in European society, since he recognized that antisemitism was also part of a broader spectrum of reaction and the general suppression of national liberties. On the other hand, the question of territory was secondary to Bernard Lazare, though he certainly favored the establishment of a Jewish homeland. However, he did not unilaterally specify Palestine as its predestined locus. "A Jew who today may declare 'I am a nationalist' will not be saying in any special, precise or clear-cut way, 'I am a man who seeks to rebuild a Jewish State in Palestine and who dreams of conquering Jerusalem.'" Nevertheless, Lazare believed that the establishment of new Jewish colonies in Palestine was *desirable*—not so much for the sake of the 120,000 Jews in France (and French Algeria) but for the millions of destitute, impoverished Jewish proletarians ground down by their misery in Eastern Europe. Already in November 1894, through the intermediary of the Russian Jewish journalist Avraham Ludvipol (then resident in Paris), Lazare had been made aware of Ahad Ha'am's Zionist ideas and the new settlements in Palestine.[54]

Lazare's Zionism clearly expressed an inner revolt against the spiritual and psychological dependence produced by liberal assimilation. It was above all a defiant reply to the time-honored role of scapegoat which the nations of the world had assigned to the Jew:

> We are through with being eternally exploited by all peoples, a troop of cattle, of serfs, the butt of every lash, a flock to which men even deny a stable, a horde of people denying themselves the right to have a free soil to live and die in liberty.[55]

The Jews would have to stand up to their enemies and say in a clear voice,

> We are ever the ancient stiff-necked people, the unruly and rebel nation; we want to be ourselves, and we shall know well how to conquer the right which is ours, not only to be men but also to be Jews.[56]

Lazare saw no contradiction between an inalienable human right to national freedom and the socialist internationalism to which he was still firmly committed. If socialists in 1900 demanded autonomy for Cubans, Cretans, Armenians, Finns, and other small nationalities, then why should the Jews be any less entitled to their sympathy? In order to be genuinely internationalist the exploited proletarian Jewish masses must first possess their freedom to struggle as a nation. "What do we want? We are constantly saying: give to this nation of the poor, the suffering, the proletarians, consciousness of what it is."[57] This consciousness involved firstly an honest recognition by Jews that they could not rely on others if they were to resist oppression. They must consciously assume the burden of their pariahood. "We must see what we can extract from ourselves, and to this end we must not Christianize Judaism, but on the contrary, judaize the Jew, teach him to live for, and to be himself."[58] In order to achieve this revolution of self-consciousness the chimerical ideology of assimilation would have to be repudiated. As a result of this corrupting influence, French Jews had become more papist than the Pope in their professions of jingoism. With bitter irony (and some exaggeration) Bernard Lazare characterized their role in the Dreyfus Affair:

> As in all countries where the Jews have been emancipated, they have voluntarily shattered the solidarity which existed among them. . .so that even if some three dozen of them were to be found to defend one of their martyred brothers, thousands would have been found to mount watch around Devil's Island, along with the most devoted champions of the fatherland.[59]

Lazare's painful experience in defending Alfred Dreyfus in the teeth of hostility from many of his coreligionists obviously contributed to this sour verdict. He had always belonged to that select group of intellectuals like Georges Clemenceau, Emile Zola and Charles Péguy who consistently demanded an unequivocal revision of the original sentence. After the Presidential pardon accorded to Dreyfus, following his second trial at Rennes in September 1899 (where he was again found guilty but "with extenuating circumstances"), Lazare was among those who initially wished to continue the struggle. As he told his friend, the Dreyfusard socialist and Catholic poet, Charles Péguy: "Dreyfus must appear before another court-martial, all his life if need be, but he must be declared innocent like everyone else."[60] This principled standpoint, driven by moral intransigence, contributed still further to Lazare's political isolation. The rich Jews (mindful of his attacks on the Jewish bourgeoisie) viewed him with special horror, and even made stipulations, according to Péguy, that he should not be allowed to write for any paper that they helped to finance.[61] They were only too glad to let such a troublesome gadfly fade into obscurity and oblivion. For his part, Lazare retained an unquenchable loathing for the Jewish "plutocracy" in France, which he literally regarded as a curse for the oppressed masses of his people. "This Jewish bourgeoisie, rich and not Jewish, is our garbage, our rubbish; we must rid ourselves of it; and if it is unable to protect itself against anti-Semitism, it is not our job to help it."[62]

Bernard Lazare's fight for Dreyfus, his anarchism, revolutionary libertarian Zionism, and war on the Jewish bourgeoisie were all part of a self-conscious strain of Hebraic prophetism running through his later writings.

> It is faith in the reign of this justice that has animated my people from the time of the Prophets and the poor poets who sang the psalms to those who, like Marx and Lassalle, have asserted the rights of the proletariat. . . . All my ancestors and my brothers desired fanatically that each man be granted his rights, and that the scale never be tipped in favor of injustice. For that they cried out, chanted, shed tears, suffered, despite outrages, despite insults and public contempt.[63]

Bernard Lazare initially embraced Zionism with the enthusiasm of a modern Jewish prophet convinced that only a great popular movement of the proletarian masses could redeem a downtrodden Israel. In May 1897 he had written to Theodor Herzl, identifying fully with his aim of rallying and strengthening the bonds of the scattered Jewish nation.[64] During the next two years he would direct the French section of the multi-lingual publication *Zion* produced in Berlin. In 1898 Lazare founded a new Zionist review in France called *Le Flambeau* (The torch) which preached his own radical brand of Jewish nationalism. He also contributed to two other French periodicals of a social-Zionist character, *Kadimah* and *L'Écho Sioniste*. In 1898 he was one of the stars of the second Zionist Congress, where he received a standing ovation from delegates and served on the Actions Committee. But within less than a year he had resigned, disillusioned by Herzl's *Realpolitik* and the "autocratic government [which] seeks to direct the Jewish masses as though they were ignorant children."[65] In his letter of resignation, published in *Le Flambeau* in March 1899, Lazare explained that he could not identify himself with a form of government that ignored the real economic, intellectual, and moral needs of the Jewish masses. "It is not the one of which the ancient prophets and humble folk who wrote the psalms have dreamed."[66]

Lazare nonetheless acknowledged the unforgettable services of Theodor Herzl to the national movement, and on a personal level he continued to admire the man who "knew how to stir the depths of Israel."[67] But differences in temperament, political style, social conviction and general outlook between the two men made a parting of the ways seem almost inevitable. In a letter written on 4 February 1899 Lazare reproached Herzl with mistakenly instituting "a government with social and diplomatic commitments" before "creating a people."[68] The roots of this misconception lay, according to Lazare, in Herzl's "bourgeois" limitations in understanding the social needs of the Jewish masses.

> You are bourgeois in thought, bourgeois in feeling, bourgeois in ideas, bourgeois in social content. And yet you wish to lead a people, our people, a poor, unfortunate, proletarian people. You can only do it in an authoritarian way, leading them to what *you* think is their good.[69]

The letter of rupture reflected the revolt of the anarchist against the diplomat, of the revolutionary against the statesman—of *mystique* against *politique*—to adopt Charles Péguy's famous saying about the Dreyfus Affair. Bernard Lazare saw himself as a prophet displaying all the ulcers of the Jewish people to themselves and the world—"poor Job on his dungheap" as he pungently put it. Herzl, on the other hand, thought in terms of *Realpolitik*. Hence, Lazare's stinging reproach probably struck Herzl as irrelevant: "Like all governments, you wish to disguise the truth, to be the government of a people which looks clean and the height of duty becomes for you not to display our national shame."[70] In January 1902 Lazare gave vent once more to his anger, this time at Herzl's silence (like that of the European Powers in general) over the Armenian massacres. Here was a concrete example of where Zionist courtship of the Turkish Sultan and other despots, would inevitably lead.[71]

Lazare also opposed the creation of the Jewish Colonial Trust, intended as a national bank which would organize the colonization of Palestine. "But a bank is never, and can never be an instrument of national regeneration. What an irony to make a bank the founder of the Jewish nation!"[72] Behind this objection stood Lazare's long-standing animus against the Jewish plutocracy and his fear that they would ultimately sabotage any genuine popular movement that developed among the Jews. From the beginning he had distrusted Herzl's efforts to woo wealthy Jewish bankers and philanthropists to support his schemes. But Lazare did not propose any convincing or realistic alternative to this modus operandi,[73] nor did he explain how Herzl could have significantly advanced the cause of a Jewish homeland without any support from the Great Powers, such as Imperial Germany, tsarist Russia, or Great Britain. Moreover, some minimal cooperation from the Ottoman government would clearly be vital if any serious progress were to be made. Lazare, however, saw the Turkish Sultan above all as the oppressor of Christian national minorities in his Muslim Empire. Moreover, he genuinely feared that there could be an extermination of the Armenians in the future—a prophecy that would be tragically vindicated in 1916. Lazare would not accept any political bargains with the Devil or the cool calculation of Zionists like Herzl that a Jewish State might help transform previous enemies of the Jews into allies.

Although Bernard Lazare had broken with the official Zionist movement by early 1899, he continued to fight for the liberation of the Jewish people, protesting vehemently against the persecution of Jews in the Balkans and Eastern Europe. He visited Austrian Poland, Turkey, Germany, the Czech lands, and above all Romania, where his presence almost caused a riot and led to his temporary arrest. Lazare, more than any other man of the Left, was to make the world conscious of the nightmare of legalized oppression which afflicted the lives of Romanian Jews.[74] By 1900 Lazare had become a kind of roving ambassador of his oppressed brethren, virtually ostracized in republican France but warmly admired for his defense of Dreyfus by the poor Jews of Eastern Europe. Péguy would leave an immortal portrait of Lazare in these last years of his increasing poverty, isolation, and debilitating cancer. He wrote that Lazare had "a heart which bled in Romania and in Hungary, everywhere where the Jew is persecuted, which is, in a certain sense, everywhere."[75] He described his friend as a man "consumed by a fire, by the fire of his people"—an atheist who had "aspects of a saint, of sanctity"—a true prophet of Israel.[76] Péguy's journal, *Les Cahiers de la Quinzaine,* was where Lazare's last sociological study, *Les Juifs en Roumanie,* would be published. It was here that Lazare also denounced the anti-clerical exploitation of the Dreyfusard victory by the Radical Republican regime under Emile Combes which came to power in France in 1902.[77]

Both Lazare and Péguy shared a common revulsion against the manipulation of the Dreyfusard mystique by "radical" politicians. They expressed a no less uncompromising dislike for the modern world, parliamentary corruption, opportunist political parties, and demagogic socialism. Their vision was based on the quasi-messianic belief that only an *inner* revolution, a moral transformation of man, could bring about the new humanity envisaged by Dreyfusard socialism.[78]

One of the factors which undoubtedly heightened Lazare's alienation from the mainstream of the French socialist movement even before 1900 was his awareness that it was still tainted by anticapitalist antisemitism. During the Dreyfus Affair most of the French Left (until the threat to the Republic became palpable) had been very reluctant to take any stand. Some socialists encouraged antisemitism by their overly discreet silence and ambivalence, while others even adopted an anti-Dreyfusard position.[79] This was pointed out in a little pamphlet entitled *Le Prolétariat Juif,* written in 1898 by the Groupe des Ouvriers Juifs Socialistes Français and addressed to the French socialists. It was signed by Karpel (head of the hatmakers' union) and Dinner, librarian of the Yiddish-speaking Jewish Workers Library of Paris, but the text suggests the strong influence of Bernard Lazare. We know that by the beginning of 1898 his revolutionary brand of Jewish nationalism had found an echo among immigrant Jewish workers and students from Russia and Eastern Europe, living on the margins of Parisian society.[80] These immigrants were certainly aware of his libertarian ideals. They also emphasized that there was a world-wide Jewish proletariat hitherto ignored by the French Left, yet constantly threatened by poverty, persecution, and pogroms.[81] It was this proletariat which had to bear the brunt of antisemitism because of the general hatred for Jewish bankers, encouraged by the Left as well as the nationalist Right. The pamphlet sharply criticized the French socialists for equivocation in dealing with the antisemitic campaign preceding the Dreyfus Affair and for believing that "class-hatred could be superimposed on to Jew-hatred."

In an article published in *La Grande Revue* in September 1899 Bernard Lazare expanded this critique into a frontal attack on the "social concept of Judaism" held by most of his comrades on the French Left. He noted that Fourier, Proudhon, Toussenel, and Bakunin had already denounced the Jews for usury and parasitic middleman activities.[82] This was erroneous enough, but

> it is likewise the view of men who would vehemently protest were you to attribute to them the least hint of prepossession, it is the view of intellectuals enlightened in all things save this, it is even the view of some socialists, notably Jaurès, and that is why it must be answered.[83]

A short time before this polemic Jaurès had indeed written a reply in *La Petite République* to Drumont's campaign against the Jews which was highly equivocal in tone. Although already a leading Dreyfusard, Jean Jaurès agreed that Jews exercised "an inordinate and formidable influence in our society";

he further suggested that "the social concept of the Jew, based on the idea of trade, is in perfect harmony with the mechanism of capital."[84] Had Drumont merely confined himself to pointing this out, then Jaurès implied that he would have supported him—"such a socialism, tinted with anti-Semitism, would scarcely have raised any objections among *les esprits libres*."[85]

Bernard Lazare strongly objected to this profoundly disturbing remark of Jaurès. He regarded it as symptomatic of a pernicious trend of opinion on the French Left to which he had at one time subscribed but now emphatically repudiated. "They [the socialists] regard capitalism as a Jewish creation, and just as does Drumont after Gougenot des Mousseaux, so does Jaurès after Marx speak of the judaization of the Christian peoples."[86] Lazare concentrated his fire on this one-sided and (to his mind) cripplingly dogmatic stereotype of the Jew which ran like a red thread through modern socialism. Marx, with his call to *de-judaize* the Jews in order to complete their emancipation, had been one of the prime culprits. As a young man Marx had indulged himself in "empty religio-economic metaphysics" at a time when he knew almost nothing about the Jews.[87]

With this critique of Marx and the socialists Lazare had come full circle in his spiritual odyssey. The man who had once ignorantly vilified the "mercantilism of the Talmud" now proceeded to show that the social concept of the Talmudists in fact glorified *manual* work. The great Talmudic scholars and medieval rabbis had themselves been artisans and "anti-mercantile" in outlook. The Talmud, like the Bible, regarded agriculture as a preeminent activity. One could not find any social concept based on trade in Rashi, Maimonides, or Joseph Caro. Nor was there any basis in the Hebrew Bible for such a concept. On the contrary, the prophets and psalmists consistently defended the poor, the humble, and the small freeholders against the encroachments of the wealthy and powerful. It was the Phoenicians and Greeks, not the Children of Israel, who had been the middlemen and carriers of trade in the ancient Middle East. In more recent times, philosophers and economists of Jewish origin were primarily remarkable for their opposition, indifference, or hostility to commerce. Spinoza, in the best rabbinical tradition, had preferred to earn a living grinding lenses rather than seeking fame, honors, and wealth in the Courts of Europe. Even David Ricardo's economic theories were scarcely an apologia for capitalism; while Marx and Lassalle, who had based their economic analysis on Ricardian concepts, arrived at impeccably socialist conclusions. It was French, Scottish, and English political economists such as Turgot, Adam Smith, David Hume, and Jeremy Bentham (all of them non-Jews) who had established the foundations of laissez-faire economics, with their hard-headed advocacy of the profit-motive and utilitarian market philosophies.[88]

Socialists not only ignored these facts when they mistakenly identified the Jews with capitalist usury, but they also completely overlooked the class-struggle within the Jewish communities. In Russia, Poland, Holland, France, England, and America, the Jewish worker stood in open conflict with his employers. "Of all proletarians, the Jewish proletarian is the most wretched, having against him not only the rich and poor of the peoples in whose midst he lives."[89] In his last writings, Bernard Lazare emphasized this class-struggle *within* Jewish society and "the rottenness of the Jewish upper classes" as a fundamental barrier to full national emancipation.[90] More than any other people, the Jews would have to rid themselves of their servility to the rich and cease to be "revolutionaries in the society of others" instead of their own.[91] This is one of the main themes in *Le Fumier de Job* (Job's dungheap)—a collection of aphorisms written shortly before his early death at the age of thirty-eight in 1903. This little fragment gives one a glimpse of the last stage in Lazare's aborted journey back to the sources of Jewish consciousness. Though written by an unrepentant atheist and anarchist revolutionary, it contains a moving awareness of the universal, transcendent aspects of the Jewish experience and the first seeds of a national renewal of Jewish identity despite the steamroller impact of republican assimilation. Nevertheless, there is no basis for the wildly inflated claim made by the historian Michael Marrus many years ago, that Lazare, Max Nordau, and their few supporters instituted a "Zionist Revolution" in fin-de-siècle France.[92]

Lazare was, however, unique among French left-wing intellectuals in the vehemence of his denunciations of antisemitism as a reactionary doctrine after 1895.[93] A year later he came to stress the noxious clerical role in French antisemitism which sought to return Jews to the equivalent of the medieval ghetto or (in the case of the racists) to expel them. It was an engine of war not only against the Jews but a threat to the French Republic and its revolutionary tradition—directed against dissenters, radical free-thinkers, Protestants, socialists, and anarchists. The leading French impressionist painter, Camille Pissarro (himself an anarchist, a Jew, and a Dreyfusard) was one contemporary who was powerfully struck by Lazare's 1896 brochure *Contre l'Antisémitisme.*[94] He expressed agreement and also pleasure at the thought that "a Semite should so eloquently defend these ideas."[95] He singled out for praise Lazare's conviction and courage in exposing so many anti-Jewish myths and falsehoods.[96] Lazare had by this time realized the degree to which he had previously *underestimated* the Catholic Church's decisive role in the propagation of antisemitism. Indeed, he planned a number of works (that were never to be written) on ritual murder, the blood-cult, and the use of the Judas legend, which would have amplified these points.[97] In his posthumous *Le Fumier de Job,* antisemitism is perceived above all as a *Christian* religious pathology. The devastating role of the deicide charge is also fully recognized. So, too, is the demoralizing influence on Jews themselves of having to conform themselves or adapt to Christian prejudices, stereotypes, and irrational myths.[98]

French antisemites, it should be said, continued to maintain a certain ambivalence towards Lazare throughout his life. Drumont, as we have seen, admired the "impartiality" and "objectivity" of Lazare's *History of Antisemitism.* Despite their subsequent duel, Péguy claimed in 1910 that the "Pope of French antisemitism" had always recognized Lazare's greatness of character, dignity, and devotion to Israel.[99] Other Judeophobes after Drumont would repeatedly recommend Lazare's history as the only book on antisemitism, written by a Jew, that was worth reading. This view was clearly expressed by Charles Maurras, the intellectual founder and moving spirit of Action Française. Maurras was the leading nationalist antisemite in France during the first half of the 20th century. He certainly admired part of Lazare's work, especially the section which he described as the "World Dictionary" of the "Jewish Socialist International." A radical right-wing chauvinist, Maurras quickly grasped that Lazare's emphasis on Jewish "revolutionism" along with his depiction of Judaic "exclusivism" fitted his own view of the Jews as a "State within the State" and the embodiment of "Anti-France." For Maurras's disciples, Lazare was important because he had exposed the endemically subversive character of Judaism in any Catholic society and hierarchical State. Significantly, in 1907, the royalist Action Française brought out a selected edition of Lazare's study of antisemitism, underlining his harsh judgments on the eternally unsociable Jew—"anarchist, cosmopolitan, a revolutionary agent but conservative towards himself."[100]

At the same time, despite such apparent enthusiasm, most French antisemites also saw the militant Dreyfusard Lazare as their sworn enemy. The Action Française described the monument erected in his memory at Nîmes in 1908 as "*la statue infâme*"—a symbol of anarchy, disorder, and ruin. It was mutilated several times by hooligans of the ultra-nationalist movement, the *Camelots du Roi.*[101] Indeed, ever since he had entered the fray in 1895 with his call for a revision of the Dreyfus trial, Lazare would be a target of abuse without ever attaining the notoriety of other Dreyfusards such as Zola, Picquart, or Joseph Reinach. Nonetheless, he was regarded as a key intermediary in the so-called Jewish syndicate—the connecting link between a "Semitic conspiracy" of high finance and the street agitation organized by corrupt Dreyfusard traitors.[102] Thus the antisemites implicitly recognized that Lazare had changed his spots, even if he never managed to rewrite the work that they professed to admire and from which they readily quoted. His biographer, Nelly Wilson put it well when she wrote: "Although *Antisemitism. Its History and Causes* was never rewritten in book form, Bernard Lazare's life was a passionate rewriting of it in action, and the first stage came with the Dreyfus Affair."[103]

The second stage in Lazare's odyssey would be the dramatic revision of his earlier antipathy to East European Jewry. From an initial posture of assimilationist arrogance and cultural superiority, Bernard Lazare would become by 1897 the most intrepid defender in France of Jewish immigrants from the East. Where he had once glorified the elitist patriotism of well-established and hard-working "*Israélites,*" he now lacerated the French Jewish bourgeoisie for abandoning their ill-fated co-religionists in the (illusory) belief that they might thereby escape the rigors of antisemitism. Where Lazare had once believed that antisemitism could actually accelerate the proletarian revolution, he now knew that such expectations were delusional. Where he had once been bewitched by socialist and anarchist stereotypes concerning "Jewish capitalism," he now began to flay these myths which had poisoned the left-wing vocabulary. No revolutionary in France during the mid-1890s grasped better than Bernard Lazare the urgent need for a militant struggle against antisemitism as a threat to human rights in general and to Jewish dignity in particular.[104] Through his crusade for Dreyfus, he would acquire a new self-knowledge and the indomitable courage to fight for truth, social justice, proletarian *and* Jewish national emancipation as complementary ideals.

Notes

1. Jean-Denis Bredin, *Bernard Lazare. De L'Anarchiste au Prophète* (Paris, 1992).

2. See Robert S. Wistrich, *Revolutionary Jews from Marx to Trotsky* (London, 1976), 34–53.

3. Jean-Maurice Muslak, "Bernard Lazare," *Revue des Études Juives* (1946): 39ff.; see also the fine biography by Nelly Wilson, *Bernard Lazare. Antisemitism and Jewish Identity in late Nineteenth-Century France* (Cambridge, 1978), which is still the best single account of his life and ideas.

4. Edouard Drumont, *La France Juive* (Paris, 1886), 1: xvi ff.

5. See Frederich Busi, *The Pope of Antisemitism. The Career and Legacy of Edouard-Adolphe Drumont* (London, 1986).

6. Bernard Lazare, "Juifs et Israélites," *Entretiens politiques et littéraires* 1 (Sept. 1890): 176–79. See also the perceptive analysis by Nelly Jussem Wilson, "Bernard Lazare's Jewish Journey: From Being an Israelite to Being a Jew," *Jewish Social Studies* 26, no. 3 (July 1964): 146–68; Wistrich, *Revolutionary Jews,* 135–36.

7. Bernard Lazare, "La Solidarité juive," *Entretiens politiques et littéraires* (Oct. 1890): 228 ff.

8. Ibid.; see also Muslak, "Bernard Lazare," 44, who aptly remarks, "Il répresente ici très typiquement le Juif français tel que l'avait fait un siècle d'assimilation."

9. Bernard Lazare, "La Solidarité juive," 231.

10. Ibid.

11. Ibid.

12. Ibid., 230. Also Bredin, *Bernard Lazare,* 107–12; and Philippe Oriol, *Bernard Lazare* (Paris, 2003).

13. See Zeev Sternhell, *Maurice Barrès et le Nationalisme Français* (Paris, 1972); and idem, *La Droite Révolutionnaire 1885–1914. Les Origines Françaises du Fascisme* (Paris, 1978), 177–214; also the massive work by Stephen Wilson, *Ideology and Experience. Antisemitism in France at the Time of the Dreyfus Affair* (London, 1982).

14. Bernard Lazare, *L'Antisémitisme, Son Histoire et Ses Causes* (Paris, 1969). See also my introduction to the most recent English-language edition, Bernard Lazare, *Antisemitism. Its History and Causes* (Lincoln, Neb., 1995), v–xx.

15. Lazare, *L'Antisémitisme,* 12.

16. Ibid., 143–44.

17. Ibid., 148.

18. Ibid., 149.

19. Ibid., 114.

20. Ibid., 168–69; see also Bernard Lazare, *Juifs et Antisémites* (Paris, 1992) edited by Philippe Oriol.

21. Gougenot des Mousseaux, *Le Juif, le judaïsme et la judaïsation des peoples chrétiens* (Paris, 1869), xxv; and Bernard Lazare, "L'esprit révolutionnaire dans le judaïsme," *Revue bleue,* 20 May 1893; see also idem, *Juifs et Antisémites,* 83–125 for the revision of some of his earlier views about Judaism and antisemitism.

22. Bernard Lazare, *L'Antisémitisme, Son Histoire et Ses Causes,* 152–53.

23. Ibid., 154.

24. Ibid., 157.

25. Ibid., 192.

26. Ibid., 166; see also Bredin, *Bernard Lazare,* 112–13.

27. Lazare, *L'Antisémitisme,* 170: "Ils n'en ont pas moins subi, ataviquement et éducativement, l'influence nationale juive."

28. Ibid., 176. Also Bredin, *Bernard Lazare,* 129.

29. Lazare, *L'Antisémitisme,* 179–80.

30. Ibid., 198.

31. Ibid., 199.

32. Wilson, *Bernard Lazare,* 206–21.

33. As late as 31 December 1894 Lazare could still praise Drumont in *L'Écho de Paris* for his "Jewish" (!) prophetism in denouncing the rich. "C'est un homme doué d'une violente et excellente haine instinctive; il est animé d'un vif desir de justice, et agité d'une horreur toute évangelique et toute juive des riches—je dis juive, car nul plus que les prophétistes et les psalmists n'a attaqué la richesse, et on trouve dans l'Évangile l'écho de ses colères."

34. Edouard Drumont, *La Libre Parole,* 10 Jan. 1895, 1. "C'est un livre fort nourri de faits et dominé d'un bout à l'autre, par un bel effort d'impartialité. . . ."

35. Edouard Drumont, *La Libre Parole,* 22 Oct. 1895; and Bernard Lazare, *Contre L'Antisémitisme* (Paris, 1896), 25–26, letter to *La Libre Parole* dated 23 Oct. 1895.

36. Bernard Lazare, *La Justice,* 17th Nov. 1894; see also Robert S. Wistrich, "Three Dreyfusard Heroes: Lazare, Zola, Clemenceau," in *Les Intellectuels Face à L'Affaire Dreyfus. Alors et Aujourd'hui,* edited by Roselyne Koren et al. (Paris, 1998), 13–41.

37. Bernard Lazare, "Lettres Proletariennes. . . ," *Antisémitisme et Révolution* (Paris, 1895), 12; also Michel Dreyfus, *L'Antisémitisme à Gauche* (Paris, 2009), 86–89 for other views on the French Left.

38. Bernard Lazare, *Contre l'Antisémitisme,* 8, a collection of polemical articles which originally appeared in *Le Voltaire* during May–June 1896; also Lazare, *Juifs et Antisémites,* 91–122.

39. Bernard Lazare, *Contre L'Antisémitisme* (Paris, 1896), 6.

40. Bernard Lazare, *Une erreur judiciaire: la vérité sur l'affaire Dreyfus* (Brussels, 1896), 9.

41. Alexandre Zévaès, "Une apologie de Dreyfus," *La Petite République,* 10 Nov. 1896.

42. Ibid. Zévaès, it would appear, was a latent antisemite whose prejudices were still manifest in the Vichy period. See M. Dreyfus, *L'Antisémitisme à Gauche,* 80.

43. See Harvey Goldberg, "Jean Jaurès and the Jewish Question," *Jewish Social Studies*, 20, no. 2 (Apr. 1958): 67–94, and Robert S. Wistrich, "French Socialism and the Dreyfus Affair," *Wiener Library Bulletin* 28, new series, nos. 35–36 (1975); also M. Dreyfus, *L'Antisémitisme à Gauche,* 22–27, 74–78, 116–24.

44. Bernard Lazare, "Lettre ouverte à M. Trarieux," in *L'Aurore,* 7 June 1899.

45. Ibid.; see also Bredin, *Bernard Lazare,* 250–51 for the embarrassment and displeasure Lazare's protest provoked among Dreyfusards like Picquart or Trarieux.

46. Philippe Oriol, "Zadoc Kahn et l'affaire Dreyfus," in *Zadoc Kahn. Un grand rabbin entre culture juive, affaire Dreyfus et laïcité,* edited by Jean-Claude Kuperminc and Jean-Philippe Chaumont (Paris, 2007), 153–70.

47. Bernard Lazare, "Le Nationalisme et Émancipation juive," *L'Écho Sioniste,* nos. 9–10 (20 Mar.–5 Apr. 1901): 134 (lecture delivered in the winter of 1899).

48. *L'Écho Sioniste,* no. 11 (20 Apr. 1901): 150–51. "En effet, quand le Juif eut rompu les barrières qui le separaient du monde, il se déjudaïsa lentement et de plus, . . . il se corrompit au contact de la société chrétienne; il perdit ses vertus propres, et ne gagna que les vices de ceux qui l'entouraient."

49. Nelly Wilson, *Bernard-Lazare,* 228–34.

50. Bernard Lazare, "Nationalisme et Émancipation," *Kadimah* (15 Aug. 1898): 2–3.

51. See Steve Uran, "La Réception de l'Affaire Dreyfus en Algérie," in *L'Affaire Dreyfus de A à Z,* edited by Michel Drouin (Paris, 1994), 521–29.

52. Lecture by Bernard Lazare, 6 March 1897, for the Association of Russian-Jewish Students in Paris; reproduced in idem, *Job's Dungheap* (New York, 1948), 70.

53. Ibid., 73.

54. *L'Echo Sioniste* 5 (20 Apr. and 5 May 1901): 169; see also Oriol, *Bernard Lazare,* 156–58.

55. *L'Echo Sioniste* (Mar.–Apr. 1901): 135.

56. Ibid.

57. *L'Echo Sioniste,* nos. 12–13 (May 1901): 168.

58. *L'Echo Sioniste* (Mar.–Apr. 1901): 134.

59. *L'Echo Sioniste,* no. 11 (Apr. 1901): 152.

60. Charles Péguy, *Notre Jeunesse* (Paris, 1957), 117.

61. Ibid., 97–98. "Quand on faisait des pourparlers pour créer un grand quotidien. . .et qu'on demandait de l'argent aux juifs. . .les capitalistes, les commanditaires juifs n'y mettaient guère qu'une condition: c'était que Bernard-Lazare n'y écrivit pas."

62. Bernard Lazare, *L'Écho Sioniste* (20 Apr. 1901): 152; see also his vitriolic article entitled "Capitalisme juif et Démocratie," in *L'Aurore,* 20 May 1901, which attacked the Jewish bourgeoisie of France—"la pire de toutes," for their indifference to their persecuted brethren.

63. Bernard Lazare, *L'Aurore,* 7 June 1899. Also Bredin, *Bernard Lazare,* 299–306.

64. The correspondence between Herzl and Lazare in the Zionist Central Archives (Jerusalem) is reproduced in Edmund Silberner, "Bernard Lazare and Zionism," *Shivat Zion* (Jerusalem, 1953): 350–61. On 14 May 1897 Lazare wrote to Herzl: "Je crois plus que jamais à la force de la nation juive, plus que jamais à la nécessité de la voir s'affirmer en tant que telle et j'y aiderai de toute ma force."

65. Lazare to Herzl, 24 Mar. 1899, in ibid., 360.

66. Ibid.

67. Lazare to Herzl, ibid., 359. "Vous avez su remuer les profondeurs d'Israël, vous lui avez apporté votre amour et votre vie, vous l'aurez réveillé. . . ."

68. Ibid., 360.

69. Lazare to Herzl, 4 Feb. 1899, in ibid., 357–60.

70. Ibid.

71. B. Lazare, "Le Congrès Sioniste et le Sultan," *Pro Armenia,* 10 Jan. 1902.

72. Lazare to Herzl, in Silberner, "Bernard Lazare and Zionism," 358.

73. See Muslak, "Bernard Lazare," 62; Hannah Arendt, "From the Dreyfus Affair to France Today," *Jewish Social Studies* (1946): 173–217; and Nelly Wilson, *Bernard Lazare,* 245.

74. Muslak, "Bernard Lazare," 52. "Tribun du people dispersé, il est reçu comme un sauveur." The Jews of Romania were especially grateful for his constant intercessions on their behalf. See Bernard Lazare, "Les Juifs en Roumanie," *Cahiers de la Quinzaine,* series 3, no. 8 (Paris, 1902); and three articles in *L'Aurore* (4 July 1900, 20 July 1900 and 9 Aug. 1900)—all devoted to the plight of Romanian Jewry.

75. Charles Péguy, *Notre Jeunesse,* 101.

76. Ibid., 102.

77. Ibid., 108–9. "Bernard Lazare s'opposait de tout ce qu'il avait encore de force à la dégenération, à la deviation du dreyfusisme en politique, en démagogie combiste." See Bernard Lazare, "Pour et Contre les Congrégations," *Cahiers de la Quinzaine,* series 3, no. 21 (Paris, 1902).

78. See Jacques Viard, "Péguy et la mort de Bernard-Lazare," *Les Nouveaux Cahiers,* no. 21 (Summer 1970): 45–48.

79. See *Jaurès, les Socialistes et l'Affaire Dreyfus* (Le Colloque de Montreuil, 3 Dec. 1994, published by *Cahiers Trimestriels Jean Jaurès* (Oct.–Dec. 1995).

80. *Lettre des ouvriers juifs de Paris au parti socialiste français* (Paris, 1898); quoted in E. Tcherski, "Die Dreyfus-Affare, die Arbeter-Immigranten, un die französische-yiddische Firers," in *Yidn in Frankraich* (New York, 1942), edited by E. Tcherikower, 2 vols., 165–68. See also Henry Bulawko, "Les Socialistes et l'Affaire," *Les Nouveaux Cahiers,* no. 27 (1971–1972): 26–30.

81. *Lettre des ouvriers juifs de Paris au parti socialiste français,* 17–18; see also Léonti Soloveitschik, *Un proletariat méconnu: étude sur la situation sociale et*

économique des ouvriers juifs (Paris, 1898). This sociological study was an important breakthrough in making the labor movement in France aware of the existence of a worldwide Jewish proletariat.

82. In his 1897 lecture on nationalism and Jewish emancipation (see *L'Écho Sioniste,* nos. 12–13 [May 1901]: 167), Lazare observed that "Drumont s'appuie sur Proudhon, sur Fourier, sur Toussenel et il peut invoquer Bakounine qui ne parlait jamais de Marx qu'en l'appelant le Juif allemand."

83. Bernard Lazare, "Judaism's Social Concept and the Jewish People," in *Job's Dungheap,* 109. This essay was a reply not only to Jean Jaurès but also to Lazare's anarchist colleague, Augustin Hamon, whose writings were antisemitically tinged. Hamon had published a French translation of Karl Marx's "Zur Judenfrage" in *L'Humanité Nouvelle* (1898), 580–85.

84. See Jean Jaurès, "L'embarras de M. Drumont," *La Petite République,* 13 Dec. 1898, for the original source.

85. Ibid.

86. Bernard Lazare, *Job's Dungheap,* 109–10. For Jaurès's reaction to the charge that he had flirted with antisemitism, see Marc Jarblum, "Démocratie, question nationale et sionisme en Europe centrale: qu'en pensait Jaurès," *Le Mouvement Social,* no. 52 (July–Sept. 1965): 85–97. Jaurès also made an interesting comment about Zionism in connection with Lazare: "Je n'ai connu qu'un Juif français qui ait défendu cette cause: Bernard Lazare. Mais il était seul ou presque. Il s'est heurté à une opposition violente de la totalité des intellectuels juifs, bourgeois aussi bien que socialistes."

87. Bernard Lazare, *Job's Dungheap,* 113.

88. Ibid., 121–22.

89. Ibid., 128.

90. Ibid., 41; see also Philippe Oriol's introduction to his edition of Lazare's *Le Fumier de Job* (Paris, 1998), 8–18.

91. Bernard Lazare, "Capitalisme juif et Démocratie," *L'Aurore,* 20 May 1901.

92. See Michael Marrus, *Les Juifs de France à L'époque de L'affaire Dreyfus* (Paris, 1972), 279–321.

93. Robert S. Wistrich, "French Socialism and the Dreyfus Affair"; and M. Dreyfus, *L'Antisémitisme à Gauche,* 43–98.

94. Bernard Lazare, *Contre l'Antisémitisme* (Paris, 1896), 4–7.

95. Ibid., 6.

96. See Central Zionist Archives, Jerusalem, K 22/77; and Wistrich, introduction to Lazare's *'Antisemitism. Its History and Causes,* xix.

97. See Wilson, *Bernard Lazare,* 207–13; also Robert S. Wistrich, *Antisemitism: The Longest Hatred* (London, 1991), on Christian antisemitism.

98. Bernard Lazare, *Le Fumier de Job* (Paris, 1998), 51–60.

99. Charles Péguy, *Notre Jeunesse* (Paris, 1969, reissue), 91.

100. See *Action Française,* t. xix, 1907, 177; also Charles Maurras, "Bernard-Lazare," *Action Française,* 15 Sept. 1908, and idem, *Au Signe du Flore. La Fondation de l'Action Française, 1898–1900* (Paris, 1933), 51–52, 87–89.

101. Wilson, *Bernard Lazare,* 272–74.

102. See Nelly Wilson, "Bernard-Lazare et le Syndicat," in *Les Écrivains et l'Affaire Dreyfus,* edited by G. Leroy (Paris, 1983), 27–33.

103. Wilson, *Bernard Lazare,* 109; Wistrich, "Introduction" to Lazare's history, xvi–xvii.

104. Claude Sahel, "Comment Bernard Lazare est-il devenu dreyfusard? Génèse d'une décision," in *Comment devient-on dreyfusard?* Janine Chêne et al., eds. (Paris, 1997), 115–26.

CHAPTER 8

Social Democracy and Judeophobia in Imperial Vienna

In the Austro-Hungarian Monarchy around 1910 there were more than two-and-a-quarter-million Jews—a concentration exceeded in Europe only by that of the Tsarist Russian Empire. However, in contrast to absolutist Russia where Jews suffered from fierce discrimination, persecution, and pogroms, Austro-Hungarian Jewry since 1867 had enjoyed full emancipation. In the Imperial capital of Vienna, where there were 175,000 Jews by 1910 (about 10% of the total population), they had become the driving force of economic and cultural life. Their presence was heavily felt in the free professions, in banking, commerce, industry, and journalism (especially in the liberal and socialist press). Indeed a brilliant galaxy of Jewish talent would transform the life of the capital city in fin-de-siècle Austria and helped to shape the contours of 20th-century culture. At the same time, antisemitism in Vienna was significantly stronger than in any other European metropolis and led to the election in 1897 of the populist antisemite and Christian-Social Party leader, Karl Lueger, as Mayor—a "democratic" mandate which he held until his death in 1910.

Jewish intellectuals played a major role in the foundation of the Austrian Social Democratic Party (SPÖ) in 1889. Its first leader, Victor Adler, a Jewish-born physician, dominated the party for almost thirty years. Gifted with rich political intuition and a sense for tactical improvisation, Adler was the great "unifier" of the Party who knew how to navigate his way through the complexities of a "pseudo-constitutional" State. The son of a wealthy Jewish businessman from Moravia, Adler had been educated at the Schottengymnasium—an elite and predominantly Catholic school in Vienna. At the University of Vienna he studied medicine in the 1870s (Sigmund Freud, in his *The Interpretation of Dreams,* recalled a clash with Adler during those years)—and he developed a markedly pan-German oppositional and democratic outlook. At the age of 26, Adler seemingly resolved his conflicted identity problem by converting to Protestantism—the minority Christian religion in Catholic Austria. Nevertheless, the "Jewish Question" would continue to haunt Adler and the Socialist Party which he founded, until his death in 1918—which coincided with the collapse of the Danubian Monarchy.

The Austrian socialist position on the Jewish issue was a logical continuation of established liberal theories of human equality and the desirability of full Jewish integration into the national body politic. It was a position whose origins dated back to the French Revolution of 1789. At the same time, Socialists since the 1830s had developed a more hostile attitude to Jewish social and economic activity than their liberal predecessors. In France and Germany, Jews had been identified on the Left with petty huckstering and "parasitic" middleman occupations. Karl Marx had made it clear in his *Zur Judenfrage* (1844) that "Emancipation from *haggling* and *money,* from practical, real Judaism would be the self-emancipation of our time."[1] Marx's anti-Jewish stereotypes had some influence on the leaders of the SPÖ, by reinforcing pre-existing prejudices and a certain distaste for the masses of *Ostjuden* on the fringes of the Empire. For the Austrian Marxists the economic role of Galician Jews, in particular, seemed a microcosm of everything that was "unproductive" in the decomposing feudal society gradually being infiltrated by capitalism.

The southern Polish province of Galicia, annexed in the late 18th century to Austria, was the home of two-thirds of Habsburg Jewry a century later. Already in the early 19th century it had been regarded by Austrian bureaucrats (as well as some Jewish "enlighteners") as a symbol of backwardness. The Austro-German liberal and prominent Jewish writer, Karl-Emil Franzos, referred to this "Half-Asia" (*Halb-Asien*) in the 1860s as a realm of darkness, sordid barbarism, clerical fanaticism, and violent hatreds.[2] The Jewish ghettos were equated by such authors with obscurantist superstitions, the futile clinging to obsolete customs and to the Yiddish language (invariably considered by the *maskilim* or liberal "enlighteners" as a corrupt and vulgar jargon). Viennese Jewish liberals could not abide the incorrigible ethnic particularism of Jewish Galicia. To this "defect," the socialists would add their horror of those Jews who "lived from the air" (*Luftmenschen*)—primarily engaged in haggling and petty trade. Like the assimilated Jewish bourgeoisie of Vienna from which he came, socialists like Victor Adler had fully internalized anti-Jewish stereotypes concerning ghetto Jews and traditional Judaism from their Gentile environment. Precisely because they considered themselves as the vanguard of "progress," socialist leaders like Victor and (his son) Friedrich Adler, Otto Bauer, Friedrich Austerlitz, and Wilhelm Ellenbogen—all of them highly assimilated and

Germanized Jewish middle-class intellectuals—shared the revulsion of most Gentile Austrians against the shabby external appearance, stubborn Orthodoxy, insular customs, and national separatism of traditional Jewry. This affected their response to the rise of Austrian antisemitism.

Austrian socialists of Jewish origin were by no means blind to the real perniciousness of modern antisemitism. But their opposition to anti-Jewish agitation was in some respects paralyzed by their hostility to the *Ostjuden* and the unconscious self-hatred it engendered. As elsewhere, many Austrian Socialists of Jewish origin had arrived at their new credo through a rejection of Judaism and their own ethnic background. In this they were preceded by such iconoclastic German-Jewish radicals as Karl Ludwig Börne, Heinrich Heine, Karl Marx, and Ferdinand Lassalle. Like these forerunners (with the exception of the repentant Heine) they regarded "Judaism" in the socio-economic sense as a symbol of alienation and the antithesis of the universal dialectic of human emancipation. Jewry was misleadingly perceived as the embodiment of greed, egoism, and the capitalist ethic as well as being one of the pillars of European feudal reaction. In their hostility to the Rothschilds, to the Jewish *Finanzaristokratie* (finance aristocracy), or the *Ostjuden,* for example, there was little to distinguish the socialists of Imperial Vienna from the Austrian antisemitic parties.

In a famous passage on the Galician *Ostjuden* who had settled in Vienna's Second District, the Leopoldstadt, during and after the First World War, the Austrian novelist Joseph Roth observed:

> It is terribly difficult to be an East European Jew; there is no harder fate than to be an East European Jewish alien in Vienna. . . . For the Christian-Social party, they are Jews. For German Nationalists, they are Semites. For Social Democrats, they are unproductive elements.

Both the Christian-Social Party and the German nationalists, Roth pointed out, "include antisemitism as an important point in their programs." The Social Democrats, on the other hand, "fear being labeled as a 'Jewish party.'"[3] This perceptive summing up of the situation in the early 1920s reflected a remarkable continuity with the prewar period.[4] The Social Democrats in late 19th-century Austria, influenced by classic leftist prejudices against Jews and Judaism, had already become entangled in a defensive and largely futile war to prove that they were not a *Judenschutztruppe* (Jewish protective guard). From this starting-point they could scarcely wage an effective battle against militant political antisemitism. The fact that the Austrian Social Democrats did eventually take a stand against the Catholic and pan-German varieties of antisemitism in 19th- and 20th-century Imperial Austria should not obscure the extent to which the party leadership itself contributed to the growth of the phenomenon.[5]

The discussion of socialist and Marxist attitudes to antisemitism (whether in Austria or elsewhere) has often been confused by the erroneous and illogical assumption that left-wing parties are immunized against racial, religious, or ethnic prejudice.[6] The theory and above all the *praxis* of the Austrian workers' movement are a good illustration of how unfounded this assumption is when closely examined in concrete historical situations. Not only was the labor movement far from immune to the cultural and political antisemitism that began to pervade broad strata of German-Austrian society from the early 1880s onward, but it was from the outset permeated with prejudices against Jews.[7] This was true at the mass level, as it was in the upper reaches of the Austrian party. However, in contrast to German Nationalist or Christian Social Judeophobia, "socialist" prejudices were never really activated or used as a major strategic weapon in politics. Antisemitism did not feature in official party platforms, nor was there any intention of deliberately and actively discriminating against Austrian Jews, though calls to limit their presence and influence were heard on several occasions within the Socialist party.[8] As in Imperial Germany, socialist animus was expressed primarily in the highly ambivalent stance adopted toward the rise of the populist antisemitic movement in Vienna after 1890. The seeds of the failure to adequately resist and combat the propaganda of this movement were already apparent in a letter from Vienna by Karl Kautsky (dated June 1884) in which he complains to Engels: "We are having trouble preventing our own people from fraternizing with the antisemites. The antisemites are now our most dangerous opponents, because their appearance is oppositional and democratic, thus appealing to the workers' instincts."[9]

Karl Kautsky, a Marxist of Czech-German background, was not mistaken in his assessment of the appeal of Georg von Schönerer's pan-German nationalists (*Deutschnationale*) to a section of the Austrian workers, who were increasingly alarmed at the consequences of Czech and Jewish immigration to Vienna. Other Austro-Marxists like Wilhelm Ellenbogen (a middle-class intellectual and physician of Jewish origin) saw this xenophobic appeal more as a reaction of déclassé petit bourgeois strata to the impact of large-scale capitalist methods of production.[10] This explanation had a certain validity for Vienna, where the artisanal character of local industry and the crisis of the craftsmen were indeed central to the *origins* of the antisemitic movement in the 1880s. It is also true that in the early phases of Austrian industrialization there was less of a clear dividing line between the lower *Bürgertum* and the proletariat. This lack of a developed class consciousness made it easier for antisemitic stereotypes in the early 1880s to infiltrate the nascent working class.[11]

The classic Marxist schema, according to which antisemitism was a reaction of "medieval, declining strata against modern society," would prove, however, to be only partially applicable to Austria-Hungary in the late 19th century.[12] Furthermore, such views, while ostensibly intended to demonstrate and warn against the "reactionary" character of antisemitism, proved quite insufficient in ensuring the immunization of the labor movement against ethnic prejudices.[13] The Marxist assumption that modern capitalism must inexorably lead to the disappearance of premodern, preindustrial lower middle strata in the population (and thereby to the collapse of the antisemitic movement) was also to prove illusory in the Central European context. Such fatalistic determinism was, moreover, a decidedly flimsy basis on which to wage a successful resistance to antisemitic demagogy. Equally vain was the new Marxist dogma in the 1890s that historical development would inevitably drive the antisemitic *Kleinbürgertum* into the arms of the Austrian Social Democrats.[14]

In their reliance on such a mechanistic concept of social change, Austro-Marxist theoreticians did not substantially diverge from their colleagues in most other European social democratic parties. The social, economic, and political context in which they operated *was,* however, substantially different. It is this that best explains why the concessions made to Judeophobic terminology and attitudes appeared to go far beyond what was necessary. In the first place the "Jewish Question" in Vienna had become significantly more acute by the 1890s than elsewhere in Western or Central Europe, though parallel developments were occurring all over the Continent. Between 1869 and 1880 the Jewish population had risen from 40,227 (6.10 percent of the total population) to 72,588 (10.06 percent). By 1910 there were 175,818 Jews in Vienna where fifty years earlier there had been only 6,217 (2.16 percent)—a stupendous rate of growth. When these demographic data are related to the occupational structure of Viennese Jewry and the historic traditions of Judeophobia in Catholic Austria, the dramatic rise of political antisemitism seems less surprising. From the socialist standpoint, moreover, the economic structure of Viennese Jewry, and in particular its crucial role in banking, industrial capitalism, commerce, department stores, the liberal press, and the free professions hardly made the relatively prosperous Jewish community appear as the natural ally of a proletarian movement.[15]

Even among the poorer Jews of the Leopoldstadt, who had immigrated after 1860 from Hungary, Galicia, or Moravia, there were serious social and cultural obstacles to participation in the labor movement. Most of the immigrant Jews of lower status were not genuine proletarians, and very few were factory workers.[16] Unlike the lower-class Czech immigrants to Vienna, they did not live in the typical proletarian quarters of Ottakring, Hernals, or Favoriten, and a far greater proportion of Jews than Gentiles, even at the lowest levels of society, were independent (*selbstständig*).[17] The poorer Jews were far from assimilated, retaining in many cases their distinctive language (Yiddish), their dress, mannerisms, mores, and what were perceived as bizarre religious customs. At the turn of the 20th century, with the increased immigration to Vienna of more traditionalist and Orthodox *Ostjuden* from Galicia, the *cultural gap* between this Jewish sector of the population and modern Social Democracy began to widen still further.[18] The rise of Jewish nationalism in fin-de-siècle Vienna was a further factor alienating an important part of the Jewish population from the Austrian Social Democrats; the latter were noticeably unsympathetic to Zionism or even to more modest claims for Jewish cultural-national autonomy in Galicia and Bukovina.[19]

On the other hand, by the end of the 19th century there were also the first clear signs of active Jewish participation in the Austrian labor movement. The most striking feature of this new trend was the role played by a growing section of the Jewish intelligentsia in the leadership of the Social Democratic party, in the party press, and in its myriad cultural, youth, and sport organizations. This intelligentsia was already thoroughly Germanized and identified strongly with both the national and the social objectives of the pan-Austrian labor movement.[20] Along with this assimilated stratum of middle-class intellectual Jews, there was also a palpable drift toward Social Democracy among the new class of commercial employees (*Handelsangestellten*), who constituted a significant proportion of Viennese Jews by the turn of the century.[21] There was also a more nationally minded sector among these commercial employees who became attracted to labor Zionism after 1900, rather than to an independent "Bundist" Jewish workers' movement which had little attraction for poorer Viennese Jews. The Poalei Zion organizations in Austria before 1914, it should be noted, recommended voting for the Social Democrats wherever Jewish national candidates were not available.[22] After the First World War the shift of Vienna Jews toward the Social Democrats, which had occurred before 1914 largely among the educated bourgeois and intellectual strata of Jewry, became a flood. As a result, the image of "Red Vienna" literally fused in antisemitic circles with that of

"Jewish" subversion.[23] In the eyes of Catholic and nationalist antisemites, Jews who identified with Marxism came to be regarded as sworn enemies of traditional Catholic society and culture.

The seeds of this postwar clerical and fascist propaganda against Red Vienna can be found, however, in the late Habsburg period. It was no accident, for example, that in his autobiography, *Mein Kampf* (1924), the young Adolf Hitler explicitly related his hatred of Jews and Social Democrats to experiences in turn-of-the-century Vienna.[24] The fear and anxiety induced by the *Judensozi* (or "Jewish" Social Democrats) were rooted in the class distinctions that continued to pervade Gentile Austrian society and were exacerbated by the impact of the Christian-Social agitation after 1900. Having finally conquered the city of Vienna in 1897, the new Catholic populist rulers under the charismatic leadership of Karl Lueger turned the burden of their propaganda against the rising Social Democratic party. Christian Socialism sought at the turn of the century to become *the* party of the Viennese German bourgeoisie and the supreme defender of *Mittelstand* interests against the "Red Menace." Karl Lueger, who in the 1890s had so successfully united the middle and lower *Bürgertum* against the decaying liberal order in the name of traditional ideals of Austrian *Bürger* culture, now found a new rallying cry in his crusade against the "Judaized" Social Democracy.[25]

The "Red Menace" and the "Jewish Question" merged in the propaganda of Lueger's movement, intensifying from the moment he achieved office. Anti-intellectualism, *Mittelstand* phobias concerning proletarianization, anxiety over socialist atheism, and petit bourgeois fears of Jewish competition were cleverly exploited by the Christian Socials to mobilize their bourgeois clientèle. It was in this atmosphere of anti-Marxism, antisemitism, and rampant anti-intellectualism that déclassé elements like the young Adolf Hitler concocted their crackpot theories of a satanic conspiracy by Jewish Marxists against the German *Volk*. "The names of the Austerlitzes, Davids, Adlers, Ellenbogens, etc.," Hitler histrionically recalled in *Mein Kampf*, "will remain forever engraven in my memory."[26]

Hitler's assumptions, which ultimately led to the mass murder of European Jewry, were of course utterly remote from the actual theories of Austro-Marxism or from the praxis of the Social Democratic movement in Austria-Hungary. Not only did Hitler completely ignore the pronounced *German* character of the Austrian Social Democratic party and its strong emotional attachment to the idea of *Anschluss* (union with Germany), but he clearly knew little about the anti-Jewish and anti-capitalist attitudes of the most prominent leaders in the labor movement. Far from favoring "Jewish" interests or identifying with other Jews—whether in ethnic, religious, or class terms—the "Jewish" leadership of the Austrian Social Democracy bent over backwards to *dissociate* themselves from their former co-religionists. In order to refute the antisemitic attacks on their leadership, they indulged in strategies either of avoidance, trivialization of antisemitism, or even sophisticated justifications that only revealed the extent of their alienation from Jewry.[27] This tradition had begun with the Party's founder, Victor Adler, a fervent German nationalist in his younger days. Adler would set the tone after 1886 on this as on other major issues. He resolved his own personal "Jewish Question" by adopting an official façade of neutrality in the so-called war between philo- and antisemites. In practice, with the spectacular rise of Karl Lueger in the 1890s, this meant favoring the Judeophobes as against their liberal "philosemitic" opponents—who were by no means great defenders of the Jews.

Victor Adler's classmates at grammar school in Vienna had included the famous Austrian historian Heinrich Friedjung (an assimilated Jew and an extreme German nationalist) and the man who would become his life-long friend, the future socialist leader, Engelbert Pernerstorfer. At Gymnasium and university in Vienna, Adler suffered intensely from his Jewishness. He was anti-religious, regarding Judaism as a relic of the past which had no place in the modern secular world. But he would soon discover that even his conversion to Protestantism for pragmatic reasons, was no solution to the problem of antisemitism.[28] Like Freud and Schnitzler, Victor Adler was attracted to psychiatry, a study which he was to put to good use in later years when he became embroiled in the madhouse of Austrian politics. The abundance of Jews in the medical profession was however already creating a backlash of academic antisemitism in the late 1870s when Adler was a student at the university. For example, the distinguished surgeon, Theodor Billroth, had in 1875 deplored "the flooding of the faculty by proletarian Jews from Galicia and Hungary." Billroth claimed that German Jews were "only German-speaking by chance, accidentally educated in Germany, even though they may write or think in the German language more beautifully than many pure Teutons," He considered it undesirable that they should become German academics. Billroth (who, ironically enough, later became a defender of the Jews) wrote in 1876 that the "abyss between purely German and purely Jewish blood" was as deep as that between the ancient Teutons and the Phoenicians.[29]

Stung by these remarks which challenged the core of his own assimilationist credo, Victor Adler discussed them publicly in the *Leseverein* of German national students in Vienna. While rejecting the attacks of the liberal press on Billroth and not questioning his thesis that Eastern Jews were inundating the medical profession, Adler passionately objected to the racialist view that the Jewish "tribal" character was fixed and unalterable. "Jewish blood," he pointed out, "has flowed in German battles," though he added that "the present of German culture is not easily repaid" and the Jews could not expect the gratitude of the German nation. Nevertheless, he was convinced that the bond already formed "would tie the next generation of Jews again more firmly to the German nation." Hence the Germans would have to decide whether they "preferred the thorn in the flesh or whether they would assimilate these remnants of a tribe."[30] All-too-conscious of his own vulnerability, Adler characteristically added: "I don't know whether my personal relation to this question is obscured by the fact that I am myself a Jew."

Victor Adler's Pan-German nationalism in his student years was shared by a coterie of recently emancipated Jews in Imperial Austria.[31] Karl Kautsky, then a young socialist student in Vienna, observed in his memoirs that the Austrian Jews at that time were the most ardent representatives of the *Anschluss* idea which called for the union of German-speaking Austrians to the Second German Reich of Bismarck. Kautsky noted that the *German* cultural nationalism of young Jews like Adler and his circle, who despised the Habsburg dynasty while admiring the Bismarckian Reich, was the one thing which separated him from them.[32] One can best interpret Adler's student Pan-Germanism as an over-compensatory outgrowth of Jewish emancipation and the belief that the *removal* of Catholic influence would break down the last barriers separating Jews from Germans in Imperial Austria. German nationalism in the late 1870s, except in the universities, had not yet turned *völkisch* (ethnic) and still retained strong links with the republican, anti-clerical traditions of 1848. The *grossdeutsch* (Greater German) ideology of this cultural orientation went together with a romantic passion for Wagner's music, the philosophy of Schopenhauer, and the iconoclastic thinking of the young Nietzsche. Even as a socialist, Victor Adler continued to believe in the "civilizing" mission of German *Kultur*. The peak of his political involvement in pan-Germanism came, however, with his co-authorship of Georg von Schönerer's Linz Program of 1882. Together with Heinrich Friedjung, Pernerstorfer and Otto Steinwender, Adler was responsible for an official party program which called for the integration of all the German-speaking parts of the Habsburg monarchy into an autonomous German commonwealth to be joined to the neighboring German Reich by a customs union. The Linz Program envisaged an end to the dualistic Austro-Hungarian State, the incorporation of Bosnia and Herzegovina into Hungary, and autonomy for Galicia and Bukovina. German was to be the *Staatssprache* (language of State) in the new commonwealth which would still be ruling over substantial non-German populations in Bohemia and Moravia, Silesia, and territories that would become part of Yugoslavia after 1918. Adler and Pernerstorfer formulated the more radical social demands calling for a progressive income-tax, a tax on Stock Exchange transactions, obligatory trade unions, nationalization of railways and insurance companies, the limitation of working hours and of child and female labor.[33] These measures, a few years later, would be at the heart of the political program put forward by the Austrian Social Democrats.

The break between von Schönerer and his assimilated Jewish collaborators, Adler and Friedjung, was inevitable once the Pan-German movement became committed to exclusivist *racial* antisemitism. Already in July 1883 (two years before he introduced the notorious "Jew paragraph" into his Linz Program), in the first issue of his *Unverfälschte Deutsche Worte* (Unadulterated German Words), von Schönerer declared that the help of the Jews was not necessary in the struggle against the Slavs. "If some of the Jews want to join our ranks, they may do so for all I care, but only as simple privates, not in any leading position."[34] Even such humiliating "tolerance" disappeared once Georg von Schönerer announced that antisemitism was "the mainstay of our national ideology. . .the most essential expression of genuine popular conviction."[35] Victor Adler's close friend, Pernerstorfer, also found von Schönerer's racism unacceptable, though in his case the influence of German nationalism would prove to be much deeper and carried over more intensely into his career as a leading Austrian Social Democrat.

From 1889 to his death in 1918 Victor Adler would be widely recognized as the undisputed leader of Austrian Social Democracy—a master of the art of tuning his ears to the masses and translating their often confused demands into a more coherent political language. His leadership had to overcome many centrifugal tendencies resulting from operating in a multinational Empire. Free from any fanaticism or theoretical dogma, his strength lay in conciliation and compromise. Victor Adler's view of the "Jewish Question" after leaving the pan-German movement tended to emphasize its socio-economic roots. He argued that the Jews had become dangerous economic competitors in the new liberal era of free competition. This was largely the result of hereditary qualities which had been nourished in the ghetto. Their rise to economic dominance had been made possible by the triumph of the capitalist ethic which had brought about Jewish emancipation. "During the period where the law of might prevailed, they were nothing, but when the law of exchange predominated, they emerged into the foreground."[36] But the Jews were the *products* of capitalism, not its originators, even if they had heightened some of its worst features. "If the Jews are 'the kings of the epoch,' then the epoch is responsible, not the Jews."[37] Adler was aware of the fact that only a small minority of Jews exercised economic power, while the Jewish masses were even poorer and more defenseless than many German or Slav workers. This social reality was, however, ignored by the antisemitic small tradesmen and peasants in Austria-Hungary who regarded "parvenu" Jews, alien to their customs and manners, as the primary cause of their misery. The lower middle classes were simply too backward to grasp the complexity of international economics and the effects of overseas competition on their own conditions: hence they blamed the Jews. In this respect, Adler's views in the late 1880s did not differ much from those of Engels or August Bebel.

Victor Adler, like most of his contemporaries on the Marxist Left, believed antisemitism would disappear only in a socialist society where the so-called Jewish characteristics (which antisemites identified with capitalism) would themselves become superfluous. The revolutionary working class would create a society "in which the qualities referred to, rightly or wrongly, as Jewish would not ensure anyone influence and power or a life of indulgence."[38] The workers, declared Adler, desired "to remove all exploitation, not just Jewish exploitation; to make an end of all corruption, not just Jewish corruption; to destroy all domination, not just Jewish domination!"[39] Adler concluded his Marxist analysis with the prophecy that "the future socialist society will see Ahasuerus, the eternal, wandering Jew into his grave!" Like Karl Kautsky he linked the achievement of socialism with the disappearance of Jewry through a process of natural self-dissolution.

Adler had declared that he was in favor of *neutrality* on the Jewish question. In practice, however, he directed the attacks in his newspaper *Gleichheit* (Equality) far more frequently against the liberal "philo-semites." Indeed he never tired of ridiculing the tactics of the Viennese press—especially the influential *Neue Freie Presse*—in the face of the rising antisemitic movement.[40] He suggested that the bourgeois press reported only those cases where workers spoke out against Judeophobia in public meetings, but completely ignored socialist criticism of the liberals.

> When the class-conscious workers, who are first and foremost anti-capitalist, and therefore prepared for anything but the defense of capitalist Jewry, take a stand against the ravings of antisemitism, then there is a shout of Hallelujah![41]

Gleichheit maintained that such practices served to heighten the contempt and opposition of the workers towards the Austrian middle classes. On 24 December 1887, Adler's paper gave a representative example of the technique which it deplored: German nationalists in Graz had distributed antisemitic leaflets alleging that Dr. Adler was a Jew and "therefore" had never worked in his life! Hence he had no right to speak about the conditions of the working class. *Gleichheit* reported that this ploy had failed because the workers were indifferent to the internecine conflict between Jewish and "Aryan" capital and to the contemptuous parrot-cry "*Jude hinaus!*" (Jews Out!), which was the sum-total of the antisemitic program. But, the report continued, the *Wiener Allgemeine Zeitung* (the only bourgeois paper to cover the event) had completely ignored the substance of the debate, merely concentrating on the ejection of antisemites from the meeting.

> The same paper which at every opportunity attacks the social democrats and whose ignorance is only surpassed by its impertinence, immediately begins to flirt with the same Social Democrats when there is a chance to score a point for the Jews against the antisemites.[42]

Its liberal overtures to the workers earned the *Wiener Allgemeine Zeitung* the scornful title of a "rabbinical paper" in the nascent socialist press. Its "disgusting compliments," *Gleichheit* declared, were more insulting than its enmity. Readers were reminded that the "rabbis," like the priests, sought to manipulate the workers' movement for their own selfish ends. Victor Adler and his followers had no doubt that there was an *essential unity of interests* between rich Jews and antisemites. Where money was involved, Jewish bankers and press magnates could be received at Court and even the antisemitic Don Quixotes fell silent.

> The Jewish proletarian, the poor Jewish woman pedlar is treated with all the brutality of true Aryan race-pride; while the "Jewish question" is being solved by such humane methods, monarchs are compelled to open their doors to Jewish moneylenders; and antisemitism does not rear its head! Poor Jews are hanged but rich Jews are presented at court.[43]

Under the direction of Victor Adler, the central organ of the Austrian Social Democracy, the *Arbeiterzeitung* would adopt a highly equivocal policy towards Jews. This followed the line advocated by Adler at the International Socialist Congress in Brussels (1891), to equally condemn "anti- and philo-Semitic incitement," as if these were somehow comparable phenomena. The central organ of the Austrian Socialist Party would note with pride that it "gives as little satisfaction to the Jewish exploiters as the antisemitic press. This success is sufficient for us and shows that in this matter we are moving in the right direction."[44] This strategy was partly determined by tactical considerations. At the end of the 1880s the liberals still dominated the city council of Vienna and there was little prospect that they would extend the suffrage to the working class. The interests of the middle-class Jewish community seemed closely bound up with this liberal hegemony. Moreover, Jews held important positions in the press, the free professions, and the free market economy. On the other hand, the German nationalist and Christian-social antisemites, although they represented a social class which (in Marxist terms) was doomed to disappear, were openly opposed to the status quo. Their success at the polls was gradually eroding liberal political control of City Hall and the socialists calculated that this would create conditions for a democratization of a vastly inequitable electoral system. Tactically, it appeared more astute to allow the antisemites to weaken or even destroy Austro-liberalism, thus allowing the Social Democrats to emerge as the leading opposition party. In advancing towards its Marxist goal, the Austrian labor movement was therefore prepared to acquiesce in what it assumed would be a temporary triumph of the "socialism of fools." If the Jews were to be the first victims of this detour, then that was unfortunate but a small price to pay.

Otto Bauer, who belonged to the younger generation of Austro-Marxists, and would later continue this policy, wrote in 1910 that "Marx's essay on the Jewish question [of 1844] already differentiated us sharply from liberal philosemitism."[45] But the reluctance of the Viennese Social Democrats to recognize the specificity of the "Jewish Question" was by no means purely a question of theory or ideology. The issue was fundamentally *political*—a matter of organization, tactics, and electoral strategy in what had become an intensely antisemitic environment by the late 1890s. For example, at the 1897 Austrian Social-Democratic Party congress, delegates found themselves dragged, as a result of Karl Lueger's brilliant electoral triumph in Vienna, into an unexpectedly frank discussion of the Jewish question. A rank-and-file socialist Jew from Moravia—Jakob Brod—challenged Victor Adler's official policy of indifference to antisemitism as being one of the causes of the socialist failures in the 1897 Reichsrat elections.

> The party's strategy, thus far, has been to remove at all cost any suspicion that it is Judaized. We simply wished to demonstrate that we are not slaves of the Jews. But I say to you that even if we live a hundred years, we will never convince the petite bourgeoisie. What have the comrades from the party leadership done to persuade the unenlightened elements that there is a Jewish proletariat alongside the Jewish bourgeoisie? In Vienna, "Jew" and capitalist are synonymous terms. I have never known it mentioned in the *Arbeiterzeitung* or at any meeting (shout: Oho!) that the Jewish proletariat is the most oppressed, miserable, and backward of all (Shout: but yes!). I mean, it has not been discussed enough.[46]

Brod's criticisms, angrily rebuffed at the Party congress, pointed to one of the fundamental weaknesses in Austrian socialist efforts to counter antisemitic demagoguery. Instead of emphasizing the class differentiation within Habsburg Jewry, the socialists frequently equated capitalism and Jewry, along the familiar lines of Christian-Social ideology.[47] They argued that since the *Judengeist* (Jewish spirit) was identical with the "spirit of capitalism," it followed that a consistent antisemite should ultimately wish to join the only party (the Social Democrats) that was determined in both theory *and* practice to eliminate capitalism as a whole. Using this theory, the Austrian party leadership tried to appeal to an antisemitic mass constituency—presenting themselves as the most rigorous adversaries of "Jewish" (and Gentile) capital. This opportunist use of antisemitic rhetoric under a Marxist veil to undermine the Christian-Social adversaries of the labor movement was a dangerous game to play. True, it helped to mark off the Social Democratic party from the liberals. Even better, it gave a populist edge to the workers' movement. It was also in tune with the socialist tradition of concentrating fire against the liberals as the class enemy.[48] Indeed, the Social Democrats had frequently denounced the Viennese *Judenpresse* as the bastion of liberal capitalist interests and the chief opponent of working-class demands for universal suffrage.

In the eyes of Victor Adler and his colleagues the *Neue Freie Presse* and the Jewish financial oligarchy which it allegedly represented remained a more dangerous enemy of the labor movement than the rowdy antisemitic *Kleinbürgertum* of Vienna.[49] The Austro-Marxist insistence on equating the dangers of "philosemitism" (the defense of "capitalist" Jewry) with those of antisemitism reinforced this *anti-liberal* choice. As Jakob Brod put it at the 1897 party congress: "If here and there he (Comrade Dr. Adler) dealt the antisemites a blow, he made quite certain that the liberals came in for similar treatment (Cries of: Quite right!)."[50] The party leadership, including Adler, Engelbert Pernerstorfer, and the popular working-class orator Franz Schuhmeier, rejected this critique even though politically the liberals were, by 1897, a spent force. The Socialists were slow to see that the real obstacle and long-term danger to the workers' movement came from Lueger's cohorts. This was all the more surprising since Adler was a consummate politician, party leader, polemicist, and diagnostician of the human soul. Despite his penetrating analytical mind and fine-tuned sense of irony, he underestimated Karl Lueger's skill in gaining ascendancy over the Catholic masses.

The Viennese proletarian firebrand Franz Schuhmeier, a man of action and an energetic demagogue in his own right (though closer in spirit to Lueger), adopted the same class strategy as Adler, in focusing on the liberal threat more than the antisemites. "Indeed, the liberals are simply waiting for the moment," Schuhmeier declared, "when we make the antisemites the sole object of our attack, to rehabilitate themselves." Adler himself added a further rider: "We have always said: Let the Christian-Social [movement] work, for they are working for us in the last analysis. I still think so, even today." With regard to the Jews, Adler sarcastically noted: "The special feature of the Jewish question as it exists here in Vienna, is that the capitalist bourgeoisie has a Jewish complexion. That the Jews must suffer this burden is sad. But we are also tired of always finding Jews in our soup."[51]

Adler's exasperation clearly had a personal edge since his Catholic and nationalist opponents never failed to remind the public of his Jewish origins. But this attitude was also part of a deliberate socialist strategy to try and ride the rising antisemitic wave in Vienna. Rather than ally with "progressive" Austro-liberal elements against the feudal-aristocratic ruling classes of Austria-Hungary, the Social Democrats preferred to exploit the unpopularity of the Austrian liberals for their own purposes. They obviously realized that defense of the Jews was not a vote-catching cause in Vienna. In any case, they were convinced that antisemitism was no more than a temporary phenomenon of *Mittelstand* protest doomed to disappear. If so, why not welcome the Christian-Social victory over liberalism? Why not wait patiently to inherit the Promised Land once the Austrian petty bourgeoisie finally awoke from its deep slumbers and turned to the only party that was truly anticapitalist? This illusion was, after all, at the core of the revolutionary mythology so many Socialists in Central and eastern Europe had embraced.

It is true that in the greatly truncated Austria which emerged at the end of the First World War, the Social Democrats—at least in Vienna—did obtain a degree of political hegemony thanks to the democratic suffrage. At the same time, they continued to rely on older stereotypical images of rapacious "rich Jews" in their propaganda, linking the "Semites" to entrenched Christian-Social economic interests.[52] This followed the prewar policy of presenting Karl Lueger and his antisemitic colleagues as hypocritical "Jew-lackeys" who did business with wealthy Jews and cynically hoodwinked the "fools of Vienna"—the deluded petit bourgeois masses who had put them in power.[53] In the fin-de-siècle socialist press, Lueger had often been portrayed as the Roman Catholic protector of the Rothschilds and Gutmann brothers—the most prominent Jewish barons of high finance and industry. The political message was that the Christian Social party, not the Socialists, were the true "Jewish protective guard" (*Judenschutztruppe*). Indeed, Friedrich Austerlitz—editor of the Viennese *Arbeiterzeitung*—basically concurred with the antisemitic claim that the liberal press, the banks, big industry, the universities, the arts, sciences, and journalism in Vienna were in Jewish hands. At the same time his paper regularly accused Lueger of being a puppet of rich Jews. "If there is anyone to whom one can apply the word 'Judaized' (*verjudet*) it is to the Viennese mayor."[54] The editor who wrote this was himself a Moravian Jew by origin who clearly loathed the "domination" of his former co-religionists over the economic and cultural life of the Habsburg metropolis. It was a highly dubious claim that Socialists continued to make about the allegedly "sham" antisemitism of their Christian-Social political rivals, until the debacle of 1934.

Socialist use or misuse of this type of anti-Jewish rhetoric was no doubt intended to unmask Christian hypocrisy—exposing the gap between words and deeds, theory and practice which did typify some aspects of Christian-Social rule. Unfortunately, the result was that antisemitic stereotypes of radical provenance which equated "capitalist" and "Jew" received a new kind of respectability precisely because they were used by those who claimed to be fighting antisemitism. In the context of Imperial Vienna (and later in the First Republic)—far from immunizing the workers against antisemitic prejudices, it reinforced their pervasiveness. Mimicry of Judeophobic phraseology and attempts to turn it against their political rivals, proved to have only a limited efficacy. The relentless use of irony or the unmasking of antisemitic hypocrisies and follies, were not in themselves a powerful enough antidote in overcoming the indoctrination and prejudices accumulated over the centuries.

The specific features of the Austrian Socialist response to antisemitism cannot be separated from the remarkable Jewish role in the labor movement. Socialism had begun to attract Jewish middle-class intellectuals in late Habsburg Vienna for a number of reasons. For those who cared about social justice it provided a modernist and "progressive" way to integrate themselves in European society. True, it also demanded the radical casting off of any residual Jewish particularism and an unequivocal rejection of the Jewish commercial ethos. In many cases, this involved a rupture with the Jewish family and ethnic background. But most radical Jews were in any case alienated from Judaism and Jewry. They sought a revolutionary "solution" to the social question, assuming that antisemitism would inevitably decline and was at best a temporary irritation. Moreover, some socialists of Jewish origin could and did identify with parts of the prevailing anti-Jewish ethos. Nevertheless there were also important differences. Radical Jews, unlike the populist Catholic antisemites in Lueger's movement, did not desire the restoration of *Christian* society or of a Christian state under any circumstances. Nor did they remotely support the pan-German nationalist idea of imposing racial homogeneity by discriminatory legislation against foreigners or Jews. Socialists believed in the internationalism of the workers' movement and in the supranational character of the Habsburg State before 1914. The Austrian Socialist Party also held fast to the perception that antisemitism would inevitably be swept away with the collapse of bourgeois society.

Austrian Socialists never abandoned their attacks on the "Jewish" capitalist class and its extensive influence over banking, commerce, and industry.[55] Unlike populist antisemites such as Schönerer or Lueger, they did not, however, single out "Jewish" materialism as a *unique* and eternal characteristic of the "Semitic race." Socialist Jews in particular, had to negate the premise of racial antisemitism if they were not to cut out the ground from under their own feet. In this context, their own socialist commitment served as a living proof that the curse of Jewish "materialism" could be exorcised and purged. Their own lives showed, after all, that Jews could selflessly devote themselves to a universal ideal and to egalitarian values. They could follow the examples of Ludwig Börne and Karl Marx, who had first linked *de-Judaization* (or the purging of Jewish characteristics) with the general cause of human liberation. In fin-de-siècle Vienna, such self-cleansing and the radical negation of "Judaism" implied a dual assault on the economic "domination" of liberal Jewry *and* against the reactionary obscurantism of ghetto Jewry.

Karl Kraus, Vienna's foremost satirist and a thoroughly Germanized Jew, though by no means left-wing in outlook, was a prime exponent of this syndrome. This is what linked him to those Jewish intellectuals on the Left who detested the leading liberal newspaper, the *Neue Freie Presse,* despised the *Ostjuden*, and ridiculed the Zionist movement. What was striking in the socialist case was that such self-negation and internalization of the antisemitic incubus went together with openly paraded universalist pretensions. Nothing testifies more to the personal and social pressure exercised by an antisemitic Gentile environment than such glaring contradictions. The "Jewish" leaders of Austrian Social Democracy had done everything they could to eradicate Jewishness from their own identity and replace it by a revolutionary Marxian myth concerning the proletariat as the *chosen instrument* of world history. Ironically enough, this act of quasi-messianic self-negation did not resolve their identity problem or the larger "Jewish Question" in the context of antisemitic Vienna. Their origins not only placed them in a precarious position of perpetual self-denial but the constant assault on Judeo-Marxism, especially by Lueger's Christian-Social movement, pushed them on the defensive. Their vulnerability was a revealing barometer of the dilemma inherent in assimilation in the Central European context. In certain cases, their responses were unquestionably tinged with self-hatred.[56]

One cannot ignore this psychological dimension when examining the more general ambiguities of the Austro-Marxist position on the "Jewish Question." It had a firm sociological basis in Vienna, where the dominant bourgeois society and culture did indeed appear to be more specifically "Jewish" than elsewhere in Central or Western Europe. Moreover, there was a growing *Ostjuden* problem linked to the rapid internal migration of Jews from Hungary and Galicia to Vienna that complicated the general Jewish response to antisemitism. Finally, in the Habsburg capital antisemitism was already a popular cause which would triumph politically in the 1890s—a phenomenon that happened nowhere else in Europe at that time. These were mitigating circumstances that help to explain why Austrian socialists were so hesitant in engaging in any head-on confrontation with antisemitism, but they do not justify the policy adopted. Victor Adler was evidently aware of the depth of the problem. At the Austrian Socialist congress of 1898, the Party leader told his proletarian comrades with a characteristic touch of irony and world-weary resignation: "The last anti-Semite will disappear with the last Jew."[57]

Notes

1. Karl Marx, "On the Jewish Question" (1844), in idem, *Early Writings,* introduction by Lucio Colletti (London, 1975), 236.

2. The Austrian journalist and novelist Karl-Emil Franzos (1848–1904) wrote tales and sketches, entitled *Aus Halb-Asien,* which were first collected in two volumes in 1876. Franzos understood by *Halb-Asien* not only a geographical area (including Romania and southern Russia as well as Galicia and Bukovina) but a condition in which European culture and Eastern "barbarism" coexisted.

3. Joseph Roth, *Juden auf Wanderschaft* (Berlin, 1927), quoted in his *Romane-Erzählungen-Aufsätze* (Cologne, 1964), 559ff.

4. Robert S. Wistrich, *Socialism and the Jews: The Dilemmas of Assimilation in Germany and Austria-Hungary* (London, 1982). See also for the interwar period, Margit Reiter, *Unter Antisemitismus-Verdacht. Die österreichische Linke und Israel nach der Shoah* (Innsbruck, 2001), and Bruce E. Pauley, "Politischer Antisemitismus in Wien der Zwischenkriegszeit," in *Eine zerstörte Kultur,* edited by Gerhard Botz et al. (Buchloe, 1990), 221–46.

5. See Robert S. Wistrich, "Sozialdemokratie, Antisemitismus und die Wiener Juden," in Botz, *Eine zerstörte Kultur,* 169–80.

6. Paul Massing, *Rehearsal for Destruction; A Study of Political Antisemitism in Imperial Germany* (New York, 1949), 151. See also, for examples of this viewpoint, Peter Pulzer, *The Rise of Political Anti-Semitism in Germany and Austria* (London, 1964), p. 259; and Reinhard Rürup, "Sozialismus und Antisemitismus in Deutschland vor 1914," in *Juden und Jüdische Aspekte in der Deutschen Arbeiterbewegung, 1848–1918,* edited by Walter Grab (Tel Aviv, 1976), 207–27.

7. See Robert S. Wistrich, "Austrian Social Democracy and Antisemitism, 1890–1914," *Jewish Social Studies* 38 (1975): 323–33.

8 See, for example, *Verhandlungen des sechsten österreichischen Sozialdemokratischen Parteitages* (Vienna, 1897), 91–92; and the discussion in Wistrich, *Socialism and the Jews,* 265–68. Among the first to note this phenomenon was Edmund Silberner, *Sozialisten zur Judenfrage* (Berlin, 1962).

9. Karl Kautsky to Friedrich Engels, 23 June 1884, *Friedrich Engels Briefwechsel mit Karl Kautsky,* edited by Benedikt Kautsky (Vienna, 1955), 125. On Kautsky's general view of Jews, see Jack Jacobs, *Sozialisten und die "jüdische Frage" nach Marx* (Mainz, 1994), whose interpretation is at times overly charitable.

10. Wilhelm Ellenbogen, "Der Wiener Antisemitismus," *Sozialistische Monatshefte* (Sept. 1899): 418–25.

11. See Enzo Traverso, *Die Marxisten und die Jüdische Frage. Geschichte einer Debatte (1843–1943)* (Mainz, 1995).

12. For the full text of Engels's letter of 21 March 1890, written to Isidor Ehrenfreund, a Jewish bank employee in Vienna, see *Arbeiterzeitung* (Vienna), 9 May 1890; and *Marx-Engels Werke* (East Berlin, 1963), 22: 570.

13. I sharply disagree on this point with the views of John Bunzl, "Arbeiterbewegung, 'Judenfrage' und Antisemitismus: Am Beispiel des Wiener Bezirks Leopoldstadt," in *Bewegung und Klasse: Studien zur österreichischen Arbeitergeschichte,* edited by Gerhard Botz, Hans Hautmann, Helmut Konrad and Josef Weidenholzer (Vienna, 1978), 760.

14. Wistrich, *Socialism and the Jews,* 250–56.

15. For an elaboration of this point, see Robert S. Wistrich, "Victor Adler: A Viennese Socialist against Philosemitism," *Wiener Library Bulletin* 27, n.s. no. 32 (1974): 26–33.

16. On the occupational structure of the Jewish and Gentile population in the Leopoldstadt, see Bunzl, "Arbeiterbewegung," 743–50.

17. For further details, see the demographic study by Marsha L. Rozenblit, *The Jews of Vienna, 1867–1914: Assimilation and Identity* (Albany, 1983), 78–79, who argued that Jewish residential distribution in Vienna did not depend on class: "Poor Jews shunned residence in the lower-class outer districts in order to live side by side, if not with wealthy Jews, certainly with middle-class Jews in the Leopoldstadt (II) and the Alsergrund (IX)."

18. Ibid., 43. Rozenblit claimed that the Galician Jews were not only the most recent and the most religious of the Jewish immigrants to Vienna around 1890 but also had a keen sense of themselves as a distinct group—"an East European outpost in a sea of Central European Jews."

19. Wistrich, *Socialism and the Jews,* 309–43. See also Robert S. Wistrich, "Austrian Social Democracy and the Problem of Galician Jewry, 1880–1914," *Leo Baeck Institute Year Book* (hereafter *LBIYB*) 26 (1981): 89–124. On the growth of Jewish nationalism in Habsburg Austria, see Adolf Gaisbauer, *Davidstern und Doppeladler. Zionismus und jüdischer Nationalismus in Österreich 1882–1918* (Vienna, 1988).

20. Wistrich, *Socialism and the Jews,* 332–34.

21. Rozenblit, *Jews of Vienna,* 48–70, pointed out that Viennese Gentile *Angestellte* generally worked for the imperial and municipal civil service, while Jewish employees more often served as clerks, salesmen, or managers in the business world.

22. For further details, see the Hebrew edition of the articles by Ber Borochov, *Ktavim* (Tel Aviv, 1955–1956), 3: 496–500, 534, 536. Borochov, the founder of Marxist Zionism in Russia, lived in Vienna for a number of years before World War I.

23. See Bruce E. Pauley, *Eine Geschichte des österreichischen Antisemitismus. Von der Ausgrenzung zur Auslöschung* (Vienna, 1993).

24. Brigitte Hamann, *Hitlers Wien. Lehrjahre eines Diktators* (Munich, 1996) has provided an exhaustive compendium of Hitler's experiences in Imperial Vienna and they way they shaped his outlook.

25. See John W. Boyer, "Karl Lueger and the Viennese Jews," *LBIYB* 26 (1981): 139–40; and Robert S. Wistrich, "Karl Lueger and the Ambiguities of Viennese Antisemitism," *Jewish Social Studies* 45 (1983): 251–62.

26. Adolf Hitler, *Mein Kampf,* translated by Ralph Manheim (Boston, 1942), 61.

27. Dieter Binder, "Der 'reiche Jude.' Zur sozialdemokratischen Kapitalismus-Kritik und zu deren antisemitischen Feindbildern in der Ersten Republik," *Geschichte und Gegenwart* 1 (1998): 43–53.

28. Julius Braunthal, *Victor und Friedrich Adler. Zwei Generationen Arbeiterbewegung* (Vienna, 1965), 16.

29. Theodor Billroth, *Über das Lehren und Lernen der Medizinischen Wissenschaften an der Universitäten der Deutschen Nation* (Vienna, 1876), 150–54.

30. Braunthal, *Victor und Friedrich Adler,* 19.

31. Ibid.

32. See Robert S. Wistrich, *Socialism and the Jews,* 236.

33. For the Linz Program, see E. Pichl, *Georg von Schoenerer,* 1: 111ff; and Klaus Berchthold, ed., *Österreichische Parteiprogramme 1868–1966* (Munich, 1967), 198–203.

34. *Unverfälschte Deutsche Worte,* 1 July 1883.

35. Pichl, *Georg von Schoenerer,* 1: 316–17.

36. V. Adler, "Der Antisemitismus," *Gleichheit,* 7 May 1887, 2.

37. Ibid.

38. Ibid.

39. Ibid.

40. Robert S. Wistrich, "Victor Adler: A Viennese Socialist Against Philosemitism," *Wiener Library Bulletin,* 27, new series no. 32 (1974): 26–33.

41. "Arbeiterfreundlichkeit," *Gleichheit,* 17 Sept. 1887, 1.

42. *Gleichheit,* 24 Dec. 1887, 2; see also Josef Pongratz, "Adlers erste Rede in Graz," *Victor Adler im Spiegel seiner Zeitgenossen,* 155–57.

43. "Interkonfessionelle Solidarität," *Gleichheit,* 31 Dec. 1887, 2.

44. "Die Vereinigten Christen," *Arbeiterzeitung,* 1 Nov. 1889, 2.

45. Otto Bauer, "Sozialismus und Antisemitismus," *Der Kampf* 4 (1910–11): 9.

46. *Verhandlungen,* 87.

47. See Robert S. Wistrich, *The Jews of Vienna in the Age of Franz Joseph* (Oxford, 1989); also William O. McCagg, *A History of Habsburg Jews, 1670–1918* (Bloomington, Ind., 1989).

48. See, for example, Friedrich Austerlitz, "Karl Lueger," *Die Neue Zeit* 2 (1900–1901): 36–45.

49. "Die Neue Freie Presse," *Arbeiterzeitung* (Vienna), 30 June 1893.

50. *Verhandlungen,* 87.

51. Ibid., 92, 101, 103.

52. Dieter Binder, "Der 'reiche Jude.'"

53. "Christlich-sozialer Schwindel," *Volkstribune,* 21 Feb. 1906, 2.

54. Friedrich Austerlitz, "Luegers Tod," *Arbeiterzeitung* (Vienna), 11 Mar. 1910.

55. *Arbeiterzeitung* (Vienna), 6 Apr. 1900.

56. See Martine-Sophie Benoit, "Theodor Lessing et le concept de la "haine de soi juive," and Jacques Le Rider, "Otto Weininger. Le cas par excellence de "haine de soi juive," in *La Haine de Soi. Difficiles identités,* edited by Esther Benbassa and Jean-Christophe Attias (Paris, 2000), 27–58. See also Robert S. Wistrich, *Laboratory for World Destruction. Germans and Jews in Central Europe* (Lincoln, Neb., 2007).

57. Robert S. Wistrich, *Revolutionary Jews from Marx to Trotsky* (London, 1976), 98.

CHAPTER 9

The Austro-Marxist Critique of Jewish Nationalism

Left-wing opposition to Zionism and other variations of Jewish nationalism is not a novel phenomenon. Indeed, there have been some remarkably constant features in the Marxist critique of Jewish nationalism, and in particular its rejection of any special pleading or moral obligation to further a distinctively Jewish existence as a collectivity.[1] Marxists have frequently argued that the survival of the Jewish people—whether in a purely religious, a national, or state form—is politically reactionary. They have often followed the formula of the young Marx who dismissed Judaism as a wholly negative phenomenon—a reflection of the money-lending era of capitalism, doomed to disappear with its demise. The Marxist analysis of the "Jewish Question" (like that of many liberals) assumed that antisemitism was merely a temporary phenomenon. With its dissipation the last remaining factor encouraging the "illusory" national cohesion of the Jews would also fade away. The new Left of the 1960s continued to echo, often in a bizarrely dogmatic form, arguments about Zionism and Jewish peoplehood long since taken over by events.[2] These polemics have in more recent decades become ever more partisan and disconnected from reality. Nevertheless the original Marxist interpretation of the Jewish condition was not altogether devoid of plausibility, especially in central Europe. It should be remembered that around 1900, the revolutionary socialist movement found itself confronted by rival nationalist and antisemitic movements throughout Europe, as well as the emergence of political Zionism. This was an era of decisive importance for the development of European Jewry itself, torn between contradictory movements, having to choose (especially in Russia) for or against the revolutionary movement, between a class and a national orientation in politics. It was the beginning of Jewish national emergence in the Diaspora, of mass migrations from the lands of oppression to America and western Europe, an era of full emancipation, but also of dramatically rising political antisemitism.

Those Jews who joined the Marxist camp in eastern Europe and Russia fought for a socialist revolution modeled in part on liberal emancipation in western Europe. They fought not under a Jewish banner, but with Russian slogans for a Russian Revolution which would end class, ethnic, and religious discrimination. They were assimilationists on principle, who rejected as inadmissible any notion of national rights for Jews. If there was one factor that united such well-known Marxist Jews as Paul Axelrod, Julius Martov, Leon Trotsky, Rosa Luxemburg, Leon Jogiches, and Otto Bauer, it was their complete rejection of the idea of Jewish national self-determination.[3] There can be little doubt that this hostility of Marxist Jews to Zionism and the Jewish national movement greatly influenced the attitude of other revolutionaries to the problem. Faced with this antagonism, a Diaspora nationalist like the great Russian-Jewish historian, Simon Dubnow, could remark, "How much a Jew must hate himself who recognizes the right of every nationality and language to self-determination but doubts it or restricts it for his own people whose 'self-determination' began 3,000 years ago."[4] Anyone who has closely studied the personality and background of Socialist leaders of Jewish descent cannot deny the element of truth in this judgment.[5] But the theoretical source lay in the historical-materialist outlook formulated by Marx and Engels with regard to the "national question" in 19th-century Europe.

In his early essay, *Zur Judenfrage* (1844), Marx had reduced nationality to the factor of economic interest, and misleadingly identified the "illusory" nationality of the Jew with that of the merchant and money-man.[6] In the *Communist Manifesto* of 1848, national antagonisms were regarded by Marx and Engels as purely secondary, as a factor which would disappear with the expanding freedom of trade, the growing world market, and the resolution of class contradictions within individual nation-states. This was similar to the view of Cobdenite liberalism in Great Britain, which held that free trade was the road to international cooperation and the termination of national rivalries. The 1848 revolutions in Europe, which witnessed the resurrection of the German, Polish, Italian, and Slavic national movements, already cast doubt on that optimistic theory. Marx and Engels noted the development without fully understanding it. They accepted the right of "revolutionary" nations like the Germans, Hungarians, Poles, and Italians to their national independence, but denied this same right to what they termed the "historyless peoples" in southern and Eastern Europe. It was their historic duty to be absorbed by the more progressive "civilizing" influence of the big nations in Europe.[7] The founders of Marxism above all opposed the Slav movement for independence because they feared it would only serve the reactionary interests of Russian Tsarism. This nationality doctrine is significant because it anticipated arguments later used by Karl Kausky, Lenin, and other disciples of Marx in their polemics against Zionism and the Jewish national movement.

National movements were to be judged according to their "revolutionism" in speeding up the disintegration of the feudal-absolutist monarchies in central and Eastern Europe. Thus the Polish struggle for independence was supported by Marx and Engels because it fulfilled an important role in the revolutionary strategy of weakening Imperial Russia. But the South-Slav movement was rejected as the Pan-Slavist tool of Russian ambitions in the Balkans. It is significant that the future President of an independent Czechoslovakia, the liberal democrat Thomas Masaryk, underlined in his *Philosophical and Sociological Foundations of Marxism* (1899) what he saw as the specific hostility of Marxism to both Slav and Jewish national aspirations for independence.[8] Masaryk observed that Marx had ignored the cultural-historical side of the Jewish problem; that he had misunderstood the national traditions of the Jewish communities in Russia and Galicia, and ignored the forces working against assimilation in Eastern Europe. He was one of the first commentators to point to the antisemitism of the young Marx, who identified Jewry with the worst aspects of capitalism and one-sidedly stigmatized its "practical" essence.[9] Masaryk's conclusion was that Marxist historical materialism had the same defect that it ascribed to the Jews—namely, that it was too narrowly practical, objectivist, and "materialistic."

Masaryk was writing at a time when the untenability of certain Marxist propositions about the "national question" was becoming increasingly visible even to the most orthodox of Marx's disciples. Socialist ideology was forced to come to terms with the fact that the apocalyptic universalism of the Communist Manifesto had no answer to the nationalist antagonisms between France and Germany, or the nationality conflicts threatening to tear apart the Habsburg monarchy in central Europe.[10] It is not surprising, therefore, that the reorientation of socialist theory on the national question should have first emerged in the writings of the Austro-Marxists, most of whom were in fact "assimilated" Jews. The most important theoreticians of this group were Otto Bauer and the jurist, Karl Renner. Their main purpose was to resolve the fierce internecine conflicts in the Danubian monarchy by *depoliticizing* national confrontations.[11] Their solution was to offer the maximum autonomy possible in the cultural sphere to the various nationalities in conflict with the Habsburg state. Their aim was to grant each nationality the right to legislate on its own affairs, run its own schools, and use its own language—while preserving an Austrian federal parliament to decide on all political and economic issues common to the nationalities within the Empire. Renner's theories departed from one of the cardinal axioms of Marxism, the identification of nationality with the territorial principle—which he concluded was inapplicable to a multinational state of mixed populations, each asserting its "national" rights against its neighbor. In place of the territorial principle of nationality, Karl Renner (who was *not* Jewish) proposed the *personality-principle*—the right of each individual to determine to which nation he belonged and to enjoy the full right of cultural self-expression accorded to that nationality. Significantly, his rival, Otto Bauer (the son of a Jewish textile manufacturer from Bohemia) explicitly denied this right to the Jews and devoted a whole chapter of his *Social Democracy and the Nationalities Question* (1906) to proving that cultural-national autonomy was inapplicable to them.[12] The text of Otto Bauer—the most brilliant of the younger generation of Austro-Marxists—would significantly influence socialist discussion of the Jewish national question, not only in Austria-Hungary but also in the neighboring Russian Empire.

Otto Bauer's basic presupposition was that western and central European Jewry had been undergoing a process of *de-nationalization*. As an *extra-territorial* nation without a common territory, a common language or culture, the Jews were particularly susceptible to those processes of modern capitalism which were breaking down the barriers between nations and bringing about their economic assimilation and integration.[13] Precisely because they were a pariah-nation, the Jews had been obliged to adopt the culture, habits, and customs of the surrounding nations in whose midst they lived. In feudal society, they had been able to preserve a certain semblance of independence, mainly because their economic function as a moneyed class—especially their role as intermediaries between landowners and peasants—necessitated their preservation. But the evolution of industrial society was inexorably levelling the differences between Jews and Christians. It tended to eliminate the specific economic functions which had hitherto preserved traditional Jewish identity. Capitalist production, Otto Bauer argued, had made the Jews and Christians interdependent. According to Marx's famous formula, it was transforming the "Christians" into "Jews."[14] Once Jews from the more backward areas of the Austrian Empire like Galicia and Bukovina began to be irresistibly drawn into capitalist branches of production, they would gradually lose those distinctive characteristics which had given rise to the *illusion* that there was a Jewish nation. The process of capitalist penetration of economically backward areas was irreversible and it would inevitably undermine the socio-economic structure of the Jews as a "people-class."[15]

Unlike the other nationalities in the Habsburg Empire, the Jews did not have the territorial, linguistic, and cultural prerequisites for resisting that trend. As a scattered nation, they would inevitably gravitate to those areas which offered the best prospects of earning a living. In this way, they would become fully integrated into all branches of modern capitalist production.[16] This process of economic differentiation, social mobility, and freedom from the grinding poverty of the Jewish ghettos would eliminate whatever remained of specific Jewish characteristics. Hence, assimilation of the Jewish minority was, according to Otto Bauer, eminently desirable as a proof of the extent to which modern capitalism had succeeded in wiping out medieval particularism—the real secret of Jewish survival as a separate entity. In this relatively sophisticated Marxist conception, the Jews would inevitably disappear as a collective entity and their particular qualities as individuals would then merge with those of European peoples among whom they lived. Karl Renner (whose theory of personal autonomy separated the right of cultural-national autonomy more sharply from its political and economic aspects) did not—unlike Bauer—specifically deny that right to the Jews. His ideas were taken up both by Bundists and some Jewish "bourgeois" nationalists in Russia, as a justification of their own demand for Jewish national rights.[17] However, Renner, who later became Austrian Chancellor in 1919 (and again in 1945), was certainly no "philosemite." His pan-German sympathies were already visible during World War I, and in 1938 he advised Austrians to support Hitler's annexation of the country. After 1945, he was against imposing any sanctions on former Nazis from the lower classes, and showed no empathy towards Jewish Holocaust survivors.

What attracted Diaspora Jewish nationalists like Simon Dubnow to Renner's pre-1914 theory of personal autonomy was that it implied a decentralized federal system with guaranteed minority rights for non-territorial groups. Thus it potentially offered a theoretical framework for Jews to preserve their culture and identity.[18] Renner, as a leading Austrian social democrat, was well aware of the need to make concessions to national minorities in order to preserve the Habsburg Empire. Like Otto Bauer, he also believed that there would be a flowering of national differences under socialism.[19] Otto Bauer, in particular, argued that socialism was an international movement which would take on a distinctive "national" form in every country, consonant with the cultural traditions of that nation. In each case *except* that of the Jewish national movement, he insisted with confident certitude that differentiation would increase under socialism, as the working-class came to absorb the prevailing national culture.

Although he was only twenty-six at the time, Otto Bauer had established a solid reputation as the Party's foremost sociological thinker by 1907. He was the editor of *Der Kampf,* a monthly devoted to the nationality problems of the Austrian Empire, Eastern Europe, and the Balkans. His erudition in the fields of political economy, social science, philosophy, and history was remarkable, enabling him to convincingly integrate his theory of the national question into the totality of the historic process. Moreover, unlike most other socialist thinkers of his time, Otto Bauer had an intuitive feeling for tradition and the way that the past intrudes upon and shapes the present. In particular, his concept of the nation as a *Schicksalsgemeinschaft* (community of fate) enabled him to demonstrate how certain habits of thinking and feeling derived from common experience in the past. This sense of history and understanding of "national character" did not, however, lead Otto Bauer to a more profound investigation of Jewish history. Like most Marxists, his knowledge of the subject remained sketchy and superficial.

Bauer nonetheless accepted that Jews had preserved many national characteristics, even though they lacked a common territory and language. He argued that the Jews had been shaped by forces of nature and history which mould all nations from their earliest beginnings. In medieval society, he conceded that the Jews had still been a nation:

> that the Jews maintained their race as united as most European nations can hardly be doubted; nor that the fate of their forefathers, by the laws of inheritance and natural selection, determined the characteristics of future generations and welded the Jews into a tightly-knit natural community (*Naturgemeinschaft*).[20]

But this *Naturgemeinschaft* based on ties of blood and race could preserve its national characteristics only as a result of its peculiar *intermediary* function in a pre-capitalist society. As usurers and middlemen between the landowners and peasantry, the Jews had been the agents of the money-economy in a feudal order which reinforced their corporate status. However, the Jew as pedlar, moneylender, innkeeper, corn- and cattle-merchant was indispensable only until such time as the development of the market-economy began to transform European "Christians" into "Jews."[21]

Otto Bauer fleshed out Marx's theory, seeking to neutralize its antisemitic tone and to demonstrate that Jewry as a corporate entity was doomed by the process of capitalist development. His basic assumption was that as the social environment became more urban and commercial in character ("Judaized" in Marx's terms), so the Jewish world would become more "non-Jewish" in its occupational structure. From a peculiar national entity located in the pores of feudal society, the Jews were increasingly becoming socially differentiated into classes and ceasing to fulfill any unique economic function. Bourgeois emancipation had been predicated on precisely this historical process. "These [modern] Jews adjust their culture to the culture of the European nations since the money economy, once represented only by the Jews, has become the economic organization of all European peoples."[22] Capitalism, by driving Jews from the villages and dispersing them into different branches of production, was fast eroding their residual peculiarities. They had already been obliged in Western Europe to adopt the language, clothing, customs, and habits of their Gentile environment. Although more traditional Jews still retained "a strong consciousness of their individuality and their belonging together," bourgeois society did not permit them to preserve their national character: "It would perhaps be too much to say even in Western and Central Europe that the Jews are not a nation. But one can certainly assert that they are ceasing to be a nation."[23]

Otto Bauer admitted that this process of cultural assimilation in Western and Central Europe, was not yet complete. Though the majority of Jews no longer spoke Yiddish or wore distinctive clothing they could still be identified by their physical appearance or mannerisms. Though the majority had abandoned Orthodox Judaism, Western Jews still clung in many cases to a diluted, reform faith and sought to maintain a subjective sense of separate identity. But the core social and cultural issue, as Otto Bauer realized, was presented by the non-assimilated masses of Eastern Europe: "The Jewish petty-bourgeois and workers in Russia, Poland, Lithuania, in Galicia and in Bukovina, Romania, etc., today constitute the Jewish nation."[24] Into what category could they be consigned by the leading Austro-Marxist theoretician of cultural-national autonomy? Bauer's solution was to argue that the *Ostjuden* belonged, in Hegelian-Marxist terminology, to the "historyless peoples."

> In so far as the Jews still form a nation in Europe, they bear the character of a historyless nation. Because they lack those classes which in a class-society are the carriers of cultural development, their culture is stunted, their language decayed, and they have no national literature.[25]

The concept of "historyless peoples" (*geschichtlosen Völker*) had already been used by Engels in 1848 to pass a *revolutionary sentence of death* on the

Czechs, Slovaks, South Slavs, and other "ethnic trash." Both Kautsky and Otto Bauer recognized that this cruel prognosis had been invalidated by the march of events. Bauer even argued throughout his magnum opus that capitalism had roused the "historyless peoples" to new life. Why then apply this worn-out theory to the Jews, arguably the most *historical* of all peoples? Did not the denigration of traditional Jewish culture reflect that strain of Marxist intellectual "colonialism" which consigned small, backward nations to the rubbish-bin of history? Otto Bauer, to be sure, did not condemn the emergence of a new Yiddish culture based on *socialist* values which had restored a sense of pride and dignity to the oppressed Jewish proletariat in Tsarist Russia. He acknowledged that the abortive Russian Revolution of 1905 had transformed the humble ghetto-Jew into a heroic fighter for the cause of socialism. He did not deny that a Jewish cultural-national renaissance was in the process of emerging from the ranks of the oppressed East European Jewish masses. "Certainly, a new Jewish culture is in the making and would probably develop if the Jewish people had enough time left for the development of a new living culture. But this culture is in its initial stages, it is not yet manifest."[26]

In spite of this partial recognition, Bauer nonetheless argued that the dialectic of history was against the Jews. While capitalist development had raised the Czechs to the level of a "historic nation," it would inexorably consign the new Jewish culture as well as the historic Jewish nation to self-*dissolution*. The Jews lacked a "closed area of settlement" or a territorial base to preserve their "cultural peculiarities." Hence, according to Otto Bauer, "capitalist society will not permit them to survive as a nation." In other words, their extra-territoriality would push them to assimilation. "With the progressive development of capitalism and the modern State, the Jews of the East will also cease to be a particular people and they will dissolve among the nations in the same way as the Western Jews have long since been absorbed."[27] Whereas Czech immigrant workers who migrated from agricultural to industrial areas could always return to their Czech homeland, once the *Ostjuden* entered the capitalist economic system, they would be absorbed by the dominant nationality in each region that they inhabited. To be sure, Otto Bauer envisaged this as a more long-term historical evolution which would proceed at a varying tempo in different territories. Thus he acknowledged: "In the Russian Empire the economic and juridicial prerequisites for this process of this process of assimilation are still lacking."[28] It was precisely because of this social-institutional lag that the Jewish Bund with its active promotion of a proletarian Yiddish culture had been able in

Tsarist Russia to step into an existing vacuum. But even in the Russian Pale, no less than in Galicia and Bukovina, Otto Bauer was convinced that capitalism was already creating the conditions for the definitive assimilation of the Jews.

Otto Bauer's complex theory of assimilation had a concrete political goal. It provided an ideological framework for the refusal of the Austrian Social Democrats to concede the right of cultural-national autonomy to Jewish workers in Polish Galicia. In order to veil the obvious contradiction between this decision and Austro-Marxist theories of cultural-national autonomy, Bauer had reverted to an older tradition of economic determinism. He preferred to ignore the wider issue of national self-determination and the popular Jewish agitation for group rights and the recognition of Yiddish as an official language.[29] Moreover, he made no mention of the Jewish National Party which would win four seats in the pan-Austrian parliamentary elections of 1907. The rise of Polish nationalist antisemitism and its implications for Jewish workers, as well as the aspirations of the Zionist movement in Galicia, were also passed over in virtual silence. Bauer sought instead to transform Jewish autonomy from a political and economic issue into a purely educational demand. Jewish workers in Galicia would have to adapt themselves to the culture of their neighbors and above all to remove the displeasing evidence of their origins in petty trade, Jewish business, or artisanry. They would have to abandon their traditional Yiddish language and behavior patterns before they could aspire to become modern industrial workers. What the American sociologist John Murray Cuddihy once called "the ordeal of civility" was remarkably close to what Otto Bauer envisaged as the historic road to emancipation for the Jewish working class in Eastern and Central Europe. The *Ostjude* had to be re-educated for modernity, his unappealing traditional characteristics ironed out before he was fit for the socialist class struggle. Antisemitism was reduced here to an issue of understandable antipathy felt by "Christian" workers towards their Jewish "comrades." This cultural assimilation was imperative not only for practical but also for *aesthetic* reasons. Bauer emphasized that the Jewish workers, through

> the inflection of their language, their gestures, their apparel, their customs, irritated the Christian class comrade, the foreman and manufacturer. . .the economic conflict between the peasant and the Jewish merchant continued [to live on] in the form of instinctive dislike.[30]

"Even today," Bauer pointed out,

> in many establishments the Christian workers will not tolerate any Jewish co-workers; this antipathy does not stem from political anti-Semitism, but from the naïve instinctive reaction against the strange manners of the non-assimilated Jews.[31]

Otto Bauer's apologetic stance on Austrian antisemitism did not stop there. He argued that to support cultural-national autonomy for Jewish workers, especially the establishment of separate Jewish schools, would simply reinforce popular "instinctive" reactions. Yiddish-speaking schools represented a futile and harmful effort to put the clock back. They would perpetuate the "social psychology of a dead epoch" and imbue Jewish schoolchildren with "a medieval worldview and the life-habits of a Jewish innkeeper." Bauer's unflattering picture of the Galician ghetto Jew, judged from the high plateau of modern Western culture, revealed all of the embarrassment of a sober and sophisticated Austro-Marxist intellectual at the uncouth "barbarism" of his more backward co-religionists.

> Imagine Jewish children being taught in Yiddish in their independent schools! There the children will be taught the culture of a nation without a history, the culture of a people totally isolated from the mainstream of European civilization, a people held together by the heritage of an outmoded system of thought and by the dead weight of observances transmitted from generation to generation.[32]

There was no attempt to understand the culture of the *shtetl* in its own terms, to penetrate its elaborate social code of behavior, to appreciate its value-system as it was communicated through religious education. The overriding concern was to counteract the negative impression that traditional Jewish culture might make on xenophobic Austrian or Polish workers (while denying that this constituted antisemitism) and the consequent need to efface its distinctiveness as rapidly as possible.

> What Jewish schools mean for the Jews is first and foremost the artificial maintenance of their old cultural differences, which limit their freedom of movement and thus increase their misery; in the second place, they [the schools] reinforce the old ideology, the old social psychology, which must first be overcome before they are fit to take part in the class struggle.[33]

Cultural assimilation was therefore seen as an indispensable prerequisite for social mobility and the future participation of the Jews in the modern labor movement:

> Then only will he [the Jew] be able to turn to every place and every trade where the blind working of the capitalist forces may happen to create more jobs; then only will his special Jewish misery disappear and he will be left with nothing but the common proletarian misery which he will fight and conquer in the common battle, shoulder to shoulder with his Aryan colleagues.[34]

Bauer evidently felt that it was up to the Jewish proletarian to cast off all those distinctive traits which could arouse aesthetic repulsion in his "Aryan" comrades. This in itself was a notable concession to *racial* terminology. Jews would have to abandon the "semi-Asiatic outlook" and ghetto mentality which Otto Bauer equated with traditional Judaism and conform to the norms of German culture. No Jew could become a modern industrial worker as long as there was anything at all in his appearance, clothing, mannerisms, or dialect which marked him off from his non-Jewish class-comrades. In other words, Jewish emancipation (as seen through Austro-Marxist eyes) entailed the stripping away of virtually *all* Jewish characteristics and the comprehensive negation of any meaningful Jewish identity.

Otto Bauer was clearly convinced that such total assimilation was possible, desirable, and even a natural, *inevitable* process conditioned by the laws of economic development. Although less extreme than Ludo Hartmann (another Austrian Social Democrat of Jewish origin) who regarded the *coercive* absorption of minorities as a paramount obligation, Bauer did see Jewish integration as an irreversible process. Capitalist development rather than nationalist persecution or state-sponsored coercion, from above, would drive the *Ostjuden* into the progressive melting-pot of modernization. To soften the pill, Bauer suggested that assimilation would not lead to the disappearance of "natural Jewish talents" and hereditary qualities, but to their heightening and enrichment through intermarriage and fruitful cultural interaction.

> Names like Spinoza, Disraeli, Marx, Lassalle, Heine and many others prove that Jewry has always brought forth its most brilliant achievements where native Jewish gifts and European cultural traditions have cross-fertilized each other.[35]

Although the Jews as an independent people and the "Jewish cultural community" were doomed to disappear, the natural stock would remain and fructify the European peoples with its spiritual qualities. Though no one could predict the results of "the miscegenation of Jewish and Aryan blood," Otto Bauer was confident that despite the rise in mixed marriages, the "sharply distinguished physical type" and "characteristic intellectual gifts" of the Jews would survive for the benefit of humanity. This "last of all Jewish problems" would be resolved in the future by sexual selection, by "young men's inclinations and young women's choice in love."[36] Nevertheless, as Bauer subsequently admitted, in advanced capitalist societies the "racial instincts and racial prejudices outlive assimilation" and "mixed marriages between Aryans and assimilated Jews are relatively rare." Thus, even in the West, he reluctantly conceded, assimilation was by no means an automatic process.

Bauer's language with its tendency to polarize "Aryan" and "Jew," was in itself a revealing indication of how deeply *völkisch* thought permeated his conceptual approach. Although he condemned antisemitism as a "primitive expression of anti-capitalism," he was by no means averse to employing its vocabulary. He had, after all, once described Karl von Vogelsang's Christian-social assault on Austrian Jewry as a "progressive" phenomenon in so far as it contained a marked anti-capitalist tinge. In 1910 Bauer emphasized: "Marx's *Zur Judenfrage* already differentiated us sharply from liberal philo-semitism. Social democracy has never been a "Jewish protective guard."[37] To underline the point, he carried Marx's terminology a stage further by giving a racial connotation to the class struggle in Western and Central Europe in order to underline the *anti-capitalist* character of antisemitism: "The Jewish factory-owner very frequently confronts the Aryan worker, the Jewish middleman faces the Aryan craftsman, and the Jewish usurer, the Aryan peasant."[38] This was a noteworthy anticipation of the vocabulary of German National Socialism twenty years before its rise to power by the leading Austro-Marxist of his generation.

Such a predilection for superimposing racial thinking on the methodology of historical materialism was by no means unique to Otto Bauer though it gives a convoluted quality to some of his arguments for assimilation. Behind the contradictions lay Bauer's exaggerated fear that the emergence of Jewish nationalism, by reinforcing traditional Jewish identity, would only exacerbate antisemitism and make the socialist class struggle more difficult. On this point Otto Bauer fully agreed with the Polish socialists in Galicia, led by Ignacy Daszyński, that the assimilation of the Jewish masses would be impossible as long as they clung to their separate culture. In 1911 Bauer wrote about these obstacles to a common class-struggle of Polish and Jewish workers.

> There [in Galicia] the Jewish proletariat is numerous, as well as the Jewish petty-bourgeoisie which is being very rapidly

> proletarianized. The Jewish popular masses still have their own language [the *Jargon* or Yiddish—a German dialect mixed with Slav and Hebrew words] and their own customs. This is a considerable barrier to the union of the Jewish proletariat with their Slav class-comrades in the common class struggle. There, anti-Semitism does not emerge as anti-capitalism but as nationalism which divides the workers.[39]

Although very circumspect in his references to the chauvinist antisemitism of Polish proletarians who sought to prevent Jewish workers from entering the mechanized factories, Bauer was more forthcoming on the subject of Jewish nationalism. He condemned it forthwith as "petty-bourgeois" and "utopian." Indeed, he wrote in 1912: "Any attempt to artificially hinder assimilation and nurture an ideology hostile to it in Jewry is retrograde and reactionary."[40] Jewish nationalism which "seeks to separate the Jewish proletariat from its Slav brothers" was unequivocally condemned by Bauer as an obstruction more dangerous than the grudgingly admitted antisemitism of the Polish proletariat.[41]

Such an argument, to be consistent, would have had to extend to *all* nationalist solutions of social problems which segregated workers along national lines. Bauer would have had to categorically condemn the German, Czech, Polish, Ruthenian, and Slovenian "separatist" tendencies in the labor movement. To some extent, Czech working-class "separatism" was indeed sharply reproved, but there was no questioning of the legitimacy or viability of the Czech national movement. In fact the Austro-Marxist model of cultural-national autonomy rejected *only* Jewish nationalism, ostensibly because the Jews lacked a national territory. This offered a powerful argument for the Zionist movement which sought to rectify the anomaly that the Jews were indeed a nationality without a concentrated territory. Zionists had only a few years earlier designated the ancient Jewish homeland of Palestine as the place where the (future) nation of Israel must once more be reestablished. It was the Austrian journalist, Theodor Herzl, who had organized the First Zionist Congress in 1897 which first put the movement on the international political map.

Otto Bauer's theses provoked a lively debate among Jewish socialists and labor Zionists in Eastern Europe who rejected his premise that the Western model of emancipation and assimilation was applicable to the *Ostjuden*.[42] They argued that the infiltration of capitalism in Eastern Europe, far from leading to the dispersal or absorption of the Jews or to their increased social mobility, was undermining their economic position. Capitalist development was in fact making assimilation more difficult. They pointed to the process of urbanization which not only in Galicia, but also in London, New York, Vienna, and Warsaw, was creating compact Jewish ghettos in the cities. Bauer's critics, like the Zionist Socialist Berl Locker, also emphasized the extent of the gulf separating East European Jews from their Slav neighbors—the national, religious, and linguistic differences, exacerbated by antisemitism, which made a common class struggle highly problematic. Other critics underlined the fact that national competition between workers in Eastern Europe had already provoked the exclusion of Jewish workers from the factories and discrimination in employment. In Austro-Polish Galicia, as in the Russian Pale of Settlement, mass agitation and the class struggle offered no immediate solution to economic backwardness, chronic unemployment, pauperism, or antisemitic discrimination.[43] Above all, socialist Zionists complained that Otto Bauer had refused to discuss "the needs of the Jewish working class" in the only terms which ultimately mattered—the right of *all* nations to self-determination.[44]

It needs to be remembered that no Austrian social democratic forum existed in which labor Zionist theses could be objectively presented before 1914. The one partial exception was Engelbert Pernerstorfer's *Deutsche Worte,* a German-national periodical which, following its editor's adhesion to the labor movement, sought to synthesize socialism and nationalist ideology. In July 1898, Pernerstorfer published the arguments of the Russian labour Zionist Nachman Syrkin in favor of a Jewish socialist State in Palestine.[45] Syrkin, then thirty-one years old, suggested that international socialism was an assimilationist sham which placed Jews in the untenable position of negating their heritage. The assimilated Jews in the socialist movement had followed the Jewish bourgeoisie in throwing off their Jewishness as if it were an unwanted burden. But their internationalism was based on false premises. It was not the task of the labor movement to demand the suppression of the national character of any people. On the contrary, socialists should encourage the struggle for national self-determination. Syrkin deplored the fact that there was no other nation, apart from the Jews, whose revolutionary avant-garde so systematically sought to deny its origins or "preach assimilation to a dominant nationality."[46]

Syrkin insisted that the Jews remained a distinct nation although lacking "external national characteristics." They had fought a bitter, heroic struggle over the centuries to preserve their identity. A specifically Jewish socialism had now arisen which sought to rectify the historic *abnormality* of Jewish existence—its lack of a national territory. According to Syrkin, Jews required

Zionism because their singular social position excluded any effective class struggle in contemporary conditions. Socialism on its own could "solve the Jewish problem only in the remote future."[47] In Syrkin's estimation, Zionism was a movement that affected *all* classes of Jewry and sought to rebuild Jewish life from the bottom upwards. It was based on an idealistic striving to relieve Jewish suffering and to transform the ancient messianic hope of Israel into concrete political action. It did not conflict with the class struggle (as the Austro-Marxists maintained) but stood beyond it, as a creative task that involved the whole Jewish people.[48]

Engelbert Pernerstorfer, a leading Austrian Social Democrat, felt considerable sympathy for this Zionist viewpoint, since he had consistently argued that only a good German, Polish, Italian, or Czech patriot could be a genuine socialist. He had always rejected the sweeping view of the *Communist Manifesto* that nationalism was a retrograde bourgeois ideology and that the "workers have no fatherland." Like many of the Marxist "revisionists" in Germany, he believed that socialism and nationalism "necessarily belong together."[49] The cosmopolitanism of the early labor movement had unfavorably struck him as being bloodless, overly rationalist, and detached from real life. In his youth, Pernerstorfer like Victor Adler had been a passionate Pan-German, convinced that the road to the regeneration of German culture lay through a fusion of the intellectual and emotional elements symbolized in Richard Wagner's operas. Even as a socialist he was no less committed to the concept of aesthetic politics which went together with his idealization of the creative power of the German *Volk*.[50] The Zionist movement with its appeal to both head and heart, with its idealistic aspirations and reawakening of millennial longings, derived from an ethos not so remote from Pernerstorfer's *deutschnational* radicalism.

Pernerstorfer's idealistic nationalism had been strongly influenced by the classical legacy of German humanism. The ideals of Goethe, Kant, Fichte, Beethoven, and above all Schiller acted as a check on his latent chauvinist tendencies. His "aesthetic socialism" manifested an enlightened regard for the *diversity of cultures* and for the *universality* of national aspirations. Though he insisted that loyalty to the German working class and its cultural heritage was the first duty of an Austrian Social Democrat, he was no less insistent that Czechs, Poles, Slovenes, Italians, Ruthenes, and Jews should also enjoy the same right to their own cultural-national individuality. Socialism had to encourage the liberation of *all* oppressed peoples, not their disappearance. This applied especially to smaller nationalities who were in danger of absorption by their larger neighbors. As Pernerstorfer put it in

1905, "Every nation wants its home in which it is master, as every man wants a house which belongs to him alone."[51] From this standpoint, the Zionist aspiration for a Jewish national home appeared to Pernerstorfer as a completely understandable and natural sentiment. In the light of his prominence in Austrian Social Democracy during these prewar years, he was an important ally for the labor Zionists.

It was not until World War I that Pernerstorfer came out with a categorical statement in favor of Zionism. As the Dutch socialist H. H. van Kol observed, the Great War had led to a palpable

> reawakening of national feelings even in the socialist ranks, a reaction against the hyper-centralist tendencies that were dominant before. It also made clear what only a few individuals previously accepted, that the free political development of different nationalities was an ineluctable condition of international progress.[52]

Van Kol pointed out that a climate of opinion favorable to Zionism began to emerge in the socialist world around 1916. Even in Austria-Hungary, although the Austro-Marxists and their Polish allies were adamantly opposed to it, Ukrainian, Croatian, and Slovenian socialists were sympathetic to the demands of Poale-Zion. Among the German-Austrian socialists, "only Dr. Pernerstorfer, with his energetic feeling for justice, was a loyal fighter for the Jewish cause."[53] Pernerstorfer's article on the "Jewish Question" for Martin Buber's periodical, *Der Jude,* published in 1916, confirms this assessment. In this essay Pernerstorfer most emphatically pointed out that the Jews were *not* a backward, underdeveloped people. They were a strong nation of 12 to 14 million people with an ancient Hebrew tradition and a vigorous modern literature. They were the inheritors of a great cultural and religious patrimony which had enabled them to survive for two thousand years without a common soil, territory or peasantry.

> Let us not lose sight of the fact that they are indeed a nation, a nation of outstanding intellectual endowment, like every internally coherent and civilized people. They have a right to exist as a nation.[54]

In contrast to the pan-German utterances of his youth and to the intellectual condescension of the Austro-Marxists, Pernerstorfer now put forward a new credo that might best be described as humanistic nationalism .

> We must be quite clear in our minds that with the extinction of the Jewish people important cultural elements of a special kind would

> disappear. Admittedly, they would not be wholly lost through absorption by other nations, but they would be diluted and in Western Europe at any rate, they would probably disappear altogether. The enhancement of mankind cannot be achieved through external mingling but only by inner differentiation.[55]

Having pointed out, in contrast to his Austro-Marxist colleagues (many of them Jewish), that the *Jews were a nation with an undeniable right to self-determination* [my emphasis], Pernerstorfer suggested that they now had a unique opportunity to stake their claim in Palestine. He regarded Palestine as the only viable solution, in the long run, for the millions of impoverished *Ostjuden* in Russia and Galicia.[56] Moreover, he correctly predicted that the hot-blooded nationalism of the Poles would soon transform more than three million Jews into a permanent thorn in the flesh of a restored Polish nation-state. These *Ostjuden* could not be de-nationalized or "assimilated" since they were nothing but Jews. They had no desire whatsoever to become Poles, Russians, or Romanians. Zionism was therefore the only logical solution to this East European Jewish question. At the same time, Pernerstorfer also advocated national autonomy for all Jews who remained behind, wherever they lived in densely populated, compact masses.

Pernerstorfer's attitude to the "Jewish Question" was nonetheless not free of antisemitic layers from his younger days in spite of his clear sympathy with Zionism and national-minded Jews. The year before he wrote his pro-Zionist article for *Der Jude,* he had lashed out against a left-wing socialist colleague, Dr. Robert Danneberg, a prominent assimilated Jew in the Austrian Party. His outburst had been provoked by a series of articles written by Danneberg (the leader of the socialist youth organizations) in the weekly *Volkstribune* between 17 March and 8 September 1915. Danneberg, then thirty years old, had sharply criticized the German and Austrian socialist parties for unconditional support of official national defense policies. Danneberg stood on the pacifist wing of the party and together with Friedrich Adler, Max Adler, and Thérèse Schlesinger (all of them Jewish intellectuals), he appealed to anti-war sentiment and the fading internationalism of the Austrian socialist movement. As in the SPD, passions were running high between the right wing of the party and its leftist critics over issues of territorial annexation, cease-fire proposals and war aims.

Pernerstorfer's reply to the left-wing of the Party, provocatively entitled "Der Typus Danneberg," was a harsh polemic against feckless, "cosmo-politan" internationalism which denied the reality of the German nation. He also gratuitously introduced the question of Danneberg's racial origins and those of his main supporters.

> Who then are, as it were, the authoritative representatives of nationlessness (*Nationslosigkeit*), and its tireless preachers? A gang of academics who form a tightly-knit clique, who plan to take over the reins of party leadership at the crucial moment, and to constitute the Supreme Court which decides what is genuine socialism. But this gang is not only made up of academics, but also exclusively of Jews. No other socialist party would tolerate such unpatriotic elements within its ranks. Only we, the German-speaking Social Democrats, suffer such an affliction, and have to put up with Jews in prominent positions who try to make German workers ashamed of being German.[57]

The culturally pan-German Pernerstorfer tried to head off the inevitable charge of antisemitism by emphasizing that he was a "grateful pupil of Marx and Lassalle," "decidedly a philo-Semite" and fully aware of "the gifts of this race" which had contributed so much to the Socialist Party. But he considered the "internationalism" of Danneberg and his Jewish Marxist colleagues as an evasion, and ultimately a threat to the *national identity* of the German-Austrian working-class.

> I asked Danneberg on one occasion to which nation he felt himself to belong. He replied: "I am a cosmopolitan." A splendid answer for the kind of logical person Danneberg no doubt considers himself to be. Everyone is the child of a people. But Danneberg does not wish to be a German, nor does he want to call himself a Jew, which would at least be perfectly honourable. No, he himself is a "mixed subject" and wishes to drag the German worker down to his low level.[58]

Pernerstorfer's emotional tirade was not allowed to go unanswered. On 5 May 1915, the Party leader (and a personal friend of Pernerstorfer), Victor Adler, stepped into the fray and, without identifying himself with Danneberg's views, condemned the use of personal insults as the "most indefensible of all in party discussions."[59] With cutting irony, Adler accused his old comrade of branding Danneberg as an "unregenerate sinner" simply "because he is by birth and education incurably and indelibly tainted." Moreover, there was no such thing as a "Danneberg type." The most prominent opponents of the official German Socialist line on the war were Franz Mehring, Karl Liebknecht, and Clara Zetkin, none of them Jews. On the other hand, in the *nationalist* camp of German social democracy, "it simply teems with Jews, old and young, academics and non-academics, from Joseph Bloch and Cohen right through the alphabet."[60] Victor Adler was certainly correct on this point. One cannot convincingly divide the stand of either German or Austrian socialists during the First World War along ethnic lines. In the Austrian Party there were Jews like Ludo Hartmann who were as pan-German as Pernerstorfer, and even the editor of the Viennese *Arbeiterzeitung*, Friedrich Austerlitz (a convert to Christianity), had greeted the outbreak of war in 1914 with ultra-patriotic German enthusiasm.[61] Nevertheless, it remains true that the proportion of Austrian-German Socialists who eventually identified with either a left-wing or a neutralist stance during World War I was higher among Jews than among their Gentile colleagues.

Pernerstorfer's fury against the cosmopolitan pacifist Jewish intellectuals in the Austrian Socialist Party was antisemitic in tone but not really inconsistent with his positive attitude to Jewish nationalism. Both his sympathies and antipathies towards Jews were determined by a pronounced streak of romantic idealism, *völkisch* nationalism, personal friendships, and a patriotic socialist credo. Though he never completely shook off the antisemitism implanted in him by Georg von Schönerer and the *deutschnational* student movement of the early 1880s, Pernerstorfer did *not* identify with its more extreme, brutal features.[62] Moreover, he came to see in Zionism an authentic expression of his own aesthetic, cultural and national ideals. Though he distrusted assimilation on principle, he was more than willing to acknowledge the contribution which Jews had made to the socialist movement. In 1916 he underlined this debt:

> We, German socialists especially, can never have hostile feelings towards the Jews. They have given to socialism, to the German people and to the world, two men whose memory is unforgettable; Karl Marx and Ferdinand Lassalle. For us they are Germans, for the Jews they are Jews.[63]

At the opposite end of the socialist spectrum, we also need to take into account the attitude of Karl Kautsky, the most prominent theoretician of the Second International, who was skeptical of Marx's image of the Jews as a prototype of the predatory capitalist bourgeoisie.[64] Kautsky was indeed an admirer of the Jewish contribution to international Socialism. He saw in the Jewish proletariat a social class with a future, although he dismissed Judaism as a relic of the medieval past and a ghetto phenomenon in the pores of feudal society.[65] Kautsky had been born in Prague and grew up in Austria-Hungary, fully cognizant of the "nationality questions" that increasingly fractured the political life of the Habsburg Empire. As editor of the leading German Marxist periodical, *Die Neue Zeit,* he was undoubtedly a major theoretical influence on socialist opinion in the Austro-Hungarian Empire. Like the Austro-Marxists, Kautsky refused to ascribe any "national" characteristics to the Jews.[66] In his view, the existence of a non-territorial nation was a logical impossibility—which could never be reconciled with Marxist theory. The Jewish proletariat had, therefore, to be seen as a revolutionary class without a nation. Defining Jews as an anomaly, Kautsky was *unable* to accept their claims for non-territorial autonomy. In this respect, he agreed with Otto Bauer, though their definitions of national characteristics were rather different.

The rise of Zionism and the growing separatism of the Russian-Jewish Bund posed a new set of problems. Kautsky's answer came in response to a request from the Polish Social Democrats Adolf Warski and Rosa Luxemburg to comment on the bloody Kishinev pogrom in 1903.[67] In this influential article, Kautsky analyzed Russian antisemitism as a primitive reaction to the isolation of the disenfranchised Jews in the Pale of Settlement, where they constituted a mass of semi-unemployed *Luftmenschen* and impoverished artisans. Because of their physical segregation, Jews were regarded by the Russian masses as "strangers," and as convenient scapegoats by the Tsarist autocracy. The Zionist movement, by allegedly favoring "segregation," would, in Kautsky's opinion, only strengthen antisemitism. It was thereby playing into the hands of the tsarist regime, aided and abetted by the financial support of Jewish capitalists in the West. Only the most rapid assimilation and participation in the Russian revolutionary movement could help the Jews to counter their enemies. Moreover, the Socialist idea remained the sole counterweight to the blatant antisemitism of the tsarist government and the Russian *muzhiks* (peasantry). The solidarity of Jew and Gentile in the socialist movement was therefore in the vital interests of the Jewish masses, and also corresponded to the best traditions of the Jewish people. On the other hand, the claim of the Zionist movement to transcend class interests was pure illusion and a dangerous distraction from the urgent need for proletarian solidarity.

Kautsky was better informed than the Austro-Marxists about Russian conditions and he was much more sympathetic to the Bund. But his choice for the Jews between isolation and revolutionary assimilation was rigidly dogmatic. Like Otto Bauer, he believed that the development of capitalism and the decline of religion would ultimately lead to the vanishing of Judaism as the remnant of a moribund ghetto culture. If anything, his critique of

Jewish nationalism was more severe than the Austro-Marxists, since he claimed that it would perpetuate the hereditary traits of a "caste" of urban financiers, merchants and intellectuals—the real targets of antisemitism. Kautsky casually dismissed Jewish solidarity as a poor substitute for proletarian solidarity. In his view, it had no future. Moreover, as he wrote in his *Rasse und Judentum* (1914), there were no more vacant areas in the world where the Jewish national ideal could be implemented. Palestine, for practical reasons alone, was not a serious prospect.[68] The land was infertile, the Jews were hopelessly outnumbered by the indigenous Arab population, and the possibility of establishing a viable industrial base seemed remote. Indeed after the First World War, Kautsky's prognosis for Jewish prospects in Palestine remained unreservedly pessimistic. In the later English edition of his prewar book, published in 1926 under the title *Are the Jews A Race?* Kautsky predicted that the Palestinian experiment would end tragically as soon as Anglo-French domination of the Middle East collapsed. In any case, on the theoretical level, he regarded Zionism and other varieties of Jewish nationalism as irredeemably reactionary, "a spoke in the wheel of progress." It was, so he argued, based on an untenable doctrine of historical rights.[69]

Kautsky's anti-Zionist critique found echoes in the positions adopted by German, Austrian, and Russian communists after the First World War, even though he was treated in all other respects by Lenin and his Bolshevik followers as a "renegade" from socialism. The Russian communists, like the Austro-Marxists, held tenaciously to the view expressed in Kautsky's *Die Neue Zeit* as early as 1897 that Zionism was at best an ephemeral phenomenon—the last beautiful pose of a "moribund nation" before it left the stage of history.[70] Otto Heller, a leading Austrian Communist theoretician of Jewish origin, repeated Kautsky's thesis in an orthodox Leninist form in 1931. Heller predicted that the assimilation of the Jewish bourgeoisie in the West along with that of the Jewish lower middle-class and proletariat in Eastern Europe was a historically inevitable process.[71] Palestinian Zionism was dismissed by Otto Heller as the end of the road for a *bankrupt* Jewish nationalism, the symbol of the "downfall of Judaism" in capitalist society. The classical Marxists, led by Kautsky and supported by the Bundists in Russia and eastern Europe, had said much the same thing. For the Bund, the primary concern remained the class struggle of the Jewish proletariat. In that context, Zionism was perceived as a dangerous competitor in its fight for support of the Jewish masses. Zionism, it was alleged, was fundamentally *counter-revolutionary,* because it preached to Jews that they could not rely upon the solidarity of their Gentile proletarian comrades. Worse still, the

Zionists had renounced any active participation in the struggle against antisemitism, pronouncing it to be an "eternal" and irrevocable malady of the exile (*Galut*).

What the Zionists proposed in Palestine was held to be a mirage both by Kautsky and by the Bundists, the shallow dream of a Jewish state where Jewish capitalists would continue to exploit the workers.[72] This kind of argument was also put forward by "assimilationist" Jewish Marxists from Eastern Europe, who were the most hostile of all to the idea that the Jews constituted a nation. They demanded "democratic" rights for the Jews, not separate "national" interests, which were invariably portrayed as a reactionary return to the ghetto. As Max Zetterbaum, a Galician Jewish agitator, put it: the duty of Social democrats was to "raise the cultural level of the Jewish masses" by introducing Western ideas of socialism and democracy.[73] This had to be done first in Yiddish and later in the language of the country. Ultimately the Jewish workers should speak the same language as their "Christian" comrades. The goal of revolutionary brotherhood and international solidarity was clearly deemed to be inconsistent with that of Zionism or Diaspora Jewish nationalism.

The negative attitude of Marxist Jews to nationalist "deviations" like Zionism had many sources. One driving force was the *internationalist* conviction—renewed in our own day—that the nation-state was an anachronism, an obsolescent relic of the capitalist era.[74] The psychological motivation of anti-Zionism also involved a guilt-complex about devoting oneself to Jews when there seemed to be other more pressing social and political problems in the world. It stemmed from a general revulsion against integral nationalists who were frequently be found among the most prominent promoters of the persecution of Jews.[75] Whatever the underlying causes of this hostility, Jews often achieved prominence in the "internationalist" wing of the socialist movements in Europe. Not surprisingly, perhaps, Zionism touched an especially sensitive nerve for internationalist Jews by its insistence on an independent *Jewish homeland* and state sovereignty. This standpoint irritated Jewish Marxist intellectuals who sharply disapproved of anything that would distinguish Jews from other nationalities. A Jewish State would permanently establish this distinction. The resentment is palpable to this day.

In some ways, the neutrality, impartiality, and apparent objectivity of the Marxist historical method provided a perfect cover for the subtle antisemitism that expressed itself in such hostility towards Jewish interests. Rosa Luxemburg, Leon Trotsky, Karl Radek, Israel-Helphand Parvus, Victor Adler, and Otto Bauer were all classic examples of this syndrome. Anything self-consciously "Jewish" was intolerable in their eyes. Hence, it is no surprise to find that it was Russian Social Democrats of Jewish origin (including the Menshvik leader, Julius Martov—one of the founding fathers of "Bundism") who would lead the polemics against the Bund within the Russian workers' movement. They denounced with special vehemence any demands for the cultural-national autonomy of the Jewish proletariat. Similarly in the Austrian and Polish labor movements, it was acculturated Jewish intellectuals who usually led the offensive against any form of Jewish particularism.

At the same time, Gentile socialists in the labor movement, particularly those of a "revisionist" turn of mind, proved more sympathetic to the appeal of Zionism. We have already seen how the doctrine that each nation should be master in its own house gradually come to permeate socialist thought at the beginning of the 20th century. The failure of the Second International to prevent the First World War gave this trend an irresistible impulse. By 1918 Zionism had for the first time found a sympathetic ear within the Socialist International. Reformist social democrats like the Belgians Emil Vandervelde and Camille Huysmans, the Frenchman Jean Longuet, and the Austrian Pernerstorfer, and even democratic socialists of Jewish origin like Eduard Bernstein and Léon Blum, became friendly to labor Zionism and Jewish colonization in Palestine after World War I.

The principle of national self-determination for Jews (including the idea of a Jewish State) became increasingly acceptable to reformist Social Democracy following the Balfour Declaration and the establishment of a British Mandate for Palestine. The League of Nations in 1920 solemnly committed Great Britain under international law to lay the foundations for a "Jewish National Home in Palestine." A Socialist Committee for a Workers' Palestine was formed in the 1920s, which included the British labourites George Lansbury and Ramsay MacDonald, the Dutchman van Kol, as well as the Belgian socialists, Vandervelde and Huysmans. The international Communist movement (dominated by the Russian Bolsheviks) as well as the Austro-Marxists, remained, however, fixed in the mold of prewar formulas, first evolved by Kautsky and Otto Bauer. They persisted in their conviction that assimilation was the only answer to the "Jewish Question."[76] Zionism was execrated as an ideology that promoted a fictitious Jewish solidarity and ran counter to progressive ideas, since it opposed the absorption of Jews in the Diaspora. Both Zionism and antisemitism were attacked by Lenin, no less than by Otto Bauer or the "renegade" Kautsky, as two sides of the same coin—reactionary ideologies produced by declining classes in a moribund capitalist society.

The Russian Bolshevik leader, Lenin, was especially unequivocal in his condemnation of the demand for Jewish national culture, even when it was proclaimed in its most moderate form by the Jewish Bund. It was, he insisted, "a slogan of the rabbis and the bourgeoisie."[77] Jewish nationalism in Lenin's opinion was the product of "backward and semi-barbarous countries" like Austro-Polish Galicia and Russia, which had deliberately kept the Jews segregated from the rest of the population as a caste. Any manifestation of Jewish nationalism could *not* be progressive but was, by definition, motivated by a desire to perpetuate this "*caste* position of the Jews" in Eastern Europe. In espousing this dogma, Lenin was clearly echoing Kautsky. In his many polemics against the anti-Zionist Bund, Lenin ridiculed with particular vehemence the Bundist (and Zionist) bogey of "assimilation"—claiming that "only those who with reverential awe contemplate the 'backside' of Jewry shout against assimilation."[78] He cited in contrast the melting-pot of New York and the conditions more generally prevailing in the United States around 1913 as proof that modern civilization was remorselessly grinding up national distinctions. "The best Jews, famous in history, who gave the world foremost leaders of democracy and socialism" were his models of progress, and they "never shouted against assimilation."[79]

It is striking to observe that although Lenin (like Marx) supported the national liberation movements of oppressed nationalities whenever it suited his revolutionary strategy, such backing categorically did not apply to Jewish nationalism or Zionism. These were not movements which could serve any useful purpose in the break-up of the Tsarist State. Moreover, even in its proletarian form—as expressed in the demand for cultural-national autonomy—Bundism was for Lenin a prime example of the bourgeois nationalisms threatening the unity of the transnational labor movements of other oppressed nationalities in the Russian state. Stalin, writing in 1913, closely followed Lenin's critique of the Bund and of Jewish nationalism in general. Stalin emphasized that because the Jews lacked a common territory or culture, they were not, in any sense of the word, a nation.[80] At any rate, they were not a real or living nation. At best, they were the scattered remnants of an obscure religious community, lacking the economic, territorial, and psychological prerequisites for nationhood. The young Stalin could find nothing in common between Russian, American, Georgian, or west European Jews, except obsolete relics of the past.[81] At the same time he also engaged in some harsh polemics against Austro-Marxist theories favoring a democratic federated nationalities' state based on ethnic and cultural pluralism.

The Marxist conception of the national problem in general, and of the Jewish question in particular, offered no framework in which it was possible to take account of Jewish national aspirations before 1914. The premise of Jewish peoplehood was denied (especially by the Austro-Marxists), and with it the legitimacy of Jewish national rights, the creativity of the Jews as a group, their will to autonomy, and the validity of their traditions and culture. The Austro-Marxists adopted this policy despite their greater openness to modern notions of ethnic and cultural diversity. Nevertheless, after the First World War, there were some exceptions. Max Adler, one of the leading Austro-Marxist thinkers of the 1920s, expressed both sympathy and deep interest in the cause of socialist Zionism in British Mandatory Palestine. Already in 1928, addressing young Jewish socialists in Vienna, he had declared that Jewry was not a spent force and there could be no question that Marxists needed to support "a Jewish national working-class."[82] In 1931 Max Adler again affirmed his "admiration for the idealism and abnegation of the labour Zionist pioneers."[83] In his foreword to a work published by the Marxist-Zionist radical youth movement Hashomer Hatza'ir (The young guard), Adler wrote that "one cannot overlook the fact of the national rebirth of the Jews and their will to national concentration as historical factors. One should not fight this [trend]. For Marxist socialism is absolutely not an opponent of nationalism."[84] In a speech on 22 January 1933 in Vienna, Max Adler went further still, referring warmly to the achievements of the Poale-Zionists in Palestine as one of the few bright spots in the depressing landscape of mounting racism and socialist retreat around the world. Adler evidently rejected the assimilationist perspective of his Austrian socialist comrades and of many west European Marxists when it came to Zionism.

Such "heretical" views on assimilationism were even more forthrightly expressed by Julius Braunthal, a prominent Austrian Social Democrat, who had served in the late 1920s as an editor of the *Arbeiter-Zeitung* as well as running the leading Party theoretical journal, *Der Kampf*. Braunthal came from a much more traditional, Jewish religious background than other leading Party intellectuals like Otto Bauer, Friedrich Adler, or Robert Danneberg.[85] The polemical articles published in *Der Kampf* in the late 1920s (by Mendel Singer and Hugo Steiner) which were sympathetic to socialist Zionism in Palestine, were largely due to his influence.[86] Braunthal shared Max Adler's positive view of the Palestinian labor movement which brought an important sector of Zionism much closer to the Socialist International.[87] Braunthal's visit to Palestine in the 1930s reinforced his feeling that the Zionists had accomplished a socialist miracle in the Holy Land.[88] The root of the difference between such views on Zionism and that of the party leadership under Otto Bauer, clearly lay in Braunthal's strong identification with the Jewish people. Unlike the majority of the Austro-Marxist leadership, he had always felt himself to be slightly different "from my Gentile comrades," even if in an imponderable way. This sense of individuality and of belonging to a world-wide Jewish community prevented Braunthal from becoming a convinced "assimilationist." But such exceptions aside, the Austro-Marxists did not fundamentally revise their view of the "Jewish Question," even after the crushing of the Austrian workers' uprising of 1934 by Dollfuss's authoritarian Christian-social government.

There was, however, to be a poignant endnote that accompanied Otto Bauer's fading hopes for the assimilation of the Jews. He had been deeply distressed by Hitler's *Anschluss* of March 1938 and the devastating pogromist violence against Viennese Jewry which followed in its wake. His old Austro-Marxist comrade and rival, Karl Renner, had publicly called on Austrians to vote "Ja" (yes) for the union with Nazi Germany, thereby legitimizing Hitler's rule. Otto Bauer, on the other hand, as an exile in Paris, now penned a desperate appeal to "the world conscience" to save the 200,000 Jews remaining in Austria from brutal Nazi persecution. He asked the reluctant Western democracies to open their doors to the oppressed "victims of fascism," members of a "national" minority entitled to protection under the Treaty of Saint-Germain. The appeal appeared in the London *News Chronicle* on 5 July 1938—the day after Otto Bauer's death in Paris of exhaustion, and perhaps of a broken heart. It was the last article which he wrote and it represented—at least by implication—a revision of his earlier views on antisemitism and the inevitability of assimilation. Four months later, the massively destructive Crystal Night Pogrom definitively rolled down the curtain on a century of German-Jewish "symbiosis" and creativity in Central Europe. A relatively large number of Otto Bauer's Austrian compatriots, who had greeted Hitler's annexation of their homeland with rapturous enthusiasm, would now come to play a leading role in the mass murder of European Jewry.

Notes

1. See Maxime Rodinson's introduction to Abraham Léon, *La Conception matérialiste de la question juive* (Paris, 1968), *v* ff; also Shlomo Avineri, *Moses Hess: Prophet of Communism and Zionism* (New York, 1985).

2. Ernst Vogt, *Israel—Kritik von links* (Wuppertal, 1976).

3. Robert S. Wistrich, "Marxism and Jewish Nationalism: The Theoretical Roots of Confrontation," *Jewish Journal of Sociology* 17 (June 1975): 43–54.

4. Simon Dubnow, "On the Tasks of the Folks-Partay" in *Nationalism and History. Essays on Old and New Judaism,* edited by Koppel S. Pinson (New York, 1961), 230.

5. See Robert S. Wistrich, *Revolutionary Jews from Marx to Trotsky* (London, 1976); also Percy S. Cohen, *Jewish Radicals and Radical Jews* (London, 1980).

6. *Karl Marx/Friedrich Engels Werke* (Berlin, 1964), 1: 375.

7. For a detailed critique of this Hegelian-Marxist aberration, see Roman Rodolsky, "Friedrich Engels und das Problem der 'Geschichtslosen Völker,'" *Archiv für Sozialgeschichte* 4 (1964): 87–283; also Roman Szporluk, *Communism and Nationalism* (New York, 1988).

8. T. G. Masaryk, *Die Philosophischen und Sociologischen Grundlagen des Marxismus* (Vienna, 1899), 454.

9. Ibid.

10. See Annie Kriegel, *Le Pain et les roses.Jalons pour une histoire des socialismes* (Paris, 1968), 79–94.

11. Robert A. Kann, *The Multi-national Empire* (New York, 1950); see also Gerald Stourzh, "The Multinational Empire Revisited: Reflections on Late Imperial Austria," *Austrian History Yearbook* 23 (1992): 1–22.

12. Otto Bauer, *Die Nationalitätenfrage und die Sozialdemokratie* (Vienna, 1907), 366–81.

13. Ibid., 370.

14. Ibid., 368.

15. Ibid., 376. On the concept of a "people-class," see Abram Léon, *The Jewish Question. A Marxist Interpretation* (New York, 1970).

16. Bauer, *Die Nationalitätenfrage,* 378–79.

17. See Dubnow, *Nationalism and History,* 368, for a favorable reference to Karl Renner. For a useful discussion of Otto Bauer, see Jack Jacobs, *On Socialists and "the Jewish Question" after Marx* (New York, 1992): 102–17. This analysis lacks, however, any sense of wider historical context.

18. Ibid., 368.

19. Yves Bourdet, *Otto Bauer et la révolution* (Paris, 1968).

20. Otto Bauer, *Die Nationalitätenfrage,* 367.

21. Ibid., 368.

22. Ibid.

23. Ibid., 370.

24. Ibid., 371.

25. Ibid.

26. Ibid., 376.

27. Ibid.

28. Ibid.

29. See Oscar Janowsky, *The Jews and Minority Rights, 1898–1918* (New York, 1933), 136ff; and Mathias Acher, *Das Stiefkind der Sozialdemokratie* (Vienna, 1906), 6–7, 17–19; and especially Robert S. Wistrich, *Socialism and the Jews. The Dilemmas of Assimilation in Germany and Austria-Hungary* (London / Toronto, 1982).

30. Otto Bauer, *Die Nationalitätenfrage,* 379.

31. Ibid., 378.

32. Ibid., 379.

33. Ibid.

34. Ibid.

35. Ibid., 379.

36. Ibid.

37. Otto Bauer, "Sozialismus und Antisemitismus," *Der Kampf* 4 (1910–11): 94.

38. Ibid.

39. Ibid.

40. Otto Bauer, "Galizische Parteitage," *Der Kampf* 5 (1911–12): 158–59; see also Theodore R. Weeks, *From Assimilation to Antisemitism. The "Jewish Question" in Poland, 1850–1914* (DeKalb, Ill., 2006).

41. Otto Bauer,"Sozialismus und Antisemitismus," 94.

42. See Markus Ratner, "Nationalitätsbegriff und Nationale Autonomie," *Sozialistische Monatshefte* 16, 1, 1 (1910): 345–54; idem, "Die Nationale Autonomie und das jüdische Proletariat," *Sozialistische Monatshefte* 17, 3 (1911): 1339–41; Maxim Anin, "Ist die Assimilation möglich?," *Sozialistische Monatshefte* 2, (1908): 614–19; "Probleme des jüdischen Arbeiterlebens," *Sozialistische Monatshefte* (1909): 231–35; "Die Judenfrage als Wanderungsproblem," *Sozialistische Monatshefte* (1909): 849–54; Leon Chasanowitsch, "Ziele und Mittel des Sozialistischen Zionismus," *Sozialistische Monatshefte* 2, (1914): 962–73. Also Jacobs, *On Socialists and "the Jewish Question,"* 118–41.

43. Berl Locker, "Die Allgemeinen Gesetze der Assimilation und die Ostjüden," *Der Jude* 1 (1916–1917): 504–29. See also Robert S. Wistrich, "Austrian Social Democracy and the Problem of Galician Jewry 1890–1914," *Leo Baeck Institute Yearbook* 26 (1981): 89–124.

44. Ratner, "Die Nationale Autonomie," 1341. For a postwar assessment of Bauer's prognoses written from a labor Zionist standpoint, see Mendel Singer, "Zum Problem der Assimilation der Juden," *Der Kampf* 21 (1928) 295–302.

45. *Deutsche Worte,* 18, July 1898, pp. 298–313.

46. Nachman Syrkin, "The Jewish Problem and the Socialist-Jewish State (1898)," extracts reprinted in Arthur Hertzberg, ed., *The Zionist Idea* (New York, 1973), 340 ff.; and Gideon Shimoni, *The Zionist Ideology* (Hanover, 1995), 170–78.

47. Ibid., 345.

48. "Zionism is a real phenomenon of Jewish life. It has its roots in the economic and social position of the Jews, in their moral protest, in the idealistic striving to give a better content to their miserable life." Ibid., 347. See also Shimoni, *Zionist Ideology,* 170–77.

49. Engelbert Pernerstorfer, "Der Nationale und Internationale Gedanke," *Sozialistische Monatshefte* 8 (Aug. 1905): 648.

50. William J. McGrath, *Dionysian Art and Populist Politics* (New Haven, 1974).

51. Engelbert Pernerstorfer, "Der Nationale und Internationale Gedanke," 652.

52. H. H. van Kol, *La Démocratie Socialiste Internationale et le Sionisme* (Lausanne, 1919): 4.

53. Ibid., 8.

54. Engelbert Pernerstorfer, "Zur Judenfrage," *Der Jude* (1916–1917): 313.

55. Ibid.

56. Ibid., 311.

57. Engelbert Pernerstorfer, "Der Typus Danneberg," *Volkstribune,* 28 Apr. 1915.

58. Ibid.

59. Victor Adler, "Das Märchen von den 'Formeln' und dem Typus," *Volkstribune,* 5 May 1915

60. Ibid.

61. Friedrich Austerlitz, "Der Tag der deutschen Nation," *Arbeiterzeitung,* 4 Aug. 1914.

62. Engelbert Pernerstorfer, "Von Schönerer bis Wolf," *Der Kampf* 4, no. 1 (May 1911): 390–93. See also Protokoll des Parteitages in Innsbruck, 29 Sept. to 2 Nov. 1911, p. 195. Pernerstorfer argued that his German patriotism made him more sympathetic to the aspirations of other nationalities. During World War I this zeal led however to conflict with his socialist colleagues, including Victor Adler, and to sharp criticism of his political positions, especially in Kautsky's *Neue Zeit.* For Pernerstorfer's reply, see his article, "Nationalismus und Internationalismus," *Der Kampf* 9 (1916): 98–106.

63. Engelbert Pernerstorfer, "Zur Judenfrage," 315; see also Wistrich, *Socialism and the Jews,* 332–48.

64. See Robert S. Wistrich, "Karl Marx, German Socialists and the Jewish Question 1880–1914," *Soviet Jewish Affairs* 3, no. 1 (1973): 92–97.

65. Jacob Lestschinsky, *Marx i Kautskii o evreiskom voprose* (Moscow, 1907), 25–29.

66. Jack Jacobs, "Marxism and Antisemitism: Kautsky's Perspective," *International Review of Social History* 30 (1985): part 3, 400–30.

67. Karl Kautsky, "Das Massaker von Kischineff," *Die Neue Zeit* (1902–1903): 303–9.

68. Karl Kautsky, *Rasse und Judentum* (Berlin, 1914), 79.

69. Ibid., 67.

70. See Otto Heller, *Der Untergang des Judentums* (Vienna, 1931), 21–22.

71. Ibid.

72. Johann Pollack, "Der Politische Zionismus," *Die Neue Zeit* (1897-1898): 598–600.

73. Max Zetterbaum, "Probleme der jüdisch-proletarischen Bewegung," *Die Neue Zeit* (1900–1901): 368–73. For the context, see Robert S. Wistrich, "Austrian Social Democracy and the Problem of Galician Jewry, 1890–1914," *LBIYB* 26 (1981): 89–124.

74. Isaac Deutscher, *The Non-Jewish Jew and Other Essays* (Oxford, 1968), 26.

75. Ibid.

76. Marc Jarblum, "Soixante ans du problème juif dans la théorie et la pratique du bolchévisme," *La Revue Socialiste* no. 176 (Oct. 1964). See also V. I. Lenin, "Critical Remarks on the National Question," *Prosveschenive,* October–December 1913.

77. V. I. Lenin, "National Culture," *Questions of National Policy and Proletarian Internationalism* (Moscow, n.d.), 31.

78. Ibid.

79. Ibid., 35.

80. Ibid.

81. J. V. Stalin, "Marxism and the National Question," in *The Essential Stalin, Major Theoretical Writings 1905–1952,* edited by B. Franklin (London, 1973), 62–65.

82. "Genosse Dr. Max Adlers Stellung zum Zionismus," *Jüdische Arbeiter-Jugend* 2, no. 2 (March 1928): 9. This publication was the organ of the Association of Jewish-Socialist Working-Youth in Austria.

83. See the *Bulletin of the Comité Socialiste pour la Palestine ouvrière* 5 (May 1930): 27.

84. Max Adler, "Sozialismus und Zionismus," *Der jüdische Arbeiter* 7, no. 5 (March 27, 1931): 1.

85. Avraham Barkai, "The Austrian Social Democrats and the Jews," *Wiener Library Bulletin* 24, no. 2, n.s. 19 [1971]: 21.

86. Shlomo Shafir, "Julius Braunthal and His Post-War Mediation Efforts between German and Israeli Socialists," *Jewish Social Studies* 47 (1985): 269.

87. Jack Jacobs, *On Socialists and "the Jewish Question,"* 115–16.

88. Julius Braunthal, *In Search of the Millennium* (London, 1945), 306–14. I had several long discussions with Braunthal in London in the early 1970s on the history of Austro-Marxism and the question of Palestine, which helped to shape my judgments in this chapter.

CHAPTER 10

Karl Kautsky and the Controversy over Zion

During the twenty years between the emergence of political Zionism and the Balfour Declaration in November 1917, the European socialist movement for the first time had to confront the existence of a Jewish national problem. The position of German Social Democracy (SPD), the largest and best organized labor movement existing in the world at that time, was of considerable importance in influencing the attitudes of other socialists towards this new phenomenon. Moreover, the polarization of socialist attitudes towards Zionism before the First World War, in so far as it reflected a fundamental split between the traditions of revolutionary Marxism and democratic socialism, remains of some relevance to understanding the confrontations of the present.[1] Two distinctly different positions towards Jewish nationalism were adopted by the leading reviews of the SPD, the *Neue Zeit,* edited by Karl Kautsky, and the *Sozialistische Monatshefte,* founded and edited by Dr. Joseph Bloch. What we shall henceforth designate as the Kautskyian position contains in embryonic form the seeds of future Communist, Trotskyist, and the New Left critiques of Zionism.[2] The revisionist position, on the other hand, as exemplified by the contributors to Joseph Bloch's *Sozialistische Monatshefte* was much more sympathetic to the Jewish national idea and the progress of Zionist colonization in Palestine.

Orthodox Marxism in the period of the Second International was embodied in the figure of Karl Kautsky, the leading theoretician of German Social Democracy and the unofficial Pope of the international labor movement. It was Kautsky who came closest to applying the Marxist method of historical materialism in a coherent fashion to the Jewish national problem. For a number of reasons, this led him to argue that the Jews had no future as a separate national group. Though Kautsky was aware of the fact that Marx and Engels had underestimated the dynamic of the national struggles which had unfolded in Europe since 1848, he did not seek a fundamental revision of their views on the national problem. Essentially, Marx and Engels regarded the bourgeois nation-state as a *transitory* stage in historical development, which would disappear with the victory of the proletariat in each country.

This was the internationalist viewpoint adopted in the Communist Manifesto.[3] However, disappointment at the failure of the 1848 Revolution led Marx and Engels (especially the latter) to invoke the pseudo-historicist Hegelian notion of "historic" and "ahistorical" peoples to justify the right of certain nations to self-determination and to deny this same right to smaller, more backward nationalities. Thus the founders of Communism took it for granted that Germans and Italians were entitled to their national unification, but in the Balkans and Eastern Europe, they reserved this right solely for the Hungarians and Poles.[4] On the other hand, the so-called counter-revolutionary Slav nations of Austria-Hungary, which had frustrated the movement for German national unity in 1848, would be condemned by historical development to disappear.[5]

Though Kautsky and his Austro-Marxist disciple Otto Bauer recognized that the predictions of Marx and Engels concerning the Slav national movements in Eastern and South-eastern Europe were mistaken, they barely took this into account in their analysis of Jewish nationalism.[6] Instead, they depicted the Jewish "nationality" in Russia and Eastern Europe as the fossilized offshoot of an "ahistorical" people. In contrast to the analyses in the *Sozialistische Monatshefte,* they did not seriously consider the national aspirations of the huge reservoir of non-assimilated Jews in Russia and Eastern Europe. They believed that the process of *de-nationalization* visible among Jews in Germany and Western Europe was essentially irreversible and would inevitably result in the assimilation of East European Jewry. Kautsky in particular insisted that existing demographic and socio-economic trends among West European Jewry were of decisive importance and proved that the Jews, as a collectivity, were in the process of self-dissolution.

In the Kautskyian perspective, the Jews were not a race, a nation, or even a people, but a "caste" with certain quasi-national attributes, which was on the point of disappearing.

> If one wants to characterize the role played in the Middle Ages and even today by the Jews in Eastern Europe, one can do this much better by describing them as a "caste" than as a nation. It is not among the nations with which we are concerned here, but among the castes of India that we find phenomena which correspond to the status of the Jewish community as it has been constituted since the destruction of Jerusalem and the advent of Christianity. The efforts made to preserve the Jewish community as a nation are in reality nothing but attempts to perpetuate its existence as a particular caste. Such an aspiration would be

> inexplicable in a modern State. It can only develop under the thumb of the infamous domination of the Muscovite bureaucracy or the Rumanian boyars.[7]

The Jews were a unique case, not because they had preserved their "nationality" in spite of lacking a common territory or a common language, but rather because the "laws" of historical development allowed them no future as a nation. In the course of a polemic with Otto Bauer on the national problem, Kautsky observed:

> Certainly, the Jews speak many languages. But do the Jews who speak German not form part of the German nation, those who speak French, part of the French nation? It is only in Eastern Europe that the Jews feel themselves to be a particular nation, but there they speak their own language, and not Hebrew, but a corrupted German—the Yiddish [tongue] which marks them off from their surroundings.[8]

What preserved the "Jewish nationality" in the Middle Ages and later in Eastern Europe was not, however , the Jewish religion or the Yiddish language, but the socio-economic function of Jews as merchants and usurers in a pre-capitalist society. In this respect Kautsky and Otto Bauer shared a similar standpoint.

There is a clear line of continuity which runs from this Kautskyian analysis of the Jewish national problem to the theories evolved by Lenin, Stalin, Otto Heller, Abram Léon, and more recent neo-Marxian critics of Zionism.[9] Common to all the communist, Trotskyist, and new leftist exponents of anti-Zionism is their conviction that the Jews are a product of capitalism, and that with its fall, the Jews would lose their illusory national characteristics. In his seminal *Rasse und Judentum,* first published in the *Neue Zeit* in 1914, Kautsky identified the "chimerical" attributes of Jewish nationalism with the archaic heritage of the ghetto.

> Precisely the compulsory congestion in a small space—which today has created the illusion of a Jewish nationality—also produces Jewish misery. With the disappearance of the latter, the conditions for a Jewish nationality will also disappear.[10]

In other words, Kautsky was convinced that only the special conditions in the Russian Pale of Settlement had prevented the Jews from merging completely with their surrounding environment. Once they were treated as free and equal citizens, their nationality would dissolve along with the ghetto milieu that had nourished it. This would be a process in no way comparable to the tragic extinction of the Red Indians in North America or the forced assimilation of other nationalities in the Russian Empire. On the contrary, it would be a *progressive* step for the Jews, liberating them from the triple curse of poverty, pogroms, and antisemitism.

> It seems to me, however, that for the Jew himself, the ghetto, which is the form of life of Jewry, is not a phenomenon evoking nostalgic memories. The friends of human progress have even less cause than the conservative Jew to shed a tear over the disappearance of Jewry.[11]

Crucial to Kautsky's whole argument was his distinction between the Jews who "have become an eminently revolutionary factor" and Jewry (*Judentum*) or rather traditional Diaspora Judaism, which "has become a reactionary factor."[12] He was convinced that Zionism could only reinforce the legacy of medieval obscurantism and narrow-minded ghetto Judaism. He starkly contrasted its alleged separatism with the universality of the great revolutionary Jews since Spinoza—including Marx and his radical Jewish followers in the international labor movements. Kautsky's dualistic image of the Jewish people was not untypical of the attitude of most Marxist intellectuals in the German party, whether they were Jews or Gentiles. Many would probably have agreed with Kautsky's harsh verdict on ghetto Judaism as a wholly negative phenomenon:

> Judaism is even a weight of lead attached to the feet of the Jews who seek to progress; it is one of the last remnants of the feudal Middle Ages, a social ghetto which is still maintained in the consciousness after the real ghetto has disappeared. We have not completely emerged from the Middle Ages as long as Judaism (*Judentum*) still exists among us. The sooner it disappears, the better it will be for society as well as for the Jews themselves.[13]

Kautsky and those Marxists who thought like him in the *Neue Zeit* believed in the radical enlightenment distinction between the Jews as individuals and Jewry as a nation. For them the *emancipation* of Jewry entailed its *dissolution,* just as it had for leaders of the French Revolution, for the Young Hegelians, or for Karl Marx.[14] The phantom of Jewish nationhood for most Marxists was a symptom and an outgrowth of incomplete Jewish emancipation in the semi-feudal societies of Central and Eastern Europe.

For Kautsky and his disciples, advocates of Zionism postulated an artificial "Jewish solidarity" in place of the natural proletarian solidarity and universal class-struggle against capitalist exploitation. Kautsky attacked the "fictitious" idea of supra-class Jewish solidarity on many occasions. In an important article written in the wake of the Kishinev pogrom of 1903, he blamed the antisemitic massacres, in part at least, on those Jewish capitalists in the West who had advanced loans to the same Tsarist autocracy which oppressed their poorer co-religionists in Russia.

> The unscrupulousness of international Jewish and Christian capital, and its instruments, makes it an accomplice of the Kishinev infamy. Jewish solidarity, the solidarity of Jews from all classes has become an empty phrase, as soon as more than a few farthings are involved.[15]

The SPD leader, August Bebel, made a similar point in the 1906 edition of his well-known pamphlet on the attitude of German Social Democracy towards antisemitism. While denouncing the barbarity of the Tsarist pogroms in the most outspoken manner, he stressed that the Russian Jews could not count on the solidarity of their capitalist brethren in Western Europe but only on that of the international working class.[16]

Kautsky's strenuous opposition to Jewish nationalism and Zionism was one aspect of his broader rejection of the concept of "Jewish solidarity," as something intrinsically reactionary. This is particularly evident in his constantly repeated assertion that Zionism aimed at the *enforced separation of Jew from non-Jew*—a completely misleading accusation later taken up by the Russian Bolsheviks. Kautsky wrongly regarded racial separation as a cardinal doctrine of Zionism. In his *Rasse und Judentum* he even argued that Jewish nationalism was nothing but a bastardization of antisemitic race theories.[17] In advancing this favorite canard of modern anti-Zionism, Kautsky was supported by Gustav Eckstein, an Austro-Marxist contributor to the *Neue Zeit,* himself of Jewish descent, who insisted on the "inner relationship" between racial antisemitism and Zionist ideology.[18] This had been one of Kautsky's favorite themes as far back as 1903, when he attacked Zionism for accepting the antisemitic thesis that the Jews were only a *Gastvolk* (guest-people) in the Diaspora. Commenting on Herzl's controversial negotiations with the Tsarist Minister of the Interior, Count von Plehwe (who was widely held to be responsible for the Kishinev pogrom), Kautsky observed that Zionism sought to divert the Jewish masses away from their historic role of helping to overthrow Tsarist absolutism.[19] The Zionists, by stressing Jewish "separatism," would merely deepen the gulf between the Jewish and Gentile worker, thereby condemning the Jewish masses to isolation and weakening the Russian revolutionary movement. Zionism, according to Kautsky, could

> only reinforce the anti-Semitic feelings of the popular masses, in so far as it increases the segregation of the Jews from the rest of the population and brands them even more than previously, as an alien nation, which, according to its own outlook, has nothing to expect on Russian soil.[20]

In other words, Kautsky was blaming Zionism—whose main goal was to foster Jewish emigration to Palestine for increasing rather than diminishing antisemitism in Russia.

In his *Rasse und Judentum,* Kautsky carried this argument even further, openly accusing the Zionist movement of being an accomplice of the most reactionary, pogromist regime in the world. The aim of Zionism was to create an iron wall between Jews and non-Jews:

> Zionism meets anti-Semitism half way in this striving, as well as in the fact that its goal is to remove all Jews from the existing States. There is so much in common between Zionism and anti-Semitism on these points, that there have been Zionists, who expected the gracious promotion of their objectives from the head of the orthodox Russian people, from the fountain-head of anti-Semitism in the world, from the Russian Tsar.[21]

Rather than regarding Zionism as an authentic national-liberation movement of the Jewish people, Kautsky castigated it "a spoke in the wheel of progress." It was a fundamentally reactionary ideology which aimed at preserving the *racial purity* of the Jews through the creation of a "world ghetto" in Palestine that would separate Jews from other races. ("Palästina als Weltghetto zur Absonderung der jüdischen Rasse von den anderen Rassen, das ist das Ziel des Zionismus geworden."[22]) Even the emerging trend of socialist Zionism in the Tsarist and Habsburg Empires was denounced with some vehemence by Kautsky along with various Bundist contributors to the *Neue Zeit.* In 1914, Kautsky specifically wrote that socialist Zionism aimed to inculcate in the Russian Jewish masses suspicion and distrust of their "Christian class-comrades." The labor Zionists had been partially successful in their purpose because, according to Kautsky, there was no large, well-organized Jewish factory proletariat in Russia which was sufficiently amenable to the ideology of proletarian internationalism. Hence socialist Zionists had been able to exploit a groundless fear that the victorious Russian proletariat might in the future mistreat the Jews no less than did the antisemitic Black Hundred gangs.[23] This was especially ironic since after the

1917 Bolshevik Revolution, Kautsky would himself become one of the fiercest socialist critics of Soviet Communism.

Kautsky's assault on Zionism was a consistent feature of his Marxist approach to the "Jewish question," based on the dogmatic belief that proletarian internationalism must exclude any specifically Jewish struggle for *national* emancipation. Ever since 1903 he had depicted the Zionists as tools of the antisemitic Tsarist autocracy. After the First World War he came to see in Zionism primarily an instrument of British imperialism and colonialism in Palestine.[24] Writing in 1929 in the central organ of the SPD, *Vorwärts,* Kautsky was unequivocal about Zionist dependence on British power.

> Whatever intentions the Zionists might have, the foundation of the [National] Home offered to them in Palestine can be found exclusively in the military might that England has brought to bear for its own imperialist designs, not for the sake of Jewry.[25]

Kautsky was in any case convinced that the Jew, as the *archetype of urban man,* could no more be turned into a productive farmer than the "Indo-Germanic" city-dweller. The Jew as "homo urbanus" could not successfully go back to the land and reverse 2,000 years of Diaspora history. The Zionist idea was therefore completely utopian. Without agriculture, how would the new Zion be built? How could one possibly expect a hereditary caste of merchants, financiers, intellectuals, doctors, and lawyers to succeed in establishing socialist colonies in the wilderness? Moreover, under Ottoman Turkish rule, Palestine had become a backwater rather than a magnet for Jews in search of a better life.

In 1914, raw statistics appeared to favor Kautsky's argument. Turkish Palestine was indeed a backward, undeveloped land whose prospects of supporting a large Jewish immigrant population seemed remote. The industrial infrastructure of modern roads, railways, harbors, plants, and machinery was completely lacking as a result of severe government neglect over the centuries. Palestine lacked any basic raw materials like iron, timber, and coal or a large home market and the prospect of substantial capital investment. Indeed, only a thin trickle of 26,000 Jews had made their way to Palestine in the period between 1881 and 1908. This was small change compared to the 1,600,000 Jewish emigrants who had left Russia, Romania, and Austria-Hungary for the United States or the 300,000 Jews who had migrated to Western Europe in the same period. The 10,000 Jewish colonists farming on Palestinian soil seemed like a drop in the ocean compared to this great migration.[26]

At the same time, Kautsky somewhat overstated the lack of progress in Zionist colonization before 1914. He wrongly assumed that no Great Power would ever support an independent Jewish homeland in Palestine.[27] His dismissive verdict on Zionism as mere talk came only three years before the Balfour Declaration, displaying a curious lack of vision and imagination:

> Zionism at one time wished to become a movement of the Jewish proletarian masses, but it is increasingly becoming a mere sport of Jewish philanthropists and literati. . . . All that it will ever be able to produce is a lot of talk and no results.[28]

Kautsky's derisive dismissal of Zionism as a utopian petty-bourgeois movement seeking to "restore the ghetto" was shared by an influential group of socialist colleagues (mostly Jews) in the SPD. Even a "revisionist" Marxist like Eduard Bernstein remained distinctly cool until 1917 to the concept of Jewish nationalism and continued to proclaim in a pamphlet of that year that he was no Zionist. "I feel myself too much a German to be able to be one," he added, for emphasis.[29] In an article for Martin Buber's periodical *Der Jude* in 1917, Bernstein further clarified his position: "I have a sense of solidarity with Jews whenever they are treated with disdain on account of their descent," but he could not bring himself to join any "specifically Jewish association," let alone the Zionist organization in Germany.[30] Three years earlier Bernstein had written in Kautsky's *Neue Zeit* that Zionism was:

> a kind of intoxication which acts like an epidemic. It may, and presumably will, also pass away like one. But not overnight. For in the last analysis it is only a part of the great wave of nationalistic reaction which has overflowed the bourgeois world and seeks to break into the socialist world as well. And this is sufficient reason why Social Democracy should take it seriously and subject it to a fundamental critique.[31]

Eduard Bernstein did gradually become more sympathetic to the aspirations of Poale-Zion after 1917, thanks in part to the efforts of Zalman Rubaschoff (Shazar), a Poale-Zion leader then studying in Berlin.[32] By temperament and political conviction, Bernstein was much closer to the general outlook of Joseph Bloch's "revisionist" *Sozialistische Monatshefte,* of which he was one of the guiding spirits, than to Kautsky's dogmatic Marxism. But like many German-Jewish liberals and socialists, Bernstein was nonetheless cautious about efforts to foster Jewish national consciousness. Formal Jewish emancipation in Germany had in his view eliminated the need for adopting such an outlook. Indeed, in an older article for the *Neue Zeit* in 1894 Bernstein had insisted:

> every excuse for isolation, for a special Jewish solidarity as against non-Jews has been eliminated, and where anything of the kind still exists, it must be opposed as energetically as possible.[33]

Bernstein gradually drew closer to the pro-Zionist line followed by Bloch's *Sozialistische Monatshefte* as a result of his growing concern after 1900 with the deteriorating situation of Russian and Romanian Jewry. Neither of these large Jewish communities enjoyed political rights. Following his election as a socialist deputy for Breslau, Bernstein made a maiden speech in the German *Reichstag* in 1903, in which he specifically evoked the insufferable conditions of Romanian Jewry. He drew a stark picture of their plight as aliens in Romania, disqualified from the professions and ownership of land, yet obliged to do military service and subject to special taxes. Bernstein called on the German government as co-signatory of the Berlin Congress agreements of 1878 to put pressure on Romania to abide by her legal obligation to guarantee Jewish civil equality.[34]

Bernstein, like Kautsky, was appalled by the Kishinev pogroms and seemed initially to recognize that the Marxian theory of assimilation was inapplicable to more than five million Jews living in the Russian Pale of Settlement.[35] In a book review of the sociological study of Russian-Jewish workers made by Sarah Rabinowitsch in 1903, Bernstein even acknowledged that there were passages in Marx's *Zur Judenfrage* which were open to severe criticism—a point he would further develop in another essay many years later.[36] This evolution in Bernstein's views on the "Jewish Question" encouraged the Russian Zionist leader Chaim Weizmann to believe that he might perhaps succeed in winning him over to the Jewish national cause. A letter written by Weizmann in August 1902 to his future wife tells of a conversation with Bernstein in Berlin:

> I had a long talk with Bernstein (the famous one) and his daughter in Berlin. I took him to task for taking up the cause of the Armenians and not taking up the Jewish cause. He declared: "Wenn ich jüdisches Gefühl hätte, ich ware Zionist. Vielleicht kommt es." Together with him, we cursed the assimilationists. In the journal we shall be publishing Bernstein will write against the assimilationists: he is on the road to Zionism and his daughter has paid her shekel. Kasteliansky [at that time a Russian-Jewish student in Berlin] has been working on them adroitly.[37]

Indirect confirmation of this remarkable claim comes in a letter from Karl Kautsky in January 1903 to Julius Motteler, commenting on Bernstein's intercession in a dispute between the Zionists and the SPD, concerning the archives of Moses Hess. Kautsky sarcastically wrote:

> Nothing would be more convenient than if Bernstein were to turn to Zionism, and if I could help to bring this about, I should like to do so. The Zionists need a prophet, Bernstein needs believers in his prophecies and we do not need him."[38]

Kautsky's hopes of ridding the SPD of a troublesome dissenter were to prove a little premature. Bernstein was not about to join forces with Theodor Herzl and Max Nordau in order to promote the Zionist movement. Nor was he particularly supportive of the non-Zionist Jewish nationalism of Nathan Birnbaum (a rival of Herzl) which he found distasteful and ridiculous.[39] Nonetheless, during the First World War, Bernstein did change his position and adopt the opinion that Jewish national demands for special minority status in Eastern Europe were not only intrinsically justifiable but also compatible with socialist theory.[40] Bernstein's change of heart had several causes. He was certainly aware that a number of prominent German-Jewish intellectuals with whom he was in contact like Martin Buber, Franz Oppenheimer, and Richard Lichtheim were closely involved in Zionism despite their cultural assimilation to German society. He was increasingly troubled by the anti-Jewish prejudices which still persisted in German government circles, among academics, in the bureaucracy, and the army, notwithstanding the temporary decline of noisy street-corner antisemitism in the Second Reich.[41] He was undoubtedly disappointed by the failure of the Socialist International to prevent the outbreak of the First World War and by the unseemly haste with which some of his German party colleagues had supported the mass slaughter of the trenches. The ultra-patriotic stance of certain circles in German Jewry who ostentatiously rallied to the cause of the German fatherland also upset him. The result of these frustrations was his curious pamphlet of 1917, *Von den Aufgaben der Juden im Weltkriege* (The tasks of the Jews in the World War), which was written in response to a request from the socialist-Zionist paper in New York, *Yiddisher Kemfer*.[42]

A major target of Bernstein's polemic was the calculated "assimilationism" of those chauvinistic Jews who had made the cause of Pan-German imperialism and even racial incitement against the Western Allies their speciality.[43] Their outlook was completely contrary to his neo-Kantian vision of the special tasks and duty of World Jewry, to act as mediators and peacemakers among the nations. The cosmopolitan mission of Jewry meant opposition to every kind of nationalistic propaganda, precisely because as a dispersed people the Jews were citizens of all the belligerent countries involved in the World War. It was their vocation as a people, he now asserted, to renounce a specific national destiny in favor of responsibility towards the larger family of mankind. Bernstein's pamphlet was inspired by the ideal of *weltbürgerlicher Patriotismus* (cosmopolitan patriotism) which he regarded as a synthesis of all that was best in the Jewish spiritual heritage.[44] The ethical, pacifist foundations of Bernstein's socialism were now adapted to fit what he considered to be the categorical imperative of Jewish history—to "nurture what binds the nations together and to work against whatever divides and sows hatred between them."[45] Bernstein evidently saw no contradiction between this cosmopolitan world-view and his public rapprochement with Poale-Zion a year later.

Bernstein had long been a close friend of Kautsky, exercising considerable influence over him until the early 1890s. Their views on the "Jewish Question," often converged but there were subtle differences which became more visible after 1900, when Kautsky emerged as a guiding hand in Marxist discussions of issues like Zionism, antisemitism, and the Bund. Kautsky, like Bernstein, was a vigorous opponent of antisemitism which he considered to be "reactionary through and through."[46] He sharply rejected the racist underpinnings of German antisemitic theories—especially the attempt to claim that there was "an unbridgeable racial opposition" between the "Aryans" and the "Semites."[47] He strongly supported the stand of the French socialist leader, Jean Jaurès, on behalf of the falsely accused Jewish officer, Captain Alfred Dreyfus, during the high point of the Affair in 1898. Kautsky was certainly aware that Jaurès's intervention in an "internal bourgeois quarrel" went against a schematic view of the class struggle. It made the fight against antisemitism one of the symbols of socialism—a point which Kautsky undoubtedly appreciated and respected.[48] On this issue, Kautsky was, if anything, more outspoken than Bernstein.

The Kishinev bloodbath of 1903 was another visceral reminder of where brutal pogromist antisemitism of the Russian variety, could lead. Kautsky swiftly responded to a request by Adolf Warszawski, editor of *Przegląd Socyaldemokraticzny* (organ of the Polish left-wing Social Democrats) to analyse the pogrom and its political consequences.[49] Warszawski hoped that Kautsky's observations could serve his internationalist faction (of which Rosa Luxemburg was the best-known member) in their polemics against the Russian Bund. Kautsky, however, in spite of his reservations about the Bund's organizational separatism, had a great deal of sympathy for this

Jewish workers' movement, which its leaders generally reciprocated.[50] Even though the Bund had adopted a *national* program after 1901 (demanding national rights for Russian Jewry), Kautsky played down these differences, especially since Bundists did not claim to speak in the name of a world-wide Jewish nation.[51] Moreover, after 1898, the Bund had come into direct conflict with Zionism as a rival mass-movement in the Russian Pale of Settlement. In contrast to the Zionists, the Bund (like Kautsky) believed that only Socialism and the proletarian revolution would solve the "Jewish Question" in Russia by putting an end to the pogroms, the mass emigration and legal-political obstacles in the way of Jewish emancipation.[52] Bernstein was more sceptical on this issue and far from enthused by the Bund's revolutionary outlook.

Kautsky supported the opposition of the Bund to Zionism but he saw the role of the Jewish labor movement primarily as one of integrating the Jewish proletariat into the general revolutionary process and the struggle against Tsarism.[53] Despite fulsome tributes to the combative heroism of the Jewish working-class movement led by the Bund, Kautsky avoided mention of its program for cultural-national autonomy which had brought it into conflict with Russian and Polish Social Democracy.[54] Like most other German Marxists, he preferred to ignore the national dimension of the Jewish labor movement and with very occasional exceptions he did not enter into polemics with the Bund.[55] Unlike the Bundists, Kautsky believed that growing class-differentiation among Jews in Russia and Eastern Europe was the prelude to their future assimilation. But he chose to minimize such differences while highlighting Bundist attacks on the Zionist movement.

The anti-Zionist critique of Jewish socialists from Eastern Europe was based on the premise that such a supra-class "national" ideology, was fundamentally incompatible with the concept of proletarian class-struggle. According to Max Zetterbaum, a leading propagandist of the Polish socialist party among the Jewish masses in Galicia, Zionism was a "philosophy of despair." It was primarily the product of nationalist and clerical antisemitism in Central and Eastern Europe. The Jewish middle classes had found their road to assimilation blocked, especially in Eastern Europe. In their disillusion, they had mistakenly assumed that antisemitism was an *eternal* historical category. For Zetterbaum, Zionism was ultimately the panic-stricken reaction of this Jewish middle class to its threatened proletarianization, and to the general social crisis driving millions of poor Jews to mass emigration from Russia and Eastern Europe. Writing in Kautsky's *Neue Zeit* at the turn of the 20th century, he presented Zionism as a movement *contrary* to the "progressive" ideals of emancipation and enlightenment which had inspired the Jewish working class. It was deliberately fostered, in his view, by the "clerical," chauvinist outlook of the Orthodox rabbinical Jewish leadership in Eastern Europe who believed that the Jews were a "chosen people," destined to play a special role in history.[56] Zetterbaum counseled the Jewish workers to listen to lectures on Darwinism rather than to the abstruse sermons of a "Maggid," to become "thinking Europeans" rather than model themselves on the obscurantism of "clerical Asiatics."[57]

Max Zetterbaum's outspoken anti-clericalism was shared by the Lemberg correspondent of Kautsky's *Neue Zeit,* who misleadingly identified Zionism in Galicia with the obscurantist machinations of the Hassidic oligarchy.[58] Both the Zionists and the Hasidim, he claimed, sought to keep the Jewish workers under the tutelage of their employers and of the "miracle-rabbis" (*Wunderrabiner*). Medieval religious fanaticism and capitalist exploitation, the despair of the Jewish petty-bourgeoisie, the disorientation of the *lumpenproletariat* and other déclassé elements had all coalesced into the ultra-reactionary Zionist movement, which was the sworn enemy of the Jewish proletariat. The correspondent from Lemberg claimed that Jewish workers recognized Zionism to be the ideology of their employers, and had broken up meetings of the movement in Kraków, Lemberg, Kolomea, and other Galician towns.[59] An earlier critique of Zionism by a Jewish socialist from Bukovina also emphasized its *Mittelstand* character, suggesting that it was a movement which attracted those strata of Jewish society threatened with unemployment, economic decline, or loss of social status.[60] It was the peculiar social stratification of the Jewish people in Galicia and Bukovina, with its mass of petty traders, middlemen and out-of-work artisans faced with imminent proletarization, which temporarily favored the Zionist movement. Such reports, which appeared in the *Neue Zeit* in 1895, sometimes acknowledged idealistic and progressive socio-economic features in Zionism, alongside its utopian, petty-bourgeois aspects. Large-scale colonization in Palestine, however, was declared to be wholly unrealistic in view of the infertile soil, difficult climate, lack of water, and deforestation. Before the First World War, Kautsky and Bernstein would certainly have agreed on this practical assessment, despite their differing emphases.

The emergence of political Zionism, following the publication of Theodor Herzl's *Der Judenstaat* in 1896, provoked a particularly nasty response from the *Neue Zeit.* One of Kautsky's closest collaborators, a former rabbi from Württemberg, Jakob Stern, described Herzl's pamphlet as a "queer project," no less "utopian" than the bankrupt fantasy of another Viennese liberal Theodor Hertzka, to establish a model society in East Africa. Both projects were "conceived in the same spirit of negative boldness."[61] Like other Marxist critics of Zionism, Stern summarily dismissed the view that Jewish national solidarity could ever be an answer to antisemitism. This was, in his view, a childish, romantic aberration. He predicted that antisemitism would pursue the Jewish capitalists into their new State (if it were ever established) where it would abandon its mask as the "socialism of fools" and soon be revealed as the struggle of Jewish workers against their exploiters. As in other Marxist critiques of Zionism before 1914, there was no reference to the Palestinian Arab population which appeared to be a negligible factor at the time. Not only were Palestinian Arabs loyal subjects of their Ottoman Turkish rulers still beholden to the Muslim Caliphate but there was no organized Arab national movement worth speaking of in the Middle East.

Johann Pollack's discussion of Herzl's program at the First Zionist Congress in Basle in 1897 was fairly typical of the general Marxist perspective.

> All in all there is no reason for taking Dr. Herzl's Zionism as anything more than an ephemeral phenomenon, as a beautiful pose with which a nation that is no longer living steps for the last time onto the stage of history before its complete disappearance.[62]

This dismissive view of Herzlian Zionism focused on unmasking its supposedly reactionary social features and nationalist pretensions in seeking to organize Jewry on a supra-class basis. Pollack asserted, for example, that the Jews were an "artificial" nation, because there was no common language or culture linking Western and East European Jewry. He pointed out that the modern emancipated Jew generally knew no Hebrew and was remote from the national-religious tradition of Judaism. Nor could Yiddish be claimed as a "national" language. It was at best a popular dialect which varied according to different regions in Eastern Europe. From the social standpoint, Pollack considered the Zionism of Jewish workers as being comparable to the antisemitism of those Catholic proletarians who supported the Christian-social movement in Austria.

> The Zionism of this [Jewish] worker just like the "Christianity" of the Christian-social worker is the primitive form of a protest against his poverty, the causes of which he does not yet understand.[63]

Max Zetterbaum, writing nearly three years later in the *Neue Zeit,* made a similar analogy between the political Zionism of the Jewish bourgeoisie (seeking to exercise national sovereignty over the Jewish masses) and the desire of the Christian bourgeoisie to restore the glories of medieval Christendom.

> The one demands the "Christian" State of the Middle Ages, the other the "Jewish" State of Antiquity.[64]

Zetterbaum scornfully attacked Zionism as a "business undertaking" (*Befreiungsgeschäft*) of the Jewish bourgeoisie, in which Jewish capital and not the working class would direct the colonization project in Palestine. It had nothing in common with an authentic struggle for national liberation.[65] He particularly objected to Herzl's diplomatic methods and attempt to win support for Zionism from imperialist powers like Ottoman Turkey, Tsarist Russia, and Wilhelminian Germany, or from such sworn enemies of the Jewish people as the Tsarist interior minister, Count von Plehwe. Like the Bundists in Russia, he considered that Herzl had crossed a red line:

> The Jewish Social Democracy is revolutionary, it has nothing to do with Sovereigns and Diplomats, and the friends of Tsarism are its enemies.[66]

Like other Jewish socialist critics of Zionism around 1900, Zetterbaum was doubtful if a Jewish "nationality" still existed in Eastern Europe.[67] At the same time, although Karl Kautsky had pointed out that the Jews lacked a common language or territory, it was evident to Zetterbaum that in Eastern Europe they were much more than simply a religious community. He chose, therefore, to describe the Jews of Russia, Poland, Lithuania, and Romania as having the characteristics of a *Stammesgenossenschaft*. In other words, they were more akin to a "tribal community" with its own customs, moral codes, historical tradition, and folk-identity. Though he rejected the Zionist concept of pursuing Jewish "national" politics within the boundaries of another State, Zetterbaum did not rule out the possibility that the Jews might once again become a nation. Only future developments could determine whether the Jews would dissolve among the nations, but if

> this Judaism bears within itself its own negation, if it leads to an exalted cosmopolitanism, to the rule of pure spirit and an all-encompassing love, we cannot help that.[68]

After the failed 1905 Revolution in Russia, polemics against Zionism intensified in character, with spokesmen of the Bund using the columns of the *Neue Zeit* to attack Zionist-socialist efforts to win over Jewish workers in the Pale of Settlement.[69] According to the Bund, the Zionists sought to establish a class-state in Palestine and to mask the class contradictions within Jewry by spurious appeals to national unity. This had negatively reinforced the "psychology of the ghetto" and tended to encourage political indifference among the Jewish masses in Russia.[70] An article in the *Neue Zeit* in 1905 on the economic conditions of the Russian-Jewish proletariat stressed, however, that the class differences between Jewish employers and workers in the Pale of Settlement were *unbridgeable*. Russian Jewry was divided into two hostile classes and, Zionist delusions notwithstanding, the Jewish employers had good reason to fear the revolutionary militancy of the Jewish working class.[71] The Zionists might preach their ideology of class collaboration but there could never be any common interests between Jewish capitalists and proletarians, least of all in a "Palestinian" Jewish State. As one Bundist writer in the *Neue Zeit* bluntly declared:

> We do not wish to discuss this not only senseless but harmful utopia any further; we say harmful utopia, because it can only deflect the Jewish masses, with its unrealizable pretensions, away from their daily struggle for their real interests.[72]

The class interests of the Russian-Jewish proletariat could best be served by the overthrow of Tsarism. Only when the Russian people as a whole were freed from the autocratic yoke would the specific oppression and social disabilities of the Jews, which were the real cause of their poverty and unemployment, come to an end. This was also the view of another Bundist critic of Poale Zionism, who condemned as myopic its core thesis that the Jews were doomed to permanent proletarization in the Pale of Settlement.[73] Once Russian absolutism had been defeated, there would be no need to create the independent, Jewish national economic base in Palestine advocated by Ber Borochov—the leading theorist of the Russian Poale-Zion.

> With the fall of absolutism and the cessation of anti-Jewish persecution, once the libertarian movement has achieved its goal, Poale Zionism will have lost any foundation and will sink helplessly into the sea of oblivion.[74]

In any case, such Jewish critics of Zionism totally opposed the whole concept of transplantation to another country—especially Palestine—in order to achieve Socialism. The desired goal could be accomplished with far less effort by remaining in "the old country."[75] Moreover, the Zionist dream of Palestine would only sow still more suspicion in the minds of the Christian workers concerning the reliability of the Jewish masses as an ally in the common revolutionary cause.

The attacks on labor Zionism in Kautsky's *Neue Zeit* invariably branded it as a *bourgeois* ideology which sought to neutralize the class struggle until the

Jews had won a foothold in Palestine. The proposition that colonization of Palestine could halt or correct the process of stagnation, pauperism, mass emigration, and antisemitism which afflicted the Jewish masses was rejected out of hand.[76] Instead, under the editorship of Karl Kautsky, the leading Marxist review of the age consistently pursued the line that Zionism was a *divisive* and *retrograde* movement which weakened the unity of the international proletariat.[77] The Kautskyian view of the issue, strongly supported by Jewish socialists (especially Bundists) from Russia and Eastern Europe, was that only an all-Russian revolution would solve the Jewish national problem and create conditions of prosperity for the Jewish masses. The overthrow of Tsarism would sweep away feudal structures which had hindered the development of capitalism; it would abolish the Pale of Settlement and dismantle the ghettoes which had nourished Russian and East European antisemitism. In Karl Kautsky's own words, written on the eve of the First World War, the revolution would bring about the dissolution of the Jews as a community and their liberation as human beings. In the dialectical ascent of socialist society towards the creation of a "new man," the image of Ahasverus, the wandering Jew, would finally be put to rest. He would live on in the memory as a victim who had suffered unparalleled misfortune yet contributed the most to mankind.[78]

Such a messianic approach to the "Jewish Question" was emphatically *not* shared by an influential group of "revisionists" in the German party, who regularly contributed to the *Sozialistische Monatshefte*—a prestigious monthly founded in 1897 by the Lithuanian-born Joseph Bloch. The review would become a major outlet for non-Marxist socialists in Germany during the "revisionist debate" at the end of the 1890s. Among its most important associates was Eduard Bernstein, whose 1898 book, *Die Voraussetzungen des Sozialismus* (Evolutionary socialism) had sparked off the revisionist controversy. Important contributors were the right-wing socialist Eduard David, Carl Legien (the trade-union leader), the pragmatic Ignaz Auer, the neo-Kantian Kurt Eisner, Paul Kampfmayer, and Max Cohen-Reuss. Other regular participants included leading Austrian Social Democrats like Victor Adler and Engelbert Pernerstorfer; Jean Jaurès and Georges Sorel from France; Turati, the Italian socialist leader; and the moderate British socialist Ramsay MacDonald. Among contributors who dealt specifically with Jewish issues and were sympathetic to Zionism was a group of German socialists including Ludwig Quessel, Julius Kaliski, Hermann Kranold, and Gerhard Hildebrand.[79] Like Joseph Bloch, this "pro-Zionist" circle within the *Sozialistische Monatshefte* tended to adopt a German nationalist position on matters concerned with foreign policy and colonial affairs. Ludwig Quessel and Gerhard Hildebrand, along with other German socialists like Cohen-Reuss, Wolfgang Heine, and Max Schippel, backed a policy of Social Democratic imperialism on the grounds that German industrial, military, and political expansion was economically beneficial to the working class.[80] "Reformists" like Eduard David, Max Schippel, August Winnig, and the Austrian Pan-German socialist Karl Leuthner, also believed that German imperialism was historically inevitable and morally justifiable. Like most European Social Democrats in the late Victorian era, they saw no contradiction between the universal cultural mission of socialism and colonial expansion. Indeed, many Social Democrats before the First World War considered the "peaceful" penetration of backward regions of the globe by European powers to be a "progressive" phenomenon. Even Marxists like Bebel and Kautsky had defended the establishment of *Arbeiterkolonien* (worker colonies), especially in temperate zones. They regarded overseas colonization as a blessing insofar as it had liberated new energies and productive forces.[81] The Anglophile Eduard Bernstein also admired the "civilizing mission" of enlightened colonizers like the British, who had brought economic progress to far-flung undeveloped countries.

A number of prominent West European socialists like the Belgians Emil Vandervelde and Camille Huysmans, the Dutchman van Kol, and the British Fabians also strongly defended the benefits of European colonization for the mother country, the settlers and natives alike.[82] It was no accident that these socialists who stressed the blessings of European civilization for non-European societies were among the warmest supporters of Zionism. European Social Democrats like Vandervelde, Huysmans, Ramsay MacDonald, Jean Longuet, Léon Blum, van Kol, and Pernerstorfer admired Zionism as a pioneering and idealistic movement which aimed at colonizing a backward, undeveloped country through hard work, redeeming the land by modern methods of agriculture.[83] Interestingly enough, the anti-Zionist Left of the pre-1914 era did not challenge Zionism on the grounds that it was a "colonialist" movement. The potential conflict between Jewish settlers and Palestinian Arabs, for example, played no role in the controversies over Zionism before the 1917 Balfour Declaration. The differences between the Kautskyian and the "revisionist" socialist perspectives on Zionism had nothing to do with the "Arab problem" or the rights of indigenous populations to self-determination.

The majority of the articles in the *Sozialistische Monatshefte* relating to Zionism came, not surprisingly, from the pens of Jewish socialists who originated from Russia or Poland. They belonged to the *territorialist* trends within the Jewish workers' movement which in the aftermath of the 1905 Revolution in Russia had been considerably strengthened. The largest of these territorialist currents at that time were the Zionist-Socialists (S.S.), founded in Odessa in 1905. Like Poale-Zion, the Zionist-Socialists rejected the exile (*Galut*), but they did not regard Palestine as the only possible Jewish national territory. The fact of territorial concentration per se rather than its location, was central to their outlook. One of its leading theoreticians, Max Schatz-Anin (1885–1975), was certainly the most prolific contributor on the "Jewish Question" in the columns of the pre-1914 *Sozialistische Monatshefte*.[84] He had been deported from Russia, graduating in Berne (Switzerland) in 1910 with a doctoral dissertation on the nationalities' question. His socio-economic analyses stressed the abnormal occupational pyramid of the Diaspora Jewry and the inadequacy of cultural-national autonomy (the Bundist program) as a solution to the Jewish problem.[85] Like other Jewish socialist contributors to Bloch's review, he considered that the lack of territory made the class-struggle of the Jewish proletariat in the Pale ineffective. Instead he advocated planned colonization as a solution, though he did not analyze the specific problems of Palestine or designate it as the sole land of immigration.

The Poale-Zion (Workers of Zion), on the other hand, was a Jewish Social Democratic Labour Party which had always emphasized the centrality of Palestine in their program. Like the Zionist-Socialists, they also argued that without a "strategic base" (an independent territory of their own), the Jews could not develop a normal occupational pyramid and the prerequisites for a class-struggle that would realize socialism. But Poale-Zion saw no prospect at all for establishing this "strategic base" anywhere except in Palestine.[86] They were convinced that Kautsky and his followers had fundamentally misunderstood both Zionism and the condition of world Jewry. The anti-Zionists had failed to register the disastrous consequences of Jewry's material plight. They also ignored the vital need for idealism and the power of the transformative will which clearly animated the Zionist labor movement in confronting the oppression of the Jewish workers.

The third territorialist movement, the SERP (Jewish Socialist Labor party) also underlined the point that lack of a territory had seriously hindered the national development of the Jewish proletariat. The leaders of SERP, unlike the Zionist currents in Jewish socialism, considered, however, that achieving national-political autonomy for the Jewish masses (and other oppressed minorities within the Russian Empire) was a more urgent priority than the need for territorial autonomy.[87] Mark Borisovich Ratner (1871–1917), one of the leading thinkers of SERP, also provided some of the most incisive criticisms both of the Bund and of orthodox Marxist theory on the Jewish problem for the *Sozialistische Monatshefte*. In particular, he ridiculed Kautsky's "grotesque" comparison of the Jewish nation with Indian Hindu castes, both for its unhistorical character and because of its unacceptably pejorative connotations.

Each of these differing trends within the Jewish labor movement and on the left-wing of the Russian-Jewish intelligentsia offered its own specific solution to the Jewish national problem. But there were also some common factors in their analyses which are worth noting. In the first place, they all emphasized that socio-economic, political, and linguistic conditions largely *separated* the Jews from the non-Jewish Slavic environment in Russia and Poland. They observed that the low level of capitalist development in Tsarist Russia made the formation of a genuine factory-proletariat out of the declining Jewish artisan class exceedingly difficult. Moreover, Jewish workers, as a result of historic anomalies in the structure of the Jewish economy, were divorced from what the Poale-Zion theorist Ber Borochov insistently termed the "primary areas of production." They remained mainly concentrated in the final stages of production, dealing in consumer goods. Even when they lived in more industrialized regions of the Tsarist Empire like Russian Poland, the economic self-interest and antisemitism of Polish workers ensured that they were excluded from employment in the mechanized factories. The low level of mechanization among Jewish workers and the prevailing small-trader and artisan structure of Jewish life, had created a "socio-economic ghetto" (Schatz-Anin) which would remain, even if the legal and political obstacles to Jewish emancipation in Russia were removed.[88] Jewish poverty, according to the analyses in the *Sozialistische Monatshefte*, was a specific *national* syndrome which could not be resolved merely by the overthrow of Russian absolutism. Its roots lay in the *non-productivization* of the Jewish masses which could only be cured by some form of territorial concentration and planned colonization, whether in Palestine or elsewhere.[89]

Joseph Bloch, as editor of the *Sozialistische Monatshefte* provided the link between German Social Democrats and the East European Jewish socialists. He had grown up in a strictly Orthodox family in Königsberg where socialist ideas supplemented but did not altogether erase the Judaism of his home background.[90] Bloch had come to Berlin in the early 1890s to study mathematics and physics, becoming involved as a student in founding the

Sozialistische Akademiker (1895) which two years later was renamed the *Sozialistische Monatshefte*. His own world-view, like that of many German-Jewish intellectuals, were essentially ethical and humanitarian in character. The Kantian categorical imperative and belief in the freedom of the will rather than historical materialism (or a deterministic confidence in the inevitability of Socialism), brought him into the SPD. However, unlike co-religionists such as Eduard Bernstein, Kurt Eisner, or Hugo Haase, he was no pacifist and unabashedly supported the growing *nationalist* wing of the German Social Democratic party. Nonetheless Joseph Bloch believed passionately in Franco-German rapprochement which he hoped would lead to a joint hegemony over the European continent. The main obstacle to this goal was British policy, which Bloch spent his entire political life in opposing. Indeed, it was his hostility to Great Britain's "divide and rule" imperialist policies against continental Europe, and the German Empire in particular, which largely accounted for the strong support that the *Sozialistische Monatshefte* gave to the German government during the First World War. Bloch's advocacy of a protectionist *Kontinental Europa* strategy based on a separate peace with Russia, along with his deep suspicion of Anglo-Saxon imperialism, would cause a rift with the pro-British and pacifist-oriented Bernstein, with whom he had been closely associated before the Great War of 1914–18.

Bloch's publication greeted Herzl's political Zionism more positively than did their Marxist rivals. Sergej Njewsorow, writing in 1897, conceded that Russian Jewish proletarians had, at first sight, little in common with Herzl's movement led by middle-class doctors, lawyers, and businessmen from Central Europe. But Zionism was above all an *idealistic* movement, "called like nothing else to morally uplift Jewry."[91] Njewsorow did not think much of Herzl's eclectic efforts "to out-trump socialist demands" and to reconcile cooperative labor with laissez-faire liberalism, but he did acknowledge that Zionism had solid roots in Central European antisemitism. Nowhere was this more true than in fin-de-siècle Vienna, where the new Christian Social Mayor, Karl Lueger, had just scored a decisive electoral victory on a populist antisemitic platform:

> It is perhaps no accident, that this new Zionist breeze has come over from Austria and specially from Vienna. It is well known that Austria is now the classic land of anti-Semitism—the result: Jewish misery, material and moral, cannot fail to appear, and the prerequisites for a strengthening of national sentiments are

> consequently at hand—once more you have the famous trinity: Jew-hatred, Jewish misery, Zionism.[92]

Austrian antisemitism was also addressed by another writer in Bloch's journal, who commented critically on Karl Kraus's malevolently anti-Zionist pamphlet, *Eine Krone für Zion* (1898). Kraus was a notoriously anti-Jewish Jew from Vienna with a wicked wit, who had derided Zionism as little more than a hysterical Jewish reflection of antisemitism. The reviewer sharply reproached the Viennese satirist for having completely ignored "the tragic conditions of life of the Russian-Jewish proletariat" which were the real driving-force of the Zionist movement.[93] Moreover, there was a socialist element in Zionism which gave it considerable appeal to Jewish workers submerged in the poverty and exploitation of the East European ghettos. A similar point was also made by Adele Schreiber in her review of the *Lieder des Ghetto,* written by the Yiddish poet, Morris Rosenfeld.[94] Adele Schreiber observed that Zionism complemented, rather than contradicted the socialist vision of future redemption from suffering and oppression. The dual curse from which the Jewish proletariat still suffered—economic deprivation and racial persecution— required a dual form of emancipation which would fuse the national-religious messianism of the "return to Zion" with the secular proletarian dream of Socialism.

> Zionism and the labour movement, so different in their tendencies, converge in so far as they are both movements for liberty, whose strength is rooted in their revolt against unjust oppression. They are also both emanations of a longing, of sorrow at the present and an almost visionary hope for the future. Their point of departure, as with every advance of civilization, is the rousing of the masses from their hollow contentment or passive suffering.[95]

Zionism would remind the Jewish worker, trapped in the degradation and exploitation of the sweatshops, that he was also the heir of a warrior people who had once shown great heroism in defending their land and liberty.

The debate over Zionism and Jewish national aspirations intensified in the *Sozialistische Monatshefte* after the abortive Russian Revolution of 1905 which led to a further deterioration in the conditions of Russian Jewry. Virtually all the Jewish socialist movements in Russia had by this time accepted elements of nationalist ideology, seeking to synthesize them with Socialism.[96] There were also those, like Max Schatz-Anin, who began to concentrate their fire on the assimilationist theories of Karl Kautsky and Otto

Bauer.[97] In opposition to the German and Austrian Marxists, Anin asserted that the industrialization of the Russian Empire was pauperizing rather than improving the conditions of Jewish workers. They were not being hired either by Jewish or Christian employers; they faced fierce competition from the workers of other nationalities; and as Jews, they were also subject to special discrimination by the Tsarist regime. Ultimately the Jewish proletariat was being trapped in a vicious circle. Without being drawn into the developing capitalist system the Jewish workers could not assimilate, and until they had assimilated they would remain excluded from productive work. Civil emancipation on the Western European model could not solve this dilemma. Nor could the rhetoric of class-struggle adopted by the Bund disguise the structural weakness of the Jewish proletariat. Without legal rights, social mobility, the requisite technical skills and a strategic position in the process of production, the Jewish working class was condemned to permanent impotence.

> In place of the old ghetto walls, tower ever higher the walls of a socio-economic ghetto, which can in no way be destroyed by Jewish emancipation.[98]

Socialist Zionists generally argued that the Jewish workers could never solve their national problem within the Russian Pale of Settlement, since there was no possibility of absorbing the mass of Jewish artisans or restructuring the inverted Jewish occupational pyramid. Moreover, outside Tsarist Russia, Jews lacked any territorial nucleus where they formed a compact national majority. Haphazard emigration was no answer because this would soon reach saturation point without resolving the trap of poverty, unemployment, and antisemitism in which Jewish existence was enmeshed. Mass emigration was merely replicating East European urban ghettoes in America and England. As Theodor Herzl had predicted, this wave of immigration to the West was already creating an anti-alien backlash. On the other hand, the colonization of an undeveloped, free territory did offer the prospect of a successful struggle for social emancipation in the future. It would recue the Jews from their stunted ghetto economy, the misery of the sweatshops, relentless persecution and the inability to determine their own future.[99] Anin specifically quoted the views of Bebel and Vandervelde to demonstrate that *colonization* (free of the desire for profit or domination over other peoples) was not at all in contradiction to socialist principles. Nor was the principle of Jewish national self-determination at variance with the "spirit of the age":

> In a period which has seen the awakening of even the smallest, completely historyless nations, the Jewish people are also approaching, after centuries of grievous suffering and persecutions, nearer to the autonomous shaping of their destiny.[100]

Anin's theses were close to those of Ber Borochov and the Russian Poale-Zion, though he did not explicitly mention Palestine as the future land of Jewish colonization. Leon Chasanowitsch, on the other hand, was the Secretary of the world Poale-Zion movement in Vienna and a committed Marxist Zionist. In a long essay in the *Sozialistische Monatshefte* he argued that territorial concentration in Palestine was the *only* solution to the problem of the Jewish working class.[101] Along with the future president of the State of Israel, Zalman Rubaschoff (Shazar), Berl Locker, and Shlomo Kaplansky, Chasanowitsch was one of the most gifted advocates of Poale-Zion in Central Europe. His article was an important breakthrough in making the case for labor Zionism better known inside the ranks of the German Social Democracy. Chasanowitsch began by defining socialist Zionism as a movement which rejected assimilation, seeking to establish an independent Jewish community in Palestine with its own national culture as well as a functioning agriculture and industry. Socialism and Zionism were two great *modern* movements within East European Jewry which had initially fought one another, but which would eventually find their reconciliation in Poale-Zionism.[102] In the meantime, labor Zionists still had to battle on two fronts—both against bourgeois Zionism *and* the "assimilationist," cosmopolitan socialists in the international labor movement. Their long-term objective was to influence Zionism in a socialist direction while bringing socialists to a clearer understanding of the need for Jewish national liberation. Chasanowitsch pointed out that Poale-Zion had already made headway in establishing itself in Tsarist Russia, Imperial Austria, Great Britain, North America, and Palestine, as well as among immigrant Jewish workers in Western Europe. It was striving everywhere to unite Jewish proletarians dispersed in many lands into a world Jewish section of the Socialist International. This aspiration was also supported by the Zionist-Socialists and SERP, but strongly opposed by the Bund and assimilationist Jews in different European labor parties.[103] On the national question, Chasanowitsch declared himself sharply against the leveling utopia of international socialism which negated the importance of national self-determination and sought to repress the free development of national individuality.

Chasanowitsch spcifically praised the theoretical contribution of the Austro-Marxists, and in particular of Otto Bauer, for recognizing that it was

Socialism which had first raised the broad popular masses to the level of national consciousness.[104] Unfortunately, the Austro-Marxists and their Polish socialist comrades had failed to apply their own insight to the "Jewish question." Instead, there was a loud outcry among Socialists against the unholy trinity of "Reaction Chauvinism or even Clericalism" as soon as Jewish national aspirations were evoked. What was conceded to even the smallest, most obscure and backward nationalities was deemed inadmissible for the Jews of Russia and Eastern Europe. Only Jews were expected to renounce all hopes for their *national* renaissance.[105] This was a shocking double standard. Moreover, Chasanowitsch stressed that assimilation and the disappearance of the Jews from the stage of history would be a great loss to humanity. Not only that, but it was impossible to implement except for that small élite in East European Jewry who already enjoyed full social and economic mobility. The only result of unrealistic assimilationist strivings would be to deepen the rift between the acculturated Jewish intelligentsia and the non-assimilated Yiddish-speaking masses—a gulf which had already produced harmful and destructive effects for the Jewish nation as a whole.

Chasanowitsch did not deny that "in Germany, France, Holland and Italy the assimilation of the Jews was to a certain extent a necessary process." Widespread socio-economic mobility, the abolition of ghettoes and the smaller size of the Jewish communities had made the successful adaptation of Jews to the wider society in Western Europe entirely possible.[106] Nevertheless he condemned the sweeping assimilationist standpoint of most contemporary liberals and leftists as being "not only an anti-national but also in the highest degree an anti-social phenomenon."[107] In any event, in Russia, Galicia, and Romania, general political backwardness and mass impoverishment had made the social as well as economic integration of Jewry inconceivable. The draconian measures of the Tsarist regime and the Romanian authorities as well as the anti-Jewish economic boycotts in Russian Poland were already undermining the traditional basis of Jewish existence in petty trade and middleman occupations.[108] It was these broad economic and political processes which made the case for labor Zionism a matter of urgency.

Other contributors to the *Sozialistische Monatshefte* also emphasized those factors which were pointing towards a heightened Jewish national consciousness.[109] German socialists, more sympathetic to Zionism, usually stressed the cultural gap separating Jews from non-Jews in Eastern Europe. They pointed out that Jews in Russia, Poland, Romania, and Austrian-ruled Bukovina with their Yiddish mother-tongue and distinctive religious customs were regarded as members of an *alien* community by most of the indigenous population in those lands. It was not only a matter of linguistic and religious differences. There existed a special type of Jewish peoplehood (*ein besonderes Volkstum*) with its own unique spirituality (*Geistigkeit*) which was self-evident to most East European Jews.[110] The Zionist idea that the colonization of Palestine would help resolve the "social distress" of a new generation of East European Jews was grafted onto this pre-existing sense of national identity, which provided it with a special energy.

For a number of German right-wing socialists like Ludwig Quessel and the Austrian Social-Democrat, Engelbert Pernerstorfer, it seemed no less self-evident that Jewry—especially in Eastern Europe—was indeed a nation with very distinctive cultural and spiritual qualities. They pointed to the cohesive national character of the *Ostjuden* as a major factor favoring Zionist aspirations.[111] Pernerstorfer, for example, declared in 1916 that the Jews "are a nation, indeed a nation of special *Geistigkeit* (spirituality) as is every inwardly strong *Kulturnation.* They have a right to their national existence."[112] Pernerstorfer's viewpoint was close to that of the circle around Joseph Bloch. These were socialists who were convinced that the free development of nationalities was a prerequisite for authentic internationalism and that efforts to denationalize the *Ostjuden* were doomed.

Even before 1914 there had been a growing concern among some German-speaking socialists at the oppression of Russian and Polish Jewry which would be greatly reinforced by developments during the First World War. The awakening of patriotic sentiments all over the European continent during the Great War had weakened the appeal of a socialist internationalism, which had too readily identified social progress with the disappearance of national barriers. The Marxist critique of Zionism as a diversion from the class struggle began to lose some of its potency, especially for mainstream socialists, like Eduard Bernstein, disturbed by the national oppression of the Jewish minority in Russia, Romania, and Eastern Europe. Pernerstorfer correctly predicted that a Jewish national minority already numbering nearly three million souls in 1916 would become a thorn in the side of the intensely chauvinistic Poles if they ever succeeded in reestablishing their nation-state.[113] This was one of his strongest arguments in favor of supporting a Jewish homeland in Palestine. It would be echoed by Hermann Kranold writing in the *Sozialistische Monatshefte* in 1917.[114] In that same year, the Belgian socialist and Secretary of the International Socialist Bureau, Camille Huysmans, declared at a Congress in Stockholm:

> The Jewish people ought to be given the right to determine their own destiny. That is perfectly in harmony with the general principles of the right of self-assertion for all nationalities. . . .[115]

Eduard Bernstein, in an unpublished manuscript written at this time, had also come to a similar conclusion. Indeed, at the end of the war he welcomed the admission of Poale-Zion to the Socialist International.[116] By 1919 he was even ready to speak at Poale-Zion events in Berlin, publicly recognizing that "there is a specific Jewish movement in socialism that is today necessary." The Jewish national movement, especially in its labor Zionist form, was now fully acknowledged as a reality and along with it the need to recognize Jews as a nationality wherever they had developed a national life. The Poale-Zion program, Bernstein conceded, was not inconsistent with socialist internationalism. The *Sozialistische Monatshefte* had for years been advocating just such a position. It had published several articles critical of the attitude of the Second International and its anti-Zionist tendency well before 1914.[117] One of the most distinctive features of Bloch's review in this regard was its positive attitude to European colonization overseas. Gerhard Hildebrand, for example, regarded colonizing activities in social Darwinist terms as a test of the vitality and cultural strength of a nation.[118] It was an expression of developing *Volkskraft* (national power) involving the transmission of higher ethical values rather than military might to more backward areas of civilization. Zionism was an outstanding example of this thesis since it represented a concentration of the energies of the Jewish people, which would qualitatively transform Diaspora Jews into productive workers and independent farmers. Zionist efforts in Palestine deserved the special sympathy of socialists "in view of the extremely miserable condition of the Jews in Russia, Romania, Galicia and in many other places. . . ."[119] Not only that, but the Zionist project merited serious study by agronomists, economists, and politicians interested in the development of new agricultural and colonizing techniques overseas.

Ludwig Quessel, like Hildebrand, regarded Zionism as a thoroughly laudable enterprise to regenerate the Jewish nation by welding together an agriculturally productive population. Drawing extensively on a study by Curt Nawratzki of Jewish colonizing methods in Palestine, Quessel presented its successes and failures in a much more positive spirit than Karl Kautsky. He noted that the early Jewish settlers from Russia who had come to Palestine in the 1880s and 1890s had to face exceptional difficulties, due to their relative inexperience, primitive agricultural techniques, and the harsh conditions of soil and climate. Nevertheless, in spite of wanton Turkish neglect of the land,

and the presence of a non-Jewish majority, Palestine still offered great potential for large-scale Jewish settlement and economic development.[120] The deserts could be made fruitful again through Jewish industriousness, science, and technology. The waste areas bought from Arab absentee landowners could be redeemed through planned cultivation by Jewish farmers. There was ample room for a much larger population than the 600,000 "natives" and 85,000 Jews in Turkish Palestine mentioned by Quessel. He also took issue with the skepticism of many German Jews concerning the ability of Zionism to solve the "Jewish question" in Europe. In Quessel's view, their negativity was a product of unjustified fears that Zionist activities would further inflame antisemitism in Europe. This viewpoint might have been understandable during the 1890s when political antisemitism in Germany had branded the Jews as a separate and distinct "race"—a position which Zionism superficially appeared to reinforce. But the anxieties of the "so-called assimilationists" were based on a "complete misunderstanding of national psychology." The success of Zionism, Quessel believed, would only raise the prestige of Jews in Germany.[121] He argued, moreover, that the Jews had been well prepared by their entire historical experience for the task of carrying out the colonization of Palestine. No other people had shown such an energetic capacity to adapt to new environments, to displace itself physically and intellectually without losing its inner cohesion. Throughout their history in the Diaspora, the Jews had displayed a civilizing vigor unmatched even by the ancient Greeks and Romans, or German colonists in the Slav lands of Eastern Europe.[122]

Quessel emphasized that Jewish colonization in Palestine at the beginning of the twentieth century had already produced a new generation of Hebrew-speaking settlers able to revive their ancestral tongue and create the foundations for a new Jewish national culture. Although still small in number, the Palestinian Jewish settlements would, in his view, provide an inspiring example for similar colonizing efforts in other parts of the world. In a period when the Old and the New World was beginning to close their doors to the mass emigration of Jews from Russia and Eastern Europe, the significance of the Zionist experiment would only grow in importance. Palestine offered the prospect of a secure haven that would be capable of solving the East European Jewish question in the future. Quessel concluded his remarks by praising the Zionists as instigators of an idealistic national movement which was in the best interests of civilized mankind. It would, at the same time, free the oppressed East European Jews, seeking a new soil under their feet, from the feeling of homelessness, enabling them to rise up out of the depths of social and national misery to a life of freedom and human dignity."[123]

Leon Chasanowitsch echoed some of these arguments in his presentation of the historical case for Poale-Zionism in 1914. Zionism, he asserted, was a historic need of the times, in view of the rapid proletarization of the Jewish masses in Russian Poland and Galicia. Alternative solutions such as mass emigration to America and England were already being undermined by growing anti-alien agitation and more stringent immigration laws. Efforts to settle East European Jews on the land in Russia, Austria-Hungary, or Argentina had been a fiasco and only led to demoralization.[124] It was wrong to see the transforming of Jewish city-dwellers into farmers as a regressive phenomenon. For the foreseeable future, agricultural production would retain its importance in the world economy. Even the German Social Democrats would come to regret their neglect of the agrarian problem. For its part, the Poale-Zion recognized that for reasons of national and social psychology, Palestine offered the best prospect for compact Jewish agricultural settlements. The Jews as a nation were much more suited to intensive agriculture and adopted "innovations and improvements with greater facility than the peasantry of any other people."[125] As settlers, they were specially well adapted to the cooperative mode of production, which was of great importance to modern agriculture.

Such labor Zionist arguments carried precious little weight with the followers of Karl Kautsky. For them, Jewish nationalism endangered the ideological dogma of international class struggle and the commitment of the Jewish proletariat to revolutionary socialism. The Jews, it was endlessly repeated, had no future as a separate nation. Their only defense against antisemitism was to throw in their lot with the struggle of the working class in Tsarist Russia and other European lands. The perspective offered by Kautsky, Rosa Luxemburg, and other German Marxists to the Jewish proletariat was therefore unreservedly *anti-nationalist*. In Kautsky's case, this went together with a heroic idealization of the Jewish workers. In 1902 he wrote:

> If such an oppressed class as the Jewish proletariat in Russia is able to rise and overcome stupendous obstacles with a superhuman energy, then we may boldly and sure of our victory, look at the future. Socialism—that's the idea that gives to the

> feeble David of the Jewish proletarian class the strength to fight the foul goliath of the Russian despotism and capitalism.[126]

Kautsky, no less than Lenin, felt confident in 1914 that the charismatic idea of international socialism and an imminent Russian Revolution would inspire Jewish and non-Jewish workers alike with the certainty of ultimate victory. Before the Bolshevik Revolution he repeatedly insisted that Jewish destiny would be played out in Russia, not Palestine.[127] According to Kautsky, the Zionists were therefore pursuing a chimera. By seeking to revive a nation which had only survived as a result of persecutions, forced segregation in the Russian Pale of Settlement, and counter-revolution, they were vainly attempting to turn back the clock of history. Worse still, Zionism was a kind of betrayal. By diverting Jewish energies from the revolutionary class-struggle, the Zionist goal was tantamount to a "desertion of the colors."[128] It was a regression to the worst traditions of the ghetto—an amalgam of religious obscurantism and chauvinist separatism.[129]

Karl Kautsky went still further in the 1920s in his denunciation of Zionism—derisively attacking the concept of Jewish "historical rights" in Palestine as moth-eaten and obscurantist. For the first time he now claimed that it would mean a complete denial of democracy and self-determination for the Arab inhabitants of Palestine.[130] His prognosis for Jewish colonization in Palestine also became notably more pessimistic than it had been in 1914. He argued not only that the land was too barren to support large-scale Jewish immigration but that the Jews would remain permanently outnumbered in Palestine. The Zionist experiment, Kautsky wrote in 1921, was bound to come to a tragic end as soon as Western imperialist hegemony over the Middle East collapsed.

The perspective of Joseph Bloch's review was almost diametrically opposed to this gloomy assessment of the Jewish national movement. Bloch had always felt great sympathy for the tradition of enlightened, universalist nationalism which emerged at the time of the French Revolution. He regarded Zionism as a worthy descendant of this classical liberal trend in European nationalism.[131] Bloch continued to believe that Jewry must not abandon its national consciousness as the price for absorbing the highest values of West European culture. The Zionist settlement of Palestine represented the Jewish rendezvous with its manifest destiny as well as the only practical answer to a long history of persecution.

Zionism for Bloch was the perfect synthesis between European humanist universalism and the national ideals implicit in biblical Judaism. The return to Zion, according to the editor of the *Monatshefte,* would forge a new link between East and West, building a vital bridge between the dispersed fragments of World Jewry.[132] Far from being a "return to the ghetto," Bloch believed that, through its *national* emancipation, Jewry would complete the process of individual liberation from ghetto Judaism which had begun in France in 1791. The Jewish National Home in Palestine would offer an indispensible answer to the malevolent antisemitism whose recrudescence in Weimar Germany continued to worry contributors to the *Sozialistische Monatshefte*. Bernstein, for example, warned in 1925 that Germans and Jews were "living in a time of the blackest of reactions."[133] Five years later, he pointed to the mounting antisemitic wave "which is becoming ever larger" and was compelling Jews to rally around the idea of a national homeland. "The anti-Semitic wave of today is more poisonous than ever," he told a German Jewish correspondent in 1931.[134] Bernstein had, towards the end of his life, completely rejected his earlier assimilationist stance, moving closer to Jewish communal institutions as well as to the Zionist movement.

Joseph Bloch was even more adamant, convinced as he was for over thirty years that only Zionism could liberate the non-Jewish world from antisemitism. The restoration of Israel, by reconciling the Jews with the world of nations through the establishment of an independent Jewish nation-state, would represent the final and complete form of emancipation. The Jews would thereby be able to fulfill their own ethical and cultural mission, overcoming the self-estrangement imposed by centuries of exile. Bloch continued to see in socialist Zionism the only realistic hope for resolving the East European "Jewish Question." The Jewish masses in Eastern Europe, who had long suffered from endemic poverty, persecution, civil and political inequality, would find their salvation through productive labor on the land.[135] This vision of Zionism would be largely vindicated by the establishment of Israel in 1948. The persistence of the "Palestinian Question" and systematic efforts since then at delegitimizing Israel have nonetheless cast a long shadow over the more rose-tinted imaginings of peace and harmony in Zion.

NOTES

1. See Robert S. Wistrich, "German Social Democracy and the Problem of Jewish Nationalism 1897–1917," *Leo Baeck Institute Year Book* (hereafter, *LBIYB*) 21 (1976): 109–42. There is also the rather superficial treatment by Walter Z. Laqueur, "Zionism, the Marxist Critique and the Left," *Dissent* (Dec. 1971): 560–74. For the Weimar years, see Donald L. Niewyk, *Socialist, Anti-Semite and Jew. German Social Democracy Confronts the Problem of Anti-Semitism 1918–1933* (Baton Rouge, 1971).

2. For a useful though problematic analysis of Kautsky's influence on German Social Democrats and Communists between the two World Wars, see George L. Mosse, "German Socialists and the Jewish Question in the Weimar Republic," in *LBIYB* 16 (1971): 123–51. Edmund Silberner, *Kommunisten zur Judenfrage. Zur Geschichte der Theorie und Praxis der Kommunismus* (Opladen, 1983) deals briefly with German Communism in the 1920s.

3. Karl Marx and Frederick Engels, *Selected Works* (Moscow, 1962), 1: 51. In the *Communist Manifesto* (1847), Marx and Engels argued that "the supremacy of the proletariat" would cause the abolition of national differences and antagonisms. See also Georges Haupt and Claudie Weill, "Le legs de Marx et Engels sur la question nationale," *Studi Storici,* no. 2 (1974): 270–324; and Albrecht Martiny, "Marximus und nationale Frage," *Deutschland-Archiv* 8 (Nov. 1975): 1176–80.

4. On Engels's assessment of the national problem with regard to Italy, see *Marx-Engels Werke* (East Berlin), 13: 225–68. On the Polish problem, Karl Marx, *Manuscripte über die Polnische Frage (1863–1864),* edited by W. Conze ('s-Gravenhage, 1961).

5. Roman Rosdolsky, "Friedrich Engels und das Problem der 'geschichtslosen' Völker" (Die Nationalitätenfrage in der Revolution 1848–1849 im Lichte der "Neuen Rheinischen Zeitung"), *Archiv für Sozialgeschichte* 4 (1964): 87–283.

6. For Kautsky's views on the national question, see "Die moderne Nationalität," *Die Neue Zeit* (1887): 392–405, 442–51, "Das Judentum," *Die Neue Zeit* (1890): 23–30, "Der Kampf der Nationalitäten und das Staatsrecht in Österreich," *Die Neue Zeit* 1 (1897–1898): 516–24, 557–64. This article had a considerable influence on Bundist and other advocates of Jewish cultural autonomy.

7. Karl Kautsky, "Nationalität und Internationalität," *Die Neue Zeit* 1 (1907–1908) (Supplement, 18 Jan. 1908): 7.

8. Ibid.

9. For an analysis of neo-Marxist critiques of Jewish nationalism, see Robert S. Wistrich, "The Marxist Concern with Judaism," *Patterns of Prejudice* 9, no. 4 (July–Aug. 1975): 1–6.

10. Karl Kautsky, "Rasse und Judentum," *Die Neue Zeit* (Supplement, 30 Oct. 1914),: 93.

11. Ibid.

12. Ibid.

13. Ibid.

14. Ibid., 67. Kautsky believed that only the forced segregation of the ghetto with its attendant civil and political inequality enabled Jewry to maintain itself. Wherever the Jews could freely connect with their environment or were treated as equal citizens, this segregation would disappear.

15. Karl Kautsky, "Das Massaker von Kischineff und die Judenfrage," *Die Neue Zeit* 2 (1902–1903): 308–9. On the background to this article see the letter by Adolf Warszawski (Warski) to Kautsky which can be found in the *Kautsky Nachlaß* at the Amsterdam International Institute of Social History (IISH), KD XXIII, 63.

16. August Bebel, *Sozialdemokratie und Antisemitismus* (Berlin, 1906), 36.

17. Karl Kautsky, "Rasse und Judentum," 82–83. Kautsky based his equation of Zionism with racism on a book by Dr. Ignaz Zollschan, *Das Rassenproblem. Unter besonderer Berücksichtigung der theoretischen Grundlagen der jüdischen Rassenfrage* (Vienna and Leipzig, 1910). Zollschan, an Austrian anthropologist and a dedicated Zionist, had published his study specifically to *combat* the antisemitic theories of Wagner, Dühring, and Houston S. Chamberlain. This did not deter Kautsky or Gustav Eckstein from misleadingly branding him—as well as Zionism—with the stigma of racism.

18. In his review of Zollschan's book in *Die Neue Zeit* 1 (1910–1911): 60, Gustav Eckstein wrote: "Die Vertreter des Nationalitätsprinzip im Judenthum sahen sich daher geradezu genötigt, sich bei Geltendmachung ihrer Ansprüche auf dasselbe Rassenprinzip zu berufen, dass die erbittersten Gegner der Juden, die Alldeutschen als Waffe gegen sie gebrauchen." Eckstein insisted that Zionists based themselves on the same "race principle" as the antisemitic Pan-Germans.

19. Karl Kautsky, "Das Massaker von Kischineff," 308.

20. Ibid.

21. Kautsky, "Rasse und Judentum," 78.

22. Ibid., 82.

23. Ibid., 77.

24. See the English translation from the 2nd ed. of *Rasse und Judentum* (Stuttgart, 1914), published under the title, *Are the Jews a Race?* (London, 1926), 209.

25. Karl Kautsky, "Nochmals der Zionismus. Eine Antwort an Eduard Bernstein," *Vorwärts* (15 Dec.. 1929): 586, 2 Supplement, p. 1.

26. Kautsky's data came from a study by Curt Nawratzki, *Die jüdische Kolonisation Palästinas* (Munich, 1914), which arrived at much more positive conclusions concerning the viability of Jewish settlement in Palestine.

27. Kautsky, "Rasse und Judentum," 82.

28. Ibid. I do not agree with Jack Jacobs's claim that hostility from mainstream German Zionists towards the SPD contributed to Kautsky's negative attitude. See Jack Jacobs, "Marxism and Antisemitism: Kautsky's Perspective," *International Review of Social History* 30 (1985): Part 3, 412.

29. Eduard Bernstein, *Von den Aufgaben der Juden im Weltkriege* (Berlin, 1917), 32.

30. Eduard Bernstein, "Wie ich als Jude in der Diaspora aufwuchs," *Der Jude* 2 (1917–1918): 187.

31. Eduard Bernstein, "Der Schulstreit in Palästina," *Die Neue Zeit* 1 (1913–1914): 752. Bernstein's article was partly a defense of his friend Dr. Paul Nathan, the founder of the *Hilfsverein der deutschen Juden,* whose philanthropic and cultural activities in Palestine had been criticized by Jewish nationalists. Nathan was an assimilationist who unequivocally *opposed* the Zionist movement and believed that only complete assimilation with the non-Jewish population would secure full emancipation for the Jews in Russia, Eastern Europe, and other countries. In 1914 this viewpoint was still as congenial to Bernstein as it was to the Marxist wing of the SPD. On the Hilfsverein see Moshe Rinott, "The Zionist Organisation and the Hilfsverein. Cooperation and Conflict (1901–1914)," *LBIYB* (1976): 261–78.

32. For a first-hand account of Bernstein's sympathies with Poale-Zion after 1917, see Zalman Shazar, *Or Ishim* (Tel Aviv 1955), 2: 27.

33. Eduard Bernstein, "Das Schlagwort und der Antisemitismus," *Die Neue Zeit* 2 (1893—1894): 236–37.

34. See *Stenographische Berichte über die Verhandlungen des Reichstags*, X. Legislaturperiode, *II. Session 1900/03*, vol. 10 (10 Mar.–30 Apr. 1903), 8756–8759.

35. *Dokumente des Sozialismus* (Stuttgart 1903), vols. 2–3: 344–46.

36. Ibid. In his review of Rabinowitsch's *Die Organisationen des jüdischen Proletariats in Russland* (Karlsruhe, 1903), Bernstein wrote of Marx's essay on the Jews: "Wir erkennen vielmehr an, dass die Marxschen Aufsätze über die Judenfrage neben vielen tiefen Ausführungen auch recht anfechtbare, auf flachen Rationalismus hinauslaufende Sätze enthalten." See also his critical remarks in an article for a Dutch socialist periodical, "Die Joden in de Duitsche Sociaal-Democratie," *De Socialistische Gids,* no. 2 (Nov. 1921): 971ff.

37. Chaim Weizmann, *The Letters and Papers of Chaim Weizmann,* Series A (London, 1968), 1: 389. Weizmann's letter, dated 29 Aug. 1902, was written in Russian. For further details see the chapter on Bernstein in Robert S. Wistrich, *Socialism and the Jewish Problem in Germany and Austria 1880–1914* (Ph. D. diss., University of London, 1974), 419 ff.

38. Kautsky to Motteler, 9 Jan. 1903, *Motteler Nachlass,* International Institute of Social History (Amsterdam), 2222/I.

39. See Bernstein's review of *Das Stiefkind der Sozialdemokratie* (Wien, 1905), by Matthias Acher (Nathan Birnbaum), in *Dokumente des Sozialismus* (1905), 5: 298–99.

40. In his unpublished manuscript entitled "Die demokratische Staatsidee und die jüdisch-nationale Bewegung" (*Bernstein Nachlaß,* International Institute of Social History, A. 114), written during the First World War, Bernstein sought to reconcile democratic socialism with the ideas of the Jewish national movement.

41. Eduard Bernstein, "Der Schulstreit in Palästina," 751–52.

42. Bernstein, *Von den Aufgaben,* 7.

43. Ibid., 29–31; see also Eduard Bernstein, *Entwicklungsgang eines Sozialisten* (Leipzig, 1930), 49.

44. Eva G. Reichmann, "Der Bewusstseinswandel der Deutschen Juden," in *Deutsches Judentum in Krieg und Revolution 1916–1923,* edited by Werner E. Mosse and Arnold Paucker (Tübingen, 1971), 511–612. Dr. Reichmann pointed out that the organ of the C.V. (Centralverein deutscher Staatsbürger jüdischen Glaubens) considered it urgent, "auf die frivole Leichtfertigkeit des Juden Bernstein zu verweisen, der für sein von allen Seiten als vaterlandsfeindlich gebrandmarktes Treiben dem Judentum die Verantwortung zuschieben möchte." *Im deutschen Reich* 23 (Dec. 1917): 499 (quoted in Reichmann, 522). On the relations between the C.V. and Social Democracy during the two decades preceding the First World War, see Arnold Paucker, "Zur Problematik einer jüdischen Abwehrstrategie in der deutschen Gesellschaft," in *Juden im Wilhelminischen Deutschland 1890—1914,* edited by Werner E. Mosse (Tübingen, 1976), 501–4.

45. Eduard Bernstein, *Von den Aufgaben*, 49.

46. C[arolus] Kautsky, "Der Antisemitismus," *Oesterreichischer Arbeiter-Kalender für das Jahr 1885* (n.p., 1886), 101.

47. S (K. Kautsky), "Das Judentum," *Die Neue Zeit* 8 (1890): 27.

48. Karl Kautsky, "Jaurès' Taktik und die deutsche Sozialdemokratie," *Vorwärts* 172 (26 July 1899): 3.

49. On Warszawski, see J. P. Nettl, *Rosa Luxemburg* (London, 1966), 1: 79.

50. Even in the 1920s Kautsky frequently sent warm fraternal greetings to Abe Cahan and the Bundists in America. In the *Kautsky Nachlaß* in Amsterdam, many of these materials have been preserved. See also Karl Kautsky, "Di oyfgaben fun di yiddisher sotsialistn in Amerika" (The tasks of the Yiddish socialists in America), published in *Forverts,* 23 Apr. 1922, p. 6.

51. See Jack Jacobs, "Marxism and Antisemitism," 416–23.

52. Ezra Mendelsohn, *Class-Struggle in the Pale: The Formative Years of the Jewish Workers' Movement in Tsarist Russia* (Cambridge, 1970); also Henry J. Tobias, *The Jewish Bund in Russia. From its Origins to 1905* (Stanford, 1972).

53. Karl Kautsky, "Rasse und Judentum," 77. "Die Bestrebungen nach Einfügung des jüdischen Proletariats in den Klassenkampf des gesamten russischen Proletariats haben ihren sichtbaren Ausdruck gefunden im jüdischen Arbeiterbund."

54. For a discussion of this omission, see Robert S. Wistrich, *Socialism and the Jewish Problem in Germany and Austria,* 300–7; see also Moshe Mishkinsky, *National Elements in the Development of the Jewish Labour Movement* (in Hebrew) (Ph.D. diss., Hebrew University of Jerusalem, 1965), 178–86.

55. Some of Rosa Luxemburg's Polish articles on the Jewish problem can be found in German translation in Irving Fetscher, ed., *Marxisten gegen Antisemitismus* (Hamburg, 1974), 127–50. For her attitude towards the Bund see Robert S. Wistrich, "The Jewish Origins of Rosa Luxemburg," *Olam* 3 (Winter–Spring 1977): 3–10; and idem, "Rosa Luxemburg, Leo Jogiches and the Jewish Labour Movement, 1893–1903," in *Jewish History,* edited by Ada Rappoport-Albert et al (London, 1988), 529–46.

56. See Max Zetterbaum, "Klassengegensätze bei den Juden," *Die Neue Zeit* 2 (1892–1893): 4.

57. Max Zetterbaum, "Probleme der jüdisch-proletarischen Bewegung," *Die Neue Zeit* 1 (1900–1901): 329.

58. S. Häcker, "Über den Zionismus," *Die Neue Zeit* 2 (1894–1895): 760. For a fierce attack on the East European *Wunderrabiner,* see Max Beer, "Die russischen und polnischen Juden in London," *Die Neue Zeit* 2 (1893–1894): 730 ff.

59. Häcker, "Über den Zionismus."

60. B. Emmanuel, "Über den Zionismus," *Die Neue Zeit* 2 (1894–1895): 601.

61. Jacob Stern, Review of Theodor Herzl's *Der Judenstaat* in *Die Neue Zeit* 1 (1896–1897): 186.

62. Johann Pollack, "Der Politische Zionismus," *Die Neue Zeit* 2 (1897–1898): 597.

63. Ibid.

64. Max Zetterbaum, "Probleme der jüdisch-proletarischen Bewegung," *Die Neue Zeit* 1 1900–1901): 325.

65. Ibid., 326.

66. Ibid., 330.

67. Ibid., 372.

68. Ibid., 373.

69. See *Die Neue Zeit* 2 (1903–1904): 537–38.

70. *Bericht für den Internationalen Sozialistischen Kongress in Amsterdam* (Geneva, 1904), "Die Tätigkeit des Allgemeinen Jüdischen Arbeiterbundes in Litauen, Polen und Russland ("Bund") nach seinem V. Parteitag," 24–25.

71. Die ökonomische Lage des jüdischen Proletariats in Russland," *Die Neue Zeit* 1 (1905–1906): 336.

72. Ibid., 337.

73. A. Lampert, "Der Poale-Zionismus. Eine Neue Strömung im russischen Judentum," *Die Neue Zeit* 1 (1905–1906): 804–13.

74. Ibid., 809.

75. Ibid., 810; see also A. L., "Die prinzipielle Stellung des jüdischen Arbeiterbund," *Die Neue Zeit* 2 (1905–1906) 702ff.

76. B. Rosin, "Die Zionistisch-Sozialistische Utopie," *Die Neue Zeit* 1 (1908–1909): 29–34.

77. See, for example, the remarks of Vladimir Medem, the leader of the Bund, in an article on "Der moderne Antisemitismus in Russland," *Die Neue Zeit* 1(1910–1911): 263. "Und gerade der jüdische Nationalismus hat sich als total unfruchtbar erwiesen. Bald weinerlich-pessimistisch, bald träumerisch-territorialistisch pendeln seine Anhänger hin und her, ohne die Kraft zu haben, um auf eigenen Füssen zu stehen."

78. Karl Kautsky, *Rasse und Judentum,* 94.

79. For further details, see Zalman Shazar, *Or Ishim,* which also includes interesting chapters on Eduard Bernstein, Joseph Bloch, and Leon Chasanowitsch.

80. For a valuable study of German socialist attitudes before World War I to colonialism and imperialism, see Hans-Christoph Schroeder, *Sozialismus und Imperialismus. Die Auseinandersetzung der deutschen Sozialdemokratie mit dem Imperialismusproblem und der "Weltpolitik" vor 1914* (Hannover, 1968).

81. See the article by August Bebel in *Vorwärts* (19 Dec. 1897); and the pamphlet by Karl Kautsky, *Sozialismus und Kolonialpolitik* (1907); also the earlier article by Kautsky, "Auswanderung und Kolonisation," *Die Neue Zeit* (1883): 366, 393 ff.

82. For a good example of the socialist defense of colonization, see Emil Vandervelde, "Die Sozialdemokratie und das Kolonialproblem," *Die Neue Zeit* 1 (1908–1909): 737 ff.

83 See H. H. Van Kol, *La Démocratie Socialiste Internationale et le Sionisme* (Lausanne, 1919), for a sympathetic view of Zionist aspirations. Also the *Bernstein Nachlass* (International Institute of Social History) B. 10, "Zwei sozialistische Antworten auf Karl Kautskys Artikel, 'Die Aussichten des Zionismus.'" The two replies to Kautsky's attack on Zionism, by Emil Vandervelde and Camille Huysmans, both stressed the positive achievements of Jewish colonization and cooperative labor in Palestine. See also Bernstein, "Les nationalistes arabes et le mandat palestinien," *Comité Socialiste pour la Palestine Ouvrière Bulletin* 5 (May 1930): 12. Also Bernstein's review of Vandervelde's pro-Zionist *Schaffendes Palästina*. The ms. can be found in the *Bernstein Nachlass,* A 126, IISH.

84. For his view of the national question, see M. Anin, *Die Nationalitätenprobleme der Gegenwart* (Riga, 1910), which received a hostile review in the *Neue Zeit*. Anin (whose original name was Maks-Aryeh Z. Shats) was a leading advocate of Jewish socialist representation in the Second International. In 1917 he emerged as a co-founder of the United Jewish Socialist Workers Party in Russia and of the left-wing Yiddishist "Kultur-Lige." He later joined the Bolsheviks.

85. M. Anin, "Probleme des jüdischen Arbeiterlebens," *Sozialistische Monatshefte* 1 (1909): 231ff.

86. For the classic exposition of Marxist-Zionist theory, Ber Borochov, *Die Grundlagen des Poale-Zionismus* (Frankfurt, 1969). Borochov had already worked out the guidelines of Poale-Zionism by 1905 in his famous manifesto "Our Platform." See Matityahu Mintz, *Ber Borochov: Ha-maagal ha-rishon (1900–1906)* (Tel Aviv, 1976); and Gideon Shimoni, *The Zionist Ideology* (Hanover, 1995), 179–93.

87. M. Ratner, "Die Nationale Autonomie und das jüdische Proletariat," *Sozialistische Monatshefte* 3 (1911): 1333ff.

88. M. Anin, "Ist die Assimilation der Juden möglich," *Sozialistische Monatshefte* 2 (1908): 614ff.

89. M. Anin, "Die Judenfrage als Wanderungsproblem," *Sozialistische Monatshefte* 2 (1909): 849ff.

90. See the article by Charles Bloch, "Der Kampf Joseph Blochs und der 'Socialistischen Monatshefte' in der Weimarer Republik," *Jahrbuch des Instituts für Deutsche Geschichte* 3 (Tel Aviv, 1974): 257–89; also Roger Fletcher, "Revisionism and Empire: Joseph Bloch, the *Sozialistische Monatshefte* and German Nationalism, 1907–14," *European Studies Review* 10, no. 4 (1980): 459–85.

91. Sergej Njewsorow, "Der Zionismus," *Sozialistische Monatshefte* (1897): 651.

92. Ibid.

93. "Literarische Rundschau," *Sozialistische Monatshefte* (1898): 535–36.

94. Adele Schreiber, "Ein Dichter des jüdischen Proletariats," *Sozialistische Monatshefte* (1903): 449–54. Rosenfeld's poems, translated into German by Berthold Feiwel, were also reviewed by Julie Zadek in *Die Neue Zeit* 2 (1903–1904): 285, and criticized for their melancholy ghetto flavor.

95. Adele Schreiber, "Ein Dichter des jüdischen Proletariats," 453.

96. See A. Tartakower, "Zur Geschichte des jüdischen Sozialismus," *Der Jude* 8 (1942): 392ff.

97. M. Anin, "Ist die Assimilation der Juden möglich?," *Sozialistische Monatshefte* 614ff.

98. Ibid., 618.

99. M. Anin, "Probleme des jüdischen Arbeiterlebens," *Sozialistische Monatshefte,* no. 3 (1908): 231ff.

100. M. Anin, "Die Organisation der jüdischen Wanderung," *Sozialistische Monatshefte* 3 (1909): 1254.

101. Leon Chasanowitsch, "Ziele und Mittel des Sozialistischen Zionismus," *Sozialistische Monatshefte* (July 1914): 962–73.

102. Ibid., 962.

103. For an example of Bundist opposition to this project of a world Jewish section in the International, see Wladimir Medem, "Ein nationalistischer Vorschlag," *Die Neue Zeit* (1909–1910): 748–51.

104. Leon Chasanowitsch, *Sozialistische Monatshefte* (July 1914): 964.

105. See Berl Locker, "Die Allgemeinen Gesetze der Assimilation und die Ostjuden," *Der Jude* 1 (1916–1917): 504–9; and Leo Rosenberg, "Emanzipation und Zukunft des Ostjudentums," *Sozialistische Monatshefte* (1917): 681–90. Both writers, like Chasanowitsch, pointed out that the western pattern of emancipation did not apply to the non-assimilated Jewish masses of Eastern Europe.

106. Chasanowitsch, *Sozialistische Monatshefte* (July 1914): 964.

107. Ibid., 965.

108. M. Anin, "Der Judenboykott in Polen," *Sozialistische Monatshefte* 1 (1914): 350ff.

109. See, for example, Raphael Seligmann, "Über die Juden in Russland," *Sozialistische Monatshefte* (Sept. 1914):. 1084–91. Seligmann emphasized the strength of folk-consciousness in Russian Jewry, what he termed the "urwüchsige und unversiegbare nationale Kraft," manifested in movements like Hasidism, Bundism, Zionism, and the revival of Hebrew literature. Neighboring peoples like the Ukrainians, Poles, Byelorussians, Lithuanians, and Latvians had no doubt that the Jews constituted "eine eigenartige Nation" (a unique nation).

110. This point was well made by the German socialist, Dr. Ludwig Quessel, "Die jüdische Neukolonisation Palästinas," *Sozialistische Monatshefte* (June 1914): 675–76.

111. Ibid.

112. Engelbert Pernerstorfer, "Zur Judenfrage," *Der Jude* 1 (1916–1917): 313. H. H. van Kol in his *La Démocratie Socialiste Internationale et le Sionisme,* 8, observed that of all the pre-1914 socialists in Central Europe—"Seul, le Dr. Pernerstorfer, avec son énergique sentiment du droit, fut un lutteur fidèle de la cause juive."

113. Pernerstorfer, "Zur Judenfrage."

114. Hermann Kranold, "Die Juden in Polen und Palästina," *Sozialistische Monatshefte* (1917): 681–90.

115. Quoted in Lewis Rifkind, *Zionism and Socialism* (London, 1918), 14. Huysmans's favorable judgment on Zionism was published, along with similar statements of Dutch and Scandinavian socialists, by the Jewish Press Bureau in Stockholm on 30 Nov. 1917.

116. See Robert Wistrich, "Eduard Bernstein and the Jewish Problem," *Jahrbuch des Instituts für deutsche Geschichte* 8 (1979): 253; and E. Bernstein, "Die demokratische Staatsidee und die jüdisch-nationale Bewegung," K 13/26 Central Zionist Archives. The original is in the *Bernstein Nachlass* in Amsterdam, see A 114, IISH. Also Leon Chasanowitsch to Bernstein (8 Jan. 1918), *Bernstein Nachlass,* D 317, IISH.

117. See M. Anin, "Das Nationalitätsprinzip in der Sozialistischen Internationale," *Sozialistische Monatshefte* 2 (1910): 890; see also idem, "Was will die jüdische Sektion in der Sozialistischen Internationale?" *Sozialistische Monatshefte* (1911): 396–400.

118. Gerhard Hildebrand, "Kolonisation und Kultur," *Sozialistische Monatshefte* 1 (1910): 293–302.

119. Gerhard Hildebrand, "Zionismus," *Sozialistische Monatshefte* (Mar. 1910): 404.

120. Ludwig Quessel, "Die Jüdische Neukolonisation Palästinas," *Sozialistische Monatshefte* (June 1914): 680. "Es kann keinem Zweifel unterliegen, dass ein sehr grosser Teil der wüsten Gebiete in Palästina, wieder fruchtbar gemacht warden kann. Zurzeit ist das eigentliche Palästina, das an Grösse die Provinz Pommern übertrifft, ein noch ziemlich menschenleeres Land. Neben den 100,000 Juden finden wir dort eine einheimische Bevölkerung von nur 600,000 Köpfen. Es ist klar, dass durch Urbarmachung der wüsten Ländereien, die zumeist im Besitz arabischer Grossgrundbesitzer sind, dort eine jüdische landwirtschaftliche Bevölkerung angesiedelt warden könnte, die ein vielfaches der heutigen beträgt." Quessel' figure of 100,000 Jews settled in Palestine in 1914 is slightly overstated.

121. Ibid., 682. In support of his thesis, Quessel suggested that those nations which had hitherto regarded the Jews as "intruders" would be ready to welcome the rebirth of an independent Jewish nation.

122. Ludwig Quessel, "Kolonisation," *Sozialistische Monatshefte* (1913): 394.

123. Ludwig Quessel, "Die Jüdische Neukolonisation," 684.

124. See Leon Chasanowitsch, *Die Krise der jüdischen Kolonisation in Argentinien* (Stanislau, 1910). This book was also published in Yiddish and aroused considerable interest at the time. It was primarily an attack on the administration of the settlements of the Jewish Colonisation Association in Argentina, a subject on which Chasanowitsch was an expert.

125. Leon Chasanowitsch, "Ziele und Mittel des Sozialistischen Zionismus," *Sozialistische Monatshefte* (July 1914): 970–71.

126. Karl Kautsky, "A Pariah among Proletarians," *Justice*, 22 Feb. 1902.

127. Karl Kautsky, *Are the Jews a Race?,* 213.

128. Ibid., 215.

129. Ibid., 217.

130. Ibid., 207–10. Nevertheless the Palestine Arabs remained a secondary factor in the controversy over Zion for Kautsky's generation.

131. See Charles Bloch, "Der Kampf Joseph Blochs und der 'Sozialistischen Monatshefte' in der Weimarer Republik," 284–86.

132. Ibid. These ideas were expressed in Joseph Bloch's political testament, dictated to his friend and pupil Felix Stössinger. They appeared in *Selbstverlag* (Prague in 1938), two years after Bloch's death.

133 See Jack Jacobs, *On Socialists and "the Jewish Question" after Marx* (New York, 1992), 68.

134. See Bernstein's interview with Paul Kampfmeyer, "Eduard Bernstein. Zu seinem 80 Geburtstage," *C.V. Zeitung* 9, no. 1 (3 Jan. 1930):. 6.

135. Charles Bloch, "Der Kampf Joseph Blochs," 285.

CHAPTER 11

The Internationalism of Rosa Luxemburg

It is doubtful if any revolutionary Marxist before the First World War more perfectly embodied the spirit of socialist internationalism than Rosa Luxemburg, yet few displayed a greater level of disaffection from their Jewish background.[1] One of the ironies of Luxemburg's manifest alienation from her roots was the degree to which it derived from an adolescent desire to integrate into the surrounding culture that she grew up with in Warsaw and embrace a Polish identity; yet no other European social-democrat would so intransigently oppose Polish democratic demands for national self-determination. Luxemburg also went further than almost any of her contemporaries in claiming Socialism and nationalism to be two *absolutely* conflicting and irreconcilable ideas.[2] When she and a small group of friends broke out of the Polish Socialist Party (PPS) of Russian Poland in 1893, it was the *national question* which remained the main bone of contention. The SDKPiL (Social Democracy of the Kingdom of Poland and Lithuania), as it came to be called after 1900—which she co-founded and led, had adopted a consistently *anti-nationalist* position that subordinated the aspirations of the Polish proletariat to the social revolution in Tsarist Russia. Polish national independence, according to Luxemburg, was economically and politically undesirable because it would cut off Polish industry from its Russian markets and obstruct the development of the class struggle. Therefore it constituted a thoroughly retrograde step.[3] Polish Social Democracy, she insisted, must seek to realize its political aims in the framework of an all-Russian revolution. Even the Bolshevik leader Vladimir Ilyich Lenin was taken aback at the intransigence of Luxemburg's positions on Poland and the national question more generally, which he sharply criticized on the eve of the First World War.[4] Partly, his objections were for tactical reasons. He did not so much blame the SDKPiL for opposing the secession of Poland but rather for turning internationalism into a dogmatic principle that would deny any right of separation and self-determination for subject peoples.[5] Lenin realized that the adoption of such a position would limit his room for maneuver and play into the hands of the "great Russian arch-reactionary chauvinism" of the Tsarist regime which he sought to overthrow.

By 1914, after two decades of polemics against the nationalistic PPS, Luxemburg was, however, adamant that the assertion of national interests "can serve only as a means of deception, of betraying the working masses of the people to their deadly enemy, Imperialism."[6] Already in 1908, in a major exposition of the nationality question for a Polish socialist publication, she had insisted that there was no "right to self-determination" *as such.*[7] According to the rigorous "scientific" approach of historical materialism, the concept of the nation was at best temporary and would pass away with the close of the capitalist era in history.[8] It was a time-bound category of bourgeois ideology which ignored the reality of a society based on classes. There could never be any true common ground between the ruling elites and the proletarian masses as the "national-patriots" liked to claim.

The bourgeois notion of a "national fatherland" was entirely alien to Rosa Luxemburg, as was the "patriotic" consciousness shared by most socialists of her generation. Even an ardent international Marxist like Lenin, despite his revulsion at Russian chauvinism, still identified with much of Russian history, culture, and attitudes. This was not the case with Rosa Luxemburg, though, at times, she chose to assert her Polish background against some of her colleagues in the German Social Democracy (SPD). But she felt no special attachment to her native Poland or to her adopted German homeland. She had even less time for any self-conscious manifestation of Jewishness. In 1917 she sharply reproached her socialist friend Mathilde Wurm for even evoking the sufferings of the Jewish masses in the Russian Pale of Settlement:

> Why do you come with your special Jewish sorrows? I feel just as sorry for the wretched Indian victims in Putamayo, the negroes in Africa. . . . The "lofty silence of the eternal" in which so many cries have echoed away unheard resounds so strongly within me that I cannot find a special corner in my heart for the ghetto.[9]

Luxemburg did not explain why she was so annoyed by what she called "special" Jewish afflictions or in what way this diminished concern with the oppression of South American Indians or Africans. At the same time, she also evoked the rather more abstract "fatherland" of the working class in preference to any loyalty towards a concrete nation—whether Russian, Polish, Jewish, or German. In her feverish agitation against German militarism and the looming threat of a world war, her internationalist stance soon led to prosecution by the German authorities. On 20 February 1914 she was tried in Frankfurt and sentenced to a year in prison. Officially condemned by the Reich government as a woman who was "rootless," "a creature without a home," Luxemburg vigorously and effectively defended herself:

> As regards the question of being an expatriate, I would not swop with the public prosecutor on any account. I have a dearer, greater home than any prosecutor. . . . What other fatherland is there than the great mass of working men and women? What other fatherland is there than the improvement of life, the improvement of morality, the improvement of the intellectual strength of the great masses which constitute a people?[10]

Like her Bolshevik contemporary, Leon Trotsky, Luxemburg was always consistent in her Marxist credo that the proletarian revolution would erase all national boundaries, class divisions, and obscurantist religious or ethnic prejudices. She believed that these divisions—the product of a decaying capitalist order—would soon be swept away. With the collapse of capitalism, there could be no further justification for the preservation of separate national identities, least of all for the maintenance of a distinctive Jewish nationality. Remote as she was from her own ethnic roots (though she did know some Yiddish expressions), ignorant of Judaism, of Jewish history and culture, Luxemburg often acted as if she did not consider herself Jewish at all. In response to pogroms being directed against Polish Jews, she at one point retorted:

> Let them learn, speak, and think Polish, celebrate Polish holidays, and cease insisting on their Sabbath rest, for this they must learn and commit to memory—the apparatus of capitalist production and trade is under no obligation to accommodate the faith, customs and calendar of the Jews.[11]

This was an extraordinarily intolerant response to the predicament of her Polish-Jewish co-religionists. It is all the more remarkable given her own direct experience of a devastating pogrom in Warsaw in 1881, when she was only eleven years old. On her way home from school, as a terrified and helpless Jewish child, she had to hide from a violent mob which rushed past her towards the Jewish quarter, howling "kill the Jews."[12] The Warsaw pogrom began on Christmas Day, 1881, after a crowd of Poles had left the Church of the Holy Cross and (undisturbed by the Tsarist police) began to storm the Jewish area, looting, breaking windows, and throwing stones. The pogrom raged on for three days and nights in the Jewish quarter. It would have spread further were it not for those Jewish workers, peddlers, cobblers, and shopkeepers who somehow managed to improvise their own self-defense.[13] The young Rosa Luxemburg, then in her second year at the Russian Second Gymnasium for Girls, was doubly in danger—both as a Jewess and also because of her severe limp which made it virtually impossible for her to run away.

Many years later (without evoking the pogrom), she wrote to her friend Luise Kautsky:

> I imagine that again I must enter an overcrowded gigantic hall, the glaring lights, the ear-splitting noise, the mass of people pushing against me. . . and I feel an urge to suddenly run away! . . . I have a horror of crowds.[14]

Thus, even at the height of her fame, when masses of German proletarians would enthusiastically chant "Long live Rosa!," she was still frightened of the mob, traumatized perhaps by images of violence that she had once witnessed as a child in Russian Poland. One of her biographers, Elżbieta Ettinger, has plausibly argued that "the pogrom left Rosa with a permanent scar" but one which "she buried deeply." Only once did she ever explicitly mention this pogrom. This was done completely *impersonally,* in an unsigned article written in 1911 for *Czerwony Sztandar*. Significantly, she was mistaken about the date.[15] To highlight the severity of this experience was not something she cared to do. It could have exposed her vulnerability as a Jewess as well as contradicting the Marxist belief that racist antisemitism was no more than an epiphenomenon—a passing scourge on the road to socialism.

Rosa Luxemburg (née Rozalia or Róża Luksenburg) had been born in Zamość in March 1871, the youngest of five children. The city, then situated in the southeastern part of Russian Poland, had a substantial Jewish community, including a strong Hassidic and Orthodox population which fiercely opposed the rising trend of *Haskalah* (Enlightenment) in the East European Jewish world. Rosa's paternal grandfather had been a successful timber merchant. His son Eliasz inherited his father's business but evidently not his abilities, for over the years his fortunes declined. According to some accounts, Eliasz Luxemburg was determined to assimilate, and took a strong interest in Polish affairs.[16] He certainly spoke fluent Polish, which was the language of choice at home, though he frequently used Yiddish in business as well as German. Nevertheless, the Luxemburg family, while moving towards cultural assimilation, was by no means uninvolved in Jewish life. Jack Jacobs has argued that Rosa's father associated himself with the secularizing ideology of the Polish *maskilim* (enlighteners) in Zamość, who looked to a modernized form of Jewish religious practice.[17] Apparently, he also contributed to the publication of Hebrew-language works written by *maskilim* and was, for a time, even an elected official of the local Jewish community.

From letters written to Rosa by her siblings in the 1890s, it also seems clear that the family—especially her mother Lina (née Löwenstein) observed certain Jewish religious traditions. The granddaughter of Rabbi Isaac Löwenstein from Poznań, Lina descended from a most impressive line of rabbinical ancestors and Talmudic interpreters in Germany, Poland, and the Czech lands. She was as profoundly enamored of the Bible as she was well versed in Goethe and Schiller. A letter from Rosa's eldest sister, Anna, in late 1897, specifically referred to her mother's "deep religious faith" as well as her "angelic kindness" during the dreadful ordeal of her last years when she was ill with an incurable stomach cancer.

> The inhuman suffering did not stop Mother from figuring out, ahead of time, the date of the Holiday [the Jewish New Year] and insisting that the parcel reach you in time.

Another letter from Anna noted that Lina had insisted, even on her deathbed, that she prepare a traditional Rosh Hashanah meal "for Papa to know this is a home and this is a holiday."[18] Following Lina's death, Jozef Luxemburg (Rosa's brother) wrote to her:

> Now there is nothing I can do—I can only say *Kaddish* in the temple every day, as Mama would have done had I left her. Mama was religious and during her illness she asked us to pray for her recovery.[19]

Another brother, Maksymilian (Munio) wrote to Rosa from Warsaw on 30 October 1897, evoking the Jewish prayer for the dead, which the Luxemburg family had said at their mother's grave:

> A few days after the funeral we went to the cemetery to say *el mole rachamim* [in Hebrew in the original, meaning "to the Merciful God"], for each of us separately and of course for you. We are also going tomorrow to lament at her grave and relieve our suffering.[20]

Rosa Luxemburg, then living abroad, did not attend either her mother's or her father's funerals, nor (as far as we know) did she ever go to visit their graves. Her relationship to both of her parents seems to have been ambivalent. Their petty-bourgeois outlook and transparent Jewishness evidently grated on her—as did their repeatedly expressed concern for her welfare. Perhaps Rosa unconsciously blamed them for not detecting early enough her hip dislocation as a child, which had left her severely disfigured and even partially crippled, with one leg noticeably shorter than the other. She certainly did not share Lina Luxemburg's deep attachment to Judaism though on one occasion in prison she recalled her mother's stories about King Solomon understanding the language of the birds. But she never mentioned the distinguished rabbinical ancestry on her mother's side.[21] Perhaps, like Karl Marx, she regarded this fact as so much embarrassing dead weight from the past.[22] In Warsaw, the metropolis with proportionately the largest Jewish population anywhere in Europe, the adolescent Rosa Luxemburg was already too close for comfort to a world of men with long beards, yarmulkas and kaftans, Jews with earlocks, women in wigs, *schnorrers,* and street vendors constantly gesticulating in Yiddish. This was hardly the world that young Rosa yearned for; and unlike her mother, she was never able to meaningfully integrate the Jewish heritage into her broader European culture.

At her Russian gymnasium, from 1880 onwards, Luxemburg was made to feel the humiliating aspects of the inferior status of being a Jew in Tsarist Poland. She had been admitted under a quota system, and soon discovered how different she was from the bulk of her Russian and Polish fellow-students. Her classmates were mostly the daughters of impoverished Polish gentry and the intelligentsia, of middle-level officials, or Russian functionaries stationed in Warsaw, and a small number of Jews from more modest merchant families. Jewish girls like Luxemburg could not easily blend into the semi-underground Polish culture (repressed by Tsarist officialdom) which stressed the legacy of Catholicism, of the Polish kings, and exhibited a fierce, unyielding national pride. Thus, the obstacles to assimilation in her adolescent years proved considerable. They were partly overcome through Luxemburg's sheer tenacity, ambition, drive, intellectual curiosity, and a passion for the Polish romantic poet Adam Mickiewicz, whose idealism captivated her. Her subsequent involvement in Polish and German socialism was the final step towards full assimilation into the culture of the international labor movement.

Despite her genuine identification with Mickiewicz, by the time Luxemburg had left Warsaw for ever in 1889, this highly intelligent 18-year-old Jewish girl already felt remote from almost everything defined at the time as Polishness—whether by Catholic nationalists or mainstream Polish Socialists. For them she would always remain "a Jew with no roots, no tradition, and no country."[23] The fact that she was determined to escape the confines of her family and milieu, to cease being a Jew, changed nothing at all in the way she was perceived by her Polish political opponents. Her

"Semitic" features, intense deep-brown eyes, short stature, and mass of dark-brown hair, along with her sarcastic wit, strong will (bordering at times on arrogance), and superior intellect soon marked her out. Her stubborn resistance to Polish (and later German) patriotism did the rest. Nor did her own family escape her impatient chiding and sarcasm. Her ailing father, whose letters to her went unanswered, as she became more intensely involved in the internal politics of the German labor movement, was particularly shocked at her indifference towards him near the end of his life. Though proud of his daughter's achievements, he could not really fathom the world in which Luxemburg now moved.

The Jewish socialists (members of the Bundist workers movement in Russia and Poland) who came into contact with Rosa Luxemburg in the early 1890s, had decidedly mixed feelings about her political positions.[24] There were some like John Mill, who insisted that as early as 1894 Luxemburg rejected the "isolationist" tendencies of Yiddish-speaking Jewish workers in Wilno (Vilna, now known as Vilnius) as "hundred percent separatism." She had caustically denounced their aspirations as a form of "petty-bourgeois" nationalism. For her, the call for a Jewish workers' organization was a mirror-image of PPS nationalism. Jewish socialists, she lectured Mill, did not need the Yiddish language or require a separate Jewish proletarian movement. They had, above all, to learn the language of the population around them, whether Polish or Russian. The Jewish proletariat should "blend with the Christian working class." Any other road "would only lead into a nationalistic swamp."[25]

Luxemburg continued to nourish an abiding hostility to the notion of any separate Jewish ethnicity as well as to the cultivation of *Jargon* (as Yiddish was disparagingly known). After 1901, the development of Yiddish culture would become part of the Bund's formal demands for Jewish cultural-national autonomy. This obviously repelled Luxemburg. Indeed, one veteran Bundist, Jacob S. Hertz, would many years later recall:

> Luxemburg hated Jews. And even more than Jews she hated Yiddish. This is a characteristics of many assimilated types.[26]

In 1901, Luxemburg even warned a prominent non-Jewish SDKP militant that the Bund leaders were above all characterized by "idiocy and perfidy." According to her description, they were incapable of "exchanging two words with you, of looking at you, without having the hidden intent of stealing something from you."[27] She advised her correspondent to break off all relations with the Bundists. A few years later she emphatically told Leo Jogiches: "I do not agree to any alliance with the Jews. This rabble needs us, we do not need them."[28] Luxemburg evidently found Bundist demands extremely annoying and tiresome.[29] At the 1907 London Congress of the Russian Social Democratic Party, she gratuitously attacked the Bund leader Raphael Abramovich and his supporters for being "among those who speculate with the rising and falling prices of sugar. . . .[30] The Bundists (and some other delegates) protested angrily against this antisemitically-tinged remark, which compared them to sugar speculators. This slight would later be erased from the record of the proceedings.

Luxemburg's close comrade, Adolf Warszawski (Warski)—the future founder of the Polish Communist Party in 1918—fully shared her aversion towards Yiddish and her opposition to Bundist efforts to consolidate a separate Jewish workers' organization. A highly Polonized Jew, Warski (like Luxemburg) constantly complained about the Bund's use of *Jargon,* dismissing Yiddish as a throw-back to "remnants of the Dark Middle Ages." To a somewhat lesser extent this aversion was also shared by Leo Jogiches (Luxemburg's lover and de facto husband between 1890 and 1905)—who had been born in Wilno, Lithuania, in 1867. Jogiches came from a prominent and wealthy Jewish family in the Lithuanian capital. Already in his teens he had rebelled against his family's "bourgeois" life-style, opting for the conspiratorial underground and the proletarian cause before escaping to Swiss exile. The SDKPiL would become a center for his future activity. It was Jogiches who provided Luxemburg not only with the necessary funds to support her activities but also with constant political and tactical advice—which may have helped her to climb more swiftly in the ranks of the German Social Democracy (SPD) after her move to Berlin in 1898.[31] Their personal relationship was close but often tense, kept together for over fifteen years by a common commitment to the revolutionary cause.

Leo Jogiches came from *the* cradle of a specifically *Jewish* socialism in Wilno, where the great mass of impoverished Jewish workers and craftsmen did not speak either Russian or Polish. Though the movement had originated in Wilno, it gradually spread to the Ukraine and Russian Poland, especially to Warsaw and Łódź. Its development was strongly influenced by the growing industrialization of the Russian Empire (noted by Luxemburg in her doctorate), by the rise of the Polish workers' movement, the impact of Marxist ideology, and the gradual secularization of Jewish life. The more specifically Jewish features of the Bund were partly the product of its political isolation in the Pale of Settlement and the peculiar socio-economic as well as demographic characteristics of the Jewish population in the Russian Empire.[32] Jogiches, though himself a well-off "Russified" Jew, was far more familiar than Luxemburg with this Jewish socialist milieu. He continued to maintain links with the Jewish labor leaders in Wilno even after his forced departure from Tsarist Russia to Switzerland and followed the Jewish workers' movement with slightly more empathy than Luxemburg.[33]

In 1893 Jogiches published as a brochure the *Four Speeches of Jewish Workers* made in Russian and Yiddish at a May Day rally in Wilno.[34] The brochure appeared in Geneva with an introduction by Boris Kritchevsky. It was almost certainly edited by Luxemburg and Jogiches whose ideas are virtually impossible to separate at this time. The speeches were an important manifestation of Jewish working-class solidarity with the ideals of the international socialist movement. It is therefore worth looking in some detail at the article which Jogiches wrote in January 1894 for *Sprawa Robotnicza* (the organ of the Polish Social Democrats, edited by Rosa Luxemburg) about the Wilno speeches.[35] Jogiches began on an upbeat note:

> In moving words, full of feeling and in the picturesque form characteristic of the Yiddish language, the poor, persecuted Jewish proletarians paint their working-class situation and express their aims and aspirations.

Approvingly, Jogiches then quoted a Jewish worker denouncing the common yoke of capital which "oppresses his brethren as much as the proletarians of other nationalities." There was no question, Jogiches pointed out, but that "Russian Jews are the most deprived of rights and the most enslaved of all the subjects of the Tsar." "Laws exist," he added,

> which do not permit the Jews entry to a whole range of occupations, which limit their numbers in schools, forbid them to acquire property, etc. We shall not discuss that; although the laws themselves merit condemnation, they do not touch the Jewish proletariat much. But the greatest onus of persecution falls as usual on the backs of the poor working people.[36]

It was "the poor, defenseless Jewish proletarian," not the wealthy Jews (who could bribe officials to ensure their protection), who received the worst blows. Moreover, the Tsarist autocracy since the pogroms of 1881 had unscrupulously used the Jews as a scapegoat for the discontent of other subject nationalities. The most recent example had been the anti-Jewish pogrom organized by the Tsarist police in Łódź as a pretext for bloodily repressing the strikes and demonstrations by Polish workers.[37] *Sprawa Robotnicza* had praised the Polish workers of Łódź for refusing to become the accomplices of the Tsarist autocracy by participating in the pogrom.

> You have shown the whole world that for you a Jew or a German does not exist, that you know your enemies well, the capitalists of all faiths and nationalities—that a Jew like Poznanski or a German like Scheibler are your deadly enemies, but that the poor Jewish tinker or German textile worker are your comrades in misery and oppression.[38]

In a report from Warsaw (July/August 1893) the paper again noted that

> at a time when violent anti-Semitism is raging in bourgeois intellectual circles, the workers are once more demonstrating as they did last May in Łódź, by courageous actions, that they understand the meaning of class solidarity with the Jewish proletariat and that no prejudices of racial hatred exist for them.[39]

Rosa Luxemburg, Jogiches, and Warski well understood that Jewish workers could hardly be convinced of their common class interest with the Polish and Russian proletariat unless they had complete confidence in the readiness of the latter to resist antisemitism. This preoccupation becomes clear in Jogiches's commentary on the Wilno speeches. It also explains his opposition to Zionism, which already then was beginning to emerge as a possible rival to the Polish socialist movement.

> The yoke which they perpetually bear as Jews could conceal from them the yoke which they suffer as workers. In a word, they could fall into a trap and perceive their chief enemies as foreign nationalities rather than the capitalist class and the Tsarist regime.

This might occur the more easily since a "patriotic" movement had arisen among Russian Jews during the past decade under the influence of the Hovevei Zion circles, which were particularly active in Wilno. Jogiches referred in some detail to the polemics of the Jewish workers against this "Palestinian" movement, as it was then called.

> The ancestors of Jewry, say the leaders of the Palestinian movement, once lived in Palestine and had their own independent State. In order to free ourselves from the persecution of the Russian government and society, we should build up our own independent Jewish State—let us go out to Palestine, let us buy land and arrange things to suit ourselves.[40]

The "Palestinophiles" had told the Jewish workers that only in their own country could they become masters of their own fate and live in freedom and material contentment. If the Jewish workers had been won over to this program, Jogiches observed, then

> the Jewish proletariat would dissociate itself from all the Polish and Russian workers. Instead of the class standpoint, it would adopt a nationalistic one and following Jewish patriotism arrive at hatred for other nationalities. The Jewish worker would hate his brothers—the Polish and Russian workers—he would feel solidarity with every Jew, even if he were a capitalist, his enemy and exploiter.[41]

It is evident from this chain of reasoning that both Jogiches and Luxemburg considered any form of Jewish ethnic solidarity as inimical to international proletarian brotherhood. This was their fundamental objection to Zionism, even before it had been given a precise political formulation by Theodor Herzl in 1896. Jogiches noted with satisfaction that the Wilno workers did not appear to have been seduced by the nationalist program of the "Palestinophiles." With approval he quoted the argument of the speakers in Wilno that they would encounter in Palestine the same social system based on exploitation as existed in the Russian Pale, and that socialism could only be built by proletarian struggle against both Russian and Jewish capitalists.

> And so our comrades understand that the rebuilding of their own State will not destroy capitalism, that the working people will continue to be the exploited and persecuted class, that freedom to use their own language will neither feed nor clothe them. As for political freedom, which is indispensable for the improvement of the workers' welfare and for the struggle against capitalism, the Jewish comrades also understand clearly that this, not the rebuilding of a utopian Jewish State, is their goal.[42]

Political freedom could only be achieved through a common struggle by *all* the nationalities of the Russian Empire against Tsarist autocracy. The fact that Jewish workers in Wilno, "notwithstanding all the national persecution and despite the patriotic agitation," had nonetheless been able to adopt a consistent class standpoint was therefore a matter of considerable importance to Jogiches, Luxemburg, and their small internationalist group. It was concrete evidence, Jogiches remarked, of "how fertile the soil in the Russian State has become for socialistic agitation, and this fills us with confidence as regards its further development in the workers' movement." Even if the "Palestinophile" movement which "recruits its few adherents chiefly among the petty bourgeoisie and a certain part of the intelligentsia" became a movement of "social-patriotic" flavor, Jogiches and Luxemburg were sure that "our comrades will certainly give a sharp retort." The class solidarity of the international proletariat "will be the answer of our Jewish comrades if the Jewish patriots would want to combine the socialist movement among their co-religionists with national aspirations."[43] On this common platform of opposition to Jewish nationalism, Jogiches welcomed the Wilno workers as "new comrades" to the "international family of the proletariat" and to the struggle against Tsarist absolutism.

One needs to remember that Leo Jogiches, Rosa Luxemburg, and the future leaders of the Bund (established in 1897) did share a *common* belief in the need for united mass action by the Russian, Polish, and Jewish proletariat. This attitude contrasted sharply with that of the PPS, which jealously guarded its independence from the Russian Social democracy while regarding the non-Russian nationalities as its closest allies. At a time when Jogiches was welcoming Jewish workers as "new comrades" of the Polish and Russian proletariat, Józef Piłsudski, the leader of the PPS (and future strongman of interwar Poland), was seeking to win them away from "Russian" influence. Piłsudski, in his appeal to Jewish social democrats in 1893, depicted antisemitism as a product of alien *Russian* domination and recalled the historic friendship between Poles and Jews. At the same time (and this complaint was constantly echoed in PPS literature before 1914) he reproached Jewish socialists for their *indifference to Polish independence* and their preferred use of the Russian language.[44]

The PPS, like Rosa Luxemburg, (but for different reasons) was opposed from the outset to the creation of a specifically Jewish organization to protect the interests of the Jewish proletariat. At the same time, it made considerable efforts to win over Jewish workers in the 1890s by sponsoring propagandist literature in Yiddish, founding a Jewish section in its own party, and even publishing Jewish newspapers (especially in Austrian-ruled Galicia). But the PPS insisted on the unconditional assimilation of Jewish workers to Polish culture and their support for the *Polish national cause*. The cosmopolitan SDKPiL rejected such Polish "chauvinism," although it, too, favored linguistic and cultural assimilation as part of its Marxist internationalism. However, unlike the PPS, it did not initially regard the emergence of the Jewish Bund in 1897 as a serious threat to its position within the general workers' movement on Polish soil. The numerically large Jewish proletariat, including some factory workers and weavers in Łódź and Warsaw as well as craftsmen and pedlars, constituted an important social stratum in Russian Poland and Lithuania. This fact was well known to the PPS, which now found itself competing with the Bund as well as SDKPiL for their support. It was particularly angered by the *Russian* orientation which the Bund shared with the SDKPiL (in 1898 the Bund had become a constituent member of the all-Russian Social Democratic Party, which it helped bring into existence). Significantly, at its Fourth Congress the PPS attacked the policy of the Bund as lacking solidarity "with the Polish and Lithuanian proletariat in the struggle for liberation from the Russian yoke."[45]

The Bund, for its part, responded at its Third Congress in 1899 by refusing support for an *independent* Poland and accused the PPS of seeking to "weaken its independence and undermine its existence."[46] The *Yidishe Arbeter* even published at this time an article by Rosa Luxemburg *against* the PPS, though it was fully aware that she was no less critical of its own separatism.[47] Still more significant, the Bund at its Fourth Congress envisaged a federal link with the SDKPiL, something that would have been inconceivable with the PPS. John Mill, one of the leaders of the Bund who maintained particularly close contacts with Leo Jogiches and Rosa Luxemburg, summarized the reasons for the Bund's negative attitude to the PPS in his memoirs:

> We, who looked upon the common struggle of all socialist and revolutionary organizations against Tsarism as the most important task. . .could not accept the distrust of the Russian socialists by the PPS, its unfounded doubts concerning the possibility of revolution in Russia, its chauvinist language.[48]

The Bund, like Rosa Luxemburg, believed that the liberation of the Jewish masses would come not through Polish independence but as a result of the victory of socialist revolution in Russia. This remained the primary reason why both the Bund and the SDKPiL sought a federal link with the Russian Social Democratic party.

The SDKPiL was periodically critical of the way in which the PPS treated the "Jewish question," especially at its Sixth Congress in 1902. A month later, an editorial in its leading theoretical review, *Przegląd Socjal-demokratyczny,* even expressed a sympathetic attitude to the Bund. It argued that this "fraternal organization" was a valuable ally in the struggle to awaken the class consciousness of Jewish workers and defended a common cause. Through the class struggle waged by the Bund, the Jewish proletariat was becoming more aware of its common interests with the Polish proletariat. In that sense the Bund was performing an indispensable function and the fact that "this assimilation must express itself in Yiddish changes nothing."[49] The editorial further observed: "Without the Bund the Polish proletariat would not have such a valuable partner in the struggle as it now possesses in the Jewish proletariat." At the same time the SDKPiL, while recognizing the Bund as an "independent fraternal organization" and the "sole class organization of the proletariat," rejected its viewpoint on several key issues. This included the crucial question of whether the Russian Empire should be transformed into a federation of nationalities—which led to the rift between the Bund and the Bolshevik faction of the Russian Social Democratic Party led by Lenin. There was also an unbridgeable difference between the position of the SDKPiL and the Bund on the Jewish national problem.

It was no accident that in 1892 Leo Jogiches had ignored references to *the Jewish nation* and its history of glorious martyrdom made by Jewish proletarians in Wilno.[50] But by the late 1890s the *national* component in the Jewish workers' movement was clearly beginning to crystallize. Julius Martov, in a famous speech in May 1895 that has often been seen as the founding charter of Bundism, even described the national "indifference" of the Jewish masses as a hindrance to the awakening of their class consciousness.[51] Martov, the future leader of Menshevism (the moderate wing of Russian Social Democracy), urged at the time the need to stamp a definite "Jewish" character on the workers' movement and to create a specifically Jewish socialist organization. The Jewish proletariat had a national as well as a social role in the struggle for obtaining equal rights for Russian Jewry. It should no more rely on the Russian and Polish proletariat than it could depend on the Jewish bourgeoisie to secure the national rights of the Jewish masses.

The SDKPiL (like the German, Austrian, and Russian Social Democrats) appreciated the services of the Bund in so far as it *opposed* Orthodox Judaism, Hebrew culture, and especially Zionism. It was even sympathetic to the Bund in so far as it was subjected to PPS attacks for its alleged role as an agent of "Russification." It was willing to praise the contribution of the Bund to fostering class consciousness among Jewish workers, within certain limits. But as we have seen, it could not abide the championing of Jewish proletarian nationalism in the name of socialist ideals. Rosa Luxemburg, in particular, hoped that Polish Jewry would become far less separatist in its way of life and that Jewish workers would completely merge into the Polish proletariat. This program clearly entailed the abandonment of Jewish customs and national festivals as well as the adoption of the Polish language and culture. In this respect, the positions held by Luxemburg, Jogiches, or Warski were not so dissimilar from those of orthodox German and Russian Marxists. Significantly, in 1903, when the SDKPiL was seeking a rapprochement with the RSDRP (Russian Social Democratic Workers' Party), it began to condemn the Bund more strongly for its "separatism." The Bund was duly criticized for failing to see that the closest unity of the proletariat of *all* nationalities in the Russian Empire must always be the priority goal.

Although Rosa Luxemburg disagreed with Lenin's ultra-centralist, monolithic concept of party organization, and negotiations for a merger with RSDRP broke down over Bolshevik insistence on the principle of national self-determination, the SDKPiL's criticism of "Bundist nationalism" was remarkably similar to Lenin.[52] Neither Luxemburg, Jogiches, or Warski had ever been willing to recognize the Jews as a separate national group, although the issue had not come to a head before 1903. Rosa Luxemburg would certainly have agreed with Lenin's assessment in February 1903 that the autonomy provided under the rules establishing the Russian Social Democratic party in 1898 gave the Jewish working class all it needed. Lenin accepted the need for "propaganda and agitation in Yiddish, its own literature and congresses" as well as:

> the right to advance separate demands, to supplement a single general Social-Democratic programme and to satisfy local needs and requirements arising out of the special feature of Jewish life. In everything else there must be complete fusion with the Russian proletariat, in the interests of the struggle waged by the entire proletariat of Russia.[53]

Luxemburg did not object to Lenin's *condemnation* of the Bund for seeking the "complete separation and demarcation of the Jewish and non-Jewish proletariat of Russia." This was a Bundist policy which the Polish Social Democrats also considered would lead to division and the dismemberment of the working-class movement. As Lenin, Martov, and Trotsky vigorously argued at the 1903 Congress of the RSDRP, the Bund's separatism implied the suspicion that the Social-Democratic convictions of the Russian party were not completely sincere. There was, however, a double standard in the fact that Rosa Luxemburg and the SDKPiL were prepared to advocate the Bund's complete *subordination* to the centralized control of the Russian party. For one of the chief reasons that the SDKPiL itself refused to merge with Lenin's Bolsheviks was that its élite group disliked the hierarchical structure and rigid discipline which the Russians had sought to impose.[54] Rosa Luxemburg, one of the sternest critics of Lenin's bureaucratic ultra-centralism in organizational matters, was herself allergic to the kind of disciplined subordination to all-Russian interests she was advocating for the Bund.

The political attitude of the SDKPiL was moderated by its antagonism to PPS chauvinism in respect of which the Bund was still a potential ally.[55] Thus Rosa Luxemburg could afford to adopt a position of benevolent neutrality when the Bundists accused the PPS of inflaming antisemitism among Polish workers. The PPS resented the influx of Lithuanian Jews ("Litvaks") into the Kingdom of Poland and the extension of the Bund's influence among Jewish craftsmen, apprentices, and workers in Warsaw and Łódź. It continued to regard the Bund as an agent of "Russification" and even accused it of being a tool of the Jewish bourgeoisie and of the Russian Tsar. Rosa Luxemburg did sympathize with the Bund's indignation at these charges, the more so as similar accusations had been flung by PPS leaders against her own party.[56] In reviewing a Bund pamphlet against the PPS in April 1903, she pointed out, however, that the Bund's defensive nationalism was itself the reverse side of the aggressive chauvinism espoused by the PPS. She warned, as always, that every nationalism, whether bourgeois or socialist, would ultimately adopt an exclusivist or hegemonic attitude to minorities in its midst.

Rosa Luxemburg remained relentlessly critical of the Bund's self-assertiveness as a specifically Jewish organization which claimed to defend the national rights of Jewish workers as well as their class interests. She could never accept that the cultural and linguistic peculiarities of the Jewish proletariat or its special "national psychology" might justify the separatist approach of the Bund. In particular, Luxemburg opposed the Bund's position that there was any need to defend the national rights of Russian Jewry if it was to achieve full civic equality. The achievement of civil rights was an issue affecting the Russian and Polish proletariat no less than the Jewish workers. Hence with the abolition of the Pale of Settlement and the establishment of a democratic Russian republic, the raison d'être of an organization like the Bund would fade into obscurity.[57] Its only real justification was in the sphere of local agitation and propaganda among the Jewish masses in the Yiddish language. This was an area in which the Bund had indeed achieved "excellent results." But this was also a historical situation that would inevitably disappear.

Rosa Luxemburg's standpoint was echoed in June 1903 by her close associate Adolf Warski (later assassinated in the Stalinist purges of 1938), who had written to the leading theoretician of the SPD, Karl Kautsky, requesting advice. Warski urged Kautsky to write an article for the SDKPiL theoretical organ, *Przegląd Socjaldemokratyczny* (Social Democratic Review) on antisemitism and the tasks of Social Democracy, "in the wake of the recent dreadful massacre in Kishinev."[58] The SDKPiL feared that the latest pogroms instigated by the Tsarist autocracy in places like Kishinev, might divert the Polish and Russian workers away from the revolutionary movement and incite them against the Jewish population. Tsarist antisemitism had already caused an influx of "Litvaks" into Russian Poland and thereby aroused nationalistic feelings against these "alien" immigrants. "The issue has even greater significance for Polish social democracy because the bulk of the Jewish population lives in Russian Poland and Lithuania, as a result of laws which forbid them to settle in other parts of Russia."[59] The Kishinev pogroms, Warski pointed out, also had the effect of reinforcing the "isolationist" tendencies among Jewish workers and especially the national program of the Bund.

> The Bund has, for example, created a superior organization, thereby bringing much enlightenment and still more revolutionary enthusiasm to the Jewish working class, by means of Yiddish (*Jargon*) and its knowledge of Jewish life in general. But at the same time, ever more nationalistically inclined, the Bund has increasingly demonstrated the tendency towards separate party organization and the separatist removal of the Jewish working masses from the working class as a whole in the Empire and its provinces.[60]

Warski, like Luxemburg, was concerned about the impact of this trend on the united proletarian front against Russian Tsarism. "Now we fear that the recent pogroms will drive the Bund further in the same separatist direction, thanks to its theoretical confusion, though it is more than ever necessary to bind the Jewish working masses firmly to the Russian and Polish [proletariat]." Warski informed Karl Kautsky that the SDKPiL had itself issued a proclamation to the Polish workers after the Kishinev massacre, denouncing Tsarist antisemitism and calling on them "to defend the Jewish population." But this appeal was made more difficult by the Bund's exasperating insistence that it alone could defend the national interests of Jewish workers.

> Recently we have got to the point (as have our Russian comrades) that in every town we have two party organizations—Polish (or Russian) and national-Jewish—which can only complicate the tasks of social democracy with respect to antisemitism. Quite apart from the question of whether the Jews are really a nation and have a national future in Russia—as the Bund asserts—the

> problem of party organizations and the relation of the Jewish workers to the working class as a whole—must be solved according to common interests—and not according to burning national interests.[61]

Kautsky was much more sympathetic to the Bund than either Warski, Rosa Luxemburg, or Lenin. He responded to Warski by writing "The Kishinev massacre and the Jewish Question," which he promptly published in the *Neue Zeit* (the leading German Marxist journal) in 1903.[62] It also appeared in *Przegląd Socjaldemokratyczny* and in Lenin's *Iskra*, becoming a classic statement of the Marxist assimilationist position on the Jewish problem before 1914. Kautsky's immense prestige as the guardian of German Marxist orthodoxy assured his views an immediate influence. It was no accident that he did not mention the Bund in the course of the article. His polemic was primarily directed against the Tsarist autocracy (and the diversionary role of Zionism), though the implications of his line of argument could also be used against the Bund. Indeed, both the Russian and Polish Social Democrats interpreted Kautsky's article as clear disapproval of any "separatist" tendencies in the Jewish community and within the all-Russian labor movement. In a letter to Kautsky, Rosa Luxemburg reported with satisfaction that Warski was "highly delighted" with his Kishinev article.[63]

Although Rosa Luxemburg never drew any crude parallel between Bundism and Zionism as twin forms of "Jewish separatism," such as was made by Plekhanov, Trotsky, or Lenin, she undoubtedly shared their view that assimilation was the only "progressive" solution to the Jewish national problem. Any concessions to nationalism could only delay the advent of socialism and retard the class struggle. Antisemitism was not a specifically "Jewish problem," necessitating a special struggle, but only one of a whole range of social problems created by capitalist society and the maneuvers of the counter-revolution. As she put it in her vigorous polemic against the "progressive" Polish intelligentsia in Warsaw, written in 1910:

> for the followers of Marx, as for the working class, *the Jewish question as such does not exist,* just as the "Negro question" or the "Yellow Peril" does not exist. From the standpoint of the working class, the Jewish question. . .is a question of *racial hatred as a symptom* of social *reaction,* which to a certain extent is an indivisible part of all societies based on class antagonism.[64]

Only the radical transformation of the capitalist system through socialist revolution would solve the "Jewish Question" along with other manifestations of racism.

Where Rosa Luxemburg most sharply differed from the Bund was over its insistence on regarding the Jews as a distinct *national* entity with a right to full cultural autonomy. In this respect her position was similar to that of Karl Kautsky, Otto Bauer, and Lenin. Referring in 1910 to an SDKPiL polemic against the Bundist theoretician Bronisław Grosser, Luxemburg made it clear that she considered the long-term prospects for an *independent* Jewish culture in Poland to be hopeless:

> The separateness of the Jewish nationality is based in Russia and Poland on the socially backward petty-bourgeois small-scale production, on petty commerce, life in small towns and close links with the religious element. As a consequence, the separate Jewish consciousness which is supposed to be the basis of extra-territorial Jewish autonomy displays itself not through a separate bourgeois metropolitan culture—but through small-town lack of culture. All the efforts to develop a Jewish culture through the initiative of a number of Yiddish publicists and translators are futile. The only manifestation of a truly modern culture on a Jewish foundation is the Social Democratic movement of the Jewish proletariat. By its very nature, this movement can least of all replace the historical lack of a Jewish bourgeois-national culture. . . .[65]

It is clear from this passage that a key argument of Rosa Luxemburg against Bundist advocates of extra-territorial Jewish autonomy in Russian Poland was that the Jews had no *bourgeois national culture*. The "peculiarity" and irredeemable weakness of the Jewish nationality in Poland was rooted, above all, in East European small-town life. The material basis of economic existence in the shtetl was simply too narrow to perpetuate a separate and "historically backward" nationality. Its demise was therefore inevitable given the "socially backward, petty-bourgeois production and petty-commerce" of small-town life. Like most international Marxists, Luxemburg undoubtedly expected the "Jewish nationality" to be extinguished by the growth of industrial capitalism in Eastern Europe. No more than Kautsky or Otto Bauer could she imagine that its disappearance would be the result of a state-organized mass murder initiated by the German National Socialists twenty years after her own assassination in Berlin.

It is hardly surprising that Luxemburg opposed Zionism, though this was far more marginal to her concerns than Bundism. As we have seen, since the early 1890s she and Leo Jogiches had been aware of "social-patriotic" tendencies in the Jewish labor movement in Russia. This embryonic national yearning for Zion was soon shrugged off as being of marginal importance. But Luxemburg did not change her tone two decades later when the Zionists were on the verge of achieving the Balfour Declaration and official British recognition for a Jewish *national* home in Palestine. With scarcely disguised contempt she wrote in 1916 of "nations and nationlets on all sides giving notice of their right to form states." She derided "the rotting corpses" which "climb out of century-old graves filled with a new spring" and the "history-less peoples who never before formed self-determining commonwealths [and] who now feel a passionate urge to form states. Her blacklist of "rotting corpses" included Poles, Ukrainians, Lithuanians, Czechs, Yugoslavs, "and ten new nations of the Caucasus." The final barb was aimed at the Zionists who "are already establishing their Palestine-ghetto, for the present in Philadelphia."[66]

Luxemburg's attitude to antisemitism was rather more complex, for it involved partly suppressed emotional factors as well as general ideological and political principles. On one occasion she quoted Marx's "Zur Judenfrage" at some length in a polemic against "leftist" Polish antisemites. They had claimed inspiration for their racial doctrines from the founding fathers of socialism. Luxemburg, , was, however adamant that Marx

> for the first time [had] removed the Jewish question from the religious and racial sphere and given it a *social* foundation, proving that what is usually described and persecuted as "Judaism," is nothing *but the spirit of huckstering and swindle*, which appears in *every* society, where *exploitation* reigns.[67]

Like most socialists, she felt obliged to defend Marx, inferring that he had proved "that Jewish emancipation is above all an emancipation of society from *this* 'Judaism'—meaning the *abolition of exploitation*."[68] However, she did not fundamentally challenge the validity of any socialist making such a prejudiced equation between "Judaism" and capitalism in the first place.

In reply to her Polish "progressive" adversaries, Rosa Luxemburg declared that Marxism rejected any attempt to mystify concepts such as "nation" and "race."[69] International social democracy, she pointed out, divided the world into "two nations"—the exploiters and the exploited, as well as two religions—those of capital and labor. The antisemites, by contrast, argued that the nation was a *homogeneous* racial entity which existed above and beyond the class-struggle. This, she claimed, was nothing but a mythical nationalist fiction which had no "scientific" foundation. Rosa Luxemburg emphasized instead that Marxism regarded antisemitism as a specific pathology of *bourgeois* society, not as an independent issue. It was a typical manifestation of social reaction in a class-divided society.[70] The logic of this analysis was that "only a fundamental transformation of the capitalist system could ultimately eliminate the radical attacks on "Jewry."[71] Rosa Luxemburg conceded, however, that there was also another dimension to the problem in Russia—namely, the "civil equality of the Jews." But, in her view, this was simply "*one of a thousand social tasks,* whose only common solution one must seek elsewhere."[72]

From a Marxist standpoint, the "Jewish Question" as a social problem was no different in kind for Rosa Luxemburg than other issues such as education, the emancipation of women (which she refused to treat separately), the nationalities' conflict, or regional autonomy. Such questions were the result of a backward "political system" which could only be resolved by a proletarian revolution, carried out by all the oppressed nationalities in the Russian Empire. Rosa Luxemburg argued that to place the "Jewish Question" in the center of political discussion would be to fall victim to a classic maneuver of the Polish and Russian counter-revolution.[73] The aim of the antisemites was to divert attention from genuine class and political antagonisms, to paralyze the mass movement of the proletariat and mobilize the counter-revolutionary "scum of society." Herself unmistakably Jewish in appearance, sharply polemical and a constant target for antisemites in Poland and Germany, she could speak here with some authority. The antisemitic Polish "free-thinking" intelligentsia openly reviled her cosmopolitan SDKPiL as a standard-bearer of *anti-patriotism,* and a symbol of the "anti-goyism" of the Jews. Andrzej Niemojewski, one of her most virulent detractors in Poland, wrote in his *Mysl Niepodlegla* (Independent thoughts) in 1910, "As all Jews hate non-Jews, so Luxemburg's Social Democrats have a passionate hatred for Poland."[74]

The PPS papers *Naprzód* (Forward) and *Przedświt* (Dawn) were not slow in seizing their cue from Niemojewski, asserting that the SDKPiL served the "Jewish" and not the proletarian interest. Julian Unszlicht (Sedecki) and Emil Haecker led a scurrilous campaign in the PPS press against Rosa Luxemburg and her party, whom they consistently accused of seeking to "russify" Poland.[75] Sedecki openly blamed her, as well as the Bund, for "Social-Litvakism"—a pejorative reference to the overrunning of Poland by Lithuanian Jews, with their "alien" customs.[76] Rosa Luxemburg, in a series of stinging articles for the SDKPiL organ *Młot* (The hammer) in November 1910, hit back with fury at these and other antisemitic slurs, concentrating her fire against the Polish "progressive" press. She lashed out at the "mongrel" and "half-wit" Niemojewski, who symbolized to her the profound moral decay of the Polish bourgeoisie in the aftermath of the 1905 Revolution. She concluded that the political purpose of such slanders was twofold: to make the Jews a scapegoat for the growing influence of socialism, and to settle accounts with the Polish workers for the wave of strikes in 1905. She characterized the anti-Jewish campaign in the Warsaw press as a "literary pogrom," morally even more despicable than the primitive violence promoted by Vladimir Purishkevitch and the Russian Black Hundred gangs.[77] It was unforgivable that the cream of the Polish intelligentsia in Warsaw had given "free rein to their zoological instincts." Like the Russian Black Hundreds, the Polish "progressives" claimed to be against the "Jewish revolutionaries" rather than opposed to the Jews as such. But, as Rosa Luxemburg sarcastically pointed out, it was "in any case impossible to maintain strict order among the pogromist bands."[78]

The "progressive" campaign aimed to unite the whole of bourgeois society in one camp, by preaching that Jews were the enemies of the Polish nation. Luxemburg added that:

> Antisemitism has become the common platform of the Endek realists, the "Christian," clerical Reaction and the "progressive" free-thinkers—the common banner of political backwardness and cultural barbarism.[79]

The social and material foundation of this "intellectual" alliance with barbarism was a common hatred of the proletarian class-enemy. The "hooligan" elements of Polish progressivism had taken the lead in spreading the "bestial cretinism" of Black Hundred antisemitic propaganda to mask their surrender to clerical and nationalist reaction in Poland. The sheer passion and virulence of Luxemburg's language in answering the "zoological antisemitism" of Niemojewski and his followers was quite stunning. It was all the more noteworthy since like many Jewish revolutionaries, she had tried so hard *not* to make a special case out of antisemitism.[80] Moreover, in contrast to her denunciation of the literary "pogrom" in Warsaw, she had relatively little to say about the Russian pogroms themselves or their effect on the Jewish population. The SDKPiL had, of course, deplored the Kishinev pogrom of 1903 as well as the smaller-scale violence on Polish soil. Rosa Luxemburg and Adolf Warski did immediately appeal to Polish workers to rally to their Jewish comrades. But at the same time, as we have seen, they stepped up their criticism of the Bund's "separatism," even mobilizing Karl

Kautsky for the cause. Kautsky, however, chose to focus more on the Zionists than on the Bund in criticizing trends towards Jewish "isolation."

It is remarkable that Rosa Luxemburg, despite her defense of oppressed minorities like the Armenians and Poles in Germany or her robust denunciation of Polish "literary" antisemites, never expressed any genuine empathy for the Jewish victims of the Russian pogroms.[81] This fact is all the more striking when contrasted with the notable outrage which the pogroms provoked in other Marxist socialists like Lenin, Trotsky, Bebel, and Kautsky or in Russian intellectuals such as Leo Tolstoy and Maxim Gorky. Since Luxemburg regarded the Tsarist regime with no less hostility, one can only assume that she was publicly incapable of displaying any feelings of *personal* identification with the sufferings of the Jewish people. Her single reference to the Black Hundred massacres in a pamphlet entitled *Co Dalej?* (What next?) in 1906 would be difficult to surpass in its cold, analytical detachment. It reads more like a mathematical equation than an account of the murderous barbarism of the Russian *pogromschiki*.

> The Jewish pogroms, the most important method of attack by absolutism in the first phase of the Revolution, have already become a worn-out and useless weapon. Their only consistent result was to compromise Tsarism abroad. In Russia itself, and in Poland, the triggering-off of pogroms was already impossible wherever there existed enlightened and revolutionary workers. Jew-baiting was already an impossibility in Poland, [Saint] Petersburg, Moscow, Riga, in all the important centers of the Revolution. It is still possible only in small remote villages in Southern Russia and Bessarabia—namely, where the revolutionary movement is weak or non-existent. In short, pogroms are only possible where they are not needed, and impossible there where they should serve as a tool against the Revolution.[82]

Apart from the questionnable analysis, this emotionally dry comment exemplified Rosa Luxemburg's evident determination not to single out "Jewish" victims as deserving anything but marginal attention. Like not a few Jewish Marxists, she exhibited a curious mental block when it came to speaking concretely about *real* pogroms. In this respect she was very different from Leon Trotsky. Luxemburg was, however, remarkably prescient in her *political* criticism of Lenin and Trotsky after November 1917 for having established a narrow, dictatorial regime in Bolshevik Russia in which the bureaucracy would remain the only active element, once all opposition had been suppressed. "Public life," she prophetically remarked, "gradually falls asleep." A small number of "leaders of inexhaustible energy and boundless experience direct and rule. . . . A dictatorship to be sure; not the dictatorship of the proletariat, however, but only a dictatorship of a handful of politicians in the bourgeois sense. . . ."[83] The dictatorship of the proletariat, Luxemburg added, consisted "of the way one applies democracy and not in its abolition." The Bolsheviks had imposed rule by terror and a "democracy from above" which could only demoralize the masses. For freedom, as Luxemburg pungently put it, "is always freedom for the one who thinks differently." Yet this admirable insight was never consistently applied by her to the "Jewish question," antisemitism or to the nationality conflicts that were mushrooming throughout Europe and in the colonies.

Rosa Luxemburg was especially evasive with regard to antisemitism in Imperial Germany and Western Europe. True, she did follow events in France during the Dreyfus Affair with careful attention, beginning with a series of short, unsigned articles in the *Sächsische Arbeiterzeitung* (Dresden) in the summer of 1898.[84] These reports, based on material supplied to her by Leo Jogiches and Boris Krichevsky, were unconditionally pro-Dreyfusard and warmly supported the crusade of the French socialist leader Jean Jaurès for the rehabilitation of Alfred Dreyfus. Rosa Luxemburg praised his "energetic campaign against the clerico-military oligarchy" and his vehement condemnation of the "nationalist virus" spread by populist antisemites like Rochefort and Drumont.[85] But this was virtually the only allusion that she made in her analyses to the virulent anti-Jewish offensive in France being waged by the anti-Dreyfusard forces. This is all the more remarkable since racist and Catholic antisemitism was a central issue in France during the Dreyfus Affair. It was also a cause of serious dissension on the French Left which climaxed with the entry of moderate socialist Alexandre Millerand into a "bourgeois" government of "Republican defence" in 1899.

In her often perceptive articles on the events in France, written for the *Neue Zeit,* Luxemburg scarcely mentioned anything of concern to Jews.[86] Only in her reply to an international questionnaire sponsored by Jaurès's paper *La Petite République* in 1899 did Luxemburg list antisemitism in passing as one of "four social factors" (alongside militarism, clericalism, and chauvinism) which gave the Dreyfus Affair "the mark of a question involving the class-struggle."[87] Nevertheless, she saw no reason to deviate from her general policy of submerging it completely under other social and political issues. Rosa Luxemburg considered it to be a socialist obligation to intervene in the Dreyfus Affair, not because Dreyfus was a Jewish officer victimized by the French Army or even because he was the victim of a gross miscarriage of justice, but solely because the working class movement needed to challenge the arrogance of the militarist clique in France. By waging a firm campaign against "militarism, clericalism, nationalism and antisemitism," the socialists would be able to strengthen proletarian class-consciousness. However, by the end of 1899, when the political situation changed, she sharply rejected Jaurès's tactics of class-collaboration with the radical bourgeoisie, which had flowed logically from his involvement in the Affair. Luxemburg was now convinced that the orthodox French Marxists had been right all along to emphasize the primacy of proletarian class interests and to avoid any entanglement in a bourgeois government. Once she reversed her attitude to the strategy of Jaurès, the Dreyfus Affair only interested her as a stick with which to beat the hell out of the "revisionists" of Marxism in both France and Germany.

It is therefore misleading to imply that "she felt particularly concerned by the struggle against antisemitism" as a Jewess.[88] The evidence suggests precisely the opposite. Nor was Luxemburg's reluctance to discuss antisemitism in France and Germany due to any lack of provocation since Rosa Luxemburg was well aware "of the peculiar reception" which she and "other non-Germans" had received in the SPD almost from the outset. She had arrived in Berlin on 12 May 1898 (having obtained German citizenship by a sham marriage) and henceforth her main political aim was to become a force in German party affairs. The SPD was the leading socialist party of the Second International, and it was from its left wing that she sought to influence international socialism. Although the SPD had a reasonably creditable record in combating antisemitism, the reaction to Rosa Luxemburg in the more conservative circles of the party was frankly xenophobic, displaying a scarcely disguised hostility to her personality and politics. Some of this criticism was antisemitically tinged, although this was by no means the only prejudice to which she was subject. As an ambitious woman, an ultra-revolutionary and an "Easterner," the odds were already stacked against her. Her meteoric rise in the party, her passionate temperament, intellectual superiority and biting sarcasm—allied to her indelible "foreignness"—ensured that she would make enemies.

It would be mistaken to imagine, as her biographer Peter Nettl once implied, that the response she provoked was a "matter of indifference" to someone as sensitive as Rosa Luxemburg.[89] Unconsciously it probably reinforced her anti-Establishment position within the Social-Democratic party, and the acidity with which she answered political opponents. In a letter to Leo Jogiches, nearly a year after her arrival in Berlin, she gave vent to her frustration at the way she was being treated by the party executive. Quoting a Polish antisemitic proverb, she remarked, "*Jak bieda to do żyda, po biedzie precz zydie*" ("to the Jews for help—and when it is over, away with you, Jews").[90] This bitter comment certainly did not reflect any positive Jewish identification in Rosa Luxemburg. She always preferred to stress her Polishness far more than her Jewish identity in the Second Reich in order to to differentiate herself from the German comrades, many of whom she evidently disliked.[91] The remark therefore testified more to her feeling of being an outsider in the SPD, which could only have been strengthened by allusions to her origin, made by her opponents on the right wing of the party. By throwing herself into the "revisionist" controversy in 1898 and becoming the spearhead of revolutionary Marxism against the social-reformist theories of Eduard Bernstein, she undoubtedly provoked intense resentment, even if these polemics proved to be the springboard to her celebrity.

At the Party Congresses of 1898 and 1899 Luxemburg had unmercifully flayed Wolfgang Heine as a scapegoat for the absent Bernstein, and admonished the German trade unions in a dismissive manner for their "Sisyphus-work" in the class-struggle.[92] Her insistence on the *final* aims of socialism and support for militant strike-agitation also alienated the moderate Bavarian wing of the party: they particularly resented the intellectual superiority and tactlessness of this impulsive woman and "foreigner," with her sharp, lecturing tone. The powerful trade union bureaucracy also lashed back at the ultra-leftist intellectual gadfly from the East who downplayed their organizational achievements and chided them with quotations from Marx. Resentment towards Frau Dr. Luxemburg and even more against her fellow Russian Jewish émigré, Alexander Israel Helphand (Parvus), increased as the "revisionist" controversy stirred up passions in the German party. Shortly before the Lübeck Congress of 1901 the German socialist leader Bebel wrote to Karl Kautsky,

> You cannot imagine the animosity against Parvus and also La Rosa in the Party, and even if I am not of the opinion that we should be guided by such prejudices, we cannot at the same time afford to ignore them completely.[93]

The barrage of angry criticism directed at Rosa Luxemburg and Parvus during the Lübeck Congress confirmed this judgment. The "new arrivals from the East" were angrily attacked by Richard Fischer, business manager of *Vorwärts*, as a pair of "literary ruffians," intolerant of any criticism.[94] Wolfgang Heine, a leading supporter of Bernstein's revisionism, declared that the "Russian and Polish Jews" by their tactless statements had abused

German hospitality.[95] He suggested that their behavior had "made the struggle against antisemitism more difficult," and had strained the internationalism of the SPD to its limits. He even compared the behavior of Parvus and Rosa Luxemburg to that of guests who "come to us and spit in our parlor." The mood of other delegates reflected a growing Russophobic and antisemitic undercurrent in the German party. Only Clara Zetkin rose to defend the absent Rosa and Parvus as "party comrades" who "stand with us for the same program and share our struggles."[96]

Though Rosa Luxemburg was not present when the personal attacks were made against her, she was far from indifferent to such personal slurs. In a letter to Kautsky—who had refused to publish her reply to Richard Fischer in the *Neue Zeit*—she upbraided him for personal cowardice and gave vent to her wounded feelings.

> Well, I am sickened at the thought of having to insist upon rights if these are only to be granted amid sighs and gnashing of teeth, when people not only grab me by the arm and thus expect me to "defend" myself, but try in addition to beat me to a pulp, in the hope that I may thus be persuaded to renounce my rights.[97]

But Luxemburg chose *not* to engage either privately or publicly with the xenophobia, antisemitism, or misogynistic comments directed at her in Imperial Germany. In public debate, she tried to remain outwardly "impervious" to the blatant aspersions on her womanhood and ethnic origins which she had to endure in the SPD and outside it. She generally presented such assaults as proof that, politically, her opponents had a weak case. This may have been partly true. But it is nonetheless revealing that she made so few allusions in her voluminous German writings or in her private correspondence to the widespread antisemitism in Imperial Germany.[98] The contrast between her silence on this issue and the very public *anti-antisemitism* of Bebel, Wilhelm Liebknecht, Bernstein, or Kautsky is noteworthy.

In 1905, when she sought to draw more general lessons from the Russian Revolution for the benefit of the German working class, the campaign against "bloody Rosa" in the bourgeois press took on a more openly antisemitic coloring. Repellent caricatures of her and other prominent Jewish members of the SPD like Paul Singer and Arthur Stadthagen, now appeared under captions insinuating a conspiracy of "The Great Sanhedrin."[99] Her physical imperfections were grossly accentuated, and long-nosed "Rosa with the snout" was depicted as being the center of this "Semitic" plot, in the rabid style later adopted by *Der Stürmer*.[100]

The conservative and antisemitic press called for the expulsion from Germany of this subversive Polish Jewess and "vagrant" revolutionary. Even in the SPD, her emphasis on the need for mass strikes was earning her growing notoriety; while in German "revisionist" circles she was regarded as a "Russian patriot" following her enthusiastic praise for the 1905 Russian revolution.[101] Gustav Noske, the SPD expert on military and naval affairs, felt a particular and scarcely disguised antipathy towards this déclassé Easterner, who had stepped forward, as he put it, to "instruct the German proletariat." In his memoirs, published in 1947, Noske insisted that it had "nothing to do with antisemitism" when he observed that East European Jewish Marxists in the SPD had a special gift for "transforming socialism into a dogma and platitudes into articles of faith.[102] Noske sarcastically claimed that the East European Jews had evolved a "secret science" of Marxism, which "remained incomprehensible to the German workers."[103] Like some other right-wing socialists in the SPD, he obviously resented the presence of cosmopolitan Jewish revolutionaries in the German party, who appeared to have won the confidence of its centrist leadership. He clearly felt that their moral pathos, vibrant internationalism, and self-proclaimed rootlessness in the name of the Revolution was completely "alien" to the average German party functionary preoccupied with real everyday issues.

In 1919, when Noske became people's commissar for military affairs in the new Socialist Government, Rosa Luxemburg and Karl Liebknecht were brutally murdered by *Freikorps* officers, called in to quell the Communist-led Spartacist revolt. Whether he was directly complicit in her execution is not certain, but Noske did nothing to stop his henchmen carrying it out. Luxemburg, as co-founder of the *Spartakusbund* and of the fledgling German Communist Party (KPD), had only reluctantly gone along with the Spartacus-led workers' uprising in Berlin in January 1919. According to Captain Waldemar Pabst, who was personally responsible for carrying out her assassination, the original intention was that Luxemburg should be murdered pogrom-style by a furious mob. Elżbieta Ettinger puts it even more starkly: "Liebknecht was to be shot—he was a German. The mob murder was reserved for Luxemburg—she, a Jew, should perish in a pogrom."[104] The killing was carried out in the end by the same ultranationalist paramilitary organization from which Hitler's Storm Troops would soon find some of their most promising recruits. Luxemburg's battered body would be summarily thrown into Berlin's Landwehr Canal.[105]

Within two years the German military and far Right fanatics had deliberately murdered a significant number of leading Socialists of Jewish origin including Leo Jogiches, Hugo Haase, Kurt Eisner, Eugen Leviné, and Gustav Landauer. In 1922, the highly assimilated, conservative Foreign Minister and Prussian patriot, Walter Rathenau—from a leading Jewish industrialist family—would also be killed by far Right radicals who believed him to be one of the "Elders of Zion." The murder of Rosa Luxemburg was thus a disaster and a major turning-point for what was to come in the freshly-minted and ill-fated Weimar Republic. It irrevocably poisoned the relationship between the German Social Democrats (who were held responsible for the deaths of Luxemburg and Karl Liebknecht) and the Communists. The resulting fratricidal hatred and disunity on the Left made Hitler's Nazi triumph fourteen years later that much easier to achieve.

Rosa Luxemburg, like Karl Marx and Leon Trotsky, to the bitter end would fail to understand the driving power of modern nationalism. The First World War had conclusively demonstrated the falsity of Marx's slogan in the *Communist Manifesto* that "the workers have no fatherland." Luxemburg's own utopian dream of a revolutionary "proletarian" democracy was also buried in the carnage of the trenches and the Bolshevik terror after 1918. None of the 20th-century revolutions which brought Communists to power—whether in Russia, China, Vietnam, or various other Third World societies, could have happened without harnessing nationalism to the proletarian cause. The establishment of Israel in 1948 was yet another nail in the coffin of the Luxemburgist negation of the right to national self-determination. Rosa Luxemburg's last article in *Rote Fahne* (January 1919), entitled "Order reigns in Berlin," acknowledged the "temporary" defeat of Spartacus and of the German Revolution. A message of defiant millennial hope nonetheless lit up the debacle as if echoing across the centuries some strange Yahwist incantation:

> "Order rules in Berlin!" You stupid lackeys! Your "order" is built on sand. Tomorrow the revolution will rear its head once more and announce to your horror amid the brass of trumpets: "I was, I am, I shall always be!"[106]

NOTES

1. See Israel Getzler, "Martov ve-Luxemburg. Internationalistim Yehudim" in *Yehudim be-Tnuot mehapkhaniot* (Jews in revolutionary movements), edited by Eli Shaltiel (Jerusalem, 1982), 119–24.

2. Peter Nettl, *Rosa Luxemburg* (London, 1969), abridged edition, 500–19.

3. Rosa Luxemburg, *Die industrielle Entwicklung Polens* (Ph.D. diss., Leipzig, 1898) developed these economic arguments at considerable length.

4. Lenin, "Critical Remarks on the National Question" (1913; in Russian), in *Sochineniya,* 4th ed., 35 volumes (Moscow, 1941–50), 20: 1–34.

5. Lenin, "On the right of nations to self-determination," in *Sochineniya,* 20: 400.

6. Rosa Luxemberg, *Die Krise der Sozialdemokratie* (Zurich, 1916). This short book by Rosa Luxemburg—published under the pseudonym Junius—later appeared in the English collection of her *Selected Works,* vol. 1. It was a violent rejection of the official German Social Democratic Party's position on World War I. See Nettl, *Rosa Luxemburg,* 505.

7. Rosa Luxemburg, "The question of nationality and autonomy," *Przegląd Socjaldemokratyczny,* no. 6 (Aug. 1908), reproduced in *Wybór Pism,* edited by Bronisław Krauze (Warsaw, 1959), 2: 114–66.

8. Ibid., 147–48.

9. Rosa Luxemburg, *Briefe an Freunde,* edited by Benedikt Kautsky (Hamburg, 1950), 48–49.

10. Quoted by Nettl, *Rosa Luxemburg,* 518.

11. Judd Teller, *Scapegoat of Revolution* (New York, 1954), 164.

12. Ibid., 165.

13. See Elżbieta Ettinger, *Rosa Luxemburg: A Life* (London, 1988), 14–15.

14. Rosa Luxemburg, *Briefe an Karl und Luise Kautsky,* ed. Luise Kautsky (Berlin, 1923), 181.

15. Ettinger, *Rosa Luxemburg,* 15.

16. Stephen Eric Bronner, *A Revolutionary For Our Times: Rosa Luxemburg* (London, 1981), claims that the Luxemburg family "had no ties to the strong and cultured community of the town," thereby exemplifying "the cosmopolitan attitudes of 'enlightened' Jewry." This is somewhat overstated. Like earlier Marxist biographers, Bronner is too eager to adjust Luxemburg's family background in a "progressive" direction.

17. Jack Jacobs, *On Socialists and the Jewish Question after Marx* (New York, 1992), 71–85.

18. See ibid., 75–76. Also Ettinger, *Rosa Luxemburg,*, 303–4, 316–17.

19. See the appendix to Ettinger, *Rosa Luxemberg* (p. 311) for Józef's letter, dated 30 October 1897.

20. Ibid., 316.

21. Avraham Bick (Shauli), *Merosh Tsurim* (From the lofty heights), (Jerusalem, 1972). The subtitle is *Metaknei Chevra al Taharat Hakodesh Shalshelet Hayichusim shel Avot Hasotsialism* (Social reformers in the spirit of sanctity—the family tree of the fathers of socialism). It includes an essay on Luxemburg's ancestry called "Nesher

Ha-Mahapecha" (The eagle of revolution), 76–90, which looks at parallels between the ethical teachings of her rabbinical ancestors and her own beliefs.

22. On Marx's own amazingly impressive rabbinical ancestry, see Shlomo Barer, *Doctors of Revolution* (London, 2000), 108–51, 1170–78.

23. Ettinger, *Rosa Luxemberg,* 12–13.

24. Robert S. Wistrich, "Rosa Luxemburg, Leo Jogiches and the Jewish Labour Movement 1893–1903," in *Essays in Honor of Chimen Abramsky,* edited by Ada Rapoport-Albert and Steven J. Zipperstein (London, 1988), 529–46.

25. John Mill, *Pioniern un boyer* (Pioneers and builders) (New York, 1946–1949), 1: 225.

26. See Samuel A. Portnoy, ed., *Vladimir Medem. The Life and Times of a Legendary Jewish Socialist* (New York, 1979), 486–87. The comments were made in a taped interview by the editor with Jacob Hertz on 23 April 1973.

27. Nettl, *Rosa Luxemburg,* 1: 53.

28. See Jack Jacobs, *On Socialists,* 78–79.

29. Robert S. Wistrich, *Revolutionary Jews from Marx to Trotsky* (London, 1976), 76–94.

30. B. Michaelevich, *Zichrones fun a Yidishen Sotsialist* (Warsaw, 1929), 149–50; and Portnoy, *Vladimir Medem,* 428.

31. Elżbieta Ettinger, ed., *Comrade and Lover. Rosa Luxemburg's Letters to Leo Jogiches* (Cambridge, Mass., 1979) for a portrait of Jogiches.

32. See Ezra Mendelsohn, *Class Struggle in the Pale: The Formative Years of the Jewish Workers Movement in Tsarist Russia* (Cambridge, U.K., 1970); Henry J. Tobias, *The Jewish Bund in Russia* (Stanford, 1978) and Jonathan Frankel, *Prophecy and Politics. Socialism, Nationalism and the Russian Jews 1862–-1917* (Cambridge, 1981). Also Joshua D. Zimmerman, *Poles, Jews and the Polish Socialist Party* (Madison, Wisc., 2004).

33. Robert S. Wistrich, "Rosa Luxemburg, Leo Jogiches," 531.

34. Leo Jogiches, *Pervoe maia, 1892. Chetyre rechi evreiskikh rabochikh* (Geneva, 1893), re-edited with parallel texts in Russian and Hebrew under the title *Arba'at ha-neumim shel poalim yehudim* (Jerusalem, 1967), introduction by M. Mishkinsky.

35. See L. Jogichesa-Tsyszki, "Nowi towarzysze," in *Socjaldemokracja Królestwa Polskiego i Litwy. Materialy i Dokumenty: Volume 1: 1893-1903,* edited by H. Buczek and F. Tych (Warsaw, 1957), 146–52. These passages from the Polish, which I have personally translated, have not previously appeared in English.

36. Ibid., 148.

37. Ibid.

38. Ibid., 157. From a report entitled "Świeto I Maja 1892 Roku w Łodzi," *Sprawa Robotnicza,* no. 38 (1894).

39. From "Korespondencje z kraju," *Sprawa Robotnicza* (Warsaw), no. 16 (July–Aug. 1893).

40. See Buczek and Tych, *Socjaldemokracja Królestwa Polskiego i Litwy,* 149.

41. Ibid.

42. Ibid., 150.

43. Ibid., 152.

44. See *Przedświt* (May 1893), where Piłsudski appealed to the "Jewish socialist comrades in the stolen Polish provinces," by which he meant the region that once belonged to the Grand Duchy of Lithuania before annexation by Tsarist Russia.

45. *Robotnik,* nos. 5–6 (1894).

46. John Bunzl, *Klassenkampf in der Diaspora. Zur Geschichte der judischen Arbeiterbewegung* (Vienna, 1975), 92.

47. *Yidishe Arbeter,* no. 8 (Dec. 1899). The article, originally entitled "Der Sozialismus in Polen," first appeared in the *Sozialistische Monatshefte* (Dec. 1897). Its appearance in a Bund newspaper did not of course signify that Rosa Luxemburg's views on Polish independence were officially supported by the Bund leadership.

48. J. Mill, *Pioner un boyer* (New York, 1946), 1: 116 ff.

49. "W Kwestii żydowskiej," *Przegląd Socjaldemokratyczny,* no. 3 (July 1902), 21–25, in *Socjaldemokracja Królewstwa Polskiego i Litwy: materially i dokumenty* (Warsaw, 1961), 2: 85–90.

50. The same omission was made by I. Ignatieff (pseudonym of Alexander Israel Helphand-Parvus) in his article on the Wilno speeches, "Russisch-jüdische Arbeiter über die Judenfrage," *Die Neue Zeit,* vol. 1 (1892–93), 176 ff.

51. On Martov's role in the early history of the Bund, see his *Povorotnyi punkt v historii evreiskogo rabochego dvizhenia* (Geneva, 1900), 17–19. Also I. Getzler, *Martov. A Political Biography* (Cambridge, 1967).

52. The differences between the SDKPiL and the Bolsheviks over the question of national self-determination persisted after the October Revolution. See Nettl, *Rosa Luxemburg,* 2: 699–700, 796–97, 851–59.

53. V. I. Lenin, "Does the Jewish Proletariat Need An 'Independent Political Party'?," *Iskra,* no. 34, 15 Feb. 1903.

54. R. Luxemburg, "Organisationsfragen der russischen Sozialdemokratie," *Die Neue Zeit,* vol. 2 (1903–1904): 484–92, 529–35.

55. On the Bund's attitude towards Polish independence, see M. G. Rafes, *Ocherko po istorii Bunda* (Moscow, 1923), 45; N. A. Bukhbinder, *Istoriya evreiskogo rabochego dvizhenia v Rossii* (Leningrad, 1925), 87. During the 1905 Revolution in Russia, the SDKPiL and the Bund did in fact collaborate and theoretical disputes were temporarily forgotten. In sharp contrast to the PPS, both parties stressed more than ever the need for unity with the Russian social democracy.

56. See Rosa Luxemburg's review of the Bund pamphlet, *Polska Partia Socjalistyczna o żydowskim ruchu robotniczym* (London, 1903) which appeared under the heading "Krytyka i bibliografia" in *Przegląd Socjaldemokratyczny,* no. 4 (Apr. 1903): 159–63.

57. Ibid.

58. Adolf Wars(zaws)ki to Karl Kautsky, 20 May 1903 (unpublished letter in the Kautsky Nachlass D XXIII, International Institute of Social History, Amsterdam).

59. Ibid.

60. Ibid.

61. Ibid.

62. K. Kautsky, "Das Massaker von Kischineff und die Judenfrage," *Die Neue Zeit,* vol. 2 (1903): 303–9. For a detailed discussion of Kautsky's views on the Jewish national problem and their influence, see Robert S. Wistrich, *Socialism and the Jews. The Dilemmas of Assimilation in Germany and Austria-Hungary* (London, 1982).

63. R. Luxemburg to Karl Kautsky, 6 June 1903, in *Briefe an Karl und Luise Kautsky.*

64. R. Luxemburg, "Diskusja," *Młot,* no. 14 (5 Nov. 1910): 5–7. *Młot* (The hammer) was the organ of the SDKPiL in Warsaw for which she wrote four unsigned articles during October–November 1910 sharply attacking the "progressive" antisemitism of Andrzej Niemojewski and the free-thinking Polish intelligentsia.

65. See the extract by Grosser, "From Pole to Jew," written in 1911, shortly before his death, in *The Golden Tradition. Jewish Life and Thought in Eastern Europe,* edited by Lucy S. Dawidowicz (New York, 1967), 435–41. The Luxemburg quote comes from her Polish article, "The National Question and Autonomy," *Przegląd Socjaldemokratyczny* (Dec. 1908); it is reproduced in German translation in Irving Fetscher, ed., *Marxisten gegen Antisemitismus* (Hamburg, 1974), 138.

66. Rosa Luxemburg, "Fragment über Krieg, nationale Frage und Revolution," in *Gesammelte Werke,* 2nd ed. (Berlin, 1979), 4: 367–68.

67. Idem, "Dyskusja," *Młot,* no. 14 (5 Nov. 1910), 5–7 for the Polish original.

68. See Fetscher, *Marxisten gegen Antisemitismus,* 144.

69. Ibid., 145.

70. Ibid., 147–148.

71. Ibid., 14.

72. Ibid.

73. Ibid., 149.

74. See Theodore R. Weeks, *From Assimilation to Antisemitism: The "Jewish Question" in Poland, 1850–1914* (DeKalb, Ill., 2006), 116, 134, 156–58, 177. Niemojewski, after 1905, fulminated in particular against Jewish religious practice, especially the Talmud. But the real targets were acculturated Jews who were allegedly

"judaizing" Poland. On Luxemburg's response, see Georges Haupt and Pawel Korzec, "Les socialistes et la campagne antisémite en Pologne en 1910: un episode inédit," *Revue du Nord,* 57, 225 (1975): 185–94.

75. See Julian Unszlicht (Sedecki), *O program Ludu Polskiego: rola socjal litwactwa w niedawnej rewolucji* (Kraków, 1919).

76. Julian Unszlicht (Sedecki), *Social-litwactwo w Polsce: z teorii i praktyki SDKPiL* (Kraków, n.d.) and *Młot* (29 Oct. 1910).

77. Rosa Luxemburg, "Po Pogromie," *Młot,* no. 10 (8 Oct. 1910).

78. Ibid.

79. Ibid.

80. Ibid. See also the interesting textual discussion of Luxemburg's anti-antisemitic fury at the Polish "progressives," by Lars Fischer, *The Socialist Response to Antisemitism in Imperial Germany* (Cambridge, U.K., 2007), 218–27. However, this account suffers from a serious lack of understanding of the Polish context.

81. See Rosa Luxemburg, *W obronie narodwosci* (Poznań, 1900). She wrote nothing comparable in defense of the Jewish minority in Russia and Poland.

82. Róży Luksemburg, "Co Dalej?" (Warsaw, 1906) in *Wybór Pism,* 1: 469.

83. Rosa Luxemburg, *The Russian Revolution,* edited by Bertram D. Wolfe (Ann Arbor, 1961), 76–77.

84. "Aus Frankreich," *Sächsische Arbeiterzeitung,* 23, 26, 27, 28, 30 July 1898; 4, 9, 18 Aug. 1898; 13, 14, 18, Sept. 1898. Some of these articles have been collected together in Rosa Luxemburg, *Le Socialisme en France 1898–1912,* edited by Daniel Guérin (Paris, 1971), 50–61.

85. *Sächsische Arbeiterzeitung,* 28 July 1898.

86. See Rosa Luxemburg, "Die sozialistische Krise in Frankreich," *Die Neue Zeit,* vol. 1 (1900–1901): 495–99, 516–25, 548–58, 619–31, 676–88.

87. "Consultation internationale sur l'affaire Dreyfus et le cas Millerand," *Cahiers de la Quinzaine,* no. 2 (Paris, 1899): 76–82.

88. For this misplaced remark, see Daniel Guérin's introduction to Rosa Luxemburg, *Le Socialisme en France (1898–1912),* 18.

89. See Nettl, *Rosa Luxemburg,* 1: 33.

90. Róży Luksemburg, *Listy do Leona Jogichesa-Tsyzki* (Warsaw, 1968), edited by Feliks Tych. Letter dated 27 April 1899.

91. Nettl, *Rosa Luxemburg,* 2: 860.

92. *Protokoll über die Verhandlungen des Parteitages der Sozialdemokratischen Partei Deutschlands* (Stuttgart, 3–8 October 1898), 99–100, 117–18; (1899), ibid., 171–75, 219, 265–67, 290–91.

93. See Victor Adler, letter dated 4 Sept. 1901 in *Briefwechsel mit August Bebel und Karl Kautsky* (Vienna, 1954), 1377.

94. *Protokoll über die Verhandlungen des Parteitages der Sozialdemokratischen Partei Deutschlands,* 22–28 Sept. 1901 (Berlin, 1901), 191.

95. Ibid.

96. Ibid., 202. See also Robert S. Wistrich, *Revolutionary Jews*, 88–89.

97. Rosa Luxemburg, 3 Oct. 1901, in *Briefe an Karl und Luise Kautsky,* 68-69.

98. The one exception I have found is contained in an unsigned article she wrote for the Berlin socialist newspaper *Vorwärts,* 27 Sept. 1910, entitled "Freidenkertum und Sozialdemokratie." Significantly, in this polemic against Andrej Niemojewski, Rosa Luxemburg remarked that the vulgarity of Polish "free-thinking" antisemitism made German antisemites like Adolf Stöcker and Hermann Ahlwardt appear as "most respectable" (*höchst anständig*) by comparison.

99. See Gernard Beier, "Rosa Luxemburg. Zur Aktualität und Historizität einer umstrittenen Grösse," *Internationale Wissenschaftliche Korrespondenz* (June 1974), 2: 184–88.

100. Ibid., 188.

101. See Nettl, *Rosa Luxemburg,* 2: 510–13, for an interesting discussion of her Russian orientation.

102. Gustav Noske, *Erlebtes aus Aufstieg und Niedergang einer Demokratie* (Offenbach-am-Main, 1947), 27.

103. Ibid.

104. E. Ettinger, *Rosa Luxemburg,* 245–51.

105. Ibid., 251. The body was recovered on 31 May 1919.

106. Rosa Luxemburg, "Die Ordnung herrscht in Berlin," *Rote Fahne,* 14 Jan. 1919, reproduced in *Ich war, ich bin, ich werde sein!* (East Berlin, 1958), 142–43. This formula "I was, I am, I shall *always* be!" is curiously reminiscent of Exodus III:14, where God defines himself to Moses as *Ehyeh asher ehyeh*—"I will be what I will be." The divine name was meant to assure the Israelites of their eventual deliverance, though its precise manner was not yet revealed. For Rosa Luxemburg the certainty of the "final victory of the revolution" was based on the romantic notion of the eternal creativity of the masses, while accepting that the advent of socialism must pass through a series of inevitable defeats. Her messianism was, of course, entirely secular in spirit, with the role of Providence rationalized by a voluntarist theory of historical dialectics.

CHAPTER 12

Leon Trotsky—A Bolshevik Tragedy

In his memoirs, the international revolutionary and poet, Victor Serge, left behind a striking portrait of Leon Trotsky, describing the Bolshevik leader as he appeared at the apex of his power, popularity, and fame in 1920.

> No one ever wore a great destiny with more style. . . . He was forty-one. . .leader of the Petrograd masses in two revolutions; creator of the Red Army, which (as Lenin had said to Gorky) he had literally "conjured out of nothing; . . ." the acknowledged organizer of victory in the Civil War. . . . [He] outshone Lenin through his great oratorical talent, through his organizing ability, first with the army, then on the railways, and by his brilliant gifts as a theoretician. . .his bearing was superbly martial, with his powerful chest, jet-black beard and hair, and flashing eye-glasses. His attitude was less homely than Lenin's, with something authoritarian about it.[1]

Serge, as a critical Communist with anarchist leanings, did not disguise his concern, even then, about Trotsky's dictatorial character and the inflexibility manifested in some of his proposed political solutions to Soviet Russia's difficulties. He was dismayed by Trotsky's stern advocacy of the militarization of labor and his ruthless suppression of the Kronstadt sailors' rising. He admired the Bolshevik leader's outstanding vision and insights but not his systematic "schematizing of old-time Bolshevism."[2] Trotsky, he observed, could never altogether shake off the authoritarian, intolerant tradition of turn-of-the-century Russian Marxism. In the 1930s, as the Trotskyists were being ground into powder by Stalin's violent repression in the USSR, Serge added that "in the hearts of the persecuted" (including Trotsky himself) "I encountered the same attitudes as in their [Stalinist] persecutors."[3]

Lev Davidovich Bronstein (to use his original name) was born on October 26, 1879 in Yanovka, a small isolated village on the steppes of the Southern Ukraine. By a strange twist of fate, the boy's birthday coincided precisely with the date, thirty-eight years later, when under his pen name of Leon Trotsky, he established the Bolshevik Power in Petrograd. Two months later, his deadly adversary Josef Stalin (Djugashvili) would be born in the squalor and poverty of a small Georgian county town. The boy was named Lev (the Russian word for "lion") after his grandfather who, some twenty-five years earlier, had left a small Jewish town in the province of Poltava for the free and open steppes of the Province of Kherson. It was in this rural Russified environment far removed from the traditional mores of the *shtetl* that young Bronstein had grown up. According to his own account of his childhood and adolescence, he did not speak Yiddish, though his grandparents had come from the urban, Yiddish-speaking heartland of the Russian Pale. The language in Bronstein's immediate family was a broken mixture of Russian and Ukrainian. In his father's case, the preponderant tongue appears to have been Ukrainian.[4]

This cultural background is important for understanding why Trotsky—who later came to personify for millions the figure of the revolutionary Jewish internationalist—seemed so distant and indifferent towards his coreligionists. No other Russian revolutionary would more obviously appear to illustrate the paradox of being an alien to the Jews and a "Jew" to the Gentiles. Vladimir Medem, the leading light of the Jewish Socialist Bund, recalled that after a debate in Switzerland in 1903, Trotsky loftily told him that he did not regard himself either as a Russian or as a Jew, but simply as a Social Democrat.[5] The Bundist leader also noted Trotsky's visible anger when he [Medem] had dared to accuse the Russian Social Democrats of consistently neglecting the important task of fighting antisemitism. Trotsky categorically denied the charge but added that "to make the Jews a *special* subject of discussion among the broad masses was superfluous."[6] Antisemitism, to the young Trotsky, was merely the consequence of a universal lack of consciousness in the masses. Once they were brought to a higher state of general awareness, it would simply fade away as a problem. Medem grudgingly acknowledged Trotsky's brilliance as a speaker and writer (as well as his acidic tongue in personal polemics) but dismissed his opponent's arguments as nothing more than self-serving rationalizations.

Trotsky's relations with his father, David Bronstein—a frontier type of Jewish farmer made sturdy by physical labor—were somewhat tense. He despised his "petty-bourgeois" life-style and habits dominated by the "acquisitive instinct."[7] In his autobiography, Trotsky records:

> Father did not believe in God from his youth and in later years spoke openly about it in front of mother and the children. Mother

> preferred to avoid the subject, but when occasion required, would raise her eyes in prayer.[8]

Although on holy days his parents journeyed to synagogue and his mother abstained from sewing, ceremonial observance declined with the years into religious inertia and indifference. When he was seven, Lev Davidovich was sent to a Yiddish-speaking *heder* (Jewish religious school) in Gromokley, a few miles from Yanovka. This was an unhappy experience for young Bronstein, who (unfamiliar with Yiddish) could understand neither his teachers nor his classmates.[9] He was repulsed, moreover, by the sight of the Jews of Gromokley humiliating a woman of loose morals, whom they had driven out of one of the main village streets.[10] This unpleasant memory of Jewish squalor and intolerance contrasted strikingly for Lev Davidovich with his recollection of the tidy, neat cottages of the German colonists in Gromokley.

From Trotsky's memoirs we learn that in 1888 he went to Odessa to stay with his cousin Moissei Filipovich Spentzer, a translator, journalist, and cultivated middle-class liberal who polished his manners, taught the boy Russian, and sent him to St. Paul's Realschule. Bronstein lost a year because of the *numerus clausus* which limited the number of Jewish pupils in Russian secondary schools to 10 percent, but on this subject he was distinctly reticent. What did make a deep impression on him was rather the cosmopolitan atmosphere and heterogeneous national composition of his Lutheran gymnasium, with its Russians, Germans, Poles, Ukrainians, and Jews. Religious education was given in the Greek Orthodox, Roman Catholic, Lutheran, and Jewish faiths. Trotsky recalled that

> a good-natured man by the name of Ziegelman instructed the Jewish boys in the Bible and the history of the Jewish people. These lessons, conducted in Russian, were never taken seriously by the boys.[11]

Young Lev Bronstein was equally dismissive in his comment on the private lessons he received in the Bible from an elderly Hebrew teacher in Odessa: "My studies lasted only a few months and did little to confirm me in the ancestral faith."[12] Bronstein, who was "always at the top of the grade," claimed to have been unaffected by any restrictions which existed on the Jews at his gymnasium. Altogether his account of life in a Russian secondary school in the early 1890s differs markedly from that of his somewhat older socialist comrades Julius Martov and Paul Axelrod, who vividly recalled the anti-Jewish persecution to which they were subjected. Martov (the leader of

Russian Menshevism) had indeed been traumatized as a child by the 1881 pogroms in Odessa. Not that the young Bronstein was totally indifferent to the nationality question; his eye was caught by the indignities to which Germans, Ukrainians, and Poles were subjected. Thus he singled out the baiting of a Polish Catholic boy by a Russian Orthodox priest as an example of national inequality: this, he reflected,

> was one of the underlying causes of my dissatisfaction with the existing order, but it as lost among all the other phases of social injustice. It never played a leading part—not even a recognized one—in the list of my grievances.[13]

One cannot rule out the possibility that here, as elsewhere, Trotsky was deliberately playing down his Jewishness. Nevertheless, his account of his school experiences in the more tolerant, multiracial atmosphere of Odessa is not altogether implausible. What emerges is that for the self-image of the young Bronstein, Jewish experiences did not play a significant role at this stage of his life. His intellectual brightness and general sophistication, encouraged by his model showing as a pupil in Odessa, had rapidly alienated him from the coarseness and narrow horizons of life on the farm in Yanovka. Already, well before his conversion to Marxian socialism, he began to see his family, and especially his father, as a privileged "kulak," a "hoarder" who mistreated the servile laborers on the farm.[14]

As a proud, sensitive adolescent, Bronstein was pushed more by circumstances than by any predestined "Jewish" fate, towards socialism. Like Marx, he was initially repulsed by the "socialist utopia," distrusting what he felt to be a formula for "mob rule." But it was not long before he abandoned class, religion, and upbringing for the revolutionary cause. It was in the Black Sea port of Nikolayev that the 17-year-old Bronstein first made contact with radical students and workingmen and was exposed at the end of 1896 to Populist doctrines. His progress was rapid, and by the end of 1897 he had become a Marxist and helped to organize the Southern Russian Workers Union in Nikolayev, which had some two hundred members. From this revolutionary initiation— which earned him the customary punishment of imprisonment and later exile to Siberia—he would never look back. With regard to his religion and nationality, Trotsky remained an unrepentant rationalist.

> Even in my early youth, the national bias and national prejudices had only bewildered my sense of reason, in some cases stirring in me nothing but disdain and even a moral nausea.[15]

This comprehensive, all-embracing rationalism, deepened by his Marxist education and acquaintance with different political systems and cultures, never left him.[16]

> The feeling of the supremacy of general over particular experience, of law over fact, of theory over personal experience, took root in my mind at an early age and gained increasing strength as the years advanced.[17]

Marxism was attractive because it claimed to offer a universal, *scientific* solution to the problems of mankind as a whole. Here was a class doctrine which served to transcend national and religious frontiers, and which was interpreted by Trotsky as an inevitable outcome of the dialectic of history. In effect, Marxism would become for him a kind of revolutionary religion, an *Idea* of captivating power, subsequently embodied in the dictatorship of the proletariat, the class struggle and the undisputed leadership of the Bolshevik Party.[18] His blind, fanatical devotion to this Idea sometimes had an apocalyptic edge in the defiant belief that history would justify all the sacrifices required to bring about a new social order of harmony and justice.

The 21-year-old Lev Davidovich would greet the 20th century from his Siberian exile with fighting words that could well have been the epitaph for his stormy career.

> As long as I breathe I shall fight for the future, that radiant future in which man, strong and beautiful, will become master of the drifting stream of his history. . . .[19]

By the time he escaped from Siberia he had inserted into his false passport the name Trotsky, by which he was to become known for the rest of his life. It was a curious choice—the name of the heavy-set chief guard of the Odessa jail where he had been briefly imprisoned—a majestic dominating figure symbolizing the arrogance of power. At the same time the name which he had chosen was also synonymous in German with boldness, defiance, and disdain—fighting qualities which the young Marxist revolutionary was to consummately display in the future. It was almost as if Bronstein-Trotsky had unconsciously taken into himself a part of that power he was fighting against. These early ambiguities in his search for a new identity—and especially in his attitudes to authority—would be even more important in the struggles that lay ahead.

The young Trotsky confronted the Jewish problem for the first time as a political issue at the Second Congress of the Russian Social Democratic Workers' Party in London in 1903. The conflict with the Jewish Workers'

Bund which emerged there was to have important repercussions on the history of Russian social democracy. The struggle between the *Iskra* board and the Bund brought to a climax a series of problems involving the Jews and their role in the Russian revolutionary movement.[20] Were the Russian Jews to assimilate, or did they require a separate Yiddish culture and an independent organization to represent their interests? Was the Jewish Bund to have a special autonomous status in the party and the right to frame its own policy with regard to the Jewish proletariat? Was it justified in demanding schools in the Yiddish language and cultural-national autonomy for Jewish workers? Finally, could the Russian Social Democratic Party accept that the Bund was the sole representative of the Jewish working class in Russia?[21] Beyond these specific demands raised by the Bund lay a crucial problem for the founder and leader of the Bolshevik wing of Russian Social Democracy, Vladimir Ilyich Lenin. Was the Russian revolutionary party to be a centralized, disciplined, cohesive unit or a federation of autonomous national groupings as for example in the neighboring Austrian Empire? On the former issue it was the assimilated Jews around Lenin, led by Martov, Axelrod, and the 23-year-old Trotsky who fiercely opposed the Bund and tabled their signatures to a resolution rejecting its demands. Trotsky was already sufficiently established to play an important part in the debate.

Representing the makeshift Siberian Social-Democratic Workers' Union, Trotsky was in fact Lenin's hatchet-man in forcing the Bund to abandon the London Congress thereby (unintentionally) helping, with Martov, to forge a Bolshevik majority at the proceedings. Trotsky particularly provoked the Bundist delegates with his aggressive manner and insistence on speaking as a *Jew* in order better to refute their demands. He accused the Bund of endangering the cohesion of the anti-Tsarist revolutionary forces and encouraging Jewish workers along the retrograde path of nationalism and separatism. He supported Martov's resolution, calling for the "closest unity of the Jewish proletariat with the proletariat of those races among whom it lives,"[22] and took the floor no less than ten times to speak in the debate. He declared that the twelve Jewish comrades who had signed Martov's resolution while working in the all-Russian party "regarded and still regard themselves also as representatives of the Jewish proletariat." This claim, coming from a revolutionary who had previously disdained all affiliation to the Jewish people, not surprisingly made the Bundist delegates indignant. Mark Liber, the Bundist spokesman, described Trotsky's statement as a piece of "gross tactlessness" and demanded its retraction.[23] This was refused by Georgii Plekhanov, the veteran founder of Russian Marxism and Chairman of the conference, no admirer of Trotsky, but even less sympathetic to the Bund. Lenin himself, in a memoir of the meeting, recalled Plekhanov's "phenomenal intolerance" towards the Bund, accusing its members of exploiting the Russians. The Jews, Plekhanov declared, were "all chauvinists and nationalists," a "serpent-tribe"—hence the Bund should be summarily thrown out of the Party.[24]

The hard-line Bolsheviks and the "softer" Mensheviks alike rejected the claim of the Bund to any special place in the Russian Social Democratic party, though they did not wish to curtail its local work among the Jewish proletariat. Trotsky, for his part, regarded the Bund as a *parochial* organization whose leaders had undeniably achieved much in the past, but who would obtain better results in the future if they looked beyond the Pale of Settlement. Instead of representing the Social Democratic Party among Jewish workers, the Bund was wrongly defending them against it, casting a vote of no confidence in the Russian comrades. The Bund, he alleged, had allowed a *national* viewpoint to predominate over class-interest. Fortunately, this provincialism had been rejected by the Second Russian Social Democratic Congress. In Trotsky's words, this was a triumph for Marxist universalism over the narrow Jewish particularism of the Bundists.[25]

Trotsky never went back on this harsh judgment of the specifically Jewish labor movement. He would always regard Bundists with a certain disdain and aristocratic hauteur. Like Rosa Luxemburg, who held remarkably similar views (though she expressed them more prudently), he despised the Bund as a nationalistic outgrowth of Jewish "isolationism," founded on an outmoded ghetto psychology. But there was a deeper psychological dynamic at stake in Trotsky's polemic against the Bund, which extended to his rejection of Zionism. Not merely was the notion of a Jewish "nationality" unacceptable to him, it directly offended his evolving self-image as a Russian revolutionary and as a progressive Marxist. Chaim Weizmann recalled that Lenin, Trotsky, and Plekhanov all exuded a similar contempt for the Zionist students in the Russian colonies of Switzerland who were moved by a love of Jewish tradition and concern for the fate of the Jews.

> *They* could not understand why a Russian Jew should want to be anything but a Russian. *They* stamped as unworthy, as intellectually backward, as chauvinist and unmoral, the desire of any Jew to occupy himself with the sufferings and destiny of Jewry.[26]

Had not Lenin himself written in October 1903 that the "idea of a Jewish nation was Zionist in inspiration and therefore false and reactionary."[27] But at that stage, the Zionists were peripheral to his concerns. The campaign was really about Lenin's implacable determination either to swallow the Bund or else drive it out of the Social Democratic Party.

Trotsky was no less scathing than Lenin or other Russian comrades in taking both the Bund and Zionism to task. In an article in *Iskra* (January 1904) on "The Decomposition of Zionism and its Possible Successors," he asserted that the Sixth Zionist Congress was proof that Theodor Herzl's Zionist movement was about to collapse.[28] In this article, ironically enough, Trotsky echoed the opinions of Bundist leader Vladimir Medem who had also attended the Sixth Congress in Basle (1903) when the British offer of Uganda for future Jewish settlement had indeed nearly wrecked Zionism.[29] Trotsky outdid even Medem in his vituperative attack on Herzl for seeking "the aid of the princes of the world" on behalf of "his" people. In Trotsky's mocking eyes, Herzl was nothing but a "repulsive figure" and a "shameless adventurer" who had the impudence and "devilish perfidy" to try to obtain a fatherland for the Jews.[30] Zionism itself, he arrogantly dismissed as a reckless enterprise doomed to defeat. With characteristic sarcasm, he evoked the sense of betrayal among delegates at the Zionist Congress, angry at Herzl's acceptance of the Uganda project, describing their objections as the "hysterical sobbings of the romanticists of Zion." For good measure, Trotsky added:

> Though intrigue-mongers and hundreds of simpletons may still go on supporting his adventure. . .Zionism as a movement is already doomed to a deprivation of all its rights for the future.

What ultimately interested the young Trotsky was not the fate of Zionism but whether Social Democracy would benefit from its inevitable (!) collapse in Russia. He confidently predicted that Poale Zion (the Zionist-Left) would be driven by Tsarist police repression and the need for self-defense against pogroms, into the *general* Russian revolutionary ranks, not towards the "nationalist" Bund.[31]

Trotsky's initial reaction to the Kishinev pogrom of 1903 reflected the view of most Marxist revolutionaries, that there was no necessity for a *special* struggle against antisemitism.[32] Nevertheless he did not ignore the extent to which the reactionary Tsarist regime, local authorities, and the police used pogroms to divert mass discontent, break strikes, and counter the revolutionary mood following the Russian defeat by Japan. His graphic descriptions of the pogroms—the murder, rape, and arson practiced by drunken bands in the name of the Tsar, God, and fatherland—were undoubtedly an impassioned and deeply felt indictment of the regime.

Trotsky unsparingly depicted the horrors of the "black October bacchanalia," in which "hundreds of towns suffered from 3,500 to 4,000 dead and up to 10,000 maimed."[33] He also drew attention to the fear and panic of the Jewish population, even in St. Petersburg. In a famous speech of October 1906, defending his central role the previous year as the Chairman of the Petersburg Soviet, the 26-year-old Trotsky cited the pogroms as the living proof that the Tsarist regime was "an automaton for mass murder," cutting the living flesh of the people to pieces.[34] In his book on the 1905 Revolution, he paid close attention to the mobilization of the counter-revolutionary Black Hundred pogromists. With searing indignation and narrative skill he described the activities of these hooligans who represented the brutal revenge of the old order against the revolutionary challenge. Recruited from every alley and slum, among petty shopkeepers, beggars, publicans, police spies, professional thieves, dumb *muzhiks,* and brothel doorkeepers, the pogromists burst into Russia's townlets, transforming them into living hells. Their basic props, as Trotsky observed, were "the Tsar's portrait, a bottle of vodka, a tricolor flag." The ragged Black Hundred army, embittered by ignorance and poverty, was organized around a disciplined nucleus, "receiving its slogans and watchwords from above." The scene was set by pogrom proclamations, special articles in local newspapers, sinister rumors, the arrival of visiting "specialists" and a special service for the hungry mob in which "the bishop makes a solemn oration." In his description of the patriotic procession, it is the clergy which is out in front, and churches along the way ring their bells in anticipation. A military band plays without cease while at the sides and rear of the procession march the police. Here is an extract from his account:

> The governor salutes, the police chief publicly embraces the leading members of the Black Hundreds: . . . To start with a few windows are smashed, a few passers-by beaten up; the wreckers enter every tavern on their way and drink, drink, drink. The band never stops playing "God save the Tsar," that hymn of the pogroms. . . . The doss-house tramp is king. A trembling slave an hour ago, hounded by police and starvation, he now feels himself an unlimited despot. Everything is allowed him, he is capable of anything, he is the master of property and honor, life and death. . . . There exist no tortures, figments of a feverish brain, maddened by alcohol and fury at which he need ever stop. He is capable of anything, he dares everything. God save the Tsar.[35]

No other Marxist revolutionary, it should be said, matched the passionate quality of Trotsky's evocations of the pogromists in all their hideous savagery. Nor did he downplay the suffering of the victims—some of whom, after a few hours of the pogrom in Odessa, had "sunk into the eternal night of madness." Images of unimaginable suffering, of pain, degradation, and death were fused in Trotsky's prose into a searing indictment of the "whole infernal morality of the pogrom policy." The pogrom mentality perfectly mirrored the reactionary character of Tsarism, of the Russian nobility, the bureaucracy, the Orthodox clergy, and the Black Hundred thugs. Though the Jews are never specifically mentioned *qua* Jews, they are clearly the *victims*—"bloodstained, charred, driven frantic, still searching for salvation within the nightmare."[36]

Trotsky's vivid account of the 1905 pogroms echoed his fierce feelings of hate and vengeance towards the Tsarist regime. Even the horrors of the 16th-century St. Bartholomew's Night massacre of French Protestants, or the agitation over the Dreyfus Affair seemed to him like harmless theatrical effects in comparison. At his trial in 1906, Trotsky minced no words about Tsarist complicity in the pogroms, noting that "behind the façade of the Black Hundreds was the powerful fist of the ruling clique." Trotsky's sensitivity to pogromist violence also played a part in his sharp response to the notorious Beilis case in Kiev (the proceedings began in September 1913) in which a poor Ukrainian Jewish shoemaker had been charged with ritual murder. At the time Trotsky was living in Vienna (he resided there between 1907 and 1914) where he wrote for the German and Russian press. He noted that the Russian Ministry of Justice, headed by a notorious antisemite Shcheglovitov, was determined to frame the Jew Mendel Beilis, for the murder of a local Kiev youth called Andrei Yuschinsky. The storm of indignation throughout Western Europe and the United States prompted Trotsky to write a long essay (published in the German Marxist periodical *Die Neue Zeit*) denouncing the efforts of the reactionary ruling forces in Tsarist Russia to revive the medieval blood-libel. In particular, he lambasted the efforts of the antisemitic Union of the Russian People (*Soyuz Russki Narod*) to turn the alleged Ukrainian victim of "ritual murder" into a saint canonized by the Greek Orthodox Church.

From the outset Trotsky emphasized the stunning, deliberate falsity of the charges laid against an "ordinary Jewish worker," indifferent to religion, who had suddenly found himself accused of draining out the blood of a living child. The most primitive superstitions and prejudices were being used to instill in the Kievan jurors "hatred toward Beilis as a Jew." Trotsky also slammed the perfidious role of ignorant monks and converts from Judaism in the prosecution's case, who had proceeded to cast aspersions on the Bible, Talmud, and other Jewish sources allegedly at the root of Beilis's "ritual" crime. He insisted that the Beilis case was far worse than the accusations of military treason made against Captain Dreyfus in France nearly 20 years earlier. There was a fundamental difference between the outlook of cynical, erudite French statesmen who neither believed in God nor the Devil and Tsar Nicholas "who is still convinced that at night witches dash out riding on brooms through chimneys." There was an even greater difference "between the French drawing-room-Jesuitic anti-Semitism and the Russian criminally pogromist Black Hundredism. . . ."[37]

Trotsky regarded the Beilis case as decisive confirmation of the "depravity of the [Romanov] court-monarchy and bureaucratism"—proof of the utter corruption of the Imperial Russian justice system. The proceedings in the case could only arouse a feeling of utter *physical nausea* given that the entire apparatus of government was determined to make a single innocent human being the scapegoat for its own criminal decadence. The Beilis Affair exposed, in Trotsky's view, the sheer hollowness of repeated claims that Russian antisemitism was a spontaneous mass phenomenon. On the contrary, he argued, the Beilis case was an "eloquent confirmation that pogroms take place only when the government wants them."[38] Trotsky was confident that millions of urban Russian workers would be even more strongly motivated by the Affair to bring down the morally bankrupt despotism of the Romanov dynasty.

Trotsky's awareness of the "Jewish Question" was further sharpened by his experiences as a reporter in Romania in August 1913. In a series of three articles for a Russian journal, he noted that antisemitism had successfully established itself in Romania as "a state religion—the last cementing factor of a feudal society rotten through and through." Nothing held up the mirror more revealingly to the total corruption and mismanagement of this backward Balkan country than its attitude towards Jews. It was an agrarian society ruled by Purishkeviches (the name of an extreme right-wing antisemitic deputy in the Russian Duma)—which exploited Jews as middlemen while depriving them of any civil or political rights and making them targets for the revenge of the downtrodden peasantry. No less than a third of the urban population in Romania, Jews were already hated as potential competitors by lawyers, government officials, and army officers; they were also easy scapegoats for teachers and priests, intent on maintaining the traditional ethos of national serfdom. The press, too, consistently indoctrinated ordinary Romanians with the fiction that their "misery and bondage originate with the Jews."[39]

Trotsky wrote down these observations as the Balkans correspondent in Vienna for the liberal Russian paper *Kievskaya Mysl*. He did not fail to notice the shocking fact that almost 300,000 Jews in Romania, though they and their parents had been born in the country, had no citizenship rights.

> Any Jew can at any moment be thrown out of the country, like a roaming vagabond. . .although they are excluded from citizenship, the government nonetheless imposes on them the whole burden of civic obligations including taxes and military service.[40]

The "Jewish Question" in Romania was symptomatic of a corrupt social organism dominated by a "Boyar" clique who lorded it over "servile" peasants. The ruling class in Romania hated the Jews, but could no longer survive without them. Whether as a leaseholder, moneylender, middleman, or hired journalist, the Jew was simply indispensable. He was the vital intermediary between landlord and peasant, the agent of feudal exploitation, instructed to "fulfill the dirtiest assignments of Purishkevich."[41] Trotsky concluded that Romanian antisemitism was "the last psychological cement of a completely decadent feudal society, covered up with a gold leaf—the strictly qualified constitution."[42] Nevertheless, the Romanian ruling class retained a healthy respect for the influence of high finance and the "Jewish" press in Western Europe. Was it not Otto von Bismarck, the Iron Chancellor of Germany, who had personally taken up the cause of the miserable Moldavian Jews under proddings from his Jewish financial adviser, the banker Gerson von Bleichröder? German financial interests and various *Realpolitik* machinations had made the fate of Romanian Jewry a pawn in the game of European diplomacy.[43]

The outbreak of the First World War found Trotsky still living in Vienna, watching in disbelief as festive crowds in the Ringstrasse greeted the news of mobilization with hope and joy. The war was in his opinion primarily a struggle for imperialist hegemony between the powerful German Reich and the British Empire. The task of the proletariat was, however, to create "a new, more powerful and stable fatherland—the republican United States of Europe, as a transition to the United States of the World."[44] By 1916, Trotsky confidently anticipated a Russian Revolution which would act as a prologue to the social revolution of the European proletariat."[45] The workers would first have to liquidate the old Socialist International, whose national party framework had bound it too closely to the defense of conservative state structures and of "social-imperialism." Returning to Russia in 1917, Trotsky would play a decisive role in the October Revolution, as its foremost orator and mass spellbinder.[46] However, between 1917 and 1924 the architect of the Bolshevik insurrection and creator of the Red Army would pay relatively little attention to the "Jewish Question."[47] During this brief era of *internationalist euphoria,* Trotsky must have felt reinforced in his earlier belief that assimilation was the only viable solution for the Jewish masses. His more immediate political problem lay elsewhere—in his lack of any solid organizational base within Russian social democracy. His position in the Bolshevik Party—which he only joined in 1917—would never be truly secure. This had little directly to do with his Jewish origin, but went back to his ideological differences with Lenin.

Since 1903, the young Trotsky had become increasingly convinced that in matters of organization and political philosophy Lenin was a "dull caricature of the tragic intransigence of Jacobinism," a Bolshevik parody of Maximilian Robespierre. Lenin's intransigent outlook, he argued, could only lead to a form of dictatorship *over* the proletariat.[48] The logic of Bolshevism would end up with the guillotine and terror and "Marx's lion head would be the first to fall"—Leon Trotsky wrote (more prophetically than he could ever realize) in 1904.[49] The 25-year-old Trotsky still veered at that time towards the Menshevik views of Paul Axelrod, to whom his own venomous attack on Leninism would be dedicated. He felt alienated by what was specifically Russian in Bolshevism—especially its links with the native autocratic tradition of violence and its distrust of Western democratic methods. Trotsky was fundamentally a Westerner in outlook who disliked the endemically conspirational atmosphere of the Russian revolutionary movement—the intrigues, squabbles, and splits of party politics in exile.[50] Between 1905 and 1917 he remained ostentatiously aloof from the Bolshevik party. During the abortive 1905 Revolution, as Chairman of the Petrograd Soviet, the energetic Trotsky had nonetheless been the only Marxist leader of note to play a major directing role in the upheavals of the time.

In 1905, on the basis of this practical experience, Trotsky with the help of Israel Helphand Parvus (another prominent Russian-Jewish revolutionary) evolved a novel theory to describe the future tasks of the socialist revolution. The next uprising in Russia would have to be a *permanent revolution* which would telescope together in one unbroken continuum the aims of both the bourgeois and socialist revolutions. The theory of permanent revolution would turn Russian backwardness into a springboard for mass action, under proletarian leadership. By 1917 Lenin had come round to a similar point of view from a different starting-point. This convergence enabled both Lenin and Trotsky to encourage an immediate link and transition from the bourgeois-democratic to the proletarian-socialist order in Russia.[51] For Trotsky, "permanent revolution" ultimately meant that the Russian revolution would not compromise with any form of class rule and would aim at the "complete liquidation of class society." It was the October Revolution which brought Lenin and Trotsky together, despite the bitterness of their past polemics. Unlike other Bolsheviks who resented Trotsky's sudden rise to eminence as that of an upstart and adversary, Lenin was ready to forgive and forget the past. Trotsky's Jewish origin seemed insignificant to him in the heady euphoria of the Bolshevik triumph. This does not mean, however, that antisemitism had disappeared or that it ceased to play any part in the dramatic events which followed the October uprising. Trotsky himself was well aware that his Jewishness might be held against him. In his autobiography he rationalized this fear as follows:

> If, in 1917 and after, I occasionally pointed to my Jewish origin as an argument against some appointment, it was simply because of political considerations.[52]

Like Lev Kamenev, Grigorii Zinoviev, Karl Radek, Steklov, Sverdlov, and Uritsky, he had severed all his ties with Judaism, with the Russian Jewish community, the Jewish masses, and with Jewish history. But Trotsky also knew that he was perceived by many of his opponents as an "alien" or outsider to Russian traditions. His consummate mastery of Russian would make little differences to the antisemites, for whom he would always remain the *Zhid* Trotsky. In that respect his fate was similar to that of Rosa Luxemburg and other Jewish revolutionaries of his generation.

The "Jewish Question" under Bolshevik rule first arose when Lenin offered Trotsky the post of Commissar for Home Affairs in the new Soviet Government. He instantly declined on the grounds that this appointment would play into the hands of the "White" counterrevolutionaries, whose antisemitism was already proverbial. Lenin initially dismissed this argument as an unjustified concession to the "socialism of fools."[53] But he eventually backed down and accepted Yaacov Sverdlov's suggestion that Trotsky should head the new Soviet Foreign Ministry. Subsequently, he would be called upon to establish and command the new Red Army, summoning the Russian masses to prodigious efforts during the Civil War against the White Armies. As the embodiment of the October insurrection, Trotsky successfully mobilized and rallied war-weary workers and peasants to the defense of Soviet Russia, acting as an inspiring catalyst for dormant revolutionary energies. In his autobiography he even quotes from a White Guard writer, reporting a Cossack's defiant reply to taunts that he had accepted the command of the "Jew" Trotsky.

> Trotsky is not a Jew, Trotsky is a fighter. He's ours, he is Russian! . . . It is Lenin who is a communist, a Jew, but Trotsky is ours, a fighter, a Russian.[54]

Despite its tainted source and antisemitic content, the anecdote obviously flattered the vanity of the Bolshevik leader.

In the flush of victory during the Civil War, Trotsky probably felt confirmed in his messianic hopes for world revolution and dismissal of such trifles as the sufferings of Jewry. What did *he* have in common with Judaism or the Jewish masses in Russia, to whom he devoted a mere four sentences in his *History of the Russian Revolution*? Their fate, like that of his own father, seemed like a minor ripple in the storm of world history. With the death of Lenin, however, anti-Jewish prejudices would rapidly resurface. Trotsky did not deny this. On the contrary, he was the first to inform the parties of the Communist International, and then a skeptical world, that his main rival Joseph Stalin had introduced antisemitism as a weapon against him and the "Trotskyist" Left Opposition within the Russian Bolshevik Party. "Anti-Semitism raised its head with that of anti-Trotskyism. They both derived from the same source—the petty bourgeois reaction against October."[55] This was a simplistic view, though humanly understandable from Trotsky's standpoint.

For the mass of Russian Jewry—merchants, traders, shopkeepers, and pedlars—the new Communist regime meant economic ruin. The Jewish masses only began to swing towards the Bolsheviks in 1919 out of an instinct of physical self-preservation against the murderous pogroms of the White armies.[56] Jewish assessments of Trotsky at this time were compounded of mixed feelings of pride and fear; on the one hand, he seemed like an avenger of Jewish humiliations under Tsarism, bringing fire and slaughter to their worst enemies. On the other hand, in the Ukraine where Trotsky's Red Army had put down aspirations for national independence and peasant revolts, as well as the anarchist Makhnovite bands, resentment and hatred was rife. The pogroms of 1917—1919 in the Ukraine, fed by White propaganda (including the notorious *Protocols of the Elders of Zion*), were at least in part a reaction against the *Zhid* Trotsky and the Bolshevik armies under his command.[57] One Zionist Hebrew writer who witnessed the Revolution and Civil War even held the Communists of Jewish origin responsible for the pogroms.

> Trotsky is more to blame than a thousand Denikins and Petliuras. Even before 1917, some of the Zionist leaders warned the Jews against sticking their noses into the Russian Revolution. . . . For

> Trotsky's throne as minister of war. . .Russian Jewry has paid dearly.[58]

The prominence of other Jews not only in the Bolshevik political leadership in the period from 1917 to 1922 (15–20 percent of the delegates at party Congresses were Jews) but especially in the Cheka (secret police), clearly nourished antisemitism. Jews were suddenly conspicuous as local Commissars, bureaucrats, and tax officers, as well as police officials. The eminent Russian Jewish historian Simon Dubnow, writing in his diary in early January 1918, anticipated the likely consequences:

> We shall never be forgiven for the share that the Jewish speculators of the revolution have taken in Bolshevist terror. The Jewish companions and fellow workers of Lenin—the Trotskys and Uritskys—eclipse even him: the Smolny Institute [H.Q. of the Revolution in Petrograd] is secretly called *Centerzhid* [Yid Center]. Later on this will be talked about aloud, and anti-Semitism will be rooted deeply in all parts of Russian society. The soil is ready for cultural anti-Semitism.[59]

Even Trotsky himself appears to have been worried at this turn of events, encouraging a greater number of Jews to go to the battle front—to counter "chauvinist agitation" among Red Army men. At the same time, he opposed the idea of separate Jewish battalions:

> I suggest that the Jewish battalions enter those regiments where there are also battalions of other nationalities. In this way we can avoid the chauvinism which results from the estrangement of the different nationalities, and which unfortunately arises when entirely independent national military units are formed.[60]

Trotsky remained, however, fundamentally indifferent to the plight of the Jewish masses in Russia, whom he continued to identify with the despised petty-bourgeoisie. At the pinnacle of his power he invariably sent Jewish delegations away, repeating that he was an internationalist and a social democrat, unconcerned with their problems.[61] This cold indifference also extended to his own father, David Bronstein, who, at the height of the Civil War found himself menaced by the Whites because of his son, and by the Reds because he was a rich "kulak." Having lost all his savings during the Revolution, the elder Bronstein (who was too illiterate to read any of his son's works) had to walk hundreds of miles to find shelter in Odessa. In his autobiography Trotsky rather callously observed:

> My father died of typhus in the spring of 1922, at the very moment when I was reading my report at the Fourth Congress of the Communist International.[62]

When the chief Rabbi of Moscow Jacob Mazeh desperately pleaded with Trotsky to intercede for the starving Russian Jews in 1921, he replied with some emphasis that he was a revolutionary Bolshevik and not a Jew. Mazeh is alleged to have commented: "The Trotskys make the revolutions, and the Bronsteins pay the bills."[63]

Trotsky's revolutionary career totally alienated him from his family, his religion, and national origin. During the Civil War he occasionally concerned himself with administrative and propaganda aspects of the "Jewish Question" such as the recruitment of Jewish youth to the revolutionary forces. Trotsky suspected that these recruits joined the Bolsheviks for national rather than class reasons, but he nonetheless encouraged them, if only to counter the widespread belief that Jews shirked military service.[64] But with the end of the Civil War and the emerging struggle for Lenin's succession Trotsky swiftly discovered that his Westernism, his European Marxist cosmopolitanism, and Jewish background made him a renewed target for hostility. He was, after all, a latecomer among the Bolsheviks, even though he had emerged after 1917 as Lenin's trusted lieutenant and a true hero of the Revolution. Nor did his personality traits of intellectual arrogance, pride, maverick individualism, his incapacity for intrigue, or the fear of his envious colleagues that he might establish a military dictatorship, help his case. Worse still, Trotsky was out of touch by 1924 with the mood of the Russian people, grown weary of endless sacrifice and bloodshed after the orgy of destruction unleashed during the Civil War. He undoubtedly underestimated the sheer exhaustion of the Soviet working class, the demoralization and chaos caused by the collapse of the Russian economy. He initially failed to see that the party's new General Secretary, Joseph Stalin, appealed to a general craving for peace, stability, and safety. By contrast, Trotsky was acting out the role of an unwanted heroic "savior" who would recklessly involve the Soviet Union in unpredictable new adventures and dangers. His warning that a backward Russia could never achieve socialism alone seemed defeatist. The idea that the Soviet fortress existed only to spark off an *international* revolution, without which world capitalism would inevitably destroy the socialist island in its midst, offended the *amour propre* of many Russians in the 1920s.[65]

Stalin's slogan of "socialism in one country" appeared as an emotionally more compelling reaction to Russian isolation than the seemingly impossible burdens of revolutionary internationalism conducted in a void. Trotsky seemed to ignore the socioeconomic realities of a hungry nation desperately seeking to recover its equilibrium after seven years of massive upheaval. The apathy of a post-revolutionary period did not favor his messianic activism, his impatience with anything but world revolution. It was not difficult for Stalin and his allies to accuse Trotsky of pessimism, of underestimating the peasantry, "anti-Leninism," lack of faith in the Soviet proletariat, and of irresponsible adventurism.[66] Moreover, Trotsky underestimated Stalin when he denounced his policy as the triumph of self-satisfied mediocrity. Stalin to him always symbolized the upstarts, the kulaks, bureaucrats, careerists, and the Nep-Men who had risen in the post-revolutionary order of the mid-1920s.[67] This was something of a caricature, completely dismissing Stalin's political skills and organizational talents. But beyond ideology and temperament, what part, if any, did Trotsky's Jewishness play in his defeat during the struggle for power? Winston Churchill, for one, had no doubt that it was crucial to his failure.

> He was still a Jew. Nothing could get over that. Hard fortune when you have deserted your family, repudiated your race, spat upon the religion of your father, and lapped Jew and Gentile in a common malignity, to be baulked of so great a prize for so narrow-minded a reason![68]

Was the choice, then, between Stalin and Trotsky ultimately that between a budding Great-Russian Bolshevik nationalist of Georgian background and an international Jewish Marxist? Certainly, those like Trotsky, who had absorbed internationalism into their very flesh and blood, could scarcely stomach Stalin's new *orthodoxy* of socialism in one country. Significantly, there were relatively few Jews to be found in the Stalinist or pro-peasant Bukharinist factions which appealed in the 1920s to ancient Russian messianic reflexes of national self-sufficiency. Trotsky's own messianism, which was militant, atheist, and supranational in its Marxist form—missionary and salvationist in its underlying content—had a more apocalyptic flavor. It was predicated on a passionate and unswerving faith in the imminence of worldwide revolution. It was this credo which enabled Trotsky to overcome the psychic inhibitions imposed by his residual Jewishness and the reflective intellectuality associated with it. It was a messianism steeled in the Bolshevik-Leninist teaching of revolutionary violence that Trotsky had enthusiastically embraced in October 1917. From that moment, Trotsky had indeed become an *armed* prophet, breaking the last chain linking him to the Jewish tradition which he had so ostentatiously spurned from his childhood. Only when stripped of his power and later condemned to lonely opposition as a pariah and outcast did fate cast Trotsky once more in a more familiar though unwelcome role: that of a wandering Jew and arch-heretic—the "Judas" of world Communism.[69] But already in the mid-1920s Trotsky suspected that Stalin was surreptitiously fomenting antisemitism within the Bolshevik ranks against him. In a letter to Bukharin on 4 March 1926 he strongly protested against anti-Jewish undertones in the whispering campaign being encouraged in Moscow.

> Is it true, is it possible, that in *our party*, in MOSCOW, in WORKERS' CELLS, anti-Semitic agitation should be carried on with impunity?![70]

He repeated the same protest two weeks later, at a Politburo meeting, but his colleagues merely shrugged and professed to know nothing. Stalin's campaign gathered momentum, and in 1927 the "Jews" in the opposition led by Trotsky, Zinoviev, and Kamenev were denounced for agitating against Leninism. Trotsky openly challenged this campaign before the Presidium of the Central Control Commission, which was considering his expulsion, together with that of Grigorii Zinoviev—formerly President of the Communist International. He reiterated that questions worthy of Black Hundred antisemitism were constantly being posed in "workers and peasants' cells" about the "opposition." In his *Platform of the Opposition,* written in 1927, Trotsky for the first time publicly linked this issue with careerism and bureaucratism in the party. Later, in his 1937 pamphlet *Thermidor and Anti-Semitism*, he would develop the idea that Stalin's bureaucracy was actively promoting antisemitism in the USSR, despite the legal ban on it imposed during Lenin's rule.[71]

It was only in defeat and exile that Trotsky began to more fully grasp the reality of Soviet antisemitism, which he had tended to shrug off in the aftermath of the Bolshevik Revolution. He also came to a better understanding of the Jewish workers movement which he had derided in the past. For example, in the 1930s Trotsky established contact with several immigrant Jewish workers' organizations in France and America that published Yiddish-language newspapers. Trotsky not surprisingly insisted that the most important task of Jewish workers in France, as elsewhere, was "to participate in the workers' movement of the land in which they live, work and struggle."[72] He also added, "Sixty thousand Jewish workers in Paris is a great force" (!) and could contribute to shake up "the country's strong conservatism." As foreigners sharing the bottom layers of society with the indigenous proletariat, the Jewish workers were "of an immigrant spirit, more mobile, more receptive to revolutionary ideas!"[73] Their historic mission was to act as a catalyst and to fructify the French working class in a revolutionary manner. At the same time, he emphasized the need for the new immigrants to acquire the French language and fully integrate themselves into French society.

Trotsky's greetings to Jewish workers in America in 1932 were conceived in a similar spirit. He affirmed that:

> Historical conditions have made the Jewish workers susceptible to the ideas of scientific Communism. The very fact of the dispersement of the Jewish workers in a number of countries should instill in them, and does instill in them, the ideas of *internationalism*. In view of this alone, the Communist Left opposition has every reason to count on a big influence among the Jewish proletarians in the United States.[74]

The Jewish workers, precisely because of their "pariah" status, their lack of civil rights and economic situation were "a weak link of the proletariat." Trotsky evidently hoped and believed that this fact would make them receptive to the ideas of the Left opposition which he was seeking to rally against the Stalinist policies of the Comintern.

Trotsky's fundamentally negative view of Zionism was somewhat modified by the menacing situation facing the Jews in the 1930s. On the one hand, he periodically repeated the mantra that the rise of Nazism and the Arab-Jewish struggle in Palestine proved "that the Jewish question cannot be solved within the framework of capitalism."[75] At the same time he did not deny the possibility that Jewry might exist as an independent nation though this could only happen in the context of an international proletarian revolution. However vaguely, he was allowing that large-scale Jewish immigration to Palestine and the establishment of a territorial base there, was not out of the question—either on the basis of a mutual understanding, or with the aid of a kind of international proletarian tribunal which should take up this question and solve it."[76] This hesitancy confirms Trotsky's own admission that he was "not thoroughly familiar with the facts" about Palestine. Asked to comment on official Comintern policy, following the Jewish-Arab clashes in Palestine in 1929, he tentatively suggested that there were mixed elements behind the Arab riots—"such as national liberationists (anti-imperialists) and reactionary Muslims and anti-Semitic pogromists."[77] It seemed to him that all these elements were present—an analysis which was clearly opposed to the official Comintern line advocating unconditional support for the Palestinian Arab struggle. For the Stalinists of that era, there was evidently no problem about justifying Arab pogroms as part of a revolutionary "liberation" struggle.

In 1934, in *Reply to a Question about Birobidjan,* Trotsky again reconsidered his position on the "Jewish Question." Predictably, he still condemned Zionism because it "draws away the workers from the class struggle by means of unrealizable hopes of a Jewish state under capitalist conditions."[78] But he also affirmed that "a workers' government is duty-bound to create for the Jews, as for any nation, the best circumstances for cultural development." This included, by Trotsky's own definition, Jewish schools, press, theater, and a "separate territory for self-administration and development," if they so desired.[79] Clearly, unlike many postwar Trotskyists, the exiled Russian Bolshevik leader had no difficulty in characterizing the Jews as a "nation" nor was he congenitally incapable of revising some of his past dogmas in the light of changing circumstances.

After his arrival in Mexico, in January 1937, Trotsky answered a further series of questions from correspondents of the JTA (Jewish Telegraphic Agency) and *Der Weg* about his attitude to Birobidjan, antisemitism in the Soviet Union, assimilation, and the Palestine problem. The revision of his previous standpoint had become more evident without necessarily implying a deep change in his opposition to Zionism. Nevertheless, Trotsky did acknowledge that his original belief in the "quasi-automatic" disappearance of the Jewish question had proved *unfounded.* Decaying capitalism had everywhere (and especially in Germany) "swung over to an exacerbated nationalism, one part of which is anti-Semitism."[80] Moreover, he now accepted that the rise of a Yiddish language culture had led to the development of a *Jewish nation,* though one which still lacked a territorial base. Zionism sprang from this lack of a common territory, but it would, he believed be incapable of solving the Jewish question. Against the background of the 1936 Arab revolt in Palestine, Trotsky ominously added that the confrontation between the Jews and the Arabs in Palestine was daily acquiring a more tragic and menacing character. Again, he repeated that the Jewish-Arab conflict could not be resolved within the framework of "rotting capitalism" and "under the control of British imperialism."[81]

Trotsky did not foresee that within ten years Great Britain would evacuate Palestine, partly as a result of fierce Zionist resistance to its policy of deporting Jewish survivors of the Holocaust who reached its shores. At the same time he emphasized that the "Jewish nation" was a reality with which one must reckon "for an entire epoch to come." This was undoubtedly an important theoretical shift that some of his followers did not fully internalize.

So, too, was the vision of Jews becoming a *territorial nation* under the condition "of the most developed technique and culture"—utopian though this inevitably sounded.[82] Trotsky was trying to imagine a socialist world with no compulsory migrations or displacement of nationalities, no "creation of new ghettoes"—a freely consented reassemblage of peoples as "part of the planned economy." In other words, only in the context of "the complete emancipation of humanity" would the Jewish issue be laid to rest. "To work for international socialism means also to work for the solution of the Jewish question."[83] These somewhat abstract formulas showed, however, that Trotsky still remained imprisoned within the straitjacket of Marxist dogma.

On the issue of Soviet antisemitism Trotsky was more realistic. He noted that the omnipotent Stalinist bureaucracy in the USSR did not hesitate

> to resort in a scarcely camouflaged manner to chauvinistic tendencies, above all the anti-Semitic ones. The latest Moscow trial, for example, was staged with the hardly concealed design of presenting internationalists as faithless and lawless Jews who are capable of selling themselves to the German Gestapo.[84]

Trotsky himself had been demonized in absentia at the Moscow show trials in 1937 and this must have strengthened still further his personal sense of revulsion at the tactics of Stalin's henchmen. Once again, he traced the emergence of antisemitic demagogy in the USSR back to 1926, emphasizing that it was camouflaged and manipulated "with a cunning skill in order to canalize and to direct especially against the Jews the existing discontent against the bureaucracy."[85] It was an incontrovertible expression, for Trotsky, of the "Thermidorian reaction" under Stalin, a symptom of the "unbridled chauvinist passions" which the Moscow show trials had helped to unleash. Yet this plain statement of the facts aroused strong resentment in some left-wing American Jewish quarters. B. Z. Goldberg, a columnist on the New York Yiddish daily *Der Tog,* publicly objected to Trotsky's "discovery" of antisemitism only after he had lost power and been removed from the Kremlin. The USSR, he insisted, did not oppress its nationalities, nor was there any antisemitism in the Soviet State.[86] Trotsky's views on this issue were, however, more perceptive than those of his critics. In his article entitled "Thermidor and Anti-Semitism," written in February 1937, Trotsky accused his detractors of "vulgar non-dialectical thinking."[87] In their eagerness to counterpose a "kingdom of national harmony" in Stalin's Russia to the "absolutist kingdom of anti-Semitism" in Hitler's Germany they mistook their illusions for reality.[88] Trotsky recalled that the Bolshevik Revolution of 1917 had abolished the outlawed status of the Jews without eliminating the national prejudices deeply rooted in the backward social strata of "Mother" Russia. It was naïve to think that in less than twenty years the Soviet regime could wipe out all the legacies of Tsarism, the "national and chauvinist prejudices, particularly anti-Semitism."[89] In this matter he was certainly correct.

Trotsky insisted on relating the emergence of Soviet antisemitism to the "bureaucratic deformation" of the workers' state. Hatred of the Stalinist bureaucracy by the workers and peasants was "a fundamental fact in Soviet life," and it was all too common to deflect this against the Jewish officials. Fearful of their privileges, Soviet bureaucrats exploited "the most ingrained prejudices and the most benighted instincts" of the populace. For Trotsky the new antisemitism in the Soviet Union was a symptom of this general corruption of the Stalin regime, one of its preferred means "to divert the indignation of the working masses from itself to the Jews."[90] Ever since the mid-1920s Stalin's clique had "purposely emphasized the names of Jewish members of casual and secondary importance." Once Kamenev and Zinoviev joined with Trotsky the situation had rapidly worsened. Jews were removed from responsible party positions even if they supported the general line, and the opposition was depicted as being led by three "dissatisfied Jewish intellectuals."[91] Trotsky categorically stated that the baiting of the opposition in Moscow, Leningrad, and elsewhere "often assumed a thoroughly obvious antisemitic character," and that he had received hundreds of letters deploring this fact.

The slogan "Beat the opposition" took on, in Trotsky's own words, the complexion of the old Tsarist-era slogan "Beat the Jews and save Russia"—the more that Stalin's campaign gathered in intensity.[92] It was in Trotsky's view a carefully calculated and premeditated campaign which did not shrink from dividing the opposition into "orthodox" (i.e., Russian) and "Jewish" factions. Trotsky also emphasized Stalin's exposure of the original *Jewish* names of his opponents Zinoviev (Radomislyski) and Kamenev (Rozenfeld), at the time of the Moscow show trials. He had no doubt that this was intended to foster an antisemitic mood. He was particularly sensitive to the use of such tactics against his own son, Sergei Sedov, whose "real" name had been "unmasked" by the Soviet press as Bronstein. Trotsky bitterly complained at this fact, possibly exaggerating its importance and thereby exposing his own unconscious "Jewish" complex.

> If these falsifiers wished to emphasize the connection of the accused with me, they would have called him Trotsky, since politically the name Bronstein means nothing at all to anyone. But

> they were out for other game; that is, they wished to emphasize my Jewish origin and the semi-Jewish origin of my son. I paused at this episode, because it has a vital and yet not an exceptional character. The whole struggle against the opposition is full of such episodes.[93]

In reply to critics who attacked him for "suddenly" raising the Jewish question, Trotsky conceded that in the past it had "never occupied the centre of my attention." But this was no argument for silence and blindness to a problem "which exists and demands solution." The creation of a Jewish Autonomous Region in Birobidjan was not, however, the answer. Birobidjan was "a bureaucratic farce" which could never succeed, since it was organized by Stalinist methods. Only under a Soviet democracy and "completely *voluntary* migrations" within a federal socialist regime could a territorial solution to the Jewish problem have any chance of success.[94] Trotsky was apparently prepared to envisage an "independent Jewish republic" in a more democratized USSR on the lines of a free and independent Ukraine.

Since the early 1930s Trotsky had also become increasingly aware of the mounting threat of Nazism for the future of the European proletariat and the agenda of the world revolution. Indeed his analyses of National Socialism stand out as one of the more incisive attempts in Marxist literature to understand "this stupendous phenomenon of social psychopathology." To be sure he never altogether freed himself from the limitations of Marxist ideology in addressing this issue or from his excessive optimism concerning the revolutionary mission of the working class. Hence his romantic illusions concerning the ability of the German or Russian proletariat to resist, let alone overthrow totalitarian dictatorships like Nazism and Stalinism, from within. Moreover, like most Communists, he tended to ignore the extent to which the *political* power structure (the single Party, the secret police, the bureaucracy) constituted an autonomous dynamic force more weighty than property relations. Trotsky was as mistaken as the Stalinists in regarding fascism as serving the interests of big capital in the last resort. Equally restrictive and reductionist was the insistence on analyzing fascism only in the context of capitalist crisis. Nevertheless, Trotsky's critique of Communist as well as Social Democratic strategies in confronting German National Socialism was exceptionally perspicacious for its time.[95] The German Communist Party (KPD), following Stalin's orders, had after 1928 begun to concentrate its fire more against the "fascist social democrats" (the SPD) than against the Nazis. Indeed, the Communists even claimed that Hitler could not be defeated without the total destruction of the SPD. At the same time, the KPD leader

Ernst Thaelmann brashly told the Comintern Executive in April 1931 that the Nazi party was set on an irreversible downward spiral. This did not prevent the KPD from flirting with "the phraseology of German nationalism" while seeking to undermine working class support for the Social Democrats. Their grossly mistaken premise was "that Hitler would add nothing new; that there was no cause to fear Hitler; that Hitler will only clear the road for the communists."[96]

This Communist strategy revealed to Trotsky an "utter misunderstanding of mass psychology and of the dialectics of revolutionary struggle." For once Hitler gained power no amount of speeches about the future "Soviet Germany" would sweep him away.[97] Worse still, the Stalinist approach had demoralized the German proletariat which was being "paralyzed from above" by its own misguided leadership. Nor were the German Social Democrats, with their blind faith in the Weimar Constitution and in the norms of bourgeois legality, much better in a time of acute crisis. Their ineffectual politics of reform and timidity had merely prolonged the agony of the capitalist regime, depriving the German proletariat of its capacity to lead the petty-bourgeois masses, thereby strengthening the social base of Nazism.[98] Since 1918, the Social Democrats, instead of mobilizing the German workers to conquer power, had been issuing vain appeals to the existing state apparatus, the police and even the Army. They, too, had a historic responsibility in the abysmal failure to organize joint proletarian action against Hitler.[99] Without this fighting unity, Trotsky warned the workers, as early as December 1931, Nazism in power would exterminate the flower of the German proletariat, destroy its independent organizations, and "ride over your skulls and spines like a terrific tank."[100] This was heady stuff and unfortunately it proved to be only too accurate.

As we have suggested, Leon Trotsky attributed the dramatic growth of Nazism after 1930 to two crucial factors:

> a deep social crisis, throwing the petty-bourgeois masses [in Germany] off balance, and the lack of a revolutionary party that would today be regarded by the popular masses as the acknowledged revolutionary leader.[101]

This conjuncture had given German fascism the initiative over the Communists and turned it into a *real* danger by 1931, as the bourgeois parliamentary regime began to crumble. The German fascist leadership also proved superior to its opponents on the Left. Trotsky did not ignore Hitler's role in becoming the focus of "anonymous historic forces" or deny his ability to express the exasperation of the pauperized masses, the upstarts from the old army, and the decaying *Mittelstand* in German society. Trotsky unmistakably despised Hitler as a "pretentious misfit with a sick psyche," who exuded monomania while vilifying Jews and Socialists on his long climb to the top. At the start of his political career, Hitler had stood out primarily because of his fiery temperament, his harsh booming voice, and "intellectual mediocrity." But he had shrewdly exploited the powerful grievances against the Versailles *Diktat* and the high cost of living, the resentment against bankers and Jewish journalists. Better than all the other demagogues he had known how to give voice to a mass of "ruined and drowning people with scars and fresh bruises." Hitler's endless harangues resounded "now like commands, and now like prayers" addressed to inexorable fate. Even his sentimental formlessness and the absence of disciplined thought in his utterances had ultimately turned into pluses, enabling him "to unite all types of dissatisfaction in the beggar's bowl of National Socialism. . . ."[102]

Trotsky acknowledged that the Nazis had successfully won over sections of the German proletariat, a layer of the unemployed masses (from the Communist ranks), many salaried employees, technical and administrative personnel, petty traders, hawkers, and *lumpenproletarians*. The National Socialists had skillfully whipped up the frustrations of the petty bourgeoisie to a white heat. Everything in Nazism was "as contradictory and chaotic as in a nightmare." Five months before the Nazi seizure of power, Trotsky perceptively summed up some of the glaring contradictions in the movement:

> Hitler's party calls itself socialist, yet it leads a terrorist struggle against all socialist organizations. It calls itself a workers' party, yet its ranks include all classes except the proletariat. It hurls lightning bolts at the heads of the capitalists, yet it is supported by them. It bows before Germanic traditions, yet it aspires to Caesarism, a completely Latin institution."[103]

Fascism, for Trotsky, compellingly demonstrated the inexhaustible reserves of human savagery, darkness, and ignorance in the lower depths of society. In June 1933 the exiled Bolshevik leader would give a particularly devastating depiction of this barbaric side of National Socialism:

> Everything that should have been eliminated from the national organism in the course of the unhindered development of society comes out gushing from the throat; capitalist society is puking up the undigested barbarism. Such is the physiology of National Socialism.[104]

Nevertheless, Trotsky's impassioned logic had its limitations. He alluded in overly simplistic terms to "the immense poverty of National Socialist philosophy"—ignoring its solid ideological foundations and intellectual base of support. He hyperbolically dismissed Hitler's millions of followers as "human rubbish."[105] Like so many Marxists he despised the "social consciousness" of the fascists as being far inferior to that of the proletariat. Their race theories were mocked as "zoological materialism borrowed at second hand" without explaining why they had achieved such resonance, even among renowned artists, academics, and scientists. In practice racism, according to Trotsky, boiled down to economic liberalism, freed from the constraints of political liberty. It was "a vapid and bombastic variety of chauvinism," expressing the deluded fantasies of the pauperized petty bourgeoisie. This was vulgar Marxism at its worst, a superficial and reductionist analysis of the role that antisemitic race theories played in National Socialism.

Trotsky's approach to Nazi racism revealed that he was far too much of a rationalist to grasp the power of mythical ideas in modern dress. Like most Marxists he was prone to dismiss such ideologies as being the impotent ravings of a confused *Kleinbürger* mentality. His view of Nazi Jew-baiting in 1933 hardly moved beyond conventional Communist perceptions except perhaps in its (sardonic) willingness to invoke the concept of evil.

> The Nazis abstract the usurious or banking capital from the modern economic system because it is the spirit of evil; and as is well known, it is precisely in this sphere that the Jewish bourgeoisie occupies an important position. Bowing down before capitalism as a whole, the petty bourgeois declares war against the evil spirit of gain in the guise of the Polish Jew in a long-skirted caftan and usually without a cent in his pocket.[106]

By January 1937, in an interview with Jewish correspondents in Mexico City, Trotsky clearly understood that these earlier assessments of antisemitism and the "Jewish Question" were no longer adequate. After the Nazi triumph, all his long-held assumptions about Jewish emancipation and assimilation were rapidly being overtaken by events.

> During my youth I rather leaned towards the prognoses that the Jews of different countries would be assimilated and that the Jewish Question would disappear in quasi-automatic fashion. The historical development of the last quarter of a century has not confirmed this perspective. Decaying capitalism has everywhere

> swung over to an exacerbated nationalism, one part of which is anti-Semitism. The Jewish Question has loomed largest in the most highly developed capitalist country of Europe, in Germany.[107]

Trotsky in this 1937 interview acknowledged that the very core of the Marxist analysis of the Jewish question had been misconceived. Jews, far from becoming more deeply integrated as a result of capitalist development, were being brutally squeezed and excluded from nation-states across the globe. Antisemitism, far from merely being the product of semi-feudal social structures (as in prewar Tsarist Russia or Romania) had reached new heights in advanced modern societies like Germany, at the very apex of scientific, technological, and business efficiency. Nationalism, far from diminishing in the era of global markets, had grown more intense, violent and extreme. What then was left of the theoretical edifice concerning the "Jewish Question" erected by the disciples of Marx, Engels, and Lenin?

Trotsky, admittedly, still clung to the classic Bolshevik illusion that racism and antisemitism were ultimately malignant convulsions of the *capitalist* death-agony. The Fourth International, which he had recently founded, adopted in its transitional program his call for an "uncompromising disclosure of the roots of race prejudice and all forms and shades of national arrogance and chauvinism, particularly anti-Semitism. . . ."[108] These were conventional and somewhat wooden slogans. But Trotsky's own analysis of Stalinist antisemitism had already implied that antisemitism was hardly restricted to the capitalist world. Moreover, the former Bolshevik leader was himself underlining, by 1938, the "gigantic dimension of the evil burdening the Jewish people." Indeed, with astonishing prescience Trotsky even predicted the impending global catastrophe of the Jews which has come to be known as the Holocaust. Contrary to an influential body of post-Shoah commentary which includes historians like Jacob Katz, Walter Laqueur, Michael Marrus, and Yehuda Bauer, who have emphasized the impossibility of predicting the Holocaust, Trotsky spoke unequivocally of the forthcoming *annihilation* of the Jews.[109] His appeal to American Jews, written in December 1938 clearly pointed to the "physical extermination of the Jews."

Trotsky could not, of course, be expected to specify the exact form in which such a Holocaust might occur, but he related its *certainty* to what were observable trends at the time.[110] He noted that "the number of countries which expel the Jews grows without cease," while those ready to accept refugees was rapidly diminishing.[111] He recognized the dire predicament of world Jewry which demanded the audacious mobilization of the workers against fascism and antisemitism as well as concerted action by the Jewish people, especially American Jewry. Trotsky added a chilling prophecy:

> It is possible to imagine without difficulty what awaits the Jews at the mere outbreak of the future world war. But even without war the next development of world reaction signifies with certainty the *physical extermination of the Jews*.[112]

Two months later, on 30 January 1939, Adolf Hitler himself would, for the first time, declare to the German Reichstag that in the event of a second world war, the result would be "the destruction of the Jewish race in Europe" rather than the "Bolshevization" of the earth. Trotsky had uncannily anticipated Hitler's own self-fulfilling *genocidal* prophecy. It seems to me that Trotsky, with all his many flaws, was more perceptive on this point, than most of his contemporaries and many historians of the Holocaust. Beyond his unusual powers of intuition, Trotsky's all-too-accurate warning revealed his awareness that Nazi antisemitism was in fact far more than merely a petty-bourgeois backlash against modernity. Nor was it simply a marginal symptom of "decaying capitalism," though Trotsky could never quite free himself from this traditional Marxist cliché.[113] Nevertheless, by 1939, he felt in his bones that Nazi Jew-hatred was a culminating point of contemporary barbarism with *genocidal consequences* for the Jewish people.

Trotsky's last general comment on the "Jewish Question" would come in May 1940, when he drafted a manifesto to the world proletariat, presented at an Emergency Conference of the Fourth International. It briefly analyzed, among other things, the relationship between imperialism and antisemitism. In the "monstrous intensification of chauvinism and especially of antisemitism" Trotsky discerned the final bankruptcy of moribund capitalism.

> Today decaying capitalist society is striving to squeeze the Jewish people from all its pores; seventeen million individuals out of the two billion populating the globe, that is, less than one per cent, can no longer find a place on our planet! Amid the vast expanses of land and the marvels of technology, which has also conquered the skies for man as well as the earth, the bourgeoisie has managed to convert our planet into a foul prison. . . .[114]

In the same text, Adolf Hitler's "zoological" antisemitism was described as the "chemically pure distillation of the culture of imperialism." Trotsky pointedly observed that since the Nazi-Soviet pact there had not been even a "single word of condemnation about the destruction of Czechoslovakia and

Poland, the seizure of Denmark and Norway and the shocking bestialities inflicted by Hitler's gangs on the Polish and Jewish people!"[115]

In July 1940, only a month before his assassination in Mexico City by an agent of the Soviet secret police, Trotsky also expressed his views on the Palestine problem. His remarks came in response to the draconian British White Paper drastically restricting Jewish immigration to the National Home. The prognosis was dire though accurate enough in its assessment of Great Britain's massive betrayal of its promises to Zionism. Where Trotsky erred was in his dogmatic linkage of the Jewish fate to the development of capitalism.

> The attempt to solve the Jewish question through the migration of Jews to Palestine can now be seen for what it is, a tragic mockery of the Jewish people. Interested in winning the sympathy of the Arabs who are more numerous than the Jews, the British government has sharply altered its policy toward the Jews, and has actually renounced its promise to help them found their "own home" in a foreign land. The future development of military events may well transform Palestine into a bloody trap for several hundred thousand Jews. Never was it so clear as it is today, that the salvation of the Jewish people is bound up inseparably with the overthrow of the capitalist system.[116]

Trotsky's negation of Zionist prospects to establish a Jewish State in Palestine was not new. Ever since the days of Herzl (nearly forty years earlier) he had seriously underestimated Zionist will, tenacity,and idealism. Moreover, his ignorance of Jewish religion and culture made him virtually tone-deaf to the profound historical connection between the Jewish people and the land of Israel. Indeed he was notoriously allergic to nationalist appeals of any kind. Moreover, he knew very little about the situation on the ground in British-controlled Palestine, though since 1929 he had sporadically collected and received material on the Jewish labor movement and the Arab population in Palestine. In 1934, when asked specifically if Palestine could be a possible Jewish homeland, he expressed skepticism while not excluding the idea of a territorial base for Jewry in a post-capitalist international order. According to a Russian-born Zionist socialist, Bela Idelson, who visited him in June 1937 in Mexico City, he listened attentively to her detailed insider account of Jewish settlement in Palestine. He even seemed to be moved by her descriptions of the collective settlements and eager to learn more. Idelson was asked, however, to keep their conversation secret—which she did for 19 years. By way of explanation, Trotsky told her:

> The world will not understand. People will seek in this, too, grounds for accusing me of harboring alien views, and perhaps even sympathy for Zionism.[117]

Idelson, for her part, was struck by the sense of Trotsky's otherness: "a feeling accompanied me all the time that he was a Jew, a wandering Jew, without a fatherland."[118]

On the other hand, there have been historians such as Baruch Knei-Paz who argued that there was no "Jewishness" detectable in Trotsky's works or actions.[119] This seems more than questionable in the light of our analysis, even though the Bolshevik leader sought in different ways to downplay his Jewish background after October 1917—ultimately to no avail.[120] A desire to suppress Jewishness is not, however, always identical to self-loathing. For example, Trotsky never used Karl Marx's *Zur Judenfrage* to bolster whatever latent anti-Jewish prejudices he may have harbored. Nor (unlike some other Jewish revolutionaries) can one find any *overt* manifestations of self-hatred in his conduct.[121] Nor could one accuse Trotsky of deliberately downplaying antisemitism of the Stalinist variety. On the contrary, in January 1937 he told the New York *Jewish Daily Forward* that Soviet bureaucrats played "a double game in the Jewish question. . . ." Thus they might periodically make official statements against antisemitism, they would even bring "bigoted pogromists" to trial and sometimes decided to shoot them. But he quickly added that "they systematically exploit anti-Semitic prejudices in order to compromise every opposition group."[122] He recalled that in 1927 Stalin had gone out of his way to state that he was "struggling against Trotsky, Zinoviev, Kamenev and others, not because they are Jews but because they are Oppositionists." Trotsky mocked this declaration. "The intention," he told his American Jewish interviewer, "was to clearly indicate that at the head of the Opposition stand Jews."[123] This interpretation was consistent with his more general assessment that the political methods of Stalin and Hitler differed little from each other. Nonetheless, Trotsky stopped just short of classifying Stalinism as a species of Red fascism. But he did avow that nobody (not even Hitler) struck so ferociously at fellow Communists as had Stalin and his "willing executioners." Moreover, Soviet antisemitism was a symptom of profound societal "degeneration." So, too, was the willingness of Stalin's USSR, after September 1939, to hand over to the Gestapo a large group of German anti-fascists and Jews who had escaped from Nazi persecution.[124]

Trotsky's residual Jewish identity had been strictly subordinated for almost twenty years to the international Communist ideal. He had embraced

Bolshevism with uninhibited zeal and ardor only in the summer of 1917. As Angelica Balabanoff perceptively remarked, his prewar history of ideological conflicts with Lenin had made him, if anything, even more intransigent, revolutionary, and Bolshevik after October 1917 than his peers.[125] It was then that Trotsky's harsher traits became more manifest in his way of fiercely condemning any sign of weakness, vacillation, or indecision in others. To some extent he appeared to associate these traits with the Jewish, "petty-bourgeois" and intellectual background from which he came. In his own self-image, even before his conversion to Bolshevism, he had sought to incorporate what were then considered as non-Jewish characteristics of boldness, steel-like resolution, *machismo,* and heroic grandeur far removed from the ways of the *shtetl.* This "overcompensation" was manifest, too, in his derisive treatment of a fellow Russian Jewish revolutionary, Julius Martov (Zederbaum), the founder of Russian Menshevism – with whom he had once been friendly. Martov was no less Russified a Jew than Trotsky and for a time they had even shared a common antipathy to Lenin's centralism and his insistence on a conspiratorial underground party of professional revolutionaries.[126] Trotsky subsequently came to despise Martov's "soft" approach to revolution, which tried to align Russian Social Democracy with the more liberal-democratic credo of its Western parliamentary counterparts. Martov's prescient warnings against the Bolshevik *putsch* in 1917 were mocked by Trotsky as signs of weakness, reflecting the passivity, capitulation and lack of courage supposedly endemic to Menshevik thought.

Martov's "indecision" would become a codeword for the vulgar "philistinism," shopkeeper mentality, compliancy, and cowardice that Trotsky (the Bolshevik neophyte) henceforth associated not only with the Russian bourgeois intelligentsia but with reformist Social Democrats in general. These were also features, in Trotsky's eyes, of a specifically Jewish "petty-bourgeois" mentality that throughout his Bolshevik career he repeatedly denigrated. At the 2nd Congress of Soviets in Petrograd (October 1917) Trotsky had imperiously consigned Martov to the *rubbish bin of history.* Elsewhere he deprecatingly satirized Martov's dialectic as "the thought of a watchmaker in politics." Martov represented, in effect, that whole cluster of petty-bourgeois stereotypes tinged with antisemitism that Trotsky was determined to banish from his horizon. They included "physical weakness, irresolution, softness, subtlety, effeminacy, and Jewishness."[127] These were negative "Jewish" characteristics which the young Trotsky wished to repudiate and overcome in himself. Martov as a Menshevik leader, unconsciously epitomized for the "Bolshevik" Trotsky, the weak, indecisive

Jew, the Hamlet personality which had to be eradicated. That was the kind of Jew that Trotsky most definitely did not want to be, a personality lacking the instinct, the energy, will-power and leadership ability to make "hard" and ruthless decisions. Ironically, as Trotsky's own ambivalences and political failure in the struggle for power with Stalin during the 1920s were to amply demonstrate, he never fully succeeded in shaking off this shadow Jew in his own unconscious. Indeed he would frequently be charged by his adversaries with doctrinaire intellectualism. The most intransigent of revolutionary Bolsheviks would himself fall victim to a "man of steel" (Stalin's adopted Russian name)—who was even harder than himself. Ironically, in the last decade of his stormy career, it was Leon Trotsky—hero of the Revolution and the Civil War—who would be unceremoniously cast into another "rubbish bin of history." He would become the arch-heretic of the Stalinist theocratic universe institutionalized by the Comintern—the scapegoat for all its reversals, failures, and defeats.

NOTES

1. Victor Serge, *Memoirs of a Revolutionary 1901–1941* (paperback, Oxford, 1967), 140.

2. Ibid., 348.

3. Ibid., 349.

4. Leon Trotsky, *My Life* (New York, 1930), 5.

5. See Vladimir Medem, *Fun mein Lebn* (New York, 1923), 2: 9. Also Leon Trotsky, "A Social Democrat Only," in *The Golden Tradition: Jewish Life and Thought in Eastern Europe,* edited by Lucy S. Dawidowicz (London, 1967), 441.

6. Samuel A. Portnoy, ed., *Vladimir Medem. The Life and Soul of a Legendary Jewish Socialist* (New York, 1979), 268–69.

7. Trotsky, *My Life,* 5–6.

8. Ibid., 84.

9. See Joseph Nedava, *Trotsky and the Jews* (Philadelphia, 1972), 35; and Joel Carmichael, *Trotsky: An Appreciation of His Life* (London, 1975), 17. Both skeptically regard this claim as part of Trotsky's affected indifference to Jewishness.

10. Bertram D. Wolfe, *Three Who Made a Revolution* (London, 1966), 205–6.

11. Leon Trotsky, *My Life*, 86.

12. Ibid., 85.

13. Ibid., 86–87.

14. Ibid., 81–84.

15. Ibid., 340–41.

16. Ibid., 86–87.

17. Ibid., 110–11.

18. See Robert Wistrich, *Trotsky. Fate of a Revolutionary* (New York, 1982); also Albert Glotzer, *Trotsky. Memoir and Critique* (Buffalo, N.Y., 1989) and Dmitri Volkogonov, *Trotsky. The Eternal Revolutionary* (New York, 1996).

19. Isaac Deutscher, *The Age of Permanent Revolution: A Trotsky Anthology* (New York, 1964), 64.

20. See Henry J. Tobias, "The Bund and Lenin until 1903," *Russian Review* 29, no. 4 (Oct. 1961); *Vtoroi S'ezd RSDRP Protokoly* (Moscow, 1959), 50–123; see also Portnoy, *Vladimir Medem,* 272–89.

21. R. Abramovich, *In Tsvei Revolutsies* (New York, 1944), 1: 115. "The contention between Iskra and the Bund was to a certain extent a struggle between assimilationists and national-Yiddishists within the Jewish people itself. The struggle revolved around the question of whether the Jewish people in Russia would assimilate or not."

22. *Vtoroi S'ezd RSDRP Protokoly, Otchet Sibirkoi Delegatsii* (Geneva, 1903), 57.

23. Ibid.

24. Quoted in Glotzer, *Trotsky,* 211.

25. See Nedava, *Trotsky,* 96–98.

26. Chaim Weizmann, *Trial and Error* (Philadelphia, 1949), 50.

27. V. I. Lenin, "Polozhenie Bunda v Partii," *Iskra*, no. 51 (22 Oct. 1903).

28. Leon Trotsky, "Razlozhenie Sionizma i ego vozmozhnye preemniki," *Iskra* (1 Jan. 1904); see also Nedava, *Trotsky,* 196–97.

29. See Vladimir Medem, *Shestoi Sionistichesky Kongress v Bazele* (London, 1903), 29–30. "One thing is clear to us: political Zionism is bankrupt. . .the liquidation of Zionism has begun." Also Medem, *Fun mein Lebn,*2: 33ff.

30. Trotsky, "Razlozhenie Sionizma."

31. Ibid.

32. Vladimir Medem, *Fun mein Lebn,*2: 8–9.

33. Nedava, *Trotsky*, 54–57.

34. Ibid., 61.

35. See Robert Wistrich, *Trotsky,* 145–47.

36. Ibid., 146–47.

37. Nedava, *Trotsky,* 75–77. Beilis was eventually released after a worldwide outcry.

38. Ibid., 77.

39. L. Trotsky and C. Rakovsky, *Ocherki Politicheskii Ruminii* (Moscow-Petrograd, 1923), Ch. 9, p. 82 (*Evreiskii Vopros*, 17–21 Aug. 1913, *Kievskaia Mysl,* nos. 226, 229, 230 [1913]).

40. Ibid.

41. Trotsky, *Evreiskii Vopros,* 83

42. Ibid., 84.

43. Ibid., 85–88.

44. *Age of Permanent Revolution,* 74.

45. Ibid.

46. See Joel Carmichael, *Trotsky*, 148–84; Wistrich, *Trotsky,* 76–93.

47. Nedava, *Trotsky,* 199–200. Trotsky took little interest in the activities of the Yevsektsiia—the Jewish sections of the Russian Communist Party.

48. Leon Trotsky, *Nashi Politicheskie Zadachi* (Geneva, 1904), 95.

49. Ibid.

50. E. H. Carr, *Socialism in One Country* (New York, 1958), 1: 139–52, observed that Trotsky was the most Westernized and Stalin the least European among the Bolshevik leaders. He pointed out that Trotsky emphasized with special zest "the nullity of the Russian contribution to civilization."

51. Leon Trotsky, *The Permanent Revolution* (New York, 1962), 6–10; see also Volkogonov, *Trotsky,* 196–211.

52. Trotsky, *My Life,* 341.

53. Ibid., 340. Lenin's angry reply, as recorded by Trotsky, was to say: "We are having a great international revolution; of what importance are such trifles?"

54. Ibid., 361.

55. Ibid.

56. Avraham Yarmolinsky, *The Jews and Other Minorities under the Soviets* (New York, 1928), 50; see also Zvi Y. Gitelman, *Jewish Nationality and Soviet Politics* (Princeton, 1972), 117–18; also Oleg Budnitskii, ed., *Evrei i Russkaya Revoliutsiya* (Moscow, 1999), and idem, "The Jews and Revolution: Russian Perspectives, 1881–1918," *East European Jewish Affairs*. 38, no. 3 (Dec. 2008): 321–34.

57. E. Tcherikover, *Antisemitizm un Pogromen in Ukraine 1917–18* (Berlin, 1923), 103–4. See also Nedava, *Trotsky,* 156, 162–66.

58. Abba Ahimeir, *Yudaika* (Tel Aviv, n.d.). See Nedava, *Trotsky,* 166.

59. Budnitskii, *Evrei,* 7, 18. Dubnow's diary entry was dated 7 Jan. 1918. See S. N. Dubnow, *Kniga zhizhi. Vospominaniia i razmyshleniia. Materialy dlia istorii moega vremeni* (Riga, 1935), 2: 222–47.

60. Leon Trotsky, *The Trotsky Papers,* Vol. I: *1917–1919,* edited by Jan M. Meijer (The Hague, 1964), 361–63. This statement appeared in a cable dispatched by Trotsky as head of the Military Revolutionary Committee, on 10 May 1919. It was in response to requests by Poale Zion and was sabotaged by the Yevsektsiia. On Trotsky's general attitude to Jewish recruits in the Red Army, see Nedava, *Trotsky,* 110–15; also Budnitskii, *Evrei,* 339–40.

61. See G. A. Ziv, *Trotsky-Kharakteristika po Lichnym Vospominiam* (New York, 1921), 46; also the *Jewish Chronicle,* 28 Dec. 1917, 7. The Chief Rabbi of Petrograd quoted Trotsky as saying to him just after the Balfour Declaration, "I am not a Jew; I am an internationalist."

62. Leon Trotsky, *My Life,* 20.

63. Nedava, *Trotsky,* 167.

64. Ibid., 112–13.

65. Isaac Deutscher, *The Prophet Unarmed. Trotsky: 1921–1929* (London 1970), 259, 286–88.

66. J. V. Stalin, *Works* (Moscow, 1953–1955), 6: 350–352; Robert C. Tucker, *Stalin as Revolutionary 1879–1929* (London, 1974), 380–90.

67. Leon Trotsky, *Stalin* (New York, 1958), 393–94; L. Trotsky, *The Revolution Betrayed* (New York, 1945), 277.

68. Winston Churchill, *Great Contemporaries* (London, 1937), p. 202.

69. Robert Wistrich, *Trotsky,* 99.

70. Quoted in Robert S. Wistrich, *Revolutionary Jews from Marx to Trotsky* (London, 1976), 201.

71. "Leon Trotsky, "Thermidor und Antisemitismus 22nd February 1937," in *Marxisten gegen Antisemitismus,* edited by Iring Fetscher (Hamburg, 1974), 179–88.

72. See Leon Trotsky, *On the Jewish Question* (New York, 1970), 14–15. The letter referred to here was written by Trotsky from Prinkipo (Turkey) and published in *Klorkeit,* no. 3 (May 1930). Its subject was "The Role of the Jewish Workers' Movement within the General Workers Movement in France."

73. Trotsky, *On the Jewish Question,* 15.

74. Ibid., 16. From a letter of 9 May 1932 to *Unser Kamf,* a Trotskyist Yiddish-language paper in New York.

75. Ibid., 18. Letter of 7 Aug. 1932 to Lazar Kling, editor of *Unser Kamf.* These letters can be found in the YIVO Institute in New York.

76. Ibid.

77. Ibid.

78. Trotsky, *On the Jewish Question,* 19.

79. Ibid.

80. See *Writings of Leon Trotsky (1932–33)* (New York, 1972), 133–36, 246–57; Also Isaac Deutscher, *The Prophet Outcast. Trotsky: 1929–1940* (London, 1970), 132–54; and Wistrich, *Trotsky*, 176–94.

81. Trotsky, *On the Jewish Question,* 20. From the interview given in Mexico on 18 Jan. 1937 which appeared in the Yiddish socialist paper *Forverts,* 24 Jan. 1937.

82. Trotsky, *On the Jewish Question,* 21.

83. Ibid.

84. Ibid.

85. Ibid.

86. *Der Tog*, 26 Jan. 1937, quoted in Nedava, *Trotsky,* 186.

87. "Leo Trotzki, Thermidor und Antisemitismus," in *Marxisten gegen Antisemitismus,* edited by Irving Fetscher (Hamburg, 1974), 179–88.

88. Ibid., 179.

89. Ibid., 180.

90. Ibid., 181.

91. Ibid.

92. Robert S. Wistrich, *Revolutionary Jews,* 205.

93. Ibid.

94. Trotsky, *On the Jewish Question,* 28–29.

95. See Leon Trotsky, *The Struggle against Fascism* (London, 1975).

96. Idem, "What Next?," in *Struggle against Fascism,* 148.

97. Idem, "The German Catastrophe. The Responsibility of the Leadership," in *Struggle against Fascism,* 402 (28 May 1933).

98. Idem, "The Only Road," in *Struggle against Fascism,* 273.

99. Idem, What Next?,"in *Struggle against Fascism,* 116–17, 123.

100. Idem, "For a Workers' United Front against Fascism" (8 Dec. 1931), in *Struggle against Fascism,* 109.

101. Idem., "The Turn in the Communist International," in *Struggle against Fascism,* 13–14.

102. Idem, "What Is National Socialism?" (June 10, 1933), in *Struggle against Fascism*. 408-409.

103. Idem, "The German Puzzle" (Aug. 1932), in *Struggle against Fascism,* 252.

104. See Robert Wistrich, *Trotsky,* 176–77.

105. Leon Trotsky, "Before the Decision," in *Struggle against Fascism,* 341.

106. Idem, "What Is National Socialism?," in *Struggle against Fascism*, 412.

107. Leon Trotsky, *On the Jewish Question* (New York, 1973).

108. Wistrich, *Trotsky,* 190–91.

109. See Jacob Katz, "Was the Holocaust Predictable?," in *The Holocaust as a Historical Experience,* edited by Y. Bauer and N. Rotenstreich (New York, 1981), 23–41; Walter Laqueur, *The Terrible Secret* (London, 1980), 1–10; Michael Marrus, *The Holocaust in History* (London, 1987), 156–64. Y. Bauer, *The Holocaust in Historical Perspective* (Seattle, 1978), 15–22 even suggests that nobody predicted the Holocaust—in the sense of the mass murder of millions of human beings. That is not quite the case. See Robert S. Wistrich, *Hitler and the Holocaust* (New York, 2003).

110. See Norman Geras, "Marxists before the Holocaust," *New Left Review* 224 (July–Aug. 1997): 19–20.

111. Leon Trotsky, "An Appeal to American Jews, menaced by Fascism and Anti-Semitism," written on 22 Dec. 1938 and printed in *Fourth International* (Dec. 1945).

112. Ibid.

113. See Enzo Traverso, *Les Marxistes et la question juive* (Montreuil, 1990), 155–56, 219–22; and Geras, "Marxists before the Holocaust, 26–27.

114. Extract from a manifesto of the Emergency Conference of the Fourth International held in May 1940. Reprinted in *Writings of Leon Trotsky (1939–1940)* (New York, 1969) and Fetscher, ed., "Leo Trotzki, Imperialismus und Antisemitismus," 189–90.

115. Ibid.

116. Quoted in Trotsky, *On the Jewish Question,* 12.

117. Her recollections were eventually published in the Tel Aviv Hebrew daily *Davar,* 6 July 1956. Some extracts were reproduced by Nevada, *Trotsky,* 206–7.

118. Ibid., 206.

119. Baruch Knei-Paz, *The Social and Political Thought of Leon Trotsky* (New York, 1978), 541–43.

120. Ibid.

121. Robert S. Wistrich, *Revolutionary Jews,* 192–207.

122. "Interview with Trotsky," *Jewish Daily Forward,* 18 Jan. 1937; see also A. Glotzer, *Trotsky,* 222–23.

123. Ibid.

124. Sergei Kudriashov, "L. D. Trotsky and the Second World War," in *The Trotsky Reappraisal,* edited by Terry Brotherstone and Paul Dukes (Edinburgh, 1992), 90.

125. Wistrich, *Revolutionary Jews,* 189.

126. On Martov, see Wistrich, *Revolutionary Jews,* 176–88.

127. Philip Pomper, "Trotsky and Martov," in Brotherstone and Dukes, *Trotsky Reappraisal,* 166–76.

PART III

Anti-Zionist Mythologies

CHAPTER 13

From Lenin to the Soviet Black Hundreds

The month of November 1917, which witnessed both the Balfour Declaration of the British Government and the Bolshevik Revolution in Russia, was a watershed in European, Jewish, and world history. For the next 72 years until the fall of the Berlin wall there would be no abatement in the historic antagonism between the ideologies of Communism and Zionism, despite periodic efforts to find some common ground. Except for a brief period immediately preceding and following the creation of the Jewish State in 1948, considerations of ideology and *Realpolitik* dictated a pro-Arab and anti-Zionist Soviet policy in the Middle East. Similarly, with the crucial exception of the Second World War when the Soviet Union was prepared to exploit "Jewish solidarity" for its own purposes (to raise funds and win political support in the West) considerable efforts were made to repress all spontaneous manifestations of Jewish nationalism within its own borders. Nevertheless, it would be mistaken to regard Communist attitudes to Zionism as constituting a monolithic, unbroken line of development which never underwent any adaptation or change. The historic situations of 1917, 1947, and the immediate post-1967 period, to take only the most important turning-points before the actual collapse of Communism, were strikingly different and they produced a diverse pattern of Jewish challenge and Soviet response.

It is important to note that a strong, well-organized Zionist movement had already developed among the Russian and Ukrainian Jewish communities well before the First World War. Opposition to this trend was most intense in the Jewish socialist Bund, thus giving early Russian anti-Zionism the character of an internal, Jewish family quarrel. Again, in the first decade of Soviet rule it was local, Jewish communist officials of the *Yevsektsiia* (a special section of the People's Commissariat for Nationality affairs) who were most active in harassing and denouncing the Zionist movement as "counter-revolutionary," "clerical," and "nationalistic."[1] Given the role of establishing the "Dictatorship of the Proletariat in the Jewish street," these officials (many of them former militants of the Bund) far outstripped the Soviet government in their energetic, anti-Zionist zeal. The early Bolshevik leaders, ironically enough, showed proof of greater tolerance. Indeed, they did not decisively clamp down on Zionist organizations before 1924. In this respect it is interesting to recall that neither Lenin, Trotsky, nor Stalin paid much attention to Zionism before 1917 though they unanimously repudiated the concept of a "Jewish nationality" as unscientific and reactionary.[2] In Lenin's polemics, in particular, one finds a fierce critique of the Bund, its organizational concept, and its claim to exclusively represent the Jewish proletariat. This was repeated in Stalin's theoretical writings before 1914. Little, however, was said by Lenin or Stalin about the Zionists. This fact would later be distorted in postwar Soviet literature on the subject which misleadingly equated Bundism with Zionism, as if they were two identical nationalist "heresies."

After 1914 Lenin came to modify his earlier assimilationist perspective on both the national and the "Jewish" questions, seeing in movements for national liberation a potential lever for the overthrow of Tsarism. Recognizing that the Russian Jewish masses were far from assimilated, Lenin also saw the need (perhaps in response to the Zionist challenge) for granting full civic *and* national rights to the Jews who were henceforth designated as a "nationality." The Bolsheviks in the 1920s, ironically enough, took over some aspects of the Bundist policy of cultural-national autonomy even as they outlawed the Bund and all opposition parties, condemned as obsolete remnants of the *ancien régime*.[3] One temporary consequence of the Leninist policy in the 1920s was a flourishing socialist-oriented Jewish culture, mainly expressed in the Yiddish language, with its own network of Jewish schools, scientific institutes, publishing houses, newspapers, and theatrical companies. But after 1930, the disbanding of the Yevsektsiia heralded the beginning of a sharp decline in the Yiddish revival. This development coincided with Stalin's ruthless drive for industrialization, his gradual conversion of the Soviet Union into a monolithic, totalitarian State, and with the disintegration of the compact communities of the old Russian Jewish shtetl.

It is important to remember that the anti-Zionism of the first, post-revolutionary years was relatively untainted with antisemitism. The Resolution of the Soviet government "On the Uprooting of the Antisemitic Movement" (27 June 1918) and Lenin's famous speech against the pogroms (recorded on a phonograph in March 1919) with its ringing cry "Shame on those who sow enmity towards Jews, who sow hatred towards other nations," had been unequivocal in tone.[4] Lenin's emphasis on the "progressive" and internationalist role of the Jewish intelligentsia and on the class solidarity of Jewish "toilers" with the proletariat of other nationalities was based on sympathy as well as a hard-headed analysis of the objective situation.[5] He had been genuinely outraged by the anti-Jewish libels of the Tsarist regime and revolted by the pogroms of the White counter-revolutionaries, with whom the Bolsheviks were engaged in a merciless struggle.[6] While he and other leading Communists did on occasion reproach Zionism for preaching class-collaboration instead of class-struggle, this also has to be seen in the domestic context of the Russian Civil War.[7] The impact of the Balfour Declaration on Russian Jewry, with pro-British articles appearing in the Russian Jewish press and pro-British demonstrations in Odessa and Petrograd, helped to feed the suspicion that Zionism could become a dangerous anti-Bolshevik weapon in the hands of the Western powers.[8] Furthermore, the attraction of Palestine as a rallying cry might weaken the recruitment of the Jewish masses into the Red Army during a critical period of the Civil War. Equally, there was an irredentist threat posed by movements of national separation at a time when the new Soviet regime was desperately fighting for its very survival against foreign interventionists. Though Zionism was far less dangerous than Ukrainian separatism, it is not surprising that on the domestic front it could be viewed as a "bourgeois" and potentially counter-revolutionary movement. Nevertheless, the founder of the Soviet secret police (Cheka), Feliks Dzierżyński, was pragmatically opposed to the "persecution of the Zionists," given their "considerable influence in both Poland and America."[9]

The Bolshevik assessment of the "colonial question" in the Middle East was also an important factor in early attitudes to Zionism, especially after the British conquest of Palestine in 1917 and the Anglo-French partition of the entire region. Such actions seemed to confirm Lenin's theory of the division of the globe among the rapacious imperialist powers. The Bolsheviks were fundamentally hostile to Western "annexationism." Indeed, one of the first acts of Leon Trotsky as Commissar for Foreign Affairs had been to publish the secret Sykes-Picot treaty in order to embarrass the Western Powers and expose the hollowness of their "democratic" promises to the Arabs. The fact the Zionist movement under Chaim Weizmann was intent on cooperating with the British government further reinforced the Bolsheviks in their belief that it was a "tool of imperialism." Their hostility was also enhanced by the fact that the British were indubitably the dominant colonial power in the Middle East, and the most determined to overthrow the Soviet regime. Hence, it is not surprising that the Bolsheviks should try to stir up revolutionary ferment among those backward colonized populations that found themselves predominantly under British control, which included a substantial part of the Arab and Muslim "toilers" of the East. At the Congress of the People of the East in Baku (September 1920) Grigori Zinoviev, president of the Communist International, openly called for a "holy war" by Muslim toilers against the British and French capitalists. Zinoviev and Radek (both of them internationalist Jews) were in the forefront of passionate appeals for a jihad against the West under the Communist banner.[10] Given the global revolutionary and anti-colonial strategy of the Bolsheviks, it was almost inevitable that they would look to Palestinian Arab workers and peasants rather than Zionist settlers as the spearhead of anti-British feeling in the area. Nevertheless, after the ebbing of world revolutionary euphoria by 1923, relatively little attention was paid by Soviet leaders to the Middle East. The riots in Palestine in 1929 and the Arab revolt of 1936–39 did admittedly encourage a flurry of local agitation against "Zionist imperialist oppression." But there was objectively no revolutionary situation in the region as a whole and the dogmatic, sectarian approach of the Comintern to colonial questions was unlikely to produce one.[11]

Soviet anti-Zionism in the 1920s was not yet a significant force beyond its unilateral support of Palestinian Arab nationalism—which further alienated Jewish settlers in Eretz Israel from the Communist Party. In contrast to the Soviet anti-Zionist crusade of the 1960s and 1970s, Jewish nationalism was largely a peripheral issue left in the hands of Yevsektsiia functionaries. The Jewish Communists showed true fanaticism in seeking to extirpate Jewish religious institutions, the Hebrew language, and Zionist sentiments from Russian Jewish life. In sharp contrast to this trend, there were also some Bolshevik leaders like Soviet president Mikhail Kalinin (himself of peasant stock) who advocated a Soviet version of "Zionism" within the borders of the U.S.S.R.[12] Kalinin believed that a dispersed national minority like Soviet Jewry could never become a nation without *territorial concentration* and extensive *agricultural colonization*. He sincerely hoped that Russian Jews would seize the opportunity to leave the big cities and settle as farmers in the Crimea, the Southern Ukraine, or some other territory in the U.S.S.R. in order to prevent their erosion as a "nationality." The creation of a Jewish autonomous region in Birobidzhan at the end of the 1920s was precisely such an effort to *normalize* the situation of Jews in the Soviet Union. By settling Jews in the Far East it was hoped that a new foundation for Jewish national existence within the U.S.S.R. might be laid.[13] In his speech in 1934, proclaiming Birobidzhan as a Jewish autonomous region, Kalinin made it clear that such a *normalization along territorial lines* would be the only way to preserve a Jewish national culture.[14]

Why then did this "Siberian Palestine" prove such a fiasco, in spite of having the support of a number of prestigious figures in Soviet public life, including not only Kalinin and Chicherin, but also Maxim Litvinov and Leonid Krassin? Why did a project backed by the People's Commissariat of Agriculture and the Commissariat for Defense so conspicuously fail? Undoubtedly, the forbidding climatic conditions—notably the near-Arctic winters, wilderness and swamps, and the geographic isolation of the Soviet Far East—did not facilitate matters. Nor did it help that the whole project was bureaucratically inspired from *above*. But there was a more serious defect. Birobidzhan was simply too far removed from the cultural background, the social aspirations and the spontaneous feelings of Russian Jewry.[15] Conceived in part for geo-strategic reasons and no doubt as a counterweight to Palestinian Zionism, Birobidzhan had no roots in Jewish history or in Jewish national-religious sentiments. True, there were Jewish Communist enthusiasts (some of them former members of Poale Zion) who ecstatically praised Jewish territorial concentration and land colonization when it was practiced in the Soviet Far East, while vilifying it as a "petty-bourgeois deviation" when carried out in Palestine. But by the end of the 1930s with the consolidation of Stalin's totalitarian rule, not only were the last vestiges of organized Zionism in the U.S.S.R. eradicated but the leaders of the Yevsektsiia and the organizers of the Birobidzhan project had themselves been exiled, imprisoned, or murdered.[16]

It was the Nazi attack on the Soviet Union which first provoked a significant change in official Communist attitudes to Jewish nationalism. Significantly, this was a period when Great Russian nationalism was itself on the upswing and antisemitism had greatly increased—stimulated by Nazi racial propaganda which had swiftly penetrated the Soviet Union. In order to strengthen resistance to the German invaders, the Soviet authorities felt obliged to encourage national and religious feelings among different ethnic groups. The Jewish Anti-Fascist Committee was set up in April 1942 with precisely this purpose—to win support among Jews at home and abroad for the Red Army.[17] Stalin clearly considered the sympathy of world Jewry important enough during World War II to outweigh the fundamental Soviet axiom that Russian Jews must have no feelings of solidarity for Jews outside the U.S.S.R. Even the so-called myth of a world Jewish people (so relentlessly attacked in Soviet anti-Zionist propaganda) was allowed public expression in order to win the political goodwill and the assistance of British and American Jewry. For the first time in August 1941 a voice could be heard over Radio Moscow (that of the famous Yiddish poet Perets Markish) addressing his "Brother Jews" all over the world as *one* people and *one* army. It was also at this time that the Red Army Colonel, Itzik Feffer, wrote his stirring poem "I am a Jew," with its heroic Maccabean and quasi-Zionist strains.[18] Similarly, the head of the Jewish Anti-Fascist Committee (JAC), the celebrated actor Solomon Mikhoels, felt able to speak freely of a "community of fate" binding all Jews together. He even described Zionism as a "great idea" during his wartime visit to London, though it was not (he emphasized) applicable to Soviet Jewry. Even more significantly, the secretary of the Jewish Anti-Fascist Committee, Shachna Epstein, wrote in November 1944 in *Aynikayt* (Unity—the organ of the JAC), that the Jews have a "right to political independence in Palestine."[19] None of this could have been done, of course, without Stalin's blessing and it clearly seemed to presage a turn in postwar Soviet policy towards support for a Jewish State. Moreover, in 1948 there was a wave of Jewish national sentiment that followed the establishment of Israel. The visit of the first Israeli ambassador, Golda Meir (Meyerson), to Moscow's Choral Synagogue during the Yom Kippur festival on 16 October 1948 and the great enthusiasm which it generated among Russian Jews, clearly reinforced Stalin's growing paranoia.[20]

Stalinist Russia of the immediate postwar years appeared to have exactly inverted the Bolshevik position of 1917. Lenin and his closest followers had for the most part been genuine internationalists who strongly opposed antisemitism and remained cool towards Zionism.[21] On the other hand, Stalin and his entourage between 1945 and 1953 acted as Great Russian cultural imperialists who were "anti-Zionist" and strongly antisemitic at home while pursuing a tactically pro-Israel policy in the Middle East. How can one explain this seemingly schizoid Stalinist policy? And why should the brief Soviet-Israeli honeymoon which dramatically reversed thirty years of Communist opposition to the Yishuv as a "counter-revolutionary tool of British imperialism," have coincided with the "Black Years" of Soviet Jewry? What were the underlying reasons for Moscow's sudden volte-face on the raison d'être for a Jewish State in Palestine? More puzzling still, how can one reconcile the bizarre (yet partially accurate) image of Joseph Stalin as "godfather" of the Jewish State with his hateful campaign against both "Jewish nationalism" and "rootless cosmopolitanism" during those same years?

The media attack on "Jewish nationalism" (which was part of a broader onslaught against "bourgeois nationalism" in general) had already been initiated in 1946 in the Soviet press. This campaign which declared Jewish nationalism and Zionist sentiments to be wholly incompatible with Soviet patriotism would later be used to justify the complete destruction of Soviet Jewish culture. Already with Mikhoels' assassination at the beginning of 1948, it was clear that Stalin had no further need for the support of world Jewry or what remained of a Yiddish-speaking Jewish Communist intelligentsia. Though the "rootless cosmopolitans" in literature and the arts suffered a less brutal fate, they, too, would be sharply denounced as "alien" to communist ideology and as enemies of Soviet culture.[22] This was the death-knell for the Leninist tradition of anti-antisemitism to which Stalin had still paid lip-service before 1939. Stalin's campaign in 1949 against the *assimilated* Jewish intelligentsia deliberately focused on its alleged *lack of Soviet patriotism* and implied the disloyalty of Russian Jewry. Then, in 1952, the accusations of "Jewish nationalism" and "cosmopolitanism" were fused together by means of an explicit Zionist conspiracy theory, which linked Israel and Western imperialism to the "Doctors' Plot" against the lives of Soviet leaders. The Soviet dictator could now organically link his "anti-Zionism" to visceral antisemitism. Had things gone according to plan, the surviving remnant of Soviet Jewry might have been mercilessly repressed and its existence imperiled. The rabid antisemitic character of the plot would have had devastating consequences for Soviet Jews and led to widespread purges.[23]

The pro-Israel turn in Stalin's foreign policy during 1947 coincided with the suppression of Jewish nationalism at home. At first sight this might appear somewhat strange. A clue to the paradox is suggested by Ilya Ehrenburg's well-known article published in *Pravda* on 21 September 1948 which clearly reflected the official standpoint and was intended as a warning to Russian Jewry not to become emotionally involved in the resurrection of the Jewish State. Ehrenburg was close to Stalin and widely recognized as one of the most popular writers and publicists in the U.S.S.R. An active member of the Jewish Anti-Fascist Committee, he had been exceptionally well informed about Hitler's policy towards the Jews during the Holocaust. He had worked as a journalist for *Krasnaya Zvezda*—the daily paper of the Soviet Defense Ministry—throughout the war years. In collections of his wartime writings published under the title *Voyna* (The war), Ehrenburg's denunciations of Nazism stood out for their sheer vehemence. Between 1942 and 1944, while visiting areas liberated from Nazi occupation, he began to collect material on the German extermination of the Jews. These documented testimonies were eventually put together as *The Black Book*.[24] Ehrenburg was especially impressed by the stories about the valour of the Jewish partisans and the fighting members of the ghetto underground. On 1 May 1944 he was awarded the U.S.S.R.'s highest decoration, the Order of Lenin. Many Soviet Jews in those tragic years looked up to him as an outstanding representative of their people and hoped (somewhat naively) that he could help them.[25]

After the war, Ehrenburg was sent to Germany to observe the Nuremberg trials of the leading Nazi war criminals. It is striking that he did not avoid discussion of the extermination of the Jews—a theme which featured prominently in many of his reports. This was all the more remarkable since antisemitism was unmistakably on the rise in the U.S.S.R. after 1945 and had again become a sensitive topic for the Soviet authorities. Ehrenburg was well aware of this reality. He did not flinch from it, urging the Jewish Anti-Fascist Committee to focus more attention on combating antisemitism in the U.S.S.R. The prize-winning Soviet author also pointedly observed that antisemitism had become the international language of fascism.[26] Some of his wartime experiences and his intense concern with antisemitism would be reflected in his novel, *The Storm* (1947), which earned him the Stalin Prize. Hence, the selection of Ehrenburg as Stalin's messenger to Soviet Jewry, during Israel's War of Independence, was a logical choice. The Soviet authorities highly valued his services as an internationally renowned and respected writer whose views would be listened to by Russian and also Western Jews. When he stressed that the U.S.S.R. sympathized with Jewish aspirations for statehood in Palestine, he was following the Stalinist line. So, too, when he insisted on the duty of the Israeli working class to repulse not only the Arab invaders but also their own "bourgeois" government which exploited them and acted like a tool of Anglo-American imperialism. Ehrenburg now denied that there was any such thing as a "Jewish people" or even any affinity between Jews in different countries. This, he claimed, was solely the invention of bourgeois Zionist "mystics" and Jewish nationalists whom he sharply condemned in classic Soviet fashion. The warning to Soviet Jews against any flirtation with Israel could not have been plainer.

Ehrenburg's views on Zionism were not far removed from those of Stalin. Already in 1913, as a Bolshevik militant, the young Stalin had predicted that the Jews would disappear through assimilation and he vigorously denied that they constituted a nation. After all, Jews lacked any single common language, territory, economic life or culture.[27] Yet, in Palestine by 1947, these same prerequisites made the emergence of a new "Israeli" people seem perfectly compatible with the classic Stalinist definitions of the nation. But an Israeli nation-state should have nothing to do with Russian Jews, whose aims and future must be solely linked to the building of communism in the U.S.S.R. Though this viewpoint sharply contradicted Zionist assumptions, it did not initially diminish the enthusiasm of many left-wing Israelis for the victorious, postwar U.S.S.R. as a model society and the true fatherland of socialism. They failed to understand that Soviet support for the Jewish State in 1948 was not motivated by a common ideology or values but by a naked drive for greater Soviet power and influence in the Middle East. It was a perfectly logical decision in terms of Soviet *raison d'état* at a time when the U.S.S.R. still had no allies in the Middle East, least of all among the Arabs—very much under the British imperial tutelage.[28] At the same time, Soviet representatives knew that the Israeli struggle for national independence in Palestine was primarily directed *against* the British Empire. Hence, the Jews of Palestine objectively stood in the forefront of the *anti-colonial* struggle to weaken what was still the dominant Western power in the Middle East.

With the onset of the Cold War, it had become increasingly important for Soviet Russia to enter the Middle East. Her southern flank (Iran, Turkey) was exposed at a time of rapidly growing East-West tension; she feared that the Persian Gulf and Middle East oil might fall completely under Anglo-American domination; and above all it was in the Soviet interest to split or undermine the Western alliance. The Middle East seemed to provide the best prospect between 1945 and 1948 of inflaming Anglo-American rivalry. The "Palestine question" offered a perfect opportunity to divide the British from the Americans and prevent a further consolidation of their Cold War partnership against the Soviet Union. The acrimony sensed between American President Harry S. Truman and the new Labour government in Britain over Jewish immigration to Palestine had grown considerably since the end of World War II. In this context, the toleration by the Soviet Union of the *Brichah* (illegal emigration to Palestine) from Eastern Europe was certainly significant. The issue of displaced persons (DPs) had become highly sensitive in the aftermath of the Holocaust and world public opinion would sharply condemn Great Britain for persisting in its cruel policy of closing the gates of Palestine after 1945 to the traumatized survivors of the concentration camps. The Soviets had every interest in further embarrassing Britain by encouraging the stream of Jewish refugees to Palestine who would then be intercepted on the high seas by the Royal Navy. Anglo-American disagreements could be reinforced at a critical time when Great Britain was already overextended in India, Pakistan, Ceylon, Greece, and Turkey, seriously dependent on American economic assistance, and hoping for US diplomatic support over Palestine. Stalin also knew that the British—while seeking to keep the U.S.S.R. at all costs out of the Middle East—were determined to abort the creation of a Jewish State in Mandatory Palestine. He fully intended to frustrate these aims in order to weaken Britain.

For propaganda effect, the Soviet Union also needed to show that it was acting out of something more than naked political interest. Hence its carefully orchestrated pose of a compassionate Great Power concerned to make amends to the Jewish people for the terrible sufferings it had endured at the hands of the "Nazi-fascist hordes." The postwar *prise de conscience* about the Holocaust made it an expedient and shrewd decision for the U.S.S.R. to present its sympathy for a Jewish homeland in Palestine as a *moral* decision rather than an act of conventional power politics.This was a rare example of Stalin's *Realpolitik* appearing to coincide with the "world conscience." Andrei Gromyko's famous "Zionist" speech of 14 May 1947 which evoked the "unparalleled torture and torments" of the Jewish people during the Second World War, might best be described as Stalin's Balfour Declaration in reverse—intended to *eject* the British from Palestine. "No nation in Western Europe," Gromyko solemnly reminded the United Nations, "was able to extend the required help to the Jewish people in defending its rights and physical survival against the violent deeds of the Hitlerites and their allies. This explains the aspiration of the Jews to their own State. It will be unjust if we ignore this aspiration and deny the Jewish people the right to realize it."[29]

It is important to note that neither in this speech nor elsewhere, did Gromyko or any other Soviet leader refer to the *Zionist* movement as the inspiration of the Jewish struggle for independence in Palestine. This was no accident given Stalin's basically anti-Zionist attitudes which had decried Jewish nationalism since 1913 as a "moribund" and "reactionary" ideology. What then had changed? Clearly the Holocaust theme in Gromyko's speech at the UN in 1947, was intended as an explicit *anti-Western* reproach. The U.S.S.R. was condemning the passivity of the Western powers in face of the Nazi "Final Solution." This argument was, of course, highly selective. The Soviet government itself had collaborated with the Nazis between 1939 and 1941. It had generally played down the Jewish identities of the victims of Nazi atrocities on Soviet soil. The number of Jewish civilian casualties on the Eastern Front had in fact been proportionately greater than in Western Europe. Furthermore, direct *collaboration* with the Nazi genocide (especially through the murder of Jews by Ukrainians, White Russians, Latvians, and Lithuanians) had been very extensive in the U.S.S.R. In other words, the Soviet Union proved no more capable than the Western Allies of defending the lives of defenseless Jewish citizens during the Holocaust. Had this been admitted, of course, then Gromyko's whole argument could have been turned against the Soviet Union and used to justify Jewish immigration to Palestine from the U.S.S.R.—something absolutely inadmissible to Stalin. But these unpleasant facts were dwarfed in 1947 by the positive, heroic image in the wider world of the Red Army which had broken the back of the Nazi war machine.

The Soviet desire to weaken the West and undermine British interests in the Middle East at a time of mounting Cold War confrontation was obviously paramount in Stalin's calculations. It is also possible that he may have believed that in return for Russian diplomatic and military support, the new Jewish State could be transformed into a Soviet-style "people's democracy"; that it would eventually become a communist base in the Middle East. The idea was not altogether farfetched in those years. It was given considerable credence by the British Foreign Office and the American State Department in the late 1940s. After all, the founding fathers of Israel were nearly all Russian Jews, many of them imbued with Russian culture and familiar with Marxist socialism. There were, too, Zionist leaders like Moshe Sneh, chief of the Haganah from 1940–46, who genuinely believed that the Yishuv should politically orientate itself to the Soviet Union for the sake of the anti-British struggle. This was also the conviction of the left-wing Hashomer Hatzair kibbutz movement and its successor, Mapam (the United Workers' Party) founded in late 1947, which tried hard to reconcile Zionism with Marxist doctrine. Furthermore, socialist-Zionist circles in the Palmach (the élite force of the Haganah) were openly sympathetic to the Soviet Union and felt inspired by the heroic victory of the Red Army over the Wehrmacht during World War II.[30] None of these parties, groups or trends had a broad mass base in Israel. But they counted for considerably more than the Israeli Communist Party, which in the first Israeli national elections of 1949 polled only 3.44% of the votes.

The U.S.S.R. undoubtedly underestimated the basic pro-Western orientation of the mainstream socialist-Zionist leadership under David Ben-Gurion. At the same time it had little to lose by supporting the underground Jewish struggle in Palestine to terminate the British occupation. The Zionist success did damage British prestige in the Middle East and set in motion a broader anti-colonial momentum for national liberation. In 1948 this was still in its infancy. Arab nationalists were tainted by Nazi and fascist associations ever since the 1930s and early 1940s. Key Arab nationalist leaders like the Palestinian Grand Mufti of Jerusalem, Haj Amin el Husseini were notorious anti-Communists who had actively served the Axis Powers in Berlin during

World War II. Husseini's world-view was unambiguously pro-Nazi, virulently antisemitic, anti-Western, and anti-Soviet.[31] This was an outlook shared by a number of other Arab leaders in Iraq, Egypt, and Syria who had been strongly attracted by fascist ideology and electrified by the example of Hitler's Germany. Moreover, in 1945, the Arab world was still controlled by reactionary monarchs, effendis, and feudal cliques, mostly tied by treaties and alliances to British imperial interests. Hence there was scarcely any reason for Stalin to take the Arabs seriously as potential allies. When Arab armies under the orders of the Egyptian ruler King Farouk, Nuri Said Pasha of Iraq, and King Abdullah of Transjordan attacked Israel in 1948, with what appeared to be British connivance and backing, it made plenty of sense for the Soviets to sharply condemn this "reactionary war conducted by the chieftains of the Arab League under British control." Stalin had no intention of allowing Great Britain to regain control of Palestine through the back door, in the event of a successful Arab invasion to destroy Israel.

Support for the establishment of Israel in 1948 was a shrewd chess move—the best way for the U.S.S.R. to penetrate the Middle East at a time of heightened Cold War tensions. The relatively "normal" relations with Israel between 1948 and 1952 would continue just as long as the Arab world was deemed to be lacking any serious revolutionary potential. During this period the Soviet Government preferred to adopt a neutral policy of non-intervention in Middle Eastern affairs.[32] The crisis in Soviet-Israeli relations which began in January–February 1953 was not in fact directly related to the Middle East. It was the result of Stalin's increasingly irrational antisemitism revealed by the arrest of six Jewish physicians falsely accused on 13 January 1953 of seeking to liquidate the top Soviet leadership. It was officially alleged that they were "Zionist spies" linked with the American Joint Distribution Committee as well as being agents of the British and American secret services. When the U.S.S.R. broke off diplomatic relations with Israel in February 1953 (they were restored in July), antisemitic, anti-Zionist and anti-Israel motifs had fully coalesced.

This unholy trinity of Soviet propaganda remained in force under Stalin's successor, Nikita S. Khrushchev, despite his bold de-Stalinization policy. The main difference was that after 1955 Khrushchev's aggressively pro-Arab strategy in the Middle East granted greater primacy to the *anti-Israel* theme.[33] With the expansion of the Soviet fleet and a more dynamic policy towards the Third World, the U.S.S.R. under Khrushchev could see new opportunities in the Middle East, where a new generation of anti-Western Arab nationalists like Gamal Abdul Nasser, had arisen by the mid-1950s. A fundamental reorientation now took place in attitudes towards Third World national liberation movements. In contrast to Stalin (who was skeptical about most non-aligned and non-communist nationalist leaders), Khrushchev believed that "radical" anti-imperialist regimes in the developing countries were the natural allies of the U.S.S.R.[34] The new Soviet interest in these nations coincided with the rising tide of Third World Non-Alignment symbolized by the Afro-Asian Conference at Bandung in 1955. In the same year Khrushchev decided to grant military assistance to Nasser's Egypt. The Sinai campaign of 1956 in which Israel was publicly identified with the Anglo-French invasion of Egypt greatly reinforced the anti-Israeli orientation in Soviet foreign policy. The tone of the note sent by the Soviet Prime Minister to the Israeli government on 5 November 1956 was particularly menacing and claimed that the "very existence of Israel as a state" was now in jeopardy.[35] Henceforth, until 1967, the Jewish State would be regularly characterized in the Soviet press as a "puppet" of Western imperialism, in constant readiness to launch unprovoked attacks on its Arab neighbors.[36]

In contrast, Arab leaders like Nasser, General Kassem in Iraq and Ahmed Ben Bella in Algeria were extravagantly hailed in the U.S.S.R. as "progressive," even when (as in Iraq) they savagely repressed the Communist parties in their own countries. Although the Soviet Union liked to portray itself as the patron saint of national liberation movements in the Middle East, it did not hesitate to sacrifice local Arab Communists—persecuted by nationalist regimes—as long as this served its immediate foreign policy interests. Both Ben Bella and Nasser were praised as "progressives" despite their repressive measures. They were awarded the title of "Hero of the Soviet Union" in 1964 and exalted as "revolutionary democrats," who were taking the road to socialism.[37] Competition with the Chinese Communists for influence in the developing world contributed still further to this radical trend in Soviet global strategy. After the fall of Khrushchev, a more cautious policy emerged, which was less blind to the economic and political backwardness of the Third World. But this shift under Leonid Brezhnev had no discernible impact on Soviet assessments of the Arab-Israel conflict.[38]

With regard to Zionism, antisemitism, and the internal Jewish problem, Soviet policy under Khrushchev had continued some of the discriminatory techniques familiar from an earlier period. In spite of de-Stalinization, the Soviet leadership kept silent about its liquidation of the cream of the Yiddish-speaking intelligentsia between 1948 and 1952. Nor did it permit any references to Stalin's antisemitism. Khrushchev's personal distaste for Jews may well have played a role in this ominous silence.[39] Popular broadcasts, magazines and pamphlets in the late 1950s invariably found a "Zionist hand" at work in any attempt by Soviet Jews to assert their Jewish identity, let alone to express sympathy for Israel or Jews in the Western world. It was under Khrushchev that Trofim Kichko's racist diatribe *Judaism without Embellishment* was published by the Ukrainian Academy of Sciences in October 1963. Accompanied by crudely antisemitic illustrations, this text which openly identified Judaism with the usury of Jewish bankers, aggressive Zionism, warmongering Israel, and greedy Western capitalism was exceptionally virulent even by Communist standards. It was eventually withdrawn from circulation as a result of worldwide protests, led by the radical intelligentsia and communist parties in the West. Nevertheless, in the course of Khrushchev's atheistic onslaught against religion, the Soviet media continued to vilify Judaism as a subversive, parasitical, repulsive, and conspiratorial faith. In the early 1960s, antisemitism also appeared in a particularly crude form in the U.S.S.R. with a high-profile campaign against "economic crimes" in which the Jewish origins of those sentenced and executed were frequently underlined in the press. This, together with the various quota devices discriminating against Jews in employment, belied Khrushchev's claim that Western charges of antisemitism were a "vicious slander on the Soviet people."[40]

Khrushchev's ostentatious indifference to Jewish suffering during the Holocaust was another striking feature of his hostile approach to Jewry. He was especially infuriated by the publication of Yevgenii Yevtushenko's celebrated poem "Babi Yar" in *Literaturnaya Gazeta* (21 September 1961)—lyrics which movingly commemorated the bestial massacre by the Germans of more than 30,000 Kiev Jews in only two days, on 29–30 September 1941. Such memorialization had been deliberately discouraged by the Soviet regime for twenty years. Local authorities had even planned to transform the killing site of Babi Yar into a sports stadium. One poem had nonetheless thrown a spanner in the works. Khrushchev angrily reproached Yevtushenko for his *chutzpa* and for having raised the issue of Soviet antisemitism. Yet under Khrushchev, there had been an unmistakable trend to limit the number of Jews in prominent positions (*numerus clausus*). This was true in politics, culture, and the universities. "Popular" antisemitism in the form of vandalism against synagogues and Jewish cemeteries, as well as crude verbal aggression directed against Jews was also on the rise. In Margelan in the Uzbek Republic there was actually a small pogrom in September 1961 following blood libel allegations directed by Soviet Muslims against an innocent Jewish woman. The local Communist authorities did nothing to alleviate the sense of insecurity and fright that this incident generated among Uzbek Jews.[41]

But it was only after 1967 that antisemitism and anti-Zionism would assume a truly systematic and organized character. It began with the need for the Soviet Union to explain away the Arab debacle of June 1967. It was decided to politically delegitimize Israel by denouncing its "treacherous aggression" as an assault on all peace-loving forces in the world. Already in the summer of 1967 Soviet media began to denounce Israel's so-called genocide against the Palestine people. Within days of the Israeli victory, the Soviet press would brand Israeli Defense Minister Moshe Dayan as a "pupil of Hitler" and execrate world Zionism as a racialist, criminal conspiracy. Soviet leader Leonid Brezhnev told military graduates in July 1967: "The Israeli aggressors are the worst of bandits. In their arrogance against the Arab population, it seems they want to copy the crimes of the Hitler invaders."[42] The tone had been set for what would become a veritable tsunami of articles, lectures, broadcasts, and films vilifying Judaism, Zionism, and Israel in the Soviet mass media. The only comparable analogy would be the monstrous specter of *Das Weltjudentum* in Nazi propaganda of the 1930s and 40s—this time with the roles reversed.[43] In place of the relentless Nazi myth about "Jewish Bolshevism," the Soviet Communists began to fabricate the equally mendacious thesis of "Jewish Nazism." According to Yevgeny Yevseyev, a leading exemplar of this licensed state pornography and author of *Fascism under the Blue Star,* the octopus-like tentacles of World Zionism were actually more far-reaching and dangerous than those of all the major varieties of European fascism (German, Italian, Spanish) put together.[44] The villainy of the Jewish bourgeoisie, which lay behind the Zionist monster, was also unrivalled throughout the capitalist world.

According to these and other racist Soviet pamphlets published between 1967 and 1989, Zionism was the great invisible power whose influence extended into every nook and cranny of politics, finance, religion, and the communications media in the Western world. This "international Mafia," allegedly controlled by big Jewish bankers and capitalists, was deemed to have a vast intelligence network and unlimited financial resources at its disposal. As early as 4 October 1967, *Komsomolskaya Pravda* was making the fantastic claim, with the aid of utterly bogus statistics, that "the adherents of Zionism in the USA number from 20 to 25 million people. . .Jews and non-Jews." According to this popular Soviet Communist youth organ, Zionists owned 80% of local and international news agencies, comprised 70% of American lawyers, 60% of the physicists and 43% of the industrialists in the United States. Yury Ivanov in his *Beware! Zionism!* first published in 1969 and hailed by the Soviet press as a major "scientific" work on the subject, would provide the guiding concept. Zionism, he explained, was "the ideology, the ramified system of organization and the political practice of the big Jewish bourgeoisie that has merged with the monopolistic circles of the USA and of other imperialist powers. Its basic content is militant chauvinism and anti-communism. . . ."[45]

A new breed of Soviet pseudo-Marxist hacks was given the "patriotic" task of rewriting history in order to demonise Zionism and expose the origins and goals of this "fascist, criminal conspiracy." A clear illustration of the methods employed by these propagandists can be found in the book by Vladimir Begun, *Creeping Counter-Revolution* (1974). In his introduction to this work, A. M. Malashko pointed out that Soviet historians had in the past accepted an unjustifiably benign view of the role of Zionism—one which regarded antisemitism as its basic cause. Begun's study had corrected this fundamental error by presenting Tsarist antisemitism as "the spontaneous reaction of the oppressed strata of the toiling population to their barbarous exploitation by the Jewish bourgeoisie."[46] The unsuspecting Soviet reader learned that Polish, Ukrainian, and Byelorussian peasants "reduced to despair by merciless exploitation" had "avenged themselves" on their [Jewish] oppressors, making no exceptions whatsoever "on grounds of nationality." The Khmelnitsky massacres of the 17th century in the Ukraine and later anti-Jewish pogroms had been *understandable* reactions against economic exploitation, "the personification of which were the rapacious Jewish tenant-farmers, money-lenders and publicans."[47] A reviewer of Begun's book in the mass circulation periodical *Ogonyok,* fully agreed with this line of argument, claiming that the antisemitism of the Russian masses was indeed a justifiable form of class-struggle.[48] Thus, the monarchist *pogromchiks* who had mobilized the ultra-reactionary Black Hundreds around 1905 in defense of Tsarism, were now being rehabilitated as precursors of a new and better socialist world.

There was a sharp difference between such interpretations and the sixty-year-old Leninist decree of the Council of People's Commissars (27 July 1918) which had declared that "the anti-Semitic movement and anti-Jewish pogroms are fatal to the cause of the workers' and peasants' revolution." But such classic denunciations of antisemitism written by founding fathers like Lenin or the great Russian proletarian writer, Maxim Gorky, no longer suited the Black Hundred psychology developing in certain circles close to the Kremlin. Most revealing in this regard was the reproduction by the journal of the Soviet embassy in Paris in 1972, of extracts from a pamphlet originally published nearly seventy years earlier by the antisemitic "Alliance of the Russian People."[49] The only significant divergence in the modernized Soviet version of Black Hundred antisemitism was the substitution of the code-word "Zionist" for "Jew." The article consisted of largely fabricated quotations from Jewish religious writings, designed to prove that Judaism was a *man-hating* religion which claimed divine sanction to massacre Gentiles. On 24 April 1973 a Paris Court found the French Communist publisher of the Soviet Embassy's journal guilty of incitement to discrimination, hatred and racial violence.[50]

During the 1970s a wide variety of classic anti-Jewish motifs became virtually obligatory in so-called academic Soviet publications. Ostensibly concerned with Zionism, these writings insistently slandered Judaism as a creed that calls for genocide and the enslavement of non-Jews. They followed the lead of the recently rehabilitated Kichko, who, in his *Judaism and Zionism* (Kiev 1968), had claimed that the Jewish faith at its very core was based on the doctrine of a "superior race." Kichko railed against the "chauvinistic idea of the god-chosenness of the Jewish people." Intoxicated by the "Judaic propaganda of messianism" and the prospect of ruling over the peoples of this world, the Zionists sought to educate Jews "in the spirit of contempt and hatred towards other peoples." Ultimately this ideology was founded to justify the "extermination" of the Palestinian Arabs. According to Kichko: "Judaism teaches that Jews should force the subjugated people in the invaded lands to work for them as a people of priests." In the writings of Kichko, Ivanov, Yevseyev, Begun, and other Soviet specialists, the cruel, vindictive Hebrew God, Yahweh, and the dogma of the "God-chosen nation" constituted the very essence of Zionist "criminality." Thus Vladimir Begun could write in his *Creeping Counter-Revolution* that "Zionist gangsterism. . .has its ideological roots in the scrolls of the 'holy' Torah and the precepts of the Talmud."[51] The sources of Zionist "racism" and Israeli "aggression" in the Middle East lay in the utterly reactionary and corrupt character of Judaism as a faith and in its inhuman code of conduct. Twenty years after the collapse of Soviet Communism, this antisemitic trope still lives on, mutating into the lowest common denominator of contemporary left-wing hostility towards Israel and the Jews.

A glowing review of Begun's book entitled "The Ideology and Practice of Violence," appeared on 12 October 1974. In the style of medieval Jew-baiting it evoked the "cruel approach of the Talmud that taught the religious Jews to hate the non-believers, the 'goyim,' to cheat them by all means, and if possible to destroy them."[52] The author, Dmitri Zhukov, held that man-hating "Talmudism" explained why "Zionist hooligans in Israel erase whole villages, rape little girls and force defenseless Arabs to crawl for hours on their knees."[53] Yair Tsaban, then Secretary of the Central Committee of Maki (the Israeli Communist Party which had been repudiated by Moscow), sarcastically commented: "Not just fifty years divide Lenin from Zhukov, but an ethical and philosophical abyss divides them, and no use of any Marxist vocabulary and no adornment with Lenin-quotations will manage to bridge the gap."[54]

Writing in a familiar tone of dogmatic contempt in March 1975, the Soviet publicist Vladimir Kiselev pithily summarized the theoretical base of Zionism as being a fusion of "anti-Marxism, national chauvinism and mysticism. . .bellicose anticommunism, adventurism and terrorism."[55] The false theory of a "world Jewish nation" and the myth of the "chosen people" had been fabricated by Zionists to "substantiate an attitude toward other people as 'inferior'" and representatives of a "lower race." Zionism deliberately intended to provoke hostility against "Gentiles" as a whole, branding them all as inveterate "antisemites."[56] Not to be outdone by his fellow propagandists, Kiselev claimed that the Zionists had established "direct contacts with the fascist regimes in Italy and Germany" because they recognized them as objective allies. Naturally, Kiselev ignored the extensive collaboration of Stalin with Hitler between 1939 and 1941. Nor was there any mention of the close ties between Arab nationalists and the fascist regimes in Europe—especially the alliance of Haj Amin el-Husseini and Rashid Ali with Nazi Germany. Another striking omission was the silence surrounding Communist support for Israel in 1948. History was being radically rewritten under Brezhnev to show that "the policy of aggression and expansion was adopted by Israel's Zionist leaders from the very start."[57] It belonged, so to speak, to the violent and evil *essence* of the Zionist ideology.

In the new dispensation, "Zionism" had indeed become a bogeyman. Thus it was supposedly international Zionist machinations which had subverted socialist Czechoslovakia in 1968.[58] Equally, Zionists had acted as a "Trojan Horse" for Western Imperialism in Asia and Africa in order to divide or weaken the solidarity of Third World nations. Communist propaganda invariably portrayed "World Zionism" as an all-pervasive, menacing, and perfidious force threatening the cohesion of the socialist camp, all newly independent states, and a wide variety of movements of national liberation. Indeed, so extensive were the tentacles of international Zionism that it represented a *universal peril*. On 22 July 1977 a Tass commentary announced the publication by the prestigious Academy of Sciences of a 176-page book entitled *International Zionism: History and Politics*. In this so-called scientific work, which can fairly be described as an updated Soviet version of the *Protocols of Zion,* not only the international banking-system and the military-industrial complex, but key industries throughout the capitalist world were described as being under the control of the Jewish bourgeoisie, for whom Zionism represented the perfect cover.[59] The ultimate aim of this stealthy penetration by "Zionists" of key strategic positions in the global economy was to establish a Jewish-dominated "super-government" consistent with the conquering ideology of Jewish "messianism," which aspired to "mastery over all mankind." Behind the pseudo-Marxist phraseology it was not too difficult to detect the familiar strains of the "Jewish world-conspiracy"—a sinister plot to enslave all non-Jews through a secret government built on limitless financial power.[60]

Soviet publicists in the late 1970s (including the Jews among them) were also innovators in the systematic "Nazification" of Zionism. A case in point was offered by articles in *Soviet Weekly* written by Ruvim Groyer, explaining that Zionism was indeed a "racist" doctrine and that Zionist leaders in Europe had "collaborated" with the Nazis in the liquidation of Polish Jewry. In an article of 1 October 1977, Groyer brazenly asserted: "There is no doubt that top-echelon Zionists and Hitlerites were drawn together by their common social nature."[61] In his second piece on 10 October, the author, after grossly exaggerating the "racism" in Israel towards Palestinians and "Oriental" Jews, pompously concluded that the Israelis were "worthy heirs to Hitler's National-Socialism." Such articles were only the tip of the iceberg in the relentless campaign of the Soviet media to totally identify Zionism with Nazism. The "anti-Zionists" laid particular stress on the "bestial hatred" of Gentiles supposedly inculcated by Torah Judaism.[62] Some, like Lev Korneyev, focused more on the alleged monopolistic control exercised by Zionists in the West which was "threatening world peace." According to Korneyev, Zionism was backed by enormous resources

> that are being pumped out from the gold, diamond and uranium mines of South Africa, the workshops and industrial plants of Europe, America and Australia. Zionists are trying to infiltrate into all the spheres of public life, into ideology, science, commerce. Even "Levi's" jeans are part of their operation; the profits from selling the pants are used to help the Zionists. Most of the major monopolies producing arms are controlled by Jewish bankers. The business built on blood grants them huge profits.

> The bankers Lazard and Loeb count their profits as bombs and shells explode in Lebanon. Piles of dollars multiply in the safes of the Lehmans and Guggenheims while bandits in Afghanistan poison schoolchildren with gasses. It is understandable that peace in the world is the main enemy for Zionism.[63]

Korneyev's diatribe, published on 10 October 1980 in the main organ of the powerful Komsomol youth organization, was typical of the broad trend to brand Zionism as a war-mongering force of "world reaction" and "counter-revolution." Such outpourings openly embraced the language of the *Protocols* and did not shrink from *Stürmer*-like Nazi caricatures which had acquired free rein in the Soviet media after 1967.[64] Only fifty years on from the Bolshevik Revolution it appeared that the antisemitic traditions of the autocratic Russian State were being successfully revived and slowly devouring the class-struggle doctrines of Marxism-Leninism. The mass media clearly had instructions from above to encourage this torrent of demonization against Zionism, Jews and Judaism—unprecedented in its scale and duration.[65]

What was the motivation for this antisemitic cascade in the U.S.S.R. during its last two decades of existence? One might see it as a symptom of deep internal tensions and the beginnings of terminal decay within the Soviet system as a whole. After 1967, "National" Communism, closely linked to antisemitism and xenophobia, was gradually filling the almost hollow shell of Marxist-Leninism with its own toxic content. It was exacerbated by Soviet imperial expansionism in the 1970s which viewed Israel as a powerful base and the staunchest ally in the Middle East of the rival American superpower. Domestic motives were probably even more crucial. Thus it is striking how virtually all the nonconformist, dissident, or nationalist trends within the Soviet empire which could become potential sources of disaffection or disintegration were quickly linked to "Zionist subversion." At times the "Zionist" and the "dissident" became overlapping categories. "Zionists" could, however, be more easily portrayed as a visible, concrete, *internal* enemy with foreign associations—thereby helping to discredit the dissident phenomenon as a whole.[66] Xenophobic, anti-intellectual, and antisemitic feelings, solidly anchored in the population of the Soviet Union, were readily manipulated to this end. The fixation on "World Zionism" as a vast center for subversion, espionage, anti-communist propaganda, and slander of the Soviet system was symptomatic of Communist paranoia. So, too, was the obsession that "Zionists" in East European socialist countries had infected the Soviet bloc with liberalism and "revisionism"—ideological deviations that were perceived as life-threatening to the totalitarian system. Since Jews did indeed play a prominent role in dissident movements both in Russia and eastern Europe, hard-liners in the Kremlin doubtless regarded the "anti-Zionist" scarecrow as an indispensable weapon to discourage non-Jews from any association with such dangerous "instruments of imperialism."

No less important since the late 1960s was the impact of the pressure for Jewish emigration, dramatized so effectively by Israeli and world opinion—which posed a very serious problem of principle and prestige for the Soviet leadership.[67] The Zionist revival within the U.S.S.R. after the Six-Day War and the bold, defiant methods of the Jewish activists, with their stream of petitions and appeals to the West, was not something that could ever be honestly discussed in the Soviet mass media. On the ideological level it exposed the hollowness of the core Communist claim to have "solved" the Jewish question in the Soviet Union. In foreign policy, the Jewish demand for "repatriation" to Israel aroused strong objections from the Arab States and the Palestinians who angrily protested that the U.S.S.R. was reinforcing the economic, scientific, and military potential of Israel at their own expense. The Zionist call for a *return* to the historic Jewish homeland of Palestine/Eretz Israel also raised the old Bolshevik specter of ethnic separatism within the multinational Empire—threatening to reopen a whole Pandora's box of unresolved national grievances. The Jewish emigration movement and the resurgence of Jewish nationalism exposed the bankruptcy of the Leninist nationalities' policy which had become little more than a façade behind which stood the cultural imperialism of Great Russian chauvinists. This nationality policy did not only fail the Jews; it could no longer satisfy the national aspirations of most Ukrainians, Georgians, Armenians, Volga Germans, Uzbeks, Crimean Tartars, or the Baltic peoples. But it was Israel's spectacular triumph in 1967 and the blow it inflicted on the U.S.S.R.'s Arab allies which first opened up the breach.

The Soviet regime undoubtedly had grounds to fear that mass Jewish emigration could spark off similar demands from other non-Russian nationalities. Hence one could interpret the demonization of "Zionism" and the unmasking of its organic links with Western "imperialism" as an (ultimately vain) attempt to keep other forms of "bourgeois nationalism" in check. This was especially the case in the Ukraine where the "anti-Zionist" campaign aquired unique virulence. Zionism and Ukrainian "bourgeois nationalism" were deliberately coupled together by the Russian Communists as reactionary tools of "White" counterrevolution. Soviet policy in the Ukraine followed the classic imperial strategy of "divide and rule," constantly seeking to fuel the historic enmity between Jews and Ukrainians.[68] The anti-Zionist crusade, by reinforcing traditional Ukrainian antisemitism and Jewish suspicions of their neighbors (heightened by memories of Ukrainian collaboration with the Nazis during the Holocaust) intensified already existing tensions and thereby served a crucial diversionary purpose.

The anti-Zionist campaign also had the important function of intimidating activists in the Jewish community. They were constantly being harassed, persecuted, exiled, threatened with punitive trials, and imprisoned in order to discourage them and others from persisting with demands for Jewish emigration. Rabid anti-Zionist slander had the further goal of seeking to isolate Jews from other Soviet nationalities and potential allies within the Russian intelligentsia who might wish to press for more liberal domestic policies. By depicting Zionists as the willing accomplices of the Nazis and architects of a *criminal conspiracy* against the Soviet motherland, the authorities clearly hoped to destroy any residue of sympathy in the broader Soviet population for the absence of Jewish national rights. At the same time, assimilated Soviet Jews were mobilized to support the anti-Zionist campaign and provide an alibi against accusations of antisemitism. As in the West today, some of the most prominent crusaders against Zionism were individuals of Jewish origin.[69] Indeed, the Jewish Anti-Zionist Committee in Moscow would become, after 1983, a vital conduit for the Kremlin's special propaganda on Jewish questions both inside the U.S.S.R. and abroad. The Establishment Jews at the forefront of the campaign naturally insisted that they were all patriotic citizens immune to "Zionist falsehood and slander against the socialist homeland." They vehemently denied that there was any "Jewish problem" in the Soviet Union. They denounced Zionists as "rich exploiters" of other Jews and Zionism itself as "a concentration of extreme nationalism, chauvinism and racial intolerance" used to justify territorial seizures, annexations, and "armed adventurism."[70]

Jewish "anti-Zionists" were also required to defend Soviet restrictions on exit visas for Jews. Thus, General David Dragunsky, a wartime Hero of the Soviet Union who headed the Committee, and his deputy, Samuil Zivs, publicly justified the Soviet policy of drastically reducing the number of permits for Jewish emigration. They deplored the "psychological war" against the U.S.S.R. initiated by "international Zionism." From the beginning of 1984, the Committee's anti-Zionist propaganda statements became ever sharper, echoing the theses of the veteran Soviet journalist, Vladimir Bolshakov, who had declared Zionism to be the moral and political equivalent of Nazism. Dragunsky himself was especially active—against the background of the Lebanon War (1982)—in promoting the Zionist-Nazi equation. Not only had Israel institutionalized Nazi-like terror as its State policy but under the mask of "defending Soviet Jews" it was pursuing relentless subversive activity against the great motherland of Socialism.[71] At the same time, Dragunsky mendaciously contrasted the bravery of "non-Zionist" Jews who had fought heroically in the Red Army, in the partisan units and for the Western Allies with those traitors (the Zionists) who had unforgivably "collaborated" with the Nazis—avoiding the fight against fascism altogether.[72] This was the kind of Soviet "Big Lie" which might have amused Joseph Goebbels.

Even with the accession of Mikhail Gorbachev to the apex of the Soviet leadership in 1985, the Jewish Anti-Zionist Committee (and especially its vice-Chairman, Yuri Kolesnikov) continued for a time with their malign vituperation against Israel and Zionism. In August 1985 wide publicity was given by a TASS broadcast to the *White Book,* sponsored by the Anti-Zionist Committee, which held Zionist leaders responsible for the annihilation of thousands of Jews by the Nazis. According to the Soviet news agency, it was "precisely the Zionists who assisted the Nazi butchers," helped them "to make up the lists of the doomed inmates of the ghettoes," and escorted them to their places of extermination.[73] In the view of the Anti-Zionist Committee, Soviet Jews had long been misled, deceived and even blackmailed by the Zionists who remained a threat to the entire world and to civilization itself. Only with the new policy of détente and dialogue with the United States that began after 1987, did the Soviet Public Anti-Zionist Committee begin to lose some ground and appear increasingly anomalous.

Antisemitism itself did not of course disappear with the advent of President Gorbachev's new policy of *glasnost* (openness). On the contrary, it initially even intensified as a key weapon in the ideological war of the Russian nationalist opposition to Gorbachev's "restructuring" (*perestroika*) of the Soviet Union and his bridge-building towards the West. But for the first time, there were official Communist acknowledgements of the dangers of Black Hundred-style antisemitism. It was admitted in the Soviet press that tainted sources like the *Protocols of the Elders of Zion* lay behind much of the "anti-Zionist" falsehoods. Criticism was now openly directed against hate-mongers such as Begun, Yevseyev, Skurlatov, Emelianov, Bolshakov, Kiselev, Korneyev, and many others—who were still writing for Soviet publications. On 22 July 1990 an editorial in *Pravda*—less than a year before the collapse of Communism—made an astonishing confession: "Considerable damage was done by a group of authors who, while pretending to fight

Zionism, began to resurrect many notions of the anti-Semitic propaganda of the Black Hundreds and of fascist origin. Hiding under Marxist phraseology, they came out with coarse attacks on Jewish culture, on Judaism and on Jews in general."[74]

By 1990 it was clear that at the highest levels of the Communist Party there was growing concern that antisemitism might be getting out of hand. This was hardly surprising after two decades during which "anti-Zionism" had become such a cardinal element in Soviet ideology and hate propaganda directed at Israel which was being assiduously promoted and even encouraged. The demonology of Israel, Zionism, Judaism, and the Jews, disseminated throughout the Soviet mass media, could not fail to have dire consequences. Repeated incantations against the mysterious ghost of Zionism—the hidden, all-powerful, and perfidious international enemy—decisively exposed the ideological bankruptcy of Marxist-Leninism in the Soviet Union. In the Soviet military, since the early 1970s, the most flagrant kind of Black Hundred antisemitism had been openly defended or shamelessly exalted. Within the Writers' Union, by 1990, viciously antisemitic authors already formed a powerful faction. In the reception room to the main hall of the Writers' Congress in December 1990, one could find a large number of copies of Hitler's *Mein Kampf,* the *Protocols,* and various other antisemitic works openly on sale. At the Congress itself, some antisemitic speakers publicly appealed to the Army and the Communists to save what was left of a disintegrating Soviet Union that was sinking into oblivion under the sheer weight of a new "Jewish-Zionist yoke." During a visit to Moscow in 1990 I witnessed such trends at first hand.

Fortunately for the Jews of the ex-U.S.S.R., the anti-*perestroika* forces in the Soviet Union who had hoped to seize power and restore authoritarian Communist rule, were defeated in 1991. Their anti-democratic perspectives, linked to the full-blown encouragement of a hysterical antisemitism reminiscent of the late Tsarist era—could have had disastrous consequences for Soviet Jewry. Instead, in the post-Communist Russia that emerged under Boris Yeltsin, former Soviet Jews would enjoy something of a cultural and national renaissance under an admittedly erratic and rarely sober Russian President. Though they still suffered from deep-seated Russian chauvinism, Judeophobia, and the anti-Western populism that had long been an organic part of Russian history, for the first time they were truly free to make their own choices. A small elite became extremely wealthy "oligarchs"; a minority returned to Judaism. Others found their niche in the professional middle classes. Above all, no less than a million ex-Soviet Jews opted for the land of

Israel in the 1990s—greatly strengthening its scientific, technological, and educational base. It was above all this mass migration which most dramatically testified to the failure of the Communist experiment and represented a remarkable symbolic victory for Jerusalem over Moscow.[75]

NOTES

1. On the role of the Yevsektsiia, see the comprehensive study by Zvi Y. Gitelman, *Jewish Nationality and Soviet Politics. The Jewish Sections of the CPSU, 1917–1930* (Princeton, 1972).

2. See Theodore H. Friedgut, "Soviet Anti-Zionism: Origins, Forms and Development," in *Anti-Zionism and Antisemitism in the Contemporary World,* edited by Robert S. Wistrich (London, 1990), 26–45.

3. M. Rafes, "Evreii i Oktiabr'skaia Revolutsia," *Zhizn Natsionalnostei,* no. 1 (Jan. 1923): 237.

4. See V. I. Lenin, *O. Evreiskom Voprose v Rosii* (Moscow, 1924), Introduction by S. Dimanshtein, 6.

5. Ibid., 17.

6. V. I. Lenin, *On the Jewish Question* (New York, 1934), 3. "only entirely uneducated and completely oppressed people can believe the lies and slanders which are being spread about Jews. . . ."

7. See Zvi Gitelman, "The Evolution of Soviet Anti-Zionism: From Principle to Pragmatism," in Wistrich, *Anti-Zionism,* 11–25.

8. Joseph Ariel, "The Good Tidings of the Balfour Declaration in Odessa" (in Hebrew), *Heawar* 15 (May 1968): 120.

9. Michael Beizer and Vladlen Izmozik, "Dzerzhinskii's Attitude Toward Zionism," *Jews in Eastern Europe,* no. 23 (Spring 1994): 64–70.

10. Stalin's article "Don't forget the East," *Zhizn Natsionalnostei,* 24 Nov. 1918 (included in *Sochinenia* [Moscow, 1949] 4: 171–73) indicates the hopes which the Bolsheviks attached to a rising of Muslim "toilers" in the East. See also Laurent Murawiec, *The Mind of Jihad* (Cambridge, U.K., 2008), 208–16.

11. Jane Degras, *The Communist International 1919–1943, Documents* (London, 1956), 1: 143–48. Also Paul Novick, *Palestine: The Communist Position on the Colonial Question* (New York, 1936).

12. See Jack Miller, "Kalinin and the Jews: A Possible Explanation," *Soviet Jewish Affairs* 4, no. 1 (1974): 61–65.

13. Henry Bulawko, *Mise Au Point. Les Communistes et la Question Juive* (Paris, 1971), 85–88 for statements by Kalinin on the Jewish Question and Birobidzhan.

14. Zvi Gitelman, *Jewish Nationality,* 416–18.

15. C. Abramsky, "The Biro-Bidzhan Project, 1927–1959," in *The Jews in Soviet Russia since 1917,* edited by Lionel Kochan (London, 1970), 62–75.

16. On the harassment and persecution of Zionists in the U.S.S.R., see Arieh Leib Tsentsiper, *Eser Sh'not R'difot* (Tel Aviv, 1930); and Guido Goldman, *Zionism under Soviet Rule: 1917–1928* (New York, 1960).

17. Leonard Schapiro, "The Jewish Anti-Fascist Committee and Phases of Soviet Anti-Semitic Policy During and After World War II," in *Jews and non-Jews in Eastern Europe 1918–1945,* edited by Bela Vago and George L. Mosse (Jerusalem, 1974), 283–300.

18. Itzik Feffer, "I am a Jew," translated from the Yiddish by Joseph Leftwich, in *Calling All Jews to Action* (London, 1943), 9.

19. Quoted in J. B. Schechtman, "The USSR, Zionism and Israel," in Kochan, *Jews in Soviet Russia,* 114; see also Shimon Redlich, *War, Holocaust and Stalinism* (Luxembourg, 1995)—a documentary history of the Jewish Anti-Fascist Committee in the Soviet Union.

20. On the mood among Russian Jewry at this time, see Yehoshua A. Gilboa, "The 1948 Zionist Wave in Moscow," *Soviet Jewish Affairs* 1, no. 2 (1971): 35–39.

21. Yehoshua A. Gilboa, *The Black Years of Soviet Jewry* (Boston, 1971); and the important article by Benjamin Pinkus, "Soviet Campaigns Against 'Jewish Nationalism' and 'Cosmopolitanism,' 1946–1953," *Soviet Jewish Affairs* 4, no. 2 (1974): 53–72; also Gennadi W. Kostyrtschenko, "Kampanija borbe s kosmopolitis-mom w SSSR," *Voprosi Istorii,* no. 8 (1994): 47–60.

22. For earlier Soviet campaigns in the 1920s *against* antisemitism, see Michael Beizer, "Antisemitism in Petrograd/Leningrad, 1917–1930," *East European Jewish Affairs* 29, nos. 1–2 (Summer–Winter 1999): 5–28.

23. Jonathan Brent and Vladimir P. Naumov, *Stalin's Last Crime. The Plot against the Jewish Doctors, 1948–1953* (New York, 2003).

24. See Leonid Smilovitsky, "Ilya Ehrenburg and the Holocaust in Byelorussia," *East European Jewish Affairs* 29, no. 1–2 (Summer–Winter 1999): 61–74.

25. Mordechai Altschuler, et al., eds., *Sovetskie evrei pishut Ilye Ehrenburgu 1943–1966* (Jerusalem, 1993).

26. Joshua Rubinstein, *"Tangled Loyalties." The Life and Times of Ilya Ehrenburg* (New York, 1996).

27. J. V. Stalin, "Marksizm i Natsionalni Vopros," in *Sochinenia* (Moscow, 1949), 2: 300.

28. Yaacov Ro'i, "Soviet-Israeli Relations, 1947–1954," in *The USSR and the Middle East,* edited by Michael Confino and Shimon Shamir (Jerusalem, 1973), 123–46.

29. See Arnold Krammer, *The Forgotten Friendship: Israel and the Soviet Bloc 1947–53* (Urbana, Ill., 1974).

30. Peter Brod, *Der Antizionismus und Israelpolitik der UdSSR* (Baden-Baden, 1980).

31. See Jeffrey Herf, *Nazi Propaganda for the Arab World* (New Haven, 2009) on the success of Axis propaganda in the Middle East.

32. Yaacov Ro'i, *From Encroachment to Involvement. A Documentary Study of Soviet Policy in the Middle East, 1945–1973* (Jerusalem, 1974), 115.

33. Walter Laqueur, *The Struggle for the Middle East, the Soviet Union and the Middle East 1958–1968* (London, 1972). Although dated, this study is still useful.

34. Uri Ra'anan, "Moscow and the 'Third World,'" *Problems of Communism* 14 (Jan.–Feb. 1965).

35. For the text of Bulganin's note, see Ro'i, *From Encroachment to Involvement,* 190ff.

36. See, for example, K. Ivanov and Z. Sheinis, eds., *The State of Israel. Its Position and Policies* (Moscow, 1958).

37. Morton Schwartz, "The USSR and the Leftist Regimes in Less Developed Countries," *Survey* 19, no. 2 (87) (Spring 1973): 217.

38. David P. Forsyth, "The Soviets and the Arab-Israeli Conflict," *World Affairs* 134 (Autumn 1971): 132–42.

39. Benjamin Pinkus, *The Jews of the Soviet Union* (Cambridge, U.K., 1988), 219–20.

40. Matthias Messner, *Sowjetischer und postkommunistischer Antisemitismus* (Konstanz, 1997), 89–119.

41. Ibid., 99–100.

42. *Pravda,* 6 July 1967.

43. See Mikhail Agursky, "Russian Neo-Nazism—A Growing Threat," *Midstream* (Feb. 1976): 35–42.

44. Yevgeny Yevseyev, *Fascism under the Blue Star* (Moscow, 1971); and idem, "Zionism in the System of Anti-Communism," *Nauchny Kommunizm,* no. 1 (1974).

45. Y. Ivanov, *Ostrozhno! Sionizm!* (Moscow, 1969). For extracts see the *Bulletin on Soviet and East European Jewish Affairs* (London), no. 3 (Jan. 1969).

46. Vladimir Begun, *Polzuchaya Kontrrevolyutsiya* (Minsk, 1974), 79. Extracts in English from this work were published as *Creeping Counter-Revolution* (London: Institute of Jewish Affairs, 1975), translated by Howard Spier; see also William Korey, *Russian Antisemitism, Pamyat, and the Demonology of Zionism* (Chur, 1995), 27–45.

47. Begun, *Creeping Counter-Revolution,* 29.

48. Dmitri Zhukov, "The Ideology and Practice of Violence," *Ogonyok,* 12 Oct. 1974. For the parallel text in Russian and English of this review, see *Israel at Peace* (organ of the Communist Party of Israel [(MAKI]), no. 1 (Jan. 1975). Also Korey, *Russian Antisemitism,* 35–37.

49. The article first put out by the semi-official Novosty Press on 22 Sept.r 1972, appeared in the French-language journal of the Soviet Embassy, *URSS.*

50. See Emmanuel Litvinoff, *Soviet Antisemitism: The Paris Trial* (London, 1974) for the full story.

51. V. Begun, *Creeping Counter-Revolution,* 151.

52. Zhukov, "Ideology and Practice of Violence."

53. Ibid.

54. For Tsaban's sharp protest, *Israel at Peace.* Zhukov's article also prompted the American Communist organ, *Daily World,* 10 May 1975, to reluctantly comment that it "clearly propagates anti-Semitic stereotypes and it violates the precepts of Soviet socialism and Leninist principles. It is unquestionably deserving of the severest criticism."

55. Vladimr Kiselev, "Zionism. Weapon of Anti-Communism," *Soviet Weekly,* 15 Mar. 1975.

56. "Zionism. The Link with Imperialism," *Soviet Weekly,* 22 Mar. 1975.

57. Vladimir Kiselev, "Zionism—Imperialism's Trojan Horse," *Soviet Weekly,* 5 Apr. 1975. Cf. *Bolshaya Sovetskaya Entsiklopediya* (Moscow, 1972), 10: 325 which claimed that the Arab-Israeli war of 1948 was caused by Anglo-American imperialism and the intrigues of international Zionist circles.

58. In connection with Czechoslovakia, great emphasis was placed on the Zionist role in the mass media and its espionage techniques. See V. Bolshakov, "Anti-sovetizm-profesiya sionistov," *Pravda*, 19 Feb. 1971.

59. William Korey, "Protocols Revived," *Jewish Chronicle* (London), 23 Sept. 1977.

60. See Shmuel Ettinger, "Anti-Zionism and Anti-Semitism," *Insight* 2, no. 5 (May 1976); and Robert S. Wistrich, *A Lethal Obsession. Anti-Semitism from Antiquity to the Global Jihad* (New York, 2010), 129–53.

61. Ruvim Groyer, "Why We Condemn Zionism?," *Soviet Weekly*, 1 Oct. 1977.

62. See, for example, "Zionist Heirs of the Gestapo," *Za Rubezhom,* 3 Oct. 1973.

63. Lev Korneyev in *Pionerskaia Pravd*a, 10 Oct. 1980.

64. On the visual manifestations of this propaganda, see Judith Vogt, "Old Images in Soviet anti-Zionist Cartoons," *Soviet Jewish Affairs* 5, no. 1 (1975): 20–38.

65. Shmuel Ettinger, "Anti-Zionism and Anti-Semitism," pointed out that "no other subject has been given so voluminous attention by the mass media of the Communist bloc." In this context, the hour-long documentary about Zionism, entitled

"Traders of Souls" shown on national television in the U.S.S.R. on 22 Jan. 1977, was significant. See William Korey, "The Smell of Pogrom," *Jewish Chronicle,* 18 Mar. 1977. The best-selling antisemitic novels by the former naval officer Ivan Shevtsov, published in the 1970s, were also symptomatic of this licensed popular antisemitism.

66. See Emmanuel Litvinoff, ed., "Jews, Dissent and the Future," *Insight* 2, no. 4 (Apr. 1976); also the personal testimony of Roman Rutman, "Jews and Dissenters: Connections and Divergences," *Soviet Jewish Affairs* 3, no. 2 (1973): 26–37.

67. Jonathan Frankel, "The Anti-Zionist Press Campaigns," *Soviet Jewish Affairs* no. 3 (May 1972): 1–26 persuasively argued that this was a decisive factor in the anti-Zionism of the 1969–1971 period.

68. Israel Klejner, "The Soviet Ukraininan Press on Zionism and Israel," *Soviet Jewish Affairs* 4, no. 2 (1974): 46–53. See also idem, "The Present-Day Ukrainian Movement in the USSR and the Jewish Question," *Soviet Jewish Afairs* 11, no. 3 (1981): 4.

69. "Soviet Anti-Jewish Jews," *Insight* 3, no. 7 (July 1977).

70. See William Korey, *Russian Antisemitism,* 86–114.

71. *Pravda,* 17 Jan. 1984.

72. Korey, *Russian Anti-Semitism,* 107–8.

73. TASS, 15 Aug. 1985; also the review of the *White Book* in *Ogonek* 36 (31 Aug.–7 Sept. 1985).

74. Sergei Rogov, "Sushchestvie-li nash yevreiskii vopros?" (Is there a Jewish problem here?), *Pravda,* 22 July 1990.

75. Korey, *Russian Antisemitism,* 198–99.

CHAPTER 14

The Holocaust Inversion of the Left

The Soviet specter of "Zionist Nazism" was an almost perfect mirror-image of the Nazi propaganda myth of "Jewish Bolshevism." In the Nazi world-view, Bolshevism was a central part of the international Jewish conspiracy, linking Moscow with Wall Street and the City of London. For the neo-Stalinists, "Zionist Nazism" was the sinister agent of imperialism and a clique of international financiers seeking to subvert the socialist camp led by the U.S.S.R. The great difference is that the Holocaust inversion of the Left, which execrates Zionism as a form of Nazism is still very much with us today. Indeed its rapid spread into the Western world during recent decades suggests that it still has a future before it. The twinning of the Nazi Swastika and the Star of David as symbols of genocidal fascism (today a commonplace) was, however, at one time an exclusive Soviet preserve.[1] In other words, it is a totalitarian fabrication. It appeared for the first time during the Slánský trial, which depicted leading Czech Communists of Jewish origin not only as crypto-Zionist traitors but as *fascist shock-troops* for the subversion of the "popular democracies."[2] Joseph Stalin, the inventor of this particular post-Holocaust "anti-Zionist" mythology, had himself learned from Hitler the value of presenting the corporate Jew as an invisible, omnipotent enemy whose machinations justified eternal vigilance and internal repression. Hitler's conqueror by a cruel irony of history became his most adept disciple in the matter of antisemitism. It should also be remembered that both Hitler and Stalin have had many imitators since the 1940s in the Arab and Muslim worlds.[3] Similarly, in the liberal West, the inversion of the Holocaust which transforms contemporary Jews/Israelis into "Nazis" has become increasingly routine.[4]

The Prague show trial of 1952 was especially important as the first public anti-Zionist spectacle of its kind in the Communist bloc. It indicated a radical shift by Stalin from vigorous support for Israel four years earlier to its unbridled vilification. The most prominent Jews in the Czech Communist Party and government leadership were accused of close links with "the Zionists" for the purpose of espionage and treason. The Kremlin deliberately targeted the only country which in 1948 had sold vital arms to Israel during the War of Independence (with Stalin's agreement) at a time when the United States and the West imposed a strict embargo on arms sales to the Jewish State. Czechoslovakia was at the time one of the least antisemitic countries in East-Central Europe. It was among the first states (after the U.S.S.R. and the United States) to recognize Israel. Did Stalin intend it to expiate this "sin" by forcing Czechoslovakia to become the first European country to publicly denounce Israel? Was the Prague trial a signal to the world (and especially to the Arabs) of the coming shift in Soviet foreign policy in the Middle East? Since the trial was clearly orchestrated from the outset by Soviet advisers, who introduced a blatantly antisemitic tone into the interrogations, this seems likely. According to Eugen Löbl (the first high-ranking Czech Communist to be arrested) the Soviet adviser, Likhatchev, said to him early on:

> You are a Communist, and you are not a Czechoslovak. You are a dirty Jew, that's what you are. Israel is your only real fatherland and you have sold out Socialism to your bosses, the Zionist imperialist leaders of world Jewry. Let me tell you: the time is fast approaching when we'll have to exterminate all your kind.[5]

This pattern of brutal antisemitic insult (thinly masked by "anti-Zionism") accelerated with the arrival of more Soviet security officials in Prague. They drummed into the heads of their Prague counterparts that the Rockefellers [*sic*], the Rothschilds, and other "Jewish" bankers were behind the "treasonous" activities of Rudolf Slánský, the recently demoted Czech Communist Party leader. They told their Czech opposite numbers that the greatest enemy of Socialism was not Western imperialism but "international Zionism" with its powerful espionage network. By November 1951, the Czech Stalinist leadership was coming round to this view. The investigations of the arrested suspects (eleven out of fourteen were Jews) focused on their "petty-bourgeois, Jewish nationalist, and Zionist past," their links to the West, their efforts to subvert the economy, and above all, on the alleged directives they received from "World Zionism" and the State of Israel. The prosecutors labeled the three Gentile suspects as "non-Jewish Zionists," and the eleven of Jewish origin as "Zionist Jews." This was particularly outrageous since all of the accused (but especially the Jews) were out-and-out *anti-Zionists* and, to a degree, even anti-Jewish. Meir Cotic writes:

> They were ardent advocates of pure Communism, according to which Zionism is a reactionary-nationalist movement. They

> turned their backs on their Jewish past and their Jewish families, and distanced themselves from all Jewish circles.[6]

Slánský, for example, was a sworn enemy of Israel and the whole Zionist enterprise, who had blocked the sale of heavy weapons to the Jewish State after 1948. Bedřich Geminder, another of the accused, also hated his Jewish origins and past—as did Otto Šling—who always considered Socialism, not Zionism, the ultimate solution to the "Jewish Question." The bitter irony is that all of these self-hating Jewish Stalinists now found themselves execrated and forced to confess that they were "bourgeois nationalist Jews" treasonously collaborating with the State of Israel to undermine the Communist bloc. Dr. Otto Fischl (ex-deputy finance minister), another Czech Jew charged with helping Israel, was, in fact, notorious for his deliberate and cruel persecution of any Jews emigrating to the Jewish State. Yet none of this was of the slightest help once the Kremlin decided to liquidate them as "traitors," guilty of the unpardonable heresy of "Jewish bourgeois nationalism."[7] As Max Lerner put it in the *New York Post* in November 1952:

> The fact that the men on trial never were Zionists doesn't bother a Red Commissar. The idea of the Big Lie is that the bigger the lie, the better.[8]

At every stage of the Slánský trial, the use of antisemitic epithets was rampant. It was present in the preliminary investigations, in the preparations for indictment, the proceedings of the tribunal, and in the rabid press and radio incitement against Jews. Artur London, a former deputy foreign minister, was frequently subjected to hysterical Hitlerian racial abuse by his interrotators. Mordechai Oren, one of the leaders of the Israeli left-wing Mapam party (who was arrested and also put on trial) recorded an interrogator telling him: "You, Slánský, the Jews that Slánský smuggled into the party and government machineries, and all the others. You are the scum of the human race."[9] So scurrilous was the officially permitted antisemitic vituperation that Czech public opinion became seriously infected. Statements like "Hitler should have wiped out all the Jews" became commonplace as the trial approached.[10] Even the *New York Times,* notorious for its own liberal Jewish anti-Zionist tradition, acknowledged that Jews were now in grave danger throughout the Communist bloc as Stalin "sought to emulate Hitler." On 23 November 1952, a perceptive article in the *New York Times* commented on the Slánský trial:

> Here we have the infamous Protocols of the Elders of Zion again, but in a Stalinist version for which the ground was laid four years

> ago in Soviet Russia's own campaign against "cosmopolitanism," a campaign whose victims were predominantly Jews. . . . [T]he Prague trial may well mark the beginning of a major tragedy as the Kremlin swings further and further towards anti-Semitism masked as anti-Zionism.[11]

The Prague trial did indeed exhibit a new style of antisemitism with the State of Israel and "world Zionism" at the center and Middle East politics in the wings. Venomous incitement against Jews was fused with the execration of "Zionists" as spies, subverters, and saboteurs. The Czech Communist press in commenting on the death sentences inflicted on the defendents did not shrink from simultaneously calling them "cosmopolitan Jews without a homeland," Trotskyists, Titoists, Zionists, war criminals, swindlers, and "Gestapo agents."[12] As for the prosecutor, in his attack on the defendents, he had also struck a more "modern" note by suggesting that the Jews "exploited" the Czech distaste for antisemitism and Hitlerite racism:

> This fact was exploited by Jews owning shady businesses, factory owners, and bourgeois elements of every variety to infiltrate our party. The emphasis on the suffering that the Jews underwent in the period of the Nazi rampage served these elements as armour against any criticism and as a mask covering their true face. . . . When the [Czech] nation raised its voice against Zionism, they cried "anti-Semitism" in order to cover the help they were giving to the class interests of the Jewish bourgeoisie and their ties with the imperialists through World Zionism.[13]

Only six years after the Holocaust it was already possible in a public trial to assert that Israel and Zionism manipulated antisemitism as a mask to cover up their own crimes. The Prague trial set a precedent which has had countless imitators on the Left and in the Muslim-Arab world ever since.

In the wake of the Kastner trial in Israel, the Soviet press in the mid-1950s escalated matters a stage further. Zionist leaders were accused of having had contacts with Nazi officials in German-occupied Europe.[14] The growing ties between West Germany under Konrad Adenauer were presented in the U.S.S.R. as the continuation of a prewar Nazi-Zionist alliance. Israeli Prime Minister David Ben-Gurion was "a tool of the Bonn revanchists." According to Moscow, the price of West German economic aid to the Jewish state had been an Israeli government promise of silence concerning the presence of former Nazis in Chancellor Adenauer's government and civil service. This charge of collusion was aggravated still further after the capture of Adolf

Eichmann in Argentina by Israeli secret agents and his public trial in Jerusalem for crimes against the Jewish people. The Eichmann case now became the pretext for a peculiarly convoluted conspiracy theory. Its real goal was supposedly to remove from circulation "the principal witness of world Zionism's deals with the Gestapo."[15] By sentencing Eichmann to death, his silence over the secret dealings between Zionists and "Hitlerites" during the Second World War could be *permanently* ensured. As the Soviet publicist Lev Korneyev summed it up many years later, the Zionists wanted "to pull off a big political *coup* by presenting aggressive and racist Israel in the eyes of world public opinion as a 'fighter for justice' and 'chastiser of war criminals.'"[16]

The Eichmann Affair enabled the Communists to insinuate that already in the 1930s there had been close "collaboration" between the Nazi and Zionist secret services.[17] Eichmann's brief visit to the Middle East in 1937, according to Soviet and East German writings, was primarily "to secure an agreement on the creation there of a pro-Nazi Jewish State of 'Palestine' and the strengthening of reciprocity between Hitlerite Germany's special services and the Tel Aviv Jewish Agency."[18] But it was primarily in conjunction with the Rudolf Kastner [Rezsö Israel Kasztner] case (which had already shaken Israeli public opinion in the mid-1950s) that Eichmann's activities were of particular interest for Soviet and East European disinformation efforts. A Tass foreign broadcast on 1 February 1978 presented the matter as follows:

> In 1944 Eichmann and one of the Zionist leaders, Kastner, signed an agreement on Hungarian Jews. The agreement guaranteed the lives of 600 "prominent" Jews, while condemning to death 800,000 Jews without sufficient money to pay for their lives. The Zionists' collaboration with the Nazis. . .led to a catastrophe which cost the lives of nearly 6,000,000 Jews. This shatters the myth that the Zionists defend and express the interests of the Jewish people.[19]

The purpose of these sweeping propagandist statements was not to criticize Kastner's highly controversial role in trying to save a remnant of Hungarian Jewry in 1944 but rather to demonstrate that the Zionists were *traitors* to their own people. This slander was given a Marxist ideological wrapping by suggesting that it corresponded to the "class interests" of rich Jews. According to Soviet propaganda, the wealthy Jewish millionaires and Zionist leaders had themselves supported the rise of Hitlerism and then cynically abandoned the Jewish masses to their fate. In a review of the Soviet antisemitic film "The Secret and the Overt," *Kino* wrote in August 1975 that it was no accident that

> the leaders of Zionism and the big Jewish bourgeoisie were in collusion with the Hitlerites. . . . It is no longer a secret today that Zionist capital helped to strengthen the Hitler regime in Germany and the fascists' preparations to attack the Soviet Union. And notwithstanding the fact that the Hitlerites had murdered and burned in gas chambers hundreds of thousands of Jewish workers and poor people, the Zionist leaders continued to collaborate with the fascists. The leaders of Zionism took care only of chosen persons of the rich families.[20]

Tsezar Solodar, a particularly repellent representative of the Jewish anti-Zionist clique employed by the Soviet regime for such tasks, even alleged that the Zionist leadership regarded millions of Jews in Eastern Europe as nothing more than "economic and moral dust." The Zionists had no intention whatsoever of rescuing Jews from Hitler.[21] Solodar singled out Chaim Weizmann as the *arch-criminal* and "Nazi accomplice." Six million Jews in Europe were allegedly considered by Weizmann as "useless for Israel's future." All that the Zionist leaders were interested in were "young people filled with the poison of fanatical nationalism and fit for armed attacks on the native population of Palestine."[22] Having written off the poor and defenseless Jewish masses as "human dust," the Zionists then tried to ensure the defeat of the anti-Hitler coalition, in order to "block the advance of the Soviet armies and save the fascist regime from complete rout. . . ." These criminal plans, according to prominent Communist publicists, were only frustrated by the heroism of the Red Army.[23] Nevertheless, in their boundless treachery and villainy towards their own people, the Zionists directly "took part in the mass extermination of Jews," singling out and surrendering their brethren to the fascists. According to D. I. Soyfer, a prolific Soviet Jewish anti-Zionist, writing in 1976: "The Zionists doomed the Jews, including children, to death in the gas chambers whereas Soviet soldiers rescued the children who were threatened with death."[24] The *Judenräte* (in Soviet literature wrongly equated with Zionists) did not touch the rich, but they "sent the poor to their deaths." The "chosen" ones, Vladimir Semenyuk claimed, were removed from the transports to the death camps in order to save "the cream of the nation."[25] Driven by their boundless rapacity and cold-blooded cruelty, the Zionist millionaires, wrote Yuri Ivanov in 1970, "in accordance with an agreement with the Hitlerites, helped the latter herd Jews either into the ovens of the concentration camps or the Kibbutzes [*sic*] in the 'Land of Canaan.'"[26]

During the orchestrated Soviet anti-Zionist campaign of the 1970s such vile falsehoods were echoed in hundreds of letters from "loyal" Jews to the Soviet press, written in the same frantic, semi-hysterical tone of righteous indignation. Even the tragedy of Babi Yar (whose Jewish content had been deliberately erased by the Soviet authorities) was described in *Pravda Ukrainy* not only as a symbol of "Hitlerite cannibalism" but of "the indelible disgrace of their accomplices and followers, the Zionists."[27] In the Soviet Ukraine, where real collaboration by the local population with the Nazi invaders, especially in anti-Jewish *Aktionen,* had indeed been extensive, such falsehoods had a particularly grotesque ring. But from a Communist viewpoint there was much to be gained by "exposing" the anti-Soviet alliance of Zionists and Ukrainian bourgeois nationalists as well as their "joint" collaboration with the Nazis.[28] The Ukrainian-language pamphlet *Zionism and Its Class Essence* (1973), written by R. M. Brodsky, was an excellent example of the genre. He pointed to Zionist dealings with the pogromist Ukrainian Petlyurites and with the anarchist Makhnovites, who were also accused of pogroms during the Russian Civil War. Brodsky (himself Jewish) emphasized Zionist "collaboration" with fascist regimes in interwar Poland, Romania, and Italy while singling out for special consideration their "common language with the Hitlerites." Without a shred of evidence he asserted: "It has been established that many fascist criminals avoided the punishment they deserved only thanks to their Zionist protectors."[29] These blatant libels would find in the 1980s a broad and enthusiastic reception among Western Leftists (especially Trotskyites), including a growing number of Jewish intellectuals.

In Soviet propaganda there was a clear link between the myth of Nazi-Zionist "collaboration" and the slanders against contemporary Israel as a "Nazi" state. For if, as *Pravda* insisted at the beginning of 1984, the Zionists had helped the Nazis to send their own co-religionists to the gas ovens and had joined hands with the Gestapo, it stood to reason that Menachem Begin and Yitzhak Shamir would continue to use Hitlerite methods" to massacre "sub-human Arabs" in Lebanon.[30] What could be more natural than that the allies of Hitler in the past should also be his foremost imitators, successors and heirs in the present? This link had already been made at least twenty years earlier in Soviet cartoons juxtaposing Zionism and Nazism. In an *Izvestia* drawing (12 November 1964) depicting West German arms sales to Israel, the Star of David had morphed into a symbol of death and destruction. Two Nazi officers were shown selling arms to an Israeli. The caption read: "I recommend these first-class weapons. They have been tried and tested and used in Auschwitz and the Warsaw Ghetto."[31]

An early herald of what was to come was the stance taken by the Soviet Union in the Third Committee of the United Nations on 14 October 1965 in which it demanded that Zionism, Nazism, and neo-Nazism, *in that order,* should be classified as "racial crimes."[32] This Soviet amalgam came in response to a motion by the United States and Brazil proposing that the UN Charter of Human Rights contain a clause banning antisemitism. Afraid that this clause might be used against itself, and more than ready to pander to the Arab states' resolve to uproot Israel from the Middle East, the Soviets countered with what can retrospectively be seen as their opening gambit in the war of defamation and delegitimization against Israel. But it was undoubtedly the outbreak of the Six Day War and the crushing defeat by Israel of Moscow's Arab allies which would be the decisive trigger for the Soviet campaign of Holocaust inversion. The Soviet Union's Permanent Delegate to the UN, N. T. Fedorenko, like the Arab delegates, insisted on hammering away at the similarity between Israel's policies and those of the German Nazis. The representative of Jordan, for example, had already stated that both Israelis and Nazis "have the concept of race, both have the concept of force, of acquiring lands by invasion and the use of force, and both have fifth columns." Fedorenko, however, was more vehement and explicit:

> The overweening aggressors have taken over the notorious Nazi theories of geopolitics, of *Lebensraum,* of establishing a "new order" and "vital frontiers" in the Middle East. The peoples are familiar with these ultimatums, these insensate theories, this talk of a "new order" and of recarving the political map. It was the Nazi conquistadors that set out to recarve the map of Europe and the world, and attempted by armed force to impose what they called a "new order". . . . How monstrous that these devices of the Nazi brigands, condemned by the International Military Tribunal in 1946, have now been revived by a government claiming to represent a people which suffered so bitterly at the Nazi butchers' hands![33]

Fedorenko's lurid charges were repeated by Moscow Radio. On 6 June 1967, the government newspaper, *Izvestia,* also informed its readers that "even western correspondents compare these crimes with those the Nazis perpetrated in the occupied countries during World War II." A leading article in *Pravda* on 17 June 1967 entitled "This is Genocide" made it abundantly clear that branding Israel as a Nazi State was now the official Soviet

Communist Party line. For the next few years, Moshe Dayan, Israel's Defense Minister, with his unmistakable eye-patch, would be transformed into the favored hate-symbol of Soviet cartoonists. He was consistently portrayed as an outstanding pupil of Hitler's *Lebensraum* theories and of German Field Marshal Erwin Rommel's *Blitzkrieg* methods. A notorious cartoon in *Kazakhstanskaya Pravda* (21 June 1967) showed a subdued Adolf Hitler literally cringing before a superior, sinister-looking Dayan who summarily orders him to "Move On!"[34] Dayan was constantly accused of following in the footsteps of the SS and the "mad Führer," sowing death and destruction in the Middle East. Labor Prime Minister Golda Meir, the "fascist-imitating protectress of the Jews," received similar treatment. She was denounced by *Sovetskaya Moldavia* (10 March 1970) for having "proclaimed the nightmare idea of 'Greater Israel' and for bringing back the "rotten theory of racial superiority.'" Even the dovish Israeli Foreign Minister, Abba Eban, found himself compared to Hitler and attacked by *Radianska Ukraina* (3 March 1970) for "meeting near the walls of Dachau with the ideological heirs of Eichmann." Eban, it should be said, had once compared Israel's slim 1949 Armistice borders (at some points only nine miles wide) to "Auschwitz lines"—since they so obviously left the country exposed to a swift annihilatory blow by its enemies. This may have been a slight exaggeration, but it hardly justified turning Eban into a Nazi.

After 1967 Israel itself would repeatedly be presented as a "successor state" of the Third Reich in Soviet propaganda. Moreover, as we have seen, a direct line of continuity was established between mythical Zionist "collaborators" with the Gestapo and the no less imaginary "genocide" of the Arabs. In this witches' brew of state-sponsored mendacity, the Israelis had been allocated the role of masters and the (West) Germans were merely modest disciples. As one of the leading Soviet "anti-Zionists" Yevgeny Yevseyev, pointed out in October 1967, the old wartime roles had been completely reversed: "Now it is the German revanchists and militarists who are performing services for Zionism in practical affairs."[35] It was also Yevseyev who wrote in May 1970: "The Zionists should put up a memorial to Hitler. After all, it was the raving Führer in his *Mein Kampf* who asserted the basic dogma of Zionism—the existence of a 'world-wide Jewish people' and of the 'Jewish race.'"[36] Indeed, the Nazis were increasingly demoted after 1967 to the position of merely anticipating or borrowing from Zionists rather than the other way round. Thus an article in *Sovetskaya Belorussia* (April 1970) produced a rather startling innovation in historical research:

> When Hitler proclaimed his hate policies of the war for "living space," for a "Greater Germany" in which only Aryans would live, then in this particular case he was simply repeating the idea of the Father of Zionism, T. Herzl, on the need for a colonial struggle against barbarism.[37]

In other words, in matters of genocide, Hitler was the humble pupil and a pale copy of the Viennese journalist and politician, Theodor Herzl. A cartoon in *Bakinsky rabochy* (22 December 1971), entitled "Champions Among Professionals," displayed a more familiar agitprop style. It had SS Chief Heinrich Himmler raising the blood-stained left arm of a Dayan-like general in victory; the Israeli "champion" is holding a napalm rocket and barbed wire in his right hand.[38]

The Soviet media in these years compulsively blended the Star of David and the Swastika—as did their Arab counterparts. Sometimes a resurrected Nazi would be shown offering plans for a gas chamber to a militaristic Israeli while hapless Arabs in the background awaited their fate.[39] At other times the Israelis were offered and accepted the assistance of neo-Nazi mercenaries; or else, as in *Vechernayaya Moskva* (11 March 1970), the Nazi figure would be shown as an admiring spectator observing how the "ugly Israeli" constructs his new concentration camps. The caption on the cartoon read:

> The rulers of Israel operate today with Fascist methods. Israeli Zionists wipe out Arab houses, settlements and cities in occupied territory, throw people into concentration camps and apply terrorist methods towards Communists.[40]

The Communist campaign was constantly being amplified and would reach a large international audience in the 1970s. Ten years before Menachem Begin came to power, Israel was already accused in the Soviet media of bombing and wiping out Arab villages, just as the Nazis had flattened Lidice and Oradour during the Second World War, murdering their defenseless inhabitants.[41] Prime Minister Golda Meir's speeches were already compared in the Army newspaper *Krasnaya Zvezda* in 1970 with the rantings of Adolf Hitler. Communist propagandists also liked to compare "the pure blooded warriors of Israel" to the "executioners of Hitler in the last war" and to "the American aggressors in Vietnam." No effort was spared to make sure that the belligerent Israelis were endowed with classic "Jewish" traits such as a pot-belly, bow legs, flat feet, and a protruding *Stürmer*-like nose. The "Zionists" were depicted as potential "destroyers" of the world, rabid militarists, Satanic figures, money-grubbing parasites, serpentine and spider-like occupiers clasping Arab lands. At times, in more overtly Nazi fashion, they were demonized as poisonous mushrooms taking root in occupied territories. The theme of an international Jewish conspiracy was also present. The Zionist occupiers were tentacles of a giant octopus seeking to encompass and control the globe.

The pseudo-Marxist gloss on this Judeophobia was provided by periodic reminders that Israeli Zionism was the *organic* product of Western imperialism. Anti-Zionism was mobilized to explain that Israel's policies were the inevitable result of its alliance with "the most reactionary and aggressive force in the world today—US imperialism." In itself this was not so unusual. Soviet propaganda periodically treated "colonial oppression" in Africa, Asia, and Latin America as something akin to Hitlerism. Thus it was by no means unprecedented that Zionism should be categorized as a form of fascism or Nazism—a strategy which had begun in Stalin's last years. What was striking, however, was the very explicit antisemitism involved in stressing "the old ties of Jewish financiers and Zionist leaders with big monopoly capital, with the Rothschilds and Kuhn-Loebs."[42]

No less remarkable was the intensity, longevity, and virulence of the post-1967 campaigns. The Soviet media did not relate to Zionism as just one more manifestation of Nazism in the contemporary world. They were adamant that Zionist terror and repression of Arabs had resulted "in a policy of genuine genocide," and that the misanthropic racist doctrine of Judaism led to "direct extermination."[43] They repeatedly insisted that just as Hitlerite theories concerning the "racial superiority of the Aryans" had produced the gas chambers, so, too, Zionist racism was already provoking "mass genocide." S. Astakhov, writing in the Moscow daily, *Selskaya Zhizn* (16 November 1975), even asserted that genocide had been practiced in Israel "from the first days of the establishment of the State." Vladimir Bolshakov, a veteran "anti-Zionist," writing in *Pravda* (1 August 1982), particularly stressed the historical continuity of Zionist "genocide" policy. Menachem Begin and Ariel Sharon, he emphasized, were in no sense departing from Israeli norms. "The policy of genocide being carried out at this time by the Zionists in Lebanon," he observed, "is inseparable from Zionism as an ideology and the criminal practices of the Jewish bourgeoisie."

During the 1982 Lebanon war, the same atrocity stories, false quotations, antisemitic imagery, and Nazi-Zionist parallels were being frenetically peddled as in the past. There were nevertheless moments when the campaign reached an exceptional intensity and volume only comparable with Soviet propaganda against Nazi Germany during the Second World War. The huge difference was that Stalin's U.S.S.R. between 1941 and 1944 was indeed fighting for its existence against the mighty Wehrmacht and in opposition to a Nazi occupation that *did* practice a genocide policy on Soviet soil. The very fact that the small state of Israel (in no way a military threat to a massively armed superpower like the U.S.S.R.), could be compared, even in passing, with the life-and-death danger to the Soviet Union during World War II, was in itself a mark of unbridled anti-Zionist hysteria. At the same time, this onslaught was also coldly calculated, serving the political objectives of a semi-totalitarian regime. Within the Soviet government and the KGB there were plenty of hard-liners who regarded "anti-Zionism" as an indispensable tool for demoralizing and crushing all forms of dissidence and dissent. Displacing the tensions seething beneath the surface of Russian society against the Jews was, after all, a time-honored diversionary method. Anti-Zionism was also a valued instrument for promoting Soviet influence in the Third World and discrediting American policy in the Middle East. The anti-American component was particularly visible in the wake of Israel's invasion of Lebanon.[44]

Moscow publicly denounced the 1982 invasion as part of "a global offensive on the 'Third World' liberation forces" sponsored by Washington.[45] The United States was consistently presented during the Lebanon War not only as Israel's mentor and manipulator, but as the key supporter of political gangsters, Mafiosi, and fascist "exploiters" all over the world. As Moscow's domestic TV service breathlessly announced on 18 July 1982: "Serving as the supports for this bridge have been McCarthyism, the American aggression against Vietnam, the crimes there by American soldiers, the killing of Martin Luther King, Hitlerite criminals taken into the service of the United States, the Hitlerite saboteurs who have been training their Israeli counterparts and Washington's direct support for fascist forces and dictators throughout the entire world."[46] The "extermination" of Palestinians and "enslaving" of Arab states was seen as an integral part of the strategic alliance between the United States and Israel in which the latter was blindly "carrying out the will of American hegemonism."[47] The Israeli aggression was obviously being performed at the behest of the American "monopolies," in order to impose their *diktat* not only on the Arab world but also on Western Europe. "By destroying Beirut, and Lebanon in general, Israel and the United States hope to destroy the advanced post of West European capital in the Near East."[48] By sparking anti-Israel outrage in Western Europe, the U.S.S.R. and its Communist supporters evidently hoped to drive a wedge in the Western alliance, which was less than rock-solid at the time.

Nazi-Zionist parallels were frequently evoked in the early 1980s in an anti-American context. A cartoon in *Pravda* on 5 August 1982 entitled "Familiar Handwriting" had Tel Aviv goosestepping arm in arm with Hitler's skeleton over a field strewn with Arab bodies. In the left hand of the Israeli was an axe and in the right a rocket labeled "Made in the USA." Viktor Mikhayev, in a Moscow broadcast two days later, stated that according to "the basic cannibalistic theory of Zionism, the chosen people of Israel must prosper even at the expense of the death of the lower races."[49] The Tass news agency added that Tel Aviv had embarked on its plan "for a physical destruction of the Arab people of Palestine, for a giant Holocaust." On 5 August 1982 it further elaborated that "concentration camps and prisons staffed by sadists, who are drawing on the experience of Nazi criminals, have been set up for them. The number of Lebanese and Palestinians sent to these 'death factories' is growing with every day."[50] A *Vremiya* newscast on 7 August 1982 drove the point home, describing Israel's then Prime Minister, Menachem Begin, as "a maniac and fanatic like Hitler, and probably no less a racist than the Führer. . . ."[51] There have been all-too-many echoes of this extreme defamatory campaign among Communists and pro-Palestinian Leftists in the West to this very day.

Such libels continued well after Begin's resignation as Israeli Prime Minister in 1983 and the drastic scaling down of Israel's involvement in Lebanon. Thus, on 17 January 1984 when Vladimir Bolshakov published an authoritative article in *Pravda* equating Zionism with fascism, he insisted that the Israelis were perpetrating a deliberate "genocide" in Lebanon, based on the ideology of racial purity.[52] He added that Zionists had always collaborated with fascists and Nazis in recruiting Jews from all over the world to support their crimes. This last comparison implied that pro-Israel Diaspora Jews were part of a criminal Nazi-like conspiracy. Many of these charges would be echoed in the West by new Leftists and Trotskyists – who in their hatred of Israel proved no less venomous than the neo-Stalinists they claimed to despise.

A case in point was the play *Perdition* (1987), published by the Irish-born working-class Trotskyite author from Manchester, Jim Allen.[53] Allen had sent this play to London's prestigious Royal Court Theatre in mid-1985. It proceeded to the production stage just over a year later. At the heart of the drama was, once more, the Kastner Affair, and the tragedy of Hungarian Jewry during the Holocaust. Rudolf Kastner's deal with Adolf Eichmann in 1944 to save a limited number of wealthy Jews, relatives, and Zionist functionaries from wartime Budapest had long been a source of bitter controversy. Kastner had been accused in Israel in a notorious 1953 court case of betraying Hungarian Jewry. A few years later he was assassinated by Israeli right-wing extremists, who believed that he had "sold his soul to the devil."[54] Ironically, it was right-wing writers like the famous American Jewish playwright Ben Hecht who in 1948 had first highlighted the "treason" of Kastner (a prominent Hungarian labor Zionist) as a way of attacking Ben-Gurion's ruling Mapai party in Israel. Allen's purpose was, however, very different. His objective was to "prove" the identity of interests between Zionism and Nazism. In his fictional "J'Accuse" one can find all the standard left-wing anti-Zionist clichés of the age. These include the charge that Zionists systematically oppose any struggle against antisemitism; that they advocate racial separateness; or that they sought out a special relationship with the Nazis. Allen, like many Communist propagandists before him, also repeated groundless smears against top Israeli leaders like Ben-Gurion, Weizmann, Gruenbaum, Sharett, and others, based on fabricated claims or misleading quotations torn out of context. He even suggested that the top Zionist leaders thought "the spilling of Jewish blood would strengthen their demand for a Jewish State after the War."[55]

For Trotskyites like Allen, the Zionists were indisputably Hitler's "favorite Jews." All the complexities, ambiguities as well as the agonies of the Holocaust—questions of morality and human behavior in extreme situations—were reduced to a single demagogic slogan, "The Zionists are guilty!" His play was less about the tragedy of Hungarian Jewry than about placing the contemporary State of Israel in the dock—as a racist, expansionist, and militarist "ghetto State." According to Allen (who was in fact more than a decade ahead of most mainstream western leftists in his anathemas) it was self-evident that Israel "commits outrageous crimes, then silences its critics by invoking the Holocaust." The chief protagonist in his play, *Perdition,* the Zionist Dr. Yaron, readily repeats the supposedly indisputable truth that Israel is "a nation built on the pillar of Western guilt," a racist entity whose only *raison d'être* is to illegally expropriate Palestinian land. From such premises one can better understand Allen's vainglorious boast that *Perdition* was a "lethal" attack on Zionism because it touched the heart of "the most abiding myth of modern history, the Holocaust."[56]

In Allen's left-wing "revisionism," the Holocaust had become a highly serviceable political myth to discredit, defame, and dehumanize the "Zionist enemy" on "humanitarian" grounds. The dead "Jews of Hungary murdered by the Nazis at Auschwitz" (to whom Allen dedicated the play) were one more convenient tool with which to indict the Israeli State. Naturally, Allen and his supporters were silent about the fact that the Zionist movement in 1944, wholly dependent on the Western Allies as it was, remained powerless to shape Nazi or Allied policy. To cover the author against any charges of antisemitism, Allen's publishers (the left-wing Ithaca Press) made sure to produce as witnesses for his integrity a short list of the "usual suspects." Such veteran *Jewish* intellectuals as the ubiquitous Noam Chomsky, the French Arabist Maxime Rodinson, the Austrian-born poet Erich Fried, the Trotskyite American author Lenni Brenner, and an anti-Zionist expatriate Israeli author Akiva Orr, predictably gave Allen a clean bill of health. In the play itself, there was also an array of anti-Zionist Jewish witnesses proclaiming different variations on the Trotskyist "solution" to antisemitism—namely the overthrow of the capitalist system and the assimilation of the Jews.

The presence of the well-known linguist Noam Chomsky (an established icon of left-wing politics in America) among the supporters of Jim Allen was not really surprising. Chomsky's involvement with open Holocaust deniers like Robert Faurisson or "inverters" like Allen was no accident. It was not only about the issue of free speech. Indeed it cannot be separated from his vitriolic anti-Americanism and visceral hostility to Israel. While careful not to explicitly justify Hitler, Chomsky's work over many decades conveys the general impression that the Nazis were certainly no worse than the "war criminals" of the United States and Israel today.[57] Vituperative abuse of "fascist" behavior by contemporary Israelis seems to have been the main way for Chomsky to connect to the mass murder of European Jews during World War II. This all-too-apparent lack of empathy may well have contributed to Chomsky's enthusiastic defense of Robert Faurisson—a former professor of literature at the University of Lyon and an intellectual who has been France's leading Holocaust denier for the past thirty years. It is nonetheless remarkable that Chomsky should be unfazed by Faurisson's denial that the gas chambers ever existed; or that he failed to see anything objectionable in proclaiming the Holocaust to be a "historical lie" or, in Faurisson's own words, a "gigantic political-financial swindle" whose principal "beneficiary" was the State of Israel and whose main victims were the Palestinians.[58] Nor was Chomsky apparently bothered by Faurisson's dismissal of any Holocaust eyewitnesses, historians, investigators, scholars, writers, or magistrates as being at all credible if they were "Jewish"—a blatantly antisemitic position. Faurisson naturally made an exception in Chomsky's case.

Chomsky may also have been influenced in favor of Faurisson by allegations that he was subjected to some harassment, intimidation and physical violence in France at the end of the 1970s when he first began to make public his obnoxious Holocaust denial theses; no less importantly, Faurisson was vigorously supported by a small group of radical French leftists around *La Vieille Taupe* (The old mole)—a publishing house run since the 1960s by Pierre Guillaume.[59] Chomsky was in close contact both with Guillaume and subsequently with another French anarcho-Marxist intellectual and Holocaust denier, Serge Thion.[60] He even agreed to write a preface to one of Faurisson's publications. Quite misleadingly, he described the Holocaust denier as "a sort of apolitical liberal." This intervention did much to give the cause of historical "revisionism" public credibility in France. Not only that, but Chomsky in 1982 rejected any suggestion that denying the Holocaust was "antisemitic"; there was, he insisted, "no hint of anti-Semitic implications in Faurisson's work"; and it was, moreover, a fact that the Holocaust had been "viciously exploited by apologists for Israeli repression and violence."[61]

France, it should be said, was unique among Western countries in having a revolutionary left-wing form of "negationism," combining Holocaust denial *and* inversion. The ultra-left followers of Faurisson claimed to support Holocaust denial on an "anti-capitalist" basis while rejecting the "legend of the gas chambers" as a product of Allied victors' justice at Nuremberg.[62] They owed much (like all Holocaust deniers) to the pioneering work in the 1950s of an ex-Communist Paul Rassinier. He had joined the French Socialist party in 1934—embracing pacifism and a pro-German line towards the Third Reich. Captured by the Nazis and interned in Buchenwald (from where he was released in 1945), Rassinier combined visceral anti-Communism with a pacifist left-wing denunciation of postwar French colonialism. Initially, he did not deny the existence of the gas chambers or embrace open antisemitism. Nor could he be described as a neo-Nazi though he ardently defended the German people against charges of being a "barbaric nation" that had invented mass extermination. But through the 1950s his work became more extreme and was increasingly applauded by far-right circles in France and beyond.[63] Rassinier in effect became the first Holocaust denier to offer a synthesis of right-wing anti-capitalist, anti-Communist and antisemitic ideas with libertarian pacifism.[64]

During the year following Rassinier's death in 1967, the French Left had been radicalized by the May student revolt in Paris and increasingly infiltrated by anti-Zionist ideas. Intellectuals on the far left began strongly attacking Israeli policy and some even claimed that the Jewish State had fabricated the Holocaust to win greater financial and diplomatic support. Others set about obfuscating the unique features of Nazism and of the Holocaust in comparison to other massacres.[65] The left-wing lawyer Jacques

Vergès (who in the late 1980s would defend one of the more notorious surviving Nazi war criminals, Klaus Barbie) insisted that there had been several holocausts in history. Jews should not, therefore, claim any monopoly on suffering. Moreover, the Holocaust "offended only the consciousness of white people." Vergès adamantly opposed any effort to single out the Holocaust as being worse than the atrocities committed against Third World peoples by "colonial barbarism." And since the Third World was, as he put it, "the herald of progress," its enemies were "the logical successors of Nazism: the Americans in Vietnam, the French in Algeria, the Israelis in the West Bank."[66] From this Third Worldist perspective, any mention of Holocaust uniqueness was perversely transformed into a way of obscuring and obstructing adequate recognition of colonial oppression. Jews and their "anti-fascist allies," by emphasizing primarily *Jewish* victims, were guilty of exploiting unjustified power and privilege. Both Israelis and Diaspora Jews stood accused by Vergès and other leftist intellectuals in France of the egoistic, self-interested manipulation of Holocaust memory.[67]

Conspiracy theorists on the ultra-left, along with anti-globalists and a variety of post-1968 *gauchistes* added their own versions to this mantra. But in each case the Palestinians were always lionized as the definitive example of *colonisés* (colonized people) under the proto-Nazi jackboot of Israel. In this Manichean world-view, capitalism begat fascism which begat imperialism which begat Israel and its proxy Zionism—the ultimate form of racist domination—sponsored, of course, by the "Great Satan"—the United States of America. On the antisemitic wing of this ultra-left, however, America was a mere puppet in the hands of a sinister neo-con Jewish cabal.[68] At the same time, among the left-wing Holocaust deniers, the starting-point remained as always the relationship between Auschwitz, the demise of bourgeois capitalism and democracy. Like the postwar Trotskyists, ultra-leftists assumed that Fascism and Nazism were transient expressions of the capitalist order. The Hitler regime was fundamentally no worse than everyday liberal democracy.[69]

The "myth of the gas chambers" having mystified this basic truth, had acted as a disastrous brake on modern revolutionary consciousness. In the name of "anti-fascism" it had distracted the working-class from the crucial struggle against the "capitalist mode of production that dominated the planet." Stalinist Communists, as much as Social Democrats or the Western Allies were guilty of the "anti-fascist" swindle which had singularized Nazism as the prime enemy of the revolutionary proletariat. The left-wing Holocaust "revisionists" insisted that only the complete destruction of capitalist commodity production, of the wage-system and existing State structures would bring racism and all other forms of political insanity to an end.[70] The "Auschwitz Lie," on the other hand, was nothing more than a smokescreen (transformed into a taboo) to disguise the fact that the *whole of bourgeois society* had become a concentration camp. In short, the Holocaust "myth" was masking the crimes of the democratic capitalist world and the Communist tyrannies. The myth functioned like a "universal religion." It exploited all the resources of the modern communications media in order to drown out any remaining revolutionary perspectives in the working class. As a result, Auschwitz had become *the* "anti-fascist" dam against the Revolution. By the same token, the denial of the gas chambers was a liberating and subversive truth that would awaken the masses from their stupor.

The left-wing followers of Faurisson in France categorically rejected any view of the World War II as being a genuine struggle of the democracies against fascism or humanity against barbarism. They also opposed any highlighting of antisemitism or Hitler's racist ideology. The persecution of Jews had indeed existed after 1933, but it was entirely due to the twisted nature of the capitalist system. At the same time, the ultra-leftists focused on how Jews had allegedly manipulated the myth of Auschwitz to justify the State of Israel and its "crimes" after 1948. Thus, the Eichmann Trial of 1961, it was asserted, had been orchestrated to milk the bad conscience of the West, and draw a veil over the Israeli expulsion of Palestinians in the War of Independence. The aim of the "Zionist Fascists" was to block any criticism of Israel by appealing to the new religion of "genocide"—a cynical and mendacious "exploitation of corpses" for political ends.[71] Serge Thion, in particular, stressed the link between Israel's "barbaric occupation" after 1967 (which he compared to German rule in France during World War II), its "Nazi-like" racism and the basing of its artificial legitimacy on the myth of the Holocaust.[72]

Thion was perhaps the best example around 1980 of a French Third Worldist militant indulging in the new-style ultra-left, "anti-racist" Judeophobia. In this world-view, Israel was by definition an expansionist state dependent on a fake "genocide" as its ideological pillar. To delegitimize this racist state par excellence, the Left had first of all to expose the "great lie of the 20th century"—namely the Holocaust. At the same time, Thion pointed to events like Deir Yassin (where some 250 Palestinian Arabs were "massacred" by Israelis during the bitter 1948 Arab-Israeli war) as if it were "a kind of Auschwitz."[73] The results of such massive distortions long ago became evident. An *absolute* anti-Zionism, driven by "anti-imperialist" and "anti-racist" assumptions, steadily fused in the work of Thion and Guillaume with the theses of Holocaust Denial, advocated by Faurisson. The resulting "synthesis" created a new and particularly toxic version of anti-Jewish mythology on the radical Left.[74]

Left-wing "revisionists" in France, as we have seen, did not shrink from using the argument that Zionism was engaged in a vile conspiracy against the Palestinians. They shared the belief of many on the Left that the Zionists were powerful, ruthless and diabolically cunning—stopping at nothing in the pursuit of their ends. This is today increasingly the mainstream leftist and liberal view, especially in Western Europe. Israel is seen as a bloodthirsty, racist State whose dealings with the Palestinians are characterized by betrayal, cruelty and double-dealing. Indeed it is not difficult for a partisan observer to portray the Israeli State, with its massive firepower and post-1967 image of cold, calculating, efficient and superior force as a heavily armed "Goliath." The Palestinians, on the other side, are invariably depicted in equally simplistic terms as poor, "homeless" and downtrodden. In this Manichean schema of the contemporary Left, the Palestinians—as victims of Western or Israeli "colonialism"—are a priori right. For many pro-Palestinian militants in the West they have even assumed the mantle of a "crucified people." The Jews in this narrative not only killed Christ two thousand years ago, but are repeating their dastardly crime today against the people of Palestine. They are in effect combining the ultimate crimes of deicide and genocide.

The resonance of such historical inversions and lethal myths should not be underestimated. To many of the generation born after 1945, racism and fascism are indeed the ultimate "crimes against humanity." By the same token if Zionism comes to be widely defined as "racist," "fascist" or a "Western colonialist sin, it is irredeemably beyond the pale. Thus the more Israel has been depicted as *the* inheritor of Europe's colonial heritage, the more readily it finds itself saddled with metaphors from this same Western past such as the image of an all-conquering *Herrenvolk*. This is exactly what has happened in the past forty-five years. On the radical Left, especially its Trotskyist and Maoist wings after 1967, a militant anti-Zionist ideology began to call for the violent overthrow or dismantling of the Jewish state. In its methods, argumentation and aims this style of anti-Zionism has closely resembled both Soviet and radical Arab propaganda, libelling Israel as a racist, "Nazi" state whose destruction was the sine qua non for socialist revolution in the Middle East.[75] Unconditional solidarity with the PLO acted as a major incentive for the Far Left in Western societies to equate "the struggle against racism and antisemitism" with the destruction of Israel as a "progressive" goal.[76] In West Germany, fanatical anti-Zionism resulted over forty years ago in some particularly macabre actions. A leaflet signed by the anarcho-communist "Black Rats" in November 1969 justified the bombing of the communal hall (*Gemeindehaus*) of West Berlin's Jewish congregation, on the anniversary of the *Kristallnacht* pogrom, by denouncing German guilt-feelings. It declared that the time had come to stop doing penance for the gassing of Jews in the Second World War. "This kind of neurotic, backward-looking anti-Fascism, obsessed as it is by past history, totally disregards the non-justifiability of the State of Israel." True anti-Fascism consisted in an "explicit and unequivocal identification with the fighting *Fedayin*." Solidarity with the Palestinians "could no longer be satisfied by purely verbal protests of the Vietnam variety, but would pitilessly combat the combination of Fascism and Israeli Zionism. . . ."[77]

The Berlin trial in December 1972 of Horst Mahler, a left-wing lawyer heavily involved in the Baader-Meinhof anarchist movement (which engaged in deliberate urban terror against the West German Establishment), brought to the surface some of the latent antisemitism in extreme Left "anti-Fascism." Mahler read a polemical declaration of the Red Army Faction (RAF) in court, justifying the murder of Israeli athletes at the Munich Olympic Games by Palestinian terrorists. The action was supposedly "anti-fascist. . .because it was in memory of the 1936 Olympics." Killing Israel's sportsmen was apparently a blow against the strategy of imperialism and the Federal Republic's law-and-order state. "Israel weeps crocodile tears. It has burned up its sportsmen like the Nazis did the Jews—incendiary material for the imperialist extermination policy."[78] (Horst Mahler, it should be noted, a couple of decades later, metamorphosed into perhaps the leading neo-Nazi and antisemitic ideologue in a newly unified Germany.) Ulrike Meinhof, who gave evidence for Mahler, was still insisting in 1972 that unless the German people were pronounced "not guilty" of fascism, they could not be mobilized for the revolution.

Red Army Faction leaders argued that the Left and the Communists had failed to explain Auschwitz properly to the German masses. In reality, antisemitism was popular *anti-capitalism*; it expressed the unconscious longing of the people for Communism. Their justified hatred of finance-capital and the banks had been diverted by the Nazis on to the Jews. According to Ulrike Meinhof: "Auschwitz means that six million Jews were murdered and carted on to the rubbish dumps of Europe for being that which was maintained of them—Money Jews" (Auschwitz heisst, das sechs Millionen Juden ermordet und auf die Müllkippen Europas gekarrt wurden als das, als was man sie ausgab—als Geldjuden).[79] By implication, there was nothing so terribly wrong with the Jews being murdered as *Geldjuden,* except that this had unfortunately been an action based on racism, not class-hatred. Meinhof insisted that the German people must be pronounced "not guilty" of genocide and better indoctinated in the future for their apocalyptic mission of destroying capitalism. Interestingly enough, while standing the history of the Third Reich on its head and whitewashing the German people in convoluted fashion, Ulrike Meinhof at the same time felt compelled to express a "historical identity" with the Jews of the Warsaw ghetto. Her own terrorist group, it was implied, was suffering from the same treatment at the hands of the West German bourgeois State as the Jews had experienced under the Third Reich.[80] The desire for martyrdom, a highly developed persecution-complex and "anti-Zionist" guilt projections were uneasily blended together in a mind-boggling inversion of political reality.

The concrete meaning of the RAF's "anti-fascist" identification would soon be exposed in the Entebbe hijack drama. A member of Ulrike Meinhof's radical terrorist group, Wilfried Böse, was directly involved on 27 June 1976 in the hijack of the Air France airbus flying from Tel Aviv to Paris. He and his comrades forced the plane to land at Entebbe Airport in Idi Amin's Uganda as part of a terrorist operation masterminded by the notorious Venezuelan leftist "Carlos the Jackal." The Jewish passengers were swiftly separated by Böse and his colleagues from the non-Jews, who alone were released. Some of the Entebbe hostages were actually survivors of Nazi concentration camps. One of the captives even showed Böse the camp number indelibly branded on his arm and told his captor that he found it difficult to see any difference between the new German generation of radical leftists and the Nazis. Jews were again being *selected* by Germans to die, even though the Baader-Meinhof group claimed that they were fighting for world-revolution.[81] The real difference, as the brilliantly executed Entebbe rescue of the hostages by Israeli paratroops would demonstrate, was the existence of a Jewish state capable of decisive action to prevent any return to the catastrophic era of Jewish passivity and powerlessness during the Shoah.

This "Zionist" lesson has, however, been turned on its head by the contemporary Left during the past three decades. *Holocaust inversion* which pictures Palestinians as "the Jews of today," has been especially resonant in Germany (and in Europe more generally) as a way to escape any responsibility for the Nazi past. By branding Israel as a "Nazi State," the uneasy German and European conscience can be temporarily assuaged. More than thirty years ago, a former member of the German new Left, Henryk Broder, pointed to the psychological functions of the widespread pillorying of Israel ("the Super-Jew") on whom all European guilt for the past could be so conveniently offloaded.[82] Israel, he argued in 1980, was being judged by altogether different standards from non-Jewish states. It alone was constantly depicted as the living incarnation of what the Third Reich had once represented—namely *racism-in-action*.[83]

Broder pointed out that this diversionary tactic and the accompanying campaign of self-delusion was largely driven by escapism. He sharply admonished his former comrades on the German new Left: "So you make it easier for yourselves by projecting on your parents' victims, the debates and the arguments you never had with your parents. And it works: the Jews are the Nazis, the Palestinians are the victims of the Jews—and your parents are out of the picture (and you, too). You don't have any more problems. At last, you can look them in the face, because you now know where the Nazis, who were never here [i.e., in Germany] really are."[84] Just as Hitler had needed "the Jew" to assign blame for capitalism, Communism, inflation, unemployment and the humiliating Versailles Peace Treaty to a single enemy—so, too, the contemporary Left was addicted to the State of Israel as their scapegoat for world problems. Without the Jewish State, there would supposedly be no more strife in the Middle East, no further obstacles to peace and socialism in our time. The logical conclusion was that "the Jewish State must not be."[85]

Similar attitudes have been all too common among those radical Left groups in the Western world in recent decades who embraced the destruction of Israel as a cardinal point in their program.[86] They reject any *national* rights of Jewry, including its historical continuity, ethnic dimensions, and the integrity of its cultural traditions. They also specifically negate the right to self-determination of over five million Jewish citizens in Israel, who alone among the nations of the world are seen as an *organic* obstacle to revolution, peace, and progress. This stunning act of *discrimination* and *exclusion* is carried out in the name of "anti-racism" and a universalist revolutionary utopia. According to this "anti-racist" world-view, the Jewish state in its essence and existence represents the principle of absolute injustice. It therefore *deserves* to be destroyed.[87] In practice, the "anti-racist" Left is justifying genocide in advance.

Leftist anti-Zionism is so insidious precisely because it claims to oppose the brutal antisemitism of the Nazis and all those trends which sought to abolish the civic equality of Jews in bourgeois society, to confiscate their property, expel them from the country, or to physically extirpate the foundations of Jewry. The Holocaust did indeed discredit this type of *racial* antisemitism. But it did so, only to give birth to a new anti-Jewish ideology focused against Israel as the central political expression of collective Jewish identity in the postwar era. To paraphrase the noted French sociologist Annie Kriegel: anti-Zionism came to fulfill the same negative identity role in the 1970s and 1980s for Communism and the Left as did antisemitism for the Nazis and the Right in the 1930s and 1940s.[88] The parallel was not so much one of words, declarations or ideologies but existential. The essence of the Hitlerian project *and* now of its postwar successors—above all in the Islamic world and among its left or right-wing collaborators—remains the physical uprooting of the Jewish collectivity as a people and a state. The ferocious slogan of the Nazis was *Judah Verrecke!* (Perish Judah), that of radical anti-Zionism is the destruction of Israel.[89] As far as the *security* of the Jewish people is concerned, there is little difference. Nearly six million Jews destroyed in Israel by an Iranian or Islamist terrorist nuclear attack would amount to a Holocaust—even if Israel were able to retaliate and exact severe retribution from the enemy in such a scenario.[90]

Militant left-wing anti-Zionists would no doubt claim that they only seek to negate the *national* expression of Jewish identity in a Zionist State. But that is small consolation, given the flirtation of so many leftists with Islamic radicalism and their downplaying of any threat to the existence of the Jewish State. Israeli historian Moshe Zuckermann is one of many who has repeated the accusation that the "Zionist regime" instrumentalizes antisemitism and the Holocaust as a means to silence criticism of the Jewish State.[91] At the same time, leftists like Zuckermann have little if anything to say about the way the Left has, for decades, justified tyrannical dictatorships in the name of "anti-colonialism" while pillorying Zionism as the "fascism of our time." Many so-called liberals and leftists still continue to applaud the "progressive" content of Arab terror organizations like Hezbollah and Hamas even as they vilify "reactionary" Zionism or prophesy its imminent demise. Moreover, they ignore how easily the obstinate negation of the national dimension in Jewish existence has turned in the post-Holocaust era into the focal point for attacks on Jewry as a whole. It is a fact that today the centrality of Israel in Jewish life makes it virtually impossible to differentiate between anti-Zionism and antisemitism. Thus, whether intended or not, the "anti-Zionist" campaign on the Left strikes not only at Israel but at the security and standing of *all* Jews—a reality that has become ever more apparent during the first decade of the 21st century.

Diaspora Jews regularly find themselves accused by radical organizations of complicity in "crimes" allegedly committed by Israel, and they remain a potential target at all times for terrorist attacks. For militant anti-Zionists—whether of the radical Right, the far Left, or the Islamist persuasion—Diaspora Jews are virtually a fifth column. They are perceived as the reservoir of a vast tentacular organization whose geo-political center is the State of Israel. Every Jew thereby becomes transformed into a potential *enemy,* unless he or she overtly opposes Zionism. The Dispersion itself becomes the object of suspicion, the visible manifestation of an intangible yet omnipresent secret "Zionist" empire. Already in the early 1980s, bomb attacks in Paris, London, Brussels, Berlin, or Vienna against Jewish targets appeared to the Arab terrorist perpetrators as the natural extension of their anti-Zionist crusade to its more vulnerable hinterland. The Palestinian and Islamist Holy War against Israel turned (with the complicity of neo-Nazi and left-wing extremists in the West) into an assault on the very principle of Jewish solidarity. This terrorist war began in the 1970s under the mask of "anti-fascism." It subsequently revealed its more macabre aspect in Paris in outrages like the attack on the liberal synagogue in Rue Copernic in October 1980 and the machine-gun assault on the Goldenberg restaurant in the Rue des Rosiers on 9 August 1982. The Middle East background to these murderous crimes was only too apparent though minimized by both Left and Right. Less obvious at first sight was the ideological inversion of history that permitted such terrorist actions to be considered expressions of "resistance to imperialism and Zionism." For if Jews really were Nazis as the radical Left was claiming, then it could become as natural and "moral" to kill them as it would be to assassinate Hitler and his henchmen. All that was required would be the rewriting of modern Jewish history in the light of the so-called Israeli "Final Solution" of the Palestinian problem, thereby justifying bloody acts of revenge that could be glorified as "resistance to Nazism." The Jewish tragedy of yesterday would become the pretext for Arab or Iranian retribution in the present and the herald of a future apocalypse in which Israel would finally be extinguished.

The demonization of Israel as a "Nazi State" has in recent years become a crucial plank in the constantly mushrooming efforts to delegitimize it. Those who do not actively resist Israel are by implication no better than Nazis—which is equivalent to saying that they should be shunned, isolated, boycotted, and eventually eliminated. This is especially true for Diaspora Jews who are tainted with guilt by association. Such rhetoric, spearheaded today by the militant Left, is often antisemitic as well as anti-Zionist in character. A pro-Palestinian demonstration at Ford Lauderdale, Florida, against Israel's war on Gaza in early 2009 produced repeated examples of this type of Holocaust inversion. One demonstrator screamed: "Murderers! Go back to the Ovens! You need a big oven!"[92] In San Francisco, a week later, protesters were burning Israeli flags and carried banners reading "Zionist Nazism," "Gaza Holocaust" or "Zionazis." Similar incidents have repeatedly occurred in Britain, Norway, Sweden, France, Spain and other West European countries in recent years.

The Nazi-Zionist parallel has never, of course, been confined to the Communists or the radical Left. It is a staple of Arab propaganda and increasingly encouraged by seemingly respectable academics, journalists, and sometimes by politicians, priests, and even so-called Middle East experts. Repellent comparisons between the Warsaw Ghetto and Gaza are legion today. Such distorted propaganda has become self-reinforcing through the immense power of the mass media, amplified still further by the Internet and the sheer force of repetition. The Left, which still prides itself on its "anti-racism," has played a singular role in advancing this obscene equation. The Swastika is for many so-called progressives around the world rapidly turning into a new Yellow Star to be pinned onto the Jews. For example, the popular Brazilian caricaturist Carlos Latuff—a leading left-wing anti-globalist—does not hesitate to present Israeli leaders like Ariel Sharon and his successors as *vampires* or as the *devil incarnate*; or to plaster onto the helmets of Israeli soldiers captions like "Born to Kill Babies"; or to unilaterally appropriate Holocaust imagery for the Palestinian cause. In his work, the Arab people of Palestine are the new "people of Christ," innocent proletarians martyred by wicked Israeli "child-killers."[93] The "Satanic Jew" has in fact returned in much leftist and anti-globalist vocabulary as the archetypal "imperialist criminal." Palestine, itself, is depicted as one large concentration camp—the embodiment of the absolute evil represented by Israel and its "fascist" rulers. This is becoming the new unifying cultural code of a post-modernist and anti-globalist Left for whom "the Jews" are guilty of having become racist-imperialist vampires, ethnic cleansers and perfect Nazis.

There is another related specter which continues to haunt contemporary left-wing discussion of Israel and the Holocaust—the ghost of the Palestinian *Naqba* (Arabic for "disaster"). For much of the Left has in recent years embraced the Palestinian national narrative about Israel's creation as being a "catastrophe," as if it were gospel truth that Israel was built on the "original sin" of dispossessing the native people of Palestine. The Naqba is today routinely equated by much of the Left with the Holocaust. This completely distorted narrative is widely celebrated across the globe, reinforcing the cult of the Palestinians as the quintessential "Other." They are iconized as the victims par excellence of Western and Zionist "racism." Yet the Naqba is a problematic myth, recognized as such in 1948 by most of the Left, which had strongly championed the creation of a Jewish State in Palestine as a fundamentally *just cause*. Left-wing writers like I. F. Stone had no doubts then, that Israel's creation was an epic struggle against the odds and that Arab leaders had intended to carry out "a war of extermination" (in the words of Abdul Rahman Azzam, Secretary of the Arab League) against the fledgling Jewish State. Stone, and other eyewitnesses in 1948, knew that much of the Palestinian exodus was induced by the empty promises and genocidal threats of Arab leaders; and that the Palestinian Arab refugees were deliberately kept locked up in refugee camps to dramatize the revanchist myth of the Naqba, instead of being integrated in neighboring Arab lands. The fact that Stone, like Chomsky and a number of other American-Jewish radical leftists, became scathing Israel-bashers after 1967, does not change the basic validity of the original eyewitness reports and assessments at the time. There is no foundation to the Arab legend that the Israelis committed a "racist crime" in displacing between 500,000 to 700,000 Palestinians in 1948.[94] But it has reinforced the current "Holocaust inversion" rhetoric in which Zionists are automatically caricatured as "Nazis" and Palestinians as "Jews" in defiance of any sound historical judgment. The cult of the Naqba sanctifies the status of Palestinians as "eternal victims" who are not responsible for their fate; it locks them and the international Left into a view of history where empirical facts are continually bent to the ephemeral whims of politics and narrative fashions. It binds participants and observers alike into a stifling "tyranny of guilt" that precludes any serious or critical inquiry into controversial historical events.

NOTES

1. Robert Wistrich, "The Anti-Zionist Masquerade," *Midstream* (Aug./Sept. 1983): 8–19.

2. See Meir Cotic, *The Prague Trial. The First Anti-Zionist Show Trial in the Communist Bloc* (New York, 1987).

3. See Meir Litvak and Esther Webman, *From Empathy to Denial. Arab Responses to the Holocaust* (London, 2009), 215–42.

4. Klaus Holz, *Die Gegenwart des Antisemitismus* (Hamburg, 2005), 79–99.

5. Cotic, *Prague Trial,* 219.

6. Ibid., 223.

7. "Prague Purge," *New Statesman and Nation,* 6 Dec. 1952.

8. *New York Post,* 24 Nov. 1952.

9. Cotic, *Prague Trial,* 231. The facial contortions and manual gestures in the air made by the interrogator reminded Oren of *Stürmer*-style antisemitic caricatures.

10. See Arnold Krammer, "Prisoners in Prague," in *The Left against Zion. Communism, Israel, and the Middle East,* edited by Robert S. Wistrich (London, 1979), 71–86.

11. "Tragicomedy in Prague," *New York Times,* 23 Nov. 1952; for eyewitness accounts, see Mordechai Oren, *Prisonnier Politique à Prague, 1951–1956* (Paris, 1960); Shimon Orenstein, *Aliyah be-Prague* (Tel Aviv, 1968); and Eugene Loebl, *Sentenced and Tried: The Stalinist Purges in Czechoslovakia* (London, 1969).

12. *Rude Pravo,* 28 Nov. 1952, 30 Nov. 1952; Cotic, *Prague Trial,* 143.

13. Cotic, *Prague Trial,* 124–25. The prosecutor repeatedly insisted that Zionism was the "lackey of American imperialism" and "a military outpost of the American aggressors," bent on "world conquest." Wall Street was the cement linking the "cosmopolitanism" of the U.S. monopolies with "Jewish bourgeois nationalism" and the Slánský conspiracy.

14. R. Scholom, "Telltale Trial," *New Times,* no. 23 (1955):. 20–22.

15. L. Korneyev, "The Sinister Secrets of Zionism" (Part 2), *Ogonyok,* no. 35 (1977).

16. Ibid. On Korneyev, see William Korey, *Russian Antisemitism, Pamyat, and the Demonology of Zionism* (Chur:, 1995), 50–52, 82–83.

17. L. Korneyev, "Sekretnye Sluzhby mezhdunarodnogo sionizma i gosurdarstva Izrail," *Narody Azii i Afriki,* no. 1 (1976).

18. L. Korneyev, "Shpionsky sprut sionizma" (The Zionist espionage octopus), *Ogonyok*, 29 Jan. 1977.

19. See Robert Wistrich, *Hitler's Apocalypse. Jews and the Nazi Legacy* (London, 1985), 217–18.

20. Ibid., 218.

21. Ts. Solodar, *Dikaya polyn* (Wild wormwood) (Moscow, 1977), 34.

22. Ibid. Also idem, "The Hunt for Youth," *Komsomolskaya Pravda,* 3 Aug. 1983.

23. V. A. Semenyuk, *Natsionalisticheskoe bezumie* (Nationalistic madness) (Minsk, 1976), 47.

24. D. I. Soyfer, *Sionizm—orudie antikommunizma* (Dnepropetrovsk, 1976), 50.

25. Semenyuk, *Natsionalisticheskoe bezumie,* 94.

26. Y. Ivanov, *Ostrozhno! Sionizm!* (Moscow, 1969).

27. *Pravda Ukrainy,* 13 Mar. 1970.

28. See Israel Klejner, "The Soviet Ukrainian Press on Zionism and Israel," *Soviet Jewish Affairs* 4, no. 2 (1974): 46–52.

29. Ibid., 49.

30. *Pravda,* 17 Jan. 1984; see also the report by Richard Owen from Moscow, "Israel savaged by Pravda," *The Times,* 18 Jan. 1984.

31. For a demonstration of how the Zionist-Nazi amalgam was generally used in Soviet visual propaganda, see Judith Vogt, "Old Images in Soviet Anti-Zionist Cartoons," *Soviet Jewish Affairs* 5, no. 1 (1975): 20–35.

32. Ze'ev Ben-Shlomo, "Soviets and Zionism," *Wiener Library Bulletin* 20, no. 1, n.s. no. 2 (Winter 1965–66): 7–9.

33. N. T. Fedorenko, "Perfidy and Aggression," *New Times,* 28 June 1967. For an eloquent reply, see the pamphlet published by the Anglo-Israel Association entitled *The Diplomatic History of the Six Day War,* a lecture by Gideon Rafael delivered on 25 Sept. 1975 at the Royal Society of Arts. Mr. Rafael was Israeli Ambassador to the United Nations in June 1967 and related to me some of his experiences.

34. See Vogt, "Old Images," 26.

35. Y. Yevseyev, "Lackeys at Beck and Call," *Komsomolskaya Pravda,* 4 Oct. 1967.

36. Y. Yevseyev, "Fashizm pod goluboy zvezdoy" (Fascism under the blue star), *Komsomolskaya Pravda,* 17 May 1970.

37. B. M. Fikh, "Sionizm i fashizm," *Sovetskaya Belorussia,* 2 Apr. 1970; quoted in Jonathan Frankel, "The Anti-Zionist Press Campaigns in the USSR 1969–1971: An Internal Dialogue?," *Soviet Jewish Affairs,* no. 3 (May 1972): 22.

38. Vogt, "Old Images," 27.

39. "The Well-Known Assortment," *Sovetskaya Rossiya,* 11 Aug. 1967; quoted in Vogt, "Old Images," 25.

40. Ibid., 26–27.

41. See, for example, V. Ladeikin, "Criminal Policy of the Israeli Extremists," *International Affairs,* no. 1 (1972): 43. *Za Rubezhom* on 3 Oct. 1973, carried an article on the "Zionist Heirs of the Gestapo" illustrating the Zionist-Fascist symbiosis. There were thousands of similar articles published in the Soviet media through the 1970s.

42. For a representative example among many see K. Ivanov, "Israel, Zionism and International Imperialism," *International Affairs* (June 1968): 20.

43. G. Kuznetsov, "Zionism in the Pillory," *Za Rubezhom,* 21 Nov. 1975; Y. Valakh in *Pravda Ukrainy,* 15 Nov. 1975; V. Korotev, "The Zionist Witches' Sabbath," *Gudok,* 15 Nov. 1975; Lydia Madzhoryan, "The Criminal Policy of Zionism and International Law," *Moscow News* (English-language daily), 22 Sept. 1973, insisted on the organic link between the "man-hating racial conception of Jewish superiority" and the so-called Israeli praxis of genocide.

44. See Nicolas Spulber, "Israel's War in Lebanon through the Soviet Looking Glass," *Middle East Review* (Spring/Summer 1983): 18–27.

45. "Tragedy without an Epilogue," *Novoe Vremiya,* 27 Aug. 1982.

46. Quoted in Spulber, "Israel's War in Lebanon," 21.

47. "Crusade by Washington and Tel Aviv," *Selskaya Zhizn,* 26 June 1982.

48. Spulber, "Israel's War in Lebanon," 22.

49. Ibid., 20.

50. "In the Footsteps of the Nazis," Tass, broadcast quote in Nicolas Spulber, "Israel's War in Lebanon," 21.

51. Quoted in Robert Wistrich, *Hitler's Apocalypse. Jews and the Nazi Legacy* (New York, 1985), 224.

52. V. Bolshakov, "Fascism and Zionism: The Roots of Kinship," *Pravda,* 17 Jan. 1984. See also *IJA Research Report*, "*Pravda* Equates Zionism with Fascism" (Mar. 1984); and "Israel Savaged by *Pravda*," *The Times,* 18 Jan. 1984.

53. Jim Allen, *Perdition, A Play in Two Acts* (London, 1987).

54. Robert S. Wistrich, *Between Redemption and Perdition* (London, 1990), 242–45; also David Cesarani, "The Perdition Affair," in *Anti-Zionism and Antisemitism in the Contemporary World,* edited by Robert S. Wistrich (London, 1990), 53–62.

55. Wistrich, *Between Redemption and Perdition*, 245.

56. Cesarani, "The Perdition Affair," 54.

57. See Werner Cohn, *Partners in Hate. Noam Chomsky and the Holocaust Deniers* (Cambridge, Mass., 1995). See http://wernercohn.com/Chomsky.html.

58. On Faurisson, see Pierre Vidal-Naquet, *Les Assassins de la mémoire* (Paris, 1987) and idem, *Holocaust Denial in France* (Tel Aviv, 1993), 1–17.

59. Robert Faurisson, "Revisionism on Trial: Developments in France, 1979–1983," published in the "revisionist" organ called the *Journal of Historical Review* 5, no. 2 (1985): 133–82; also the pamphlet by Pierre Guillaume, *Droit et Histoire* (Paris, 1986). Guillaume became a committed follower of Faurisson from the early 1980s. On the broader philosophical issues, see Elhanan Yakira, *Post-Zionut, Post-Shoah* (Tel Aviv, 2006), 9–62.

60. See Serge Thion, *Vérité Historique ou Vérité Politique?* (Paris, 1980); also Nadine Fresco, "Les redresseurs de Morts," *Les Temps Modernes,* no. 407 (June 1980): 2150–2211; and Alain Finkielkraut, *L'Avenir d'une Négation* (Paris, 1982). Chomsky himself characterized Thion (Faurisson's associate) in positive terms as a "libertarian socialist scholar" despite the latter's brutal characterization of the Shoah as a Jewish lie.

61. W. D. Rubinstein, "Chomsky and the Neo-Nazis," *Quadrant* (Australia) (Oct. 1981): 8–14; see also the reply and correspondence in the April 1982 issue.

62. Valérie Igounet, *Histoire du négationnisme en France* (Paris, 2000), 282. The first Holocaust denier in France, the fascist Maurice Bardèche, had argued similarly in his "pioneering" *Nuremberg ou la terre promise* (Paris, 1948).

63. See Deborah Lipstadt, *Denying the Holocaust: The Growing Assault on Truth and Memory* (New York, 1993).

64. See Limor Yagil, in Vidal-Naquet and idem, *Holocaust Denial in France* (Tel Aviv, 1993), 31–38.

65. Ibid., 40–41.

66. See Robert Wistrich, *A Lethal Obsession. Anti-Semitism from Antiquity to the Global Jihad* (New York, 2010), 635.

67. Ibid., 535–636. These charges were also made by prominent intellectuals in France like Tzvetan Todorov and Alain Brossat.

68. Ibid., 606–7.

69. Igounet, *Histoire du négationnisme en France,* 289.

70. This theory derived from ultra-left Italian Communists (Bordigists) in the early 1960s. See ibid., 186–89.

71. Ibid., 300ff.

72. Serge Thion, *Vérité Historique ou Vérité Politique* (Paris, 1980). In the preface to the Arabic edition, two years later, Thion emphasized the role of the Six-Day War in his gradual conversion to Holocaust denial.

73. Igounet, *Histoire du négationnisme en France,* 303.

74. Pierre-André Taguieff, *La Judéophobie des Modernes* (Paris, 2008), 358–76.

75. Robert Wistrich, *Hitler's Apocalypse,* 229–30.

76. Ibid., 229.

77. Rudolf Krämer-Badoni, "Zionism and the New Left," in *The Left against Zion. Israel, Communism and the Middle East,* edited by Robert S. Wistrich (London, 1979), 226–35. For a general assessment, see Stefan Aust, "Terrorism in Germany: The Baader-Meinhof Phenomenon," *German Historical Institute Bulletin,* no. 43 (Fall 2008): 45–47. Aust's book, *Der Baader-Meinhof Komplex* was first published in Hamburg in 1985.

78. Krämer-Badoni, "Zionism and the New Left," 234.

79. Quoted in Wistrich, *Hitler's Apocalypse,* 230–31.

80. Ibid.

81. Ibid., 231.

82. Heinrich Broder, "You Are No Less Anti-Semites than Your Nazi Parents," *Forum* 42/3 (Winter 1981): 109–17.

83. Ibid., 112.

84. Ibid., 113.

85. Ibid., 118.

86. Wistrich, *Hitler's Apocalypse,* 232.

87. Ibid.

88. Annie Kriegel, *Israël est-il coupable?* (Paris, 1982), 41.

89. See Jacques Givet, *Israël et le genocide inachevé* (Paris, 1979).

90. Wistrich, *A Lethal Obsession,* 908–38.

91 Moshe Zuckermann, "Zionismus als Staatsdoktrin," *Junge Welt,* 7 Oct. 2010. See also his recent book, "*Antisemit!*" *Ein Vorwurf als Herrschaftsinstrument* (Vienna, 2010) which piles up standard leftist clichés, now repeatedly recycled and given the kosher imprint by Israeli anti-Zionists.

92. Wistrich, *A Lethal Obsession,* 938.

93. See Joël Kotek, *Cartoons and Extremism: Israel and the Jews in Arab and Western Media* (London, 2008).

94. See Sol Stern, "The Naqba Obsession," *Australia-Israel Review* (Oct. 2010): 30–33.

CHAPTER 15

Bruno Kreisky, Israel, and the Palestinian Question

It was during the Holocaust years which he spent in the Swedish capital of Stockholm that Bruno Kreisky—the young exile from Vienna who would radically transform postwar Austrian Social Democracy—first honed many of the diplomatic skills which marked his later ascendancy as a political leader.[1] At the same time, it was also in the safety of neutral Sweden (where he lived between 1938 and his postwar return to Austria) that Kreisky could distance himself not only from the Nazi reign of terror but from any serious reflection concerning the mass murder of European Jewry. The apparent indifference of the future Socialist Chancellor of Austria (who lost twenty-one relatives to the horrors of German Nazi barbarity) in the face of the ravages of genocidal antisemitism should not, however, be ascribed primarily to his Swedish environment. Though Sweden's wartime record during the Shoah was far from being exemplary, it did at least produce one truly unique Holocaust hero in the shape of Raoul Wallenberg. Kreisky's attitude to issues of Jewish identity both before, during, and after the Holocaust could not have been more different. It was, if anything, distinctively Austro-Marxist and Jewish-assimlilationist rather than typically Scandinavian. Kreisky had, after all, already been socialized in an Austrian labor movement (he was twenty-seven years old by the time he reached Stockholm) that was decidedly ambivalent about Jews.

Though Kreisky subsequently insisted that he had never once suffered from antisemitism in his youth, this is simply not a credible claim. But it was one of many assertions by Bruno Kreisky which would subsequently heighten his popularity as the one Jew who could grant Gentile Austrians full exculpation from a latent sense of guilt over their prominent role in the Holocaust. Kreisky was destined to become the *Entlastungsjude* (exonerating Jew) freeing Austrians of the burdens of complicity in the German mass murder. In effect, twenty-five years after the end of World War II, he emerged as the star witness for the defence of Austria against "troublemakers" like Simon Wiesenthal and a multitude of critics abroad.

Nobody seemed better suited than Kreisky to reinforce the Austrian cult of historical amnesia from within. Not only that, but Kreisky in the 1970s insisted on pushing the Socialist International and the European community towards full recognition of the Palestine Liberation Organization (PLO)—then still a self-avowed terrorist organization—as the sole legitimate representative of the Palestinians. Moreover, his polemics against Israel as an "undemocratic," "clerical" and militarist State (unusual assertions for a leading European Social Democrat in the 1970s) ensured continuous confrontations with world Jewry as a whole. It should be remembered that Kreisky began to brand Israel as a "semi-fascist" or an "apartheid" State well before this turned into a respectable mainstream opinion or trendy sport in the West.[2] In his provocative Middle Eastern foreign policy, Kreisky was generally supported by his own party (though some had reservations about his highly personalized feud with Nazi-hunter Simon Wiesenthal) and by the broad mass of Austrians—with whom Kreisky certainly appeared to be in tune at the peak of his career.

Kreisky did not shrink from using his Jewish descent (which he never denied) to argue that he could be more "objective" than others in his relationship to Israel and Zionism. He had no hesitations, for example, in reproaching his friend, the West German Chancellor and SPD Chairman, Willy Brandt, for excessive "loyalty" to Israel. Nor did he draw back from asserting the essential commonality of interests between antisemites and Zionists—a recurring theme in his pronouncements which was guaranteed to arous the ire of many Jews.[3] In bending over backwards to prove his total separation from anything "Zionist," "Israeli," or overtly Jewish, Kreisky undoubtedly reinforced his popularity in Austria, but he also ensured the enmity of most mainstream opinion among Jews. True, there were always some exceptions to the rule, like the maverick Israeli left-wing politician Uri Avnery, who not only maintained close relations with Kreisky, but reinforced his jaundiced opinions of Israel; or his friend, the extremely wealthy Austrian Jewish industrialist, Karl Kahane, who shared many of the Chancellor's views on the Middle East and other matters. But for the majority of Diaspora Jews and especially Israelis, Austria's socialist leader seemed like the epitome of Jewish self-loathing. Bruno Kreisky was, however, much admired as a far-sighted statesman by many of his contemporaries, including American Secretary of State Henry Kissinger. For Arab notables like Egyptian President Anwar el-Sadat and Libyan dictator Muammar Gaddafi, the Austrian Socialist Chancellor was highly regarded as a friend, and ally. Yasser Arafat, head of the PLO was especially grateful to Kreisky as the first

Western leader to have politically legitimized the Palestinian cause in Europe. In 1980, under Kreisky's prodding, Austria became indeed the first Western country to fully recognize the PLO. This did not have the positive consequences that Kreisky had hoped for. Only one year later, a terrorist splinter from the PLO, the Abu Nidal group (supported by Syria, Iraq, and Libya) would attack a synagogue in Vienna causing several fatalities. This was not the only embarassment the Austrian leader would suffer at Palestinian hands.

Bruno Kreisky remained Chancellor of Austria for thirteen years, steering the Austrian Socialist Party (SPÖ) to five successive electoral triumphs. In three of those campaigns (1971, 1975, and 1979) Kreisky achieved an absolute majority—an unprecedented achievement for a Socialist leader. Thanks to his pragmatism, shrewdness, and personal popularity, the Social Democrats convinced a traditionally conservative electorate that they could manage a modern capitalist society more efficiently and democratically than their political rivals. There were parallel successes in Sweden, West Germany, Britain, and France, but rarely did any democratic socialist leader dominate his party and national politics as much as Kreisky during the years of his ascendancy. Moreover, his remarkable political success was achieved despite his cosmopolitan, *grossbürgerlich* Jewish background. It is true that in contrast to Victor Adler and Otto Bauer, his best-known Jewish forerunners as leaders of the Socialist movement, Kreisky was spared the vicious antisemitic invective which accompanied their political activity.[4] Nevertheless, the "Jewish Question" did not disappear from postwar Austrian life. There is a story told by former Austrian President, Rudolf Kirschläger, which illustrates its persistence and Kreisky's own awareness of it. At a meeting of SPÖ leaders in 1967, shortly before the election of a new Party Chairman, Kirschläger noticed the heavy gold cufflinks Kreisky was wearing, inscribed with his initials BK. Teasingly he asked whether Kreisky was already expecting to become Federal Chancellor (*Bundeskanzler* or BK for short!). Kreisky shot back: "Come on, you don't believe they're going to elect a Jew to be Chancellor."[5]

Although Kreisky always asserted that the "Jewish Question" had no *personal* significance for him, his emotional reactions to Israel and Zionism would all-too-frequently contradict this claim. In his own self-perception, things were crystal clear. He was an assimilated, *konfessionslos* (non-denominational) Jew. For him there was no living reality to Judaism or to the Jewish people.[6] In this respect, Kreisky was indubitably a disciple of the classical Austro-Marxist tradition developed by Victor Adler, Karl Kautsky, and Otto Bauer. Before 1914 they had argued that since Jews lacked a common territory or language, they could not be considered a national group entitled to cultural autonomy or an independent state.[7] Kautsky and Otto Bauer were well aware that over 5 million non-assimilated Jews lived around 1900 in the Russian Pale of Settlement with most of the attributes of a nation fundamentally distinct from the surrounding peoples. Marxist dogma was nonetheless more powerful than empirical reality.

The Austro-Marxists, like the assimilated Jewish bourgeoisie in Central Europe, firmly believed that the Jewish masses of the Pale would be integrated into mainstream European society. They looked to the classless Utopia envisaged by Socialism to bring Jewish history and Judaism to its final end. The young Kreisky certainly identified with this soft "eliminationist" perspective embraced by Otto Bauer, whom he regarded as a spiritual mentor. At the same time, after 1948, he could not ignore the existence of an independent Jewish state in the Middle East, a fact of life not anticipated by the Austro-Marxists.[8]

The charismatic idea of Socialism had framed Kreisky's personal and political world ever since 1927, when he joined the Party as a sixteen-year-old adolescent. Marxism was more than simply the theory of historical materialism or a doctrine of class war. Socialism became for young Austrian Jews like Kreisky a secular religion defining a moral commitment to serve the cause of the proletariat. It held out the universalist promise of a new world and a classless society in which mankind would be redeemed irrespective of race, religion, or nationality.[9]

Otto Bauer, the leader of Austrian socialism between 1918 and 1938 had laid the ideological foundations for this assimilationist credo, denying that the "Jewish nationality" had any future in the modern world.[10] Bauer was persuaded that with the disappearance of their special economic function as traders and moneylenders, Jews would cease to have any distinct identity.[11] At the same time he actively opposed not only to Zionism but independent Jewish schools, the teaching of Yiddish, and the demands of East European Jewry for cultural-national autonomy.[12]

Otto Bauer rationalized this position by asserting that the Jews were a "historyless" people, who had stood for centuries outside the mainstream of European civilization. He dismissed their traditions as outmoded, their religion as obscurantist, branding their social psychology as corrupt and money-centered. The task of Social Democracy was to encourage the Jewish worker to strip off his negative "ghetto" identity, abandon his Jewish characteristics, and adapt to his "Christian class-comrade." Such a radically assimilationist view of Jewish life was in the classical tradition of Marxism, but coming from a Jew it had an extra sting. Cultural individuality and national self-determination might be desirable for Slavic nationalities like the Poles, Czechs, or Yugoslavs but it became "reactionary" and harmful as soon as Jewish national autonomy was involved. This was to be the defining ideological view subsequently adopted by Bruno Kreisky.

Although the Social Democrats secured firm control of the municipal administration in Vienna by the 1920s, they were constantly on the defensive with regard to the "Jewish Question." The socialist tradition in Austria, never philosemitic, identified Jews with banking, capitalist enterprise, and profiteering. Otto Bauer and his colleagues persisted after the First World War in using the same hollow slogans about antisemitism which had failed to prevent the Christian-social demagogue, Dr. Karl Lueger, from conquering Vienna and ruling it between 1897 and 1910. The Social Democrats were still arguing in the 1920s as they had done thirty years earlier, that they had no obligation to defend Jewish capital—which was true but irrelevant.[13]

In a speech in Parliament on 6 July 1926, Robert Danneberg, a prominent left-wing deputy and close friend of Otto Bauer, described the Christian Socials as pseudo-antisemites conducting a mock war against Jewish finance, designed to hoodwink the masses.[14] In practice, as soon as capitalist interests were threatened, Jewish and "Aryan" bankers and industrialists would close ranks against the labor movement.[15] Danneberg illustrated his thesis by asserting that wealthy Jewish bankers were financing the priest Ignaz Seipel and his ruling Christian Social party. In the eyes of Danneberg and his left-wing comrades, the real representatives of Jewish interests were evidently the clerical party. This grossly misleading statement, applied at best to a tiny handful of Jewish manufacturers and bankers (some of them converts) like Mandl and Sieghart. It was a transparent socialist attempt to brand anti-semites with the "Jewish" stigma. The fact that Danneberg was himself Jewish made it even worse.

Bruno Kreisky entered the socialist youth organization one year after Danneberg's speech which had been much applauded by his parliamentary comrades. He personally witnessed the violent assault by Austrian police in 1927 against protesting workers in front of the Ministry of Justice. Kreisky was instantly "politicized" by this dramatic event which provoked many deaths. Within the Sozialistische Arbeiterjugend (Socialist Workers Youth), he soon became actively involved in organizing young proletarians. By 1933—at the age of twenty-two—he was appointed chairman of the National Committee for Educational Development within the Austrian socialist youth organizations. Following Otto Bauer's advice he began to study law, eventually obtaining a university degree, before he was forced out of Austria by the *Anschluss* with the Third Reich.

Since the early 1930s, the young Kreisky had experienced Austrian Nazi agitation at first hand, mainly on university campuses. He himself was arrested in January 1935, accused of engaging in illegal underground activity and "high treason." During the year which he spent in the prisons of the authoritarian Catholic *Ständestaat* he would encounter Nazis, under arrest, like himself, as "illegals." Some of these Austrian National Socialists were of proletarian origin. He vainly sought to convince them that antisemitism was primarily a tactical weapon of fascist movements to deflect responsibility for working-class misery away from the capitalist exploiters.

Kreisky was again imprisoned after March 1938 by the triumphant Nazis, but was fortunate enough to be released, thanks to a former cellmate and Hitler admirer, whom he had once assisted in prison. This fellow prisoner, a "typical antisemitic petit-bourgeois youth" saved him from the clutches of the Gestapo and deportation to a concentration camp. On 8 August 1938 the twenty-seven-year-old Bruno Kreisky was freed and permitted to leave for Sweden. His imprisonment in the 1930s led the young socialist émigré to distinguish sharply between the "small Nazis" for whom he had some empathy, and the brutal power-seeking elites. Nazis and Social Democrats in the 1930s seemed to have a *common enemy*—namely the "Austro-fascist" State. As a revolutionary Marxist in those years, Kreisky felt that the origins of the Austrian tragedy lay in the 1934 anti-socialist *putsch* carried out by the Catholic Social leader, Engelbert Dollfuss. By comparison, the Nazi conquest of 1938 was a much less dramatic rupture for the Social Democratic party.

The young Kreisky did not regard National Socialism as much more than a passing symptom of capitalist crisis. Equally, antisemitism was treated as relatively unimportant. Kreisky would always emphasize that before 1938 he was politically persecuted (*politisch verfolgt*) rather than victimized for racial reasons (*rassisch verfolgt*). This was a distinction which would come to have considerable importance in postwar Austria. No less significant was the emphasis in Kreisky's memoirs on the "innocence" of the Austrian masses in the rise of Nazism. To a large extent he would exculpate them from any guilt or personal involvement in the Holocaust. Hence he passed lightly over the scenes of mass jubilation at Hitler's rally in the Heldenplatz (March 1938), insisting that the great majority of Austrians never became convinced Nazis. By the same token he inflated the level of anti-Nazi feelings and political protest in his Austrian homeland—including even passive bystanders in the flattering category of "resisters."

It is intriguing to observe how Kreisky systematically highlighted his Austrianness (*Österreichertum*) at the expense of his Jewish identity. It allowed him to ignore the unpleasant fact that being a Jew in Austria after March 1938 had virtually become a death sentence. As a *political* resister, he could claim to exercise free choice and remain an autonomous individual. Hence, when he returned to Austria in 1946, it was not as a "Jew" but as an anti-fascist Austrian Social Democrat. For Kreisky, the memory of the Holocaust was relegated to little more than a historical traffic-accident. Indeed, he resumed his postwar political activity exactly where things had left off in 1934, as if the Shoah never happened. Nazism was merely a passing interlude.[16]

The Austrian socialist party was reconstituted in 1945 after eleven years of illegality. Most of its former Jewish leaders were either dead, ailing, or growing old. Of those who were in exile, only a handful would ever to return from England, America, and Sweden. The few who came back were hardly welcomed with open arms. In the first place, new cadres had arisen, steeled in the period of occupation and resistance, who tended to resent the Old Guard—those socialists in exile who had never directly experienced or suffered under Nazi rule between 1939 and 1945. Moreover, there was a significant current of working-class antisemitism which had been encouraged by the National Socialists after 1938. This is important since Kreisky's own background was hardly proletarian. His *grossbürgerlich* parents and ancestors came from the Czech part of Habsburg Austria. His father had been the director of a textile factory and his mother the daughter of an industrialist.[17] This class background did not exactly help Kreisky's political prospects as a Socialist leader. However, he derived considerable self-confidence from his family milieu, a marked attachment to the multinational Habsburg Empire of his childhood, and a strong sense of Austrian patriotism.

The Viennese-born Kreisky had never received any formal Jewish education from his German-speaking parents although at least one of his grandfathers could read Hebrew. They were all highly assimilated Jews, like other members of his close-knit family who came from Bohemia and Moravia. In his memoirs he highlights their *echte Österreichertum* (authentic Austrianism) as faithful servants of the Habsburg State and diligent schoolteachers, officials, and even parliamentary deputies. No less emphatically, he underlined their distance from the Galician *Ostjuden* (Eastern Jews) still living in ghettoes and viscerally attached to Jewish religious rituals. In Kreisky's upbeat narrative, none of his ancestors ever suffered any discrimination in Habsburg Austria. He was clearly concerned to show through his own family history that Jews could positively serve the Austrian State, the common good, and the fatherland. In other words, assimilation was a rational option whose feasibility his own family history perfectly exemplified. Had not the Kreisky clan *willed* and *accomplished* a genuine social integration?[18]

In Kreisky's autobiographical account there was no hint that he had ever experienced any insults, humiliation, or discrimination during his adolescent years in Austria. Only when describing the rowdy agitation of Nazi students at the University of Vienna in the early 1930s do we receive a brief glimpse of racist violence. Even then, rampant antisemitism is described solely as a *German* not an Austrian phenomenon. National Socialism is depicted as having been forcefully imposed by a *foreign* invasion from Nazi Germany. Austrians, according to the establishment narrative, were the *first victims* of National Socialism. Bruno Kreisky added his own Marxist gloss. The local support which the Nazis enjoyed was primarily the product of economic crisis and the social injustices inflicted by the "Austro-fascist" dictatorship of Dollfuss and Schuschnigg. This self-serving myth is still repeated by many Social Democrats until the present day.

Bruno Kreisky genuinely believed that antisemitism could be overcome if the individual was determined not to feel affected by it. He was convinced that any behavior suggesting Jews were something special—whether in a positive or negative sense—was harmful and counterproductive. Antisemitic *ressentiment,* he suggested, was primarily directed against those who *resisted* assimilation. However, the historical reality of Nazi Germany demonstrated precisely the opposite. Assimilated Jews were Public Enemy Number One. Their efforts at integration proved completely futile. Kreisky seriously underestimated the existential, irrational, and mythical power of Nazi antisemitism. Moreover, his approach implied that the (Jewish) victims of prejudice were ultimately responsible for their own persecution—especially the "caftan Jews"—who unlike Bruno Kreisky, had resisted dissolution into the (antisemitic) bourgeois milieu of Vienna.

Throughout his adolescence, these *Ostjuden* were marked out as "the other" in the eyes of the *grossbürgerlich* (upper middle class) Germanized Czech Jews from whom Kreisky originated. *Ostjuden* were the lower-class Jews who lived across the Danube Canal in the Leopoldstadt or in the Brigittenau districts.[19] The gulf between the two groups was seemingly unbridgeable. But Kreisky's own prejudices against the non-assimilated provincial Jews did not derive solely from his own class and family background. He remained convinced that any distinctive Jewish group identity—religious or national—was historically "reactionary" and responsible for provoking antisemitism.

The Holocaust clearly offered a sharp rebuttal of Kreisky's assimilationist credo. This may explain why references to the monstrous crimes against European Jewry remain astonishingly sparse in his memoirs. It is revealing, for example, that during his war years in Sweden, he either ignored or did not respond to reports about the Nazi mass murder of the Jews. At that very time he was heavily involved in helping Austrian Wehrmacht soldiers in Russian captivity to return to their Austrian homeland. Yet millions of his co-religionists were being hunted down like wild animals across the European continent or being sent to the gas chambers.[20] Kreisky showed no particular interest in their fate.

Swedish exile spared Bruno Kreisky any direct encounter with the indescribable horrors of the Holocaust. It was in Stockholm that he married Vera Fürth, a highly assimilated Swedish Jewish woman from a wealthy industrialist milieu, and established his own family. Years later he would emphasize how much closer he felt to Sweden (which he regarded as a "second fatherland") than to Israel.[21] In Social Democratic Sweden he was greatly impressed by its welfare state policies and the robust civic patriotism which he witnessed. His encounter with the democratic model of the Swedish labor movement led by Hjalmar Branting and Tage Erlander would profoundly shape Kreisky's socialist outlook. Later, in the 1970s, he would work closely with his friend, the Social-Democratic leader and future Swedish prime minister, Olaf Palme, notorious for his militant anti-Zionism and anti-Americanism.

Kreisky returned to a postwar Austria in which his fellow Austrian socialists were already seeking to recruit Nazi support, rationalizing their lack of principle by talk of "rehabilitation," "healing old wounds," and "making a fresh start." In the provincial Austrian socialist press, there was an unmistakable antisemitic slant, especially on the question of reparations to Jews. No less than in conservative or "liberal" nationalist parties, there was a strong desire to anaesthetize the Nazi past among the Social Democrats—a trend with which Kreisky fully identified.[22]

When Kreisky was elected chairman of the Socialist party in February 1967, it was paradoxically with the support of the provinces and against the advice of the Viennese party functionaries and trade union chiefs.[23] The provinces saw him as the man to lead them out of the ideological "ghetto," to unite radicals and moderates, and present a credible "modern" alternative to the Conservatives. They regarded him as a symbol of the "Great Coalition." He had, after all, served with distinction as Austrian Foreign Minister between 1959 and 1966. Moreover, he offered a modern reformist face for one of the most tradition-bound European labor movements.

Bruno Kreisky paradoxically turned out to be the ideal leader for making Socialism *salonfähig* in Catholic Austria. In 1970, he exceeded all expectations and led the Socialists to victory for the first time in their history.[24] The diplomat with the soft Viennese accent and the look of a cultured bank director of the interwar period successfully exorcised the ghost of the "Red menace." Under his leadership, the Socialists even engaged in dialogue with the Catholic Church, as well as making significant gains among the entrepreneurial middle class and peasant electorate.[25] Still, some doubts were in order. Many Jews wondered whether Austria, the cradle of modern political antisemitism, could truly change its spots. Was the election of an atheist "Jewish-born" Socialist as Federal Chancellor, proof that the shadows of the Nazi past had really been overcome?

Kreisky's attitude to Nazism was tested very soon after he entered office. On 20 April 1970, Dr. Hans Öllinger, the Minister of Agriculture in his Socialist Cabinet, was revealed by "Nazi-hunter" Simon Wiesenthal to have been a former SS lieutenant. Öllinger promptly resigned on his "doctor's advice." At a press conference, the new Chancellor vigorously defended Öllinger on the ground that he had never been a concentration camp guard or member of the Waffen-SS. Kreisky added that Öllinger had joined the National Socialists between 1934 and 1938 in the hope of a national revival and had been imprisoned together with Socialists and Communists by the "clerical" fascist dictatorship. According to the new Chancellor, everyone had the right to make a political mistake. Kreisky emphasized that he would not hesitate to reappoint Öllinger if necessary. For once, a neo-Nazi paper was not far off the mark when it claimed that Kreisky's principle was *Wer ein Nazi ist, bestimmt die SPÖ!* ("The Austrian Social Democrats decide who is a Nazi")—an allusion to Karl Lueger's cynical dictum around 1900—*Wer ein Jud ist, das bestimme ich* ["I decide who is a Jew."].[26] The new Minister of the Interior, Otto Rosch, who had been arrested as a young man in 1947 on charges of Nazi activities but acquitted for lack of evidence, was another controversial case. Kreisky also defended Rosch, insisting that he intended to ignore the Nazi background of all persons who had been reintegrated into postwar Austrian society. To prove his point he appointed yet another former member of the NSDAP, Dr. Weihs. Kreisky's handling of these appointments was taken as evidence by many that he intended "to be a Chancellor of all Austrians."[27]

Thus an extraordinarily bizarre situation had arisen. The first Socialist of Jewish ancestry to head an Austrian government was presiding over the only cabinet in Europe which included such a high number of ex-Nazis. Against this background, the feud of the Austrian Socialist government with Simon Wiesenthal after 1970 becomes clearer. The Vienna Documentation Centre run by Wiesenthal appeared to Kreisky, and indeed to most Austrians bent on forgetting the past, like a festering sore from a bygone age. The new Chancellor did not disguise his anger at Wiesenthal for having reminded Austrians of the blackest hole in their history. In the summer of 1970 he described him with contempt as a "Jewish fascist" and drove home the barb by remarking: "Happily one finds reactionaries also amongst us Jews, as well as thieves, murderers and prostitutes."[28] Another Socialist leader, Leopold Grätz, Mayor of Vienna and a former Minister of Education, added his own barely veiled threat—accusing Wiesenthal of creating "a private police and informers' organization." He alleged that there was a "grotesque alliance" between Wiesenthal and the clerical Conservatives (ÖVP) as well as the neo-Nazi *Deutsche Nationalzeitung.*[29] The Kreisky government, so it seemed, was looking for a pretext to close down the Jewish Documentation Centre.

It is difficult today to imagine the unpopularity of Simon Wiesenthal around 1970 in a country where de-Nazification had remained skin-deep.[30] There had been an astonishing number of acquittals and mild sentences passed on war criminals in Austria ever since it regained its national independence in 1955.[31] Thus Kreisky could reasonably assume that his own frontal attack on an implacable pursuer of Nazi war criminals (who was a Polish Jew to boot) would do no harm to his popularity with the Austrian electorate. On the contrary, it reinforced his image as a patriotic Austrian. So, too, did the crisis centered on Schoenau castle in lower Austria, a transit point for Jewish emigrants permitted to leave the USSR and other East European countries—many of whom subsequently went on to Israel. On 28 September 1973 three Russian Jews were taken hostage by armed Palestinians who had boarded a train from the East carrying emigrants at the Austrian border crossing. The terrorists insisted that their hostages be exchanged for Palestinians held by Israel. They also demanded the closure of Schoenau Castle and the cessation of all Russian Jewish emigration through Austria.

Within a few hours Kreisky managed to secure the release of the hostages. The terrorists were flown out of the country without any blood being spilt, and the Chancellor agreed to close Schoenau Castle down, though Soviet

Jewish emigration continued to transit through Austria. Kreisky's decision was sharply criticized at the time in Israel and in the West though his decision was widely approved in Austria.[32] One reason for public satisfaction was that the Chancellor insisted he did not want Austria to become the scene of armed confrontations between Israel and the Arabs. Moreover, he had avoided a massacre like that which occurred at the Munich Olympic Games in 1972, when German sharpshooters miserably botched an attempt to rescue Israeli athletes taken hostage by Palestinian terrorists. Nevertheless, Israeli Prime Minister Golda Meir was shocked by Kreisky's "capitulation" rushing to Vienna in early October 1973 to try and reverse the decision of the Austrian Chancellor. Legend has it that Kreisky refused her even a glass of water. Tragically, Israel would shortly afterwards be taken by surprise as the Egyptians and Syrians launched the Yom Kippur War intended to destroy the Jewish state. Golda Meir would never forgive Kreisky for his coolly detached, "neutral" position in the Arab-Israeli conflict and his barely disguised hostility to Zionism which came to the surface after 1973.

This antipathy had its roots in his dismissal of Judaism as the fossilized ghetto offshoot of a dispersed ethno-religious group lacking any national characteristics.[33] Only antisemitic persecution had, in his view, preserved any measure of artificial unity among the diverse branches of the "Jewish people." According to Kreisky, there was nothing in common between the highly acculturated Jews of America and Western Europe, the Ashkenazic *Ostjuden,* or the Sephardic masses from Islamic lands. At best one could define the Jews as a *Schicksalsgemeinschaft*—a "community of fate"—a term borrowed from Otto Bauer, which was also widely used by the Nazis. But Kreisky was emphatic that Jews were *not* a worldwide people as Zionists claimed. Indeed, the concept of Jewish peoplehood remained anathema to Kreisky, evoking as it did, the specter of dual loyalties. The Austrian Chancellor's repeated efforts to equate Zionism with the Nazi fiction of a "Jewish race" was a symptom of how threatening to him the whole idea of a Jewish nation had personally become.[34]

Ignoring the fact that mainstream Jewish nationalism was far removed from racial thinking, Kreisky arbitrarily charged Zionists with "anthropological mysticism," or a "mysterious racism in reverse." He even claimed that Zionism had embraced the *Blut und Boden* (Blood and soil) mythology of the Third Reich.[35] Disregarding the historical continuity of the Jewish people, its religious vocation, and national self-understanding, Kreisky fell back on accusations about "race" that demonstrated his ignorance of Jewish halakhic Law.

Kreisky also wrongly equated the nationalist ideology of Israel's ruling Likud party with Fascism and with the racist doctrines of South African apartheid.[36] Such denigration was never applied by Kreisky to the overtly racist character of much Arab nationalism. Kreisky never once evoked the history of collaboration before and during the Holocaust of Arab nationalists or pan-Islamic leaders with German National Socialism. He also avoided any public criticism of the grandiose, proto-fascist pretensions of Arab Socialism, whether in its Nasserist or Baathist versions. Such double standards were becoming increasingly common among European Socialist leaders in the late 1970s. This was especially true of those influenced by an anti-American, Third Worldist orientation, like Olaf Palme, then Prime Minister of Sweden, and a virulent Israel-hater of purest Social Democratic vintage, who remained until his assassination a close personal friend of Bruno Kreisky.[37]

There were also important economic interests at stake. Kreisky's courtship of the Arab world intensified after the 1973 oil crisis which accentuated European and Austrian dependence on the goodwill of the Arab petroleum producers.[38] But his outlook on the Arab-Israeli conflict crystallized above all in the framework of his Middle East fact-finding missions on behalf of the Socialist International. A wide variety of friendly contacts with Arab leaders encouraged him to develop a markedly benign interpretation of their attitudes towards Israel.[39] His views were a curious combination of prescience and prejudice. Thus in the late 1970s Kreisky was ahead of his time in favoring the creation of an independent Palestinian state in the "occupied territories." At the same time, his equation of Israel's settlements in the West Bank with the Soviet occupation of Afghanistan was deliberately insulting, unnecessary, and completely wrong.[40]

Kreisky spared no effort (along with his friend, the former West German Socialist Chancellor Willy Brandt) to make Yasser Arafat respectable (*salonfähig*) in the West. He did everything to present the PLO leader as a man of peace—which was emphatically *not* the case. Similarly, he was the first Western leader to grant Libya's Colonel Gaddafi, the red carpet treatment, although he knew full well that the Libyan leader was a ruthless dictator who financed many terrorist groups and was dedicated to Israel's destruction. What particularly angered many Israelis and Diaspora Jews was the Austrian Chancellor's insistence on presenting terrorist leaders like Gaddafi and Arafat as admirable "patriots" and "freedom-fighters." This conjuring trick occurred at the very time that Kreisky was publicly reviling Israeli Prime Minister Menachem Begin as a criminal "fascist" and "a little Polish lawyer or whatever he is."[41]

Kreisky's diatribes against Begin during the latter's term of office as Israeli Prime Minister went far beyond the question of his settlement policy or the Likud's nationalist commitment to the whole land of Israel. For Kreisky, Begin embodied the warped mentality of the *Ostjuden,* "alienated from normal ways of thinking." This was the kind of remark that gained the Austrian Chancellor a growing reputation for Jewish self-loathing. Much to his own anger and dismay, Kreisky found himself compared in Jewish circles to such pathological *Selbsthasser* (self-haters) as Karl Marx, Otto Weininger, or Simone Weil.[42] The Mayor of Jerusalem, Teddy Kollek, sarcastically declared that Kreisky required the kind of psychiatric treatment pioneered by his fellow Viennese Jews Sigmund Freud and Alfred Adler. The Israeli satirist, Ephraim Kishon, writing in September 1978 went further still, drawing the conclusion that "our big brother has decided he's got a hump, and therefore he hates all humpbacks." There was no doubt in Kishon's mind that Kreisky was "a first class antisemite," going around "like an angry bull with his own private red flag, for all that it's blue-and-white in your case."[43]

Kishon's vitriolic satire came in response to an interview given by Kreisky to the Dutch Protestant newspaper *Trouw* in which he had castigated Israeli chauvinism and "apartheid" on the West Bank. The Chancellor mocked the "refined hooliganism" of the Israeli army, the primitiveness of its diplomats, and the stupidity of the Jews in general.[44] These were things, Kishon observed, which were no longer publicly heard in the West except on scratched forty-year-old-records. Kreisky, however, insisted that his fierce criticism of Israeli government policy was perfectly legitimate and that he was the innocent victim of Zionist abuse. His hostility and anger came out clearly in an interview with *Ma'ariv* in July 1979, following the royal welcome which he had granted Arafat in Vienna. Asked what they had talked about, he hit back:

> One talks about the extraordinary arrogance of Israeli behavior. Obviously—and this should be made clear to you—the central idea of these talks tends towards a comparison between Israel and South Africa.... Israel intends to set up a "Bantustan" on the West Bank—an area in which the Arab population would have no effective rights, with Israel controlling all the resources.[45]

The mainstream presentation of Israel as an "apartheid State" was at that time still in its infancy, though it was already an integral part of Soviet, Trotskyist, and new Left propaganda. Kreisky's insistence on using this highly offensive analogy was curious since he was so eager to put himself forward as a mediator between Israel and the Arabs. He always maintained that he had worked hard to convince Palestinians to be more flexible and realistic towards the Jewish State, just as he sought to persuade Israelis that they should accept a small demilitarized Palestinian state. So why deliberately antagonize Israel by compulsively stigmatizing its alleged "racism"?

The contrast between Arab and Jewish responses to Kreisky's efforts as an "honest broker" was revealing. Arafat repeatedly called the Austrian Chancellor "my friend" and a "friend of the Palestinian people." Partly, this was simple gratitude for official Austrian recognition of the PLO—a process which began in the summer of 1979. But the PLO also perceived an *ideological affinity*. Kreisky had argued that Nazism nourished Zionism and even suggested a resemblance between the two movements. He repeatedly stated that Zionist thinking towards Arabs was arrogant and chauvinist; that a Palestinian state was historically necessary; and that opposition to it was unforgivable political stupidity. Israeli settlement policy, to his mind, was not only vainglorious but also *the* major obstacle to peace. In this perception one would have to say that Kreisky was thirty years ahead of the currently prevailing conventional wisdom. At the same time, Arab rejectionism was simply ignored as if it had never existed or was irrelevant to the present. Naturally, this was music to Palestinian ears. When Chancellor Kreisky announced that "there is no Jewish nation, only a Jewish religious community (*Religionsgemeinschaft*) or community of faith", his declaration was identical to the view in the Palestinian National Covenant of 1974. For Kreisky this was indeed his personal credo.

Although he never explicitly denied Israel's right to exist, Kreisky's *visceral* anti-Zionism was undoubtedly seen by Arafat and the Palestinians as sapping the legitimacy of the Jewish state. They, too, insisted that "Judaism, in its character as a religion, is not a nationality with an independent existence" (Article 20 of the Palestinian National Covenant) and that Jewish nationhood was an unreal, artificial concept. Kreisky profoundly agreed with this anti-Zionist dogma, telling *Die Presse* (January 1978) in an interview for a special supplement on the Arab world:

> In my opinion, the Jews are no nation. For me, the different Jewish groups are communities of fate. . . . Jews live everywhere in the world. They have much more in common in both appearance and way of life with their host peoples than they have with each other. . . . There exist jet-black Jews, Indian Jews, and Mongolian Jews.

Ethnic diversity among Jews had become another Marxian stick with which to beat Zionism. The Arab media purred with pleasure at such provocative statements and lapped up Kreisky's public denunciations of "Zionist" political pressure to make him change his Middle Eastern policy. They well remembered that he had closed Schoenau castle in October 1973 as a transit camp for Soviet Jews; that he negotiated with Arab terrorists during the Organization of Petroleum Exporting Countries hostage crisis in Vienna (December 1975) organized by the Venezuelan left-wing terrorist "Carlos"; and that he regarded the PLO massacre of innocent Israeli citizens on the Tel Aviv highway in March 1978 as an inevitable result of "Israel's shortsighted policy."[46] His statements, approvingly quoted by the London-based *Free Palestine* in December 1975, were perfectly in tune with the Arab propaganda campaign against Zionism, on an upswing since the November 1975 UN resolution condemning Zionism as a form of "racism." The Austrian Federal Chancellor did not mince words:

> I don't submit to Zionism. I reject it. It is true I am of Jewish origin and that my family is Jewish, but this does not mean I have a special commitment to the Zionist State and the Israelis, I reject that completely. . . . When Zionists ask those of Jewish faith outside Israel to be bound by a special commitment to the State of Israel and to work for it as though they were Israeli citizens, they are adopting a wrong political line which leads to the isolation of these Jewish citizens from their national motherland and leaves them forever isolated in their communities. . . . [T]here is nothing which binds me to Israel or to what is called the Jewish "people" or to Zionism.[47]

Kreisky periodically evoked the theme of "Zionist blackmail," which enthused not only Arabs but also neo-Nazis in postwar Germany and Austria. The key factor in their enthusiasm was the Austrian Chancellor's determination to let sleeping Nazis lie while business went on as usual.[48] Unlike Willy Brandt, his closest international ally, the Austrian Socialist leader ostentatiously dismissed what West German politicians called "the overcoming of the past" (*Bewältigung der Vergangenheit*) as "empty words" (*ein Gerede*).[49] No doubt the political, social and numerical weight of nearly 700,000 *ehemaligen* (or former Nazi Party members) in a small nation like Austria with only seven million people, played its part in forming his attitude and that of his party.

The comparison of Kreisky on these and other points with Brandt (Germany's first Socialist Chancellor since the end of the Weimar Republic) is revealing. Like Kreisky, Brandt had spent the war years in Scandinavia and had been an anti-fascist from his youth. However, though a Gentile German, he seemed more affected by the racial antisemitism that had led to the Holocaust, and was more sympathetic to Zionism than his Viennese comrade-in-arms. As mayor of Berlin after 1957, Brandt cautiouly developed ties with Israel as well as with the Arab world, particularly with Nasser's Egypt. Appointed German foreign minister in the CDU-led coalition government (1966–1969), Brandt continued to seek a balance between Israeli and Arab interests. During his five years as West Germany's leader (1969–1974), Brandt became the first German Chancellor in office to visit the Jewish State though his relations with Israeli Premier Golda Meir were becoming tense. Partly it was Brandt's strategy of rapprochement with the U.S.S.R. which worried the Israelis, but also the creeping pro-Palestinian trend in German foreign policy. Nevertheless, Brandt rejected (both before and after his years in office) the radical anti-Zionist positions of the German New Left which were prevalent among some of the Young Socialists (JUSOS) in his own party. Similarly, he did not share Kreisky's ideological antagonism towards Zionism though he certainly believed that Israel should show more openness towards the Palestinians and the Arab states.[50]

Willy Brandt, as German Chancellor, had humbly bowed down before the Warsaw Ghetto monument in Poland in 1969. This was not an action that Kreisky could ever have taken, given his determination not to arouse old wounds or divisions and to avoid alienating former Nazis.[51] His defense of the youthful "political mistakes" of those ex-Nazis whom he included in his first Cabinet in 1970 was indeed warmly greeted by the neo-Nazi and radical right.[52] They were fascinated by the new Chancellor's willingness to crush their old *bête noire,* Simon Wiesenthal, and to brand him as a dangerous "reactionary."[53] In Kreisky's eyes, Wiesenthal's meticulous, patient search for Nazi war criminals was not merely quixotic. It was *detrimental* to Austria's self-image. Far from being an act of justice and a necessary education for future generations, these activities were regarded by Kreisky as "vengeful," divisive, and politically inexpedient. Hence, the Chancellor and his ruling Socialist party determined to stop Wiesenthal, even if it meant relying on fabrications from the Soviet Bloc (especially in Russia and Poland)—countries in which Wiesenthal's Documentation Centre had already been branded a tool of the CIA, British Intelligence, and the Israeli Secret Service.[54] The Polish Communists, in particular, issued deliberate falsehoods maintaining that Wiesenthal himself had been a Nazi "agent" during the war and that he manufactured disinformation about antisemitism in Communist

Eastern Europe. Kreisky encouraged this defamatory campaign, several times suggesting that Wiesenthal was indeed a "collaborator" whose own past warranted close investigation.[55] At a Press Conference held at the Concordia Press Club in Vienna on 10 November 1975, an East German Communist correspondent warmly endorsed Kreisky's charges: "Herr Bundeskanzler, was Sie über Wiesenthal und seine Methoden gesagt haben ist vollkommen richtig." (Mr. Chancellor, what you have said about Wiesenthal and his methods is perfectly correct.)

Matters came to a head in the wake of the spectacular Socialist victory at the polls in October 1975. Before the elections, most observers assumed that the Austrian Social Democrats would have to form a coalition with the small Freedom Party led by Friedrich Peter, which had increasingly abandoned right-wing extremism for a more liberal orientation. However, just before Election Day, Simon Wiesenthal revealed that Peter had been involved in Nazi war crimes as a tank commander in the 1st SS Infantry brigade which was responsible for the murder of 10,513 innocent men, women, and children on the Eastern front. Peter admitted to having been a member of this Waffen-SS unit, but denied any personal involvement in shootings or "illegal acts."[56] Though Kreisky no longer needed Peter's support, he furiously attacked Wiesenthal as the agent of an organized Israeli campaign "to bring me down." The "conspiracy" against the Austrian Chancellor had been launched, so he claimed, because he had not fulfilled his task "in the service of Israel." Kreisky denounced the "Zionist ideology" about his alleged indifference to Israel as a "posthumous assumption of Nazi ideas in reverse."

An irrational and unmistakably paranoid element now emerged in Kreisky's responses to Wiesenthal. This became apparent in an interview with the Israeli journalist Zeev Barth, reproduced in *Der Spiegel* on 17 November 1975. After explaining that he came from a "quite different milieu" from Wiesenthal. Kreisky lost control, declaring that "the man [Wiesenthal] must disappear" (*Der Mann muss verschwinden*). When Barth questioned him further about his allegation that Wiesenthal had used "political Mafia" methods, Kreisky thundered back that he would not stand trial before the Israeli or Jewish public. His parting salvo, "If the Jews are a people, then they are an ugly people" (*Wenn die Juden ein Volk sind, so ist es ein mieses Volk*), aggravated an already embittered situation beyond repair.[57] As a commentator in the respected German Socialist newspaper *Vorwärts* ironically put it in December 1975, it appeared that "Superman Kreisky also has a problem which he has not quite overcome—his Jewish origin."[58] In his anxiety to prove himself more Austrian than the Austrians and demonstrate his total separation from everything Jewish, Kreisky seemed to be undermining his own case. He now came under fire from a strange alliance of the independent weekly, *Profil,* the anti-fascist resistance organizations, the Communist Party in Austria, the local Jewish community, as well as a good part of the international press. Even in his own Socialist Party there was a distinct uneasiness about the Chancellor's insistence on a court battle with Wiesenthal and a growing desire to cool tempers.[59]

On the other hand, old and new Nazis in Central Europe could scarcely conceal their delight at the spectacle of an Austrian Chancellor of Jewish origin seeking to destroy the reputation of Simon Wiesenthal. By the end of 1975 Kreisky had become an honorary "Aryan" par excellence in the eyes of pan-German nationalists. They loudly applauded his repudiation of any loyalty to specifically Jewish concerns and his outbursts against "boundless Zionist intolerance."[60] German neo-Nazis had no doubt at all about the meaning of Kreisky's attacks on Wiesenthal: "Kreisky wants a reconciliation with the ex-Nazis," trumpeted the *Deutsche Nationalzeitung,* hoping that it might finally gain some respectability thanks to the efforts of the Socialist Chancellor. Peter Michael Lingens, writing in the left-wing *Profil* on 18 November 1975, sarcastically observed that for people like Kreisky "to be accepted by former Nazis is apparently the ultimate form of dream fulfillment."[61]

During the Wiesenthal-Peter affair, Kreisky had acted as if the mass murder of European Jewry was merely a side issue and his main duty as Federal Chancellor was to whitewash Austrian consciences, liberating them from the sins of their fathers! The fact that a Jew played out this expiatory and apologetic role provided the Austrian population with a powerful alibi, acquitting them of the need for any serious confrontation with the Nazi legacy. Such unexpected *absolution* greatly enhanced Kreisky's personal standing in Austria, despite the criticism to which he was subject to in some circles.[62] Even after his retirement as Austrian Chancellor in 1983, Kreisky did not change his attitude to Simon Wiesenthal, gratuitously attacking him and other Austrians of Jewish origin who had supposedly been "ardent Fascists."[63] Though unforgiving with regard to the alleged wrongdoings of his "co-religionists," Kreisky seemed to take pride in the fact that he absolved almost everybody else (especially ex-Nazis) during his term of office. Israelis, of course, did not escape Kreisky's vindictive wrath. In the *Kronenzeitung* at the end of May 1986 he scathingly attacked Prime Minister Yitzhak Shamir as a "terrorist leader," accusing him of seeking to mobilize the West against the newly elected Austrian President Kurt Waldheim and of trying to falsely paint Austria as an antisemitic state.[64] Nevertheless, privately Kreisky recognized that the Waldheim Affair was a disaster for Austria, wrecking his years of hard work to improve the country's international image.

Bruno Kreisky persistently downplayed Austrian antisemitism throughout his career, while unnecessarily and gratuitously criminalizing the actions of Israel. The "grotesque Mr. Kreisky," as the *Jerusalem Post* once called him, was certainly a pioneer in these and other respects.[65] He was also the first European statesman outside France, to unequivocally embrace the Palestinian cause.[66] At the same time, the Austrian Chancellor had his moments of lucidity, warning Israel that unless it solved the Palestinian Question in an equitable manner, it would reap the whirlwind of Islamic fundamentalism. Israel, he insisted, could not survive as a "Crusader State." If it wanted binding declarations from the PLO it would also have to respect Palestinian *national* rights. Unfortunately, such declarations were not balanced by any public disavowal of Palestinian terror against Israeli or Jewish civilians.

Kreisky's insistence on negotiating with terrorists usually ended in a surrender to their demands. In 1975, for example, an Austrian policeman was shot and killed during the OPEC siege in Vienna. Kreisky said little about the actual victim but he was vocal in maintaining that resistance to terrorism was useless.[67] In the same vein, he opposed American counterterrorist retaliation against Libya's Colonel Gaddafi in 1986.[68] Similarly, with regard to Yasser Arafat, the Chancellor preferred to turn a blind eye to Palestinian extremism, insisting—publicly at least—that Arafat's "peaceful" intentions towards Israel were beyond doubt.[69] Privately, however, he knew that this was false.

Ever since the fact-finding mission of the Socialist International to the Middle East in 1973, in which he had been the chief mediator, Kreisky placed his main hope for Middle East peace in drawing closer to "progressive" Arab forces. Since 1977 he consistently advocated recognition of the PLO as the sole spokesman of the Palestinians and sought to consolidate support for a Palestinian state.[70] But the Palestinians did *not* renounce terrorism in favor of peace; and there was little prospect in the 1970s of nourishing a "progressive" Arab socialism, overthrowing Middle Eastern military dictators, reforming authoritarian one-party states, or changing the outlook of the oil sheikhs in the Persian Gulf. As a consequence, Kreisky's new course accomplished little for the Socialist International, the Palestinians, Israel, or the peace process.[71] If anything, his "soft" line reinforced the intransigence of Palestinian terrorism while alienating most Israelis and Diaspora Jews.

Kreisky was privately far more critical of Arafat's policies than he ever indicated publicly. Already in 1974, during a fact-finding mission of the Socialist International in Cairo, Arafat made an "unfavorable impression" on him with his cliché-ridden revolutionary phraseology and pro-Soviet outlook. He was also disturbed by the PLO leader's lack of any strategic plan. The correspondence between them reveals that despite effuse and flattering professions of friendship from Arafat, Kreisky was aware of the Palestinian leader's deceptions and character weaknesses.[72] Moreover, the Austrian Chancellor disliked Arafat's repeated comparisons of Israeli policy with the Nazi Holocaust and his references to Israeli leaders as "neo-Hitlers"—though, as we have seen, Kresiky was also given to hyperbole on this issue. He shrewdly warned Arafat that he must decide whether he wanted to remain a revolutionary guerilla fighter or become a statesman. Time would show that this was indeed a fatal flaw in Arafat's leadership.

In their correspondence, Kreisky severely reproached Arafat for a series of Palestinian terror attacks on Jewish targets in Europe which had taken place in Frankfurt, Paris, Brussels, Antwerp, and Vienna between 1979 and 1982. He was shocked and depressed by "this self-destructive activity" and the "Massada-type attitude" that it revealed. Such "senseless" acts of terror, so he feared, would rob the Palestinian cause of its justification.[73] Kreisky added that he was "personally deeply hurt" by the assault on the synagogue in Vienna. Although Dr. Isaam Sartawi (who was the closest of all the Palestinian leadership to Kreisky), assured him that the attack was carried out by a non-Palestinian group, the Austrian Chancellor was not fooled. He pointedly emphasized that this terrorism had been perpetrated under the Palestinian flag, by a group (Abu Nidal) linked to the PLO, something that was completely unacceptable. But there was no hint of these recriminations to the broader public.

The same pattern continued with the murder by the same Palestinian terror group of the Socialist municipal councilor and President of the Austrian-Israeli friendship society, Heinz Nittel. The killing took place in the spring of 1981 during a May Day parade to the Rathausplatz in Vienna.[74] Kreisky was shaken to the core by this assassination and his trust in Arafat was further eroded by another terror attack in which two visitors to a Vienna synagogue died. If that were not enough, the PLO ambassador to Austria, Ghazi Hussein, was caught at Vienna airport with two suitcases of weapons, delivered from Beirut. Once more, the Austrian Chancellor felt "deeply betrayed."[75] The assassination by Islamic fundamentalists in October 1981 of Anwar el-Sadat, the Egyptian leader who had signed the Peace Treaty with

Israel, was yet another source of friction between the two leaders. Arafat was overjoyed by the news—a reaction which Bruno Kreisky found shocking and incomprehensible. Whatever the Chancellor's misgivings about Sadat's policy, he knew that the murder of the Egyptian President was a serious blow to peace.

Despite this growing tension, Arafat continued to express "great appreciation and gratitude" for Kreisky's activities on behalf of the Palestinians. He warmly thanked the Chancellor for his formal recognition of the PLO and participation in events like Palestine Solidarity Day. In response to Kreisky's reproaches, he insisted on the PLO's right to undertake military actions in face of what he called Menahem Begin's "neo-Nazi" regime and the Israeli "genocide" against the Palestinian people. Arafat's overheated rhetoric was, however, becoming too much even for a veteran anti-Zionist like Kreisky.

The point of no return in the relationship between Kreisky and Arafat was reached with the murder of Dr. Isaam Sartawi (the most moderate of the PLO leaders) by radical elements within Arafat's organization. Kreisky had spent many hours discussing Middle Eastern problems with Sartawi in Vienna. They both argued that Arafat's *public* acceptance of the need for Israeli-Palestinian coexistence would be a crucial test case for the PLO's future relationship with the West European democracies and the Socialist International.[76] However, at a meeting of the Palestine National Council in 1983, Arafat had forbidden any declaration that would have proposed recognition of Israel's right to exist. A few weeks later Sartawi was shot dead in Portugal by killers from the Abu Nidal group. The murder coincided with a meeting of the Socialist International which Kreisky attended. This was literally the last straw. Kreisky held Arafat personally responsible for having withdrawn his protection from Sartawi. By 1983, when Kreisky resigned as Austria's Chancellor for reasons of ill-health, his relationship with the PLO leader had effectively ended.

The Kreisky era, despite its many modernizing achievements and social reforms on the Austrian domestic front, as well as in foreign policy, did not exercise a positive influence on Austrian attitudes to Israel, Judaism, and the Jewish people as a whole. One symptom of this failure in communication was the Chancellor's protracted vendetta against Simon Wiesenthal, which ended with a humiliating defeat for Kreisky in the Vienna courts.[77] But Wiesenthal was only the symptom of a deeper problem. Kreisky's outbursts against *Ostjuden,* international Jewry, or "Zionist" interference in Austrian internal affairs, went far beyond what was necessary. Indeed, they may have helped prepare the ground for the antisemitic rhetoric of a number of Austrian Conservative politicians during the Waldheim Affair. In this context it is worth recalling that Simon Wiesental claimed in 1986: "If Bruno Kreisky were chancellor today, Waldheim would be the joint candidate of both big parties. And Kreisky would defend Waldheim against the World Jewish Congress and the Jews with all his power."[78]

Bruno Kreisky remains an enigmatic, sphinx-like figure in many respects. Though not a great orator, he was a charismatic politician with the adaptability of a chameleon, gifted with an intuitive sense for symbolism and mobilizing public emotions. He was exceptionally skillful in handling the mass media. In foreign affairs he was pragmatic, often astute and statesmanlike in navigating the crises provoked by the Cold War. Though in favor of détente with the Soviet bloc, he was never soft on Communism. His relations with Israel and the Jewish world were, however, a disaster area. This is all the more striking since Bruno Kreisky is to this day the only Jewish politician to have ever governed a German-speaking country. This was a feat which he pulled off for thirteen years without ever losing a single election. Furthermore, it was achieved in one of the most antisemitic countries of Europe which had been heavily implicated in the mass murder of European Jewry and of his own family.

On his way to the top, Kreisky managed to surmount the prejudices in his own Socialist party as well as the pervasive Judeophobia in Austrian society. Despite losing more than twenty of his relatives in the extermination camps and being forced out of Austria by the Gestapo, he never revised his assimilationist views or hostility to Zionism. Since the age of sixteen, Kreisky had jettisoned Judaism, removing his name from the rolls of the Viennese Jewish community (*Kultusgemeinde*). At the same time, being Jewish was never something he denied or sought to cover up. However, he continued to regard himself as a convinced secularist (*konfessionslos*), a Marxist socialist and an Austrian patriot. As far as his public profile was concerned, he probably regarded his Jewishness as a political liability. He had no obvious interest, therefore in advertising it vocally. Moreover, he knew that the post-1945 Socialist party leadership under Adolf Schärf, did not want Jews in a prominent party role. Even in February 1967, when Kreisky unexpectedly became leader of the SPÖ it was only after an acrimonious debate in which cutting references were made to his non-proletarian background and (by implication) to his "Jewish" antecedents. During the elections of 1970, latently antisemitic insinuations by the conservatives that only their candidate was a "true Austrian" could only have heightened his sensitivity to the issue.

Antisemitism remained an irritant but it was largely disregarded by Kreisky, once he was in power. He was determined to put Austria's Nazi legacy behind him at almost any price. Yet this deliberate amnesia would rebound against him with the force of a boomerang. His explosive conflict with the Nazi-hunter Simon Wiesenthal which began in 1970 was the most visible expression of this "return of the repressed." Wiesenthal's battle against Austrian historical forgetfulness and his very public defense of the Jewish memory of the Holocaust remained anathema to Kreisky. So, too, were Israel's policies and their Zionist foundations. He did not hesitate to insult Israel, repeatedly branding it a "police state," run by men with a "fascist mentality."[79] Such vilification, along with his selective flaunting of "Jewishness" only in order to execrate Israel and legitimize the PLO, earned him a reputation among many Israeli and Diaspora Jews of being a "renegade" and an outstanding exemplar of self-hatred. Elements of truth and exaggeration were almost equally mixed in this assessment.[80]

Bruno Kreisky undoubtedly had a blind spot when it came to his own Jewish identity, the Nazi Holocaust and the State of Israel. In many respects he seems like the emblematic *Grenzjude* (marginal Jew) aspiring to become the golden *goy*. A child of the decaying Habsburg Empire, he successfully mutated into Kaiser Bruno—a new kind of people's Emperor. Kreisky embodied an extraordinary blend of elements between old and new, tradition and modernity, Austrian patriotism and socialist cosmopolitanism, Viennese wit and Jewish intellectuality. But the "Jewish question" proved to be the Achilles heel in his otherwise brilliant political career. It was the dark corner where neither reason nor experience sufficed to master the inner demons in his troubled soul.

NOTES

1. Oliver Pink, "Mythos Bruno Kreisky: Der Mann mit Eigenschaften," *Die Presse,* 28 Feb. 2010.

2. See Robert Solomon Wistrich, *Anti-Zionism and Antisemitism: The Case of Bruno Kreisky,* Vidal Sassoon International Center for the Study of Antisemitism ACTA series, no. 30 (Jerusalem: 2007); also idem, *A Lethal Obsession: Antisemitism from Antiquity to the Global Jihad* (New York, 2010), 221–26.

3. Margit Reiter, *Unter Antisemitismus-Verdacht. Die österreichische Linke und Isräel nach der Shoah* (Vienna, 2001).

4. See Günter Bischof and Anton Pelinka, eds., *The Kreisky Era in Austria* (New Brunswick, 1994). On Victor Adler and Otto Bauer, see Robert S. Wistrich, *Socialism and the Jews. The Dilemmas of Assimilation in Germany and Austria-Hungary* (London, 1982), 232–61, 332–48.

5. Herbert Pierre Sacher, "Kreisky and the Jews," in Bischof and Pelinka, *Kreisky Era,* 29.

6. Bruno Kreisky, *Die Zeit in der wir leben: Betrachtungen zur internationalen Politik* (Vienna, 1989), 59ff.

7. Wistrich, *Socialism,* 151–57 on Kautsky and the latter's pamphlet, *Rasse und Judentum* (Berlin, 1914), as well as Otto Bauer, *Die Nationalitätenfrage und die Sozialdemokratie* (Vienna, 1907), 376ff.

8. See, for instance, his revealing remarks in a long interview with a French left-wing weekly: "Bruno Kreisky et les Juifs," *Le Nouvel Observateur,* 23 Apr. 1979, 119ff, where he evokes the Austro-Marxists; also the highly critical comments of Nathan Rothenstreich, "A Working Politician and What is Beyond Him," *Forum* (Fall/Winter 1979): 1–10.

9. Josef Buttinger, *In the Twilight of Socialism* (New York, 1954), 80–81, on the appeal of socialism to many Austrian Jews: "The charismatic idea of socialism superseded the faith of the fathers."

10. Otto Bauer, *Die Nationalitätenfrage und die Sozialdemokratie* (Vienna 1907), 376.

11. Ibid.

12. Ibid.

13. For Austro-Marxist views on the Jews and antisemitism after 1918, see Jacques Hannak, "Das Judentum am Scheidewege," *Der Kampf* 12 (1919): 619ff.; "Die Judenfrage. Der Antisemitismus in der Theorie und in der Praxis," *Sozialdemokratisches Wahlhandbuch,* no. 10 (1923); and Christoph Hinteregger, *Der Judenschwindel* (Vienna 1923).

14. Robert Danneberg, *Die Schiebergeschäfte der Regierungsparteien. (Der Antisemitismus im Lichte der Thatsachen)* (Vienna 1926), 11, 17–18.

15. Jack Jacobs, "Austrian Social Democracy and the Jewish Question," in *The Austrian Socialist Experiment 1918–1934,* edited by Anson Rabinbach (Boulder, Colo., 1985) 157–66.

16. For Kreisky's years as a young Socialist, see Oliver Rathkolb and Irene Etzerdorfer, eds., *Der junge Kreisky. Schriften—Reden—Dokumente 1931–1945* (Vienna, 1986); H. Pierre Secher, *Bruno Kreisky. Chancellor of Austria* (Pittsburgh, 1993), 1–75, and Kreisky, *Zwischen den Zeiten,* 308ff.

17. Kreisky, *Zwischen den Zeiten,* 49.

18. Ibid.

19. See Ruth Beckermann, ed., *Die Mazzesinsel: Juden in der Wiener Leopoldstadt, 1918–1938* (Vienna 1984); and Harriet Pass Freidenreich, *Jewish Politics in Vienna, 1918–1938* (Bloomington, Ind., 1991).

20. Secher, *Bruno Kreisky,* 49.

21. See "Kreisky et les Juifs," *Le Nouvel Observateur,* no. 754 (23–29 Apr. 1979): 134.

22. See Margit Reiter, *Unter Antisemitismus-Verdacht,* 21–60.

23. Hanni Könitzer, "Leben bei den österreichischen Sozialisten," *Frankfurter Allgemeine Zeitung,* 3 Dec. 1967.

24. Hanni Könitzer, "Die Überraschung in Österreich," *Frankfurter Allgemeine Zeitung,* 2 Mar. 1970.

25. Barbara Coudenhove-Kalergi, "Jeder Zoll ein Liberaler," *Die Zeit,* 6 Mar. 1970; see also Felix Kreissler, "Bruno Kreisky. Aperçu politico-biographique," *Austriaca* (June 1986): 16–17; and the contributions by Oliver Rathkolb and Anton Pelinka in the same volume, 65–76, 81–90.

26. Franz Kirchberger, "Kreisky in der NS-Falle," *Deutsche Wochenzeitung,* 29 May 1970.

27. *New York Times,* 2 June 1970; see also Robert S. Wistrich, "The Strange Case of Bruno Kreisky," *Encounter* (May 1979): 78–85, and idem, "The Kreisky Phenomenon: A Reassessment," in *Austrians and Jews in the Twentieth Century,* edited by Robert S. Wistrich (New York, 1992), 234–51.

28. "Besorgnis über Dokumentationszentrum," *Frankfurter Allgemeine Zeitung,* 9 July 1970.

29. Grätz described Wiesenthal's Centre as a "Feme- und Spitzelorganisation." The Moscow Communist youth organ *Konsomolskaya Pravda* was more specific: it alleged that Wiesenthal was running an Israeli espionage centre supported by the CIA and the British secret service.

30. "Problematik der Naziprozesse in Österreich," *Neue Zürcher Zeitung,* 15 Aug. 1972.

31. *Frankfurter Allgemeine Zeitung,* 9 July 1970; also a letter by Wiesenthal addressed to friends of his Centre abroad, dated 16 June 1970. See Ingrid Böhler, "'Wenn die Juden ein Volk sind, so ist es ein mieses Volk.' Die Kreisky-Peter-Wiesenthal Affäre 1975," in *Politische Affäre und Skandale in Österreich,* edited by by Hubert Sickinger (Vienna, 1996), 502–31; Herline Koelbl, *Jüdische Portraits* (Frankfurt a.M., 1989); and Ruth Wodak et al., *"Wir sind alle unschuldige Täter," Diskurshistorische Studien zum Nachkriegsantisemitismus* (Frankfurt a.M., 1990). On the Wiesenthal Affair as a whole, see Martin van Amerongen, *Kreisky und seine unbewältigte Gegenwart* (Graz, 1977); Paul Blau, "Das Nazi-Dilemma der SPÖ," in *Wer war Bruno Kreisky?,* edited by Franz Richard Reiter (Vienna, 2000), 41–51.

32. Secher, *Bruno Kreisky,* 153–57. Western media reaction at the time was one of shock and indignation that Kreisky had "capitulated" to terrorist demands. Israelis were particularly angry at his apparent pliancy.

33. See Robert S. Wistrich, "An Austrian Variation on Socialist Antisemitism," *Patterns of Prejudice* 8, no. 4 (July-Aug. 1974): 1–10.

34. Kreisky, *Die Zeit in der wir leben,* 67; also the interview with the Beirut daily, *al-Safir,* 16 June 1980, reproduced in "Austria and the Palestine Question," *Journal of Palestine Studies,* 10, no. 2 (Winter 1981): 167–74.

35. Ibid. Also *Neue Zürcher Zeitung* (henceforth *NZZ*), 5 Sept. 1978, and *Jewish Telegraphic Agency* (*JTA*), 17 Aug. 1979.

36. "Kreisky et les Juifs," *Le Nouvel Observateur,* 151.

37. See Carl Gershman, "The Socialists and the PLO," *Commentary* (Oct. 1979): 36–44, for an account of the Third Worldist orientation that began to dominate the Socialist International from the mid-1970s with its pro-PLO and anti-Israel consequences.

38. See *Der Spiegel,* no. 29 (1979), where Kreisky explicitly linked the change in policy of the Socialist International with the Arab oil factor, vulgarizing Marx by suggesting that "gewisse Existenzfragen sensibilisierend wirken."

39. *Report of the Socialist International Fact Finding Mission to the Middle East,* Circular No. B 14/7 (London 1977), Introduction by Bruno Kreisky. The report claimed that the Arab States were ready to recognize Israel's right to exist within the 1967 borders and that the creation of an independent Palestinian State in the West Bank and Gaza was the only answer to the conflict. More than thirty years later this is a very widely held position in Europe and most of the world, even though there is no compelling evidence that the underlying assumptions are valid.

40 *Free Palestine* (May 1976); *The Observer,* 27 Feb. 1977; *Der Spiegel,* no. 48 (1979); and *NZZ,* 15 Mar. 1980, 78–82, where Kreisky drew a particularly unpleasant parallel: "Wer sagt: Russen raus aus Afghanistan muß auch sagen: Israelis raus aus der Westbank!" See also Robert Wistrich, "Kreisky, Arafat and Friends," *Encounter* (Nov. 1980).

41. *Jerusalem Post,* 3 Sept. 1978; *NZZ,* 7 Sept. 1978; on Gadaffi, see Thalberg, *Von der Kunst,* 480.

42. See Martin van Amerongen, *Die Samenzwering tegen Simon Wiesenthal* (The conspiracy against Simon Wiesenthal) (Amsterdam, 1976) and the remark of Jerusalem Mayor Teddy Kollek (himself of Viennese origin) quoted in *Die Welt,* 6 Sept. 1978: "Kreisky kann nur noch von einem Psychiater, wie es Alfred Adler oder Sigmund Freud war, geholfen werden." Also Heinz Galinski, "Ein Fall politischer Psychopathologie. Zum jüdischen Selbsthass Dr. Bruno Kreiskys"; and *Jüdische Rundschau,* 14 Sept. 1978.

43. Ephraim Kishon, "Schlage uns, Bruno, wir sind deine Trommel," *Der Spiegel,* no. 37 (11 Sept. 1978): 142–45 and Wistrich, "The Strange Case of Bruno Kreisky," *Encounter* (May 1979): 78–85 for an earlier discussion of these statements.

44. *NZZ,* 5 Sept. 1978. In this report Kreisky referred to the Israeli army as "eine verfeinerte Form des Banditentums" (a refined form of banditry). He later tried to repair the damage by suggesting that his "off-the-record" comment had been quoted out of context. He declared himself ready to apologize if he had offended anyone but stood by his political views. See *Jüdische Rundschau,* 7 Sept. 1978, and *Jewish Chronicle,* 8 Sept. 1978; see also Bruno Kreisky, *Im Strom der Politik. Der Memoiren,* vol 2. (Berlin, 1988), where he again condemned Israel's "unbounded intolerance" towards the Palestinians and its alleged "refusal to create the preconditions for peaceful co-existence with the Arab States." Extracts in English appeared in *Austria Today,* 4, no. 88 (1988): 51–52.

45. Interview in *Ma'ariv* (in Hebrew), 5 July 1979.

46. On the Schoenau affair, see Thalberg, *Von der Kunst,* 419. Kreisky nevertheless continued to permit Soviet Jews to transit through Austria with full freedom of choice concerning their ultimate destination: see *JTA,* 25 Mar. 1977 and 26 Nov. 1984 for his pride in this humanitarian policy. For the PLO terrorist assault in Israel, see "Kreisky blames Jerusalem": *Jewish Chronicle,* 17 Mar. 1978; *JTA,* 16 Mar. 1978; and "Umstrittene Aeusserungen Kreiskys und Pahrs. Israelische Selbstschuld am Massaker von Tel Aviv," *NZZ,* 16 Mar. 1978. On the hostages, "Die Geiselnahme von Wien," *Vorwärts,* 25 Dec. 1975.

47. Kreisky made his remarks in the course of a stinging attack on Wiesenthal, "Kreisky Accuses Top Zionist of Nazi Collaboration," *Free Palestine* (Dec. 1975), and *Palestine,* 2, no. 8 (Jan. 1976): 35–37.

48. *Deutsche Nationalzeitung,* 21 Nov. 1975; *Deutsche Wochenzeitung,* 5 Dec. 1975; also "Vorwand Wiesenthal," *Wiener Tagebuch,* no. 12, (Dec. 1975): 2.

49. Robert Knight, "The Waldheim Context: Austria and Nazism," *Times Literary Supplement,* 3 Oct. 1986. On Brandt, see Shlomo Shamir, "Willy Brandt, die Juden und Israel," *Jahrbuch für Antisemitismusforschung* (Berlin) 19 (2010): 379–404.

50. Shamir, 400–401. See also idem, "Helmut Schmidt: Seine Beziehungen zu Israel und den Juden," *Jahrbuch für Antisemitismusforschung* 17 (2008): 297–320.

51. "Problematik der Nazi-Prozesse in Oesterreich," *NZZ,* 15 Aug. 1972; and Wistrich, "An Austrian Variant on Socialist Antisemitism," 10.

52. Franz Kirchberger, "Kreisky in der NS-Falle" *Deutsche Wochenzeitung,* 29 May 1970.

53. *Vrij Nederland,* 1 July 1970.

54. See, for example, Izydor Lucki, "Szymon Wiesenthal, na szląku agentur, wywiadu i zdrady," *Perspektywy* (Warsaw), no. 25 (30 Jan. 1970). The series in *Profil*

(Vienna) entitled "Wer ist Simon Wiesenthal?," beginning with no. 44 (28 Oct. 1975) answers these slanders and provides a generally reliable account of the whole background.

55. *Profil,* 18 Nov. 1975, 22–25. On the same occasion Kreisky emphasized that he and Wiesenthal "kommen aus ganz verschiedenen Kulturkreisen, aus verschiedenen Religionsgemeinschaften überhaupt." He also used for the first time the threatening phrase "Der Mann muß verschwinden" in relation to Wiesenthal.

56. "Der Fall Peter," *Profil,* 14 Oct. 1975, 10, 12–16; "Peter und die Mordbrigade," ibid., 21 Oct. 1975, 18–23; and Peter Michael Lingens, "Grenzen des Opportunismus," ibid., no. 47, 18 Nov. 1975. Also *Die Presse,* 8 Nov. 1975, 11 Nov. 1975, 22 Nov. 1975; and *Der Neue Mahnruf* (Dec. 1975).

57. "Kreisky: Die Juden—ein mieses Volk," *Der Spiegel,* 17 Nov. 1975.

58. Ulrich Brunner, "Kratzer am Kanzler" (Kleinkrieg Kreisky-Wiesenthal und kein Ende), *Vorwärts,* 18 Dec. 1975.

59. "Sozialistische Schutzmauer um Kreisky gegen Wiesenthal," *FAZ,* 4 Dec. 1975; Hanni Konitzer, "Nach der Wiener Affäre: Eine miese Geschichte," *FAZ,* 5 Dec. 1975.

60. "Kann Kreisky Wiesenthal stoppen?," *Deutsche Nationalzeitung,* 7 Nov. 1975;"Wiesenthal ein Agent," ibid., 14 Nov. 1975; "Wie weit reicht Israels Macht?," ibid., 28 Nov. 1975; and "Israels Rächer in Deutschland. Ist Wiesenthal am Ende?," ibid., Dec. 1975. Wiesenthal himself seemed resigned in an interview, "Nur Don Quijote würde weitermachen," with *Der Spiegel,* 12 Jan. 1976.

61. "Neonazis: Von Kreisky lernen," *Profil,* no. 39 (21 Sept. 1975), 13. "Versöhnung mit den Nazis—aber wie?," ibid., 21 Oct. 1975, 18–23, and Peter Michael Lingens, ibid., 18 Nov. 1975: "Von ehemaligen Nazis akzeptiert zu werden, ist demnach die extremste Form der Traumerfüllung."

62. It is certainly significant that according to one poll almost 60 per cent of the Austrian population supported Kreisky's position at the end of 1975 as against only 3 percent who were in favor of Wiesenthal, with the rest either neutral or unconcerned: see *Profil,* no. 6, 3 Feb. 1976. For a recent description of the Viennese Jewish community's acute anxiety throughout the Kreisky years at the Chancellor's hostile comments, see Martin Engelberg, "Jüdische Perspektive: Unser Schmerz mit Kreisky," *Die Presse,* 22 Jan. 2011.

63. *Profil,* 21 Apr. 1986.

64. *Kronenzeitung,* 28 May 1986.

65. "The grotesque Mr. Kreisky," *Jerusalem Post,* 4 Sept. 1978 for earlier editorial comment.

66. Interview with Chancellor Bruno Kreisky, *Der Spiegel,* no. 29 (1979).

67. *New York Times,* 22 Dec. 1975.

68. See Kreisky, *Im Strom der Politik,* 339–40, 347–51, for his benign view of the mercurial Ghaddafi.

69. Henry Delfiner, "The Socialist International and the Rise of Yasser Arafat," *Midstream* (Nov.-Dec. 2002): 4–8.

70. Ibid., 6.

71. Delfiner, "Socialist International," 6; see also Carl Greshman, "The Socialists and the PLO," *Commentary* (Oct. 1979); and Yoram Peri, "Fall from Favor, Israel and the Socialist International," *Jerusalem Quarterly* (Summer 1982).

72. See "Kreisky-Arafat. Die unveröffentlichte Korrespondenz. Dokumente von Freundschaft und Weltpolitik," *Profil,* no. 47, 15 Nov. 2004, 35–44, based on 30 unpublished letters in the Kreisky Archives in Vienna that were exchanged with Yasser Arafat.

73. "Mein lieber Freund," *Profil,* no. 47, 15 Nov. 2004, 38.

74. Ibid., 40.

75. Erwin Lanc interview, ibid., 39, Lanc was Kreisky's Foreign Minister at the time.

76. Letter of 24 Dec. 1979, in *Profil,* ibid., 36.

77. On 19 Oct. 1989 Kreisky was convicted of malicious slander in a libel initiated years before by his old adversary. He received a three-year suspended sentence and was obliged to pay 270,000 Austrian schillings (about $20,000) in compensation; *Jerusalem Post,* 24 Nov. 1989; and the interview with Simon Wiesenthal in *Der Spiegel,* no. 47 (1989), 260 ff.

78. Wiesenthal's comment to Ilona Henry as reported in the *Jerusalem Post,* 23 May 1986.

79. Secher, "Kreisky and the Jews," in *Kreisky Era,* 10–33.

80. Robert Solomon Wistrich, *Anti-Zionism and Antisemitism* (2007).

CHAPTER 16

Anti-Zionist Myths on the Contemporary Left

The *ideological* war against Zionism which began long before 1948 has never really subsided for a single day of Israel's existence as a nation-state. This intense opposition to Zionism has had many sources and expressed itself in multiple ways. It has never been uniform or monolithic. It has been one of the pillars of the Palestinian Arab national movement since its birth after the First World War; and it has enjoyed overwhelming support among Arab nationalists, Pan-Arab radicals, and Islamic fundamentalists until the present day. But although the "Palestine Question" has been at the heart of political anti-Zionism, it is hardly synonymous with it. The reality of Palestinian grievances is quite inadequate to explain the global reach or intensity of anti-Zionist ideas or feelings. For example, the relentless attacks on the miniscule State of Israel at the United Nations and in the world's media, or the frequency with which it is reified as a symbol of absolute evil, suggests that something much more than "justice for the Palestinians" may be at work.[1] So the question has to be asked: Why is this conflict different from all other conflicts? Why the focus on Zion? Why the Jews? Is the irrational and obsessive pillorying of Zionism simply a disguised form of antisemitism—as many Jews tend to believe? Is the near universal impact of anti-Zionism a sign that Israel has indeed become the "Jew of the nations," as if fulfilling some kind of dark preordained fate as an eternal scapegoat? Is the war against Zion to be seen as a war on the Jewish people, a "war against the Jews," to borrow the pregnant term that historian Lucy Dawidowicz used many years ago to characterize the Nazi genocide?[2]

This is one of the more difficult questions that I tried to address in my last book, *A Lethal Obsession. Antisemitism from Antiquity to the Global Jihad*.[3] Although I make it clear that anti-Zionism has a different origin (historically speaking) from antisemitism—which long preceded it—nevertheless there has often been considerable overlap and even convergence between the two phenomena. Anti-Zionism, like antisemitism, has developed its own version of occult, sinister Jewish influences working to undermine the international political order. Thus, among Islamists as well as on the far left, it has increasingly become an ideology imbued with irrational conspiracy theories, mythical symbols, and a culture of hatred. Whether the rhetoric of anti-Zionism happens to be Marxist, Muslim, Christian, Third Worldist, fascist, or openly neo-Nazi, it is replete with stereotypical notions of the perfidy and diabolical cunning of the Jews; their corrosive, manipulative will-to-power; their insatiable love of gold and intrigue, mastery of hidden forces and domination of the international financial system. The more radical anti-Zionists no less than the classical antisemites are obsessed with the ubiquity and malignant impact of the Jews on the modern world.[4]

This compulsive and paranoid world-view did not suddenly burst forth with the beginning of the second Palestinian intifada in September 2000, or in the wake of the al-Qaeda assault on the Twin Towers in Manhattan a year later. It first assumed a *major* resonance among Muslims and radical leftists following Israel's lightning victory over three neighbouring Arab states who had sought to extinguish its sovereign existence in May/June 1967.[5] One of the long-term results of that fateful war was to free certain "critics" of the Jewish State from the unwritten taboo on openly anti-Jewish aspersions following the revelation of the Nazi death camps.[6] A much harsher anti-Israel rhetoric soon emerged from both the Right and Left, which permitted the revival of what had been a temporarily dormant antisemitism in the early 1960s. President Charles de Gaulle's notorious "Sermon to the Hebrews" at his November 1967 press conference in Paris, where he referred to Israel and the Jews as "an elite people dominating and sure of itself" was one important landmark in what was soon to become a seismic shift.[7] Left-wing "progressives," too, began to attack Israel as if it were a European colonial project based on a *Herrenvolk* (master race) ideology.[8] Israel was increasingly bracketed during the 1970s with such widely execrated apartheid regimes as South Africa and Rhodesia or with dictatorial and repressive military juntas in Chile or Argentina. Its policies, too, were branded—especially on the Left—as being the inevitable outcome of being a "white" colonialist settler-state. Zionism was vilified as a peculiarly pernicious, supremicist vision of the world and the lackey of American imperialism in the Middle East.[9]

In the view of many radical leftists who ritually condemn Zionism, the displacement of most of the indigenous Palestinian Arab population in 1948 was a "crime against humanity."The goal of Zionist ideology was defined according to this narrative, as the *racial separation* of Jew from non-Jew. Zionism came to be seen as being an inherently *isolationist,* segregationist world-view dependent upon the strengthening and even encouragement of antisemitism to implement its aims.[10] The desire of Israel to be a "Jewish" state was itself deemed to be inherently unacceptable, because the Jewish people was a religious group rather than a nation. The Law of Return was attacked with special vehemence as intrinsically racist, since it grants to immigrant Jews from the Diaspora rights of Israeli citizenship that are denied to exiled Palestinians. It is also claimed that Israeli Arabs and Oriental Jews (*Mizrachiim*) suffer from institutionalized racism within Israeli society.[11] Finally, contemporary anti-Zionists—many of them Jewish and/or Israeli—point to the so-called theocratic character of the Jewish state which by definition discriminates against the Arab minority inside Israel.

Such a distorted image of Israel in contemporary anti-Zionist discourse has itself assimilated conspicuous features of European antisemitism. The idea, for example, that Zionism aims at racist hegemony or domination over the non-Jew has long been a classic focal point of anti-Jewish propaganda. The concept of the "chosen race" is a typically antisemitic, *not* a Jewish notion. The belief that the Jews are misanthropes hostile to the rest of humanity is an ancient myth with roots in classical Antiquity.[12] The Arab-Israel conflict is difficult enough, one might have thought, without the injection of such irrational stereotypes from the arsenal of European antisemitism. But that is exactly what has happened in recent decades.

Some of the poison had already entered the Arab Middle East as a result of intense Nazi propaganda in the 1930s and during World War II.[13] Hence it is less than surprising that the Christian and Nazi demonology of the Jew could be so easily adopted by Islamist ideologues, with the focus of the attack being directed at the Israeli nation-state in the Middle East. Contemporary anti-Zionism repeats on a collective level and within the international arena the discriminatory principles of traditional antisemitism which traditionally branded the Jews as an *alien* element unassimilable into European Christian society. It is worth recalling that Jews in Europe both before and after legal emancipation had been condemned by antisemites as "Oriental" or "semi-Asiatic" hybrids in Western culture, who were culturally and biologically the ultimate "other." In the contemporary Middle East, too, the Zionists are still perceived as intruders who cannot be absorbed into the dominant framework of the Muslim Arab world.[14] The Jews, having achieved their *national* emancipation through Israel and the Zionist movement, have found themselves branded as European colonialist "strangers" despite the fact that at least 50 percent of the Israeli population originate from the Middle East. In both the leftist and Islamic narratives it is Jewish and/or Zionist "racism" which is blamed for the non-integration of Jews in the larger Middle Eastern environment. The truth is that far from being "racist," Zionism, historically speaking, has shown remarkable indifference to race as a factor in shaping the character and ethos of Israeli society. In contrast to typically white colonial societies like South Africa and Rhodesia, Australia or New Zealand, neither race nor color was ever of major importance in Israel as an indicator of social status. Nor was there any need to use race as a legitimizing ideology—as in the American Deep South—to exploit slave labor. On the contrary, many of the Jewish pioneers came to Palestine in order to create their own working-class. They were hardly attracted to mystical doctrines of race-purity (a typically antisemitic obsession) nor did they believe in a hierarchy of "superior" and "inferior" races. Such doctrines, which presuppose a belief in the hereditary differences of distinct and immutable races or in the virtues of the "blood," are completely alien both to Judaism and Zionism—despite all antisemitic claims to the contrary from both right and left.[15]

The Zionist movement, far from being oriented to the ideology of "race," arose as a direct *response* to the racist antisemitism created by reactionary forces in European, and later in Middle Eastern societies. It was external antisemitic pressure, analogous to foreign domination over other oppressed peoples, which became a major factor in obliging Jews to seek their own path towards auto-emancipation. Territorial concentration in Palestine (the traditional focus of Jewish national aspirations) building on older messianic visions of redemption, eventually became the platform of all Zionist groups—secular and religious—across the political spectrum.[16] Moreover, a modern movement that originally began as an offshoot of late-19th-century European liberal nationalism, would fifty years later become the first successful *anti-colonial* liberation struggle in the Middle East. By the mid-1940s, Zionism—whose more ancient roots lay deep in the Jewish religion and an unparalleled history of suffering from racial and religious persecution—had become a leading pioneer of postwar *decolonization* and the liberation of oppressed peoples in the Third World. Furthermore, the emergence of Zionism as the dominant ideology in Jewish life after 1945 corresponded to the harsh reality of the Jewish condition in the postwar world, to the plight of a *homeless* people, of Holocaust survivors in their hundreds of thousands, as well as nearly a million "Sephardic" or Middle Eastern Jews shortly to be expelled or ejected from an increasingly inhospitable Arab World.

In seeking to solve this crisis, the Zionist movement between 1945 and 1948 had to fight against the full might of the British Empire, which had slammed shut the gates of Palestine. In this desperate battle for survival, the Zionist resistance movement was struggling for Jewish national independence *against the British occupation of Palestine*. In 1948 Israel primarily depended on Czech arms and Soviet political support, as well as the strength and bravery of its own citizens. At that time Arab potentates like King Farouk of Egypt, Nuri Said Pasha of Iraq, and King Abdullah of Transjordan attacked Israel (in defiance of international law) with British connivance and backing. Although U.S. President Truman did swiftly recognize Israel's independence in 1948, other key decision-makers in the American State Department, the Pentagon, the intelligence community, and among the pro-Arab oil lobby in the United States were very much opposed to a Jewish State.[17] Contrary to the prevailing left-wing mythology about Israel's creation being a Western Zionist-imperialist conspiracy, *official* American support for Israel was comparatively lukewarm. Moreover, the American arms embargo on Israel remained in force until 1964. The great turning-point came only in 1967 as a result of the Six-Day War and the gradual emergence of a de facto American-Israeli strategic alliance in the Middle East.[18] For the crucial first twenty years of its existence, the United States scarcely considered Israel as an important ally and its material interests in the Arab world were infinitely greater.

The collective amnesia of the Left in this regard is especially striking since in the late 1940s, most Communists and socialists in the West enthusiastically hailed the "anti-colonialist" nature of the Israeli war of independence. Indeed they followed the USSR in strongly supporting the establishment of Israel as a blow against "Anglo-American domination of the Middle East."[19] Typical was the attitude of the British Communist *Daily Worker* which denounced the "reactionary war conducted by the chieftains of the Arab League under British control" against the newly-founded Jewish state. Here is how it described the composition of the Arab armies that invaded Palestine in flagrant contravention of the UN partition scheme:

> There are Iraqi Fascist bands, reluctant Syrian and Lebanese regulars, professional Transjordan Legionnaires, Egyptians, Britishers, a few German Nazis, Anders Poles and even Yugoslav Royalists.[20]

Such examples expose the historical vacuousness of so much contemporary leftist vilification of Israel. What today is eulogized as the Palestinian "struggle against Zionism" was considered by most Communists or Socialists in 1948 as utterly reactionary. As former Israeli Foreign Minister Abba Eban wittily remarked: "Truth does not change simply because those who proclaim it become tired of their own veracity."

The hysterical incitement in Arab capitals preceding the Six-Day War of 1967 and the genocidal calls for the elimination of Israel were, however, ignored by the Communist world. Ahmed Shoukeiry, leader of the recently created Palestine Liberation Organization (PLO), openly proclaimed in 1967 that "there would be no survivors" after the reconquest of Palestine.[21] True, this prompted Cuba's Communist dictator Fidel Castro to point out that advocating genocide had nothing in common with revolution, socialism, or national liberation.[22] But in the U.S.S.R., Communist Eastern Europe, and Maoist China, it was Israel which was accused of "aggression" and harboring genocidal aims. Only a few years later, Cuba, too, would become a leading exponent of the Zionism=racism mythology in its Third World incarnation. More recently, however, in an interview with Jeffrey Goldberg of the *Atlantic Monthly,* the 84-year-old Fidel Castro did sharply criticize President Ahmadinejad of Iran for denying the Holocaust and advised him (and others of his ilk) to acknowledge the "unique history of anti-Semitism" if they wished to serve the cause of peace. "The Iranian government should understand the consequences of 2000 years of theological anti-Semitism" and why Israelis had ample reason to fear for their existence. Castro pungently added:

> I don't think anyone has been slandered more than the Jews. I would say they have been slandered much more than the Muslims because they are blamed and slandered for everything. No one blames the Muslims for anything.[23]

Castro went on to remind people that the Jews "were expelled from their land, persecuted and mistreated all over the world, as the ones who killed God." Their existence had been made much harder than that of others yet "their culture and religion kept them together as a nation."[24] Moreover, there was nothing in the annals of human suffering, he insisted, that was comparable to the Holocaust. Castro also emphasized that Israel had an unequivocal right to exist.[25] It is an ironic comment on the idiosyncracies of our time that Fidel Castro's unexpected deviation from the ever-proliferating lies of Israel-negationists on the left should in the year 2010 become a newsworthy item.

Forty years ago one could, however, already see the beginnings of the shift by the Western Left towards embracing the completely partisan narrative of the Palestinian Liberation Organization (PLO) whose new leader, Yasser

Arafat hardly disguised his *politicidal* goals. On 16 December 1974 he declared:

> We shall never stop until we can go back home and Israel is destroyed. . . . The goal of our struggle is the end of Israel, and there can be no compromises or mediations. We don't want peace, we want victory. Peace for us means Israel's destruction, and nothing else."[26]

Such declarations hardly troubled the sleep of many Western "humanist" intellectuals four decades ago any more than do the spine-chilling genocidal pronouncements of the Palestinian Hamas movement, the antisemitic diatribes of the Lebanese Hezbollah, or Iranian President Ahmadinejad. The PLO in its National Covenant of 1968 already identified as one of its central aims the elimination of the "racist" State of Israel, linking this goal with the ongoing world struggle against Imperialism. Article 22 of the Palestinian Covenant, vilified Zionism as "a racist and fanatical movement in its formation: aggressive, expansionist and colonialist in its aims, and Fascist and Nazi in its means." It went on to categorically state that "Israel is the tool of the Zionist Movement and a human and geographical base for world imperialism."[27] Article 20 of the Palestinian National Covenant made it equally clear that Israel was to be viewed as a *non-nation* and that Jewish nationalism had always been a *false, artificial,* and *reactionary* phenomenon.[28] Echoing well-worn Soviet Marxist dogmas, the same article claimed that "Judaism, in its character as a religion, is not a nationality with an independent existence."[29] There is no doubt that what the PLO envisaged was an *Arab* Palestine in which Islam would be the dominant faith and only Palestinian Arabs would possess *national* rights.[30] Article 1 of the Palestinian National Covenant made this crystal clear: "Palestine is the homeland of the Palestinian Arab people and an integral part of the great Arab homeland, and the people of Palestine is a part of the Arab nation."[31] This *exclusivist* nationalist vision of Al-Fatah and the PLO did not, however, prevent many liberal and Western leftist commentators from embracing Palestinian integral nationalism as a "progressive" cause unlike "reactionary" Zionism. The explanation for this stunning double-standard is rarely forthcoming and it usually relies on a blindly uncritical view of the Palestinians as having no responsibility for the conflict or for their own actions—which have indeed only led to disaster.

Article 6 of the PLO Covenant regarded as "Palestinians" only those Jews who were physically present in the land of Israel before 1917—a definition which would exclude almost all of the Israeli Jewish population from any right to remain in their own country.[32] Hence, the posture of the PLO for the next two decades would be built upon a *total denial* of the Jewish right to national self-determination. This exclusionist (not to say racist) concept has been at the root of the Palestinian, pan-Arab and Islamist refusal to accept the legitimacy of the *Jewish* State of Israel until the present day. This intransigent rejectionism is especially visible in the 1988 Sacred Covenant of the Palestinian Hamas—a brazenly antisemitic, as well as a jihadi fundamentalist, document. Hamas (or to use its full name, The Movement of Islamic Resistance) is a Palestinian offshoot of the Egyptian Muslim Brotherhood. It is thoroughly imbued with an anti-Jewish ideology based on the discredited conspiracy theories contained in the *Protocols of the Elders of Zion*.[33] While the Western Left does not embrace the *Protocols,* it has to some extent bought into the mythic Palestinian structure of thought which is not so dissimilar. Thus, the radical Left persists in obsessively pillorying Israel as a central *symbol* of the evils of world Imperialism. Zionism is continually conceptualized as a *criminal conspiracy* whose dimensions are *global*.[34] Israel is seen as a base from which the West has repeatedly sought to liquidate the Palestinian people. This is the position not only of Hamas (which rules the Gaza Strip) but of most Arab nationalists. What has given this ideologically twisted narrative a certain legitimacy has been the theoretical and practical support which it receives from Western intellectuals who continue to define themselves as "progressive."

One of the prominent pioneers of the New Left mythology that has contributed to undermining Israel's legitimacy was the Polish-born historian and biographer of Trotsky, Isaac Deutscher. Shortly before his death in July 1967, Deutscher fiercely attacked what he called Israeli "propagandists" for seeking to justify a war of conquest in the Middle East by conjuring up "biblical myths and all the ancient religious-national symbols of Jewish history."[35] The Israeli government had deliberately whipped up a "frenzy of belligerence, arrogance and fanaticism." According to Deutscher, ordinary Israelis in 1967 blindly accepted their government's "doctrine" of reducing Arab states to impotence by deliberately provoking wars. The ex-Trotskyite Deutscher contemptuously dismissed Israel as nothing but an anti-communist Western outpost in the Middle East, designed to block Arab national aspirations. Though he had himself been brought up in the Polish Orthodox Jewish tradition, Deutscher could not refrain from libelling Israel as a bastion of "racial-talmudic exclusiveness and superiority." Sarcastically, he branded Israelis as "the Prussians of the Middle East," imbued with "the same absolute confidence of their arms, chauvinistic arrogance, and contempt for other peoples."[36] Israel's maverick existentialist philosopher Yeshayahu Leibowitz, a real practising Orthodox Jew, went still further in 1968, pillorying his country as a "Judeo-Nazi" State. Unlike Leibowitz, however, Deutscher had come to loathe Judaism and singled out for special opprobrium the medieval scenes of hassidim "jumping with joy at the Western Wall."[37]

Nor did Deutscher shrink from accusing Israel of willfully perpetuating the causes of antisemitism. In Europe, according to his astonishingly reductionist analysis, antisemitism had attained its paroxysm as a backlash against the *Jewish role* in the capitalist economy.[38] The lesson for the present seemed obvious

> Yet they [the Jews] now appear in the Middle East once again in the invidious role of agents not so much of their own relatively feeble capitalism, but of powerful Western vested interests and as protégés of neo-colonialism. This is how the Arab world sees them, not without reason. Once again they arouse bitter emotions and hatreds in their neighbours, in all those who have ever been or are still victims of imperialism.[39]

For Marxists like Deutscher, Jews were therefore to blame for the hatred of their Arab neighbors outraged by Israel's role as an imperialist "stooge." Such one-sided views anticipated and influenced the outlook of the newly minted pro-Palestinian radical Left in America and Europe. It fitted the trend of leftist support for Third World "liberation" struggles in Cuba, Algeria, and Vietnam. Not only the far Left but also the far Right and black separatists in the United States were beginning to use a similar language in denouncing "kosher fascism" and deploring the "white" Israeli oppression of "black" Arabs.[40] The Black Panthers, for example, unequivocally praised Palestinian terrorist actions against the "Israeli pigs" after 1967 while stridently calling for the abolition of the Zionist "racial state."[41] The John Birch Society and other propagandists of white America's radical Right spewed out equally vile denunciations of Israeli "aggression," while shedding crocodile tears over imaginary Israeli massacres of Palestinian Arabs. These white racist supremacists shamelessly denounced Israel as a predatory state built on "stolen land," whose strength was a function of the wealth, power, and influence of world Jewry, especially its American branch. The neo-Nazis and most of their successors today on the extreme Right have come to share a common loathing for Israel with radical Islamists and the militant anti-Zionist Left.[42]

In West Germany, after 1967, support for the Palestinian cause was soon apparent not only on the neo-Nazi far Right but also among militant left-wing students who were ideologically committed to the ideal of "world revolution." The path from Berlin left-wing student politics to El-Fatah terrorism would be quickly traversed in 1969 by a small group of German anarchists belonging to the extra-parliamentary opposition. They planted a bomb on 10 November 1969 (the anniversary of the *Kristallnacht* Nazi pogrom) in the communal hall of West Berlin's Jewish congregation house in the Fasanenstrasse. During their investigation, the police soon found incriminating leaflets, proclaiming under banner headlines "Shalom and Napalm" and the intent to deface Jewish memorial stones with this ugly slogan. Such drastic action, according to the German anarchists, was required to overcome bourgeois West Germany's *Judenkomplex*.

> We admittedly gassed Jews and, therefore, feel obliged to protect them from further threats of genocide. This kind of neurotic, backward-looking anti-Fascism, obsessed as it is by past history, totally disregards the non-justifiability of the State of Israel. True anti-Fascism consists in an explicit and unequivocal identification with the fighting *fedayin*. Our solidarity with them will no longer be satisfied by purely verbal protests of the Vietnam variety, but will pitilessly combat the combination of Fascism and Israeli Zionism.[43]

Over 40 years ago, the destruction of Israel was already openly contemplated by the more extreme sections of the German New Left in the name of "international socialist solidarity."[44] Already then, Israel, with its newly displayed military efficiency, was caricatured as a heavily armed Goliath facing the Palestinian David, and as the "spearhead" of Western neo-colonialism in the Middle East. The stark geo-political reality in 1970 of three million Jews concentrated on a tiny sliver of territory (barely ten miles wide in the middle) threatened by one hundred million Arabs, was either dismissed out of hand or simply ignored. Instead, leaflets distributed by *internationale solidarität* culminated in the highly inflammatory slogan of *Schlägt die Zionisten tot, macht den Nahen Osten rot* (Beat the Zionists dead, make the Near East red).[45] The Palestine Committees founded by German New Left and Arab students (predominantly Palestinians) consistently blurred the increasingly thin dividing line between anti-Zionism and unabashed antisemitism. Predictably, the murder of Israeli athletes during the Munich Olympics of 1972 would be enthusiastically justified by radical German Leftists as a "brave and resolute action of the Palestine revolutionaries." Leaflets at the University of Frankfurt praised the terrorist murders while ridiculing "official crocodile tears" and attacking pro-Israel journalists who by their mendacity, encouraged "the guilty conscience demanding restitution for Jews."[46]

More than a decade later, during the 1982 Lebanon War, the radical German Left (like so many of its European counterparts) once again demonstrated its remoteness from any lucid reflection about Auschwitz and its own "Jew-complex." Israel's actions in Lebanon were almost immediately greeted as an attempted "Final Solution of the Palestinian Question" and as a "genocide in Lebanon." Menachem Begin mutated into Adolf Hitler, the Israel Defense Forces into the Wehrmacht, and Israeli Jews found themselves metamorphosed into Nazi Germans. The script for this scenario could have been written in Moscow, but using the terminology of the Holocaust clearly had a different connotation in Berlin or Frankfurt. If Jews were guilty of nakedly stealing land, of military occupation, of carrying out *Lebensraum* policies, or brutally expelling Palestinians, then perhaps German crimes were not so unique after all. Embracing the cause of Palestine could retrospectively become an effective method for Germans to overcome their burdensome Nazi past. By turning Israelis into ugly "perpetrators" and Palestinian Arabs into wholly innocent victims, Germans could place themselves in the more virtuous position of supporting the underdogs.[47]

Anti-Zionism in the 1970s and 1980s increasingly began to look like the leftist functional equivalent of what classical antisemitism had once represented (in the interwar period) for the fascist Right.[48] Not only was anti-Zionism clearly the historical heir of earlier forms of antisemitism, but it was steadily emerging as the lowest common denominator between sections of the Left, the Right, and Islamist circles.[49] This has become even more true today than it was several decades ago. In the current context anti-Zionism has indeed become a powerful point of connection between the latent anti-Americanism of many European intellectuals and the endemically anti-Western attitudes in the Arab Middle East."[50] It offers a bridge between the Christian churches and fundamentalist mosques, between left-wing radicals and conservative nationalists, between the "chattering classes" in Western Europe and the more militant protesters on the streets who scream "Death to Israel!"[51]

Anti-Zionism as a leading component in leftist ideology is a relatively recent phenomenon. For example, before 1945, the subject scarcely assumed *major* importance for the Old Left. Neither Marx, Engels, Kautsky, Lenin, Trotsky, nor Rosa Luxemburg had ever dreamed that Zionism or the *Judenfrage* could become a *central world problem,* or an ideological issue on a par with the class struggle or the fight against capitalism, imperialism, and globalization.[52] The leaders of the pre-1914 Socialist International and their Communist successors generally regarded Zionism as no more than a minor irritant, an annoying obstacle to full assimilation that would vanish in the classless society of the future created by socialist revolution. Zionists, so the argument ran, were engaged in the hopeless endeavor of trying to revive a fossilized "ghetto" Judaism and perpetuate a reactionary "medieval caste" (Kautsky/Lenin) which had no place in modern society. Such nationalist "chimeras" could only retard the common struggle against antisemitism. But no classical Marxist seriously imagined that Zionism could one day be presented as a major pillar of "world reaction" or *the* biggest threat to peace on earth, as a majority of Europeans appeared to believe in 2003.

Jewish liberal and left-wing intellectuals have been prominent in recent years in making such grossly inflated accusations. At times it seems as if only by lacerating the State of Israel can they overcome their own social marginality, intellectual mediocrity, or unresolved individual neuroses as Jews. As highly-prized anti-Zionists they can enjoy the flattering though largely fraudulent status of "heroic dissidence" in the West. Not only that, but anti-Zionism has become the indispensable entry card for any self-respecting "right-thinking" man or woman of the Left, especially if they are of the Jewish persuasion. Armed with such *bona fides* one can speedily acquire (especially in Europe and on American campuses) the (unmerited) status of being a "good Jew" in the Hebrew prophetic tradition. Some radical Israeli academics have eagerly jumped on this seductive bandwagon.

The anti-Zionism espoused by left-wing Jews has long been couched in a peculiarly vitriolic language, especially when directed against co-religionists from the right of the political spectrum. This was already true before the Holocaust. Thus the radical Jewish journalist, William Zukerman, writing in 1937, attacked the immigrant Polish Jewish middle class in Palestine for "transplanting the ghetto" to the Middle East and creating "its own fascist party, with Brown Shirts, Storm Troops, and all the paraphernalia of Fascism." He venomously castigated the right-wing Zionist followers of Vladimir Zeev Jabotinsky for opposing the Palestinian Jewish labor movement "in the best Nazi manner." Zukerman lashed out against what he termed the unrestrained militarism, anti-Arab racism, narrow fanaticism, and nationalist zealotry of Jabotinsky's supporters.[53] On the other hand, Zukerman (*unlike* his left-wing heirs today) did at least recognize that "the majority of Palestine Arabs are now under the influence of fascist leaders compared with whom the Zionist-Revisionists are moderates and liberals." He readily acknowledged "that practically the entire Arab world outside

Palestine has perceived an enmity for all Jews the world over."[54] Arabs, he observed, had been poisoned in the 1930s by European-style Jew-hatred, which cynically exploited their fears that they would lose Palestine to the Zionists.

Zukerman was certainly more honest than most of his leftist contemporaries in admitting that fascist and Nazi influences had penetrated deeply into the Arab world. He knew that the Third Reich aroused great enthusiasm among pan-Arab and Islamic fundamentalist leaders in the Middle East. They were dazzled by Hitler's nationalist fervor, as well as his opposition to British and French colonial hegemony. They genuinely admired the militarism, order, discipline, and aura of power exuded by the German Nazis.[55] As the former Syrian Baathist leader, Sami al-Jundi recalled in his memoirs, a whole generation of pan-Arab nationalists in Damascus were fascinated by Nazism and strongly impressed by Hitler's *Mein Kampf*.[56] In Iraq, this influence was especially powerful in the late 1930s, with the nationalist press hailing Nazi Germany as the Arabs' patron in the struggle against Great Britain and World Jewry. The arrival of the Palestinian leader, Haj Amin el-Husseini (himself a genocidal antisemite), in Iraq shortly after the outbreak of the Second World War, further exacerbated an already tense situation, encouraging an increasingly fanatical antisemitism.[57] The immediate consequence was the devastating pogrom against the Jews of Baghdad that followed the overturning of the pro-Nazi regime of Rashid Ali al-Gailani in Iraq (1–2 June 1941). Several hundred Jews were killed, many more wounded, hundreds of houses destroyed, and many Jewish business premises ransacked.[58] This happened several years *before* the creation of the State of Israel and it would set the stage for the state-organized expropriation and expulsion of Iraqi Jewry a decade later.

Iraqi nationalists considered the horrific massacre (*Farhūd*) of 1941 to be the just revenge of the Muslim majority against the Jews of Iraq. In reality, the pogrom was a wholly unprovoked and brutal assault on an unarmed, innocent and well-integrated minority who had faithfully served Iraq.[59] The role of Nazi propaganda, Arab nationalist incitement, and of the Palestinian exiles (who constantly vilified Iraqi Jews as a "fifth column" of the British and Zionists) in whipping up a mood of religious and nationalist incitement was decisive in bringing about the *Farhūd*. This event (and others like it) has been airbrushed out of the pro-Palestinian anti-Zionist narrative of the Western Left. If the *Farhūd* is evoked, it is merely in order to pretend that Muslims were the chief victims of the pogrom or that they sprang to the defence of their Jewish neighbors. But mostly the events in Iraq remain a taboo subject much like Haj Amin's Palestinian antisemitism and his uncontestable ideological affinities with the German Nazis.[60] Indeed, the entire topic of Muslim antisemitism—crucial for understanding Israeli and Arab perceptions of the Middle East conflict—is rarely discussed or else is treated in a propagandist, apologetic, or trivializing manner. The result is a massive distortion of the causes of the Arab-Israeli confrontation as well as the omission of a vitally important element in understanding the clash between radical Islam and the West.

Much the same applies to the forced exodus of Sephardic or "Oriental" Jews from Arab lands in the Middle East.[61] In 1945 there were approximately a million Jews in Muslim countries, including North Africa. As a result of Arab persecution, pogroms, and harassment, a majority of these Middle Eastern Jews were driven to seek refuge in the newly created State of Israel where they would enjoy full political rights and the prospect of socio-economic mobility for the first time as a group. In the Arab world the Jewish communities could not possibly survive the rise of a militant Arab nationalism with strong Islamic overtones. As Norman Stillman put it:

> It made little difference whether Jews abjectly mouthed the Arab anti-Zionist line as in Syria, donated generous sums of money to the Palestinian cause as in Iraq, publicly proclaimed their loyalty as in Egypt, openly declared their allegiance as in Tunisia and Libya, or completely identified themselves with a colonial power as in Algeria. In the end they all shared a similar fate and chose to emigrate or flee from the lands of their birth.[62]

This forced mass exodus of Jews from Arab lands after 1945 has been erased by those left-wing ideologues who brand Zionism with the stigma of being a *Western* colonialist movement. While endlessly evoking the "injustice" towards the Palestinian Arabs, they studiously *ignore* the ethnic cleansing of Middle Eastern Jews from Arab states.

Post-1945 Zionism is as much a Middle Eastern as a European phenomenon. It is no less a product of the Muslim intolerance towards non-Muslims than it is of Christian or Nazi persecution of the Jews.[63] Along with the Russian pogroms and the Nazi mass murder, the mob assaults of Arabs against "Oriental" Jews contributed a great deal to forging the "Zionist" consciousness of what is today half of the Israeli Jewish population. This is the deliberately suppressed reality that many liberals and leftists—with their guilt-complex about Western colonialism and their ambivalence towards Jews—are unable to deal with. They invariably repeat the Arab mantra that *European* Zionism is the root of all evil, *the* factor which upset a pastoral (though largely fictitious) Arab-Jewish harmony in the Middle East. To the extent that the presence and the real-life experiences of Middle Eastern Jews are ever acknowledged by European liberals or leftists, they are insultingly patronized as passive objects or duped "victims" of a Western colonialist and Zionist ideology. This condescending assumption completely sidesteps the deeply-rooted attachment of Sephardic and Oriental Jews to the Land of Israel. It also ignores the humiliation suffered by Middle Eastern Jews at the hands of Arab and Muslim rulers over many centuries.

In whitewashing this record, Western Marxists even ignore Marx's own journalistic writings on the misery and wretchedness inflicted upon the Jews of mid-19th-century Jerusalem by Ottoman Muslims.[64] Marx had few illusions about the religious fanaticism of the East or the tyranny of "Oriental despotism." The contemporary Left has also forgotten that the first Zionists came as agricultural immigrants at the end of the 19th century to what was a very neglected province of the Ottoman Empire, fleeing from persecution and pogroms in Russia and Eastern Europe. They came not as "colonial settlers" but to work and plow areas which were largely wasteland, to drain swamps and marshes, to forest the dunes, and water the desert. Today such reminders are treated derisively as nothing but Zionist propaganda. But the fact remains that Jewish pioneers bought land in Palestine at extortionately high prices, reclaiming it through back-breaking labor in order to make it cultivable. The money for purchasing this land—mainly bought from absentee Arab landowners—did not come from wealthy Jewish capitalists or "colonialist" agencies.[65] It was acquired by the Jewish National Fund, whose capital emanated from millions of petty Jewish artisans, shopkeepers, workers, and professional people living in Central and Eastern Europe. The Zionist colonization of Palestine was the *antithesis* of a "colonialist" enterprise. It deliberately sought to *avoid* the capitalist exploitation of indigenous labor and the acquisition of private property. The unique social vision behind the activities of the early Zionist pioneers (*halutzim*) who came to Palestine lay in their will to create a new society and a new man inspired by constructivist revolutionary ideals. To quote the Israeli political scientist Shlomo Avineri:

> The typical *halutz* was a young middle-class Jew, usually quite well-educated for the circumstances of his age and society, who in going to Palestine turned his back both on the Diaspora and on bourgeois society, and set out to find personal and communal redemption by becoming a worker or peasant.[66]

Nothing could have been further removed from the typical attitudes of white colonial settlers in Africa and Asia, than the mind-set of East European and Russian Jews arriving in Palestine in the first half of the 20th century. They were in revolt against all the social and national conventions of their time. In their own minds, they had returned to Palestine to restore a lost homeland for a scattered people, to redeem themselves and the Jewish nation through manual labor. In the *kibbutzim,* these Jewish settlers sowed the seed of a *socialist* (not a colonialist) society, based on the common ownership of the soil, economic equality, and the abolition of wage-labor. The labor movement within the Zionist enterprise (which dominated Israeli politics until 1977) looked to the development of a self-sustaining peasantry and working-class as the most important social base of a renascent nation.[67] The demographic, economic, and political changes in Israel since 1967 do not alter these historical facts. Nor does the current collapse of the Israeli Labour Party alter the seminal role in Zionist colonization which it played. It is revealing that before 1945, Jewish immigration to Palestine, far from being perceived as "imperialist," was labeled as "subversive" by the traditionalist Arab leadership. They themselves regarded the Zionists as dangerous "Bolsheviks" rather than "Western" colonialists. At a popular level, there was also a more general Arab backlash against the *modernization* of Palestine, fear of the erosion of traditional customs through the incursion of a highly literate, mobile Jewish population with a different culture, life-style, and social attitudes. It was precisely the democratic, socialist, and *egalitarian* character of the predominantly Russian Jewish immigration after 1905 which had alarmed the Palestinian Arabs most of all—already under Ottoman Turkish rule.[68] Following the Third Aliyah after the 1917 Bolshevik Revolution, this anxiety greatly intensified. Not by accident, anti-Communism became a central plank in the anti-Zionist and antisemitic agitation of Haj Amin el-Husseini (the undisputed leader of the Palestinian Arab national movement) in the interwar years.

Anti-Zionist ideologues of the Right and Left have either rubbed out or demonized this history just as they ignore Zionist readiness to compromise over the British partition plan of 1937 and the U.N. partition of 1947. The pro-Palestinian narrative disregards the fact that it was Arab leaders who unilaterally insisted that Palestine must be an *Arab state in its entirety.* It glosses over the failure of the Palestinian Arabs to capitalize on the progressive whittling-away of the British commitment to the Jewish National Home in Palestine after 1917. The British White Paper of 1939 (a virtual death-sentence on European Jewry once other avenues of escape were blocked) gave the Palestinians a future veto against Jewish immigration, which would have throttled the entire Zionist enterprise. Great Britain had broken most of its promises to the Zionists well before then. Indeed, from the outset it tended to favor the local Arab elites over the Jewish settlers. In 1922 it had rewarded its Hashemite Arab allies by arbitrarily severing Transjordan from the Palestine Mandate, in order to establish a throne for the Emir Abdullah. The ultimate British betrayal of Zionism would come after 1945 with the advent of a Labour Government under Attlee and Bevin, which managed to combine together the uglier traditions of British Imperial *Realpolitik,* an irrational anti-Zionism, and a nasty strand of antisemitism.[69]

The traditional antipathy of the British Foreign Office to Israel—like that of many other Great Powers—was not disconnected from the Jewish State's lack of any natural resources of great economic value to offer to the major capitalist powers. For precisely this reason Saudi Arabia, Iraq, Libya, and the Gulf oil-producing Arab States have always been far more important to the West than Israel—a critical point often buried in discussions of Palestine. So, too, for economic and geo-political reasons, the Arab world would be assiduously courted by the Soviet Union after 1955, which soon established its military influence and found allies in key Arab countries like Egypt, Iraq, and Syria. A mixture of economic and political interests also prompted France to reverse its earlier pro-Israel policy in favour of close collaboration with the Arabs.[70] De Gaulle's pro-Arab policy after 1967 was an essential part of his strategy to establish French influence in the Third World as a counterweight to American hegemony. Nevertheless left-wing anti-Zionist mythology barely addresses this consistent Great Power support for the Arab world, while vastly exaggerating its much more modest help to Israel. There is an ever-mushrooming literature about all-powerful "Jewish" lobbies and imaginary networks of "Zionist" financial, banking, and capitalist interests which back Israel. But remarkably little has been written about the Saudi lobby in the United States or the very tangible Arab oil interests that influence international money-markets and the economies of the free world. This is all the more striking since major oil producers like Saudi Arabia, Iraq, or Iran have at times nurtured or bankrolled terrorist movements, jihadism, and Islamic fundamentalisms around the world. The Arab "lobby" appears, however, to be of minimal interest to left-wing conspiracy theorists.[71]

The success of tiny Israel as a thriving Western-style democracy and high-tech economy in an ocean of brutal Arab dictatorships has plainly been intolerable to the radical Left. Arab "socialism" produced only a grim blacklist of despicable tyrannies, repression, ethnic conflicts, religious hatreds, and genocide. To acknowledge this contrast would be to underline the bankruptcy of a post-colonial world-view built on the Manichean polarization between the vices of Western capitalism and the superior "virtues" of backward, non-Western peoples. Instead, Third World "liberation movements" like the PLO have invariably been seen by the post-colonial Left as absolute *victims* of America and Israel—countries who supposedly embody the inherently "Western" sins of greed, aggression, and racism.

In this context it is revealing that Palestinian national and fundamentalist movements like Fatah or Hamas which represent nothing socially "progressive" enjoy such unquestioning support by the contemporary Left. It is as if almost any movement of vehement protest against America and Israel can be presented as a desirable ally for the post-modern Left.[72] Not only that, but even the Arab-Muslim holy war against the Jewish State, which denies its right to exist becomes fully acceptable. The vile language used today by most of the radical Left against the "Nazi-apartheid State" of Israel and the fantasies concerning imaginary Jewish "cabals" in America and Britain clearly reflect the increasingly antisemitic trend within pro-Palestinian circles.

We have moved a long way from the days of a de facto alliance of the Left and the Jews in the 1930s against the rising tide of fascism. Even then, there was more than a tinge of leftist antisemitism in the air, especially in European pacifist circles. Nevertheless, until the early 1970s what might be loosely and ironically described as "progressive mankind" had not yet turned its back on Israel or Zionism. It was only after the New Left project began to slowly fragment into several disparate semi-ideologies that the scene was set for the heterogeneous anti-Zionisms of our own day. Third Worldism, feminism, the Green movement, Black Power, and various countercultural trends of the 1970s have all contributed to this centrifugal process on the Left which accelerated still further following the collapse of the broader Marxist revolutionary project after 1989. A revamped and eclectic ideology of Human Rights, mixed with transnational "progressivism," post-national cosmopolitanism, and a new type of identity politics stepped into the vacuum left by the "bankruptcy of Marxism."[73] Anti-Americanism together with anti-globalization (sentiments shared by much of the far Right) coalesced with anti-Zionism to generate a morally relativist and *nihilist* version of leftism—viscerally hostile to the world as it is. Anthony Julius has called this kind of contemporary left-wing anti-Zionism a *boutique movement* in which the cause of Palestine appears to many militants as a worthy successor to the decomposing "fight for socialism."[74] Unrelated to any large-scale project of human liberation, such a cause seems intrinsically more vulnerable to flirting with Jew-hatred.

The constant charges of Israeli "war crimes," "human rights violations," or infringements of international law, provide a broad liberal support for the pro-Palestinian narrative that Israel is solely to blame for the continuing conflict in the Middle East. By completely erasing the jihad (holy war) and Palestinian intransigence from the picture, no further analysis is required, let alone any fair-minded or cogent peace strategy for the Left. Anti-Zionism serves here as an *ersatz*—a substitute religion as well as a magnet for all the post-1989 Marxist debris—the orphaned causes of what Bernard-Henri Lévy picturesquely described as "all these dark little stars fallen from doctrinaire galaxies."[75] The anti-Zionist amalgams of the New Age seem to curiously resemble antisemitism in their tasteless blending of moralizing hysteria, emotional indignation at unproven Jewish "crimes" and their intellectual confusion. At times it even appears that the very existence of Israel has itself become "a crime against the Left."[76] A real peace in the Middle East metamorphoses into an imagined peace "without Israel"—the kind of *liquidationist* position more openly and brutally espoused by Iran, Hezbollah, Hamas, and some parts of Fatah. This has not prevented some Trotskyists and anarchists in Britain, for example, from manifesting an unquenchable enthusiasm for finding common ground with the Islamists.[77] Distinctions between Islam and secularism, jihad and class-war, tend to collapse in the name of revolutionary solidarity against America and Israel. On the extreme Right, too, despite the xenophobia towards Muslim immigrants, there is an unmistakeable tinge of admiration for radical Islamist violence against a decadent and "judaized" West.

The denial or playing down of antisemitism have become almost *de rigueur* on the anti-Zionist Left even when it is invoking conspiracy theories in its own defense against such charges. Thus, Jew-hatred is dismissed as an "invention" or cynical ploy by the Israeli Government in order to try and immunize itself against any criticism of its policies towards the Palestinians. According to such an iconic figure of the British Trotskyist Left as the Pakistani-born activist Tariq Ali, antisemitism today is no more of a threat to Jews than Arabs or Muslims represent any danger to Israel.[78] This is, of course, an insult to the intelligence. So, too, is the effort by many contemporary leftist commentators in the West to dismiss the *genocidal* antisemitism emanating from President Ahmadinejad's Iran or from the Palestinian Hamas as if it were mere rhetoric. Such obfuscation has now become one of the defining traits in the more general Western appeasement of Islamism. Some, like the British journalist Jonathan Cook, go further still. According to his analysis it is Israel that is deliberately creating and promoting the "new" antisemitism, just as it is presumed to have encouraged the "Clash of Civilizations." According to such cynical conspiracy theories, Israel's role is not merely to stifle any criticism of itself or to incriminate Muslims; more importantly, the Jewish State desperately needs antisemitism as a *marketing strategy*—in order to encourage *aliyah* and make its case to a sceptical Diaspora.[79]

The derision and contempt towards Israel and the Jews contained in such discourse is by no means confined to the Left. The false analogies, misleading amalgams, and Orwellian doublespeak that long ago replaced reasoned thought in the anti-Zionist camp can be found right across the political spectrum. For example, the unceasing attempts to equate Zionism with racism, colonialism, ethnic cleansing, apartheid, or Nazism belong to a more general and pervasive pollution of the contemporary political vocabulary. On the Left, however, such trends are more hypocritical precisely because their language is ostentatiously "anti-racist" and directed at the State of Israel in the name of "human rights." The "humanitarian" perspective is all the more jarring when combined with the use of a peculiarly aggressive, stigmatizing and dehumanizing vocabulary against the Jewish State.[80] Such a discourse in the media, on-line, in the universities, and in public life more generally, has already had an undeniably damaging effect. It usually involves the feverish recycling of antisemitic stereotypes, continued resolutions to boycott Israel (especially by trade unions and left-wing academics), endless excuses for Palestinian terrorism, and the harassment of pro-Israel students on university campuses.[81] The intention, as in the South African apartheid analogy, is to completely isolate Israel within the international community as an illegitimate or pariah State.[82] The methodology—defamation, double standards, and relentless boycott resolutions—recalls the more noxious and time-honored techniques of classic antisemitism. The vilification of "Zionism" by many contemporary Leftists is indeed all-too-reminiscent of the execrations of "the Jews" (or "the Jew" per se) in the 1930s. In such cases the desire is not merely to wound with words but to negate, to efface and to *symbolically* wipe out the adversary—a necessary prelude to his future physical annihilation.

Despite vehement denials by its practitioners to the contrary, the entire Jewish people is ultimately targeted by this negationist anti-Zionist ideology and practice. Zionism, after all, is a *Jewish* national movement, and Israel from its inception has been a Jewish State. Some left-wing anti-Zionists may perhaps still differentiate between "good" (universalist) and "bad" (particularist) Jews, but this is an empty distinction within the broader Middle

Eastern environment where radical anti-Zionism seeks the total eradication of Israel as a collective Jewish entity. What is crucial here is that the current negation of Jewish national identity is no less *discriminatory* than earlier forms of anti-Judaic hostility directed against Jews as a religious, "racial," or social group. By denying to the Jews of Israel or the Diaspora the elementary freedom to define themselves as a group on their own terms, to enjoy their inalienable right to full self-determination and *political* independence, the anti-Zionist Left is in fact guilty of betraying core principles of liberty, equality, and fraternity. Worse still, it is trying to turn the clock back to the dark days shortly before the Holocaust and Israel's creation, when Jews were chronically divided, dispersed, disorganized, partly ghettoized, stateless, and ultimately powerless to determine their fate. The results of that tragically anomalous status in which Jews were at the mercy of predatory imperialist states were cataclysmic and devastating. Anti-Zionism, like anti-Judaism and antisemitism which preceded it, is beginning to acquire the same toxic aura of bullying paranoia as Israel is pilloried in international forums and treated as if it were a leper among the nations.[83] The continued complicity of the contemporary Left, including some of its more prominent intellectuals, in such a degrading witch-hunt, is one of the more abject spectacles of our time.

Notes

1. See Georges-Elia Sarfati, *L'Antisionisme. Israël/Palestine aux miroirs d'Occident* (Paris, 2002).

2. Lucy Dawidowicz, *The War against the Jews, 1933–45* (London, 1983).

3. Robert S. Wistrich, *A Lethal Obsession. Anti-Semitism from Antiquity to the Global Jihad* (New York, 2010).

4. Pierre-André Taguieff, *La Judéophobie des Modernes* (Paris, 2008), 353–406.

5. Bernard Lewis, *Semites and Anti-Semites. An Inquiry into Conflict and Prejudice* (New York, 1986); Yossef Bodansky, *Antishemiut Islamit Ke-Machshir Politi* (Tel Aviv, 1988); and Robert S. Wistrich, *Antisemitism. The Longest Hatred* (New York, 1994), 195–268.

6. See Robert S. Wistrich, *The Politics of Ressentiment: Israel, Jews and the German Media* (ACTA Series, no. 23, Vidal Sassoon Center for the Study of Antisemitism, The Hebrew University of Jerusalem, 2004).

7. Wistrich, *A Lethal Obsession,* 279–81.

8. Alain Finkielkraut, *Au Nom de l'Autre. Réflexions sur l'antisémitisme qui vient* (Paris, 2003).

9. Taguieff, *La Judéophobie,* 407–24.

10. Robert S. Wistrich, *The Myth of Zionist Racism* (London, 1976), 12–14; also Lenni Brenner, *Zionism in the Age of the Dictators* (New York, 1983), 1–25.

11. See, for example, the views of Roger Garaudy—a French pro-Islamic ex-Marxist, in his *The Case of Israel. A Study of Political Zionism* (London, 1983), 89–122.

12. John G. Gager, *The Origins of Anti-Semitism: Attitudes Towards Judaism in Pagan and Christian Antiquity* (Oxford, 1985); also Peter Schäfer, *Judeophobia: Attitudes towards the Jews in the Ancient World* (Cambridge, Mass., 1997).

13. Jeffrey Herf, *Nazi Propaganda for the Arab World* (New Haven, 2009), 179–93; also Klaus Gensicke, *The Mufti of Jerusalem and the Nazis: The Berlin Years* (London, 2010).

14. Robert Wistrich, *Anti-Zionism as an Expression of Anti-Semitism in Recent Years* (Jerusalem: Study Circle of the President of Israel, 1985).

15. These claims have been more recently revived (in the most unconvincing fashion) by Shlomo Sand, *The Invention of the Jewish People* (London, 2009)—a fairly representative product of post-Zionist left-wing Israeli academia. Typically, for our time, such shallow works are enthusiastically received by the compact anti-Israel majority abroad and taken seriously even in Israel.

16. See Gideon Shimoni, *The Zionist Ideology* (Hanover, 1995), 333–88.

17. John Loftus and Mark Aarons, *The Secret War against the Jews* (New York, 1994), 219–58.

18. Conor Cruise O'Brien, *The Siege. The Saga of Israel and Zionism* (New York, 1986), 400–18; see also Michael B. Oren, *Six Days of War* (New York, 2002).

19. Arnold Krammer, *The Forgotten Friendship: Israel and the Soviet Bloc, 1947–1953* (Urbana, Ill., 1974).

20. *Daily Worker* (London), 29 June 1948.

21. Wistrich, *A Lethal Obsession,* 712.

22. Ibid., 623.

23. See http://www.theatlantic.com/international/archive/2010/09/castro-no-one-has-been-slandered-more-than-the-jews/62566.

24. Ibid.

25. Jeffrey Goldberg, "Fidel Castro and Israel's Right to Exist." See http://www.theatlantic.com/international/archive/2010/09/fidel-castro-and-Israels-right-to-exist/63369. Castro was asked "Do you think the State of Israel, as a Jewish State, has a right to exist?" Fidel Castro answered, "Si, sin ninguna duda"—"Yes, without a doubt."

26. See *The New Republic,* 16 Nov. 1974; also Jillian Becker, *The PLO: The Rise and Fall of the Palestinian Liberation Organization* (London, 1984); and John Laffin, *The PLO Connections* (London, 1982), 85–96.

27. See Bernard Lewis, "The Palestinians and the PLO," *Commentary* (Jan. 1975) for the complete text of the Palestinian National Charter; it is also reproduced by Harris Okun Schoenberg, *A Mandate for Terror. The United Nations and the PLO* (New York, 1989), 467–75.

28. See Schoenberg, *Mandate for Terror,* 470–71. Article 20 of the Covenant describes the Balfour Declaration and the League of Nations Mandate for Palestine as null and void; it insists that "claims of historical or religious ties of Jews with Palestine are incompatible with the facts of history" and contrary to "the true conception of what constitutes statehood." Judaism is merely a religion, not an independent nationality. Finally, the PLO Covenant insists that Jews do not constitute "a single nation with an identity of its own"—a position shared by the anti-Zionist Left.

29. Ibid.

30. Y. Harkabi, *The Palestinian Covenant and Its Meaning* (London, 1979).

31. Schoenberg, *Mandate for Terror,* 467 for Article 1.

32. Ibid., 468. Article 6 reads: "The Jews who had normally resided in Palestine until the beginning of the Zionist invasion will be considered Palestinians. Internal discussions in the PLO reveal that 1917 (the year of the Balfour Declaration) was considered the onset of the "Zionist invasion."

33. See "Charter of Allah: The Platform of the Islamic Resistance Movement," 18 Aug. 1988, http://www.palestinecenter.org/cpap/documents/charter.html ; see also Wistrich, *A Lethal Obsession,* 731–62.

34. Ibid., 684–730.

35. Deutscher's text, "The Israeli-Arab War, June 1967," appeared in his *The Non-Jewish Jew and Other Essays* (London, 1968) and can be found in Adam Schatz, ed., *Prophets Outcast* (New York, 2004), 168–86. It was based on an interview he gave to the *New Left Review* on 23 June 1967.

36. Schatz, *Prophets Outcast,* 178.

37. Ibid., 184. Deutscher spoke with disgust of the "displays of the conquerors' pride and brutality," the "wild celebrations of the inglorious triumph," without even reflecting on how things would have looked if Israel had lost the war—which would have led to some indescribable and *real* horrors.

38. Ibid., 185.

39. Ibid., 186.

40. On black American antisemitism and the Jewish response, see J. J. Goldberg, *Jewish Power. Inside the American Jewish Establishment* (New York, 1996), 141–42, 328–31.

41. See Paul Berman, *Blacks and Jews: Alliances and Arguments* (New York, 1994); also Jonathan Kaufman, *The Broken Alliance: The Turbulent Times Between Blacks and Jews in America* (New York, 1988).

42. On this topic, see Mark Weitzman, *Magical Logic: Globalization, Conspiracy Theory and the Shoah* (Posen Papers, no. 10, Vidal Sassoon International Center for the Study of Antisemitism, The Hebrew University of Jerusalem, 2009).

43. Quoted by Rudolf Krämer-Badoni, "Zionism and the New Left," in *The Left against Zion. Communism, Israel and the Middle East,* edited by Robert S. Wistrich (London, 1979), 234–35. According to the *Frankfurter Allgemeine Zeitung* (13 Nov. 1969), the leaflet was signed by "The Black Rats."

44. See Gerd Langguth, "Anti-Israel Extremism in West Germany," in Wistrich, *The Left against Zion,* 257.

45. Ibid.

46. Ibid., 257–58; see also Ernst Vogt, *Israel—Kritik von Links* (Wuppertal, 1976), a valuable anthology of left-wing German critiques of Israel.

47. Wistrich, *A Lethal Obsession,* 503–6; also Martin Kloke, "Israelkritik und Antizionismus in der deutschen Linken: ehrbarer Antisemitismus," in *Aktueller Antisemitismus—ein Phänomen der Mitte,* edited by Monika Schwarz-Friesel et al. (Berlin, 2010), 73–92.

48. Annie Kriegel, *Israël est-il coupable?* (Paris, 1982), 19–27, 104–12.

49. Robert S. Wistrich, "Some Reflections on Contemporary Antisemitism," *Midstream* (Fall 2009): 18–20.

50. Philipp Gessler, *Der neue Antisemitismus* (Freiburg, 2004), 91–111.

51. Klaus Holz, *Die Gegenwart des Antisemitismus* (Hamburg, 2005), 79–99.

52. See my article "Left-Wing anti-Zionism in Western Societies," in *Anti-Zionism and Antisemitism in the Contemporary World,* edited by Robert S. Wistrich (London, 1990), 46–52.

53. William Zukerman, *The Jew in Revolt* (London, 1937), 151–55, 168–71.

54. Ibid., 166.

55. See Matthias Küntzel, *Jihad and Jew-Hatred, Islamism, Nazism and the Roots of 9/11* (New York, 2007).

56. Wistrich, *A Lethal Obsession,* 676–79.

57. Shmuel Moreh, "The Role of the Palestinian Incitement and the Attitude of Arab Intellectuals to the Farhūd," in *Al-Farhūd. The 1941 Pogrom in Iraq,* edited by Shmuel Moreh and Zvi Yehuda (Jerusalem, 2010), 119–58.

58. Elie Kedourie, "The Sack of Başra and the Farhūd in Baghdad," in *Al-Farhūd,* 83–118.

59. Zvi Yehudah, "The Pogrom of 1941 in the Light of New Sources," in *Al-Farhūd,* 9–25.

60. See Robert S. Wistrich, "Antisemitism: The European and Islamic Legacies," *Antisemitism International,* nos. 5–6 (2010): 144–53.

61. See the valuable scholarly study by Norman A. Stillman, ed., *The Jews of Arab Lands in Modern Times* (New York, 1991); also Bat Ye'or, *The Dhimmi. Jews and Christians under Islam* (London, 1985).

62. Stillman, ed., *The Jews of Arab Lands,* 180.

63. Andrew G. Bostom, *The Legacy of Islamic Antisemitism* (New York, 2008), 663–84.

64. See Shlomo Avineri, ed., *Karl Marx on Colonialism and Modernization* (New York, 1968), 134–43.

65. The classic Marxist view has usually presented Zionism as a form of European colonialism, organically linked to imperialism. See, for example, Maxime Rodinson, *Israel. A Colonial Settler State* (New York, 1973). Rodinson was a French Arabist of Jewish origin and a former member of the French Communist Party who later became an independent Marxist.

66. Shlomo Avineri, "The Palestinians and Israel," *Commentary* (June 1970); and idem, *The Making of Modern Zionism* (New York, 1981).

67. G. Shimoni, *Zionist Ideology,* 166–235.

68. See Jonathan Frankel, *Prophecy and Politics. Socialism, Nationalism and the Russian Jews, 1862–1917* (New York, 1981), 377–452 for the seeds of the conflict.

69. On Bevin's antisemitism, see Richard Crossman, *A Nation Reborn* (London, 1960), 69–72.

70. Paul Balta and Claude Rulleau, *La politique arabe de la France: de De Gaulle à Pompidou* (Paris, 1973).

71. John Mearsheimer and Stephen Walt, "The Israel Lobby," *London Review of Books,* 23 Mar. 2006, virtually ignore the topic in their incredibly simplistic and misleading analysis. See the astute critical comments of Bernard Harrison, *The Resurgence of Anti-Semitism. Jews, Israel, and Liberal Opinion* (Lanham, Md., 2006), 194–203.

72. Harrison, *Resurgence of Anti-Semitism,* 182–92.

73. Anthony Julius, *Trials of the Diaspora. A History of Anti-Semitism in England* (Oxford, 2010), 452–53.

74. Ibid., 455.

75. Bernard-Henri Lévy, *American Vertigo* (New York, 2006), 9.

76. Phyllis Chesler, *The New Anti-Semitism* (San Francisco, 2003), 87.

77. Julius, *Trials of the Diaspora,* 467.

78. Tariq Ali, "Notes on anti-Semitism, Zionism and Palestine," *Counterpunch,* 4 Mar. 2004.

79. Quoted by Julius, *Trials of the Diaspora,* 530.

80. Robert Wistrich, "Some Reflections on Contemporary Antisemitism," 18.

81. See Manfred Gerstenfeld, ed., *Academics Against Israel and the Jews* (Jerusalem, 2007).

82. David Hirsh, *Anti-Zionism and Antisemitism. Cosmopolitan Reflections* (Yale Working Papers Series, 2007).

83. Wistrich, *A Lethal Obsession,* 604–7.

CHAPTER 17

Great Britain: A Suitable Case for Treatment?

The self-congratulatory and somewhat sanitized history of Anglo-Jewry since the mid-17th century "return" of the Jews to Britain traditionally depicted as a triumphal passage from servitude to freedom or from darkness to light. In the spirit of the Passover festival, Great Britain—mother of parliaments, land of religious and civic toleration, cradle of the Industrial Revolution, and possessor of a great overseas empire which protected its minorities—was extending its liberties to the Jewish community which had every reason to love Britain precisely because it is British. So if things have been so good, how come they are so bad? Why are there so many dark clouds building up on the horizon? Why is Anglo-Jewry the only important ethnic or religious minority in contemporary Britain that has to provide a permanent system of guards and surveillance for its communal institutions, schools, synagogues, and cultural centers?

Antisemitism in the British Isles is certainly not a new phenomenon. It has a long history which should surprise only those who naively think of the English as being a uniquely tolerant, fair-minded, and freedom-loving nation. There were periods like the 12th century, as the historian Anthony Julius recently noted, when Anglo-Jews were being injured or murdered without pity or conscience—at times in an atmosphere of public revelry. Over 150 people were killed in March 1190 during the massacre of the Jews of York. This nasty wave of violent persecution (which included the first anti-Jewish blood libels in Christian Europe) culminated in the unceremonious expulsion of Jewry in 1290. This, too, was another starred first for medieval Britain. Nor did popular antisemitism vanish during the succeeding centuries when Jews were physically absent from British shores. It was faithfully preserved in visual art, folklore, mystery plays, the sermons of the clergy, and canonical works of English literature from Geoffrey Chaucer's "Prioress's Tale" in the Middle Ages, through to Shakespeare's *Merchant of Venice* and Charles Dickens' *Oliver Twist*. Stereotypes of Jewish bloodthirstiness, rapacity, petty legalism, cunning, and dishonesty continued to recur well into the 20th century. Literary "modernists" like the politically ultra-conservative T. S. Eliot and the Fabian socialist H. G. Wells were as mistrustful or hostile to Jews in the 20th century as most of their illustrious predecessors before them. Today this genteel (though often deeply unpleasant and insulting) form of antisemitic prejudice "with the boots off" is more often expressed as an implacable antipathy towards the Jewish State. An elite and prestigious fortnightly magazine like the *London Review of Books* (*LRB*), for example, has consistently portrayed Israel for over a decade as a bloodthirsty and genocidal regime, while publishing generally sympathetic portraits of jihadi terrorist and antisemitic organizations like Hamas and Hezbollah. This unswerving hostility to Israel in what is said to be the most widely circulated of European literary magazines is expressed in many ways. Thus Israeli leaders are constantly defamed in the *LRB,* the actions of the Jewish State are relentlessly denigrated and its security concerns almost never acknowledged or else airily dismissed.

Virtually no mainstream Israeli viewpoint has ever been represented in the pages of the *LRB* although more than half of the articles on the subject are actually written by Jews (and more than a third by Jewish Israelis with a marked animus towards their country). As in other liberal-left publications in Great Britain, this strong presence of Jewish anti-Zionists and Israeli "post-Zionists" provides the perfect alibi against charges of antisemitism, even while feeding the sickness itself with repulsive images of Israel's alleged "war-crimes."

The three-week Israel-Hamas conflict in Gaza that ended in January 2009 provided a plethora of opportunities for many other Britons—especially on the Left and among local Muslims—to vent their spleens. The far Left anti-Israel activist and former MP, George Galloway, publicly expressed at a demonstration in 2009 a widely-held but ludicrously misleading British view of Gaza as a modern-day concentration camp. "Today the people in Gaza are the new Warsaw Ghetto, and those who are murdering them are the equivalent of those who murdered the Jews in Warsaw."[1] In other words, the Israelis are all-powerful Nazis and Palestinians are the powerless "Jews." Such stereotypical depictions, constantly reinforced by the media, have been central to the revival of anti-Jewish sentiments in contemporary Britain. They take full advantage of the heavily pejorative connotations currently attached to the word "Zionism." Moreover, through bodies like the Palestine Solidarity Campaign (PSC) which specializes in demonizing and isolating Israel, the anti-Zionist movement to boycott Israel (economically, academically, and culturally) has been able to acquire considerable momentum. This swelling tide of anti-Zionism with its built-in hysteria, deception and distortions is not only reminiscent of earlier waves of pre-Shoah antisemitism but contributes to its resurgence. One result has been to transform the Jewish State into a leper among the nations in the eyes of many British (and West European) intellectuals. At best Israel is depicted in this hateful discourse as an intolerable anachronism; more often as a racist colonizing implant and "apartheid State" in the Middle East, or in some cases as a contemporary reincarnation of Nazi Germany. Not surprisingly, in such a relentlessly hostile atmosphere, antisemitic incidents are rising significantly in Great Britain.[2]

According to the annual report of the Community Security Trust (CST), which tracks antisemitic incidents in Britain, 2009 was indeed the worst year of antisemitic violence, vandalism, and harassment since it began keeping statistics in 1984. Between January and June 2009, 303 antisemitic incidents were recorded in London, and 143 in Manchester—the two largest Jewish communities in the British Isles. In January 2009 alone, there were 286 incidents reported—an all-time statistical peak in antisemitism for Great Britain. During the first six months of 2009, no less than 609 instances of antisemitism were recorded by the CST. This was all the more shocking since the previous *annual* high had been 598 antisemitic incidents in 2006.[3]

Yet Britain is unusual not simply in the frequency and severity of antisemitic incidents. Many other European countries have come to associate antisemitism with the forces of the extreme Right, the radical Left, or the increasingly vocal Muslim minorities. In Britain, however, antisemitic sentiment is also a part of *mainstream* discourse, continually resurfacing among the academic, political, and media elites.[4] Matters have reached a point where anti-Zionism or hostility to Israel (and as a consequence, to Jews) enjoy greater tolerance in public life, than in most countries of Western Europe. While the French state, for example, has in recent years marshaled its resources to fighting antisemitic words and actions, in Britain the response before 2006 was far less decisive. Public condemnations of antisemitism were rarely supported by institutional or government sanction.[5] This only began to change after the publication of the British All-Party Parliamentary Inquiry into Anti-Semitism in 2006 initiated by Labour MP John Mann. It was the first time in the postwar era that British political leaders had recognized the gravity of the problem.

There are several possible explanations for the unusual quarter that antisemitism in Britain currently enjoys.[6] Whereas the efforts to combat antisemitism in France, Germany, or Poland are intimately connected with the memory of the Holocaust that took place on their soil, Britain has never had to undergo a similar kind of soul-searching. Moreover, Britain in recent years has become the hub of an assault on Israel's legitimacy based on Arab and Islamist ideology but coordinated primarily by the political Left. London has indeed become a world center for the propagation of Muslim antisemitism and the demonization of Jews (and especially of Israel) that accompanies it. Already in September 2003, columnist Melanie Phillips (partly in response to these trends) could write with some anguish:

> It is not an exaggeration to say that in Britain at present it is open season on both Israel and the Jews. . . . I no longer feel comfortable in my own country because of the poison that has welled up toward...the Jews.[7]

Seven years later, hating Israel had even become a valid criminal defense. A jury acquitted five people who had vandalized an arms factory in Brighton on the grounds that it did business with the Israeli Army. Incredibly, the judge George Bathurst-Norman had instructed the jury that Gaza was a hell on earth (for which Israel was held exclusively responsible) thereby almost licensing the actions of the accused in breaking the law.

To understand the peculiar nature of British antisemitism, and the alarming degree of legitimacy it currently enjoys in public discourse, it is important to recognize some of its deeper roots in more recent British history. While it is true that, unlike Germany, Austria, France, Russia, Romania, or Poland, Britain did not become a major stronghold of antisemitism in the modern era, its liberal democratic tradition has nonetheless been far more ambivalent toward Jews than is often assumed.[8] This was already apparent following the immigration of Jews from Eastern Europe after 1881. The population of Anglo-Jewry rose from 65,000 in 1880 to 300,000 by 1914, of whom two-thirds settled in London.[9] These predominantly Russian immigrants were at times the target of malevolent antisemitic incitement; they were seen—especially by conservatives—as breeders of anarchism, socialism, and other subversive doctrines. The 1905 Aliens Act, intended to restrict further waves of Jewish immigration, reflected this tense climate of opinion, which also found strong echoes in the British labor movement. It should be remembered that only a few years earlier, during the Boer War (1899–1902), a left-wing, populist antisemitism had erupted in Britain. It demonized wealthy Jewish capitalists and greedy financiers for having "engineered" a crooked imperialist war to seize the gold-rich Transvaal in order to advance the hidden agenda of world Jewry. Through their presumed control of the British press and high finance, a "golden international" of Jews was said to be "poisoning the wells of public information."[10] Prominent figures on the British Left including Labour MP John Burns and various trade union leaders, as well as Britain's leading Marxist, Henry Hyndman, attacked the sinister conspiracy of foreign "cosmopolitan" Jews (of German origin) who had clandestinely seized control of British foreign policy, recklessly dragging the Empire into its disastrous South African adventure.

Twenty years later, however, Jews in Britain came to be associated as much with communism as with capitalism. The Bolshevik Revolution of November 1917 exacerbated broad fears of a world revolutionary upheaval instigated by Russian Jews—purportedly engaged in a conspiracy against England.[11] This was the murky background to the popularity that the *Protocols of the Elders of Zion* initially attained in post-1918 Britain.[12] In the aftermath of World War I, and with the establishment by the League of Nations of a British Mandate for Palestine, anti-Jewish feelings found yet another trigger. The right-wing *Morning Post,* for example, exhibited extreme hostility to Zionism, perceived as being engaged in a broad Jewish conspiracy to achieve world domination. Even the London *Times* was concerned at this prospect. Jews were portrayed in the early 1920s by anti-Zionists in Britain as expropriating the Palestine Arabs' land under the protective cover of British bayonets and at the expense of British taxpayers. Anti-Zionism and antisemitism became an integral part of the rhetoric used by right-wing newspapers against the liberal Lloyd George government and British rule in Palestine. But it was also present in a more subtle form in the writings of such prominent British socialists as H. G. Wells, who loathed all forms of Jewish religious, cultural, and national particularism. Wells even blamed Hitlerism on the Jewish "refusal to assimilate" (a grotesque misperception) while sharply attacking Zionism as an irrational form of nationalism.[13]

With the emergence of Oswald Mosley and his British Union of Fascists in the 1930s, a new antisemitic motif rose to the surface—one that still carries a decidedly contemporary resonance. Jews were accused of trying to drag Britain into an unnecessary war with Nazi Germany.[14] Mosley, originally a man of the Left, called for the preservation of the British Empire and for "peace with honor," while directing anti-capitalist populist appeals to lower-class antisemitic sentiment, which was especially pervasive in London's East End. The residues of his Blackshirt campaigns carried through into World War II, making the British government feel that it had to continually demonstrate that it was *not* fighting a "Jewish war." During World War II, an obsessive fear of "fifth columns" and "enemy aliens" existed in Britain, alongside a perceived linkage of Jews with black-marketeering, spying, and subversion.[15] This undercurrent of antisemitism, linked to anti-Zionism, probably contributed to Britain's refusal after 1939 to undertake any serious effort to save European Jewry from the Nazis. It also helps to explain why Prime Minister Winston Churchill almost never used his powerful position during World War II to concretely help the Zionists or indeed the Jews of Europe. The notorious White Paper policy of the British Government which had virtually blocked Jewish immigration to Palestine from 1939 until the foundation of Israel, was never lifted by Churchill. Nor was British officialdom seriously interested in rescue schemes proposed during World War II if it meant that Jewish survivors might reach Palestine. This inhuman policy reached its climax with the advent of a Labour government in Britain in 1945.

Despite the Holocaust, antisemitic attitudes had, if anything, grown worse in official and Army circles, even resonating at the highest levels of the British government. The first American ambassador to Israel, James G. McDonald, writing in his diary on 3 August 1948, was aghast at the "blazing hatred" of Labour's Foreign Secretary Ernest Bevin for "the Jews, the Israelis, the Israeli government" as well as for the new U.S. president Harry S. Truman.[16] Richard Crossman, a young Labour MP who knew Bevin intimately, concluded in 1947 that British policy in Palestine was excessively influenced by "one man's determination to teach the Jews a lesson."[17] Ernest Bevin had been General Secretary of the Transport and General Workers Union between 1922 and 1940. In 1945, as Foreign Secretary, he favored the *repatriation* of Jewish refugees already in Britain. He was as opposed to Holocaust survivors being admitted into Britain (only 5,000 were allowed into the country between 1945 and 1948) as he was to their going to Palestine. At a time when postwar Socialist Britain was suffering an acute labor shortage, the Attlee government issued more than half a million work permits (including to war criminals and East European Nazi collaborators) but acted mercilessly towards Jewish DPs in postwar Europe. Bevin publicly warned the Holocaust survivors not to get too much "to the head of the queue." He reinforced the British naval blockade of Palestine against "illegal" Jewish immigration and had the desperate Jews who ignored it herded into congested barbed wire camps in Cyprus or sent back to Germany. According to Crossman, the obstinate refusal of Palestinian Jewry to conform to British plans for them tipped the former trades union leader Bevin over into "overt anti-Semitism." The Labour foreign secretary was by now convinced that "the Jews were organizing a world conspiracy against poor old Britain" in which the Zionists, together with the Soviet Union, would seek to bring down the British Empire.[18] The last British High Commissioner for Palestine, General Sir Alan Cunningham, also took a very dim view of Zionism as a Nazi-like nationalist movement which (accompanied by the "abnormal psychology of the Jew") had produced something perverse and unresponsive to rational treatment.

Jewish resistance to British rule in Palestine in the summer of 1947 soon triggered anti-Jewish riots at home. They erupted after the hanging of two British sergeants by the Irgun. But this cruel act did not occur in a vacuum. It came in retaliation for the execution of Dov Gruner, an Irgun member, by the British authorities. Nevertheless, British public reaction to the events in Palestine was violent. On 1 August 1947, mobs of youths rampaged through Jewish districts in Liverpool, Manchester, Glasgow, East London, and other cities. Jewish property was looted, synagogues attacked, and cemeteries desecrated.[19] Palestine—not for the first or last time—had become a catalyst for British hostility to Jews.

A striking example of the ways in which anti-Zionism could merge with antisemitism can be found in the person of the conservative John Bagot Glubb, the British supreme commander of the Jordanian Arab Legion which fought against Israel in 1948. This Arabophile Englishman regarded the creation of Israel as an unforgivable crime. Glubb was an unabashed antisemite, who firmly believed that the "unlikable character" of the Jews had provoked their persecution throughout history; that most Russian and East European Jews were really Khazar Turks with no connection to the promised land—a discredited theory now revived by left-wing Israeli anti-Zionists like the historian Shlomo Sand. Glubb Pasha also believed that the Jews were by nature aggressive and stiff-necked; and that the "vengeful" mentality of the Jewish people had been "passed down without a break from generation to generation."[20] Since biblical times, Jews had allegedly been indoctrinated with "the idea of a superior race," whose blood must not be contaminated "by inter-mixture with others." According to Glubb, not only did Jews invent the idea of the "master race," but their behavior towards Arabs had been driven from the outset by Hitlerian ruthlessness.[21]

In a secret July 1946 memorandum to London, Glubb described the new Jews in Palestine as fusing the ancient, hateful Hebrew tradition with "a layer of up-to-date Eastern European fanaticism." He asserted, without any evidence, that they had copied Nazi techniques—embracing "the theories of race, blood and soil, the terrorism of the gunmen, the inculcation of hate into the young, and the youth movements." The young Sabra Jew of Palestine,

Glubb concluded, was "as hard, as narrow, as fanatical, and as bitter as the Hitler youth on whom he is modeled."[22] At least four decades before it became fashionable to do so on the British Left, General Glubb Pasha was busy defaming Zionism as a combination of "Judaism and Nazism."

The intellectual pioneer in the 1950s of the idea that Zionism is a form of Nazism was, however, another eminent member of the British establishment, the renowned philosopher of history Arnold J. Toynbee. His monumental *A Study in History* unequivocally and relentlessly indicted the Zionists as "disciples of the Nazis." According to Toynbee, they had even chosen "to imitate some of the evil deeds that the Nazis had committed against the Jews."[23] Completely ignoring the Arab determination to strangle the infant State of Israel at birth, Toynbee suggested that Jews had gratuitously murdered and expelled peaceful Arabs in a bloodthirsty and unprovoked frenzy. This outright falsehood, born on the Right and embraced by liberals like Toynbee, would eventually become a mantra of the British Left. After the Six-Day War, such comparisons would also become commonplace in the Soviet Union and on the New Left, with its dogmatic "anti-racism." The new Leftists often pilloried Zionist policy toward the Palestinian Arabs after 1967 as "genocide" and upbraided British Jews for being the reactionary accomplices of Israeli "fascism."[24] The Young Liberals in Britain adopted a similar agenda on British campuses in the 1970s. This was a crucial formative period during which a malevolent hostility towards Israel within parts of the British intelligentsia first began to definitively crystallize.

During the first Lebanon war of 1982, the far-Left Trotskyite *News Line* led the pack in falsely accusing the Zionists of employing "horrendous gas weapons" (previously used against the Jewish people by the Nazis), and of trying to carry out a "Final Solution" against the entire Palestinian people.[25] Another organ of the British Left, the *Labour Herald* (co-edited by Ken Livingstone), published a cartoon in 1982 that anticipated the present-day assault on Israel down to the last detail. A bespectacled, ostentatiously Jewish Menachem Begin (then Israel's prime minister) was shown wearing Nazi jackboots, a Death's Head insignia, and a Star of David armband as he raised his right arm in a *Sieg Heil* salute over a mountain of skull bones. Lebanon lay bleeding at his feet. The headline, in Gothic script, simply read: "The Final Solution."[26]

Then, as now, prominent British writers could be found in the vanguard of demonizing Israel, inverting the Holocaust, while spinning an intricate web of implicitly antisemitic allusions and innuendoes. Best-selling children's author, Roald Dahl, for example, did not hesitate to brand Begin and Sharon in 1983 as "almost the exact carbon copies in miniature of Mr. Hitler and Mr. Goering."[27] They were "equally shortsighted," "bloodthirsty," and as deserving as their Nazi models to be arraigned by a war crimes tribunal. "Never before in the history of mankind," Dahl claimed, "has a race of people switched so rapidly from being much pitied victims to barbarous murderers."[28] For good measure he added that the Jews had been "cowards" in World War II.[29] It was not for nothing, he suggested, that Hitler had scapegoated them.

Today, antisemitic expression in Britain—especially on the Left—often assumes a similar mode of almost hysterical, wholly disproportionate vilification of the Jewish state. It is of course the case that not all disagreement with Israeli policy can or should be considered antisemitic or illegitimate. But in much of the British media, such criticism all-too-frequently abandons any pretence of civilized debate, indulging in demonization, flagrant double standards, and the implicit or explicit denial of Israel's right to defend itself—thereby transforming itself into an updated form of antisemitism.

A major venue for anti-Israel views has been the state-owned British Broadcasting Corporation—itself completely dominated by employees of a liberal-left persuasion. While generally downplaying the jihadist motivations of militant Islam, the BBC has shown no such reticence in misrepresenting Israel's efforts at self-defense. In many current affairs programs during the Second Intifada, the image of a bloodthirsty, implacable Ariel Sharon would be contrasted with a relatively benign Yasser Arafat, portrayed until his death as the amiable, grandfatherly leader of the Palestinians. In BBC interviews, Palestinian spokespeople would usually be treated to soft and respectful questioning, whereas Israelis, unless they explicitly repudiated Israeli government policies, were liable to be handled far more harshly. This blatant partiality extended to vocabulary. The BBC consistently refers to the Hamas and Islamic Jihad terrorists as "militants" or "radicals."[30] The word "terror" is almost never used, even for the most brutal Palestinian assaults and atrocities against Israeli civilians—though the network had no qualms about describing the September 11 attacks in New York and Washington, the Bali bombing, and other jihadi assaults in Djerba, Casablanca, and Istanbul as "terrorist" acts.[31] The same pattern of bias was revealed when the BBC quoted verbatim from libellous and unsubstantiated Palestinian accusations—such as the harvesting of Palestinian organs by the Israeli army, or the use of poison gas and depleted uranium by Israel—while calling into doubt the authenticity of any evidence Israel might present in its own defense. Israeli sources cited by the BBC usually "allege" while Palestinians "report." Bias was also apparent in many documentaries, including the screening of "Israel's Secret Weapon" on 17 March 2003—which depicted Israel as a rogue regime, Ariel Sharon as a Jewish Saddam Hussein, and Dimona, rather than Baghdad, as the rightful target of UN weapons inspectors.[32]

Media prejudice is not just a matter of bias among individual editors and reporters, but appears to be a consistent pattern throughout the BBC. Media Tenor, an independent, Bonn-based research group, conducted a 2003 study which found that the BBC's Middle East coverage was 85 percent negative, 15 percent neutral, and 0 percent positive toward Israel.[33] The Jenin affair offered a prime example of Israel-baiting in Britain during the Second Intifada. Many British journalists hailed without question the grossly inflated claims of 3,000 Palestinian dead made after Israel's assault on the refugee camp in April 2002 in the course of Operation Defensive Shield. The well-known author, A. N. Wilson, a leading columnist of the London *Evening Standard,* confidently informed his readers that "we are talking here of massacre, and a cover-up of genocide."[34] The liberal-left *Guardian* malevolently compared Israel's incursion into Jenin with al-Qaida's attack of September 11 on the World Trade Center in New York. The Israeli action, it said, was "every bit as repellent in its particulars, no less distressing, and every bit as man-made." The incursion, it added, "already has that aura of infamy that attaches to a crime of especial notoriety."[35] The *Times*' correspondent, Janine di Giovanni, went completely overboard, claiming that rarely had anyone seen "such deliberate destruction, such disrespect for human life."[36] Phil Reeves of the more radical *Independent* spoke of Cambodia-style "killing fields," quoting without any verification Palestinian claims of "mass murder" and wholesale "executions." His dispatch began thus: "A monstrous war crime that Israel has tried to cover up for a fortnight has finally been exposed."[37] Even months after a UN investigation concluded that there was *no massacre* in Jenin, and even Palestinian leaders had conceded the point, BBC anchors and its website were still implying that there were doubts about what had really happened.[38]

A particularly insidious example of the link between anti-Israel defamation and classical antisemitic imagery was afforded by Dave Brown's sensationalist cartoon in the *Independent,* depicting Ariel Sharon in the act of devouring the flesh of a Palestinian baby. Sharon was shown, nearly naked, wearing a Likud fig leaf, while in the background Apache helicopters fired missiles and blared out the message, "Vote Likud."[39] This cartoon would not have looked out of place in *Der Stürmer*. It also recalled older images of the medieval blood libels.[40] Nevertheless, the Press Complaints Committee in the United Kingdom dismissed all protests. This ignoble caricature was subsequently awarded first prize in the British Political Cartoon Society's annual competition for 2003.[41]

It was in such an increasingly toxic atmosphere that the journalist Julie Burchill (in an opinion piece published on 29 November 2003) explained why she was leaving the *Guardian*: Burchill was frankly dismayed by the British press's "quite striking bias against the State of Israel." For all its faults, she retorted, Israel was still the "only country in that barren region that you or I, or any feminist, atheist, homosexual or trade unionist, could bear to live under."[42] Burchill, who is not Jewish was particularly scathing about Richard Ingrams, former editor of *Private Eye* and a veteran columnist for the *Observer,* who had demanded that Jewish journalists declare their racial origins when writing about the Middle East. Ingrams had smugly boasted to his readers: "I have developed a habit when confronted by letters to the editor to look at the signature to see if the writer has a Jewish name. If so, I tend not to read it." Six years later Ingrams was complaining about "the pro-Israeli bias of Sir Martin Gilbert and Sir Lawrence Freedman, who had both supported the 2003 invasion of Iraq, which was now the subject of a British parliamentary inquiry.[43] For Ingrams there was no doubt that the Iraq war was a plot by American "neo-con" Jews and ardent Zionists to protect the security of Israel. Hence British Jews like Gilbert should not have been appointed as part of a British parliamentary investigative panel looking into the war.

Since 2003, this kind of commentary has become ever more brazen. There is a widespread and justified perception among Anglo-Jewry that antisemitic canards, the demonization of Israel, and the rationalization of terrorism against Israeli civilians have become legitimate in much British reporting and commentary on the Middle East. For example, in 2005, a British play called *My Name is Rachel Corrie* glorified the young American activist who was accidentally killed in the Gaza Strip in 2003. Rachel Corrie had been attempting to prevent a bulldozer from destroying a home used to supply Palestinian terror networks and her death was clearly a tragic accident. The play, however, presented her as a martyr of Israeli ruthlessness and inhumanity. Rather than challenge the play's undisguised bias or discuss its controversial moral perspective, British theater critics enthusiastically hailed it as comparable to dramatizations of the lives of Primo Levi and Anne Frank, thereby trivializing the suffering of Holocaust victims.[44] Even more disturbing was the ten-minute play (for Gaza) by Caryl Churchill, entitled

Seven Jewish Children, performed at the Royal Court Theatre in 2009. The text provided a popular though very ugly version of how contemporary Jews—particularly in Israel—have supposedly lost any moral compass. The impression is created that they have brought up their children on a diet of lies, deceit and false justifications for criminal behavior.

It is striking that moralizing British "critics" of Israel have almost no interest in the suicide bombings against Israeli *civilian* targets. These outrages are invariably explained away as a product of the general misery induced by Zionist policies. Such assumptions, for example, led Cherie Blair, wife of New Labour's prime minister at the time, to remark at a charitable event in London in June 2002 that young Palestinians "feel they have got no hope but to blow themselves up."[45] She made the comment only hours after a Hamas suicide bomber had blown up a bus packed full of Israelis, including schoolchildren—killing 19 and injuring dozens. Worse still, Jenny Tonge, a Liberal Democrat British legislator who was back-benched in 2005, after expressing open sympathy for Palestinian suicide bombers and comparing Arabs in Gaza to Jews in the Warsaw Ghetto, was nominated to serve in the House of Lords.[46] In September 2006, Baroness Tonge, addressing a meeting of the Palestinian Solidarity Campaign, went one step further, declaring that the "pro-Israel lobby has got its grips on the western world, its financial grips." Since Baroness Tonge had included her own Liberal Democrat Party in these allegations, she earned a sharp rebuke from her own Party leadership for the "clear anti-Semitic connotations" of these remarks.[47] This did not deter the Baroness (in February 2010) from calling for an inquiry into whether Israeli rescue teams sent to Haiti had not been trafficking organs from earthquake victims. The Liberal Democratic spokesman for international affairs, Lord Wallace, nonetheless found it appropriate to defend her position on the Palestinians while attacking Israel for its alleged intolerance of "criticism."

In the Labour Party, too, the thin boundary between "criticism of Israel," antisemitism and anti-Zionism has increasingly been breached—especially during the eight-year incumbency of London's left-wing populist mayor, Ken Livingstone. In February 2005 Livingstone had angrily and gratuitously compared a Jewish reporter for the *Evening Standard* to a concentration camp guard. Instead of later apologizing, Livingstone then criticized the reporter's newspaper for what he called its history of racism, scare-mongering and antisemitism. Shortly thereafter, Livingstone published a piece in the *Guardian* claiming that Ariel Sharon "is a war criminal who should be in prison, not in office," adding that "Israel's own expansion has included ethnic cleansing." Subsequently, the Muslim Public Affairs Committee, responding to Jewish critics of the mayor, published an article in support of Livingstone on its website, entitled "Zionists Want Their Pound of Flesh."[48]

Passions in London were further stirred by the 2005 election contest in the city's Bethnal Green district, the second-most populated Muslim area in Britain. The highly charged electoral race pitted sitting Labour MP Oona King, a black Jewish woman, against George Galloway, a former Labour MP who at that time was already the candidate for the anti-war Respect Party, a curious blend of far-Left and Islamist politics. After youths threw eggs at King as she honored East End Jews killed in Nazi bombing raids, one young Muslim told the *Daily Telegraph*: "We all hate her. She comes here with her Jewish friends who are killing our people and then they come to our backyards."[49] King lost by 823 votes.

After the election, the climate in London grew still more antagonistic for Jews who felt supportive of Israel. On 21 May 2005, a major rally was held in Trafalgar Square, with the crowd waving Palestinian flags and anti-Israel banners despite the heavy rain. Speakers included Palestinian representatives and local Muslim leaders, but most notable was the presence of non-Muslim left-wing public figures. Jeremy Corbyn, a backbench Labour MP, called for the British government to "cease all trade with Israel," while Tony Benn, a former Labour MP, an icon of the radical Left and a veteran of the British political scene, called George Bush and Ariel Sharon the "two most dangerous men in the world." Paul Mackney, president of the country's second-largest union of teachers, advocated the widespread boycott of Israel by British academia, while Andrew Birgin of the Stop the War Coalition demanded the dismantling of the Jewish state. "The South African apartheid state never inflicted the sort of repression that Israel is inflicting on the Palestinians," he said to enthusiastic cries of *Allahu akbar!* from the audience. "When there is real democracy, there will be no more Israel."[50]

The rally's most prominent speaker, however, was George Galloway, fresh from his election victory over Oona King. Galloway promptly used the rally as an opportunity to launch the call for an international boycott of Israel. "We will join them," he said, referring to the Palestinians, "by boycotting Israel. By boycotting Israeli goods. By picketing the stores that are selling Israeli goods." To cheers and applause, Galloway added, "It's about time that the British government made some reparations for the Balfour Declaration."[51] Since then Galloway has chosen to embrace the groundless libel that Israel has harvested the organs of Palestinian prisoners in its jails. At the end of

December 2009, he shamelessly accused the Jewish State of "playing mini-Mengele" with incarcerated Palestinians.

Given the legitimacy that such rhetoric enjoys in Britain today, it should not surprise us to discover considerable support among the intellectual elites in Britain for actions like the boycotting of Israeli products and people. It is these activities which have turned the public atmosphere in Britain into one of the most uncomfortable for Jews in all of Europe. In this area Great Britain has proved itself to be a world leader and innovator in promoting the "new antisemitism." First came the much-publicized Mona Baker affair, which involved her removal of two Israeli colleagues from the board of a scientific publication she edited in Manchester. The Egyptian-born Baker claimed to have been inspired by the boycott initiative of two left-wing British academics, Steven Rose (who is Jewish) and his wife, Hilary. Supporters of the original boycott petition included the AUT, NATFHE (the lecturers' union), and over 700 academics. Matters escalated when Andrew Wilkie, a professor of pathology at Oxford University, flatly rejected the application of an Israeli student simply because of his nationality. On 23 June 2003, Wilkie had told the student that he had "a huge problem with the way that Israelis take the moral high ground from their appalling treatment in the Holocaust, and then inflict gross human rights abuses on the Palestinians."[52] Oxford University promptly slapped Prof. Wilkie with the punishment of two months of unpaid leave, although the same institution failed to take any action against the poet Tom Paulin. A radical lecturer and TV personality, Paulin had published a scandalous poem in 2002 that branded the Israeli army as the "Zionist SS."[53]

Matters only worsened in April 2005 when the AUT, which had some 40,000 members, voted by sizable majorities to impose a boycott on two Israeli universities, Bar-Ilan University and the University of Haifa, in solidarity with the Palestinian cause. According to the AUT secretary general, this ban would "take the form described in the Palestinian call for academic boycott of Israeli institutions." The rushed vote was held on Passover eve, preventing most Jewish members from taking part, and opponents of the motions were denied right of reply due to "lack of time." Just before the vote, speakers addressing the AUT's executive union meeting declared Israel a "colonial apartheid state, more insidious than South Africa," and called for the "removal of this regime." While some British institutions, such as Oxford, considered action to override the ban, it was mainly international pressure, rather than repercussions within British society, that ultimately led to the reversal of the boycott a month later.[54]

Boycotts against Jews arouse painful associations. Attempts to remove Israeli products from Selfridges, Harrods, Tesco, Marks & Spencer, and other British chains, under the slogan "Isolate the Racist Zionist State," have been both a symptom and a rallying point for the resurgence of antisemitism in Britain.[55] Demonstrators involved in such actions, generally collect money and signatures, sell pamphlets comparing Israeli leaders to Hitler, or shout slogans at passersby. Carol Gould has offered a telling example of one such experience of a demonstration outside the Marks & Spencer on Oxford Street, London, in November 2003. Gould described how the Moroccan conductor of her double-decker bus harangued his passengers about "all Marks & Spencer money that goes to the 'Zionist murderers.'"[56] Once outside the store, Carol Gould encountered "an hysterical crowd of hate-filled people," in which English people outnumbered those of Middle Eastern origin. The scene was clearly one of anti-Jewish incitement. One woman in religious Muslim attire was screaming, "You Jews destroyed my country, Iraq." Others shouted, "You people invented terrorism in Palestine!"; "Israel is expanding every day and will soon own the whole Middle East!"; "Israel is slaughtering thousands of Palestinians every day!"[57] An elegantly dressed English businessman told Gould: "I love and revere the suicide bombers. Every time I hear of a suicide bomb going off I wish it had been eighty or ninety Jews instead of a pitiful handful."[58]

It needs to be emphasized that this kind of "new" antisemitism in Britain is not exactly the same kind of hatred that prevailed in Europe seventy years ago. The complex multicultural society of Great Britain will not readily tolerate cries of *Sieg Heil,* jackboots, or the openly racist mythology that was irrevocably stained by the Holocaust. Nor is the classic blend of British aristocratic snobbery, genteel middle-class distaste for Jews or working-class dislike of "bloody foreigners" as politically correct as it used to be.

Instead one finds an obsessive focus on Israel, often linked to a deep loathing for the United States and the "neo-colonialist" West. The spearhead of this assault has been the "anti-racist" Left in Great Britain which now attributes to Jews and the state of Israel the worst sins of the West—racism, ethnic cleansing, "crimes against humanity," and even genocide. This conscious attempt to "Nazify" Judaism, Zionism, and Israel deserves to be regarded as one of the most scandalous inversions in the history of the longest hatred.[59] It has also coincided with the extraordinary indulgence shown by the British Left towards the havoc wrought by radical Islamists in British society in pursuing their jihadi agenda against Israel and the West. Invariably, much of the Left has found mitigating factors in excusing jihadi terrorism and its anti-Western incitement, even when expressing cautious disapproval of its violent methods. When a former Labour Minister, Dennis McShane, did speak out against Muslim terrorism and later criticized Islamist antisemitism, this aroused a storm of protest.[60] In contemporary Britain, even to mention that Islamic fundamentalists have been spewing out antisemitic and anti-Christian poison for many years, is likely to provoke charges of Islamophobia or racism. On the other hand, to denounce fictitious Israeli "war crimes" has become a necessary qualification for being considered a part of the so-called progressive camp. Anti-Israelism has now become the position of the 6.5 million-strong Trade Union Congress (TUC) which in September 2009 called for a consumer-led boycott and sanctions campaign against Israel at its Conference. It demanded the removal of the separation wall and "illegal" settlements" as well as ending an EU agreement, which provided preferential trade facilities for Israel. The War on Want charity, which in 2007 had already advocated a world-wide boycott of Israel, has been no less militant. It organized an event in East London in July 2009 vilifying Israel as an "apartheid state" and damning it as guilty of "massive human rights abuses." The gathering featured rabidly anti-Israel speakers like Ben White, a freelance writer who in 2002 had accused the Israeli government of ethnic cleansing. For good measure White added that he understood why people in Britain were antisemitic.[61]

Labour MP John Mann (who is not Jewish) but who chaired the British All-Party Parliamentary Group against Anti-Semitism, was particularly concerned by the accelerating anti-Jewish hostility on the Left, which he found more sinister and dishonest than the blatant antisemitism of Muslim or far-Right extremists. Mann noted the widespread perception inside the British Parliament that "Jews are rich and therefore are 'good for donations.'" He deplored the prevalence of "disgraceful and outrageous anti-Semitism in Parliament, including statements from those who are meant to be bastions against racism."[62]

In this context, it might be appropriate to quote from an interview on British antisemitism which I gave to Manfred Gerstenfeld early in 2008 at the Jerusalem Institute of Public Affairs. Here is a brief extract:

> What is interesting is that in Britain, as in much of Europe, the proclaimed anti-racism of the left-wing variety often feeds the new antisemitism—which is directed primarily against the State of Israel. Of course, if one suggests that such leftists are anti-semites in disguise, they are likely to become enraged, retorting that one is "playing the antisemitic card." This has become a

> code-word for saying, as it were, "you are a dishonest, deceitful, manipulative Jew" or a "lover of Jews." Zionists supposedly use the "accusation of antisemitism" to disguise, to hide, to silence the fully justified criticism of Israel and its human rights abuses. The word "criticism" in this context is misplaced—it is a euphemism or license for the demonization of Israel. And that in turn is a major form of antisemitism in our time.[63]

In my recent book, *A Lethal Obsession: Antisemitism from Antiquity to the Global Jihad* (2010), I also point out that Great Britain has become a European pioneer in several areas of anti-Zionism and antisemitism.[64] The British undoubtedly lead the pack when it comes to the academic isolation of Israel and in initiating trade union economic boycotts of Israeli goods; and there is no other Western democratic nation where jihadi radicalism, closely linked to anti-Americanism and antisemitism is so violent and intertwined with left-wing attitudes.

The prevalence of Trotskyite anti-Israel attitudes has been a significant influence on the Left since 1967, representing a particularly obtuse and dogmatic form of anti-Zionism. In the Trotskyite concept, Zionism has always been identified with "decaying" capitalism and since 1945 bracketed with American imperialism. In the 1970s, British Trotskyites (some of them Jewish) organized the Socialist Workers' Party (SWP) into a particularly active force in demonizing Israel. They were still a major factor in the huge antiwar demonstrations in London in February 2003.[65] The SWP has systematically savaged Israel as America's "attack dog" and agent in the Middle East—picking on it as the more vulnerable, isolated and easy-to-demonize surrogate for their anti-American rage. Periodically, the Trotskyists and other sections of the British Left have also presented the Israel/Jewish lobby as having a stranglehold over American foreign policy.

The theme of the omnipresent and all-powerful Jewish lobby has indeed become something of a leitmotif attracting much attention in the mainstream British media as well as on the Left. The veteran Labour MP, Tom Dalyell, caused considerable controversy when he declared in an interview for *Vanity Fair* back in 2003 that then-British Prime Minister Tony Blair was surrounded by a sinister "cabal" of Jewish advisers. This small clique had allegedly dragged him into the unpopular Iraq war. According to Dalyell, the cabal was linked to hawkish neo-conservative intellectuals (a code-word for Jews influential in the Bush administration) in Washington, D.C. who had supposedly masterminded the invasion of Iraq. Both President Bush and Prime Minister Blair, according this far-fetched leftist conspiracy theory, were instruments of a pro-Likud, pro-Sharon Jewish Zionist plot designed to protect Israel by forcefully removing Iraqi dictator Saddam Hussein. Dalyell bizarrely included as "Jews" the then-British Foreign Secretary Jack Straw and the New Labour spin doctor Peter Mandelson (neither of whom even define themselves as Jewish). Under the Nazi race laws, however, their partial Jewish ancestry might possibly have qualified them for Auschwitz.[66]

The only "conspirator" is Dalyell's trio of villains who could indisputably qualify as Jewish was Blair's personal envoy to the Middle East, Lord Levy—a wealthy British Jew, New Labour's most important fundraiser at the time, and also a favorite target of British media innuendo. Levy's integrity and impartiality was fiercely attacked by the Australian-born John Pilger, a leftist pro-Palestinian crusading journalist who has never lost an opportunity to lash out at Israel's "greedy expansionism" and its supposed trampling of human rights.[67] Pilger, like many on the British Left, in pro-Palestinian circles, or in the Muslim media, appears convinced that there really is a dangerous Jewish/Zionist lobby that manipulates British and American foreign policy. This belief, broadly shared by a third of Britons according to a 2007 opinion survey, is also periodically aired by the BBC. The Channel 4 investigative series, *Dispatches,* featured, for example, "Inside Britain's Israel Lobby"—a documentary screened in November 2009, replete with repulsive innuendos about the power of pro-Israel "moneybags." Viewers were treated to speculations about the lobby's supposed control of the British Labour and Conservative parties and their "pro-Israel" intimidation of the British media. The documentary predictably criticized the "pro-Israel" abuse of antisemitism as a weapon to deflect unwelcome criticism of the Jewish State. It also contained sinister music accompanying photos of "lobby" members blurred across a background of British and Israeli flags.[68]

The theme of an occult Jewish/Zionist conspiracy is not new in Britain. But before 1948 (and during the early period of the Israeli state), most active British anti-Zionists tended to be members of the Establishment—former army officers, colonial officials, Conservative politicians, Christian missionaries, or Arabists who came from elite schools. Today, on the other hand, we are more likely to find a bizarre unwritten alliance of "peace" activists, left-wing radicals, anti-globalists, and Islamists spearheading the anti-Zionist forces. Many of these activists are linked to the Palestine Solidarity Campaign (PSC), which has built an effective mass campaign and constantly organizes protests that aim to isolate and delegitimize Israel. The PSC played a central role in mobilizing British opinion to divest from any companies (like the heavy machinery manufacturer Caterpillar) which provide services, products, or technology that helps maintain "the occupation of the Palestinian territories."[69] The PSC sponsors the Boycott Israeli Goods campaign, which has targeted Israeli agricultural and high-tech exports to Britain; and in 2005 it began to offer extensive support to anti-Zionist academics seeking to convince the AUT (then the largest university teachers' union in the UK) to break all ties with Israeli universities.

The PSC has also strongly backed those in the Church of England who favor disinvestment from Israel and it cooperates with fiercely anti-Zionist Christian groups like the Sabeel Ecumenical Liberation Theology organization headed by the Reverend Dr. Naim Ateek.[70] The Palestine Solidarity Campaign has, not surprisingly, developed close links with the Muslim Council of Britain (MCB), the leading organized representative body of British Muslims, and with the more radically anti-Zionist Muslim Public Affairs Committee. A closer examination of the literature, activities, and networks of the PSC confirms the view that it is far more concerned to delegitimize Israel than to genuinely right any Israeli "wrong" towards the Palestinians; that its intense and even irrational hatred of Israel is more intimately connected with its opposition to a *Jewish* state than with securing a genuine peace in the Middle East. As David Hirsh has pointed out, much the same is true of the UCU (University and College Union) efforts to boycott Israeli universities (but no other universities in the world) since 2003. The UCU record reveals a flat refusal by the British academic Union to examine its own institutionalized antisemitism, discrimination against Israeli academics, unlawful insistence on boycott motions at its Congresses, and "antiracist" racism towards Jews objecting to its policies.[71] As a result, Jews in the UCU—feeling themselves bullied, excluded, and silenced—have increasingly resigned in recent months.

The PSC's influence on the decision of the Trades Union Congress (TUC) to promote a boycott, divestment, and sanctions campaign against Israel has been particularly striking. In collaboration with the hard Left within the TUC, they have done everything in their power to execrate Israel as a racist apartheid state. The Gaza invasion of January 2009 undoubtedly strengthened popular support for the Boycott Israel Movement in the unions, the media, among prominent NGOs, as well as mobilizing some British politicians. The boycott drive, with its uniquely antagonistic attitude towards the Jewish State (while ignoring massive and far graver human rights violations elsewhere) is without doubt an extreme case of double standards with clearly antisemitic implications. As Anthony Julius and Alan Dershowitz noted in 2007, "the boycott has been an essential tool of anti-Semites for at least a thousand years."[72]This did not, however, stop prominent left-wing British film-makers like Ken Loach from recently advocating a more sweeping cultural boycott of Israel as well as condemning the British and American governments for their support of the Jewish State. Nor did it prevent the largest trade union in the UK, Unite, from passing a resolution in favor of boycotting Israel. The main effect of such actions has been to mainstream still further the British delegitimization of Israel.

The essence of the boycott is to economically and politically damage the Jewish state, denying it the freedom and rights enjoyed by other nation-states. Its negative physical and psychological impact on British Jews is an important side-effect of such activities. While the New Labour government in Britain opposed both the trade union and academic boycotts (as did the major national newspapers), it nonetheless supported the discriminatory labeling of goods from West Bank settlements. The previous Labour administration of Gordon Brown also arbitrarily cancelled export licenses for Israeli warship parts. Whether the new Conservative-led government will continue down this path remains to be seen.

British foreign policy (always mindful of its important interests in the Arab world) has never been particularly pro-Israel. But government policy is much less antagonistic than that of influential NGOs such as Oxfam, Christian Aid, or the War on Want. In June 2010, these organizations were joined by the Methodist Church of Britain (with 70 million members worldwide) whose official report on the Palestinian issue was, according to the *Jewish Chronicle,* "so deformed that it could almost have been written by the Hamas leadership."[73]

The radicalization of Anglicans and Methodists on the Palestinian issue is an important symptom of the sea-change that has taken place in British attitudes to Israel. The churches, like the NGOs, have been infiltrated by the prevailing mantras of cultural relativism and a thick layer of "colonial guilt" from the long-gone days of the British Empire. Israel with its distinctive national identity, patriotism, and readiness to use force when faced by threats to its existence, does not fit the prevailing "pacifist" British ethos. Its national particularism flies in the face of the nominal liberal-left consensus of integration into Europe and reverence for international organizations. Zionism in this context is perceived by the British Left as being at best a 19th-century anachronism belonging to the vanishing era of the nation-state.[74] Israel is caricatured as a nasty form of "Jewish supremacism" (a similar vocabulary also exists on the far Right) and branded as a particularly vicious offshoot of the Western imperialist project. Not only is it deemed similar to

European racism, Nazism, colonialism, and apartheid, but the entire Zionist enterprise is also defamed as being *uniquely* evil.

This overblown, hyperbolic language clearly brings with it an inevitable escalation in the direction of anti-Jewish rhetoric.[75] It is also a narrative driven by historical amnesia. It has removed from its collective memory a series of crucial circumstances surrounding Israel's creation in 1948. First, the fact that the Jews won their independence in a national-liberation struggle against the British Empire, followed by a defensive war of survival against the *illegal* invasion of Palestine by neighboring Arab states, has been flushed down the memory-hole. Equally overlooked is the truth that Communist Czechoslovakia (with Soviet blessing) provided the crucial arms which enabled Israel to win the 1948 war; or that the U.S.S.R. was more supportive of Israel at that time than the United States, which slammed an arms embargo on the fledgling Jewish State. The British Left is also silent about the "ethnic cleansing" of Jews by Arab rules between 1945 and 1970—many of whom subsequently found refuge in Israel. These Middle Eastern Jews, almost half of Israel's population, were hardly "imperialist" interlopers from Europe, any more than the Holocaust survivors who came to Palestine after 1945.

Such historical amnesia has helped the spread of slanders against Israel as well as lurid fantasies about Jewish power and manipulation behind the scenes. At the same time, it has become almost an article of faith on the Left that there is no real Judeophobia in Europe or the Middle East. Instead, the *talk about antisemitism* is deemed to be the problem—one supposedly being exploited by Israel and its Zionist supporters. The columnist Johann Hari, writing in *The Independent,* even suggested there was an organized Jewish campaign in America and Britain to smear anybody who evoked the Palestinian plight as an "antisemite." This wholly unfounded allegation came in the wake of angry responses to an earlier article of his that had falsely accused Israel of deliberately depositing "raw untreated sewage" on Palestinian lands in order to poison the drinking water. Hari's obscene diatribe came as part of a particularly vitriolic commentary on Israel's 60th anniversary in May 2008. Hari wrote that whenever he thought about Israel, "a remembered smell fills my nostrils, the smell of shit."[76] Incredibly enough, this liberal-left columnist who seems to specialize in smearing his critics as "racists" was awarded the prestigious George Orwell prize for political journalism. A little bit of Israel-bashing, it would seem, does no harm at all in furthering the pursuit of Britain's glittering prizes in the field of journalism or political cartoons. Indeed it appears to be almost a necessary requirement.

Other journalists and public figures have preferred to focus on Islamophobia (allegedly the "real racism" of the present) as a way of downgrading antisemitism. This is a highly questionable concept, despite the growing backlash against the large Muslim presence in Western Europe today. In contrast to paranoid antisemitic fantasies, the fear of terrorism as well as of creeping "Islamization" in Europe is not devoid of foundation or simply a demented product of religious or racial prejudice. Equally, it would be quite wrong to present Jew-hatred as if it is simply a problem of the past.[77] Such claims exhibit astonishing ignorance and amount to a deeply disturbing *denial* of the reality of antisemitism as a contemporary social, cultural, and political phenomenon. They indicate that British society, including some of its elite institutions and representatives, remains singularly ill-equipped to deal with the spreading pathology of antisemitism in its midst. The patient is not only in denial but increasingly intent on projecting the guilt for his deteriorating condition on extraneous factors like the crimes of America, the assumed "wickedness" of Israel or the mythical power of the "Jewish" Lobby.[78] The British Left, with its entrenched hostility to Israel (and towards any Jew who does not utterly repudiate its actions) has played a singularly destructive role in accelerating the ravages of the disease.

The last word in this sorry tale should perhaps be given to the Anglo-Jewish author Howard Jacobson, whose award-winning novel *The Finkler Question* has wittily encapsulated some of the issues we have discussed here, in the form of a dark satire of contemporary British society. In a probing article for *The Independent* (18 February 2009) Jacobson dissected the increasingly poisoned atmosphere surrounding present-day discussions of Israel in Great Britain as follows:

> A discriminatory, over-and-above hatred, inexplicable in its hysteria and virulence whatever justification is adduced for it; an unreasoning, deranged and as I can see irreversible revulsion. . . . You can taste the toxins on your tongue.
>
> But I am not allowed to ascribe any of this to anti-Semitism. It is, I am assured, "criticism" of Israel, pure and simple. . .and you are either not listened to or you are jeered at and abused, your humanity itself called into question. . . .[79]

Jacobson went on to address the obsessive and perverse trend in "tolerant old England" of defaming Israelis as Nazis or comparing Gaza to the Warsaw Ghetto.

> It is as though, by a reversal of the usual laws of cause and effect, Jewish actions of today prove that Jews had it coming to them yesterday. Berating Jews with their own history, disinheriting them of pity, as though pity is negotiable or has a sell-by date, is the latest species of Holocaust denial. . . .[80]

Jacobson similarly minced no words about what he saw as the almost casual antisemitism underlying Caryl Churchill's previously mentioned short play *Seven Jewish Children*. This pro-Palestinian "progressive" work climaxes in an Israeli character's racist monologue rejoicing in the slaughter of Palestinian children: "They're animals. . . . I wouldn't care if we wiped them out. . . . we're chosen people." Jacobson's response to the play was sharp and surely to the point.

> Once you repeat in another form the medieval blood-libel of Jews rejoicing in the murder of little children, you have crossed over. This is the old stuff. Jew-hating pure and simple.[81]

During the last decade Britain, led by its liberal-left elites, has been sleepwalking into a morass of anti-Israel and anti-Jewish bigotry, while vehemently denying that anything is amiss. Even more distressing is to witness the nihilistic folly of "progressive" Jews—driven by self-congratulatory narcissism as much as self-loathing—assuming prominent roles in directing the suicidal charge into the abyss. For that particular malady there may be no treatment, only a post-mortem.

NOTES

1. Quoted by Jonny Paul, "Widespread use of anti-Semitic themes in mainstream British circles," *Jerusalem Post,* 12 Nov. 2010.

2. Robin Shepherd, *A State Beyond the Pale: Europe's Problem with Israel* (London, 2009).

3. Community Security Trust, *Antisemitic Incidents, January–June 2009* (London, 2009). See also idem, *Antisemitic Discourse in Britain in 2008* (London, 2009).

4. Efraim Sicher, *Multiculturalism, Globalization, and Antisemitism: The British Case*, ACTA series, no. 22 (Jerusalem, 2009).

5. *Report of the All-Party Parliamentary Inquiry into Antisemitism* (London: HMSO, 2006).

6. Robert S. Wistrich, *A Lethal Obsession: Anti-Semitism from Antiquity to the Global Jihad* (New York, 2010), 362–434.

7. Melanie Phillips, "London: A Leftist Axis of Anti-Semitism," *Hadassah Magazine,* 4 Sept. 2003.

8. Colin Holmes, *Anti-Semitism in British Society 1876–1939* (New York, 1979).

9. Ibid.

10. See Claire Hirschfeld, "The British Left and the 'Jewish Conspiracy': A Case Study of Modern Anti-Semitism," *Jewish Social Studies* (Spring 1981): 95–112.

11. Sharman Kadish, *Bolsheviks and British Jews: The Anglo-Jewish Community, Britain, and the Russian Revolution* (London, 1992).

12. Gisela Lebzelter, *Political Anti-Semitism in England 1918–1939* (London, 1978), 13–28. The London *Times* took the *Protocols* very seriously until its correspondent in Istanbul, Philip Graves, exposed it as a forgery in August 1921. See Norman Cohn, *Warrant for Genocide* (London, 1970), 78, 166–71.

13 Henry Defries, *Conservative Party Attitudes to Jews, 1900–1939* (London, 2001). On Wells, see Bryan Chayette, "H. G. Wells and the Jews: Antisemitism, Socialism and English Culture," *Patterns of Prejudice* 22, no. 3 (1988): 22–35.

14. See W. F. Mandle, *Anti-Semitism and the British Union of Fascists* (London, 1968); Richard Thurlow, *Fascism in Britain: A History, 1918–1985* (Oxford, 1987).

15. Tony Kushner, *The Persistence of Prejudice: Anti-Semitism in British Society during the Second World War* (Manchester, 1989), 78–133.

16. James G. McDonald, *My Mission in Israel, 1948–1951* (London, 1951), 22–24.

17. Richard Crossman, *A Nation Reborn* (London, 1960), 69–72.

18. Ibid.

19. *Jewish Chronicle,* 8 Aug. 1947; see also 15, 22, and 29 Aug. reports. Most of the British press did deplore the weekend violence.

20. Benny Morris, *The Road to Jerusalem: Glubb Pasha, Palestine, and the Jews* (London, 2002), 23.

21. From a Glubb speech of 6 May 1949, quoted by Morris, *Road to Jerusalem,* 23.

22. Ibid., 81–82.

23. Arnold J. Toynbee, *A Study of History* (London, 1954), vol. 8, and vol. 12: 290; see also Yaacov Herzog, *A People that Dwells Alone* (London, 1975), 21–47. Herzog convincingly refuted Toynbee's claims in a 1961 debate at McGill University, Montreal.

24. Robert S. Wistrich, *Hitler's Apocalypse* (New York, 1985), 228.

25. *The News Line,* 11, 18, 30 June, 1982, 10 July 1982.

26. *Labour Herald*, 25 June 1982, 7.

27. Roald Dahl, *Literary Review* (Aug. 1983); the article was reprinted in the mass circulation *Time Out* (18–24 Aug. 1983).

28. Dahl, *Literary Review*.

29. *New Statesman,* 26 Aug. 1983.

30. See the 28-page critical study by Trevor Asserson and Elisheva Mironi, *The BBC and the Middle East,* www.bbcwatch.com/old.html; and a 39-page BBC Watch report on the Iraq War, also by Asserson, at www.bbcwatch.com/fullReport3.htm. Both BBC reports indicated a marked and consistent pro-Palestinian bias.

31. See "Friends Survive Bomb Terror," www.bbc.co.uk, 14 Oct. 2002, http://news.bbc.co.uk/1/hi/england/2328233.stm.

32. See Bret Stephens, "Anti-Semitism in Three Steps," *Jerusalem Post,* 3 July 2003.

33. Tzvi Fleischer, "Beeb Outdoes Itself," *The Review* (Sept. 2003): 8.

34. A. N. Wilson, "A Demon We Can't Afford to Ignore," *Evening Standard,* 15 Apr. 2002; see also idem, "The Tragic Reality of Israel,"*Evening Standard,* 22 Oct. 2001. In this latter article Wilson basically repudiated Israel's "right to exist," called it an aggressor, and claimed that "it never was a state" and was in any case doomed to failure.

35. "The Battle for Truth," *Guardian*, 17 Apr. 2002, lead editorial. After the release of the UN report, the *Guardian* pretended that its findings confirmed "what we said last April"—namely, that "the destruction in Jenin looked and smelled like a crime." This was quite untrue. See the issue of 2 Aug. 2002 for the paper's justification.

36. Janine di Giovanni, "Inside the Camp of the Dead," *Times,* 16 Apr. 2002.

37. Phil Reeves, "Amid the Ruins, the Grisly Evidence of a War Crime," *Independent,* 16 Apr. 2002. The utter absurdity of this comparison can be easily exposed by a few basic facts: at least 100,000 Chechens died in Russia's brutal suppression of their fight for independence since the mid-1990s. In Bosnia between 1991 and 1995, 250,000 people were killed. The documented death toll in Jenin on both sides was about 80, which included twenty-three Israeli soldiers.

38. See Greg Barrow, "Jenin Report Reflects UN Dilemma," BBC Online, 1 Aug. 2003, http://news.bbc.co.uk/2/hi/middle _east/2166871.stm.

39. See *Independent,* 27 Jan. 2003 (which is National Holocaust Remembrance Day in Britain). The newspaper's editor, Simon Kelner, is Jewish.

40. "Independent Cartoon Sparks Protests over 'Anti-Semitism,'" *Jewish Chronicle,* 31 Jan. 2003.

41. Editorial, "Cartoon Jews," *Jerusalem Post,* 1 Dec. 2003.

42. Julie Burchill, "Good, Bad and Ugly," *Guardian,* 29 Nov. 2003. Burchill made it clear she did not swallow "the modern libel line that anti-Zionism is entirely different from anti-Semitism."

43. Ibid.; see also Richard Ingrams, "Will Zionists' Links to Iraq invasion be brushed aside?" *The Independent,* 28 Nov. 2009.

44. Yaakov Lappin, "Corrie Compared to Anne Frank," *Jerusalem Post,* 9 May 2005. Writing in the *British Theater Guide,* Philip Fisher compared the Corrie play to Anthony Sher's dramatization of the life of Holocaust survivor Primo Levi, who was deported to Auschwitz in 1944: "Like Sir Anthony Sher's 'Primo,' 'My Name is Rachel Corrie' is a remarkably moving 90-minute solo piece about human dignity and suffering. Corrie was little more than a girl and while she could be naïve, she also had a saintly aspect, meeting death with the beatific happiness of a martyr."

45. *The Independent,* 19 June 2002; and the *Guardian,* 19 June 2002, predictably defended Mrs. Blair. See also Trevor Kavanagh, *Sun,* 20 June 2002, who rubbished Mrs. Blair's remarks and lambasted "the brainwashed suicide zombies [who] want to wipe the State of Israel off the map of the Middle East. . . ." See also "Cherie Blair's Suicide Bomb Blunder," *Times,* 19 June 2002; and "What Cherie Really Thinks," *Daily Telegraph,* 19 June 2002, which reminded Mrs. Blair that "hope" rather than "despair" motivated the martyrs; first, the hope they would go to heaven if they murdered Jews; second, the hope they would destroy Israel; and third, the hope that their families would receive a $25,000 reward from the Iraqi and Saudi governments.

46. Michael Freund, "Fired MP Nominated to House of Lords," *Jerusalem Post,* 10 May 2005.

47. On the original Tonge affair, see "UK Baroness Accused of Anti-Semitic Comments," *Jerusalem Post,* 21 Sept. 2006, 15 Oct. 2006, and 29 Nov. 2006.

48. See Ken Livingstone, "This is about Israel, Not Anti-Semitism," *Guardian,* 4 Mar. 2005; and idem, "Zionists Want their Pound of Flesh," 24 Feb. 2005, www.mpacuk.org/content /view/369.

49. Richard Alleyne, "Jewish MP Pelted with Eggs at War Memorial," *Daily Telegraph,* 11 Apr. 2005.

50. Yaakov Lappin, "Speakers at London Rally Call for Israel's Destruction," *Jerusalem Post,* 22 May 2005. Birgin later clarified that he was referring to Israel "in the sense that it exists now," which in his view should be replaced with a "democratic secular state in which peace can move forward."

51. Lappin, "Call for Israel's Destruction." For Galloway, see also Dave Rich, "From Blockade to Boycott: The Impact on U.K. Jewry of Reactions to Gaza," *Meria* 14, No. 2 (June 2010). Website: http://www.gloria-center.

52. Robin Shepherd, "Blind Hatred," *Jerusalem Post,* 29 Sept. 2004.

53. See Neil Tweedie, "Oxford Poet 'Wants US Jews Shot,'" 13 Apr. 2002, http://news.telegraph.co.uk/news/main.jhtml?xml=news/2002/04/13/npauli13.xml&sSheet=/news/2002/04/13/ ixnewstop.html.

54. Yaakov Lappin and Talya Halkin, "Israel Fumes at UK Academics' Boycott," *Jerusalem Post,* 22 Apr. 2005; Fania Oz-Salzberger, "Israelis Need Not Apply," *Wall Street Journal,* 8 May 2005.

55. Anat Koren, "Israeli Hate Campaign Hits London's Streets," *London Jewish News,* Supplement (Sept. 2002). Slogans like "Do not buy from Marks & Spencer" recall the Nazi catchwords of 1933, "Don't buy from Jews."

56. "I Wish Eighty or Ninety Jews Would Die with Each Bomb," editorial, 30 Nov. 2003, www.jewish.comment.com/cgibin/news.cgi?=11&command=shownews &newsid=569.

57. Ibid.

58. Ibid. A policewoman finally booked this individual after he screamed: "You people have been trying to acquire land across the entire globe and will soon own every nation if you are not stopped.

59. Robert S. Wistrich, *Anti-Semitism: The Longest Hatred* (New York, 1991), where I first coined the term "the longest hatred."

60. Daniel Johnson, "Allah's England," *Commentary* (Nov. 2006), 44–45; see also Robert S. Wistrich, "Playground of Jihad? The Case of Great Britain," in *Old Demons, New Debates: Antisemitism in the West,* edited by David I. Kertzer (New York, 2005), 81–92.

61. Marcus Dysch, "Charity Plans 'Apartheid Israel' Forum," *Jewish Chronicle,* 19 June 2009.

62. "I'm shocked by MP's antisemitism. The Simon Round Interview," *Jewish Chronicle,* 13 Feb. 2009.

63. Robert Solomon Wistrich, "Antisemitism Embedded in British Culture," *Jewish Political Affairs* (Spring 2008).

64. Wistrich, *Lethal Obsession,* 381–418.

65. Ibid., 399ff.

66. "Anti-Semitism: Tam O'Slander," *Economist,* 8 May 2003.

67. Wistrich, *Lethal Obsession*, 389–90; see also Stephen Pollard, "A Massacre of the Truth," *Guardian,* 24 Sept. 2002.

68. "Britain's Channel 4 Exposes 'Power' of Pro-Israel Lobby," *Haaretz,* 21 Nov. 2009. The program triggered a wave of condemnation among Anglo-Jewish representatives, who accused the BBC of stoking antisemitism.

69. Rory Miller, "British Anti-Zionism Then and Now," *Covenant,* 1, no. 2 (Apr. 2007); see http://www.covenant.idc .ac.il/en/vol1/issue2/millerprint.html ; accessed 16 Sept. 2009.

70. See Margaret Brearley, *The Anglican Church, Jews, and British Multiculturalism,* Posen Papers in Contemporary Antisemitism, Vidal Sassoon International Center for the Study of Antisemitism at the Hebrew University of Jerusalem (Jerusalem, 2007).

71. For the text of David Hirsh's talk at the UCU Seminar in Brighton, 18 Jan. 2010, see www.EngageOnline.org.uk.

72. Anthony Julius and Alan Dershowitz, "The Contemporary Fight against Anti-Semitism," *Times Online,* 13 June 2007, http://www.timesonline.co.uk/tol/comment/columnists/guest_contributors/article 1928865.ece.

73. Winston Pickett, "UK Embraces the Boycott," *Jerusalem Post,* 14 Aug. 2010.

74. See David Hirsh, *Anti-Zionism and Antisemitism. Cosmopolitan Reflections*. Working Paper, Yale Initiative for the Study of Antisemitism, Yale University, 2007.

75. The seeds of this shift were pointed out 20 years ago in my article, "Left-wing Anti-Zionism in Western Societies," in *Anti-Zionism and Antisemitism in the Contemporary World,* edited by Robert S. Wistrich (London, 1990), 46–52. See also Dave Rich, "The Holocaust as an Anti-Zionist and Anti-imperialist Tool for the British Left," in *The Abuse of Holocaust Memory. Distortions and Responses*, edited by Manfred Gerstenfeld (Jerusalem, 2009), 218–230.

76. *Antisemitic Discourse in Britain in 2008* (London, 2009). For the original articles, see Johann Hari, "Israel is suppressing a secret it must face," *Independent,* 28 Apr. 2008; and his subsequent rant, "The loathsome smearing of Israel's critics," *Independent,* 8 May 2008.

77. See Wistrich, *Lethal Obsession,* 274–361.

78. Anthony Julius, *Trials of the Diaspora. A History of Anti-Semitism in England* (Oxford, 2010), 571–88.

79. http://www.independent.co.uk/opinion/commentators/howard-jacobson-let82175-see-the-8216criticism8217-of-israel-for-what-it-really-is-1624827.html.

80. Ibid. See also *CST Antisemitic Discourse Report* (2009), 52–53.

81. Jonathan Foreman, "The Howard Jacobson Question," *Commentary* (Dec. 2010), 45–48.

CHAPTER 18

The Marxist-Islamist Alliance

At first sight the ideologies of radical Islam and modern Marxism may seem far removed from one another. A closer examination reveals certain similarities. For example, both the Islamic and Marxist-Leninist traditions polarize the world into two opposing camps and assume that war is the natural condition of mankind. According to the classical Islamic view, the world is divided into *Dar al-Islam* (the House of Islam) and *Dar al-Harb* (the House of War); furthermore, it is the collective obligation of the former to wage a *perpetual struggle* to subjugate the world outside of Islam. As Bernard Lewis pointed out more than fifty years ago, there is a parallel here in Lenin's Bolshevik doctrine that a state of war would continue to prevail until Communism definitively triumphed over the doomed capitalist order. The content of these beliefs, as Lewis noted, might be utterly different, "but the aggressive fanaticism of the believer is the same."[1] Moreover, from the earliest days of Bolshevik rule in Russia a pattern of relations and complicities between Communism and Islam emerged, whose long-term impact has been seriously underestimated. The parallel lines that exist between the Marxists and Islamists are clearly not based on any textual similarities between the *Communist Manifesto* and the Holy Quran. Nor do Communists or contemporary leftists feel any noticeable commonality with the theocentric universe of the Muslim Brotherhood ("God is our goal / the Prophet is our leader / the Quran is our constitution / *jihad* is our way"). The Islamist cult of death and martyrdom for Allah—inextricably linked to the centrality of jihad—is at bottom fundamentally alien to the secular rationalist world-view that influenced Bolshevism and most of the Western Left. So, too, are the relentless imprecations of the jihadists that Islam must crush the "infidels" and conquer the whole world by fire, sword, and the Quran. Atheistic Communists, Social Democrats, or anti-globalist anarchists are, after all, very much a part of that army of "unbelievers" who must either be killed or coerced at some future date into salvation. Nevertheless, there have long been radical Islamists, like Ali Shariati in the 1970s (along with Ayatollah Khomeini, the leading ideologue of the Iranian Revolution), who did seek to blend their Islamic credo with a peculiar and profoundly anti-Western form of Marxism. The Paris-trained Shariati may well have imbibed his belief in the necessity of purificatory violence against the colonialist West from his reading of Algerian Frantz Fanon's seminal *The Wretched of the Earth* (1961). His own "Islamo-Marxist" version of Shiite Islam reinterpreted the Prophet Muhammad and icons of Shiism, like Ali and Husain, above all as defenders of the poor exploited masses.[2] "Red Shiism," with its gallery of redemptive martyrs, was presented by Shariati as the only answer to the toxic alienation of Western society and the Muslim loss of identity in societies like Iran under the Shah.

Ali Shariati's Islamo-Marxism unreservedly extolled the blood-sacrifice of the *mujahid*—the fighter-martyr ready to die for the sake of the Revolution. Other theorists of the Islamic revolution in Iran were no less preoccupied with the role of heroic martyrdom. Islam, in their eyes, was *the* quintessential religion of agitation, liberation, blood, and martyrdom.[4] Their obsession with death as "liberation" can also be found among the Sunni Muslim martyrs of Palestine—whether they belong to the Hamas, Fatah, or Islamic Jihad. At the heart of the Palestinian national movement lies the slogan: "With our lives and with our blood we will redeem Palestine."[5] Yasser Arafat from the beginning of his career was, for example, committed to the sacred mystique of revolutionary violence and to the motto "victory or death," which also inspired Che Guevara and the Latin American *guerrilleros* in the 1960s. Palestinian ultra-radicals like the Marxist George Habash (leader of the Popular Front for the Liberation of Palestine) no less enthusiastically glorified violent martyrdom, the hijacking of airplanes, and the killing of civilians. Habash did not, for example, shrink from the prospect of a Third World War if it would serve the Palestinian cause. Habash (a radical secular leftist from a Greek-Orthodox Christian background) declared that in today's world, "no one is innocent, no one is neutral. A man is either with the oppressed or he is with the oppressors."[6] Habash was franker than Arafat in confessing that "international Judaism" was (in his eyes) identical to Zionism and a more dangerous enemy to Palestinians than Western imperialism.[7] He also admitted in 1979 that his own radical pan-Arab wing of the PLO could draw equally on Soviet and Iranian fundamentalist sources of inspiration. "Many have been surprised," he added, "that we, as Marxists, should be on the side of a religious movement like Khomeini's. But beyond ideology, we have in common anti-imperialist, anti-Zionist and anti-Israeli elements."[8]

In the Arab world such a syncretic approach is not uncommon. The charismatic leader of the Lebanese Shiite Hezbollah, Hassan Nasrallah (a dedicated follower of the Ayatollah Khomeini), learned in the 1990s how to blend radical Islam and the cult of death with a tinge of popular Marxism and antisemitic hatred of Israel. He, too, embraced Khomeini's polarizing division of the world into "oppressors" and "oppressed," using it as part of Hezbollah's domestic political program. In Hezbollah's vision of a coming apocalyptic battle, the Jews, along with America, are aligned with the "party of Satan" (*Hizbu'shaytan*) against the exploited Third World peoples—with particular emphasis on the oppressed Shiite masses. Drawing on the Quran and an idiosyncratic version of Marxist theory, Hezbollah has striven for a "universalist" definition of "the oppressed" as potentially including all social classes and religious denominations.[9] This radical Shiite universalism does not, of course, extend to Israel (dehumanized by Hezbollah as the *ultimate* oppressor) or to the United States as the "Great Satan." Hezbollah's conflict with Israel is seen by its leaders as a continuation of Muhammad's war with the "demonic" Jews who, from the dawn of Islam, supposedly threatened the essential core of Islamic identity. For Nasrallah and other Hezbollah leaders like the late Sheikh Fadlallah, there is no real difference between Judaism and Zionism. For them the Holocaust never happened or was hugely exaggerated while the Jewish conquest of Palestine is the result of a global "Zionist" conspiracy.[10]

It is worth pointing out that in radical Shiite Islam, the ahistorical category of the "oppressed" is often used in a sense roughly analogous to Marx's revolutionary proletariat. The downtrodden masses are *good* by definition, because they are exploited, and Shiism is the true representative of all such victims. In the cosmic Manichean drama of Good battling Evil, the "Red" Shiites in Iran and Lebanon are in the vanguard of social justice, sacred rebels against a long history of persecution and they alone possess God's perfect revelation.[11] Whatever promotes the revolutionary cause in this world-view is *good*; whatever obstructs it has been and is *bad*—a classic Leninist principle. There can be no middle ground between Truth and Error in this radical millenarian revolutionary struggle to establish God's just order on earth. Such an apocalyptic vision (especially strong in Iran) looks to ultimate redemption following the appearance of a divinely inspired Muslim guide (the Mahdi) who will inaugurate the coming Golden Age. According to this radical eschatology, the Jews are currently assigned a crucial role as the helpers of the *ad-Dajjal*—the Muslim equivalent of the Antichrist.[12] The demise of Israel in the radical Shiite ideology of the Iranian President Ahmadinejad is undoubtedly perceived as the necessary prologue to the End of Times.[13] The crushing of internal democratic dissent (defined as the work of foreign and "Zionist" agents) by the present regime in Iran in no way contradicts this eschatological pespective.

Western leftists are poorly equipped to fathom such messianic religious concepts as modern Mahdism—despite the latent apocalyptic content in Marxism itself. Nevertheless, the Marxists who came to power in Russia in 1917, beginning with Lenin himself, were quick to see the tactical benefit to themselves of sparking off a Bolshevik-led *jihad* against Western imperialism in Asia and the Near East. At the Second Congress of the Communist International held in Baku (1920), its President, Grigorii Zinoviev, aggressively called for "kindling a real holy war against the robbers and oppressors. . .a true people's holy war in the first place against British imperialism."[14] The close to 2,000 delegates, representing the "enslaved popular masses of the East" (Persia, Armenia, Turkey, Russia, the Arab lands), were ecstatic. About two-thirds of the delegates were Bolshevik party members. But they made a point of "respecting the religious feelings of the masses" even while educating them (in Zinoviev's words) "to hate and want to fight against the rich in general—Russian, Jewish, German, French."[15] Zinoviev was not the only Bolshevik internationalist of Jewish origin to play a central role in such incitement to *jihad*.

No less prominent in this campaign was the Comintern's secretary, Karl Radek—a professional revolutionary already active in the pre-1914 Polish, Russian, and German socialist movements. Radek had been one of the architects of the secret anti-Western alliance between the Soviet Union and military circles in Weimar Germany, which culminated in the 1922 Rapallo Treaty. He also had excellent contacts with Turkish leaders including Enver Pasha, who advocated a "Holy War" against the West to restore their own position and bring down the Versailles Treaty. In Baku, Radek did not hesitate to appeal "to the warlike feelings of the people of the East," to "the memory of Genghis Khan" (!), to "holy war" and even "to the mercy of the great conquering Caliphs of Islam." Radek, the Polish-born "Jewish" Bolshevik, was outdoing even Zinoviev—turning to the toiling Muslim masses to repaint the East in sparkling red colors and to "create a new civilization under the banner of Communism." Of course, like Lenin, Trotsky, and Zinoviev, Karl Radek knew well enough the real contradictions between the ideologies of Islam and Bolshevism. But the defeats suffered by communist uprisings in western and central Europe between 1919 and 1923 made the Russian Bolsheviks focus their attention more intensely on the revolutionary potential of pan-Islamist anti-colonialism in Asia and the Middle East.

Lenin's jihad did not bear fruit for more than thirty years despite the common fount of seething hatred which the Bolsheviks and their Muslim counterparts shared towards the "materialist West." But it is important to note that no less than fifteen times the "Manifesto of the Congress of the Peoples of the East" would use the term "Holy War" in its calls to mobilization against imperialist Britain. Indeed, jihad became an integral part of the more general appeal to the "revolutionary workers and oppressed peasants" to rise up "against the [Western] plunderers and capitalists."[16] Significant, too, was the injection of an anti-Jewish chord alongside the anti-British tone in early Communist propaganda to the Muslim East. Here is a typical example from 1920:

> Peoples of the East! . . . What has Britain done to Palestine? There, at first, acting for the benefit of Anglo-Jewish capitalists, it drove Arabs from the land in order to give the latter to Jewish settlers. Then, trying to appease the discontent of the Arabs, it incited them against the same Jewish settlers.[17]

The Palestine Communist Party (CPP) from the early 1920s followed a very similar political line. Visceral anti-Zionism went hand-in-hand with the calls from Moscow to "Arabize" the party. Compromises with Arab nationalism were not slow in coming. The 1929 anti-Jewish pogroms in Palestine which had a strong Islamist as well as Arab nationalist coloring, were trivialized by the Comintern and the CPP, which praised the violence as an "anti-imperialist" movement against the British Mandate.[18] Objections by some Jewish members of the CPP at this definition were summarily dismissed and those who persisted in their opposition were expelled from the party.[19] The predominantly Arab leadership of the CPP in the 1930s even drove it to denounce the *entire* Jewish community in Palestine as part of a sinister "Zionist-fascist" colonial project. At the same time, the Communists supported the ultra-nationalist leadership of Haj Amin el-Husseini, who headed the Arab revolt against Britain between 1936 and 1939.[20] Amin el-Husseini's undisguised admiration for European fascism (especially his courting of Nazi Germany) and his radical antisemitism were well known to the Palestinian Communists but this did not deter them from supporting his revolt. CPP leaflets called on Arabs, as the "rightful owners of the country," to rise up against the Jews and the imperialists. Communists even denounced the immigration of German Jews (fleeing the Third Reich) to Palestine. Their main criticism of el-Husseini was that he had been too moderate. It was characteristic of the Palestine Communist Party in the mid-1930s that it could call on Arabs to march on Tel Aviv and use force against the "Nazi Histadrut" (the powerful Jewish trade union organization).[21]

El-Husseini's pan-Islamic agitation, his pan-Arabism mixed with virulent antisemitism and his subsequent calls for a Holy War of Islam (in alliance with Nazi Germany) against world Jewry, did not initially diminish communist enthusiasm for his cause.[22] Only the Jewish section within the CPP protested at this Stalinist policy of unconditional support for the Arab national movement and for pan-Islamism, both of which explicitly negated any Jewish right to national self-determination.[23] No change in this policy would take place until the German invasion of the Soviet Union in June 1941. Henceforth, in Stalin's eyes, el-Husseini's total mobilization on behalf of Nazi Germany and his use of Islamist appeals on behalf of the Axis Powers against international Communism turned him into a dangerous enemy.[24] The Palestine Communists dutifully adapted themselves to Soviet foreign policy needs which eventually included support for the establishment of Israel in 1948.[25]

Stalin, like other Soviet leaders, had by 1939 long abandoned his earlier belief that the Muslim masses outside the U.S.S.R. could be readily "Bolshevized."[26] Moreover, the Soviet Union found itself facing a semi-feudal conservative Muslim world dominated by British imperial interests—which remained strongly resistant to Communist designs. Furthermore, the atheism of the Bolsheviks still represented a formidable hindrance for many Muslims to any serious alliance. So, too, was the general awareness that Communist parties (in the Middle East as elsewhere) were essentially conveyor belts for Moscow's strategic Great Power interests.

On the other hand, there were also similarities and convergences between Islam and Communism—especially their shared hatred of the West. Moreover, Islamists, Arab nationalists, and Communists all believed themselves to have a monopoly of truth and favored authoritarian dictatorship in order to implement their ideas. Since the late 1920s Islamists and Arab nationalists had violently opposed Zionism (as well as imperialism)—regarding it as the prime enemy of the Muslim *umma*. In their agitation, they owed not a little to the Communists (especially in Palestine) who had taught them the fine arts of agitprop and indoctrinated them in Marxist-Leninist techniques of denouncing colonialism and Western imperialism. Some Muslim Arab extremists had no difficulty in fusing these Soviet slogans with their traditional jihadist views. Moreover, in Egypt, Syria, and Iraq not a few of those Arab radicals who had once collaborated with European fascism in the 1930s subsequently came to cooperate with the Communists in the

1950s.[27] It was also significant that modern Muslim and Arab anti-Zionism could so effortlessly absorb a number of the uglier themes of late Stalinist antisemitism much as it had earlier internalized the conspiracy theories of Nazi anti-Jewish propaganda.[28]

Egyptian President Nasser's advocacy of "Arab socialism" and his closeness to the U.S.S.R. after 1955, did not, however, prevent his encouragement of the antisemitic myth that Communism and Zionism were equally corrupt, subversive, and interrelated doctrines manipulated by the Jews in order to control the Middle East. The bitterly anti-communist King Feisal of Saudi Arabia—an arch-conservative—was another passionate believer in this antisemitic fantasy. Other Arab potentates and ideologues would also flaunt the fiction that Communism was nothing but an international Jewish-Zionist plot.[29] Indeed, within Islamic circles this particular antisemitic myth continued to carry enormous weight until the collapse of the Soviet Empire. The only grain of truth in these fables is that individual Jews had once been prominent among the founders of the Communist parties in Morocco, Egypt, Palestine, and Iraq during the 1920s. A few radicals like the Moroccan-born Marxist Abraham Serfaty, even persisted in their Communist militancy until the end of the 20th century, despite exile, persecution, torture, and imprisonment by Arab governments. Serfaty, like most Jewish Communists in the Middle East, was in fact a strong anti-Zionist though he did somewhat moderate his views on Israel towards the end of his life.[30] Belatedly, Serfaty also came to realize that Communism could never provide Jews with a successful path to integration into the broader Muslim Arab society—dominated as it was by pan-Arabism and Islamic fundamentalism.[31] In contrast to postwar Europe, there proved to be no place for Jews (even those of the Marxist anti-Zionist persuasion) in Arab politics.

Arab nationalist socialism and Islamic fundamentalism from the 1950s onwards was undoubtedly driven by a visceral hatred of the West and the Jews. This did not in practice prevent a tactical alliance with atheistic Communists in a variety of "anti-imperialist" fronts. Indeed, in Egypt, Syria, Lebanon, and Iran, Communism made considerable progress in the 1950s and 1960s, especially with the intellectuals, in the free professions and among Arab youth. In Iraq, too, since the 1940s, the Communists had been a significant force (particularly attractive to younger Jews) though one that was repressed by the government. Iraqi Baathism, which came to power in 1968, was, however, openly antisemitic, combining an eclectic mixture of Arab nationalist, socialist, Nazi, and Stalinist themes. This toxic cocktail would later be exemplified under Saddam Hussein's brutal hegemony from the early 1970s until his demise during the Second Gulf War of 2003. When it was expedient, Saddam (the ultimate pan-Arab neo-Stalinist) did not hesitate to wrap himself in religious colors as the defender of Sunni Islam against the hereditary Persian Shiite enemy.

It was the Iranian upheaval of 1979 which brought to the forefront the *totalitarian* revolutionary aspects of political Islam as a comprehensive socio-cultural system and a carrier of genocidal antisemitism. Earlier Sunni Muslim thinkers like Sayyid Abul Ala Maududi (founder in 1941 of Pakistan's *Jamaat-i Islami* and the spiritual godfather of modern radical Islam) as well as the Egyptian Islamist intellectual Sayyid Qutb had already shown the way in presenting Islamist ideology in an innovative way as a coherent universalist creed. Maududi, in particular, aimed to transform society as a whole through a centralized revolutionary leadership on the Leninist model.[32] He explicitly defined Islam as a universalist jihad for the welfare of mankind, taking the Prophet Muhammed as his charismatic model of a revolutionary leader.[33] For Maududi, the seizure of power by a *vanguard* Islamic party would be essential in order to implement the *world revolution* as envisaged by Islam—which transcended any national boundaries. In order to achieve their aims, the Islamist revolutionary elite would, however, have to mobilize the masses—a lesson that would be thoroughly absorbed by the Ayatollah Khomeini in Iran.

Khomeini's own ideology derived its inspiration not only from Maududi and the ferociously antisemitic Qutb but also from the input of the Iranian Islamo-Marxist Al-Shariati, the leading theoretician of "Red Shiism." Moreover, the modern political and agitational techniques of the Khomeinists owed a great deal to the Iranian Communist Party, the *Tudeh* ("Masses"). The Tudeh had emerged as a powerful movement after World War II. Indeed, in the early 1950s it became the strongest and best organized political force in Iran. There was also an influential religious-national wing in the party which sought to reconcile Islam and Marxism. During the Khomeinist revolution of 1979 the Tudeh supported the Ayatollahs (despite Khomeini's fierce polemics against Marxist materialism) only to be repressed, persecuted, and banned four years later. Nevertheless the ideology of the victorious Islamists in Iran shared something with its Marxist rivals, including the utopian belief in ultimate human redemption and a perfect society to be established through violent revolution. Khomeinism would not have been the same without the often volatile and explosive dialogue between itself and the Communists. There was a sense in which to win the Iranian youth away from Marxism,

Islam had to adopt its own style of Marxist-Leninist rhetoric and to partially "Marxify" itself. The result, to quote Laurent Murawiec, was to create "an Islamo-Marxist hybrid -a monstrous laboratory experiment that was unleashed on the body of Iran and thence the rest of the world of Islam."[34]

In the West, there would be no shortage of "useful idiots" (Lenin) especially in the bourgeois intelligentsia, who hailed the Islamic revolution as a true liberation of the masses. They even included such distinguished radical thinkers as Michel Foucault. The political reality, of course, was very different from their libertarian fantasies. The totalitarian apparatus which the Islamic revolution created was all-too-reminiscent of the dictatorial methods of Lenin, Stalin, and Mao Tse Tung—still heroes for an important sector of the Western Left. True, it was clerics who were now running the Iranian Republic but through effective mass mobilization, constant propaganda, and an Islamic "cultural Revolution" (with echoes of Mao) they were challenging the West and building the kind of monolithic *ideological* State that leftist intellectuals tend to admire. Moreover, the Iranian Shiite Islamists were taking a leaf out of the Leninist playbook—peppered with a dash of Trotsky—by proclaiming an *international* revolution, a modern jihad on all fronts. They also focused quickly on Palestine. One of Khomeini's first actions would be to totally break all ties with Israel, establishing instead a PLO Embassy in Tehran. It was no accident that on arriving in the Iranian capital early in 1979, Yasser Arafat would solemnly declare his kinship with Khomeini:

> The path we have chosen is identical; we are moving forward on the same path; we are fighting the same struggle: the same revolution; our nation is one, we have always lived in the same trenches for the same goal and the same slogan. Our slogan is: we are all Muslims, we are all Islamic revolutionaries, all fighting for the establishment of one body of Islamic believers. We will continue our struggle against Zionism and move towards Palestine alongside the Iranian revolutionaries.[35]

Not long after this revealing confession of his jihadist goals, Arafat was given a royal red-carpet reception in Vienna by Austrian Social-Democratic Chancellor Bruno Kreisky and the leader of the Socialist International, West Germany's Willy Brandt. This was the first time that major European socialist leaders had so publicly legitimized the Palestinian jihad as if it were really a secular democratic enterprise.

Despite the fact that Islamists and Palestinian nationalists continue to embody so many values antithetical to their own socialist creed, western leftists seem incapable of criticizing the terrorist agendas of jihad. Marxist radicals in the West have preferred to excuse or rationalize such pathological phenomena as the Palestinian suicide bombings in Israel and across the Muslim Middle East. They invariably invoke "root causes" such as poverty, alienation, or Western and Israeli "occupation" while studiously ignoring the self-proclaimed ideological motivation and Islamic inspiration of the terrorists. None of the predominantly Saudi 9/11 hijackers were in fact impoverished, poorly educated, or under "occupation." Much the same could be said of most other jihadist bombers from the Islamic world. Nor should it be forgotten that Muslims themselves have been the major targets and victims of jihadi violence—as is the case in Iraq today. But then Muslims who are not direct victims of the United States, Israel, or the West are apparently of little interest to the radical Left. Even as the Arab world finally erupts in revolutionary anger against the repression and corruption of its own tyrants, the Left and many liberals in the West still cling to the outworn mantras about Palestine as the core conflict in the Middle East. Indeed Palestine even today remains "the fusion point of western radicalism and Islamic jihad."[36]

Muslim demonizers of America and the Jews often share with their leftist allies a common loathing for capitalist modernity as the source of the rootless, globalized society that they inhabit. Americans and Israelis—two energetic peoples equally convinced of their biblical mandate—are seen as evil harbingers of a brave new technical world which seems particularly threatening to devout Muslims. For the Islamist demonizers, Americans and Jews are in effect the Pharisees of the present age "who promise freedom and democracy but deliver the golden calf."[37] What Soviet propaganda in the 1970s used to routinely denounce as the "Tel Aviv-Washington axis" has now become "Nazi Israel" and all-devouring America in the terminology of radical Muslim propaganda—especially in Iran. The "Zionist Crusaders" have metamorphosed into the warmongering, rapacious imperialists of the New Age, cursed agents of neo-liberal globalization. During the Second Lebanon War of 2006, even on the European Social Democratic Left it became increasingly common to hear allegations that the foreign policy of the United States was controlled by Jews. In countries like Sweden, for example, the notion of a Jewish-Zionist-American neo-con conspiracy—widely touted by Islamists—has traversed almost all of the Left.[38] The same is true in Britain and many other West European countries.

In Great Britain, the Respect party (founded to oppose the Iraq war of 2003) has been perhaps the clearest example of a European political formation seeking to amalgamate international socialism and Islamism. It comprised elements of the neo-Trotskyite Socialist Workers Party (SWP), activists from the Muslim Association of Britain (MAB), anti-globalization militants, and pacifist protesters against the Anglo-American invasion of Iraq.[39] Intense anti-Zionism (including the explicit negation of Jewish statehood in Israel), fierce opposition to neo-liberal economics, hatred of the United States, and an anti-war platform were from the outset key principles of the party whose left-wing leader George Galloway won an impressive general election victory in 2005 over his New Labour opponent in London's Bethnal Green constituency. Trotskyists and Islamists in the movement found common ground in glorifying the "Palestinian resistance" and in branding Israel as a criminal "terrorist state." They combined forces in damning the Jewish State as even worse than apartheid South Africa and demanding a reinforcement of the Boycott Israeli Goods Campaign. Yvonne Ridley, a political editor of Britain's Islam Channel and member of Respect's National Council, bluntly declared in 2006 that Respect was a "Zionist-free party." To clarify this point beyond all possible doubt, she added:

> if there were any Zionists in the Respect Party, they would be hunted down and kicked out. We have no time for Zionists.[40]

In the world-view of Respect and its British adherents, Israel is considered an entirely *illegitimate* state, all of whose territory is defined as "Occupied Palestine." Not surprisingly, then, Respect has expressed its full support for the Islamist movements of Hamas and Hezbollah—allies of Iran who are totally committed to the destruction of Israel. In July 2006, for example, George Galloway went out of his way in an article for the *Socialist Worker* to salute Hezbollah in its battle against Israel.

> I glorify the Hizbollah national resistance movement, and I glorify the leader of Hizbollah, Sheikh Sayyed Hassan Nasrallah.[41]

The establishment of Respect marked the crystallization of the Marxist-Islamist axis which already achieved an impressive mass expression on 15 February 2003 during one of the largest political demonstrations ever held in postwar Britain. This event took place under the slogan "Don't Attack Iraq—Freedom for Palestine." Nearly a million people marched through the streets of London. The rally had been coordinated by the Trotskyite-inspired Stop The War Coalition together with the Islamist Muslim Association of Britain (MAB). The banners of the MAB included Hamas slogans like "Palestine from the sea to the river"—reflecting the position of an organization that has publicly justified suicide bombers and maintained close ties to the Muslim Brotherhood.[42] The Islamists might disagree with their Trotskyist and far Left allies about feminism, homosexuality, religion, secularism, and the aims of socialism, but they clearly share a common anti-Western, anti-globalist and anti-Zionist agenda.[43] Islamists in Britain are not, of course, partisans of the traditional class-struggle of the industrial proletariat. But like the far Left, they passionately hate America and regularly echo the hoary myths of a Zionist world conspiracy. In Britain, as in France, the anti-globalist Left and Islamic fundamentalists have also shared a deep suspicion of liberal modernity and the entire Enlightenment project.[44] The web-sites of the anti-globalists in Britain (like those of the Islamists) are often soaked in the most vulgar anti-Americanism, *Protocols*-inspired conspiracy theories, and outright defamation of Israel as a racist state.[45] In addition, the morbid self-indulgence of leftist victim-centered culture has been all-too-evient in the pro-Palestinian partisanship of the International Solidarity Movement. Radical Muslims, for their part, have never disguised their loathing of Israel, Western capitalism, democracy, and individual freedom or their opposition to the use of American military power in the Middle East. They detest Israel with special vehemence as a dangerously effective agent of American imperialism and carrier of Western modernity. Many militants apparently believe that Jews control the domestic and foreign agenda of the Western world—a myth that they share with neo-Nazis as well as the far Left.

The links between the radical Left and the hard-line Islamists in Western Europe took on a new lease of life during the European elections of June 2004, especially in France. The radical Left alliance of Revolutionary Communists and *Lutte Ouvrière* ("Workers Struggle") groups turned to Islamic militants to help it secure seats in Parliament. According to Arlette Laguillère, the Trotskyite passionara of the working class, "the struggle for Palestine" was an integral element in the "global proletarian revolution." Wiping Israel off the map had become part of the fight to overthrow the global economic system and American power. Muslim immigrants were eagerly designated as the new underclass who could help to realize the fading dream of destroying world capitalism. Six years later, in 2010, the French Trotskyist leader, Olivier Besancenot, was still flirting with Islamism, supporting Hamas and Hezbollah, pointing the finger at Israel and ignoring the routine violations of human rights by various dictators in the Middle East and beyond.[46] The Arab revolutions of early 2011 which took the European Left (and many others) by surprise, have once again underlined the relative indifference of Western leftists to the real sufferings of the Muslim masses wherever they could not be blamed on America, Israel, or global capitalism.

Anti-globalist agitation during the past decade has added a new dimension of militancy to anti-capitalist radicalism. A striking example was provided by the French farmers' leader José Bové. He proved to be no less vocal than the Islamists in his anti-Americanism, anti-Zionism, and assaults on symbols of corporate capitalism like McDonald's restaurant chain. For Bové, like many other pro-Palestinian advocates in Europe, Israel represents the world's last "colonialist" state, imposing "an apartheid system on the occupied territories and the [Israeli] Arab population." This exploitative system, according to Bové, had been "invented" by the Western powers nearly a century ago, to serve as a capitalist enclave in the heart of the developing world. The task of Zionism was "to integrate the Middle East into globalized production circuits, through the exploitation of cheap Palestinian labor."[47] But the conspiracy also extended to contemporary France. Bové even insisted soon after the outbreak of the Second Intifada that the Israeli Mossad had deliberately orchestrated the wave of antisemitic violence in France to distract attention from Israel's repressive actions in the Palestinian territories.

During the past decade it is worth noting that there have been a number of assaults by antiglobalization activists on Jews carrying Israeli flags (even those with peace banners) at rallies held in Milan, Paris, London, Berlin, and other cities in the West. Here is Mark Strauss's description of the World Social Forum which took place in 2003 in Porto Allegro in Brazil:

> Marchers among the 20,000 activists from 120 countries carried signs reading NAZIS, YANKEES, AND JEWS: NO MORE CHOSEN PEOPLES! Some wore T-shirts with the Star of David twisted into Nazi swastikas. Members of Palestinian organizations pilloried Jews as the "true fundamentalists who control United States capitalism."[48]

Antiglobalist demonstrators at the 2003 World Economic Forum in Davos could also be seen brandishing similar slogans. One of them wore the mask of former American Defense Secretary Rumsfeld together with a huge Star of David, "while being driven forward by a cudgel-branding likeness of Ariel Sharon, followed by an outsized golden calf."[49] The goal was evidently to highlight America as being enslaved to Mammon-worshipping Jews—the mercenary avant-garde of capitalist globalization.[50] The conspiracy theories, espoused by leftist and far-Right anti-globalists, endlessly recycle this hatred of America and Israel as powerful oppressors and warmongering "rogue states" imbued with a dangerously self-righteous sense of "divine mission."[51] The United States is repeatedly damned for advancing economic globalization, devouring local industries and jobs in dependent Third World countries. It is attacked for promoting rampant modernity and *cultural* globalism in its own image. "Americanization," with its export of popular music, blue jeans, junk food, celluloid violence, and sensationalist mass media, is routinely blamed for destroying any sense of tradition or national identity.[52] This subversive role of American-style globalization echoes the ultra-conservative view of mobile, urbanized, and "rootless" Jews in modern society according to classic antisemitic perceptions. It has been revived by Islamists today. On the far Left, anti-Americanism and antipathy to Jews reflect a range of conspiracy theories, usually wrapped up in a pseudo-Marxist terminology tinged with a Third Worldist orientation. In its contemporary leftist variant, the "Zionist" conspiracy is almost always linked to a veritable obsession with the Palestinian cause.

Nowhere has this compulsive quality been more apparent than in France during the past decade. Radical pro-Palestinian propaganda along with the stigmatization of Israel has increasingly penetrated the schools, universities, and debates in the media, often driven by a section of the Left, determined to win Muslim political support at virtually any cost.[53] The leftists have usually insisted that antisemitism in France is vastly exaggerated. Even to raise the issue is often a catalyst for denunciaions of Zionist "intellectual terrorism." The question of antisemitism—so we are asked to believe—is always being raised in order to silence justified criticism of Israel. This kneejerk accusation conveniently avoids any discussion of left-wing Judeophobia. At the same time, there is a general silence on the Left about the resentment towards Jewish success in France expressed by recent Muslim immigrants from North Africa.[54] To the extent that Muslim antisemitism on French soil is even acknowledged, it is blamed either on Israel or on the alleged ethno-religious self-segregation of the French-Jewish community (*communautarisme*). Yet French Muslims are far more "segregated," a fact deliberately obfuscated by the Left.

"Communitarianism" has gradually become *the* stigmatizing label to discredit political opponents from ethnic and religious minorities in the French Republic. It is widely used as an arm of intellectual intimidation, serving to delegitimize as "anti-republican" any coherent communal responses to the real threats that French Jewry have confronted since 2000. The charge is not only spurious but intellectually dishonest and politically motivated. What the anti-communitarians (some of them Jewish themselves) appear to be upset about is the strong identification of French Jews with Israel. The mere fact of defending the existence of Israel as a Jewish state is seen by much of the Left as *exclusivist, tribal,* and even *racist*. Behind such impoverished clichés lies the implicit criminalization of Israel and a barely concealed desire to bring about the marginalization of French Jews as a community.[55] Linked to this phenomenon is the Manichean conceptual world of "progressive" antiracism, with its glorification of hybridized identities and cultures. Those leftists, for whom multi-culturalism and "anti-racism" have become a kind of substitute ideology, usually despise Israel as a dangerous anachronism and an obstacle to their utopian vision of universal brotherhood.[56]

Since the beginning of the 21st century the cumulative intoxication of anti-Zionist mythology seems to have unhinged many French intellectuals on the Left.[57] The rise of militant Islam and its hijacking of the Palestinian cause has certainly played a part in this disorientation. A sign of the times were the statements by the celebrated Venezuelan left-wing terrorist Carlos the Jackal (Illich Ramirez Sanchez), who nearly thirty years earlier had *secretly* converted to Islam in order to better implement his dream of world revolution. Carlos, speaking from his Paris prison, gave an interview to a neo-fascist publication in November 2001 praising the attack on the World Trade Center and calling for the convergence of right-wing and leftist extremism with radical Islam in order to battle "Yankee imperialism and Zionism"—both of them qualified as "enemies of humanity." For Carlos, the jihad to liberate Palestine and the Holy Places (including Mecca and Jerusalem), as well as to bring down the American "hyper-power," was by definition a *sacred* cause demanding "heroic sacrifices" on the scale of 9/11. Submission to Allah's kingdom and espousal of the pure Communist ideal had become identical for the imprisoned Carlos—a prominent figure in Third Worldist activism and international terrorism since the mid-1970s. After 2001, Bin Laden would become his model of the *mujahid* (holy warrior) struggling for universal liberation and the apocalypse whose fulfillment required the eradication of Israel.[58] Carlos's Islamo-communism involved an eclectic synthesis and merging of different militant ideologies united by their intransigent opposition to the United States and Israel.

Carlos emphasized that "the liberation of Palestine" and of the Holy Places of Islam were central to his radical Islamist embrace of the global jihad. It had been further strengthened after 1989 by the "disintegration of the atheist socialist camp." In a collection of texts, first published in 2003, Carlos insisted on the iron consistency of his communist engagement with his pro-Palestinian and jihadist convictions.

> I am and remain a professional revolutionary, a fighter, in the purest Leninist tradition. Without the revolutionary avant-garde

> made up of permanent militants—exclusively committed to prepare, organize and set the Revolution in motion, it would never take place. . . . I have consecrated my life to the Revolution since the age of 14. A militant Communist since January 1964, . . . I continue to be one, exactly as I have remained an intransigent revolutionary. . . .

Carlos added that the decisive turning-point for him had come at the beginning of the 1970s:

> when the world Revolution embodied itself for me in the Palestinian cause. . . . Islam has reinforced my revolutionary convictions at the same time as it purified them, this time granting them a new transcendent dimension.[59]

Carlos's Islamo-Communist militancy in the cause of Palestine is by no means unique. Indeed it is typical of the fluid cross-fertilization of revolutionary ideas, practices, and tactical alliances provoked by left-wing solidarity with the Palestinians. Its equivalent on the far Right would be the Islamo-Nazism of the neo-fascist German intellectual, Horst Mahler, a veteran antisemite who in the early 1970s had achieved notoriety in the anarchist Red Army Faction. For pro-Palestinian Trotskyist revolutionaries of Jewish origin like the late Daniel Bensaïd, the Palestinians were also the ultimate "victim" and therefore beyond rational criticism. He invariably blamed Israel itself (and Jewish communal leaders) for all the problems of the Middle East. The "pyromaniac firemen" of French Jewry, Bensaïd claimed several years ago, combined Judaism and Zionism to the point where any political struggle against the Israeli "occupation" inevitably would be interpreted as antisemitic. Not only that, but the Muslims in France who physically attacked Jews (a fact which he, like other leftists, minimized as far as possible) were themselves whitewashed by the Trotskyite Bensaïd as totally innocent "victims" of French racism, Israeli Jewish oppression and the Middle East conflict.[60] This kind of reasoning was in some ways worse than straightforward apologetics and more popular than the Islamo-Communist fanaticism of Carlos. It completely obscured any Muslim responsibilities for the gratuitous violence against Jews on French soil as well as trivializing the seriousness of jihadist antisemitism.

However, the most effective apologist for radical Islam in France and Western Europe has been Tariq Ramadan—the grandson of Hassan al-Banna who founded the Egyptian Muslim Brotherhood in 1928. Ramadan, a Swiss-born philosopher with a perfect mastery of the French language, is well-placed to spread the Islamist message in the more sophisticated European idiom that appeals to many liberals and leftists. His discourse has relied on a more traditional approach to Islam, open to universal values but sharply rejecting Western materialism and global capitalism. What links him to the antiglobalist Left has been his hostility to neoliberal economics, as practised by the International Monetary Fund and the World Bank.[61] Ramadan's "Islamic socialism" undoubtedly facilitated his patronage by neo-Communist, Trotskyist, and Third Worldist circles in France, beginning with his friend, the left-wing editor-in-chief of *Le Monde Diplomatique,* Alain Gresh—himself an Egyptian Jew by origin.[62]

Ramadan has proved himself to be a shrewd master of doubletalk, not least in relation to antisemitism. Initially he condemned it as "unacceptable and indefensible," contrary to Islam, and to the teachings of the Prophet. In an article of December 2001 he even called for respect towards Judaism, for honoring the memory of the Holocaust, and recognizing the spiritual tie between Jews and Muslims. He also judiciously criticized the exaggerated sense of victimization felt by many marginalized Muslims in France and the rest of Europe.[63] However, in September 2003, Ramadan launched an astonishing attack on a number of leading French-Jewish intellectuals whom he gratuitously accused of being slavish "communitarian" defenders of Israel. The hit-list included André Glucksmann, Bernard-Henri Lévy, Alain Finkielkraut, Pierre-André Taguieff (a non-Jew), and Bernard Kouchner (later to become Foreign Minister), who is half-Jewish. Ramadan claimed that these self-proclaimed cosmopolitan and "universalist" intellectuals had become no more than narrow-minded tribalist lapdogs of Ariel Sharon. None of Ramadan's accusations were actually true. Most of the intellectuals under fire were not even identified with the Jewish community in France or Israel. Their attitudes towards the Jewish State varied considerably and none could be qualified as right-wing Likud supporters. Nor were they indifferent to universal causes. Lévy had publicly opposed the American invasion of Iraq and intervened on behalf of Muslims in Bosnia; Glucksmann had been particularly active in trying to halt the genocide in Rwanda and the massacres of Muslims in Chechnya; Kouchner had established "Doctors Without Borders"—a humanitarian non-governmental organization deeply involved in humanitarian causes in Africa. As for the non-Jewish Taguieff, he belonged to the secular republican camp and was also France's leading historian of antisemitism. To accuse him of "Jewish communitarianism" clearly strained all credulity.

Glucksmann was brief though trenchant in his reply to Ramadan, writing: "What is surprising is not that Mr. Ramadan is antisemitic, but that he dares to proclaim it openly." Alain Finkielkraut pointed out that if Ramadan's list of "Jewish intellectuals" had been published by Jean-Marie Le Pen, there would have been a universal explosion of outrage.[64] Instead, the grandson of Hassan al-Banna rapidly became a celebrity, invited to the popular TV talk show of Thierry Ardisson, *Tout le monde en parle*. Not only that, but the anti-globalist European Social Forum in November 2003 publicly hailed Ramadan as a precious Islamist ally, despite his own "communitarist" insistence that his new friends on the Left accept Muslim group specificity. Ramadan's frontal assault on French Jewish intellectuals and his blaming of the Iraq War on Paul Wolfowitz (a "notorious Zionist"), Richard Perle, and other neocon, "pro-Likud" American Jews was hardly a problem for most of his anti-globalist friends. Their unconditional pro-Palestinian positions, reinforced by radical anti-Americanism, anti-Zionism, and a transparent desire to win over young Muslims in France, made them only too willing to ignore the anti-semitic implications of Ramadan's remarks. Bernard-Henri Lévy deplored this uncritical "libertarian" reflex. He observed that Ramadan had crudely attacked his book on the gruesome Islamist-inspired assassination of the American-Jewish journalist Daniel Pearl in Karachi, as if it were part of a pro-Sharon plot to discredit Pakistan and justify an Indian-Israeli alliance. Such absurd conspiracy theories were all too reminiscent of the *Protocols of the Elders of Zion*.[65]

In France with its 600,000-strong Jewish community and a significant number of Jewish intellectuals willing to defend Israel, it was at least possible to effectively answer influential Islamists like Tariq Ramadan. This was hardly the case in Sweden, a country with only 15,000 Jews where the moralistic hectoring of Israel has long been a standard feature of political and media elite opinion. Writing on this topic in October 2003, history professor Sverker Oredsson, together with Swedish researcher, Dr. Mikael Tossa-vainen, noted that many Muslim students in Sweden were extremely antisemitic. They frequently labeled the Holocaust as "Zionist propaganda," expressed undisguised admiration for Hitler, and regretted that he had not killed more Jews. These students generally absorbed their antisemitism from the Quran, Muslim fundamentalist culture, and their own countries of origin, via satellite TV and the Internet. They were also influenced by the hostile anti-Israeli media reports about the Middle East coming from Swedish sources. The result was a sharp rise in harassment, threats, and attacks on Jews by Arabs and Muslim immigrants in Sweden. However, rather than deal with the nefarious impact of radical Islam, Swedish politicians and intellectuals, especially on the Left, preferred to pillory Israel. This trend of appeasement was particularly obvious in the Swedish Social Democratic Party whose antagonistic attitude towards Israel in recent decades has been no secret. In recent elections the Social Democrats and other left-wing groups in Sweden were clearly looking for votes from the half-a-million Muslims who heavily outnumber Jews in Swedish society. They have not refrained from making overtures to radical Islamic groups who might assist them in this endeavor.

Spain offers another example of the intense hostility of many on the Left towards Israel. The Socialist prime minister of Spain, José Luís Rodríguez Zapatero, has been one of Israel's fiercest critics inside the European Union. At a rally on 19 July 2006, Zapatero was photographed wearing a kaffiyeh at a time when Hezbollah was firing rockets at Israel. He sharply attacked Israel's policy of using "abusive force" and the U.S. invasion of Iraq for producing only "fanaticism and instability." The conservative Popular Party responded by bluntly calling Zapatero's views on Israel the product of "antisemitism, anti-Zionism, and Israelophobia."[66] Several months later, Juan José Laborda, a veteran Spanish Socialist senator, repeated these same charges, noting that antisemitism was strongly rooted in Spanish history, from the expulsion of Jews in 1492, through the Inquisition, to the pro-Arab Franco dictatorship (1939–1975), and the "infantile anti-Americanism" of contemporary leftists in Spain.[67] These sentiments were stirred up once again by the Second Lebanon War, in which Israel was blamed by the Left (and at times by conservatives) for the confrontation with Hezbollah, with some of the commentaries containing an unmistakable antisemitic slant.

Prime Minister Zapatero himself contributed to the ugly climate by referring to the Israeli-Palestinian struggle as a "cancer" that had metastasized and spilled over into all the other Middle-Eastern conflicts. He left the impression that Israel rather than Islamist terror (which he never condemned) was the cancer in question. A year earlier, in 2005, at a dinner party in the Spanish equivalent of the White House, Zapatero concluded yet another anti-Zionist tirade by expressing understanding that "someone might justify the Holocaust." Such rhetoric fitted well with Zapatero's loathing for capitalist globalization on the American model—an animus often linked on the Spanish far Right and Left with "Jewish influence." Indeed, a *majority* of Spaniards appear to believe that "Jews have too much power in international market." This is all the more striking since today there are less than 20,000 Spanish Jews (0.05 percent) out of a total population of 42 million. Yet antisemitism is notably stronger in Spain than in France, whose Jewish population is thirty times larger.[68]

Demonization of Israel and its leaders is not uncommon in the mainstream Spanish media, including its main TV channels. The "criminality of Israel," so it seems, is for many not even a topic that requires empirical proof. For example, the April 2002 events in Jenin were spoken of, almost axiomatically, as "ethnic cleansing" by Israel or, worse still, as a "Holocaust"—especially on the Spanish Left. Pilar Rahola, herself a left-wing Spanish Catalonian journalist who has courageously exposed these trends, observed in May 2003:

> The Jewish victims in Israel also end up. . .as their own killers. There are no Jewish victims, just as there are no Palestinian executioners. . . . Arab terrorism becomes comprehensible and even acceptable.[69]

As elsewhere on the European Left, it has evidently become commonplace in Spain to claim that Israel was seeking a "final solution" of the Palestinian question through Nazi-like methods. This antisemitic libel, especially rampant among Marxists and Islamists, has had a toxic effect on the discourse concerning Israel and the Jews, in recent years. The short Gaza war, followed by the flotilla fatalities in the summer of 2009, further escalated these trends.

The ideological war against Israel is equally glaring in Latin America among left-wing leaders like Daniel Ortega in Nicaragua, and, above all, in the case of Venezuela's mercurial President, Hugo Chávez. His "anti-Zionism" goes well beyond the traditional propaganda of communist parties and Third World movements in South America. It reflects the growing antisemitic influence coming from outside Islamist forces like Iran and Hezbollah since the 1990s, which has fused with local anti-American and anti-Zionist hate speech. Iranian moves to develop friendly relations with Latin American states (especially authoritarian populist Third World leaders like Chávez) are driven by ideological affinities as well as economic and geostrategic motives. They are a part of revolutionary opposition to the status quo, and the American-dominated international system. But they also have an anti-Jewish edge. Chávez, in particular, shares with the Iranian leadership the same propensity to hurl Holocaustal terminology at the Jewish State whenever the occasion presents itself. Thus in a television broadcast in late January 2009 he bluntly stated: "The Holocaust, that is what is happening right now in Gaza."[70]

Such pronouncements have led, not surprisingly, to an escalation in verbal and physical attacks on Jews in Venezuela. Indeed, the American State Department felt compelled to list the country as a state sponsor of antisemitism as well as anti-Israel hysteria.[71] There is no doubt that since Chávez came to power Venezuela's small but prosperous upper-middle class Jewish community has come under increasing threat. The August 2006 street demonstrations of *Chavistas* (Chávez supporters) included ominous slogans in Caracas such as "Jews go home," "Jewish murderers," "The US and Israel want to destroy Venezuela." Constant incitement in the government (reflecting President Chávez's own aggressive rhetoric) has presented Israel as a "genocidal State" and made Venezuelan Jews feel unwelcome in their own country.[72] The weekly *Los Papeles de Mandinga,* for example, did not shrink from ferociously attacking the head of the Caracas Jewish community, for defending the "Nazi mass murderers" who govern Israel.[73]

The relentlessly anti-American Chávez, a former military commander who heads a nation that is the world's third largest petroleum producer, is primarily responsible for this collapse in relations with the Jewish community. A self-declared socialist (who claims to emulate the 19th-century liberator of South America, Simon Bolívar), Chávez's aim to forge an axis of anti-American leftist regimes across the continent, has been largely achieved. His eclectic world-view includes a heady mix of Jesus, Marx, Lenin, Castro, left-wing nationalism, and increasingly intimate links with the Islamic Revolution in Iran.[74] The ideological inspiration for Chávez's links with the Arab and Muslim world goes back to the 1990s, when he came under the influence of the Argentine sociologist, Norberto Rafael Ceresole. Ceresole, a former Peronist who died in 2003, was much admired by the Hezbollah, with whom he developed strong links. He attributed the deadly antisemitic terrorist bombings in Buenos Aires—at the Israeli Embassy and the Jewish communal center, AMIA, in the 1990s—to "Jewish terrorism" though they were indisputably ordered by Iran and carried out by Hezbollah.[75] Already then, Ceresole had come to see Iran as "the center of resistance to Jewish aggression" and as the only state capable of destroying Israel.[76] In his view (shared by much of the far Left, the Argentine Hezbollah, and most probably by President Chávez), the struggle against the Jewish State had to include the Third world as well as the Middle East.

Ceresole soon gravitated from left-wing Peronism towards an idiosyncratic synthesis of communism, fascism, and radical Islam. Arriving in Venezuela in 1994 he became a close political adviser of Commandante Chávez while maintaining close ties with Islamic terrorists. After a temporary expulsion from Venezuela he returned in 1998, writing a glorified account of the Chávez revolution. The first chapter blamed Zionism and world Jewry for his earlier exile; subsequent chapters revealed his admiration for French Holocaust deniers Robert Faurisson and Roger Garaudy. The former Communist Garaudy (a convert to Islam, who became a Holocaust denier and a fervent anti-Zionist) was an obvious role model for Ceresole's own "unmasking" of the Holocaust as a propaganda tool ruthlessly used by Israel and the Jews. The Holocaust "myth," Ceresole insisted, had been cynically exploited to blackmail Germany, Europe and America. Since 1948 it had served to justify the rape of "Arab Palestine" and to promote the "messianic-monotheistic creed" of American-Zionist global domination.[77]

Such antisemitic rhetoric is today not uncommon in Socialist Venezuela. This is a land in which government media as well as prominent parliamentarians regularly join in frenzied accusations against Israel as a racist "genocidal" State and pillory the "Jewish-Zionist bourgeoisie" in Venezuela itself. In this witchhunt, they can safely follow the lead of their authoritarian populist President, who on 6 January 2009 accused Israel for the umpteenth time of carrying out a "holocaust" against the Palestinians in Gaza.[78] Chávez has indeed never lost an opportunity during the past decade to demonize Israel and compare its actions to those of the Nazis. His anti-Americanism is no less virulent. On visits to China and the Middle East in the summer of 2006 he continually branded the United States as a satanic, fascist-imperialist Empire of evil, and Israel as its terrorist tool. This was naturally music to the ears of his host in Tehran (and close ally), the antisemitic Holocaust-denier, President Mahmoud Ahmadinejad.[79] During a visit to Damascus that same summer, Chávez called for a new world which would "dig the grave of North American imperialism" and bring an end to Israel's "Nazi crimes" in Lebanon and Palestine. At a press conference with President Bashar al-Assad, he called Israel's control of the Golan Heights (secured in a defensive war against Syria in 1967) a "theft perpetrated against the whole world."[80] During these and other visits to the Middle East, Chávez made a point of expressing his admiration for Arab nationalist heroes like Gamal Abdul Nasser.[81]

Chávez's implacable anti-Americanism and demonization of Israel has assured him iconic status among the Hezbollah fighters and their followers in Lebanon as well as the warm embrace of Ahmadinejad in Tehran. Hassan Nasrallah saluted him as a popular hero to the Muslims of Beirut on a par with Ernesto Che Guevara and Iran's Supreme Guide, Ali Khamanei.[82] This coupling is itself revealing. Hezbollah-sponsored agitation in Latin America has learned to skillfully blend the débris from Marxist, anti-globalist, antisemitic, and Islamo-fascist concepts to serve jihadist ends. Chávez as the central figure in the "heroic resistance" of Latin American socialists to American "banditry" is as obvious an ally for the Lebanese Hezbollah as he has been for its Iranian patrons. Chávez fully reciprocated by defending Iran's nuclear program and calling his allies in Tehran "brothers who fight for a just world."[83] Indeed, the radical anti-Israeli and antisemitic motifs in Chávez's Bolivarian revolution cannot be separated from the dynamics of this international strategy. Among the immediate consequences have been the expulsion of the Israeli ambassador from Caracas in January 2009 and the exodus abroad of many Venezuelan Jews from all socioeconomic strata. These almost inevitable results of antisemitic escalation are closely linked to the inroads of Islamism into Venezuela and the strong sympathy that local Hezbollah groups have expressed for Chávez's Bolivarian revolution.

Chávez had first been introduced to the Muslim world by his antisemitic mentor, Ceresole in the 1990s. The Argentine theorist had become, as we have seen, a strong advocate of a new Latin-American and Arab alliance—the precise strategy that Chávez would pursue once in power. It is this axis with Iran and a number of Arab states (especially Syria) that has helped bolster Chávez's claims to be a major international player and leader of the anti-Yankee leftist bloc in Latin America. Scapegoating Israel is as essential to this strategic alliance as Chávez's cultivation of radical Islam. References to "the descendants of those who crucified Christ" have also been thrown in for good measure to reinforce the Marxist-Islamic connection with a dose of traditional Catholic antisemitism. In a Christmas message on 24 December 2005, Chávez said:

> The world has an offer for everybody but it turned out that a few minorities—the descendants of whose who crucified Christ, the descendants of those who expelled Bolívar from here and also those who in a certain way crucified him in Santa Marta, there in Colombia—they took possession of the riches of the world. . . .[84]

Chávez and his supporters claimed he was referring to global capitalism rather than to the Jews but this seems inherently implausible. The context makes it clear enough that it was not the (Italian!) descendants of Pontius Pilate (Roman Governor of Palestine at the time) whom he had in mind; and if capitalist globalization was the sole enemy, there was no need at all to refer to the crucifixion of Christ, which, in popular Latin American Catholic consciousness, was perpetrated solely by Jews.

The defenders of Commandante Chávez in the Venezuelan press have undoubtedly envenomed antisemitism with their unrestrained demonization of the Jewish State. The pillorying of Israel and the Jews in the name of a populist socialism (mixed with Christian, Muslim, and Third Worldist *ressentiment*) has had the inevitable effect of intimidation. The Jewish race is said to have been damned with the mark of Cain "for having destroyed Jesus Christ"; it supposedly invented the myth of its own "chosenness" to dispossess the Palestinians; it controls the economy and government of the United States; and is "conspiring in Venezuela to take over our finances, our industries, commerce, construction, government positions and politics."[85] The well-known left-wing journalist Alberto Nolia in a radio broadcast on 19 July 2006 even referred to the "assassin Zionist dogs" destroying Lebanon as being far worse than the Nazis; caricatured Israel as "a fundamentalist theocracy" and falsely asserted that there were no Arabs in the Israeli Parliament.[86] Such comments are a standard part of the systematic incitement of Venezuela's impoverished masses by an authoritarian Socialist regime and its media hounds. These masses take their inspiration from a leader, Hugo Chávez, for whom there is no question that Israel is doing to absolutely "innocent" Arabs and Palestinians "what Hitler did to the Jews."[87] Like Ahmadinejad and the Iranian leadership, the Venezuelan ruler firmly believes that both America and Israel represent the satanic face of fascist imperialism—a force doomed to disappear by the decree of God, history, and popular justice.[88] The political influence of this growing Venezuela-Iran alliance in the rest of Latin America should not be underestimated and has already influenced the trend towards embracing the Palestinian cause throughout the region.[89]

Over a decade ago, Hugo Chávez inherited the mantle of Fidel Castro as the fountainhead of anti-American sentiment in Latin America. By using a mixture of Venezuela's oil wealth, drug money, shrewd political deals, and crude populist appeals, he has indeed achieved a measure of leadership on an awakening continent, eager to emancipate itself from what is clearly perceived as the declining power of the United States. His close links with an Iranian regime relentlessly seeking strategic allies in Latin America, makes perfect sense. In the case of Chávez, the alliance of populist Marxism with messianic jihadism has been forged by the expedient combination of geopolitical need, a dictatorial will-to-power, anti-Americanism, and the common hatred of Israel. Nearly twenty years ago, the former Argentine leftist, Norberto Ceresole decisively shaped Chávez's turn toward radical Islam, Iran, and Hezbollah as future political allies in the war to overthrow

U.S. imperialism. Ceresole's vision of the Jewish international conspiracy would also become an integral part of this political turn, which is echoed in much of the rhetoric in the Venezuelan public sphere during recent years. The Chavista media has encouraged a vulgar Marxist campaign presenting "Judaism" as a mind-control device to intoxicate the Catholic masses; and damning Zionism as a sinister exploitative ideology whose ultimate aim is to accumulate wealth and power, while seeking to sabotage the success of Chávez's Socialist revolution. The language of class struggle, anti-imperialism and antisemitic hatred directed at a mythical "Jewish lobby" merges together in a poisonous synthesis.[90] The antisemitic element in Chávez's messianic socialism and Third World nationalism has been shrewdly adapted to the Latin American *caudillo* tradition. Fragments of radical populism, xenophobic nationalism, Marxist class-struggle, anti-Americanism, anti-globalism, political Islam, and Christian liberation theology are all part of the eclectic mish-mash that forms Chávez's ideology. Demonic images of "Christ killers," of rapacious capitalists who have seized the world's riches and revulsion at a Dracula-like U.S. blood-lust, accompany not only the hijacking of the Palestinian cause but the identification with militant Islamist aspirations. Old and new stereotypes have come together with malignant conspiracy theories in a Latin American version of national socialism remoulded to fit the twenty-first century.[91] Anticapitalist antisemitism underpinning radical anti-Zionism is an integral part of the Marxist-Islamist ideological axis which seeks to redeem the contemporary world from the sinister "plots" of American imperialism and the yoke of Zionist "oppression." It remains to be seen whether such a bizarre mixture of fragments from Marx, Castro, Jesus, and Muhammad can be successfully updated to fill the vacuum left by the collapse of Soviet Communism two decades ago.

NOTES

1. Bernard Lewis, "Communsm and Islam," *International Affairs* 30 (Jan. 1954): I, 9–10.

2. See Ali Shariati, *Red Shiism* (Houston, 1974) and idem, *Reflections on Humanity: Two Views of Civilization and the Plight of Man* (Houston, 1974). Also Frantz Fanon, *Les Damnés de la Terre* (Paris, 1961), a seminal text on the redemptive role of violence in the "anti-imperialist struggle of national liberation."

3. Shariati, *Red Shiism*, 8. Also Farhad Khrosrokhavar, *Les Nouveaux Martyrs d'Allah* (Paris, 2002), 72.

4. Khrosrokhavar, *Les Nouveaux Martyrs,* 76.

5. Efraim Karsh, *Arafat's War: The Man and His Battle for Israeli Conquest* (New York, 2003), 92–101.

6. Jillian Becker, *The PLO: The Rise and Fall of the Palestinian Liberation Organization* (New York, 1984), 106.

7. Robert S. Wistrich, *A Lethal Obsession. Anti-Semitism from Antiquity to the Global Jihad* (New York, 2010), 713.

8. Ibid.

9. Amal Saad-Ghorayeb, *Hizbu'llah. Politics and Religion* (London, 2002), 16–30.

10. Ibid., 168–86.

11. Ali Shariati, *Red Shiism,* 7–10.

12. Wistrich, *A Lethal Obsession,* 763–829.

13. Ibid., 879–927.

14. *Congress of the Peoples of the East, Baku, September 1920* (Stenographic Report, London, 1977), quoted in Laurent Murawiec, *The Mind of Jihad* (Cambridge, U.K., 2008), 211.

15. Ibid., 212.

16. *Congress of the Peoples of the East,* 167–73.

17. Murawiec, *Mind of Jihad,* 215.

18. Stephan Grigat, "Mit dem Mufti gegen den Zionismus—mit Gromyko für Israel. Aus der Frühgeschichte der israelischen und palästinenschen Kommunistischen Partei," *Transversal* 2 (2009): 97–127.

19. On the history of the Palestine Communist Party in the 1920s, see Jacob Hen-Tov, *Communism and Zionism in Palestine: The Comintern and the Political Unrest in the 1920s* (Cambridge, Mass., 1974); also Sondra Miller Rubinstein, *The Communist Movement in Palestine and Israel 1919–1984* (Boulder, 1985); and Musa Budeiri, *The Palestine Communist Party 1919–1948* (London, 1979).

20. See Walter Laqueur, *Communism and Nationalism in the Middle East* (New York, 1956).

21. Murawiec, *Mind of Jihad,* 237.

22. On Haj Amin's collaboration with Hitler Germany, see the detailed biography by Klaus Gensicke, *The Mufti of Jerusalem and the Nazis. The Berlin Years* (London, 2011).

23. Budeiri, 93.

24. Grigat, "Mit dem Mufti," 112–14.

25. Ibid., 115–16.

26. Early Bolshevik leaders, including Stalin, believed in the revolutionary possibilities of the Muslim world. They were much influenced by an Indian radical best known under his alias of M. N. Roy (1887–1954). Roy was, in fact, a Hindu-born

Islamophile and perhaps the leading strategist of the "Red Jihad." See Murawiec, *Mind of Jihad,* 207–23. As for Stalin, in the 1920s he sought to exploit the anti-British revolutionary potential of pan-Islamism but later cooled towards the project. In the 1930s he would purge and execute many of the Muslim National Communists in the U.S.S.R. who followed the ideas of Sultan Galiev.

27. Murawiec, *Mind of Jihad,i* 233–55.

28. See Jeffrey Herf, *Nazi Propaganda for the Arab World* (New Haven, 2009).

29. Y. Harkabi, *Arab Attitudes to Israel* (Jerusalem, 1972), 237–40.

30. Among Serfaty's writings, see *Dans les prisons du roi* (Paris, 1992), *Écrits de prison sur la Palestine* (Paris, 1992), and with Mikhaël Elbaz, *L'insoumis: juifs, marocains et rebelles* (Paris, 2001), 191–241. See also his memoirs, written together with his wife, Christine Daure-Serfaty, *La mémoire de l'autre* (Paris, 1993).

31. See Andrew Bostom, ed., *The Legacy of Islamic Antisemitism* (Amherst, 2008).

32. Sayed Abul Ala Maududi, *Jihad in Islam* (Lahore, 1998–2001) is a seminal work.

33. Ibid., 9–10, 13–14.

34. Murawiec, *Mind of Jihad,* 286.

35. Ibid., 318; see also Robert S. Wistrich, *A Lethal Obsession*, 830–78 on Khomeini.

36. David Horowitz, *Unholy Alliance. Radical Islam and the American Left* (Washington D.C., 2004), 128–31.

37. Yossi Klein Halevi, "Hatreds Entwined," *Azure* (Winter 2004): 25–31.

38. Mathan Ravid, "Prejudice and Demonization in the Swedish Middle East Debate during the 2006 Lebanon War," *Jewish Political Studies Review* 21, nos. 1–2 (Spring 2009): 79–94.

39. Eran Benedek, "Britain's Respect Party: The Leftist-Islamist Alliance and Its Attitude toward Israel," *Jewish Political Studies Review* 19, nos. 3–4 (Fall 2007): 153–63.

40. "Taleban Kidnap Victim, Yvonne Ridley, Talks to Alon Orbach," *FelixOnline* 1344: Features, 16 Feb. 2006, www.felixonline.co.uk/v2/article.php?id=293 (no longer available). Ridley, a British citizen, converted to Islam after she was released by the Taleban who had kidnapped her in Afghanistan.

41. George Galloway, "Hizbollah Is Right to Fight Zionist Terror," *Socialist Worker*, 29 July 2006, 3.

42. Dave Hyde, "Two Tribes. Europe's Other Red-Green Alliance," *The Review* (Melbourne) (July 2003): 25–27; also Nick Cohen, "The Left's unholy alliance with religious bigotry," *Guardian,* 23 Feb. 2003. Cohen, despite his name, is not Jewish but he reported receiving a flood of defamatory e-mails whenever he touched on subjects relating to Israel or Islam.

43. Mark Strauss, "Antiglobalism's Jewish Problem," *Foreign Policy,* 28 Oct. 2003, http://www.foreignpolicy.com.

44. Mick Hume, "The anti-imperialism of fools," *New Statesman*, 17 June 2002, 29–31.

45. Hume, ibid., 31, quotes Naomi Klein, a prominent Canadian Jewish critic of both the Israeli occupation and globalization, as saying: "every time I lock on to activist news sites such as indymedia.org [the main antiglobalist website]. . .I'm confronted with a string of Jewish conspiracy theories about 9/11 and excerpts from the Protocols of the Elders of Zion."

46. Joseph Macé-Scaron, "Les Soviets plus l'obscurité," *Marianne,* 6–12 Feb. 2010.

47. Wistrich, *A Lethal Obsession,* 605.

48. Strauss, "Antiglobalism."

49. Daniel Goldhagen, "The Globalization of Antisemitism," *Forward,* 2 May 2003.

50. See Josef Joffe, *Nations We Love to Hate: Israel, America, and the New Antisemitism* (SICSA, Hebrew University of Jerusalem, Posen Papers in Contemporary Antisemitism, no. 1, 2004).

51. Ibid., 11–14.

52. Ulrich Beck, "Globalisierte Emotionen: Der neue europäische Antisemitismus," *Süddeutsche Zeitung,* 17 Nov. 2003, 11.

53. See Pascal Boniface, *Est-il permis de critiquer Israël?* (Paris, 2003).

54. Wistrich, *A Lethal Obsession,* 292–93.

55. Shmuel Trigano, "Communauté juive et communautarisme," *Observatoire du monde juif,* nos. 10–11 (May 2004): 1–7.

56. See the essay by Alain Finkielkraut, "Le sionisme face à la religion de l'humanité," in *Le Sionisme face à ses Détracteurs,* edited by Shmuel Trigano (Paris, 2003), 160–70.

57. Meir Weintrater, "L'inquiétante étrangeté de l'antisionisme," *L'Arche* (May 2003): 36–41.

58. See *Marianne,* 4–10 Feb. 2002; also Wistrich, *A Lethal Obsession,* 300; and Pierre-André Taguieff, *La Nouvelle propaganda antijuive* (Paris, 2010), 522–24.

59. Ilich Ramirez Sánchez [Carlos], *L'Islam révolutionnaire,* edited and presented by Jean-Michel Vernochet (Monaco, 2003), 37–39.

60. Interview with Daniel Ben-Saïd, "Les responsables juifs sont des pompiers pyromanes," *Marianne,* 28 Jan.–3 Feb. 2002.

61. Ian Buruma, "Tariq Ramadan Has an Identity Issue," *New York Times,* 4 Feb. 2007.

62. Pierre-André Taguieff, *Prêcheurs de Haine: Traversée de la judéophobie planétaire* (Paris, 2004), 906–13.

63. Tariq Ramadan, "Existe-il un antisémitisme islamique?" *Le Monde,* 22 Dec. 2001.

64. Alain Finkielkraut, "Une réponse à Tariq Ramadan," *L'Arche* (Nov.–Dec. 2003): 28–29.

65. Bernard-Henri Lévy, "Tariq Ramadan et les altermondialistes," *Le Point,* 10 Oct. 2003.

66. "One of Israel's Biggest Critics: Spanish Prime Minister Leads Anti-War Chorus," *Jerusalem Post,* 13 Aug. 2006.

67. Wistrich, *A Lethal Obsession,* 456–57.

68. On contemporary Spanish antisemitism and attitudes to Israel, see Alejandro Baer, "Spain's Jewish Problem," *Jahrbuch für Antisemitismusforschung* (2009): 89–110; also *Estudio Sobre Antisemitismo en España. Informe de Resultados* (Casa Sefarad Israel, July 2010).

69. Wistrich, *A Lethal Obsession,* 458.

70. Ibid., 661.

71. Melanie Kirkpatrick, "The Politics of Intimidation," *Wall Street Journal,* 1 May 2009.

72. Among many examples from the Venezuelan press, see "Cianuro en Gotas," *Los papeles de Mandinga,* 19–-25 Sept. 2006; and Basem Tajeldine, "La disociación mental del Pueblo Elegido," *Rebelión,* 26 May 2008—a nakedly antisemitic article.

73. Wistrich, *A Lethal Obsession,* 625.

74. "With Marx, Lenin and Jesus Christ," *Economist,* 13 Jan. 2007.

75. See Norberto Ceresole, "La Argentina e el espacio geopolitico del terrorismo judio," Radio Islam, http://www.radioislam.net/islam/spanish/sion/terror/cap2.htm and http://www.islam-shia.org/.

76. Norberto Ceresole, "Carta abierta a mis amigos iranies," http://www.vho.org/aaargh/espa/ceres/carta.html (a Holocaust denial website).

77. Norberto Ceresole, *Caudillo, Ejército Pueblo: la Venezuela del Commandante Chávez* (Madrid, 2000).

78. Venezuela's Chávez Calls Attack 'Holocaust,' Reuters, 6 Jan. 2009, at http://www.alertnet.org/the news/newsdesk/No6437606.htm.

79. "Chavez et Ahmadinejad, unis contre les Etats-Unis," *Libération,* 31 July 2006.

80. Simon Romero, "Venezuela Strengthens Its Relationships in the Middle East," *New York Times,* 21 Aug. 2006.

81. "Venezuela President Chavez on Al-Jazeera," *MEMRI, Special Dispatch Series,* no. 1235 (8 Aug. 2006).

82. See "Entrevista a Sayyid Hassan Nasrallah, dirigente máximo de Hezbollah," *Izquierda Punto Info,* http://www.organizacionislam.org.ar/conflib/repor-sayyed.htm.

83. See Luís Roniger, *Antisemitism, Real or Imagined? Chávez, Iran, Israel, and the Jews* (Analysis of Current Trends in Antisemitism, no. 33, Vidal Sassoon International Center for the Study of Antisemitism, The Hebrew University of Jerusalem, 2009).

84. Quoted by Roniger, *Antisemitism, Real or Imagined?,* 17.

85. See the articles by Basem Tajeldine on the "Zionist Menace" in Venezuela, in *Diario Vea,* 14 Sept. 2006; also Tarek Muci Nasir, "Zionist Jews," *El Diario Caracas,* 2 Sept. 2006.

86. Alberto Nolia, *Los Papeles de Mandinga,* 19 July 2006, YVKE Mundial (Radio).

87. "Venezuelan President Chavez on Al-Jazeera: Israel Uses Methods of Hitler," *MEMRI, Special Dispatch Series,* no. 1235, 8 Aug. 2006.

88. "Venezuelan President Chavez and Iranian President Ahmadinejad on Iranian TV," *MEMRI, Special Dispatch Series,* no. 1226, 2 Aug. 2006.

89. Caroline B. Glick, "Why Latin America Turned," *Jerusalem Post,* 10 Dec. 2010.

90. Ceresole had initially come from the left-wing Peronist organization, Montoneros, before adopting Holocaust denial, the theory of the Jewish world conspiracy, and the equation of Israel with Nazism. See Roniger, *Antisemitism, Real or Imagined?,* 19–21.

91. Wistrich, *A Lethal Obsession,* 629–30.

Archival Sources and Selected Bibliography

Archival Material

Archiv der Sozialen Demokratie (Friedrich Ebert Stiftung, Bonn–Bad Godesburg). *Nachlässe*: Ludwig Frank, Ernst Heilmann, Georg Ledebour, Paul Levi, Gustav Noske, Bruno Schoenlank, Friedrich Stampfer.

Institute of Social History (Amsterdam). *Nachlässe*: Otto Bauer, August Bebel, Eduard Bernstein, Friedrich Engels, Jules Guesde, Moses Hess, Wolfgang Heine, Karl Kautsky, Paul Lafargue, Wilhelm Liebknecht, Rosa Luxemburg, Karl Marx, Julius Motteler, Georg von Vollmar.

Verein für Geschichte der Arbeiterbewegung and the *Austrian Social Democratic Party Archive* (Vienna). Materials on Victor Adler, Friedrich Adler, Engelbert Pernerstorfer, Franz Schuhmeier.

YIVO Institute for Jewish Research (New York). Abraham Cahan, Jacob Lestchinsky, Chaim Zhitlovsky.

Bund Archives of the Jewish Labour Movement (New York). Materials on the Foreign Committee of the Bund, Karl Kautsky, Vladimir Medem.

Central Zionist Archives (Jerusalem): Nathan Birnbaum, Leon Chasanowitsch, Theodor Herzl, Bernard Lazare, Berl Locker, Max Nordau.

Jewish National and University Library (Hebrew University of Jerusalem, Givat Ram Campus): Martin Buber, Albert Einstein, Stefan Zweig: archives and correspondence.

Archives of the Alliance Israélite Universelle (Paris). Archives of Bernard Lazare, Wladimir Rabi.

Préfecture de la Police (Paris). Files on Auguste Chirac, Edouard Drumont, Jules Guérin, Gérault Richard, Bernard Lazare, Fernand Pelloutier, Albert Regnard, Henri Rochefort, Edouard Vaillant.

Archives Nationales (Paris). Dossiers on the Dreyfus Affair.

In addition we have studied various private papers relating to the Dreyfus Affair at the Bibliothèque Nationale de France.

Select Bibliography of Newspapers and Periodicals

A. Before 1945

Allgemeine Zeitung des Judenthums (Leipzig and Berlin)
Arbeiterstimme, London (Yiddish)
Arbeiterzeitung (Vienna)
Archiv für Geschichte des Sozialismus und der Arbeiterewegung (Leipzig)
Berliner Volksblatt (Berlin)
Cahiers de la Quinzaine (Paris)
Der Jude (Berlin)
Der Kampf (Vienna)
Der Sozialdemokrat (Zurich/London)
Der Socialistische Gids (Amsterdam)
Deutsche Worte (Vienna)
Die Fackel (Vienna)
Die Neue Freie Presse (Vienna)
Die Neue Zeit (Stuttgart)
Die Welt (Vienna)
Dokumente des Sozialismus (Berlin)
Frankfurter Zeitung (Frankfurt a.M.)
Gleichheit (Vienna)
Iskra (Leipzig/Munich/London/Geneva)
Justice (London)
Kadimah (Paris)
L'Action Française (Paris)
L'Antijuif (Algiers)
L'Aurore (Paris)
L'Echo Sioniste (Paris)
L'Humanité (Paris)
La Bataille Syndicaliste (Paris)
La Dépêche de Toulouse (Toulouse)
La Guerre Sociale (Paris)
La Libre Parole (Paris)

La Petite République (Paris)
La Revue Blanche (Paris)
La Revue Socialiste (Paris)
Le Flambleau (Paris)
Le Journal du Peuple (Paris)
Le Libertaire (Paris)
Le Mouvement Socialiste(Paris)
Leipziger Volkszeitung (Leipzig)
Młot (Warsaw)
Neue Sozial-Demokrat (Berlin)
Österreichische Wochenschrift (Vienna)
Przegląd Socjaldemokratyczny (Warsaw)
Reynolds News (London)
Rote Fahne (Berlin)
Sächsische Arbeiterzeitung (Dresden)
Sozialistische Monatshefte (Berlin)
Sprawa Robotnicza (Paris)
Volkstribune (Vienna)
Vorwärts (Berlin)
Weltbühne (Berlin)

B. Newspaper and Periodical Sources since 1945

Annali (Milan)
Antisemitism International (Jerusalem)
Archiv für Sozialgeschichte (Bonn)
Azure (Jerusalem)
Commentary (New York)
Die Republik (Vienna)
Die Zeit (Hamburg)
Dissent (New York)
East European Jewish Affairs (London)
Economist (London)
El País (Madrid)
Encounter (London)
European Judaism (London)
Frankfurter Allgemeine Zeitung (Frankfurt)
Historia Judaica (New York)
Internationale Wissentschaftliche Korrespondenz(Berlin)
Izvestia (Moscow)

Jahrbuch des Instituts für Deutsche Geschichte (Tel Aviv)
Jewish Social Studies (New York)
Journal of Contemporary History (London)
Journal of Modern History (Chicago)
L'Express (Paris)
Le Monde (Paris)
Le Mouvement Sociale (Paris)
Le Nouvel Observateur (Paris)
Leo Baeck Yearbook (London)
Les Nouveaux Cahiers (Paris)
Libération (Paris)
Midstream (New York)
Neuer Zürcher Zeitung (Zurich)
New York Times (New York)
Pravda (Moscow)
Soviet Jewish Affairs (London)
The Daily Telegraph (London)
The Guardian (London)
The Independent (London)
The Times (London)
Wiener Library Bulletin (London)
Zion (Jerusalem)

Selected Books

Abramovich, R. *In Tsvei Revolutsies*. New York, 1944.

Acher, Mathias [pseud., Nathan Birnbaum]. *Das Stiefkind der Sozialdemokratie*. Vienna, 1906.

Adler, Friedrich, ed. *Victor Adler. Briefwechsel mit August Bebel und Karl Kautsky*. Vienna, 1954.

Adler, Victor. *Aufsätze, Reden und Briefe*. Vienna, 1929.

Alexander, Edward and Paul Bogdanor, eds. *The Jewish Divide Over Israel: Accusers and Defenders*. New Brunswick, N.J., 2006.

Allen, Jim. *Perdition, A Play in Two Acts*. London, 1987.

Altschuler, Mordechai. *Soviet Jewry on the Eve of the Holocaust*. Jerusalem, 1988.

——— et al., eds., *Sovetskie evrei pishut Ilye Ehrenburgu 1943–1966*. Jerusalem, 1993.

Amerongen, Martin van. *Die Samenzwering tegen Simon Wiesenthal* (The conspiracy against Simon Wiesenthal). Amsterdam, 1976.

———. *Kreisky und seine unbewältigte Gegenwart*. Graz, 1977.

Anin, M. *Die Nationalitätenprobleme der Gegenwart*. Riga, 1910.

Aust, Stefan, *Der Baader-Meinhof Komplex*. Hamburg, 1985.

Avineri, Shlomo. *Karl Marx on Colonialism and Modernization*. New York, 1968.

———. *The Making of Modern Zionism. The Intellectual Origins of the Jewish State*. New York, 1981.

———. *Moses Hess: Prophet of Communism and Zionism*. New York, 1985.

Bahr, Hermann. *Der Antisemitismus. Ein Internationales Interview*. Berlin, 1894.

Balta, Paul and Claude Rulleau. *La politique arabe de la France: de De Gaulle à Pompidou*. Paris, 1973.

Bankier, David, ed. *Probing the Depths of German Anti-Semitism: German Society and the Persecution of the Jews 1933–1941*. Oxford, 2001.

Bardèche, Maurice. *Nuremberg ou la terre promise*. Paris, 1948.

Barer, Shlomo. *The Doctors of Revolution*. London, 2000.

Barnikol, Ernst, ed., *Bruno Bauer, Studien und Materialen*. Assen, 1972.

Bauer, Bruno. *Die Judenfrage*. Brunswick, 1843.

———. *Das Judentum in der Fremde*. Berlin, 1863.

Bauer, Otto. *Die Nationalitätenfrage und die Sozialdemokratie*. Vienna, 1907.

Bauer, Yehuda. *The Holocaust in Historical Perspective*. Seattle, 1978.

——— and N. Rotenstreich, eds. *The Holocaust as a Historical Experience*. New York, 1981.

Bebel, August. *Sozialdemokratie und Antisemitismus*. Berlin, 1894; reissued in 1906.

———. *August Bebels Briefwechsel mit Friedrich Engels*. Edited by Werber Blumenberg. The Hague, 1965.

Becker, Bernhard. *Der Missbrauch der Nationalitätenlehre*. Brunswick, 1873.

Becker, Jillian. *The PLO: The Rise and Fall of the Palestinian Liberation Organization*. New York, 1984.

Beckermann, Ruth, ed. *Die Mazzesinsel: Juden in der Wiener Leopoldstadt, 1918–1938*. Vienna 1984.

Begun, Vladimir. *Polzuchaya Kontrrevolyutsiya*. Minsk, 1974.

Benbassa, Esther and Jean-Christophe Attias, eds. *La Haine de Soi. Difficiles identités*. Paris, 2000.

Berchthold, Klaus, ed. *Österreichische Parteiprogramme 1868–1966*. Munich, 1967.

Berlin, Isaiah. *The Life and Opinions of Moses Hess*. Cambridge, 1959.

Berman, Paul. *Blacks and Jews: Alliances and Arguments*. New York, 1994.

———. *Terror and Liberalism*. New York, 2003.

Bernstein, Eduard. *Geschichte der Berliner Arbeiterbewegung.* Berlin, 1907–1910.

———. *Von den Aufgaben der Juden im Weltkriege.* Berlin, 1917.

———. *Von 1850 bis 1872. Kindheit und Jugendjahre.* Berlin, 1926.

———. *Sozialdemokratische Lehrjahre.* Berlin, 1928.

———. *Entwicklungsgang eines Sozialisten.* Leipzig, 1930.

———. *Eduard Bernsteins Briefwechsel mit Friedrich Engels.* Edited by Helmut Hirsch. Assen, 1970.

Bick (Shauli), Avraham. *Merosh Tsurim: Metaknei Chevra al Taharat Hakodesh Shalshelet Hayichusim shel Avot Hasotsialism* (From the lofty heights: Social reformers in the spirit of sanctity—the family tree of the fathers of socialism). Jerusalem, 1972.

Billroth, Theodor. *Über das Lehren und Lernen der Medizinischen Wissenschaften an der Universitäten der Deutschen Nation.* Vienna, 1876.

Bischof, Günter and Anton Pelinka, eds. *The Kreisky Era in Austria.* New Brunswick, 1994.

Blackburn, Robin, ed. *After the Fall: The Failure of Communism and the Future of Socialism.* London, 1991.

Blackstock, P. W. and B. F. Hoselitz. *Marx/Engels: The Russian Menace to Europe.* New York, 1952.

Bodansky, Yossef. *Antishemiut Islamit Ke-Machshir Politi.* Tel Aviv, 1988.

Boehlich, Walter, ed. *Der Berliner Antisemitismusstreit.* Frankfurt a.M., 1965.

Boniface, Pascal. *Est-il permis de critiquer Israël?.* Paris, 2003.

Borochov, Ber. *Ketavim.* Tel Aviv, 1955–1966.

———. *Die Grundlagen des Poale-Zionismus.* Frankfurt, 1969.

Bostom, Andrew, ed. *The Legacy of Islamic Antisemitism.* Amherst, 2008.

Botz, Gerhard, Hans Hautmann, Helmut Konrad and Josef Weidenholzer, eds. *Bewegung und Klasse: Studien zur österreichischen Arbeitergeschichte.* Vienna, 1978.

———, et al., eds. *Eine zerstörte Kultur.* Buchloe, 1990.

Bourdet, Yves. *Otto Bauer et la révolution.* Paris, 1968.

Boyer, John. *Political Radicalism in Late Imperial Vienna. Origins of the Christian Social Movement 1848–1897.* Chicago, 1981.

Braunthal, Julius. *In Search of the Millennium.* London, 1945.

———. *Victor und Friedrich Adler. Zwei Generationen. Arbeiterbewegung.* Vienna, 1965.

Bredin, Jean-Denis. *Bernard Lazare. De L'Anarchiste au Prophète.* Paris, 1992.

Brenner, Lenni. *Zionism in the Age of the Dictators.* New York, 1983.

Brent, Jonathan and Vladimir P. Naumov. *Stalin's Last Crime. The Plot against the Jewish Doctors 1948–1953*. New York, 2003.

Brod, Peter. *Die Antizionismus und Israelpolitik der USSR. Voraussetzung und Entwicklung bis 1956*. Baden-Baden, 1980.

Bronner, Stephen Eric. *A Revolutionary For Our Times: Rosa Luxemburg*. London, 1981.

Brotherstone, Terry and Paul Dukes, eds. *The Trotsky Reappraisal*. Edinburgh, 1992.

Brumlik, Micha. *Deutscher Geist und Judenhass*. Munich, 2002.

Buczek, H. and F. Tych, eds. *Socjaldemokracja Królestwa Polskiego i Litwy. Materialy i Dokumenty*. Vol. 1: 1893–1903. Warsaw, 1957.

Budeiri, Musa. *The Palestine Communist Party 1919–1948*. London, 1979.

Budnitskii, Oleg, ed. *Evrei i Russkaya Revoliutsiya*. Moscow, 1999.

Bukhbinder, N. A. *Istoriya evreiskogo rabochego dvizhenia v Rossii*. Leningrad, 1925.

Bunzl, John. *Klassenkampf in der Diaspora. Zur Geschichte der judischen Arbeiterbewegung*. Vienna, 1975.

Busi, Frederich. *The Pope of Antisemitism. The Career and Legacy of Edouard-Adolphe Drumont*. London, 1986.

Buttinger, Josef. *In the Twilight of Socialism*. New York, 1954.

Cahan, A. *Blätter aus meinen Leben*. New York, 1926.

Calwer, Richard. *Das Kommunistische Manifest und die heutige Sozialdemokratie*. Braunschweig, 1894.

Carlebach, Julius. *Karl Marx and the Radical Critique of Judaism*. London, 1978.

Carmichael, Joel. *Trotsky: An Appreciation of His Life*. London, 1975.

Carr, E. H. *Socialism in One Country*. New York, 1958.

Ceresole, Norberto. *Caudillo, Ejército Pueblo: la Venezuela del Commandante Chávez*. Madrid, 2000.

Chêne, Janine et al., eds. *Comment devient-on dreyfusard?*. Paris, 1997.

Chesler, Phyllis. *The New Anti-Semitism*. San Francisco, 2003.

Chirac, Auguste. *Les Rois de la République*. Paris, 1888.

Churchill, Winston. *Great Contemporaries*. London, 1937.

Claussen, Detlev. *Vom Judenhass zum Antisemitismus*. Darmstadt, 1987.

Cockburn, Alexander and Jeffrey St. Clair, eds. *The Politics of Anti-Semitism*. Oakland, Calif., 2003.

Cohen, Mitchell, ed. *Class Struggle and the Jewish Nation. Selected Essays in Marxist Zionism*. New Brunswick, N.J., 1984.

Cohen, Percy S. *Jewish Radicals and Radical Jews*. London, 1980.

Cohen, Steve. *That's Funny You Don't Look Anti-Semitic. An Anti-Racist Analysis of Left Anti-Semitism*. Leeds, 1984.

Cohn, Norman. *Warrant for Genocide*. London, 1970.

Cohn, Werner. *Partners in Hate. Noam Chomsky and the Holocaust Deniers.* Cambridge, Mass., 1995.

Cohn-Bendit, Daniel. *Le Grand Bazar*. Paris, 1975.

Community Security Trust. *Antisemitic Incidents, January–June 2009.* London, 2009.

———. *Antisemitic Discourse in Britain in 2008*. London, 2009.

Confino, Michael and Shimon Shamir, eds. *The USSR and the Middle East.* Jerusalem, 1973.

Cornu, Auguste and Wolfgang Mönke, eds. *Moses Hess: Philosophische und Sozialistische Schriften 1837–1850*. Berlin, 1961.

Cotic, Meir. *The Prague Trial. The First Anti-Zionist Show Trial in the Communist Bloc*. New York, 1987.

Cottier, Georges. *L'Athéisme du jeune Marx et ses origins hégéliennes*. Paris, 1959.

Crossman, Richard. *A Nation Reborn*. London, 1960.

Danneberg, Robert. *Die Schiebergeschäfte der Regierungsparteien. (Der Antisemitismus im Lichte der Thatsachen)*. Vienna 1926.

Dawidowicz, Lucy S. *The Golden Tradition. Jewish Life and Thought in Eastern Europe*. London, 1967.

———.*The War against the Jews, 1933–45*. London, 1983.

Deák, István. *Weimar Germany's Left-Wing Intellectuals: A Political History of the Weltbühne and Its Circle.* Berkeley, 1968.

Defries, Henry. *Conservative Party Attitudes to Jews, 1900–1939*. London, 2001.

Degras, Jane. *The Communist International 1919–1943, Documents*. London, 1956.

Deutscher, Isaac. *The Age of Permanent Revolution: A Trotsky Anthology*. New York, 1964.

———. *The Non-Jewish Jew and Other Essays.* London, 1968.

———. *The Prophet Unarmed. Trotsky: 1921–1929*. London 1970.

Dreyfus, Michel. *L'Antisémitisme à Gauche*. Paris, 2009.

Drouin, Michel, ed. *L'Affaire Dreyfus de A à Z.* Paris, 1994.

Drumont, Edouard. *La France Juive*. Paris, 1886.

Dubnow, S. N. *Kniga zhizhi. Vospominaniia i razmyshleniia. Materialy dlia istorii moega vremeni*. Riga, 1935.

Elon, Amos. *The Israelis: Founders and Sons.* New York, 1971.

Engels, Friedrich. *Engels: Selected Writings*. Edited by W. O. Henderson. London, 1967.

Ettinger, Elżbieta. *Rosa Luxemburg: A Life.* London, 1986.

———, ed. *Comrade and Lover. Rosa Luxemburg's Letters to Leo Jogiches*. Cambridge, Mass., 1979.

Ettinger, Shmuel, ed. *Antishemiut be-brit ha-moatsot.* Tel Aviv, 1986.

Falk, Richard. *Human Rights and State Sovereignty*. New York, 1981.

Fanon, Frantz. *Les Damnés de la Terre*. Paris, 1961.

Farber, Seth, ed., *Radicals, Rabbis and Peacemakers: Conversations with Jewish Critics of Israel*. Monroe, Me., 2005.

Fetscher, Irving, ed. *Marxisten gegen Antisemitismus*. Hamburg, 1974.

Feuerbach, Ludwig. *Essence of Christianity*. Translated by George Eliot. New York, 1957.

Finkielkraut, Alain. *L'Avenir d'une Négation*. Paris, 1982.

———. *Au Nom de l'Autre. Réflexions sur l'antisémitisme qui vient*. Paris, 2003.

Fischer, Lars. *The Socialist Response to Antisemitism in Imperial Germany*. Cambridge, 2007.

Fischer, Klaus. *The History of an Obsession. German Judeophobia and the Holocaust*. London, 1998.

Fishman, William J. *East End Jewish Radicals, 1875–1914*. London, 1975.

———. *East End 1888*. London, 1988.

Frankel, Jonathan. *Prophecy and Politics. Socialism, Nationalism and the Russian Jews 1862–1917*. Cambridge, U.K., 1981.

Franklin, B., ed. *The Essential Stalin, Major Theoretical Writings 1905–1952*. London, 1973.

Frei, Bruno. *Im Schatten von Karl Marx: Moses Hess—hundert Jahre nach seinem Tod*. Vienna, 1977.

Gabel, Joseph. *Réflexions sur l'Avenir des Juifs*. Paris, 1987.

Gaisbauer, Adolf. *Davidstern und Doppeladler. Zionismus und jüdischer Nationalismus in Österreich 1882–1918*. Vienna, 1988.

Garaudy Roger. *The Case of Israel. A Study of Political Zionism*. London, 1983.

Garrard, John A. *The English and Immigration. A Comparative Study of the Jewish Influx (1880–1910)*. London, 1971.

Geehr, Richard S. *Karl Lueger, Mayor of Fin-de-Siècle Vienna*. Detroit, 1990.

Gensicke, Klaus. *The Mufti of Jerusalem and the Nazis. The Berlin Years*. London, 2011.

Gerstenfeld, Manfred, ed. *Academics Against Israel and the Jews*. Jerusalem, 2007.

———, ed. *The Abuse of Holocaust Memory. Distortions and Responses*. Jerusalem, 2009.

Gessler, Philipp. *Der neue Antisemitismus*. Freiburg, 2004.

Getzler, I. *Martov. A Political Biography*. Cambridge, 1967.

Gilboa, Yehoshua A. *The Black Years of Soviet Jewry*. Boston, 1971.

Gilman, Sander. *Jewish Self-Hatred: Anti-Semitism and the Hidden Language of the Jews*. Baltimore, 1986.

Gitelman, Zvi Y. *Jewish Nationality and Soviet Politics. The Jewish Sections of the CPSU, 1917–1930.* Princeton, 1972.

Givet, Jacques. *Israël et le genocide inachevé*. Paris, 1979.

Glagau, Otto. *Der Börsen und Gründungsschwindel in Berlin*. Leipzig, 1876.

Glotzer, Albert. *Trotsky. Memoir and Critique*. Buffalo, N.Y., 1989.

Goldberg, J. J. *Jewish Power. Inside the American Jewish Establishment*. New York, 1996.

Goldhagen, Daniel J. *Hitler's Willing Executioners. Ordinary Germans and the Holocaust.* New York, 1996.

Goldman, Guido. *Zionism under Soviet Rule: 1917–1928*. New York, 1960.

Goldnadel, Gilles William. *Le Nouveau Bréviaire de la Haine: Antisémitisme et antisionisme.* Paris, 2001.

Golomb, Jacob. *Nietzsche and Zion.* Ithaca, N.Y., 2004.

Grab, Walter, ed. *Juden und Jüdische Aspekte in der Deutschen Arbeiterbewegung 1848–1918.* Tel Aviv, 1976.

Graetz, Michael. *Haperipheria hayita La-Mercaz* (From periphery to center). Jerusalem, 1982.

Guillaume, Pierre. *Droit et Histoire*. Paris, 1986.

Haberer, Erich. *Jews and Revolution in Nineteenth-Century Russia.* Cambridge, U.K., 1995.

Hamann, Brigitte. *Hitlers Wien. Lehrjahre eines Diktators.* Munich, 1996; English ed. *Hitler's Vienna.* Oxford, 1999.

Hamon, Augustin. *L'Humanité Nouvelle*. 1898.

Hamon, Hervé and Patrick Rotman. *Génération. Les années de rêve.* Paris, 1987.

Harkabi, Y. *Arab Attitudes to Israel*. Jerusalem, 1972.

———. *The Palestinian Covenant and Its Meaning*. London, 1979.

Harrison, Bernard. *The Resurgence of Anti-Semitism. Jews, Israel, and Liberal Opinion*. Lanham, Md., 2006.

Haury, Thomas. *Antisemitismus von links. Kommunistische Ideologie, Nationalismus und Antizionismus in der DDR.* Hamburg, 2002.

Hegel, Georg Wilhelm Friedrich. *Vorlesungen über die Philosophie der Weltgeschichte.* Vol. 2: *Die Orientalische Welt.* Leipzig, 1924.

———. *Early Theological Writings*. Translated by T. M. Knox. Chicago, 1948.

Heid, Ludiger and Arnold Paucker, eds. *Juden und deutsche Arbeiterbewegung bis 1933.* Tübingen, 1992.

Heller, Otto. *Der Untergang des Judentums*. Vienna, 1931.

Hen-Tov, Jacob. *Communism and Zionism in Palestine: The Comintern and the Political Unrest in the 1920s*. Cambridge, Mass., 1974.

Herf, Jeffrey. *Divided Memory. The Nazi Past in the Two Germanies.* Cambridge, Mass, 1997.

———. *The Jewish Enemy: Nazi Propaganda during World War II and the Holocaust*. Cambridge, Mass., 2006.

———. *Nazi Propaganda for the Arab World*. New Haven, 2009.

Hermone, Jacques. *La Gauche, Israël et les Juifs*. Paris, 1970.

Hertzberg, Arthur. *The French Enlightenment and the Jews*. New York, 1968.

———, ed. *The Zionist Idea*. New York, 1973.

Herzog, Yaacov. *A People that Dwells Alone*. London, 1975.

Hess, Moses. *La haute Finance et l'Empire*. Paris, 1869.

———. *Moses Hess Briefwechsel*. Edited by Edmund Silberner. Leiden, 1959.

———. *Rom und Jerusalem: Die letzte Nationalitätenfrage*. Leipzig, 1862; Tel Aviv, 1935.

Hinteregger, Christoph. *Der Judenschwindel*. Vienna 1923.

Hitler, Adolf. *Mein Kampf*. Translated by Ralph Manheim. Boston, 1942.

Hobsbawm, Eric. *The Age of Extremes*. London, 1995.

———. *Interesting Times: A Twentieth Century Life*. New York, 2002.

———. *How to Change the World: Tales of Marx and Marxism*. New York, 2011.

Höhle, Thomas. *Franz Mehring. Sein Weg zum Marxismus 1869–91*. East Berlin, 1956.

Holz, Klaus. *Die Gegenwart des Antisemitismus*. Hamburg, 2005.

Horkheimer, Max and Theodor W. Adorno, *Dialektik der Aufklärung*. Frankfurt a. M., 1969.

Horowitz, David. *Unholy Alliance. Radical Islam and the American Left*. Lanham, Md., 2004.

Iggers, Wilma Abbeles. *Karl Kraus. A Viennese Critic of the Twentieth Century*. The Hague, 1967.

Igounet, Valérie. *Histoire du négationnisme en France*. Paris, 2000.

Ivanov, K. and Z. Sheinis, eds. *The State of Israel. Its Position and Policies*. Moscow, 1958.

Ivanov, Y. *Ostrozhno! Sionizm!*. Moscow, 1969.

Jacobs, Jack. *On Socialists and "the Jewish Question" after Marx*. New York, 1992.

Janowsky, Oscar. *The Jews and Minority Rights, 1898–1918*. New York, 1933.

Jay, Martin. *Dialectical Imagination: A History of the Frankfurt School and the Institute of Social Research 1923–1950*. Boston, 1973.

Joll, James. *The Second International*. London, 1955.

Julius, Anthony. *Trials of the Diaspora. A History of Anti-Semitism in England*. Oxford, 2010.

Kadish, Sharman. *Bolsheviks and British Jews: The Anglo-Jewish Community, Britain, and the Russian Revolution*. London, 1992.

Kann, Robert A. *The Multi-national Empire*. New York, 1950.

Kant, Immanuel. *Religion within the Limits of Reason Alone.* New York, 1960.

Kapp, Yvonne. *Eleanor Marx: Family Life 1855–83.* London, 1972.

Karsh, Efraim. *Arafat's War: The Man and His Battle for Israeli Conquest*. New York, 2003.

Katznelson, Berl. *K'tavim* (Writings). Tel Aviv, 1954.

Kaufman, Jonathan. *The Broken Alliance: The Turbulent Times Between Blacks and Jews in America*. New York, 1988.

Kautsky, Benedikt, ed. *Friedrich Engels' Briefwechsel mit Karl Kautsky.* Vienna, 1954.

Kautsky, Karl. *Sozialismus und Kolonialpolitik*. N.p., 1907.

———. *Rasse und Judentum.* Stuttgart, 1914; English ed. *Are the Jews a Race?*. London, 1926.

———. *Erinnerungen und Erörterungen.* Edited by Benedikt Kautsky. The Hague, 1960.

Kertzer, David I., ed. *Old Demons, New Debates: Antisemitism in the West*. New York, 2005.

Khrosrokhavar, Farhad. *Les Nouveaux Martyrs d'Allah*. Paris, 2002.

Kichko, Trofim. *Iudaizm bez prikras* (Judaism without embellishment). Kiev: Ukrainian Academy of Sciences, 1963.

Kochan, L., ed. *The Jews in Soviet Russia since 1917.* Oxford, 1970.

Kol, H. H. van. *La Démocratie Socialiste Internationale et le Sionisme*. Lausanne, 1919.

Koren, Rosleyne et al, eds. *Les Intellectuels Face à L'Affaire Dreyfus. Alors et Aujourd'hui.* Paris, 1998.

Korey, William. *Russian Antisemitism, Pamyat, and the Demonology of Zionism.* Chur, Switzerland, 1995.

Kotek, Joël. *Cartoons and Extremism: Israel and the Jews in Arab and Western Media*. London, 2008.

Krammer, Arnold. *The Forgotten Friendship: Israel and the Soviet Bloc 1947–53*. Urbana, Ill., 1974.

Kreisky, Bruno. *Im Strom der Politik.* Berlin, 1988.

———. *Die Zeit in der wir leben: Betrachtungen zur internationalen Politik*. Vienna, 1989.

Kriegel, Annie. *Le Pain et les roses. Jalons pour une Histoire des Socialismes*. Paris, 1968.

———. *Israël est-il coupable?*. Paris, 1982.

Künzli, Arnold. *Karl Marx. Eine Psychographie.* Vienna, 1966.

Kuperminc, Jean-Claude and Jean-Philippe Chaumont, eds. *Zadoc Kahn. Un grand rabbin entre culture juive, affaire Dreyfus et laïcité.* Paris, 2007.

Kushner, Tony. *The Persistence of Prejudice: Anti-Semitism in British Society during the Second World War*. Manchester, 1989.

Laffin, John. *The PLO Connections*. London, 1982.

Laqueur, Walter. *Communism and Nationalism in the Middle East*. New York, 1956.

———. *The Struggle for the Middle East, the Soviet Union and the Middle East 1958–1968*. London, 1972.

Lazare, Bernard. *L'Antisémitisme. Son Histoire et Ses Causes*. 1894; English translation, *Antisemitism. Its History and Causes.* Lincoln, Neb., 1995.

———. *Antisémitisme et Révolution*. Paris, 1895.

———. *Contre L'Antisémitisme*. Paris, 1896.

———. *Une erreur judiciaire: la vérité sur l'affaire Dreyfus*. Brussels, 1896.

———. *Job's Dungheap*. New York, 1948.

Lebzelter, Gisela. *Political Anti-Semitism in England 1918–1939*. London, 1978.

Lenin, V. I. "National Culture." In *Questions of National Policy and Proletarian Internationalism*. Moscow, n.d.

———. *O Evreiskom Voprose v Rosii*. Moscow, 1924.

———. *On the Jewish Question*. New York, 1934.

Léon, Abram. *La Conception matérialiste de la question juive*. Paris, 1968.

Leroy, G. *Les Écrivains et l'Affaire Dreyfus*. Paris, 1983.

Lessing, Theodor. *Der jüdische Selbsthass*. Berlin, 1930.

Lestschinsky, Jacob. *Marx i Kautskii o evreiskom voprose*. Moscow, 1907.

Leuschen-Seppel, Rosemarie. *Sozialdemokratie und Antisemitismus im Kaiserreich*. Bonn, 1978.

Levin, Nora. *Jewish Socialist Movements 1871–1917*. London, 1978.

Levy, Richard S. *The Downfall of the Anti-Semitic Political Parties in Imperial Germany.* New Haven, 1975.

Lewis, Bernard. *Semites and Anti-Semites. An Inquiry into Conflict and Prejudice*. New York, 1986.

Liebeschutz, Hans. *Das Judentum in Deutschen Geschichtsbild von Hegel bis Max Weber.* Tübingen, 1967.

Lindau, Paul, ed. *Ferdinand Lassalles Tagebuch*. Breslau, 1891.

Lindau, Rudolf. *Franz Mehring zu seinem 100. Geburtstag am 27.Februar*. East Berlin, 1946.

Lipstadt, Deborah. *Denying the Holocaust: The Growing Assault on Truth and Memory*. New York, 1993.

Litvak, Meir and Esther Webman. *From Empathy to Denial. Arab Responses to the Holocaust*. London, 2009.

Litvinoff, Emmanuel. *Soviet Antisemitism: The Paris Trial*. London, 1974.

Loebl, Eugene. *Sentenced and Tried: The Stalinist Purges in Czechoslovakia.* London, 1969.

Loftus, John and Mark Aarons. *The Secret War against the Jews*. New York, 1994.

Löwy, Michael *Redemption and Utopia: Jewish Libertarian Thought in Central Europe.* Stanford, Calif., 1992.

Lunacharsky, A. *Ob antisemitizme.* Moscow, 1929.

Luxemburg, Rosa. *Die industrielle Entwicklung Polens.* Ph.D. diss., Leipzig, 1898.

——— (pseud. Junius). *Die Krise der Sozialdemokratie.* Zurich, 1916.

———. *Briefe an Karl und Luise Kautsky.* Edited by Luise Kautsky. Berlin, 1923.

———. *Briefe an Freunde.* Edited by Benedikt Kautsky. Hamburg, 1950.

———. *Ich war, ich bin, ich werde sein!*. East Berlin, 1958.

———. *The Russian Revolution*. Edited by Bertram D. Wolfe. Ann Arbor, Mich., 1961.

——— [Róży Luksemburg]. *Listy do Leona Jogichesa-Tsyzki.* Edited by Feliks Tych. Warsaw, 1968.

———. *Le Socialisme en France 1898–1912.* Edited by Daniel Guérin. Paris, 1971.

Mack, Michael. *German Idealism and the Jew.* Chicago, 2003.

Mandel, Ernest. *The Meaning of the Second World War*. London, 1986.

Martov, Julius. *Povorotnyi punkt v historii evreiskogo rabochego dvizhenia.* Geneva, 1900.

Marx, Karl. *The Eastern Question.* Edited by Eleanor Marx and Eduard Aveling. 1897. New ed., London, 1969.

———. *Manuscripte über die Polnische Frage (1863–1864).* Edited by W. Conze. 's-Gravenhage, 1961.

———. "On the Jewish Question." In *Early Writings.* Introduction by Lucio Colletti. London, 1975.

Marx, Karl and Friedrich Engels. *Marx-Engels Gesamtausgabe.* Berlin and Moscow, 1927–1935.

——— and Friedrich Engels. "Manifesto of the Communist Party" In *Selected Works.* Moscow, 1962.

——— *Marx-Engels Werke.* East Berlin, 1963.

Masaryk, T. G. *Die Philosophischen und Sociologischen Grundlagen des Marxismus.* Vienna, 1899.

Massing, Paul. *Rehearsal for Destruction. A Study of Political Anti-Semitism in Imperial Germany.* New York, 1949.

Mathieu-Dairnvaell, Georges-Marie. *Historie édifiante et curieuse de Rothschild Ier, Roi des Juifs, par Satan*. 5th ed. Paris, 1846.

Maududi, Abul Ala. *Jihad in Islam*. Lahore, 1998–2001.

Maurras, Charles. *Au Signe du Flore. La Fondation de l'Action Française, 1898–1900*. Paris, 1933.

Mayer, Arno. *Why Did the Heavens Not Darken? The "Final Solution in History*. New York, 1988.

McCagg, William O. *A History of Habsburg Jews, 1670–1918*. Bloomington, Ind., 1989.

McDonald, James G. *My Mission in Israel, 1948–1951*. London, 1951.

McGrath, William J. *Dionysian Art and Populist Politics*. New Haven, 1974.

McLellan, David. *The Young Hegelians and Karl Marx*. London, 1969.

———. *Marx before Marxism*. London, 1970.

Mehring, Franz. *Herr Hofprediger Stöcker der Socialpolitiker. Eine Streitschrift*. Bremen, 1882.

———. *Kapital und Presse Ein Nachspiel zum Falle Lindau*. Berlin, 1891.

———. *Die Lessing-Legende*. Stuttgart, 1893.

———. *Geschichte der deutschen Sozialdemokratie*. Stuttgart, 1913; 2nd. ed. 1921.

———. *Karl Marx: Geschichte seines Lebens*. 4th ed. Leipzig, 1923.

———. *Aufsätze zur deutschen Literaturgeschichte*. Leipzig, 1960.

———, ed. *Aus dem literarischen Nachlass von Karl Marx, Friedrich Engels und Ferdinand Lassalle*. Stuttgart, 1902.

———, ed. *Aus dem literarischen Nachlass von Karl Marx und Friedrich Engels 1841–50*. Stuttgart, 1920.

Medem, Vladimir. *Shestoi Sionistichesky Kongress v Bazele*. London, 1903.

———. *Fun mein Lebn*. New York, 1923.

Mendelsohn, Ezra. *Class Struggle in the Pale: The Formative Years of the Jewish Workers' Movement in Tsarist Russia*. Cambridge, U.K., 1970.

Messner, Matthias. *Sowjetischer und postkommunistischer Antisemitismus*. Konstanz, 1997.

Meyer, Rudolf. *Politische Gründer und die Korruption in Deutschland*. Leipzig, 1877.

Michaelevich, B. *Zichrones fun a Yidishen Sotsialist*. Warsaw, 1929.

Michels, Robert. *Political Parties: A Sociological Study of the Oligarchical Tendencies of Modern Democracy*. New York, 1959; German ed., 1913.

Michlic, Joanna Beata. *Poland's Threatening Other. The Image of the Jew from 1880 to the Present*. Lincoln, Neb., 2006.

Mill, John. *Pionirn un Boyer*. 2 vols. New York, 1946–1949.

Mintz, Matityahu. *Ber Borochov: Ha-maagal ha-rishon (1900–1906)*. Tel Aviv, 1976.

Mishkinsky, Moshe. *National Elements in the Development of the Jewish Labour Movement*. In Hebrew. Ph.D. diss., Hebrew University of Jerusalem, 1965.

Misrahi, Robert. *Marx et la Question Juive*. Paris, 1972.

Mohrmann, Walter. *Antisemitismusideologie und Geschichte im Kaiserreich und in der Weimarer Republik*. East Berlin, 1972.
Moreh, Shmuel and Zvi Yehuda, eds. *Al-Farhūd. The 1941 Pogrom in Iraq*. Jerusalem, 2010.
Morris, Benny. *The Road to Jerusalem: Glubb Pasha, Palestine, and the Jews*. London, 2002.
Mosse, Werner E. and Arnold Paucker, eds. *Deutsches Judentum im Krieg und Revolution 1916–1923*. Tübingen, 1971.
———, eds. *Juden im Wilhelminischen Deutschland 1890–1914. Ein Sammelband.* Tübingen 1976.
Mousseaux, Gougenot des. *Le Juif, le judaïsme et la judaïsation des peoples chrétiens*. Paris, 1869.
Murawiec, Laurent. *The Mind of Jihad.* Cambridge, U.K., 2008.
Nawratzki, Curt. *Die jüdische Kolonisation Palästinas*. Munich, 1914.
Nedava, Joseph. *Trotsky and the Jews*. Philadelphia, 1972.
Nettl, J. P. *Rosa Luxemburg*. London, 1966; abridged ed., 1969.
Niewyk, Donald. *Socialist, Anti-Semite and Jew—German Social Democracy Confronts the Problem of Anti-Semitism, 1918–1933.* Baton Rouge, La., 1971.
Nochlin, Linda and Tamar Garb, eds. *The Jew in the Text: Modernity and the Construction of Identity.* London, 1995.
Noske, Gustav. *Erlebtes aus Aufstieg und Niedergang einer Demokratie*. Offenbach-am-Main, 1947.
Novick, Paul. *Palestine: The Communist Position on the Colonial Question*. New York, 1936.
O'Brien, Conor Cruise. *The Siege. The Saga of Israel and Zionism*. New York, 1986.
Oren, Mordechai. *Prisonnier Politique à Prague, 1951–1956*. Paris, 1960.
Orenstein, Shimon. *Aliyah be-Prague*. Tel Aviv, 1968.
Oriol, Philippe, ed. *Le Fumier de Job*. Paris, 1998.
———. *Bernard Lazare*. Paris, 2003.
Pauley, Bruce E. *Eine Geschichte des österreichischen Antisemitismus. Von der Ausgrenzung zur Auslöschung*. Vienna, 1993.
Péguy, Charles. *Notre Jeunesse*. Paris, 1957.
Peled, Yoav. *Class and Ethnicity in the Pale. The Political Economy of Jewish Workers' Nationalism in Late Imperial Russia.* New York, 1989.
Pinkus, Benjamin. *The Jews of the Soviet Union.* Cambridge, U.K., 1988.
Poliakov, Léon. *The History of Anti-Semitism*. Vol. 3: *From Voltaire to Wagner.* London, 1975.
———. *La Causalité Diabolique.* Paris, 1980.
Portnoy, Samuel A., ed. *Vladimir Medem. The Life and Soul of a Legendary Jewish Socialist*. New York, 1979.

Prawer, Siegfried. *Heine's Jewish Comedy.* Oxford, 1983.
Proudhon, Pierre Joseph. *Césarisme et Christianisme*. Paris, 1883.
———. *Notebooks of P. J. Proudhon*. Paris, 1960–1961.
Pulzer, P. G. J. *The Rise and Fall of Political Anti-Semitism in Germany and Austria*. 2nd revised ed. London, 1988.
Rabinbach, Anson, ed. *The Austrian Socialist Experiment 1918–1934*. Boulder, Colo., 1985.
Rabinovici, Doron et al., eds. *Neuer Antisemitismus?*. Frankfurt a.M., 2004.
Rafes, M. G. *Ocherko po istorii Bunda*. Moscow, 1923.
Raphael, Freddy. *Judaïsme et capitalisme. Essai sur la controverse entre Max Weber et Werner Sombart.* Paris, 1982.
Rapoport-Albert, Ada and Steven J. Zipperstein, eds. *Essays in Honor of Chimen Abramsky.* London, 1988.
Rapoport, Yakov. *The Doctors' Plot of 1953: A Survivor's Memoir of Stalin's Last Act of Terror against Jews and Science.* Cambridge, Mass, 1991.
Rathkolb, Oliver and Irene Etzerdorfer, eds. *Der junge Kreisky. Schriften—Reden—Dokumente 1931–1945*. Vienna, 1986.
Redlich, Shimon. *War, Holocaust and Stalinism*. Luxembourg, 1995.
Reinharz, Jehuda, ed. *Living with Antisemitism. Modern Jewish Responses.* Hanover, 1987.
——— and Walter Schatzberg, eds. *The Jewish Response to German Culture*. Hanover, N.H., 1985.
Reiter, Franz Richard, ed. *Wer war Bruno Kreisky?*. Vienna, 2000.
Reiter, Margit. *Unter Antisemitismus-Verdacht. Die Österreichische Linke und Israel nach der Shoah*. Innsbruck, 2001.
Reitter, Paul. *The Anti-Journalist. Karl Kraus and Jewish Self-Fashioning in Fin-de-siècle Europe*. Chicago, 2008.
Rennap, I. *Anti-Semitism and the Jewish Question*. London, 1942.
Rensmann, Lars. *Demokratie und Judenbild in der politischen Kultur der Bundesrepublik Deutschland.* Frankfurt a.M., 2005.
Rifkind, Lewis. *Zionism and Socialism*. London, 1918.
Robb, James. *Working-Class Anti-Semite. A Psychological Study in a London Borough*. London, 1954.
Rodinson, Maxime. *Israel. A Colonial Settler State*. New York, 1973.
Ro'i, Yaacov. *From Encroachment to Involvement. A Documentary Study of Soviet Policy in the Middle East, 1945–1973*. Jerusalem, 1974.
Rose, Jacqueline. *The Question of Zion.* Princeton, 2005.
Rose, Paul Lawrence. *German Question, Jewish Question. Revolutionary Antisemitism from Kant to Wagner.* Princeton, 1990.
———. *Wagner. Race and Revolution.* London, 1992.

Rosen, Zvi. *Bruno Bauer and Karl Marx: The Influence of Bruno Bauer on Marx's Thought.* The Hague, 1978.

Rosenbaum, Ron, ed. *Those Who Forget the Past: The Question of Anti-Semitism.* New York, 2004.

Rozenblit, Marsha L. *The Jews of Vienna, 1867–1914: Assimilation and Identity.* Albany, 1983.

Rosenfeld, Alvin H. *"Progressive" Jewish Thought and the New Antisemitism.* New York: American Jewish Committee, 2006.

Rotenstreich, Nathan. *The Recurring Pattern: Studies in Anti-Judaism in Modern Thought.* London, 1963.

Roth, Joseph. *Juden auf Wanderschaft.* Berlin, 1927.

Rothman, Stanley and S. Robert Lichter. *Roots of Radicalism: Jews, Christians and the New Left.* New York, 1982.

Rubin, Jerry. *We Are Everywhere.* New York, 1971.

Rubinstein, Joshua. *"Tangled Loyalties." The Life and Times of Ilya Ehrenburg.* New York, 1996.

——— and Vladimir P. Naumov, eds. *Stalin's Secret Pogrom.* New Haven, 2001.

Rubinstein, Sondra Miller. *The Communist Movement in Palestine and Israel 1919–1984.* Boulder, 1985.

Saad-Ghorayeb, Amal. *Hizbu'llah. Politics and Religion.* London, 2002.

Sánchez, Ilich Ramirez [Carlos], *L'Islam révolutionnaire.* Edited and presented by Jean-Michel Vernochet. Monaco, 2003.

Sand, Shlomo. *The Invention of the Jewish People.* London, 2009.

Sarfati, Georges-Elia. *L'Antisionisme: Israël/Palestine aux miroirs d'Occident.* Paris, 2002.

Sartre, Jean-Paul. *Réflexions sur la question juive.* Paris, 1954.

Schacht, Richard. *Alienation.* London, 1971.

Schäfer, Peter. *Judeophobia: Attitudes towards the Jews in the Ancient World.* Cambridge, Mass., 1997.

Schatz, Adam, ed., *Prophets Outcast.* New York, 2004.

Schleifstein, Josef. *Franz Mehring. Sein Marxistisches Schaffen 1891–1919.* East Berlin, 1959.

Schoenberg, Harris Okun. *A Mandate for Terror. The United Nations and the PLO.* New York, 1989.

Schorsch, Ismar. *Jewish Reactions to German Anti-Semitism 1870–1914.* New York, 1972.

Schroeder, Hans-Christoph. *Sozialismus und Imperialismus. Die Auseinandersetzung der deutschen Sozialdemokratie mit dem Imperialismusproblem und der "Weltpolitik" vor 1914.* Hannover, 1968.

Schwarz-Friesel, Monika et al., eds. *Aktueller Antisemitismus—ein Phänomen der Mitte.* Berlin, 2010.

Secher, H. Pierre. *Bruno Kreisky. Chancellor of Austria*. Pittsburgh, 1993.
Semenyuk, V. A. *Natsionalisticheskoe bezumie* (Nationalistic madness). Minsk, 1976.
Serfaty, Abraham. *Écrits de prison sur la Palestine*. Paris, 1992.
——— and Christine Daure-Serfaty. *La mémoire de l'autre*. Paris, 1993.
——— and Mikhaël Elbaz. *L'insoumis: juifs, marocains et rebelles*. Paris, 2001.
Serge, Victor. *Memoirs of a Revolutionary 1901–1941*. Oxford, 1967.
Shaltiel, Eli, ed. *Yehudim be-Tnuot mehapkhaniot* (Jews in revolutionary movements). Jerusalem, 1982.
Shariati, Ali. *Red Shiism*. Houston, 1974.
———. *Reflections on Humanity: Two Views of Civilization and the Plight of Man*. Houston, 1974.
Shazar, Zalman. *Or Ishim*. Tel Aviv, 1955.
Shimoni, Gideon. *The Zionist Ideology*. Hanover, 1995.
Sickinger, Hubert, ed. *Politische Affäre und Skandale in Österreich*. Vienna, 1996.
Silberner, Edmund. *Ha-Sotsialism ha-maravi ve-shelelat ha-yehudim*. Jerusalem 1955.
———. *Moses Hess: Geschichte seines Lebens*. Leiden, 1966.
———. *Kommunisten zur Judenfrage. Zur Geschichte der Theorie und Praxis der Kommunismus*. Opladen, 1983.
Slezkine, Yuri. *The Jewish Century*. Princeton, 2004.
Solodar, Ts. *Dikaya polyn* (Wild wormwood). Moscow, 1977.
Soloveitschik, Léonti. *Un proletariat méconnu: étude sur la situation sociale et économique des ouvriers juifs*. Paris, 1898.
Soyfer, D. I. *Sionizm—orudie antikommunizma*. Dnepropetrovsk, 1976.
Stalin, J. V. *Sochineniya*. Vol. 2 (*1907–1913*). Moscow, 1949.
———.*Works*. Moscow, 1953–1955.
Sterling, Eleanore. *Er ist wie Du: aus der Frühgeschichte des Antisemitismus in Deutschland, 1815–1850*. Munich, 1956.
Sternhell, Zeev. *Maurice Barrès et le Nationalisme Français*. Paris, 1972.
———. *La Droite Révolutionnaire 1885–1914. Les Origines Françaises du Fascisme*. Paris 1978.
———. *Ni Droite ni Gauche. L'idéologie fasciste en France*. Paris, 1983.
———. *The Founding Myths of Israel. Nationalism, Socialism, and the Making of the Jewish State*. Princeton, 1998.
Stillman, Norman A., ed. *The Jews of Arab Lands in Modern Times*. New York, 1991.
Stöcker, Adolf. *Christlich-Sozial. Reden und Aufsätze*. Bielefeld-Leipzig, 1885.
Stola, Dariusz. *Kampania antysyjonistyczna*. Warsaw, 2000.

Stourzh, Gerald. *From Vienna to Chicago and Back.* Chicago, 2007.

Syrkin, Marie, ed. *Nachman Syrkin: Socialist Zionist: A Biographical Memoir and Selected Essays.* New York, 1961.

Szporluk, Roman. *Communism and Nationalism.* New York, 1988.

Taguieff, Pierre-André. *Prêcheurs de Haine: Traversée de la judéophobie planétaire.* Paris, 2004.

———. *La Judéophobie des Modernes.* Paris, 2008.

———. *La Nouvelle propaganda antijuive.* Paris, 2010.

Tal, Uriel. *Christians and Jews in the "Second Reich" (1870–1914).* In Hebrew. Jerusalem, 1969.

Talmon, Jacob. *Mitos ha-Umma ve-Hazon ha-Mekhapecha.* Tel Aviv, 1981.

Tcherikower, E. *Antisemitizm un Pogromen in Ukraine 1917–18.* Berlin, 1923.

Teller, Judd. *Scapegoat of Revolution.* New York, 1954.

Thion, Serge. *Vérité Historique ou Vérité Politique?.* Paris, 1980.

Tobias, Henry J. *The Jewish Bund in Russia from Its Origins to 1905.* Stanford, 1972.

Toussenel, Alphonse. *Les Juifs, Rois de l'Époque. Histoire de la Féodalité financière.* Paris, 1845, 1847.

Traverso, Enzo. *Die Marxisten und die Jüdische Frage. Geschichte einer Debatte (1843–1943).* Mainz, 1995.

Tridon, Gustave. *Du Molochisme juif.* Paris, 1884.

Trotsky, Leon. *Nashi Politicheskie Zadachi.* Geneva, 1904.

———. *My Life.* New York, 1930.

———. *The Revolution Betrayed.* New York, 1945.

———. *Stalin.* New York, 1958.

———. *The Permanent Revolution.* New York, 1962.

———. *The Trotsky Papers.* Vol. I: *1917–1919.* Edited by Jan M. Meijer. The Hague, 1964.

———. *On the Jewish Question.* New York, 1970.

———. *Writings of Leon Trotsky (1939–1940).* New York, 1969.

———. *Writings of Leon Trotsky (1932–33).* New York, 1972.

———. *The Struggle against Fascism.* London, 1975.

——— and C. Rakovsky. *Ocherki Politicheskii Ruminii.* Moscow-Petrograd, 1923.

Tsentsiper, Arieh Leib. *Eser Sh'not R'difot.* Tel Aviv, 1930.

Tsuzuki, Chusichi. *The Life of Eleanor Marx 1855–98: A Socialist Tragedy.* Oxford, 1967.

Tucker, Robert C. *Philosophy and Myth in Karl Marx.* Cambridge, 1961.

———.*Stalin as Revolutionary 1879–1929.* London, 1974.

Unszlicht (Sedecki), Julian. *Social-litwactwo w Polsce: z teorii i praktyki SDKPiL.* Kraków, n.d.

———. *O program Ludu Polskiego: rola socjal litwactwa w niedawnej rewolucji*. Kraków, 1919.

Vago, Bela and George L. Mosse, eds. *Jews and non-Jews in Eastern Europe 1918–1945*. Jerusalem, 1974.

Vaksberg, Arkady. *Stalin against the Jews*. New York, 1994.

Vidal-Naquet, Pierre. *Les Assassins de la mémoire*. Paris, 1987

Vogt, Ernst. *Israel—Kritik von Links*. Wuppertal, 1976.

Volkogonov, Dmitri. *Trotsky. The Eternal Revolutionary*. New York, 1996.

Walter, Edward. *The Rise and Fall of Leftist Radicalism in America*. Westport, Conn., 1992.

Weeks, Theodore R. *From Assimilation to Antisemitism. The "Jewish Question" in Poland, 1850–1914*. DeKalb, Ill., 2006.

Weinstock, Nathan. *Le Pain de Misère. Histoire du Mouvement ouvrier juif en Europe*. 2 vols. Paris, 1984.

Weiss, John. *Ideology of Death. Why the Holocaust Happened in Germany*. Chicago, 1996.

Weizmann, Chaim. *Trial and Error*. Philadelphia, 1949.

———. *Letters and Papers of Chaim Weizmann*. London, 1971.

Wilson, Nelly. *Bernard Lazare. Antisemitism and Jewish Identity in late Nineteenth-Century France*. Cambridge, 1978.

Wilson, Stephen. *Ideology and Experience. Antisemitism in France at the Time of the Dreyfus Affair*. London, 1982.

Wistrich, Robert S. *Socialism and the Jewish Question in Germany and Austria 1880–1914*. Ph.D. diss., University of London, 1974.

———. *The Myth of Zionist Racism*. London, 1976.

———. *Revolutionary Jews from Marx to Trotsky*. London, 1976.

———, ed. *The Left against Zion. Communism, Israel and the Middle East*. London, 1979.

———. *Socialism and the Jews. The Dilemmas of Assimilation in Germany and Austria-Hungary*. London, 1982.

———. *Trotsky. Fate of a Revolutionary*. New York, 1982.

———. *Hitler's Apocalypse. Jews and the Nazi Legacy*. New York, 1985.

———. *The Jews of Vienna in the Age of Franz Joseph*. Oxford, 1989.

———, ed. *Anti-Zionism and Antisemitism in the Contemporary World*. London, 1990.

———. *Between Redemption and Perdition*. London, 1990.

———. *Antisemitism: The Longest Hatred*. London, 1991.

———, ed. *Austrians and Jews in the Twentieth Century*. New York, 1992.

———. *Hitler and the Holocaust*. London, 2002.

———. *European Anti-Semitism Reinvents Itself*. New York: American Jewish Committee, 2005.

———. *Anti-Zionism and Antisemitism: The Case of Bruno Kreisky*. Jerusalem: 2007.

———. *Laboratory for World Destruction. Germans and Jews in Central Europe*. Lincoln, Neb., 2007.

———. *A Lethal Obsession. Anti-Semitism from Antiquity to the Global Jihad*. New York, 2010.

Wodak, Ruth et al. *"Wir sind alle unschuldige Täter," Diskurshistorische Studien zum Nachkriegsantisemitismus*. Frankfurt a.M., 1990.

Wolfe, Bertram D. *Three Who Made a Revolution*. London, 1966.

Yakira, Elhanan. *Post-Zionism, Post-Holocaust*. Cambridge, U.K., 2010.

Yarmolinsky, Avraham. *The Jews and Other Minorities under the Soviets*. New York, 1928.

Zetkin, Clara. *Rosa Luxemburg. Karl Liebknecht. Franz Mehring. Den Führern des Spartakusbundes und Gründern der Kommunistischen Partei Deutschlands*. Moscow, 1934.

Zimmerman, Joshua D. *Poles, Jews and the Polish Socialist Party*. Madison, Wisc., 2004.

Ziv, G. A. *Trotsky-Kharakteristika po Lichnym Vospominiam*. New York, 1921.

Zlocisti, T., ed. *Moses Hess: Sozialistische Aufsätze 1841–7*. Berlin, 1921.

Zuckermann, Moshe. *"Antisemit!" Ein Vorwurf als Herrschaftsinstrument*. Vienna, 2010.

Zukerman, William. *The Jew in Revolt*. London, 1937.

Index

Robert S. Wistrich is Neuberger Professor of Modern European and Jewish History at the Hebrew University of Jerusalem, and Head of the Vidal Sassoon International Center for the Study of Antisemitism. He previously held the Chair for Jewish Studies at University College, London, and visiting professorships at Harvard, Brandeis, Oxford, and Paris. The author and editor of twenty-five books, his most recent work, *A Lethal Obsession: Anti-Semitism from Antiquity to the Global Jihad,* is widely considered the definitive study of the subject.

BOCA RATON PUBLIC LIBRARY, FLORIDA
3 3656 0579160 9